A KENTUCKY SAMPLER

A KENTUCKY SAMPLER

Essays from
The Filson Club History Quarterly
1926–1976

Edited by
Lowell Harrison & Nelson L. Dawson

THE UNIVERSITY PRESS OF KENTUCKY

ISBN: 978-0-8131-5258-5

Library of Congress Catalog Card Number: 77-76471

Copyright © 1977 by The University Press of Kentucky

A statewide cooperative scholarly publishing agency serving Berea College, Centre College of Kentucky, Eastern Kentucky University, The Filson Club, Georgetown College, Kentucky Historical Society, Kentucky State University, Morehead State University, Murray State University, Northern Kentucky University, Transylvania University, University of Kentucky, University of Louisville, and Western Kentucky University.

Editorial and Sales Offices: Lexington, Kentucky 40506

CONTENTS

A Short History of The Filson Club   1

Introduction   5

I. THE PIONEER ERA

Thomas P. Field   The Indian Place Names of Kentucky (July 1960)   11

Robert E. McDowell   Bullitt's Lick: The Related Saltworks and Settlements (July 1956)   23

Otto A. Rothert   The Harpes: Two Outlaws of Pioneer Times (July 1927)   54

Charles G. Talbert   A Roof for Kentucky (April 1955)   63

II. THE ANTEBELLUM YEARS

Nancy D. Baird   Asiatic Cholera's First Visit to Kentucky: A Study in Panic and Fear (July 1974)   87

Thomas D. Clark   The Slavery Background of Foster's My Old Kentucky Home (January 1936)   100

J. Winston Coleman, Jr.   The Code Duello in Antebellum Kentucky (April 1956)   118

Lowell Harrison   Cassius Marcellus Clay and the *True American* (January 1948)   135

Philip D. Jordan   Milksickness in Kentucky and the Western Country (January 1945)   156

Robert C. Vitz   General James Taylor and the Beginnings of Newport, Kentucky (October 1976)   168

III. THE CIVIL WAR

James Bell Benedict, Jr.   General John Hunt Morgan: The Great Indiana-Ohio Raid (July 1957)   187

Albert Castel   Quantrill's Missouri Bushwhackers in Kentucky: The End of the Trail (April 1964)   212

William G. Eidson   Louisville, Kentucky, during the First Year of the Civil War (July 1964)   221

Julia Neal   South Union Shakers during War Years
(April 1965)   236

Hambleton Tapp   Incidents in the Life of Frank Wolford,
Colonel of the First Kentucky Union Cavalry (April 1936)   241

John E. Tilford, Jr.   The Delicate Track: The L & N's Role
in the Civil War (April 1962)   260

IV. THE LATE NINETEENTH CENTURY

Nicholas C. Burckel   William Goebel and the Campaign for
Railroad Regulation in Kentucky, 1888–1900
(January 1974)   275

Louis Hartz   John M. Harlan in Kentucky, 1855–1877: The Story
of His Pre-Court Political Career (January 1940)   293

Rhea A. Taylor   Bases for Conflicts in the Kentucky Constitutional
Convention, 1890–91 (January 1972)   317

Joseph F. Wall   Henry Watterson and the "Ten Thousand
Kentuckians" (October 1950)   330

Bill L. Weaver   Louisville's Labor Disturbance, July 1877
(April 1974)   341

V. THE TWENTIETH CENTURY

J. W. Cooke   Stoney Point, 1866–1969 (October 1976)   353

Robert T. Fugate, Jr.   The BancoKentucky Story
(January 1976)   369

William Wallace Henderson   The Night Riders' Raid on
Hopkinsville (October 1950)   388

Mariam S. Houchens   Amazing Best Sellers by Kentucky Women
Writers (October 1967)   401

Robert J. Leupold   The Kentucky WPA: Relief and Politics,
May–November 1935 (April 1975)   406

John Wilson Townsend   Paul Sawyier, Kentucky Artist: Some
Recollections of Him (October 1959)   423

Allan M. Trout   The Charm of Kentucky Folklore (July 1947)   428

A SHORT HISTORY
OF THE FILSON CLUB

Many people do not consider anything worthy of historic interest until it acquires the patina of age. We are delighted with objects our ancestors lightly discarded, while we casually dispose of materials that will some day be of great interest to our descendants. Although Louisville was founded in 1778, a century passed before a permanent historical society was established.

In March 1880 Richard H. Collins, son of the Kentucky historian Lewis Collins, wrote Louisville businessman C. P. Moorman pointing out the need for a historical society in Louisville. He suggested that Moorman might be willing to provide a building and an endowment for so worthy a cause. The institution could, he observed, be called "the C. P. Moorman Historical Society of Louisville." Moorman's reply, while not extant, was apparently negative. Yet the idea had been expressed and interest demonstrated, and it did not die. On May 1, 1880, Reuben T. Durrett, Louisville lawyer, collector, and historian, read a paper before the Southern Historical Society to celebrate the one-hundredth anniversary of the founding of Louisville. In July, 1883, Durrett and several companions conducted a tour of historic sites in Jefferson County.

This interest led to the organization of a historical society in Louisville on May 15, 1884. Formed at Durrett's home at 202 East Chestnut Street by ten interested Louisvillians, including Richard H. Collins, it was named The Filson Club in honor of John Filson who wrote the first history of Kentucky in 1784. Durrett was elected the first president, serving in that capacity until 1913. When The Filson Club was incorporated on October 6, 1891, its purpose was described as "the collection and preservation and publication of historic matter pertaining to the State of Kentucky and adjacent states."

From its beginning the club drew high praise from many sources. Theodore Roosevelt, who consulted the club's collections in preparation for his famous frontier history *The Winning of the West*, acknowledged his debt by writing: "For original matter connected with Kentucky, I am greatly indebted to Col. Reuben T. Durrett, of Louisville, the founder of The Filson Club, which has done such admirable historical work of late years." In addition to collecting and preserving materials, The Filson Club also began publishing during the first year of its existence. The first series of publications consisted of thirty-six volumes appearing between 1884 and 1938. Soft-cover monographs with an average length of 260 pages, they have been widely consulted by students of Kentucky history. In 1926 the club's publishing program was expanded to include the publication of a history journal called *The Filson Club History Quarterly*.

From 1884 to 1913 club meetings were held at Durrett's home which served as the club's headquarters until his death in 1913. In 1885 the time of meetings was fixed as the first Monday night of each month from October through June. After Durrett's death the meetings were transferred to the Louisville Free Public Library. James S. Pirtle, a Louisville lawyer, became president in 1913 and served until 1917. He was succeeded by his brother Alfred Pirtle, a Louisville businessman, Civil War veteran, and important local historian, who was president until 1923.

In the early years The Filson Club made several unsuccessful efforts to secure a fireproof building to house its growing collection. R. C. Ballard Thruston, who became a club vice president in 1913 and president in 1923, continued these efforts. Born in 1858 with a distinguished Kentucky ancestry, Thruston was well qualified to lead The Filson Club. He studied at the Sheffield Scientific School of Yale University where he received a Bachelor of Philosophy degree in 1880. In 1882 Thruston began work for the Kentucky State Geological Survey. He left the survey in 1887 and entered private business. After a successful career, he devoted his time, interest, and financial resources to The Filson Club.

Thruston transferred the club's possessions to his own office in the Columbia Building at Fourth and Main streets. In 1919 he promised the club his personal library and an endowment fund of $50,000 if a building with at least one fireproof room could be acquired. A fund drive in 1926 enabled the club to purchase property and convert two residences into a fireproof building. The Filson Club moved into its present home at 118 West Breckinridge Street in June 1929.

Thruston exceeded his original pledge, for in addition to the endowment fund, he gave another $50,000 as an emergency fund. Anticipating a new era of growth, the club amended the Constitution and By-Laws and Articles of Incorporation in May 1929. These amendments reorganized the club, established an endowment fund, and created endowment and life memberships. In 1935 another gift from Thruston established the Historical Acquisition Fund for the purchase of books, manuscripts, and other historical material.

The Filson Club celebrated its fiftieth anniversary in 1934 with a garden party held on May 12—the Sunday nearest to May 15. The party proved a popular innovation and is now firmly established as an

A Short History 3

annual tradition. In 1934 the club had ten endowment, fifty-three life, and 486 annual members. The library had also grown. Thruston had given the club 5,467 books and pamphlets; Otto Rothert, longtime club secretary, had added another 926. With these gifts as a nucleus, the library consisted of over 10,000 items in 1934. The club also possessed a significant manuscript collection.

Although the rate of growth slowed during the depression and war years, the club was able to maintain itself during this difficult period. Book publication continued until 1938 when the last volume of the first series appeared. The membership increased from 525 in 1936 to 803 in 1946. By 1946 it had become apparent that the club's library and museum holdings had expanded to the point where additional space would soon become necessary.

Thruston's long tenure as president of The Filson Club ended with his death in December 1946. He was succeeded by his good friend and great admirer J. Adger Stewart who worked to increase the club's membership, establish improved administrative techniques, and expand stack and office space. Although Stewart retired after three years on the advice of his physician, he continued until his death in 1954 to work closely with Judge Davis W. Edwards who followed him as president. A building program, planned by Stewart, doubled the stack and office space. This expansion, completed in 1955, greatly improved the efficiency of the club's daily operation.

Edwards guided the club ably until his death in 1962. During his tenure as president, the club celebrated its seventy-fifth anniversary in 1959. By this time membership had risen to over 1,500. Edwards was succeeded by Leo T. Wolford, a prominent Louisville attorney, whose tenure lasted until his death in 1971. These were years of steady growth for The Filson Club as the membership, endowment, library, and manuscript holdings continued to increase. A second series of book publications was begun in 1964.

One important element of continuity in these years was Richard H. Hill, who was brought to The Filson Club in 1947 as secretary by J. Adger Stewart. He was well qualified for the position. He had enjoyed a successful legal career in Louisville and served with distinction during World War II. In 1964 he became director of the club and was elected president in January 1972. Hill himself became a Filson Club tradition and has been greatly missed since his death in February 1973.

The club's ninth president is J. Alexander Stewart, son of J. Adger Stewart, who has been an officer of the club since 1955. Further progress has been made recently. Membership continues to increase; the collections are growing steadily; the staff has been enlarged; and important innovations have improved the club's efficiency and broadened its role in the community. In 1963 The Filson Club inherited the Brennan residence, a handsome Victorian home at 631 South Fifth Street in Louisville. This residence, which was received with its original furnishings intact, is now open to the public as a house museum and has become a significant asset to downtown Louisville.

The Filson Club today stands on the brink of an exciting and challenging future. But, despite substantial progress, the club's needs remain great. The present building, adequate in 1929, has been completely outgrown, and expansion has become necessary. Due to a generous gift from the J. Graham Brown Foundation, some property adjacent to the club has been purchased, but the task of obtaining money for a new building remains. Despite this great challenge, The Filson Club, now approaching its one-hundredth anniversary in 1984, views the past with pride and the future with confidence.

INTRODUCTION

With the appearance of the October 1976 number *The Filson Club History Quarterly* completed its first half-century of publication. To commemorate that milestone, we are reprinting twenty-eight articles that have appeared in the journal since its inception in October 1926. We believe that this representative sampling will indicate why the publication is recognized as one of the best state historical journals in the country.

Although The Filson Club was organized in Louisville in May 1884, the journal was not established for forty-two years. The club published thirty-six volumes in a well-received series, *The Filson Club Publications*, but there was a recognized need for another type of outlet, one that would appear more frequently, allow shorter studies to be presented, and serve as a channel of communications to the club's members. A quarterly journal of history appeared to be the best answer to these needs. The History Department of the University of Louisville was also interested in the possibilities of such a venture, and the two groups agreed to cosponsor it. The first issue of *The History Quarterly*, dated October 1926, bore the name of Robert S. Cotterill as managing editor. He was assisted by a seven-member board of editors: Fannie Casseday Duncan, Louis R. Gottschalk, Willard Rouse Jillson, Rolf Johannesen, Anna B. McGill, Jennie Angel Mengel, and Otto A. Rothert.

The first issue contained fifty-two pages and included three articles: R. C. Ballard Thruston, "The Signing of the Declaration of Independence"; Louis R. Gottschalk, "Revoluticnary Analogies"; and R. S. Cotterill, "Kentucky in 1774." There were seven book reviews and a four-page "News and Comment" section that became a standard feature of the journal.

The journal's purpose and scope were explained in a foreword that presaged a future problem.

> In The Filson Club and the History Department of the University of Louisville, Louisville has two organized bodies of historical workers whose aims are largely identical and whose needs are the same. The primary purpose of the *Quarterly* is to serve as a vehicle of expression for them both; it is published under their joint ownership and control; its editorial board is composed of representatives of both.
>
> The Filson Club is interested chiefly in the history of Kentucky and of the Ohio Valley; the University has no preference for one

country more than another, but its facilities for study are chiefly in American history. It follows from this that the *Quarterly*, although it will not limit itself strictly to any one section, may reasonably be expected to give most of its space to American history, particularly to that of the Ohio Valley and Kentucky. After this the ambitions of the *Quarterly* are directed toward the ante-bellum South. It will hold itself free to publish papers on any phase of American history, but as a rule the only attempt it will make to deal with the history of other countries will be to publish the studies of the history faculty at the University.

The sponsors soon realized that there was a greater conflict of interest between them than had been anticipated. While most of the articles concerned Kentucky, others discussed aspects of United States history that had little connection with the Commonwealth and a few, such as "A Roman Town in Africa," held little interest for most members of the club. Starting with the October 1928 issue, The Filson Club assumed sole sponsorship of the journal with Otto A. Rothert, secretary since 1917, as managing editor, a position he filled with distinction until his retirement in 1945. The name was changed to *The History Quarterly of The Filson Club* in January 1929; a year later it was changed again, this time to *The Filson Club History Quarterly*.

When Rothert assumed the editorship, the board of editors consisted of Lucien Beckner, Fannie Casseday Duncan, Willard Rouse Jillson, Esther E. Mason, Anna Blanche McGill, Jennie Angel Mengel, and Samuel M. Wilson. Cotterill, Gottschalk, and Johannesen had left the state for notable academic careers elsewhere. No editorial board was listed in the October 1929 issue and none has been included since then, although the various editors have apparently sought advice from both club members and staff upon numerous occasions.

The Filson Club had some difficulty in finding a suitable replacement for Rothert when he retired in 1945, but the October issue carried the announcement that Colonel Lucien Beckner, another longtime member, had agreed to accept an interim appointment while the search continued. One of Beckner's major objectives was to increase the size of the *Quarterly*, which had averaged sixty-four pages in 1945. In order to meet the additional expense, advertisements first appeared in the April 1946 number, and the annual cost to nonmembers was increased from $2.00 to $4.00.

Beckner seemed much relieved when he announced in the January 1947 issue that Judge Richard H. Hill had been diverted from retirement and persuaded to accept the positions of secretary and editor. In 1964 Hill became The Filson Club's first director, and, as the club grew, his administrative duties became increasingly heavy. Robert E. McDowell, an active member of the club and a successful free-lance

Introduction 7

author, was guest editor for the July and October issues in 1970; he became managing editor with the January 1971 number. Hill continued to be listed as editor for the remainder of that year but his name disappeared from its familiar spot in the January 1972 issue. McDowell edited the *Quarterly* until his untimely death in the spring of 1975. Nelson Dawson, already a member of the club's staff, became acting editor with the July 1975 number.

The six editors have been responsible for the publication of some 800 articles during the past fifty years, in addition to numerous book reviews and such regular features as "News and Comment," "Filsonians," and the annual index and list of members. This impressive number presented serious problems when we began to look for the small number of articles that could be included in this sampler. We soon decided that certain types of material would have to be excluded from consideration: non-Kentucky studies, edited material, multipart articles, genealogical compilations. In order to provide as much variety as possible, we reluctantly agreed to use no more than one piece by an author; this decision alone eliminated dozens of possibilities, for several authors have been prolific contributors to the *Quarterly*. And we decided that as far as possible selections should reflect different periods and different aspects of Kentucky's colorful history.

These restrictions led to a quick reduction from the 800 original possibilities to several dozen; the real problem consisted of reducing that smaller number to the twenty-eight that are included in this volume. We realize that some readers may not agree with some of our selections; we are not sure that we agree with all of them either. We do not claim that these are the best articles that have been published in the *Quarterly*; we read others that are equally good but which did not fit as well into the sampler that we were trying to put together. We do believe that our selections will reveal something of the richness of Kentucky's history and of the excellence of the journal that The Filson Club has published for the past fifty years.

Except for expanded biographical statements, the articles appear just as they were published. Little editing would have been required in any case, for even the earliest articles have withstood well the tests of time and modern scholarship.

I.

THE PIONEER ERA

THE INDIAN PLACE NAMES OF KENTUCKY*

By Thomas P. Field

University of Kentucky, Lexington, Kentucky

A paper read before The Filson Club, February 1, 1960

Kentucky is constantly yielding clear evidence of long occupation by a succession of Indian cultures. Is it possible that the last Indian occupation and the beginning of white settlement had enough overlap and contact to allow the continuation of some Indian place names into the contemporary world? A casual survey of the state map creates a large measure of pessimism. Only Ohio County and the city of Paducah are evident possibilities. The Ohio, Kentucky, Tennessee, and Mississippi rivers are of certain Indian origins. Beyond this point the search must become involved with the mass of names of neighborhoods, streams, hills, historical sites and some folk lore.

The Department of Anthropology of the University of Kentucky has estimated that during the pioneer period there are recorded only a few over one hundred white-Indian contacts. As evidence of how slight the contact actually was, a Mr. Ficklin writing from Lexington in 1847 said: ". . . I have myself an acquaintance with the Indian history of the State from the year 1781 . . ."

"There is one fact favorable to this State which belongs to few, if any, of the sister States. We have not to answer, to any tribunal, for the crime of driving off the Indian tribes, and possessing their lands. There were no Indians located within our limits, on our taking possession of the country."[1]

Due to differences in the geographical areas referred to as Kentucky, the complete record does not allow such positive statements as those made by Mr. Ficklin, but the sense of his statement is essentially true. There is evidence that close to the time of his arrival in Kentucky there were some Shawnee villages on the Kentucky side of the Ohio up and downstream from the mouth of the Scioto River.[2] A village site which was occupied as late as the historical period was located at Hagerhill in Johnson County.[3] The record of a displaced band of Shawnees and their camping ground in eastern Clark County

---

*Reprinted from *Names*, Volume VII, Number 5, September, 1959, by permission of The American Name Society.

is recorded on the Gist map of 1751.[4] In the western and southern parts of the state random and refugee bands from the south, Chickasaws, Creeks, Choctaws, and Cherokees paused long enough to leave some memory of their passing. For an example instance Collins reports, ". . . . Red Bird Fork and Jack's Creek [named] from two friendly Indians bearing those names, . . ."[5]

Early in the career of Mr. Ficklin there were attempts to clear the Cherokee from the general area bounded by the Cumberland River on the north and the present Kentucky-Tennessee state line on the south.[6] In 1795 the Shawnees were confined, by treaty, to lands north of the Ohio River.[7] Such accounts clearly show why Mr. Ficklin would not be impressed by such Indians as were present, as none were legally at home in Kentucky.

The unsettled state of the Indians at this time also is in part explained in a statement by Morgan; he wrote, "As early as the opening of the 17th century the League of the Iroquois launched a period of intra-Indian warfare which reached westward to the Mississippi and southward to South Carolina and the Tennessee River. By 1700 most of the encompassed groups were, 'According to the Indian notion they were made women. . .' "[8] This general disruption resulted in the lack of permanent Indian settlements in Kentucky. And this condition when combined with land cessions and land purchases reduced the pioneer-Indian contacts, friendly or hostile, to meetings on grounds which were the home territory of neither. The pioneers were truly foreigners in the land and the Shawnee were only hunters on the neutral ground between their Ohio home and the Cherokee lands to the south in Tennessee.

The pioneers, unlike the Indians, were in the process and possessed of the means to make Kentucky their home. They proceeded to name the physical and cultural features of their habitat in a distinctly American manner. As Speed stated, "The various stations or forts which were dotted all over the level lands where the great army of immigrants spread themselves were principally named in honor of the leading pioneers. The memory of the Indian was seldom perpetuated in the names of mountain or stream, village or fort, and never in the roads and traces of the country."[9]

In Speed's statement there is left a thread of hope that some Indian place names did survive. Certainly this could not have happened often or accurately. Assuming that some of the pioneers may have wanted to perpetuate an Indian place name, there are reasonable possibilities why this did not happen in a form which can be positively identified today. Even though the Indian name for the place was known the name was really a compound word i. e., "Alananto-

Indian Place Names 13

wamiowee," the Buffalo Path,[10] or, "Nepepenine Sepe," the Salt River.[11] Such names would be difficult to incorporate into an English vocabulary. Thus, "Wepepocone-Cepewe," the Big Sandy, "Milewakene-Cepewe," the Kentucky River, "Lewekeomi," the Falls of the Ohio and other such names were never carried forward.[12] The pronunciation difficulties of such Indian names was complemented by a distaste for Indian culture and a preoccupation with the myraid problems of pioneering. It is to be expected that the continuation of an Indian name will be accompanied by some degree of alteration from the original spoken word. What are the expectations of such words as Schochoh, Ouasioto, Tyewhoppety, Helechawa, Thealka and Dango?

With the statements of Speed and Ficklin well in mind, with attention to the caution of Beeler[13] and an awareness that results would be inconclusive, a search for the Indian place names of the state was undertaken. The product of this search is the object of this paper.

The basic data used in the search for the Indian place names was contained in a card file of over thirty thousand place names compiled from various sources. The primary sources for this compilation were the topographic maps at a scale of 1:24,000 covering the entire state, 1:62,500 topographic maps covering one-half of the state, two series of county highway maps and a series of community and neighborhood maps produced by the Kentucky Agricultural Experiment Station.

For the first screening of the thirty thousand place names an "open door" policy was established. About four hundred names were selected for further consideration. A second and third review combined with research reduced the list to about one hundred and fifty "possibles." The fourth screening had as its objective the elimination of those names which were of Indian origin but which have become common property in American usage. Only if the name had strong Kentucky connections was a common Indian name retained. Removed from the list were such words as: persimmon, terrapin, hurricane, kinniconick, Mississippi, Tennessee, Cherokee and Tso-nonpow-aka. No consideration was given to any place names in English e. g., Indian Creek, Indian Fort, Yellow Creek, Eagle Creek, or Blue Licks. Sample research indicated a lack of source material in this area. The end result of the several screenings was a list of about ninety place names which strongly suggested Indian origins or about which there was an uncertainty.

The research on these ninety place names revealed that about thirty had some close Indian connection or were still unaccounted for. The following twelve names were deleted: *Catawba* (Kuttawa)

(Cuttawa), a borrowed Siouan word which in the first two instances was applied by whites to their own settlements and in the last instance went out of use before 1780; *Elkatawa,* which is possibly a corruption of the name of the "Prophet" Ellskwatawa; *Peedee,* a borrowed Siouan word of recent use in Kentucky; *Panola,* a borrowing of the Choctaw word for cotton as a place name; *Atoka,* a word said to have been borrowed from the Choctaw but which has no meaning in that language; *Okolona,* a word in the Chickasaw language which is descriptive of an Indian who impressed the whites; *Dango,* possibly a Cherokee word but unsupported by local information, if Cherokee it would mean "ground;" *Yamacraw,* a name taken from a book which referred to this band of Creeks and applied to a railroad station; *Watauga,* which was transported to Kentucky from east Tennessee and applied to two villages, in Cherokee the word means "broken water;" *Bayou,* an Indian-French generic term derived from Choctaw which is correctly and incorrectly used in at least six instances of stream names; *Chenowee* (Chenoa)[13a] (Chinoe), probably a transported Cherokee place name from Tennessee, (if Cherokee it might mean "bitter," possibly it is Choctaw in origin and if so would mean "gap,") *Wasioto* is possibly a Cherokee personal name but the use in Bell County is unsupported by reliable information. *Jellico,* from the *Tellico* branch of the Cherokees and today applied to a stream in Whitley County. The Tellicos seem to have been associated with *Watauga* (Wayne Co.).

The following place names are unexplained either as words or names. They are presumed to have no Indian origin or reference: Cutuno, Datha, Nimmo, Nisi, Sano, Sketo, Vada, and Yeadiss.

The possibility of classification of the Indian place names is limited both by the small number of names and the varying nature of the data supporting them. None of the names have escaped the effects of such erosional forces as crosscultural hazards in language always present. All are, in some measure, historically uncertain and some lose stature through disuse or uncertain revival. Because degrees of penalties are implied in the above statement the following list of Indian place names is presented in descending order of precedence:

(1) *Eskippakithiki* — A historical site in Clark County. According to Beckner the site covers an area of three thousand five hundred acres.[14] The site lies on the eastern margin of the Outer Bluegrass region and is thus flanked to the east by The Knobs and the escarpment of the Cumberland Plateau. Geomorphic and geologic evidence reveals that this area is the strath of an ancient stream and is underlain by a succession of eastward dipping strata of Ordovician, Si-

lurian, Devonian, and Tertiary formations.[15] The map reveals that much of the area is the divide between the south and west flowing Howard Creek and the south flowing Lulbegrud Creek.

The Evans-Pownall map gives an accurate location of this site early in the English period.[16] This location was occupied by Indians, to some extent, from the beginning of the Christian era until 1755.[17] Historically it is known that the site was occupied by a band of Shawnee in 1745-48 and was last occupied by a similar band of Shawnee in 1755.[18]

A Dr. T. Michaelson is quoted as saying that the first four syllables of the name undoubtedly contain the Shawnee word meaning "green." Prof. A. C. Mahr furnishes a more complete statement regarding the etymology of the name. He says, ". . . and [they] gave those lands the name *Shkipakethiki*, 'place where it is green all over'."[19]

On the geologic map of Clark County[20] the name *Kentake* is parenthetically added to the original Eskippakithiki. This name is from the pioneer tradition that the Cherokee name of the site was *Kentake*, a word translated by the settlers as "meadow land."[21] H. Kenny quoting several sources says that the word *Kentucky* is an Iroquoian word and is variously rendered as "head of the river," "prairies," "among the meadows," "big swamp," and "river of blood."[22] The last entry above could easily be in reference to the nearby Red River and the others, in spite of some conflicts, appear to say that Eskippakithiki and Kentucky are expressions of the same thought, "the place where it is green all over." Thus the appellation "Dark and Bloody Ground" appears as an erroneous translation of Kentucky and the regional use of "Bluegrass" appears as a projection of the original descriptive intent. (For further comment on *Kentucky* see the entry of that place name below.)

(2) *Eskalapia* — The use of this Shawnee name in western Lewis County is rather extensive. The topographic map records Eskalapia Mountain and Eskalapia Hollow. The county history adds by textual and map reference "Esculapia" Springs and "Esculapia" neighborhood.[23] The immediate area in which these names occur lies directly astride the Salt Lick Creek Prong of the Warrior Trail.[24]

Mahr states that *Eskalapia* is a Shawnee word.[25] His etymology of the word indicates that it means, "over and over, long stretch." The location of the Warrior Trail and the nature of the local topography strongly suggest that this name, as used for the area, is "in situ."

(3) (6) (9a) *Tywhapita* (Tyewhoppety-9a) — The first entry is the name of a neighborhood in northwestern Hancock County which is located in the bottom land of Blackford Creek.[26] The second entry,

the spelling of which is uncertain, was used in northern Hopkins County for what is now the village of Manitou.[27] The third entry is the name of a community in northern Todd County.[28] This same word, Tywappity Bottoms and Zewapeta, occurs in Missouri.[29] In Hancock County a folk etymology is given, the conclusion of which is as follows: "... the male occupants of the cabin rushed to the spot and found only a log with water slapping against it, making the sound of 'Tywhoppity-tywhoppity-tywhoppity'."[30] Mr. Boone states that the use of this word in Todd County is of uncertain origin but is locally believed to date from the 1890's.[31]

Prof. Mahr has studied this word with regard to its possible derivation from Shawnee stems. He write as follows: "Unless otherwise documented, the Shawnee treking from across the Ohio River to Kentucky and the West may have given three or more different locations in Kentucky that name of 'place of no return.' It is immaterial, therefore, whether the English transcription of *TOw/haap/ite today reads *Tywhapita* or *Tyewhoppety.*"[32]

(4) *Ouasioto* — An uncertain Indian word applied as the name of a gap on the Warrior Trail between Manchester and Station Camp Creek in Jackson County.

Originating in the Carolinas and Georgia the "Athiamiowee" was funneled through Cumberland (Cave) Gap and thus through the extremely rough country of the Cumberland Mountains and Plateau. Ouasioto Gap is, in a minor way, the entrance to easier travel for the traveler from the south. The Evans-Pownall map shows this area as occupied by the Ouasioto Mountains, a name which is no longer used though no satisfactory substitute has replaced it. None of the current maps carry the name of this gap but the name is still known in the vicinity of Gray Hawk and Bradshaw.

The etymology of *Ouasioto* is vague; however a footnote by Johnston says that the word is Shawnee and that it means "Deer Pass."[33] Prof. Mahr states that the word *scioto* is: Iroquoian (Wyandot), probably from the Wyandot och/sk' onto which mean "a deer," and, in the category of trade-and-travel words.[34]

The historical use of the word indicates an intent to perpetuate an Indian place name. The etymological difficulties do not alter its provenience from an Indian place name on the Warrior Trail.

(5) *Paducah* — A city on the south Bank of the Ohio River and the county seat of McCracken County. It is in the area of the Jackson Purchase which was taken over from the Chickasaws in 1818. Wilson records: "Its site was originally a portion of the land granted to Gen. George Rogers Clark [1752-1818], and it was William Clark, a brother

Indian Place Names

of Gen. Clark, and one of the leaders of the famous Lewis and Clark exploring expedition, who founded the settlement. There is a dispute as to the origin of the name, whether from an Indian tribe or its chief, but the personal tendency finally prevailed, and Chief Paduke[34a] the head of the tribe carried off the honor."[35]

Some insight is gained in regard to Clark's use of the word "Paduke" in the following excerpt: "Thus, Lewis and Clark, who identified the "Cattar-kah" as the "Paducar" who came to trade at the Arikara[36] villages from the region to the southwest, apparently picked up the original meaning of "Paduca" as Apache, because the "Cataka" were the Kiowa-Apache."[37]

Another approach and challenge to the foregoing is the research of Irvin S. Cobb, a native of Paducah. Using the works of H. B. Cushman, Cobb concluded, ". . . the name Paducah — and incidentally of the old chief — was derived from a compound word in the Chickasaw tongue meaning 'wild grapes hanging,' or, more properly 'Place where the grapes hang down'."[38]

An examination of Byington[39] reveals that Cobb may have been very close to the etymology of the name. The name that Clark knew from the Missouri Valley and this Chickasaw (Choctaw) word were close in sound and thus possibly joined in spelling. If this assumption is correct Paducah, as with Eskippakithiki, is a corrupted but true Indian place name "in situ."

(7) *Iuka* — A town on the Cumberland River in Livingston County. This was once the name for what is now Tama, Iowa,[40] and is currently the name of towns in Mississippi, Illinois, Missouri, and Kansas. In each instance the apparent intent was to perpetuate an Indian name the etymology and original location of which has been lost. In Livingston County the residents believe that this was the name of a refugee band of Chickasaws who camped in their locality.[41]

The prevalence of this place name suggests some substance though it is without evident historical support. Possibly the word means "place by the water." The inclusion of this place name is questionable.

(8) *Kentucky* — This familiar name is widely used in Kentucky and adjoining states and has spread as far as Southern Rhodesia and Australia; it is obscure as to original use and etymology. It appears to be of Cherokee origin. This conclusion is well supported when the word is associated with Eskippakithiki cited above. However, the research of a Tennessee historian presents equally interesting possibilities. He writes as follows: "The Emperor of the Cherokees, commonly called by the English 'Old Hop.' . . . various forms, due to the difficulty of reducing to English Cherokee gutterals in Kane-

gwati have been found by the writer in the records: Cunnicatogue, Concauchto, Connoctte, Connecocartee, Conogotocke, Canackte, referring to 'Canacaught, the great conjurer,' . . . ."[42]

A review of the literature circa 1780 would indicate that the name of the land to be settled by the followers of Boone was a matter of point of view and time. Pownall[43] and Hutchins[44] from the English point of view used the name Cuttawa for the land and the river. Other such names included Milley's (Millewakame), Cuttawba, Chenoka, Chenoa, and Little Cunaway. By 1784 Filson[45] and the settlers moving from North Carolina and east Tennessee were using some variation of the word Kentucky for the same land and river. The chronicles of the time do not relay the philosophy which caused this change in usage.

Whether "Cuttawa" or "Kentucky," both names appear as inventions of the whites rather than true Indian names. Circumstance caused the strong Cherokee influence to turn the tide in favor of "Kentucky."

(8) *Ohio* — In this instance the word "Ohio" is considered as a river name only.

The French, viewing the river first at its mouth, caused considerable confusion in names. Winsor makes the following statement in this regard, "As to this eastern affluent of the Mississippi, the French had introduced a confused nomenclature, which needs to be borne in mind in reading the early narratives. What they often called the Ouabache (Wabash) was the present stream of that name, continued in the modern Ohio below their junction."[46]

The river name, as now used, is certainly of Indian origin. Though the Shawnee name was known in a variety of spellings and meanings[47] none ever "caught on." Mahr clearly relates the transmutation of the word into its present form; he writes, "This indicates that the name 'Ohio,' evidently pronounced O/hii/o' at that time, and regardless of its probable origin among the Wyandots, had become a term of interracial travel-and-trade lingo on the all-important waterway during that era of mutual acculturation between Indians and whites, and simply meant 'the Big River' to everyone concerned."[48]

(9b) *Ootan* — The name of a creek which is tributary to Donaldson Creek in northern Caldwell County. This creek is on the evacuation route for southern Indians on their way to the West. This particular name appears only as a fragment of an Indian word.[48a] There is however, some memory of Indian words being used as place names in this immediate area. A local resident writes, "A creek north of Princeton was called 'Opicana' by the Indians that returned here to visit the graves of their dead. I have heard this stated by Mrs.

Indian Place Names 19

Ellen Dixon, now deceased."[49] It must be considered more than coincidence that the Choctaw Dictionary gives "opitama" as a word meaning "passed by." The creek referred to by Mrs. Dixon is not specified to the degree that "opitama" could be related to "ootan." All that can be said is that "ootan" is an unexplained word used as the name of a creek in the immediate area of a past Choctaw (?) use of the word "opitama" to describe a creek in northern Caldwell County.

SUMMARY AND CONCLUSIONS

The pessimism engendered by Speed in regard to finding many Indian place names in the state was well founded. The effort however, did reveal some names that were nearly lost and the status of others was established.

The moment in history allotted to the French and English to enter the bounds of the state was a period of confusion and conflict. Archaeology indicates that had the colonial period occurred at an earlier date the history and resultant influence on place names would have been considerable. As it was, the enormous wave of pioneer migrants into a nearly vacant land gave little opportunity for the continuation of Indian place names. Without the bridge of trade and mission activities it is somewhat remarkable that any form of place names of Indian origin has survived.

A partial reason for the survival of the listed names is found when these names are plotted in relation to the Indian Trails of the state. The "Warrior Trail," the Shawneetown-Russellville trail, and the river route of the Ohio were within the bounds of Shawnee influence at the time of white-Indian contact. It is thus the realization of a reasonable expectation that these routes would be dominated by Shawnee words used as place names today.

The area of the Jackson Purchase and as far eastward as the Princeton-Palmyra trail was the northern limit of the Chickasaw territory. This was also the evacuation route for both the Chickasaw and the Choctaw on their way to the West. Thus this general area is the exclusive domain of place names derived from these two languages.

The small measure of Cherokee influence at the time of settlement is amply demonstrated in the paucity of surviving Cherokee place names. Ouasioto is not clearly defined. It could be Wyandot from the north or Cherokee from the south. Other Cherokee names are either lost or have been revived by whites and used for the euphony of the word e.g., Watauga, Chenoa, Wasioto, etc., rather than perpetuating Cherokee place names "per se."

The Siouan intrusion found in the historic use of "Cuttawa" as a name for the Kentucky River is unexplained.

The absence of place names of Indian origin along the Buffalo Path, the Tennessee River-Ohio-Great Lakes trail, the Scioto Prong, the Falls of the Ohio at Louisville and the Big Sandy trail demonstrates how slender a chance it was for any name to survive. Such prominent locations in Indian and pioneer times as Big Bone Lick and Blue Licks are not recorded in regard to their Indian names.

The fact is, that in an absolute sense, there are no Indian place names in the state. There is only the hazy memory that there were a few names existent at the advent of white settlement, a mixture of isolated ephemeral adjectives and adjectival phrases.

FOOTNOTES

[1] H. R. Schoolcraft, *Information Respecting the History, Conditions and Prospects of the Indian Tribes of the United States*, Part I, Lippincott, Gumbo & Co., 1853, p. 300-301.

[2] *Christopher Gist's Journal with Historical and Ethnological Notes and Biographies of Historical Contemporaries*, J. R. Weldon Co., Pittsburgh, 1893, p. 44.

[3] W. S. Webb and W. D. Funkhouser, *Archaeological Survey of Kentucky*, publication of the Department of Anthropology and Archaeology, University of Kentucky, Sept. 1932, p. 206.

[4] Gist, *op. cit.*, p. 44.

[5] R. Collins, *History of Kentucky*, Collins & Co., Covington, 1882, p. 141.

[6] C. C. Royce, "Indian Land Cessions of the United States," *18th Annual Report of the Bureau of American Ethnology*, Smithsonian Institute, 1899, p. 648.

[7] Ibid, p. 654.

[8] L. H. Morgan, *League of the HO-DE-NO-SAU-NEE or Iroquois*, Vol. I Dodd, Mead & Co., 1851, p. 14.

[9] T. Speed, *The Wilderness Road*, Filson Club Publications No. 2, John P. Morton Co., Louisville, Ky., 1886, p. 68-69.

[10] Ibid, p. 69.

[11] ———, Trans. & Collections, American Antiquities Society, Vol. I, p. 229.

[12] Speed, *op. cit.*, p. 72.

[13] M. S. Beeler, "On Etymologizing Indian Place-Names," *Names*, Vol. V, no. 4, Dec. 1957, p. 236 et seq.

[13a] This is also a surname.

[14] Lucien Beckner, "Eskippakithiki, The Last Indian Town in Kentucky," *The Filson Club History Quarterly*, Vol. 6, No. 4, p. 355.

[15] R. P. Meacham, A. C. Munyan and G. R. Wesley, *Geologic Map of Clark County, Kentucky*, U. of Ky. Geological Survey, series IX, 1950.

[16] T. Pownall, *Map of the Middle British Colonies in North America*, 1776 and possibly 1775, reprinted in *the Horn Papers*, Vol. II, W. F. Horn, Green County Historical Society, Herald Press, Scottdale, Pa., 1945, p. 784-785.

[17] Estimate given by the Department of Anthropology, University of Kentucky.

[18] C. A. Hanna, *The Wilderness Trail*, G. P. Putnam's Sons, New York, 1911, p. 240-242.

[19] A. C. Mahr, private correspondence of 6 Dec. 1958.
[20] Mecham, Munyan and Wesley, *op. cit.*
[21] Beckner, *op cit.*, p. 1.
[22] H. Kenney, *West Virginia Place Names*, Place Names Press, Piedmont, W. Va., 1945, p. 347.
[23] O. C. Ragan, *History of Lewis County, Kentucky*, Jennings and Graham Cincinnati, 1912, p. 25-489.
[24] W. E. Myer, "Indian Trails of the Southeast," *Forty-Second Annual Report of the Bureau of American Ethnology*, Smithsonian Institution, 1928, p. 787.
[25] A. C. Mahr, private correspondence of 14 Feb. 1959.
[26] *Community and Neighborhood Map of Hancock County, Kentucky*, Ky. Agri. Exp. Station, Ext. Div., U. of Ky. Lexington, mimeographed, ed. 1941.
[27] Correspondence with B. E. Boone III, editor, Todd County Standard, who obtained this statement from an elderly lady who was born at Tywhapita, Hopkins Co., 1959.
[28] Community and Neighborhood Map of Todd County, 1942.
[29] R. L. Ramsey, *Our Storehouse of Missouri Place Names*, University of Missouri Bulletin, Missouri Handbook no. Two, U. of Missouri, 1952, p. 42-43.
[30] Correspondence with Mrs. Dorsey Thompson, Lewisport, Ky. 12 Dec. 1958.
[31] Boone, *op. cit.*
[32] Correspondence with A. C. Mahr, 7 Feb. 1959.
[33] J. S. Johnston, *First Explorations in Kentucky*. Filson Club Publications No. 13, 1898, p. 122.
[34] A. C. Mahr, "Indian River and Place Names in Ohio," *The Ohio Historical Quarterly*, Vol. 66, no. 2, April 1957, p. 140.
[34a] 18 March, 1720, baptized son of Jean Olivier and Martha Padöca [Paduca] [Padouca]. Rev. Jos. Ignatius Le Boullenger. S. J., "Kaskaskia Church Records", Trans. Ill. St. Hist. Soc., 1904, p. 402.
[35] S. M. Wilson, *History of Kentucky*, Vol. II, J. S. Clark Publishing Co., Chicago and Louisville, 1928, p. 620-623.
[36] Mooney states that they were one of three associated tribes resident along the Missouri River at the time of the Lewis and Clark expedition.
[37] F. R. Secoy, "The Identity of the 'Paduca;' and Ethnohistorical Analysis," *American Anthropologist*, Vo. 53, no. 4, part I, Oct.-Dec., 1951, p. 529.
[38] F. G. Neuman, *The Story of Paducah*, Young Printing Co., Paducah, 1928, p. 18.
[39] C. Byington, *A Dictionary of the Choctaw Language*, ed. Swanton & Halbert, Smithsonian Inst. Bureau of Am. Ethnology, Washington, 1915, p. 308.
[40] ———, *A History of the Origin of the Names in Nine Northwestern States Connected with the C & Nw, C St, PM & O Railroad*, Chicago, 1908, p. 146.
[41] Correspondence with H. Y. Martin, postmaster, Iuka, Ky., 1958.
[42] H. Timberlake, *The Memoirs of Lieut. Harry Timberlake 1756-1765*, Annotation, Introduction and Index by S. C. Williams, The Watauga Press, Johnson City, Tenn., 1927, footnote p. 39.
[43] Pownall, *op. cit.*
[44] T. Hutchins, "A new Map of the Western Parts of Virginia, Pennsylvania, Maryland and North Carolina, London, 1778.
[45] J. Filson, "Map of Kentucke," Philadelphia, 1784.
[46] J. Winsor, *The Mississippi Basin, the Struggle in America Between England and France*, Houghton, Mifflin Co., Boston, 1895, p. 17.
[47] J. S. Johnston in *First Explorations in Kentucky* records "Kitono-cepe" and John Johnston in *Indian Tribes* records "Kiskepila Sepe."
[48] A. C. Mahr, *op. cit.*, p. 138.
[48a] Possibly this is a variant of the surname Ooten
[49] Correspondence with J. E. Mason, Princeton, Ky, 1958.

THOMAS P. FIELD (1914–   ), a native of Pennsylvania, received his bachelor's degree from East Tennessee State University, his M.A. degree from George Peabody College, and his Ph.D. from the University of North Carolina. He has taught geography at the University of Kentucky since 1948 and is the author of several books including *A Guide to the Place Names of Kentucky* (1961) and *Kentucky and the Southwest Territory* (1965).

This article first appeared in *The Filson Club History Quarterly* in July 1960, vol. 34, pp. 237–47.

BULLITT'S LICK

THE RELATED SALTWORKS AND SETTLEMENTS*

By ROBERT E. McDOWELL
Louisville, Kentucky

A paper read before The Filson Club, May 7, 1956

There is a region just south of Louisville, roughly the size of a small county, that was probably the most important—the most notorious section in the entire state of Kentucky during pioneer times. Geographically it commences a little north of Fairdale and runs southward along the eastern foot of the Knobs, crossing Salt River and extending on as far south as Bardstown Junction in Bullitt County.

The heart of this region** was Bullitt's Lick and it derived its importance from salt.

Today we take salt more or less for granted. But in early days salt was a very precious, a very necessary article. For one thing, it was almost the only preservative. The early settlers had to have salt in order to pickle their beef, cure their pork, salt down their deer and bear meat. Since game was their principal source of food, without salt to preserve it they would have starved.

Even had it been practical to transport salt across the mountains, the eastern communities could not have supplied it. The Revolutionary War with Great Britain had cut off the normal sources of salt. The *Virginia Gazette* of the period is full of notices reflecting their distress: reports of planters who experimented with boiling down sea water; act after act passed by the Revolutionary legislature to encourage the manufacture of salt; bold type notices wherever a shipment of salt managed to slip through the British blockade.

In the wilderness the shortage was even more acute. The settlers were able to boil down a little at the numerous licks and salt springs for their personal use. In 1778 Daniel Boone was captured by Indians with a party of men at the lower Blue Licks as they were engaged in making salt for Boonesboro.[1] But this was only the barest trickle. Some adequate local source of salt had to be found.

Without it, the settlement of Kentucky would have been retarded for years.

---

* A preliminary report.
** See accompanying map.

This was the situation, then, when in 1779 the Saltworks was erected at Bullitt's Lick—the first commercial saltworks in Kentucky—the only saltworks west of the Alleghenies during the remaining years of the revolution—and by far the most important source of salt in the wilderness for many, many years thereafter.[2]

Bullitt's Lick appears to have been named after Captain Thomas Bullitt, a Virginia surveyor, who had led a party into Kentucky in 1773. They were engaged in locating and surveying lands on military warrants issued to officers of the French and Indian wars.[3] It isn't likely, though, that Bullitt was the original discoverer.

A salt lick was always a favorite hunting ground for both Indian and backwoodsman. Buffalo by the thousands made great roads into them and licked out deep trenches in the salt-impregnated clay, while herds of deer and elk congregated in the neighborhood. Bullitt's Lick was an unusually large lick and no doubt was known by repute at least. Captain Thomas Bullitt, however, was the first to survey it and there he located a thousand acres for Colonel William Christian, a veteran of the French and Indian wars.

The next year, 1774, James Douglas resurveyed Christian's entry on Salt River, including the buffalo lick; and it was on his survey that Christian's patent was granted. The original plat made by Douglas is still on file at the land office in Frankfort, brown and crumbling with age.[4]

When I first began this research, it never occurred to me that I couldn't find most of the information I needed in printed sources. It was a different setting for historical fiction—romantic, colorful, full of the sound of axes and the crash of falling trees, of Indian alarms, the brawling of lusty saltmakers, the tinkle of horse bells as the pack trains disappeared into the forest bearing their loads of salt. All of it dimly perceived through the swirling blue wood smoke of the furnace pits.

It was a wonderful background.

But even more important, perhaps, it was fresh and new. Millions of words have been written about Daniel Boone and the Bluegrass settlements. But this locale had never been made use of in fiction to the best of my knowledge.

I soon found out why.

Except for the scantiest mention scattered thinly through secondary sources, there was nothing. And even that nothing managed to contradict itself on almost every point. The Saltworks was established in 1778 according to one source, in 1779 according to another, or perhaps later.[5] You could take your pick. Who actually began to make

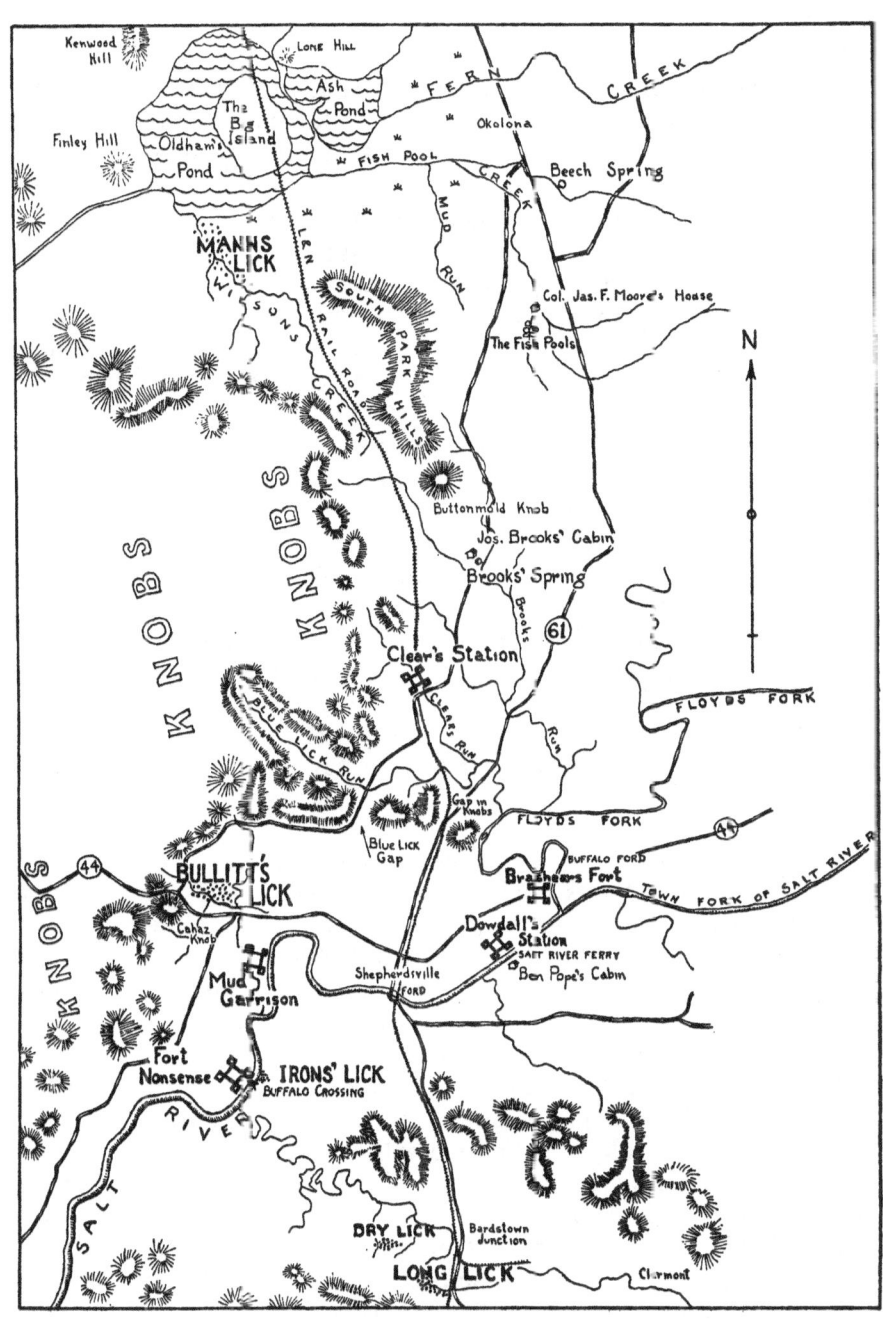

MAP OF BULLITT'S LICK REGION

salt at Bullitt's Lick or when or how was shrouded in the deepest mystery.

The same obscurity and confusion surrounded the early pioneer stations that sprang up nearby. Even the Wilderness Road—that most important of all roads in our history—went underground apparently through this region, not to emerge again until it reached Louisville.[6]

What happened that this whole district—once the most important district in Kentucky—should have passed into obscurity? Why has it been treated like a stepchild by historians until Dr. Thomas Clark, head of the History Department at the University of Kentucky, in his *History of Kentucky,* mentions the fact that salt was made in pioneer times at Big Bone Lick and the two Blue Licks and even Drennon's Lick—but doesn't mention Bullitt's Lick at all?[7]

Salt was not manufactured at the places which Dr. Clark names until later.[8] Not, in fact, until the closing years of the pioneer period in Kentucky. And even then, their scope of operations was insignificant when compared to Bullitt's Lick. In fact, at the Blue Licks, the proprietor had set up a few kettles which he would rent to anyone who cared to make a little salt for himself.[9]

Historically, Bullitt's Lick should occupy the place of foremost importance. It was Kentucky's first industry as well as its first saltworks. It was the only saltworks for a good many years. It was the hub of the salt trade in pioneer times, supplying all the salt for this state and exporting it by pack train and flatboat as far off as the Cumberland and the Illinois.

The printed histories having failed to be of much assistance—even the regional ones—I was finally driven to doing what I should have done in the first place—go to original contemporary sources.

Shepherdsville, the county seat of Bullitt County, seemed the most likely place to start. I wanted depositions, if they were to be found. Therefore, the Circuit Court appeared to be the best bet.

Mrs. Nancy Strange is the Clerk of the Bullitt Circuit Court and right here I wish to acknowledge my indebtedness to her. Without her interest and help, the job would have been almost impossible. She took me into the vault, provided me with a place to work, helped me locate the records of the first cases. The kindness, the graciousness, and very real interest that I have been shown everywhere in Bullitt County has been one of the most pleasant experiences I have had. I am only sorry that there isn't time here [The Filson Club meeting] to acknowledge everyone who has been of assistance.

But to get back to those first cases. As soon as I began to go through them, I realized that I had had a real stroke of beginner's luck. There were hundreds of depositions of the first settlers and hunters and saltmakers, taken down in their own words. There were surveys and plats, showing the location of salt licks around Bullitt's that I had never heard of, laying out the old buffalo paths and early roads, locating many of the stations. There were the original notes for salt which had circulated in lieu of money, copies of old land entries, grants, and deeds. The spelling was pretty bad. But in many cases it gave a wonderful clue to the way they spoke.

"Kittle" for kettle. "Buffaler" for buffalo. Old Isaac Skinner loses his temper. "Damn my cap and feather!" he says.

There was such a wealth of material that I couldn't hope to get through it alone. I brought my wife along and we examined it together paper by paper. If the spelling had been bad, the penmanship was worse. Moreover, the ink was faded, the old hand-made paper badly stained.

But gradually, it all began to come alive. Out of those musty records trooped the buckskin-clad company: John Burks, the hunter, who reckoned he knew the Knobs as well as any man; John McNew, who died of the smallpox; Jonathan Irons, who could handle his rowdy crew of saltmakers except when he was drunk—which unfortunately appeared to be most of the time.

They were very real people indeed. Rough and crude, perhaps, but vital; with a courage in the face of hardship that puts them in a special class. Hard men for hard, desperate times.

BRASHEAR'S STATION

The history of this region really begins with the settlement of Brashear's Station. In the early spring of 1779, a party of about 18 or 19 men left the fort at the Falls of Ohio. It is Isaac Froman who tells the story. Isaac was a young man at the time and he and his father, Jacob Froman, were members of the expedition that was starting out to build a new station.

Their pilot guided them south along an old buffalo path from the Falls almost to Bullitt's Lick. Bullitt's Lick was the hub of a great system of buffalo roads leading into it from all directions like the spokes of a wheel. Once they had passed through the Blue Lick Gap in the Knobs, though, they turned eastward away from Bullitt's Lick, falling into another buffalo path that led up Salt River on the north side. There, just below the mouth of Floyd's Fork where the buffalo path forded it, and between a quarter-and-a-half mile from the bank of Salt River itself, they selected a site and commenced building a fort.

The date is important. Early spring—March or April—1779.[10]

1777 had been the year of the bloody sevens when the settlements in Kentucky had shrunk to but three—Harrodsburg, Boonesboro, and Logan's.[11] The next spring, 1778, Clark had arrived at the Falls and a fort had been planted on Corn Island. During the fall of 1778, the settlers had built a fort on shore where they had spent the winter.[12] Then as soon as winter had broken, the party of 18 men had left to build Brashear's at the mouth of Floyd's Fork. The first station on the Wilderness Road between Harrodsburg and the Falls—antedating Bardstown, Cox's Station[13] and probably any of the stations that sprang up the same year on Beargrass Creek here in Jefferson County.[14]

Colonel Fleming, on his way from Harrodsburg to the Falls of Ohio in 1779, stopped at Brashear's Garrison, where he got some excellent "taffieo" drink—whatever that was.[15] He mentions no other stations on the road in all that vast stretch of wilderness and he was a remarkably astute observer.

Richard Collins in his history of Kentucky not only lists Brashear's Station but a "Salt River Garrison" as well on the lower waters of Salt River.[16] So does Willard Rouse Jillson in his *Pioneer Kentucky*, following Collins, I suppose.[17] Everywhere they are treated as two separate and distinct stations. As a result, I sought in vain for the location of Salt River Garrison. Then suddenly the mystery of Salt River Garrison was resolved by an old plat.

Brashear's Station and Salt River Garrison were one and the same.[18]

Confirmation followed thick and fast among the records at Shepherdsville, until there could no longer be the slightest doubt. To add further to the confusion, Brashear's Station had been called "Froman's" by some of the settlers as well as "Salt River Garrison."[19]

Brashear's, Salt River Garrison, or Froman's Station—it was referred to by all three names—is not to be confused with the Froman's Station in Nelson County, nor yet with Froman's Folly at Irons' Crossing on Salt River below the mouth of Bullitt's Lick Run.

For after helping to build Brashear's Station, Jacob Froman remained there only a couple of years. Then in 1781 he removed to a branch of Cox's Creek in Nelson County and built another fort not far from Rogers' Station.[20]

As for "Froman's Folly," there is but the briefest, tantalizing glimpse —its very existence only hinted at in a scrawled line in one of the old yellowed depositions.[21]

BULLITT'S LICK

About the time that Brashear's Station was being built, three men left the Falls to go hunting—Squire Boone, brother of the redoubtable

Bullitt's Lick

Daniel, William Moore, and James Lee. They had horses and traveled along the buffalo road, heading for Bullitt's Lick.

Squire knew the road for he had been this way before—as early as 1776, he deposes. When they reached the lick, they killed a couple of buffalo, skinned and butchered them and loading their horses with the meat, returned the way they had come.[22]

Consequently, no saltworks could have been erected at Bullitt's Lick by the spring of 1779. This seems fairly certain; for the big game invariably was driven away whenever a lick was "opened" for salt making.

However, in November of the same year, Colonel William Fleming, at the head of the land commission, was journeying from Harrodsburg to the Falls. After leaving Brashear's Station, he went through the Salt River flats to Bullitt's Lick, where he found a full scale saltworks in operation.[23]

Therefore, it would appear that the saltworks must have been erected some time between Squire Boone's visit and Colonel William Fleming's arrival. Probably in the summer of 1779.

Fleming writes in his journal:

"Nov. 13, 1779—Bullitt's Creek as it is cald is perhaps the best Salt Springs in the country ... They have a trough that holds very near 1000 gals. which they empty thrice in the 24 hours. They have 25 kettles belonging to the commonwealth which they keep constantly boiling and filling them up as the water waistes—from the trough first into kettles which they call fresh water kettles and then into others. After this management for 24 hours they put the brine into a cooler and let it stand till cold or near it and draw off the clear brine into the last boilers under which they keep up a brisk fire till they observe it begin to grain when they slacken the fire and keep them at a simmering boil till it grains. They then put it to drain. When drained they think it fit for use ... 3000 gals. of water boiled down yields from three to 4 and 4½ bushels. The dryer the weather, the better for making salt. These remarks I had from Chenith the manager."[24]

Colonel Fleming spent the night at the Saltworks and the next day he left for the settlement at the Falls, traveling along the buffalo path that was rapidly becoming one of the main traveled arteries in the wilderness.[25]

On December 25, 1779, just a little over a month later, another significant entry appears in Fleming's journal:

"We heard by a man from the Falls, the Indians had killed a man and a boy and taken two boys prisoners at the mouth of Floyd's Cr. near Brashear's Station and that the people had left the salt works and taken their kettles away, leaving the pots or kettles belonging to the publick."[26]

MUD GARRISON

Indians or no Indians, the Saltworks did not long remain idle. During the spring of 1780 the tide of emigration was running strong. The demand for salt grew greater and greater as new stations were erected. It rose in price to five hundred dollars a bushel, then to seven hundred dollars, in the depreciated currency.[27]

Sometime during that spring, the saltmakers came back; the wells were cleaned out; fires started anew in the furnace pits.[28] This time, however, they made preparations to protect their families at least against Indian depredations.

On the bank of Salt River not far from the lick, they built a fort—a double row of piles filled with earth and gravel from the river bank and enclosing about half an acre.[29]

Mud Garrison, as it came to be called, was first settled about the last of March or the first of April, 1780.[30] Not 1778, as Collins has it.[31] Nor was it located anywhere within the future environs of Shepherdsville, as Mr. Willard Rouse Jillson states.[32]

It was situated on the north bank of Salt River about a half mile above the mouth of Bullitt's Lick Run which put it very close to the Saltworks and at least a mile down river from the future site of Shepherdsville. For the accuracy of this, we have the words of old John Burks, the hunter; of Worden Pope, and a number of others—men who actually lived at the Mud Garrison or at one of the neighboring stations.[33]

Michael Teets and his wife, James Hamilton, and the Millers were among the company who built it.[34]

The garrison did not have an enviable reputation as the following passage from a deposition of James Daugherty bears witness:

"Q. Were the persons that first settled the Garrison men of respectability?

A. Mr. Teets, James Hamilton, and Mrs. Teets were people that might be relied on."[35]

Which was as far as Mr. Daugherty could be persuaded to commit himself.

They were a rough, hardy lot—these early, brawling saltmakers, the frontier levelers. The Saltworks, itself, was known as a "fair hell on earth."[36] General James Wilkinson describes them as a set of "sharpers," a classic example of the pot calling the kettle black.[37]

DOWDALL'S STATION

The third station to be established in the neighborhood was Dowdall's Garrison. Who founded the new station and when are still largely matters of conjecture. However, it was probably erected early in 1780 by settlers who found their quarters at Brashear's Station becoming cramped.[38]

Thomas and James Dowdall were among the first settlers at Brashear's Station. So were the McGees, but they all removed to Dowdall's, as well as a number of other families.

Whatever the cause, Dowdall's Station was built on the north side of Salt River about a mile below Brashear's Garrison. It was on a tract of land surveyed and patented in the name of Jacob Myers and known as Myers' 400-acre survey.[39]

The falls or rapids of Salt River begin at present-day Shepherdsville and extend a mile or more downstream, while above the falls lies a deep pool. Dowdall's had been erected on the upper bank of the river at this pool. It was an excellent site for a ferry and indeed, not long after the station was built, a ferry was established there—the first ferry across Salt River.

This ferry was to have considerable effect on the old Wilderness Road. Formerly, travelers going from the Falls to Harrodsburg after leaving Bullitt's Lick had journeyed up the north side of Salt River, fording the river about a mile below the mouth of Cox's Creek.[40] Now they could ferry across at Dowdall's and take another buffalo path that went up the south side of Salt River, ford Cox's Creek at the mouth of Rocky Run, and go up the east fork of Cox's Creek to Harrodsburg.[41] This route rapidly gained in importance.

The exact date when the ferry was first established and by whom is still pretty much a mystery. However, on the 25th of June, 1781, George Grundy leased from Jacob Myers the 400 acres including Dowdall's Garrison and the ferry. Grundy had to agree that he would respect any former indulgences that may have been given by Jacob Myers to the settlers at Dowdall's Station. But the important fact about the lease is that it reveals the ferry was in operation as early as June 1781.[42]

No description of the Salt River Ferry would be complete without some mention of Ben Pope and the McGees.

Benjamin and William Pope were brothers, who with their families had settled at the Falls of Ohio in 1779. They were shrewd, capable men, engaging in a great many pursuits—land speculation, the infant salt industry, politics, and trade—and any history of this region must take them into account.

Benjamin Pope removed with his family to Brashear's Station in 1783 where he lived a few months, then moved again, this time to Dowdall's.[43]

The McGees had arrived at the Falls about the same time as the Popes but they had gone straight inland to Brashear's Station.[44] Patrick McGee was a hunter, a land locator, and a saltmaker. The land across Salt River from Dowdall's had been entered by John Edwards, an early land speculator; it was first-rate land and Patrick McGee bought out Edwards' claim.[45]

Then in 1784, he and Ben Pope built a cabin or cabins on this tract on the south side of Salt River opposite Dowdall's Station and moved out of the protection of the garrison.[46] In 1787, Ben Pope traded some of his land on the Beech Fork to McGee for the ferry tract, as it had come to be called.[47] The Popes have owned and lived on this same tract ever since. Miss Sallie B. Pope lives there today, in the house of which the nucleus is the original hewn log cabin, built by Ben Pope and Patrick McGee.

The cabin, weatherboarded and plastered, occupies the northwest corner of the present building. It has been converted into a charming and spacious sitting room and hall. Only the thick walls hint at the time when it stood alone as a protection against Indian attack for travelers about to take the ferry across to Dowdall's. For in 1784 Patrick McGee had his house licensed as a tavern,[48] and the Popes operated the ferry there for many years.[49]

CLEAR'S STATION

I haven't been able to find out very much about the next station to be established—Clear's Station or Clear's Cabins,[50] as it was sometimes called.

Collins mentions it as being in Bullitt County.[51] He is right as far as he goes, but Bullitt County covers considerable territory. Some facts about it, however, have turned up in unexpected places.

Clear's Station was erected by George Clear well before 1783 and perhaps as early as 1780 or '81.[52] It was on Clear's Run, just a short distance above the crossing of the old Wilderness Trail from Louisville to Bullitt's Lick, and in the neighborhood of present-day Huber's Station on the L. & N. railroad.[53]

George Clear was unfortunate in picking his site; for Isaac Hite, Robert Shanklin, David Williams, Peter Casey, Ebenezer Severns, and Peter Higgins had traveled through this part of the country in company in the spring of 1776[54] and Shanklin had made an entry on the Blue Lick Run, of which Clear's Run is a branch. The conflicting claims were taken to court and Shanklin's was adjudged the better in so far as

Bullitt's Lick

their lands interfered. Clear only recovered 258 acres out of his original 1,400 acre settlement and pre-emption.[55]

Long before the case was settled, though, George Clear had employed Walker Daniel to defend his suit and had betaken himself off to the Ohio country.[56] But Clear's Cabins continued to be inhabited by settlers migrating to Kentucky. Isaac Hornbeck and his family moved to Clear's Station in 1783.[57] In 1784 the Shanklins came with their party, which included Mrs. Sodowsky and James Alexander.[58]

The road from the Saltworks at Bullitt's Lick to the Falls of Ohio ran a few hundred yards east of Clear's Cabins which nestled at the foot of the Lost Knob.[59] Colonel John Floyd in his scarlet cloak was ambushed by Indians almost within shouting distance of the station.[60] The colonel was mortally wounded. His brother, Charles, whose horse had been shot out from under him, leaped up behind the colonel and escaped, holding up his wounded brother in the saddle.[61]

What happened to Colonel Floyd after his brother had galloped off with him from the scene of the ambush has been for a long time the subject of considerable dispute.

A persistent rumor has survived that Charles carried his dying brother to the Saltworks at Bullitt's Lick which was only some three miles distant. There, the rumor goes, the colonel expired in one of the saltmaker's cabins and was buried at Bullitt's Lick.

Mr. Hamilton Tapp, however, in an article on Colonel John Floyd, denies emphatically that the wounded man was taken anywhere near Bullitt's Lick, let alone buried there. He goes on to make the statement that not one shred of evidence exists in support of the rumor.[62]

However, it's a dangerous thing to deny categorically so persistent a tradition.

As it happened, the observant Colonel Fleming was in Kentucky again and at Logan's Station when he received news of Floyd's death. On April 7, 1783, he made the following note in his journal:

". . . Gen'l. Clark and Mr. Daniels came up and informed us that Col. Floyds; One of his Brothers and another person going to the Saltworks were fired on by Indians. Col. Floyd mortally wounded, his Brother's horse shot under him, and the third person shot dead, that Col. Floyds with his Brothers assistance got to the salt works."[63]

Col. Fleming, of course, could have been misinformed.

Mr. Tapp states that Charles, bearing his mortally wounded brother, fled back the road the way they had come until they reached the cabin of a friend about five miles distant. There they stopped. Colonel Floyd died in the friend's cabin and his body subsequently was carried home to his station on Beargrass.[64]

Mr. Tapp doesn't identify the friend; however, in all fairness, Colonel James Francis Moore might have been settled at the Fishpools about five miles back the road as early as 1783. If he was, his was the only house on the road between Clear's Cabins and Sullivan's Old Station on the south fork of Beargrass.

Whether Colonel John Floyd was carried back to Colonel Moore's house at the Fishpools or ahead to Clear's Station or even to Bullitt's Lick isn't important in itself. Wherever he died, his body unquestionably was borne back to his station on Beargrass and there he was buried.

What does seem important is this invidious tendency to treat Bullitt's Lick like the skeleton in Kentucky's closet, to put it in historical coventry. Colonel Floyd can't even be allowed to die there in peace. I can't help but wonder why.

LONG LICK

The second saltworks to be erected in the neighborhood was at the Long Lick.

Long Lick Creek is a branch of Salt River. Its mouth is on the south side only a short distance below Bullitt's Lick Run. The Long Lick, itself, is about five or six miles in a general southeasterly direction from Bullitt's. Bardstown Junction lies just east of the site today and state highway 61 crosses Long Lick Creek almost at the lick.[65]

Parmenas Briscoe, a hunter at Brashear's Garrison, recognized its importance early and on November 11, 1780, he located an entry of four hundred acres in which he was careful to include the lick.[66]

Salt licks were eagerly sought out by the first settlers and land locators and the Long Lick was no exception. Besides Briscoe's pre-emption, Peter Phillips had a settlement and pre-emption right to 1,400 acres. Charles Chinn entered 1,000 acres on the Long Lick; Henry Spillman and John Cocky or "Cockeye" Owings entered 400 acres; John Bowman entered a thousand; John May and Mark Oyler entered 400; Benjamin Frye a thousand; Jacob Myer, 400, and John Friggs, 200.[67]

Most of these claims overlapped to a greater or lesser extent. It was confusion compounded. The wrangling in court was dragged out for 50 years.

However, the most important of the claims to the Long Lick was none of these, but a 250-acre warrant, which Charles Broughton had entered November 11, 1780, the same day that Briscoe had made his entry. The two entries covered almost the same ground. Nevertheless, Charles Broughton went ahead and erected a saltworks on the land some time before the 27th of October, 1785, when he had his entry surveyed. It was the first saltworks on Long Lick Creek.[38]

In 1784, Nelson County had been formed out of Jefferson. Salt River was the dividing line and the Long Lick fell in the new county.[69] Shortly after the saltworks was erected, Henry Crist and Solomon Spears acquired Briscoe's claim.

Whether Briscoe's claim was superior or not is still uncertain. In any event, Crist and Spears took over Broughton's saltworks as early as 1787 and the next year a patent for the land was issued on Briscoe's survey in their names.[70]

Henry Crist was a remarkable young man. He cannot be treated adequately in a paper of this scope. Tradition describes him as a small man, almost tiny in stature, but with an unquenchable drive, vigorous, colorful, autocratic, and contentious. Lawsuits were his ruin. At one time he laid claim to thousands of acres; when he died, he was practically penniless.[71]

He rose to the rank of General during the War of 1812 but his abiding interest was business. His life was bound up with land speculation, trading, and the salt industry generally—first at the Long Lick, then later at Bullitt's.

Henry Crist was from Pennsylvania. He was only fifteen years old when he arrived at the Falls of Ohio in 1780.[72] While still in his teens, he was acting as a land locator for another Pennsylvanian by the name of Jacob Myers.[73] Jacob Myers at one time probably claimed more land in Kentucky than any person before or since. A great many of Jacob Myers' claims lay in present-day Bullitt County—claims which Henry Crist helped to locate and for which Crist received a moiety of one half the land for his services.

He could not have been much over twenty when he and Solomon Spears bought out Briscoe's entry at the Long Lick. He was only 23 when the famous Battle of the Kettles took place on Salt River in 1788.

There is a vivid account of the battle in Collins' History and I won't repeat it here but Solomon Spears was killed and Crist seriously wounded.[74]

Close to the Long Lick proper and a little further down the creek from it was a second lick known as the Dry Lick. Charles Broughton had another entry for 500 acres which joined his 250 acres on the Long Lick. The 500-acre tract included the Dry Lick, and this he had managed to hang on to. When he lost out at the Long Lick he began to prospect for salt water on his Dry Lick property.

Luck was with him. He found an excellent vein of salt water, sunk a well and soon was back in the salt-making business. Broughton never gave up the Dry Lick. He and his heirs, the Shains, after him, continued to make salt there through all the ups and downs of the trade.[75]

The Long Lick and the Dry Lick were about a mile apart. Though separate and distinct operations, they were so closely associated that any account of one is incomplete without some mention of the other. Both of them had a long and colorful history and the names of some of the oldest families in Bullitt County are coupled with the salt trade there—Henry Crist, Adam Shepherd, Thomas Shain, James Bowman, Thomas Speed, Joshua Frye, Nacy Brashear, to mention only a few.

MANN'S LICK

The third lick to be opened was Mann's Lick. Third in point of time, perhaps, but second only to Bullitt's Lick itself in importance! Mann's Lick lay to the north of Bullitt's Lick in amongst the ponds and wetwoods near the site of present-day Fairdale in Jefferson County.[76]

There has been, perhaps, more confusion regarding the date when salt was first made at Mann's Lick than at any of the other licks. One author, in an excess of zeal, puts it back as early as 1780.[77] Fortunately the record is clear and irrefutable.

Mann's Lick was well known to the earliest settlers at the Falls. In 1780, John Todd made an entry on a military warrant for 200 acres, including Mann's Lick. James Speed entered 600 acres adjoining Todd's entry the same year. Overlapping entries followed thick and fast. George James and Daniel Sullivan, Bracket Owens, William Garrard, James Francis Moore, Levin Powell, George Slaughter, James McCawley, John Hamilton—all of them made entries there.[78]

Nevertheless, no settlement was attempted; the land remained drowned in ponds and swamps, a hunting ground only, until Joseph Brooks entered the scene in 1787.[79]

Joseph Brooks was a Pennsylvanian also. At the age of twenty-five he emigrated to Kentucky with his family, arriving at the Falls in the spring of 1780. He lived at Spring Station on the Beargrass until February 1781, when he moved to the Saltworks at Bullitt's Lick, where he remained until 1784.

In 1784, he bought a land entry at Phillips' Spring on the road between the Falls and the Saltworks. There he built a cabin and took his family to live.[80]

Phillips' or Stewart's Spring, as it was alternately called, was a famous camping place on the road.[81] In 1785, Brooks obtained a license and began to operate a tavern in his house.[82] Gradually it took the name of Brooks' Spring and is known so to this day. It is still visible on the Blue Lick Pike a short distance south of the Bullitt County line.[83]

Joseph Brooks was a shrewd, capable man. Moreover, he had lived

Bullitt's Lick

and worked at the Saltworks at Bullitt's Lick for three years. He was quick to see the possibilities of Mann's Lick.

John Todd was dead,[84] the land was in contention,[85] but in the fall of 1787, Joseph Brooks approached Todd's widow and secured her agreement to let him have the lick for a term of six years. The first two years he was to have it rent-free for erecting a saltworks there. Thereafter, he was to pay her only 100 bushels of salt per year. Brooks had a bargain and he knew it.[86]

Unfortunately the widow Todd did not have an undisputed title. William Fleming owned a quarter interest and James Speed claimed a quarter interest in addition to his own adjoining entry. In 1788, Speed rented the lick to George Wilson, who put up a saltworks close to Brooks' furnaces.[87] There was room for both, however, and they seemed to have gotten along amicably enough.

Eventually more wells were sunk, more furnaces built. Wilson bought out Fleming and became one of the proprietors. Brooks acquired part of the land outright also. The Speeds, Charles Beeler, Colonel James Francis Moore, and William Pope all were operating saltworks at Mann's Lick or engaged in the salt trade. There was an island in the Big Pond. Wells were sunk on it and more furnaces built.[88]

To Joseph Brooks, however, must go the honor of being the man who first opened Mann's Lick.

Unlike Bullitt's Lick, Mann's Lick was fortified to some extent.[89] In 1788 when Brooks moved there, the danger from savages was acute. Moreover, it occupied a peculiarly exposed situation with the knobs on one hand and the swampy wetwoods on the other. In the bitter winter months, wolves came right into the lick and pulled down the stock.

Nevertheless, a new day was at hand. From Mann's Lick on the north to Long Lick on the south, the forest was falling before the wood choppers. The furnaces devoured wood at a fearsome rate. The sound of ax strokes filled the air.

EXTENT OF SALT TRADE

The contrast between this salt-producing region that straddled Salt River and the rest of Kentucky at this early date was so great that it is hard to make it comprehensible.

Salt was beginning to be produced at a few other places throughout the state, but nowhere else was there such a concentration of wells and furnaces. Hundreds of men were employed in the actual industry as wood choppers and waggoners, kettle tenders, and water drawers. Many more, such as hunters and store keepers, coopers, and carpenters, were directly involved. People came from all over the wilderness to procure the precious salt—merchants, traders, private individuals in companies for protection against savages.

Salt was sent by pack train and flatboat and pirogue to the District Mero in Tennessee, to the Illinois, to Kaskaskia, from one end of the wilderness to the other. Bullitt's Lick must have taken on something of the nature of a boom town—a startling, unbelievable sight to the hunters in from the deep woods, to the settlers from their lonely clearings.

Louisville was a sickly place, due to ponds and swamps, and was growing painfully slowly. Lexington was only a small stockade. Frankfort had not yet been established.

Money was scarce but trade was carried on by means of barter and notes. The complications and obstacles were enormous and confusing.

It has been difficult enough to try to unravel the bewildering system of exchange. But the actual process of salt making was worse. It was an utter mystery.

It is very easy to say that the salt water was evaporated in kettles. This is so general that it is meaningless.

Let me quote from a letter written by one Thomas Perkins from Lincoln County, February 27, 1785. He is writing to the Honorable J. Palmer in Braintree, Massachusetts:

"Honored Sir: It is not from inattention or forgetfulness that I have suffered your inquiries concerning the salt springs of the country to remain thus long unanswered; but from a hope that by this time I might be able to give you some satisfactory account of them. I must, however, confess that notwithstanding all the information I am able to get I am still as ignorant of the matter as I was the moment I came into the country.

"The owners of these springs reside commonly in the old part of Virginia or Maryland and carry on the business of salt-making by negroes and ignorant people under the direction of an overseer as ignorant as themselves; so that it is impossible to learn anything from them worth hearing.

"I have seen but one spring of consequence in this district which is at a place called Bullitt's Lick on a small branch of Salt River. . . . At this spring, by the best information I could get, about 40 gallons of water will produce a bushel of salt. At the distance of a quarter of a mile from the spring is a small mountain . . . from the bottom of which the salt water appears evidently to proceed; and they now dig wells between the spring and the mountain 30 or 35 feet deep, and that the nearer they approach the mountain, the stronger the water is impregnated with salt.

Bullitt's Lick

"It is remarkable that the water from which they boil the salt is almost as black as ink, owing, as it is supposed, to its passing through a . . . pit of coal; and this idea is strengthened by the smell of the water when boiling, resembling that of the burning of coal, with a very strong mixture of sulphur. This blackness, however, disappears before the water is half boiled away; and the salt appears perfectly clean and white and is made with so much ease, notwithstanding they labor under every inconvenience, from the want of proper pans, etc., that they can well afford to sell it at $3.00 per bushel . . ."[90]

So much for Thomas Perkins. He was on the ground while the saltworks was still a going concern. I wasn't so fortunate.

Actually, as near as I have been able to determine,[91] the furnaces were long trenches dug back along the top of a bank. They were walled with slate about 15 inches thick which was laid with a mortar of clay. The kettles themselves held about 22 gallons each—sometimes they were bigger—and they sat on top of this trench in a row, with as many as fifty in the string. The furnace was fired from in front, the flames and smoke being sucked along under the kettles and out through a stone chimney at the far end of the pit. Generally they were protected from the elements by a shed roof supported on poles. It was quite common for two of these long narrow furnace pits to be under a single roof.

The water was boiled for about twenty-four hours, then transferred to a cooler—a trough, which acted as sort of a settling tank, I presume. Then the clear, saturated brine was drawn off into the kettles again, and boiled rapidly until it began to grain. Sometimes blood was added to purify the water, or the white of an egg.

When it began to grain, or form salt crystals, the fires were slackened but not so much as to stop it boiling and the salt was dipped out by hand as it formed, and put in baskets to drain.

The drippings were caught in pans, and returned to the "mother" as the water in the kettles was called. These kettles holding the mother were never allowed to boil dry. When the mother got too low, water which had been previously boiled twenty-four hours was let into them and the boiling down repeated.

However, after a certain number of boilings, the mother became so charged with impurities that it was necessary to throw it out and the whole process started over again.

The first wells were dug wells and shored with timber instead of stone. Later they were deepened by boring in them with an auger. Sometimes dikes were thrown up around them to keep out flood water and usually roofs were built over them.

The furnaces or pits were erected at some distance from the well, close to a good stand of timber, for it wasn't considered profitable to haul wood much more than a mile. It was easier to move the furnace to a new stand of trees.

If the furnace was situated close enough to the well, the water was brought to the pit by means of a covered wooden trough or flume. As wood grew scarce about the licks, the furnaces were moved further and further off. The water was conveyed to them through wooden pipes made from gum or sassafras logs. These wooden pipes were bored out by hand, fitted together, and a wooden or iron sleeve fashioned around the joints. Then a trench was dug and they were buried beneath the frost line. Some of these strings of pipes went for miles.

One string went from Bullitt's Lick all the way to Shepherdsville, crossed Salt River and ended at the furnace a half mile south of the river. Another left Bullitt's Lick following the general course of the Pitt's Point road to a furnace located well within the present boundary of the Fort Knox reservation.

These are only two examples. The pipe lines sprangled out in all directions. Miles of the old pipes must still be preserved in the ground about Bullitt's Lick and Mann's Lick, the Long Lick, and the Dry Lick.

The hungry furnaces brought about another paradox in the neighborhood. In most parts of the state, cleared land was at a premium. Sometimes a man would be given half of the land he cleared in payment for the laborious job of clearing it.

In the neighborhood of the saltworks, however, timbered land was ten times as valuable as cut-over ground. The competition for firewood grew more and more bitter all the time, until it got to be as much as a man's life was worth, if he was a landowner, to try to protect his own timber from the ravages of the saltmakers.

Poor Benjamin Stansberry, who owned 500 acres close to Bullitt's Lick, testified that the saltmakers had broken his arm when he had tried to stop them from cutting and carrying off his wood. Moreover, they added insult to injury, reviling and abusing him whenever he was forced to go into the lick on business.[92]

FORT NONSENSE

Earlier, I mentioned that a great buffalo road forded Salt River below the mouth of Bullitt's Lick Run. It led from Bullitt's Lick to Long Lick and soon became a favorite crossing for travelers going between the two licks because it was considered less dangerous during times of Indian trouble than the ford up river at the future site of Shepherdsville.[93] Sometime in 1785 or possibly earlier, a station was erected on the north side of Salt River not far from this buffalo ford. For some reason it was called Fort Nonsense.[94]

It was located within the bounds of Jacob Froman's 1,670-acre survey that joined Christian's "Bullitt's Lick Tract" on the lower side. And in one deposition it is referred to as "Froman's Folly."

William Farmer had a 700-acre claim on Salt River that lay wholly within Jacob Froman's entry and took in the site of Fort Nonsense also. Farmer's claim was superior and Jacob Froman lost that part of his land where Fort Nonsense was located.[95]

It is possible that the Fromans built Fort Nonsense on what they thought was their land only to be dispossessed by William Farmer—hence the name "Froman's Folly" or Fort Nonsense.

However, this is merely conjecture. Practically nothing is known about Fort Nonsense. Collins mentions it but gives neither the date it was established nor the location.[96]

Fortunately, salt water was discovered in the bank of the river at the buffalo ford across from Fort Nonsense or I might never have found its site.

Jonathan Irons, a salt maker at Bullitt's Lick, purchased that part of Farmer's entry which included Fort Nonsense. He acquired some land on the opposite side of the river from the old fort and commenced prospecting for salt water. In 1798, he found it almost in the bed of the river just a few steps from the buffalo ford. One of his wells was actually half in the river bed.[97]

Thus Irons' Lick was the next to be opened for salt making and was situated on the south side of the river across from Fort Nonsense. Irons moved to the site of the fort and there took up his residence.[98]

Jonathan Irons was a colorful character; illiterate, too generous for his own good, given to long drinking sprees which eventually killed him.[99]

The buffalo crossing gradually became known as Irons' Crossing, and Fort Nonsense as Irons' saltworks. In time even these names were no longer used until finally the fact that there had been a famous saltworks on the river bank was entirely forgotten.

THE SALTMAKERS

Colonel William Christian, the proprietor of Bullitt's Lick, did not come to Kentucky until 1785, and then he was promptly killed by Indians the following year.[100] In his will, he left "Saltsburg," as Bullitt's Lick had come to be called, to his son, John Henry Christian.[101] The colonel's passing made very little difference to the saltmakers.

An agent had handled Christian's interests at Bullitt's Lick before he emigrated, leasing the saltworks to various operators. John H. Christian was under age; Anne Christian, his mother, was appointed his guardian and by her direction an agent still handled affairs at Bullitt's Lick.[102]

Moses Moore leased the whole lick, subletting to half a dozen or more men who operated furnaces independently.[103] This was the general procedure at all the licks in the neighborhood. There were a score of independent operators at Bullitt's and Mann's Licks, not so many at the Long Lick and only one or two at the Dry Lick. Even Jonathan Irons was soon leasing out his new saltworks at Irons' Lick.[104]

John Christian's mother, however, died before he came of age and Patrick Henry was appointed the boy's guardian. The procedure, however, didn't change materially. Walter Warfield was Henry's agent. The independent operators banded together and tried to rent the lick themselves from Warfield, but Moses Moore went to Virginia and secured a lease directly from Patrick Henry. The case was taken to court, but Moses seems to have won out in the end.[105]

Then John Henry Christian died shortly after coming of age, leaving his sisters as heirs to the saltworks at Bullitt's Lick. The fat was in the fire, at last.

There were five sisters and each of them had a fifth share in the property. Alexander Scott Bullitt had married one sister and John Pope had married another. The Popes acquired some of the interest of the remaining sisters, so that in the end William Pope, Jr., brother of John Pope, controlled three-fifths of Bullitt's Lick and the Bullitts the remaining two-fifths. The Bullitt's Lick-Mann's Lick Company was formed and an attempt made to regulate the salt trade. "Deposits" were built to store the salt—one at Shepherdsville to accommodate the output of Bullitt's Lick, and one near South Park for Mann's Lick.[106] Old Deposit Station on the L. & N. Railroad was not a pioneer settlement but a warehouse in which to store salt.[107]

This wasn't the first time that an effort had been made to gain a monopoly in the pioneer salt industry.

General James Wilkinson, according to Dr. Thomas Clark, very nearly succeeded shortly after he came to this state.[108] And in 1792 four men—Thomas Smith, Moses Moore, Phillip Buckner, and Jonathan Owsley, under the name of Moses Moore and Company—leased the Long Lick from Adam Shepherd and Henry Crist. They already controlled Mann's Lick and Bullitt's Lick and they let the Long Lick lay idle in an effort to force up the price of salt.[109]

How successful they were I do not know.

In any event, the Bullitt's Lick-Mann's Lick Company, some ten years later, did very much the same thing. They notified the independent operators that once their current leases had expired, they would not be renewed.

Thus, during part of the year 1802, Bullitt's Lick lay idle. The first time such a thing had happened since 1779 when the Indians had caused the saltmakers to abandon their works.

Salt shot from a dollar to three dollars a bushel and it wasn't to be had then except for cash.[110]

PARAKEET LICK

Always a certain amount of prospecting for salt water went on in the neighborhood. The town of Shepherdsville had been established in 1793.[111] Then Bullitt County was formed in 1796 out of parts of Jefferson and Nelson, and Shepherdsville was made the county seat.[112] About a half mile above Shepherdsville was a pretty little lick on the north bank of Salt River known variously as McGee's Lick or the Parakeet Lick from the flocks of these colorful birds that frequented the place. Here James Burks discovered salt water and secured a lease from the McGees, who owned the tract of land it was on.

Burks was to have the lick for two years rent-free for opening it. However, he didn't have the necessary cash for the kettles.

The salt water was never too plentiful at Parakeet Lick nor was it of a very high order. It is doubtful that the lick would have been opened had it not been for the machinations of the Bullitt's Lick-Mann's Lick Company.

The scarcity of salt in 1802 and 1803, though, guaranteed the success of the venture. John Dunn, who had plenty of kettles, formed a partnership with James Burks and in 1803 they commenced making salt at the Parakeet Lick.[113]

The McGees, James Alexander, and John McDowell all subsequently made salt at Parakeet Lick.[114] It was abandoned, though, not too long after Bullitt's Lick started up again. Its later fame as a watering place completely eclipsed its earlier, rougher history. For this was the famous Paroquette Springs, one of the most fashionable spas of the old south. The sulphur well was, in reality, one of the old salt wells. Its metamorphosis must have come as a shock, indeed, to the old settlers who could remember it in its ruder days.[115]

For a while in the first years of the nineteenth century, the saltworks at Bullitt's Lick flourished like the green bay tree. It was also the heyday of the flatboatmen, and an extensive salt pork and whisky trade was carried on with New Orleans. But the coming of the steamboat was to bring an end to both the saltworks and flatboating.

Salt finally could be imported cheaper than it could be made by the crude processes in use at the licks. Better methods of extracting salt were being discovered and richer veins of salt water.

When Henry Crist bought out the Bullitt interest in the lick in 1814,[116] it was still flourishing but its years were numbered. Eventually Crist acquired the whole lick, but by that time, salt making was barely profitable.[117]

The saltmakers managed to hang on grimly for a while in spite of everything. But the odds against them had mounted until finally they were operating at a loss. In 1830 the fires were allowed to go out under the last kettle.[118] Cahaz Knob finally looked down on peaceful farm land.

It is difficult to realize how completely time and nature have obliterated nearly all evidences of the saltworks at Bullitt's Old Lick. Several years ago Ben Miller, who owns the site today, was plowing up a cornfield and uncovered the chimney remains of a few of Saltsburg's cabins. The ash banks from the furnaces have given the earth a grayish cast in places. A few metal shards can be picked up about the pits. The wells have been filled up. Even Crist's big black well is only a saucer-shaped depression.

This is a sort of plea, I suppose. A plea for Bullitt's Lick and the surrounding area to be accorded recognition—to be given its proper niche in history. A plea for markers to be placed at these sites before it is too late.

We mark battlefields, but this was more than a battle. This was an epoch in the conquest of the wilderness.

FOOTNOTES

[1] John Bakeless, *Daniel Boone, Master of the Wilderness* (New York, 1939), p. 156 ff.; Thos. D. Clark, "Salt, A Factor in the Settlement of Kentucky," *Filson Club History Quarterly*, XII (1938), p. 43; Geo. W. Ranck, *Boonesborough*, The Filson Club Publications No. 16 (Louisville, 1901), p. 64.

[2] John Filson, *Kentucke, and the Adventures of Col. Daniel Boone*, facsimile reproduction, ed. by Willard Rouse Jillson (Louisville, 1934), pp. 32-3, original published Wilmington, 1784. Filson writes, "At present there is but one, Bullitt's Lick, improved, and this affords salt sufficient for all Kentucke, and exports some to the Illinois."

Jos. Brooks Heirs vs. *Geo. Reed et. al.*, Bullitt Circuit Ct., Decrees No. 76. Depositions of Chas. Whitaker, 23 Aug. 1811; Wm. Pope, Sr., 22 Aug. 1811; Jacob Vanmeter, 23 Aug. 1811; John Tuell, 23 Aug. 1811; all say that the saltworks at Bullitt's Lick supplied the whole country with salt from about 1779 through 1783.

Sanders & Rogers vs. *Benjamin Summers et. al.*, Bullitt Circuit Ct., Decrees No. 101. Bill, filed 18 Aug. 1812, states that on the 3rd. Feb. 1783, there was no place in the present state of Kentucky where salt was made except at Bullitt's Lick. Depositions of James McCawley, 1 Mar. 1814; Benjamin Stansberry, 1 Mar. 1814; Jos. Brooks, 1 Mar. 1814; James Patton, 25 June 1814, James Guthrie, 25 June 1814, repeat in substance the above statement. However, James Welch, 2 Mar. 1814, says that he understood from information that salt was made at the Blue Licks about that time (3 Feb. 1783). Welch's information was not far wrong but is misleading. *Cf.* footnote 9 for salt making at the Blue Licks.

Equity suits tried at the Bullitt Circuit Ct. are filed in numbered bundles labeled "Decrees."

[3] Lewis & Richard H. Collins, *History of Kentucky* (Covington, 1882), II, 17-18; H. Marshall, *The History of Kentucky* (Frankfort, 1824), I, 31.

[4] State Land Office: Frankfort, Ky.

[5] Cary Robertson, "Salt and the Part It Has Played at Shepherdsville," *Louisville Courier-Journal*, Nov. 7, 1926, quotes Dr. C. G. Crist as saying that the saltworks started 1778. Hewitt Taylor, "Shepherdsville," *Louisville Herald Post*, Sept. 23, 1936, puts the first settlement back as early as 1775. Collins, *op. cit.*, II, 18, quotes a deposition by Bland Ballard who says that salt was made at Bullitt's Lick in 1780-81. By far the majority of authors, however, hazard no opinion beyond saying that salt was made at Bullitt's Lick at a very early date.

[6] A bibliography of works on the Wilderness Road would form a respectable volume, but in almost every case only the eastern leg from Virginia to Harrodsburg is treated with any thoroughness. Filson's *Kentucke*, on his map of 1784, shows it continuing on from Harrodsburgh through Bullitt's Lick to Louisville, but information about this end of it in the works of later historians is conspicuous by its absence. Thos. Speed, *The Wilderness Road*, Filson Club Publications No. 2 (Louisville, 1886) and Wm. Allen Pusey, *The Wilderness Road to Kentucky* (New York, 1921) are both excellent books, but deal primarily with the eastern leg, and the route from Harrodsburgh to Louisville is located in only the most general way. Even so fine a work as Robert L. Kincaid, *The Wilderness Road* (Indianapolis, 1947), does little to dispel the mystery surrounding this end of it.

[7] Thomas D. Clark, *A History of Kentucky* (New York, 1937), p. 9. Dr. Clark does say that salt was made at several licks near Salt River, but they are left anonymous.

[8] At Big Bone Lick, salt was not manufactured until the early 1790's; Clark, "Salt, A Factor in the Settlement of Kentucky," *Filson Club History Quarterly*, XII, p. 43; Willard Rouse Jillson, *Big Bone Lick* (Louisville, 1936), pp. 87-90.

At Drennon's Lick small saltworks were erected in the winter of 1785, Draper MSS., 12 CC 108, photostat copy in The Filson Club Library.

References to the Draper MSS. throughout this article will be either to the photostat copy of the "Kentucky Papers" or the microfilm copy at The Filson Club. For salt making at the Blue Licks, see footnote 9.

[9] "David Tanner owned the Lower Blue Licks. Settled the summer of 1784 . . . Tanner set up 4 kettles. Didn't pretend to make salt himself, but rented his kettles for the ½ that they made." Draper MSS., 12 CC 29.

[10] *Wm. Pope, Jr. et. al.* vs. *Thos. Stansberry et al.*, Bullitt Circuit Ct., Decrees No. 68; Deposition of Isaac Froman, 10 Nov. 1807.

The names of the 18 or 20 men in the party described by Froman might be among the following, all of whom were "resedenters" of *Brashear's Station* in the spring of 1779: Jacob Froman, Sr. & 2 of his sons, Isaac Froman & Jacob Froman, Jr., also his brother, Paul Froman; William Brashear, Sr. & his eldest son, Nicholas Rue Brashear; Spencer Collings & Zebulon Collings, brothers; James Daugherty; John Ray & Benjamin Ray; William Overall & John Overall; Nicholas Crist, Sr.; Patrick McGee & Thomas McGee, brothers; Thomas Phelps; David Hawkins, Sr., his two sons, John Hawkins & David Hawkins, Jr.; Andrew McMeans; James Young; Conrad Oyler; John Philips & Thomas Philips. This list is incomplete; nor does it necessarily contain the names of the *builders* of Brashear's Station. Only two are certain: Jacob Froman, Sr. & his son, Isaac.

[11] Collins, *op. cit.*, I, p. 19; Bakeless, *op. cit.*, p. 144.

[12] Wm. Hayden English, *Conquest of the Country Northwest of the River Ohio 1778-1783 and Life of Gen. George Rogers Clark* (Indianapolis, 1897), I, p. 131.

[13] Cox's Station was built and first settled in 1780, not 1775 as the marker on the outskirts of Bardstown reads. *David Collings* vs. *McGee's Heirs*, Bullitt Circuit Ct., Decrees No. 58; Deposition of Jeremiah Anderson, 1 Aug. 1820, which says that "Old David Cox & his family, Isaac Cox & his family, Joseph Inlow & his family, and Stephen Ashby, & I think Wm. Ashby, John Bennett & his family & myself [Jeremiah Anderson] & family" landed at Louisville in 1780. They came on to Brashear's Station, where Isaac Froman then piloted them up Salt River to the mouth of Cox's Creek. When asked, "Did you go to a fort when you got to Cox's Creek?" Anderson replied, "We did not. We went to where Cox afterwards built a fort." There were no improvements except token improvements to hold the land.

Anderson's testimony is borne out by depositions of other settlers, notably David Cox himself.

[14] Col. Floyd did not arrive at the Falls of Ohio until 8 Nov. 1779. Thus Floyd's Station could not have been erected until some time after Brashear's was built. Spring Station was settled in 1780, Draper MSS., 11 CC 221. This is substantiated in numerous depositions, particularly those in *Jos. Brooks* vs. *John Edwards, et al.*, Bullitt Circuit Ct., Decrees No. 45. Sullivan's Old Station, Sturgus Station, Linn's Station, the Dutch Station & Hoglin's, appear to have been established in 1780 also. See above depositions.

[15] "Colonel Wm. Fleming's Journal of Travels in Kentucky, 1779-1780," published in Newton D. Mereness, ed., *Travels in the American Colonies* (New York, 1916), p. 620.

[16] Collins, *op. cit.*, I, p. 24.

[17] Willard Rouse Jillson, *Pioneer Kentucky* (Frankfort, 1934), p. 100.

[18] *Pope* vs. *Stansberry, loc. cit., Cf.* footnote 10; surveyor's plat made by James Shanks, surveyor of Bullitt Co., 29 Aug. 1809, on which he marks the site of Brashear's Garrison at the mouth of Floyd's Fork on north side of Salt River and labels it: "Froman's or Brashear's or Salt River Garrison, alternately so called."

[19] *Brooks* vs. *Edwards, loc. cit., Cf.* footnote 14; Deposition of Wm. Pope, Sr., 6 Feb. 1817, calls it "Froman's or Brashear's Station"; Deposition of Jacob Shively, 8 Feb. 1817, calls it "Froman's or Brashear's Station"; Deposition of David Hawkins, 1 Mar. 1817, says he lived at "Froman's otherwise Brashear's Station."
Sanders vs. *Summers, loc. cit., Cf.* footnote 2; Deposition of Jos. Brooks, 1 Mar. 1814, calls it "Salt River Garrison or Salt River Fort" near the mouth of Floyd's Fork; also in same deposition he speaks of it by the name of "Brashear's Station"; Entry of Thos. Owsley, 29 May 1780, calls for "Salt River Fort or Salt River Garrison."
Collings vs. *McGee's Heirs, loc. cit., Cf.* footnote 13; Deposition of Patrick McGee, 29 Apr. 1820, who says he resided in 1779 at "Salt River Garrison," which was located where the Town Fork (of Salt River) and Floyd's Fork meet; he also says that Isaac Froman, Zebulon Collings & Spencer Collings resided there at that time. Isaac Froman, Zebulon & Spencer Collings, however, all lived at "Brashear's Station"; and Spencer Collings, 17 Apr. 1820, says he resided at "Brashear's Station" near the mouth of Floyd's Fork on the lower side of the fork in 1779, and names Patrick McGee, Thos. McGee, Zebulon Collings & Isaac Froman as being hunters at the station at that time.
Walter Brashear vs. *Henry Crist*, Bullitt Circuit Ct., Decrees No. 61; Deposition of John Overall, 9 Sept. 1816, states that he moved to "Salt River Station" at the mouth of Floyd's Fork on Salt River in June, 1779; Deposition of John R. Gaither, 18 Sept. 1816, says he was at "Brashear's Garrison" at the mouth of Floyd's Fork in April, 1780.
James Taylor & Wife vs. *Henry Hawkins*, Bullitt Circuit Ct., Decrees No. 108: Deposition of Worden Pope, 20 Aug. 1825, who says, "Froman's or Brashear's Station was near Floyd's Fork and about half a mile from the mouth." He says further that he lived at "said Froman's or Brashear's Station" a part of the spring and summer 1783.
James Taylor & Wife vs. *Richard Stringer et. al.*, Bullitt Circuit Ct., Decrees No. 109: Deposition of Spencer Collings, 15 Sept. 1820, says he settled in May 1779 below mouth of Floyd's Fork at a station generally called "Brashear's Station and sometimes Froman's Station."
Matthew Patton's Heirs vs. *Thos. Speed et. al.*, Bullitt Circuit Ct., Decrees No. 43: Deposition of John Overall, 20 Feb. 1809, states that he resided at "Brashear's Station" near the mouth of Floyd's Fork. In another deposition (see above) he calls it "Salt River Garrison."
This is only a sampling; there are many more depositions and some plats. All agree as to the site of the garrison, and by far the majority called it "Brashear's Station."

[20] *Pope* vs. *Stansberry, loc. cit., Cf.* footnote 10: Deposition of Isaac Froman, 10 Nov. 1807. For location of Froman's Station in Nelson Co. see *Taylor & Wife* vs. *Hawkins*, and *Taylor & Wife* vs. *Stringer* in the Bullitt Circuit Ct. Also cases in Nelson Circuit Ct. at Bardstown and in Jefferson Circuit Ct. at Louisville.

[21] *Brooks* vs. *Edwards, loc. cit., Cf.* footnote 14: Deposition of James Daugherty, 22 Feb. 1817, says "Froman's Folly where Mrs. Irons now lives" (1817) was settled by 1780. He is probably in error about the date.

[22] *Brooks Heirs* vs. *Reed, loc. cit., Cf.* footnote 2; Deposition of Squire Boone, 23 Aug. 1811.

[23] *Fleming's Journal*, 1779-80, *op. cit.*, p. 620.

[24] *Ibid*, pp. 620-1. Punctuation is author's.

[25] *Ibid*, p. 621.

[26] *Ibid*, p. 626.

[27] *Wm. Shannon* vs. *Admr. of Evan Hinton, Dec'd.*, Jefferson Circuit Ct., No. 248. Equity suits in the Jefferson Circuit Court are filed according to number.

[28] *Brooks Heirs* vs. *Reed, loc. cit., Cf.* footnote 2: Deposition of Jacob Vanmeter, 23 Aug. 1811, in which he says that he moved his family to Bullitt's Lick in Aug. 1780.

Brooks vs. *Edwards, loc. cit., Cf.* footnote 14: Deposition of James Daugherty, 22 Feb. 1817, says he moved to Bullitt's Lick, May 1780. Deposition of Patrick McGee, 25 Feb. 1817, says that he worked at Bullitt's Lick in May 1780. Deposition of James Welch, 28 May 1817, who testifies that he made salt at Bullitt's Lick for part of the summer 1780.

[29] *Collins, op. cit.,* II, p. 102.

[30] *Jacob Bowman* vs. *Thos. C. Brashear,* Nelson Circuit Ct., Bardstown: Deposition of James Daugherty, 27 June 1811.

Equity suits at Bardstown originally were filed in Bundles of Decrees and labeled with the year the final verdict was handed down. However, the bundles are now stored quite haphazardly and the labels missing in most cases. Suits tried in the old Supreme Court, Bardstown District, and the Nelson Circuit Court are all together. Index volumes were kept locked in a cabinet at the request of a microfilming project and were *not* made available to the author. Consequently there is no means to locate a particular suit except to go through them one bundle at a time.

[31] *Collins, op. cit.,* II, p. 21.

[32] Willard Rouse Jillson, *Pioneer Kentucky,* p. 96. Jillson says, Mud Garrison . . . "established during or shortly prior to 1778. It occupied a part of the present township of Shepherdsville."

[33] *Taylor* vs. *Hawkins, loc. cit., Cf.* footnote 19: Deposition of Worden Pope, 20 Aug. 1825, who says that it was about half a mile from the said Mud Fort or Garrison to the mouth of Bullitt's Lick Run. Worden Pope was the son of Benjamin Pope, Sr., and lived at Brashear's Station in 1783, then in Dowdall's Garrison. Worden ran the Salt River Ferry at Dowdall's Garrison. Later he became Clerk of Jefferson County. His depositions are always precise and accurate due, no doubt in part, to his legal work.

Jacob Bowman vs. *Jonathan Irons,* Nelson Circuit Ct., Bardstown: Deposition of John Burks, Sr., 3 Aug. 1804, who says Mud Garrison was about half a mile above the mouth of Bullitt's Lick Run.

John Burks, Sr., was a hunter, who arrived at the Falls of Ohio in 1779; he accompanied Geo. R. Clark's expedition to the Iron Banks, was in Fort Jefferson during the siege, and returned to Louisville in the summer of 1781 after Fort Jefferson was abandoned. It took them 32 days to come up the river.

Burks and his family then settled at Floyd's Station on Beargrass, where he was one of the principal hunters for the station. Chas. Floyd in his depositions refers to him constantly in the capacity of woodsman. About 1785 Burks removed to Bullitt's Lick.

John Burks' knowledge of the country was phenomenal and he was called on for depositions in regard to landmarks as long as he lived. The courts of Jefferson, Bullitt, and Nelson counties contain many of these depositions.

[34] *Bowman* vs. *Brashear, loc. cit., Cf.* footnote 30. The following list of settlers at Mud Garrison is far from complete and is compiled from several cases as well as the above: Michael Teets & his wife (Spring 1780); John Irwin (Spring 1780); James Hamilton (Spring 1780); James Daugherty (1781); Matthew Withers (1784) James Purcell (1781); Samuel Miller (May 1780); Nacy Brashear & family (1784), which included Robert Brashear, Thos. C. Brashear & Ignatius Brashear.

[35] *Ibid,* Deposition of James Daugherty, 27 June 1811.

[36] John Robert Shaw, *Life and Travels of John Robert Shaw,* originally published Lexington, 1807, ed. Geo. Fowler, facsimile reproduction (Louisville 1930).

[37] *Collins, op. cit.,* II, 370.

[38] The following list of settlers who resided at Brashear's Station does not pretend to be complete. It is compiled from the court records in Bullitt, Jefferson, and Nelson counties:

Wm. Brashear, Sr. & his family, which included his wife, Anne Brashear, his children: Nicholas Ray Brashear, William Brashear, Jr., Joseph Brashear, Sally Brashear, Elizabeth Brashear, Nancy Brashear & Jemima Brashear.

Jacob Froman, Sr., his brother Paul Froman, & Jacob's family which included Jacob Froman, Jr., Isaac Froman, and Absolom Froman.

Thomas Phelps & his children: Anthony Phelps, Guy Phelps, Edwin Phelps, Lucy Phelps.

John Ray, Nicholas Ray, Nicholas Crist, Parmenas Briscoe, Wm. Shain, David Hawkins, Sr., David Hawkins, Jr., John Hawkins, James Daugherty, Spencer Collings, Wm. E. Collings, Thomas Collings, Zebulon Collings, Peter Cummins & his family, John R. Gaither & Mary, his wife, Ben Pope, Sr. & Ben Pope, Jr., Worden Pope, Elizabeth Cummins, Cornelius Bogart, Wm. Overall & John Overall, Benjamin Ray, Peter Potmy & Nancy, his wife, Timothy Cummins, Fatima McClelland, Sally Thomas, Thomas Dowdall & James Dowdall, Thomas McGee, John McGee & Patrick McGee.

[39] *Guy Phelps* vs. *John McDowell,* Bullitt Circuit Ct., Decrees No. 126.
[40] *Taylor* vs. *Stringer, loc. cit., Cf.* footnote 19: Depositions of James Guthrie, 21 Aug. 1820; Geo. A. K. Pomeroy, 21 Aug. 1820; James McKeaig, 21 Aug. 1820; David Cox, 14 Sept. 1820; & other depositions in this case.
[41] Henry Crist's Papers, formerly in the possession of Mrs. W. V. Mathis, Mt. Washington, Ky. These were the personal papers of Gen. Henry Crist and contained much valuable information relative to pioneer Bullitt County, land speculations, and the salt industry. Fortunately the author was able to examine them before Mrs. Mathis' death. The present whereabouts of the Crist papers are unknown to the author. The above references, however, are from copies of depositions which H. Crist had among his papers from the case of *Thos. Rowland* vs. *Geo. Wilson & Henry Mitchel,* tried at the General Court, Frankfort, Ky.
[42] Jefferson County Court Minute Bk. "A," p. 8.
[43] *Taylor* vs. *Hawkins, loc. cit., Cf.* footnote 19: Deposition of Worden Pope, 20 Aug. 1825.
[44] *Collings* vs. *McGee's Heirs, loc. cit., Cf.* footnote 13: Deposition of Patrick McGee, 29 Apr. 1820.
[45] *John R. Gaither* vs. *Michael Troutman's Heirs,* Bullitt Circuit Ct., Decrees No. 39: Deposition of Patrick McGee, 2 June, 1817.
[46] *Ibid,* Depositions of Gordon Grundy, 2 June 1817; Levi Simmons, 2 June 1817; Patrick McGee, 2 June 1817; *Taylor* vs. *Hawkins, loc. cit., Cf.* footnote 19: Deposition of Worden Pope, 20 Aug. 1825.
[47] *Benjamin Pope, Jr.* vs. *Patrick McGee,* Bullitt Circuit Ct., Judgments No. 1. Cases tried in the common law side of the Bullitt Circuit Court are filed in numbered bundles labeled "Judgments."
[48] Jefferson County Court Minute Bk. 1, 8 Apr. 1784.
[49] *Collins, op. cit.,* II, p. 388. "Benjamin [Pope] . . . removed to Salt River, and settled about 1½ miles below Shepherdsville in Bullitt County. Near there his son Worden was engaged in running a ferry . . ."
Benjamin Pope, Sr., settled about 1½ miles *above,* not *below,* Shepherdsville, and the ferry was at Dowdall's Garrison. See deposition of Worden Pope, 20 Aug. 1825, *Taylor* vs. *Hawkins, loc. cit., Cf.* footnote 19. This is another instance of the errors which crop up repeatedly regarding this region. The Collins, both father and son, compiled a stupendous amount of material and all later historians owe them a great debt, but they could not be too critical by the very nature of their work. A great many of their statements must be carefully checked before reliance can be put in them.
[50] *Brooks* vs. *Edwards, loc. cit., Cf.* footnote 14: Deposition of Chas. Floyd, 14 May 1817, and 15 May 1817.
[51] *Collins, op. cit.,* II, pp. 18, 100.
[52] *Jos. Brooks* vs. *Geo. Clare,* Bullitt Circuit Ct., Decrees No. 4. 22 Dec. 1783, Geo. Clear assigned one-half of his settlement and preemption, including "the station commonly called *Clear's Station"* to Walker Daniel. See Bill, *Brooks* vs. *Edwards, loc. cit., Cf.* footnote 14. Deposition of James Welsh, 28 May 1817, who testifies that Clear's Station, Dowdall's, Mud Garrison and Brashear's were settled by 1780.
[53] In locating and checking the site of Clear's Station, the work has been rather involved: See depositions, surveys and plats in the following cases at the Bullitt Circuit Court, Clerk's Office, Shepherdsville:
Wm. Pope, Jr., et. al. vs. *Thos. Stansberry et. al.; Jos. Brooks* vs. *Geo. Clare; Jos. Brooks* vs. *John Edwards et. al.; Jos. Brooks Heirs* vs. *Geo. Reed et. al.; Wm. Pope, Jr., et. al.* vs. *Samuel Hornbeck et. al.; James Ferry* vs. *Thos. James; Jos. Sanders & Edward Rogers* vs. *Benjamin Summers et. al.*
The old trace from the Falls of Ohio to the Saltworks at Bullitt's Lick was roughly the same as the route of the present Blue Lick Pike. Clear's Station was on Clear's Run a short distance upstream from the crossing of the old trace.
This trace from Bullitt's Lick to the Falls of Ohio was the last leg of the original Wilderness Road. From Bullitt's Lick it passed through the Blue Lick Gap, then by Clear's Station, Brooks Spring, the Fish Pools, Moore's Spring, ran about 200 yards west of the Beech Spring, crossed Fern Creek close to where the creek emptied into the Ash Pond, went through the Flat Lick, through the Poplar Level and so on to the Falls of Ohio (Louisville). See depositions in above cases.
[54] *Patton's Heirs* vs. *Speed, loc. cit., Cf.* footnote 19: Depositions of David Williams, 10 May 1806; & Robert Shanklin, 10 May 1806. The company named were on a "tour of improving"; that is, they were selecting sites on which to locate land claims. A cabin 2 or 3 logs high would be built and some trees deadened by ringing them. These token

improvements were meant merely to hold the land, and are no indication at all as to when actual settlement took place, if ever.

[55] *Brooks* vs. *Clare, loc. cit., Cf.* footnote 52.
[56] *Ibid.*
[57] *Brooks* vs. *Edwards, loc. cit., Cf.* footnote 14: Deposition of Samuel Hornbeck, 22 Feb. 1817.
[58] Draper MSS., 11 CC 217.
[59] *Brooks* vs. *Edwards, loc. cit., Cf.* footnote 14: Deposition of Archibald Fraim, 21 Feb. 1817, who says the knob near Clear's Station was called "Lost Knob."
[60] The precise spot where Col. Floyd and his party were ambushed is shown on an old plat made by James Halbert, surveyor of Bullitt Co., 26 Feb. 1814, and filed in the case of *Sanders* vs. *Summers, loc. cit., Cf.* footnote 2. According to the plat, Floyd was ambushed about midway between Brooks Spring and Clear's Station on the trace from the Falls of Ohio to Bullitt's Lick. On a modern map it would be close to where the present Blue Lick Pike crosses the southernmost branch of Brooks Run. The site of Floyd's ambush was a landmark to the early settlers. Jos. Brooks took James Robinson along the old buffalo trace and pointed it out to him in the summer of 1785, *Brooks* vs. *Edwards, loc. cit., Cf.* footnote 14: Deposition of James Robinson, 22 Feb. 1817.
[61] Hamilton Tapp, "Colonel John Floyd, Kentucky Pioneer," *Filson Club History Quarterly*, XV (1941), pp. 21-2; Draper MSS., 5 B 66-67; Collins, *op. cit.*, II, p. 239, etc. The sources for this are numerous.
[62] Tapp, *op. cit., Filson Club History Quarterly*, XV, p. 24.
[63] "Col. Wm. Fleming's Journal of Travels in Kentucky, 1783," reprinted in Newton D. Mereness, ed., *Travels in the American Colonies* (New York, 1916), p. 672.
[64] Tapp, *op. cit., Filson Club History Quarterly*, XV, p. 22.
[65] The site of the Long Lick Saltworks is located on a plat made by James Shanks, Surveyor of Bullitt Co., 22 Aug. 1806; *Patton's Heirs* vs. *Speed, loc. cit., Cf.* footnote 19. The buffalo road from Bullitt's Lick to Long Lick is laid down also as well as the Dry Lick. The above location is borne out by a plat made by James Halbert, Surveyor of Bullitt Co., 28 Feb. 1814, *Wm. Shain* vs. *Jacob Bowman*, Bullitt Circuit Ct., Decrees No. 23. Also in numerous depositions filed with these and other cases.
The site of the Dry Lick is to be found on the farm of T. W. Hoagland, Bardstown Junction. Mr. Hoagland inherited this property from his father, R. I. Hoagland. The Dry Lick, itself, and many of the wells are still visible.
[66] *Patton's Heirs* vs. *Speed, loc. cit., Cf.* footnote 19. Copy of Briscoe's entry.
[67] *Ibid.* Peter Phillips, 15 Feb. 1780, by John Bowman, entered 1400 acres on Long Lick Creek. 11 May 1780, Charles Chinn entered 1000 acres. 9 May 1781, Henry Spillman & John Cocky Owings entered 400 acres. 27 June 1780, John Bowman entered 1000. 23 Dec 1782, John May & Mark Oyler entered 400 acres. 27 May 1780, Benjamin Frye entered 1000 acres. 13 May ——, Jacob Myers entered 400. 7 Aug. 1781 John Friggs entered 200 acres. Copies of all these entries are filed with the above case. They all were located in the neighborhood of the Long Lick.
[68] *Shain* vs. *Bowman, loc. cit., Cf.* footnote 65. Copies of Broughton's entries are filed with the case. On the 27 Oct. 1785, Broughton's entries were surveyed; the survey for the 250 acres to begin: "On the south bank of Long Lick Creek about 40 poles above where the said Broughton has erected saltworks on said creek. . . ." Thus the saltworks had to be in operation by the 27 Oct. 1785.
[69] Wm. Walter Herring, *The Statutes at Large, Virginia General Assembly* (Richmond, 1823), XI, p. 469.
[70] *John McGee's Heirs* vs. *Wm. Shain*, Bullitt Circuit Ct., Decrees No. 33. The grant to Solomon Spears & Henry Crist was issued 6 Oct. 1788 on Briscoe's entry and survey including the Long Lick and the saltworks which had been erected there.
[71] See records of numerous cases in Bullitt Circuit Ct.; the old Supreme Court, Bardstown District, as well as the Nelson Circuit Court; the General Court at Frankfort and the Court of Appeals, etc. Tract after tract of Crist's lands were sold off to satisfy debts. In his last years he was forced to transfer title of nearly all his property to friends and relatives in order to save any of it.
[72] *Taylor* vs. *Stringer, loc. cit., Cf.* footnote 19: Deposition of Henry Crist, 2 Aug. 1825.
[73] Collins, *op. cit.*, II, p. 102.
[74] *Ibid*, II, pp. 102-6. In regard to Crist and Spears, one of the most misleading statements of all is to be found in Clark, *op. cit., Filson Club History Quarterly*, XII, p. 49, in which Dr. Clark says: "In 1788 a party from Louisville under the leadership of Henry Crist and Solomon Spears went to the Mud Garrison in what is now Bullitt County, to make salt. This area was well known, for when this party arrived, they found a fortification and several saltmakers already on the ground."

The party which Dr. Clark describes was transporting a flatboat load of salt kettles up Salt River. They never did arrive for they were ambushed by Indians. Spears was killed and Crist dragged himself into Bullitt's Lick on his hands and knees. Moreover, it is highly questionable that they were going to Mud Garrison; it is much more probable that they were taking the kettles to the Long Lick where Crist and Spears had a saltworks in operation. As for finding several saltmakers on the ground, I expect they would have been dumbfounded if they hadn't. The saltworks at Bullitt's Lick in 1788 was one of the most notorious and populous regions in all the wilderness, and Henry Crist had been intimately acquainted with it since 1780.

[75] *Shain* vs. *Bowman, loc. cit., Cf.* footnote 65.

[76] Plats and Surveys showing location of Mann's Lick are quite numerous among the Chancery Cases at the Bullitt Circuit Ct. See especially: *Brooks* vs. *Edwards, loc. cit., Cf.* footnote 14.

[77] Marguerite Threlkel, "Mann's Lick," *Filson Club History Quarterly*, I (1927), pp. 169-176. Her source appears to be *Collins, op. cit.*, II, p. 242, in which Collins relates that in 1780 a party from Bryan's Station & Lexington started for "Mann's Lick" to procure salt, but were ambushed on the way and the expedition abandoned.

Willard Rouse Jillson, *Early Frankfort and Franklin County* (Louisville, 1936), p. 39, in describing the same incident, qualifies it by saying that the party intended to boil down the salt water at Mann's Lick themselves; but as no well had been dug there at that time, such an act does not seem probable, particularly in view of the fact that a saltworks was in operation at Bullitt's Lick. Indeed, Jillson has perpetuated most of Collins' errors when treating of this region.

Geo. W. Ranck, "The Story of Bryan's Station," published in Reuben T. Durrett, ed. *Bryant's Station and the Memorial Proceedings, etc.*, Filson Club Publications No. 12 (Louisville, 1897), p. 78, states correctly that the party of men from Bryan's Station & Lexington started for "Bullitt's Lick" after salt.

Jillson, *Pioneer Kentucky*, p. 121, says incorrectly that Mann's Lick was established as a salt station before 1786. *Collins, op. cit.*, II, p. 20, makes the same mistake, which is repeated again in "News and Comment," *Filson Club History Quarterly*, V (1931) p. 44.

Threlkel, *supra*, quotes James Wilkinson's letter of 19 Dec. 1786, regarding the salt trade, and infers that Wilkinson was speaking of Mann's Lick though he does not mention it by name. This letter together with a second by Wilkinson was published originally in *Collins, op. cit.*, II, p. 320, and has been reprinted scores of times since. Dr. Thos. Clark reprints it again, *op. cit., Filson Club History Quarterly*, XII, p. 44, and says that Wilkinson achieved a virtual monopoly of salt in the Lexington area and at Mann's Lick and Bullitt's Lick. But the fact is that salt wasn't manufactured at Mann's Lick in 1786. Thus Wilkinson could not have been speaking of Mann's Lick.

[78] *Wm. Garrard & Jos. Brooks* vs. *James Francis Moore*, Old Supreme Court, Bardstown District. Also *James Speed & Mary Owen Todd et. al.*, vs. *Geo. Wilson et. al.*, Jefferson Circuit Ct., No. 267.

[79] *Todd* vs. *Wilson, Supra.* See especially the Bill, filed about Feb. 1792, only four years after the first saltworks had been erected at Mann's Lick; also Jos. Brooks' Answer, 2 Mar. 1792. The facts here stated are incontestable.

See also *Brooks* vs. *Edwards, loc. cit., Cf.* footnote 14: Deposition of Joseph Sanders, 25 Feb. 1817, in which he says that Mann's Lick was first opened and worked as a saltworks about 1787 or 1788. Deposition of Chas. Floyd, 15 May 1817, says Mann's Lick was settled in the year 1787 or 1788.

[80] *Dougherty* vs. *Beall et. al.*, Jefferson Circuit Ct., No. 483: Deposition of Jos. Brooks, 17 Feb. 1818.

Brooks vs. *Edwards, loc. cit., Cf.* footnote 14: Deposition of Wm. Pope, Sr., 6 Feb. 1817, who says Jos. Brooks settled at Brooks Spring in 1784.

Brooks Heirs vs. *Reed, loc. cit., Cf.* footnote 2: Deposition of James McCawley, Sr., 18 Sept. 1815, who says, "I know your family lived at that spring [Brooks] in the year 1784 in the summer six or eight days before Walker Daniel was killed" [because] "I lay at his house all night and got my supper there." Deposition of Thos. C. Brashear, 18 Sept. 1815, says Jos. Brooks lived on the trace from the Falls of Ohio to Bullitt's Lick in the summer 1784.

[81] *Brooks' Heirs* vs. *Reed, loc. cit., Cf.* footnote 2: Depositions of James Guthrie, 22 Aug. 1811; Jacob Vanmeter, 23 Aug. 1811; Thos. Philips, 23 Aug. 1811; John Tuell, 23 Aug. 1811; James Daugherty, 23 Aug. 1811; John Philips, 23 Aug. 1811; Meshach Carter, 23 Aug. 1811; Benjamin Philips, 23 Aug. 1811; Samuel Haycraft, 23 Aug. 1811; David Standiford, 23 Aug. 1811; James Pursell, 23 Aug. 1811; Geo. Pomeroy, 23 Aug. 1811; James Stevenson, 23 Aug. 1811; Adam Shepherd, 23 Aug. 1811; Chas. Whittaker,

23 Aug. 1811; Squire Boone, 23 Aug. 1811; James Patton, 24 Aug. 1811; James Welsh, 24 Aug. 1811; & John Hundley, 28 Jan. 1812.

[82] 9 Apr. 1785—License was granted Jos. Brooks to keep a tavern at his house—Jefferson County Court Minute Book 1, p. 106.

[83] The spring is about 15 yards east of the Blue Lick Pike, while the site of Brooks' Cabins is partly on the present road bed and partly on the west side above the spring on the property of Burks Williams. Tradition has it that the cabins were fortified and the fortifications extended to include the spring. In 1785 Jos. Brooks returned to Pennsylvania and brought out James Robinson and his family, who settled at Brooks' Spring also. However, it seems questionable that it ever was a stockaded garrison such as is generally meant by a Kentucky station.

[84] Colonel John Todd was killed at the battle of the Blue Licks in 1782. Theodore Roosevelt, *The Winning of the West* (New York, 1889), II, p. 197ff. The Blue Licks here referred to are those on the Licking River in Nicholas County; and are not to be confused with the Blue Licks in Bullitt County.

[85] *Speed* vs. *Wilson*, *loc. cit.*, *Cf.* footnote 78.

[86] *Ibid*, Answer of Jos. Brooks, 2 Mar. 1792.

[87] *Ibid*, Bill, about Feb. 1792.

[88] The Big Pond was also known as Oldham's Pond. The Ash Pond and several smaller ones were adjacent and in times of high water joined in one body of water. Fishpool Creek, Fern Creek, Greasy Creek, etc., ran into these ponds just west of the present Preston St. Road near Okolona. At the lower end the ponds drained into Pond Creek. The Big Island lay in Oldham's Pond. Today the L. & N. Railroad tracks almost bisect what was the Big Island and the Medical Depot is built on it.

[89] *Collins, op. cit.*, II, p. 102.

[90] *Proceedings of the Massachusetts Historical Society 1871-1873* (Boston, 1873), pp. 38-39.

[91] The description given has been drawn from a great many fragmentary sources. Hundreds of notes, affidavits, contracts, agreements, and depositions were examined in the Bullitt Circuit Ct., the Nelson Circuit Ct., and the Jefferson Circuit Ct. *Col. Wm. Fleming's Journal 1779-80* contains a partial account previously noted. So does *The Virginia Gazette*, microfilm copies of which are at the Louisville Free Public Library. Thos. Perkins' letter contributed some additional information. Mr. T. Holsclaw, who lives on the Blue Lick Pike, was able to supply some facts regarding several of the pipe lines and the furnaces. So was Ben Miller, Shepherdsville, Ky., who owns and operates the farm where Bullitt's Lick formerly was located. T. W. Hoagland gave me invaluable help in regard to the Dry Lick.

There is an excellent account of saltmaking at Mann's Lick in Marguerite Threlkel's article, "Mann's Lick." There are also accounts in Willard Rouse Jillson's *Big Bone Lick*; Thos. Clark's *Salt a Factor in the Settlement of Kentucky*, all of which have been previously cited. The 9th edition of the *Encyclopedia Britannica* also contains an excellent article on saltmaking.

[92] *John Scott, Sr., vs. John McGee*, Bullitt Circuit Ct., Decrees No. 19: Deposition of Benjamin Stansberry, 16 May 1808.

Men were sometimes engaged by property owners to protect their timber from being pillaged by the saltmakers; John Scott received £20 per annum for preserving the timber on the Parakeet Lick Tract. See Deposition of James Burks, 16 May 1808, who says, "It was worth a good deal to keep trespassers from Bullitt's Lick off the defendant's [John McGee] land as they were continually trying to get wood off the land of others, and off his [Burks'] land, and this deponent would not have been willing to take twenty pounds per year to have taken care of the defendant's land." See also other Depositions in the above case.

[93] *Bowman* vs. *Irons*, *loc. cit.*, *Cf.* footnote 33: Deposition of John Burks, Sr., 3 Aug. 1804.

[94] *John H. Christian* vs. *Jacob Froman*, Nelson Circuit Ct. Wm. Christian had a 2,000-acre entry on Salt River joining and around his 1,000-acre grant that included Bullitt's Lick. His 2,000-acre entry was surveyed 6 Jan. 1786; the beginning corner was on the bank of Salt River near and above *Fort Nonsense*. Thus Fort Nonsense was in existence as early as 1785.

Bowman vs. *Brashear*, *loc. cit.*, *Cf.* footnote 30: Depositions of John Irwin, 3 Oct. 1810; James Hamilton, 3 Oct. 1810; Michael Teets, 3 Oct. 1810; John Overall, 27 June 1811; Wm. Chenoweth, 27 June 1811; John Ray, 26 July 1802; James Daugherty, 27 June 1811; David Hawkins, 27 June 1811; Atkinson Hill, 17 Oct. 1811; John Essery, 26 July 1802; all give information regarding the location of Fort Nonsense, the buffalo crossing & Irons Saltworks.

[95] *John McDowell* vs. *John Machir*, Nelson Circuit Ct., Bardstown. Wm. Farmer's 700 acres on Salt River opposite the mouth of Long Lick Creek was entered 29 June 1780. Jacob Froman entered 1,000 acres adjoining Wm. Christian's military survey on the lower side 13 Sept. 1780, thus Farmer's entry was superior. Froman's 1,000 acres interfered only in part with Wm. Farmer's 700-acre tract; then 16 Jan. 1784 Froman entered an additional 700 acres to join his former entry of 1,000 acres. Upon survey Jacob Froman's two entries contained only 1,670 acres, but nevertheless covered Wm. Farmer's 700 acres completely. Fort Nonsense was located in the southeastern quarter of Wm. Farmer's 700-acre survey on the north bank of Salt River and about one-fourth mile upstream from the mouth of Long Lick Creek. See also *Bowman* vs. *Brashear, loc. cit., Cf.* footnote 30; and *Bowman* vs. *Irons, loc. cit., Cf.* footnote 33.
[96] *Collins, op. cit.,* II, 100.
[97] *Bowman* vs. *Irons, loc. cit., Cf.* footnote 33.
[98] *Ibid*: Depositions of Benj. Stansberry, John McDowell, 17 Apr. 1801; John Burks, Sr., 3 Aug. 1804; James D. Young, 31 Aug. 1804; John R. Gaither, 20 Aug. 1803; Joseph Simmons, 20 Aug. 1803; John Essery, 20 Aug. 1803; David Grable, 3 Aug. 1804; Jacob Froman, 31 Aug. 1804; Wm. Overall, 1 June 1804; & Wm. Chenoweth, 1 June 1804.
[99] *Henry Crist* vs. *Jonathan Irons' Heirs et. al.,* Bullitt Circuit Ct., Decrees No. 51; *Agnes Irons* vs. *Robt. Wicliffe,* Bullitt Circuit Ct., Decrees No. 62; *Jonathan Irons* vs. *John W. Hundley,* Bullitt Circuit Ct., Decrees No. 10.
[100] *Collins, op. cit.,* II, p. 106.
[101] Katherine G. Healy, "Calendar of Early Jefferson County, Kentucky Wills: Will Book No. 1; April 1785-June 1813," *Filson Club History Quarterly,* VI (1932), p. 5.
[102] *Patrick Henry* vs. *Moses Moore,* Jefferson Circuit Ct., No. 325.
[103] *Ibid*: Bill, 2 July 1795, and Answer, 12 Aug. 1795. The names of some of the operators of salt furnaces who leased from Moses Moore are as follows: Archer Dickinson, T. W. Cochran, Witle Barrow, Daniel Banta, Wm. Hines, Nathaniel Harris, Isaac Skinner, John McDowell, James Latham, Andrew Price, Jesse Hood, Benjamin Stebbins, Samuel Hancock & John Moore.
[104] For Mann's Lick see: *James F. Moore* vs. *James Richardson et. al.,* Jefferson Circuit Ct., No. 180; *Wm. Forwood et. al.* vs. *David Wise,* Jefferson Ct., No. 99; *Christopher Burckhard* vs. *John Speed, John Lemaster & Matthew Love,* Jefferson Circuit Ct., No. 28.
For Long Lick see: *Thos. Smith et. al.* vs. *Adam Shepherd & Henry Crist,* Jefferson Circuit Ct., No. 279; also numerous small suits on the Common Law side of the Bullitt Circuit Ct.
For Dry Lick see: *Nathaniel Harris* vs. *Armstead Morehead,* Bullitt Circuit Ct., Judgments No. 1.
For Irons Lick see: *Jonathan Irons* vs. *Joshua Hobbs* etc., Nelson Circuit Ct., Bardstown.
[105] *Henry* vs. *Moore, loc. cit., Cf.* footnote 102.
[106] *Richard Bibb, Sr.* vs. *Wm. Pope, Jr.,* Bullitt Circuit Ct., Judgments No. 51.
[107] News and Comment, *Filson Club History Quarterly,* V (1931), p. 44, says incorrectly that "Brooks Station like its neighboring settlements at Bullitt's Lick, Deposit Station and Mann's Lick was probably established before 1786." The deposit for Mann's Lick Salt was built after 1800. See *Bibb* vs. *Pope, loc. cit., Cf.* footnote 106.
[108] Clark, *op. cit., Filson Club History Quarterly,* XII (1938), p. 44.
[109] *Smith* vs. *Shepherd, loc. cit., Cf.* footnote 104.
[110] *Bibb* vs. *Pope, loc. cit., Cf.* footnote 106; *Robert Luckey* vs. *Jos. Lewis,* Bullitt Circuit Ct., Decrees No. 12.
[111] Wm Littell, *The Statute Law of Kentucky* (Frankfort 1809), I, p. 183. Shepherdsville was established on a 900-acre tract of land patented in the name of Peter Shepherd. Peter Shepherd, however, died in Maryland in the year 1787. He had nothing to do with establishing Shepherdsville and does not appear ever to have been in Kentucky. The land was devised to his son Adam Shepherd who was in the state as early as 1780, looking after his father's interests. Adam Shepherd was the founder of Shepherdsville.
[112] *Ibid,* I, p. 364.
[113] *John Dunn* vs. *James Burks,* Bullitt Circuit Ct., Judgments No. 68. James Burks was the son of John Burks, Sr. The Parakeet Lick was on a 450-acre survey on Salt River between Shepherd's 900-acre tract including Shepherdsville on the west, and Jacob Myers' 400-acre tract including Dowdall's Garrison on the east.
[114] *Phelps* vs. *McDowell, loc. cit., Cf.* footnote 39.
[115] *Ibid.*
[116] *Crist's Papers, op. cit.,* Copy of contract between Henry Crist and Cuthbert Bullitt & Elizabeth Dickenson.
[117] *Henry Crist* vs. *Cosby Crenshaw,* Bullitt Circuit Ct., Decrees No. 159.
[118] *Ibid.*

ROBERT E. McDOWELL (1914–1975) was editor of *The Filson Club History Quarterly* from 1971 until his death in March 1975. Although born in Oklahoma, many of his family roots were in Kentucky, and he received his bachelor's degree at the University of Louisville. He was a successful novelist who enjoyed writing on historical subjects; his best-known historical works are *City of Conflict* and *Rediscovering Kentucky: A Guide for the Modern Day Explorer*. He was also author of the drama "Home Is the Hunter," which related the story of the establishment of Fort Harrod.

This article first appeared in *The Filson Club History Quarterly* in July 1956, vol. 30, pp. 241–69.

THE HARPES, TWO OUTLAWS OF PIONEER TIMES*

Otto A. Rothert

The story of the Harpes is more than that of mere criminals. They were arch-criminals apparently loving murder for its own sake. Any account of the barbarities they committed in Kentucky and Tennessee would be looked upon as wild fiction if the statements therein were not verified by court records and contemporary newspaper notices, or were they not carefully checked with the sketches of early writers who gathered the facts from men and women who lived at the time the crimes were committed.

It should be borne in mind that the exploits of outlaws in pioneer times greatly affected settlement of the new country. Dread of highwaymen brought peaceful frontiersmen together and thus built up communities and helped to hasten the establishment of law and order. The lives of early outlaws are therefore a part of the history of the country. The historian who passes them over as mere blood-and-thunder tales misses entirely one of the high lights in the great adventure of the settling of the Ohio and Mississippi valleys.

The atrocities of the two Harpes—Big Harpe and Little Harpe—at the close of the eighteenth century, have rarely been equaled in the annals of crime. Their motives were clouded in such mystery, and their outrages were so heartless, that Collins, the Kentucky historian, referred to them as "the most brutal monsters of the human race."

Their joint career as murderers covered a period of only two years, but it was terrible while it lasted. At that time, 1798-99, Kentucky and Tennessee were sparsely settled. The then-called West was well nigh a wilderness. Among its pioneer population were men who, as fugitives from justice, had

---
*This synopsis of the story of the Harpes was read before The Filson Club at the October, 1924, meeting. The details of the careers of the Harpes and the Masons are given in Mr. Rothert's book, *The Outlaws of Cave-in-Rock*.

deliberately sought safety away from the eastern states. The Ohio and Mississippi rivers were infested with pirates; the early rivermen themselves were a rough and violent type. Isolation led the well-meaning to be generous and confiding to those whom they had tested; but to a great degree might was right, and strangers looked askance at each other and prepared for the worst. Yet such a rude and hardy people as this was gripped with horror at the unmeaning and unprovoked atrocities of the Harpes.

It is difficult in these days of well-ordered government to realize the mysterious terror and excitement that began near Knoxville in 1798 and swept through the wilderness to the borders of the Mississippi and across the Ohio into Illinois as some sudden, creeping fire breaks out in the underbrush, and grows steadily in intensity and rage until it sweeps forests before it. All this was, in a measure, realized in the breasts of human beings as the crimes of the Harpes increased.

The Harpes were believed to be brothers. They were natives of North Carolina. Micajah, known as Big Harpe, was born about 1768, and Wiley, known as Little Harpe, was born about 1770. Their father was said to have been a Tory soldier.

The Tories who, after the Revolution, still sympathized with the King of England and continued to live in the "old settlements" were, in most sections, ostracized by their neighbors. It was to this ostracized class that the parents of the Harpes belonged; and thus it was in an environment of hatred that the two sons grew up.

About 1795 the young Harpes left North Carolina for Tennessee, accompanied by Susan Roberts and Betsy Roberts. Big Harpe claimed both women as his wives. Shortly after their arrival near Knoxville, Little Harpe married Sallie Rice, daughter of a preacher.

From cheating and trickery at horse racing the two men drifted to horse and hog stealing. Their downright criminality soon asserted itself when they set fire to houses and barns. After having been arrested several times—escaping each time before being placed in jail—they decided to leave East Tennessee. Before going they killed a man named Johnson. They ripped open his body, filled it with stones, and threw it into the Holstein River. Despite this caution the stones became loosened.

The corpse rose to the surface and was discovered a few days later. This killing of Johnson seems to have been their first murder. It was followed by many others, but the true number will never be known. Travelers vanished and left no trace, but the Harpes moved with great celerity.

We next hear of them and their women on the Wilderness Road in Kentucky. Three more victims were on their list by the time they arrived at the tavern of John Farris near Crab Orchard. No one of the tavern suspected who the new arrivals were. There they met Stephen Langford, of Virginia, who had come alone. Langford decided it would be safer to travel with companions through the wilderness than to go unaccompanied. A few days later—December 14, 1798—men driving cattle over the road leading to the Farris tavern accidentally discovered the body of a man concealed behind a log. It was identified as that of Langford. Suspicion fell on the Harpes. They were pursued and captured, and placed in the Stanford jail. On January 4, 1799, the two men and their women appeared before the judges of the Lincoln County Court of Quarter Sessions. They were held for murder, and their case was transferred to the Danville District Court.

The next day a strong guard took the prisoners to Danville, ten miles away, to await trial in April. On March 16 both Big Harpe and Little Harpe escaped, leaving their three women and three jail-born infants behind.

The jailer evidently had felt there was some likelihood that his charges would escape, for his account shows he bought, on January 20, 1799, "Two horse locks to chain the men's feet to the ground, 12 shillings, and one bolt, 3 shillings;" on February 13, "One lock for front jail door, 18 shillings," and on February 27, "Three pounds of nails for the use of jail, 6 shillings."

How the Harpes escaped is not known; the jailer's expense account shows a charge of 12 shillings for "Mending the wall of the jail where the prisoners escaped."

Such was the state of affairs when, on April 15, the trial of the women began. Five days were devoted to hearing evidence, and the trial ended in the acquittal of the women. They declared that, above all things, they desired to return to Knoxville and there start life anew. It was believed that they had obtained a happy release from their barbarous masters, and therefore a collection of clothes and money was taken among the citizens of Danville, and an old mare given, to help them on their way to Tennessee.

The jailer accompanied the three mothers to the edge of town to point out the road that led to Knoxville. It was learned later, however, that they had traveled less than thirty miles when they changed their course, drifted down Green and Ohio rivers to Diamond Island and Cave-in-Rock, and a few months thereafter rejoined their husbands near Henderson.

An organized hunt had been in progress since the two Harpes broke out of the Danville jail. It is probable that many joined the pursuing parties not because the Harpes were murderers, but chiefly because of their brutal conduct toward the three young women. No one suspected that these women had planned, should they be liberated, to meet their husbands in the lower Green River country.

Immediately after their escape the two Harpes resumed their work. On April 22, 1799, the Governor of Kentucky issued a proclamation offering a reward for the capture of either or both. Reports of killings in Kentucky were followed by others from southern Illinois, then from east Tennessee, then again from Kentucky. Among their victims was one of their own children. Declaring that Little Harpe's crying infant would some day be the means of pursuers detecting their presence, Big Harpe slung the baby by the heels against a tree and literally burst its head into pieces. During the first year of their unrestrained ferocity they had committed at least twenty murders. The whole of Kentucky and Tennessee had become terrorized by the possibility of the appearance of the Harpes at any hour in any locality.

The people of the lower Green River country, like settlers elsewhere, were on the lookout for them. In the early part of August, 1799, two suspicious newcomers were discovered prowling around some of the backwoods settlements in southern Henderson County. These strangers might be the Harpes. No one knew. The Harpes, aware that they were being hunted—and at times seen and watched—had taken the precaution never to move in the open with their women. The fact that no woman had been seen with them led the watchers to conclude that the suspects were not the widely sought murderers.

One day the Harpes left Henderson County and started toward the hiding place of their women and children—twenty or more miles away. They rode good horses, and were well armed and fairly well dressed.

That evening they arrived at the home of James Tompkins, in what is now Webster County. They represented themselves as Methodist preachers. Their equipment aroused no suspicion, for the country was almost an unbroken wilderness, and preachers, as well as most other pioneers, often traveled well armed. Tompkins invited them to supper, and Big Harpe, to ward off suspicion, said a long grace at table. After supper they bade their host farewell, saying they had an engagement elsewhere.

Late that night, August 20, they reached the house of Moses Stegall—about five miles east of what later became the town of Dixon. Stegall was absent, but his wife and their only child, a boy of four months, were at home and, a few hours before, had admitted Major William Love, a surveyor, who had come to see Stegall on business. Mrs. Stegall, expressing an opinion that her husband would return that night, invited him to remain. He had climbed up a ladder outside the house to the loft above and was in bed when the new arrivals entered the cabin. He came down and met the two men. In the conversation that followed the murderers themselves inquired about the Harpes and, among other things, stated that, according to rumor, the two outlaws were then prowling around in the neighborhood.

Mrs. Stegall, having only the one spare bed in the loft, was obliged to assign it to the three men. After Major Love had fallen asleep, one of the Harpes took an axe which he always carried in his belt and, with a single blow, dashed out the brains of the sleeping man. The two villains then went down to Mrs. Stegall's room. She, knowing nothing to the contrary, presumed Major Love was still asleep. Reprimanding her for assigning them to a bed with a man whose snoring kept them awake, they murdered her and her baby. Leaving the three bodies in the house, they set it afire.

The next morning five men returning from a salt lick found the Stegall house a smoldering ruin. Surroundings indicated that the disaster was still unknown in the neighborhood. The men proceeded to the home of Squire Silas McBee to notify him of their discovery. While they were discussing the subject

The Harpes

with Squire McBee, Moses Stegall rode up, and for the first time heard what had happened to his family.

Then began the hunt for the Harpes. Mounted and equipped, and provisioned for a few days, Squire McBee's troop of seven men started on their expedition against the murderers. They found and followed the trail until night. Early the next morning, after traveling only a few miles, they detected the Harpes standing on a distant hillside. Big Harpe was holding his horse; Little Harpe had no horse. The pursuers at once started for the hill. In the meantime Big Harpe mounted and darted off in one direction, Little Harpe ran in another—and both were out of sight. In their efforts to find traces of the Harpes the pursuers discovered the Harpe camp. They found no one there except Little Harpe's woman. When questioned threateningly she said she did not know in what direction little Harpe had fled, but that Big Harpe had just been there, hurriedly placed each of his women on a good horse, and had ridden away with them. She was left under the care of one of the men, and the chase was resumed.

A few miles farther on, Big Harpe and his two women were seen on a ridge a short distance ahead. Realizing his danger he put spurs to his horse and dashed off alone, leaving his women behind. They made no attempt to follow him, but calmly awaited their captors, two of whom took them in charge.

The other men continued the chase. Each fired a shot at the fleeing outlaw, who again and again brandished his tomahawk in savage defiance. The wild ride continued through dense woods and over narrow trails for a few miles until the fugitive, slackening his pace, was overtaken. He had been mortally wounded by one of the shots. As he lay stretched upon the ground, he asked for water. A shoe was pulled off his foot and water was brought. Moses Stegall now stepped forward. While reciting to Big Harpe how brutally he had murdered his wife and child, Stegall drew a knife, declaring he would cut off his enemy's head. Then he pointed a gun at Harpe's face. The dying outlaw, conscious of the threat, jerked his head from side to side, hoping to dodge the threatened bullet. "Very well," said Stegall, "I will not shoot you in the head, for I want to save it as a trophy." Then, aiming at his heart, he shot him in the left side. And Big Harpe died without another struggle or groan.

With the knife he had so coldly exhibited, Stegall cut off the outlaw's head. He placed it in one end of a bag, in the other end of which was a corresponding weight of provisions. The bag was slung across a horse, and the captors and their three captured women started on their return—some thirty-five miles—leaving the headless corpse to the wolves of Muhlenberg County. The head was taken to the cross roads near where the Harpes had committed their last crime. It was there placed in the fork of a tree as a warning to others. The spot ever since has been known as Harpe's Head, and the old road, now a modern highway, still bears the name of Harpe's Head Road.

The captors, leaving the outlaw's head conspicuously displayed in the tree, rode on to Henderson, some twenty miles farther, and placed the three women in jail. The prisoners were tried on September 4, 1799, before the Court of Quarter Sessions. They were found guilty of "being parties in the murder" and accordingly were ordered sent to Russellville to appear, in October, before the Logan District Court. That court found them "not guilty." After their release Little Harpe's wife returned to Tennessee; Big Harpe's women and two children continued to live in Logan County for many years.

Big Harpe was dead, and the women had again been spared through public sympathy. Little Harpe had vanished into the wilderness. No one knew where, how, or when he might reappear. All feared his return. It was not until five years later that they learned he had gone south, and under another name joined with Samuel Mason, the outlaw.

Samuel Mason stands out in pioneer history of the Ohio and Mississippi valleys as a highway robber and river pirate. He had been a useful Revolutionary soldier. The Harpes killed men, women, and children to gratify a lust for murder. Mason took to robbery solely for the purpose of getting money. He was one of the shrewdest and most resourceful robbers; nevertheless he was trapped by the younger Harpe. About two years after Little Harpe made his last flight from Kentucky —after his brother had been killed—he joined Mason's band under the name of John Setton. Mason evidently did not recognize Setton as Little Harpe.

Mason's robberies had become so frequent and so serious on the Mississippi River and the Natchez Trace that in 1802 the Governor of Mississippi offered a reward of $1,000 for the leader, dead or alive. In January, 1803, Mason and his band, including Little Harpe, who was still unrecognized under an alias, were captured near New Madrid, Missouri. After a preliminary trial before the Spanish authorities, the prisoners made their escape.

Soldiers and civilians again became man-hunters. One day two men appeared in Greenville, Mississippi (near Natchez), bringing with them a gruesome trophy—the head of Samuel Mason—and claimed the reward. The head was identified as that of Mason by a number of persons. The two heroes appeared before the judge to receive an order for the payment of the reward. They gave their names as John Setton and James May.

As the judge was in the act of making out a certificate, a traveler stepped into the court room and requested the arrest of the two men. He stated that he had alighted at the tavern, had repaired to the stable to see his horse attended to, and there saw the horses of the two men who had arrived just before him. He recognized the horses—principally because each had a peculiar blaze in the face—as belonging to parties who had robbed him and killed one of his companions on the Natchez Trace some two months before. And going into the court house, he identified the two men.

This declaration indicated that the two men had committed at least one murder and robbery, and they were therefore held under arrest. No one knew May nor the man who called himself Setton. But suspicion was aroused that Setton was actually Harpe. A notice was put up at the Natchez landing stating that it was believed Little Harpe had been captured, and persons having any knowledge of his identity were requested to come to the Greenville jail and view the prisoner. One Kentucky boatman who had seen him in the Danville jail recognized him at once. Another asserted, "If he is Little Harpe he has a mole on his neck and two toes grown together on one foot." A Tennesseean declared, "If he is Little Harpe he has a scar under his left nipple where I cut him in a difficulty we had in Knoxville." An examination showed every one of these identifying marks.

Escape was now the only hope for Harpe and May. They did break jail, but were recaptured. On January 13, 1804, they were tried, "found guilty of robbery," and sentenced to death; and on February 8 were hanged in what has been known ever since as "Gallows Field."

No attempt had been made to lynch the two condemned outlaws, but the lynch spirit evidently raged, for, after their legal execution on Gallows Field, their heads were placed on poles, one a short distance to the north and the other a short distance to the west of Old Greenville on the Natchez Trace.

The two headless bodies were buried together in one grave near the Old Trace. As time rolled on, the narrow Trace widened, as roads frequently do, and wore deeper into the slight elevation over which it led. Finally this widening and deepening process reached the fleshless bones in the solitary grave, and the two skeletons, protruding piece by piece from the road bank, were dragged out by dogs and beasts. Thus the last vestige of Little Harpe disappeared on the very highway upon which he had committed many crimes.

The terrorizing influences of the names of the Harpes gradually vanished from the South and the West, but the deeds of these outlaws and the horror they aroused have passed into the history of pioneer life.

OTTO A. ROTHERT (1871–1956) was born in Indiana, but his family moved to Louisville in 1889. After graduating from Notre Dame he began a business career but became increasingly interested in history. He served The Filson Club as secretary from 1917 until 1945 and as editor of the *Quarterly* from 1928 until his retirement in 1945. His *History of Muhlenberg County* is a classic county history. Other publications included *Madison Cawein: The Story of a Poet* and *The Outlaws of Cave-in-Rock*, as well as many articles.

This article first appeared in *The History Quarterly* in July 1927, vol. 1, pp. 155–63.

A ROOF FOR KENTUCKY

By Charles G. Talbert
Department of History, University of Kentucky

A paper read before The Filson Club, January 3, 1955

Colonel George Rogers Clark returned to Kentucky from his Shawnee campaign of 1780 with his desire to capture the British post at Detroit still unrealized. The idea, however, had caught the attention of Virginia's governor, Thomas Jefferson. The governor realized that such a project would reduce the state's support of the continental army. He referred the matter to General George Washington. Jefferson believed that the Virginia regulars under Clark's command, assisted by volunteers or by militiamen from the state's western counties, would be an adequate force for the purpose. He was confident that Virginia could furnish all necessary supplies with the possible exception of powder and asked only that Continental calls upon the state be temporarily reduced.[1]

By January, 1781, Washington had indicated that he was favorable to the plan. Jefferson then suggested to Clark that he come to Richmond to begin his preparations.[2]

Clark, upon his arrival at the capital, received a promotion to the rank of brigadier general.[3] He obtained permission to draft militiamen in several of the western counties. Orders to this effect were forwarded to the county lieutenants. Some of these militiamen were to be at Fort Pitt by March 1. There they would be joined by a battalion of Virginia regulars under the command of Colonel Joseph Crockett. Five hundred men from Lincoln, Jefferson, and Fayette counties were ordered to be at the Falls of the Ohio by March 15. It was believed that Clark would be able to advance upon Detroit at the head of two thousand men.[4]

These plans proved far too optimistic. It was not until the following August that Clark came down the Ohio to the Falls. With him were no more than 250 men.[5] Several factors had combined to produce this disappointing result. Colonel Daniel Brodhead, commandant at Fort Pitt, was not so helpful as Clark had expected him to be. Contemplating a Detroit expedition of his own, Brodhead held back men and supplies. The boundary dispute between Virginia and Pennsylvania had its effect. Men in the Monongahela region refused to volunteer for a Virginia campaign. An attempt to draft them produced a riot. The spring of 1781 brought a British invasion of Virginia. One detachment penetrated so deeply that the government was forced to flee, first to Charlottesville and then across the Blue Ridge to Staunton, for safety. Men and supplies which could have gone to Clark were needed to resist this invasion.[6]

Although Clark did not reach the Falls until August 23,[7] a report that the Detroit campaign might have to be abandoned preceded him. John Floyd, the county lieutenant of Jefferson, feared that an Indian attack upon his county was imminent. He urged Clark to hasten his return. The strength of the Jefferson County militia frequently was reduced in time of danger by the natural tendency of the people to move to safer parts of the state. As Floyd saw it, only two circumstances prevented his county from being deserted. The Indians had stolen most of the horses, and the Ohio flowed only one way.[8]

Upon his arrival Clark asked the field officers of the militia of the three counties which comprised the region known as Kentucky to meet at the Falls on September 5. He wanted them to help him and his line officers to make plans for defense.[9] The term field officer included all who held the rank of major or higher. Fayette County sent only her county lieutenant, John Todd. Lincoln County sent two representatives, Benjamin Logan, the county lieutenant, and his second-in-command, Colonel Stephen Trigg. Jefferson County, in which the settlement known as the Falls was located, was represented by her county lieutenant, John Floyd, her colonel, Isaac Cox, and her lieutenant colonel, William Pope.[10]

The meeting was held at Fort Nelson in the quarters of one of Clark's line officers, Colonel John Montgomery. Colonel Todd, the senior of the three county lieutenants, presided. Clark presented to this council a prepared statement giving his reasons for having to forego the Detroit expedition and seeking to impress upon the militia officers the seriousness of the situation. Fort Jefferson on the Mississippi already had been abandoned, and it was questionable if the garrison at Vincennes could be maintained much longer. Such withdrawals, thought Clark, would be taken by the Indians as signs of weakness. Thousands more of them would become allies of the British and eventually would descend upon Kentucky.[11]

The general asked the militia leaders to consider the possibility of taking the offensive against the enemy and to suggest possible objectives. He believed that before any expedition could be launched the Indians would have harvested and hidden their corn. In this event the frequently used method of destroying their provisions and thus forcing them to hunt instead of molesting the white settlers would not be applicable. Success would have to be measured in terms of the number of Indians killed. Since more would be encountered along the Wabash than along the Miami, Clark suggested a campaign in that region. He expressed his willingness to lead them on any expedition that offered hope for success no matter how daring it might seem.[12]

After receiving the general's opinions Todd, Floyd, Logan, and their subordinates began their deliberations. The first question which arose centered around the matter of what measures should be recommended in case an expedition should be deemed inadvisable. It was decided that fuller knowledge of the extent of Clark's authority and of his attitude toward the garrisoning of the Ohio at points above the Falls would help the council to make a wiser decision. Clark having withdrawn, Floyd and Logan were delegated to seek this information. The general made it clear that the State of Virginia had placed him in full command of its western military department, and that he was free to adopt any measures which he considered satisfactory.[13]

When Floyd and Logan returned, the question of attempting a campaign was presented to the council without further delay. There were such differences of opinion that the officers decided to have two distinct reports entered in the minutes. Logan and Todd believed that the wiser policy would be to concentrate upon defense. They suggested that a fort be constructed at the mouth of the Kentucky River. From this point small parties could harass the Indians even in winter. Such a fort also would provide a storage place for provisions for any expedition which might be undertaken in the spring.[14]

The other officers, Floyd, Trigg, Cox, and Pope, saw things differently. They favored an immediate campaign against the Shawnee. If this tribe could be forced to seek peace with the white men others might follow. All of the officers agreed that a Wabash campaign would not be popular. Most Kentuckians considered the Shawnee to be their most dangerous enemy. Furthermore, the Wabash route would be more difficult and probably too long for a successful campaign so late in the season. The officers concluded, however, by offering to furnish for Clark's use any desired number of militiamen up to two-thirds of their total strength.[15]

After he had received the report of the council of militia officers Clark called a meeting of the field officers and captains of the Virginia state troops then stationed at the Falls. This group included Lieutenant Colonel Joseph Crockett, who presided, Lieutenant Colonel John Montgomery, Major George Slaughter, Major George Walls, and eleven captains. The commander offered for their consideration his written instructions from Governor Jefferson, dated January 19, 1781, his address to the field officers of the militia, the written reply to this address, and other information prepared especially for the regular officers.[16]

This board, realizing that the total number of men available for a campaign would not exceed seven hundred, put this question to an immediate vote. Montgomery, Slaughter, and four of the captains wanted to make the attempt, but the other nine officers were opposed. It was agreed unanimously that Kentucky was of sufficient importance to the state to make its defense imperative. The regulars recommended to Clark the continued maintenance of Fort Nelson and the construction of another fort at the mouth of the Kentucky. If a third fort could be supported they would place it just across the Ohio from the mouth of the Miami. It was suggested also that Clark ask the three county lieutenants to provide militiamen to erect the forts and to assist in garrisoning them. The hope was expressed that as the terms of enlistment of the state troops expired some might be re-enlisted for garrison duty. The board closed its session with the further suggestion that the state government be asked to send out enough regulars in the coming spring to capture Detroit and to maintain it as a Virginia outpost.[17]

Before they left the Falls, Todd and Logan joined with Floyd in preparing a letter to Clark. They offered to furnish him with corn and buffalo meat in so far as they were able, but they indicated that they would expect payment. The county lieutenants knew, or believed that they knew, what decision Clark had reached regarding the defense of Kentucky. They concluded: "We wish the General success in his plan which is quite agreeable to our wishes."[18]

Although these meetings ended in a spirit of co-operation, this condition was not to last for long. Within a month Clark called upon Todd and Logan to supply militiamen for the erection of the proposed fort at the mouth of the Kentucky. Todd went over to St. Asaph's, the county seat of Lincoln, to discuss the matter with Logan. On October 13 the two militia officers sent a joint reply to Clark's request. They admitted that they had favored such a fort when they were at the Falls, but charged that the plan then proposed had been so changed that they no longer could support it. By way of explanation they added that they had expected the forts on the Ohio to be built and garrisoned chiefly by regulars. The two county lieutenants described themselves as being ready to assist, but they offered several excuses for declining to do so. They had no tools for digging trenches and constructing earthworks. Their militia forces were small and widely scattered and would not finish harvesting their crops before November.[19]

In offering some of their militiamen to Clark a month earlier Todd and Logan probably were sincere. They may have been thinking of a short campaign as had been suggested by the other militia officers. The arduous task of constructing fortifications and the boresome duty of garrisoning them would not have appealed to their militiamen. In organizations such as theirs, where a private thought himself the equal of his colonel, such objections had to be considered.

As another reason for their change of heart the two officers told of rumors that the Cherokee and Chickamauga were planning an attack upon Lincoln County. They added that it could be taken for granted that the Shawnee would attack Fayette.

A possible explanation for their reluctance can be found toward the end of the letter. They had learned that Jefferson County was not being asked to furnish men for building or garrisoning the fort at the mouth of the Kentucky. "As it is solely intended for our Defense," they wrote, "on calculating the cost we conclude that we are willing to forgoe [sic] the many advantages . . . for this season and think it better to defend ourselves near home."[20]

The only concession which the two county lieutenants did make was a promise to send provisions to Clark if this were possible. They made it clear, however, that they expected the provisions to be received "at Lees Town or somewhere on [the] Kentucky."[21]

Eight days later Todd wrote to the new governor, Thomas Nelson, explaining the position which he and Logan had taken. He criticized the state government for keeping regular troops "in the most interior and secure posts," and at the same time seeking to put "the militia on duty at a place distant from 60 to 120 miles from home . . ."[22] Logan or Daniel Boone, both of whom had sat in the Virginia Assembly in the late spring and early summer, could have told Todd that the interior regions of the state had not remained so "secure" as they were when he journeyed to Richmond as a representative of Kentucky County in the preceding year.[23]

Todd was convinced that if militiamen were sent to garrison a new post Clark would be reluctant to replace them with regulars from Fort Nelson. He was very critical of Clark's contention that the post at the Falls was "the Key of the Country." The mouth of the Kentucky, he thought, was a more logical place for regulars to be stationed. It was nearer to the route which Indians would be likely to follow if they were invading Kentucky. Also the Kentucky River provided a convenient means of transporting supplies to the garrison. It formed the boundary between Fayette and Lincoln from which Todd thought most of the supplies would have to come. The land around the Falls was filled with pools of stagnant water. This he believed to be responsible for the diseases which killed or incapacitated so many of the soldiers. "To say that the Falls is the Key to this Country seems to me unintelligible," he continued. "It is a strong rapid which may, in an age of commerce, be a considerable obstruction to . . . navigation; but as we have no trade, we neither need nor have any keys to trade."[24]

Friction between the leaders of Lincoln and Fayette on the one hand and the state officers at the Falls on the other was not new. Before Clark returned from his visit to Governor Jefferson, Colonel John Montgomery, the senior officer present at Fort Nelson, had complained of it. He had just supervised the evacuation of Fort Jefferson on the Mississippi, and he feared that if money were not provided by the government Fort Nelson too would be lost. There is "not a mouthful for the troops to eat, nor money to purchase it with," he wrote to the governor, "and . . . the credit of the government is worn bare. The counties of Lincoln and Fayette particularly, tho able to supply us, refuse granting any relief without the cash to purchase it on the spot."[25]

The idea of substituting defense for offense was approved by the Virginia Assembly in December, and the governor was urged to take the necessary steps.

The plan as it now stood was to place a roof over Kentucky by strengthening Fort Nelson at the Falls (Louisville) and by building additional forts at the mouths of the Kentucky, the Licking, and Limestone Creek. Although such a roof would have obvious holes any force which entered Kentucky from the North would risk being cut off by the garrisons of one or more of these forts. It was the opinion in the assembly that from six to seven hundred men would be enough to garrison all four posts if each post could be supported by two gunboats. The crews for the gunboats would be obtained from the garrisons.[26]

Two orders pertaining to the situation in Kentucky soon were prepared at the capital. One was a circular letter from Virginia's Commissioner of War, William Davies, to the county lieutenants of Lincoln, Jefferson, and Fayette. It directed these officers to send militiamen to Clark when he requested them.[27] Here was an indication that Virginia's new governor, Benjamin Harrison, who had taken office on November 30,[28] was going to give some attention to the defense of Kentucky, and perhaps to tackle the problem created by a divided command. Although Clark was the supreme military commander in Virginia's western department, his direct authority extended only to the regulars. When dealing with the militia he might make requests, but only during a campaign or upon the direct authority of the Virginia executive could he command.

The other order was a letter from Harrison to Clark. It enclosed the assembly's decision against offensive operations and outlined some plans for defense. Clark was authorized to ask the three county lieutenants for enough militiamen to make, when combined with his regulars, a total of three hundred and four. One hundred of these were to be stationed at the Falls and sixty-eight at each of the other defense points, the mouth of the Kentucky, the mouth of the Licking, and the mouth of Limestone Creek. Additional authority was given to Clark to increase these numbers when he felt that the situation demanded it.[29]

Harrison liked the recommendation of the Assembly regarding gunboats on the Ohio. He urged that three or four such boats be constructed. If Clark could not spare cannon for them the governor thought that a few could be sent down from Fort Pitt in the spring.

Harrison admitted that the work of building forts and gunboats would have to be done on credit. "We have nothing to depend on for the present," he added, "but the virtue of the people."[30]

In his reply to the governor, Clark spoke of having been disappointed by the government's failure to give him adequate support in the past. He denied having either money or credit, but promised to do the best that he could under the circumstances. The practice of raising money by the sale of public supplies which were not urgently needed was generally accepted at the time. Nevertheless, Clark hesitated to employ this method with no knowledge as to when such supplies could be replaced. He approved of the gunboat suggestion, but made it clear that cannon and rigging would have to be sent to him. "The Post of Licking will be Immediately established," he promised, "and the others as soon as circumstances will admit."[31]

Plans for defense continued to be affected by friction between Clark's western military department and the militia of Virginia's three western counties. Joseph Lindsay, who had served as commissary for Kentucky County, was given the same position for the counties of Fayette and Lincoln. In February, 1782, he was appointed by Clark to the post of commissary general. In this capacity he was to procure supplies for the forts which were to be erected along the Ohio.[32]

After receiving this new appointment Lindsay devoted very little attention to militia requirements. The unfortunate effects of this situation were pointed out by Logan and by his militia colonel, Stephen Trigg. Logan believed that Lindsay had in his possession provisions which actually belonged not to the regulars but to the militia. It was his opinion that Fayette County still was being supplied from this source, but that supplies which rightfully belonged to Lincoln County had been forwarded to Clark.[33]

It was unfortunate that such dissension existed at a time when Kentucky was in danger. The chiefs of some of the Indian tribes had been called to Detroit in the preceding November. They were asked to have their warriors ready to attack the Kentucky settlements in the spring. The British plan, as learned by the Americans, was to capture Fort Nelson and then to lay waste the other settlements. The Indians were urged to bring in prisoners from whom information concerning the state of Kentucky's defenses might be obtained.[34]

When news of the British intentions reached Clark, he made a change in his plans. Instead of building forts along the Ohio, which might require several months, he decided to concentrate upon strengthening Fort Nelson and upon the building of armed boats to patrol the river. Thus the roof for Kentucky, although it would contain large holes, would have movable sections which could be shifted about as conditions might require.

This new plan was referred to in a letter which Clark wrote to Governor Harrison asking that equipment for the gunboats be forwarded as soon as possible. "No vessels they can bring across the portages from the Lakes will be able to face such as we can navigate the Ohio with . . .," he explained.[35]

To implement his new plan Clark asked Logan to have a detachment of the Lincoln militia ready to march to Louisville by March 15. He told his commissary general to be prepared to supply that post with "three hundred Rations of Beef per day . . ." Lindsay was asked to be on the lookout for experienced carpenters and boatbuilders. "We are going to Build Armed Boats to Station at the mouth of [the] Miami," he explained, "to dispute the navigation of the Ohio either up or down."[36]

This time the people of Jefferson County, who stood to benefit most from the proposed strengthening of Fort Nelson, were called upon to furnish their proportionate number of militiamen for the work. Floyd informed Clark that these would be ready on the appointed day. He believed that the people of his county would be very disappointed if no forts were erected above the Falls. They may have felt that this apparent concentration upon Fort Nelson would increase the jealousy of the people of the other two counties, who already believed that Clark was not sufficiently interested in their safety.[37]

The first detachment from Lincoln County went to the Falls in March. It was commanded by Lieutenant Colonel John Logan, a brother of the county lieutenant. Upon arrival John Logan was placed in charge of all militia units which had come to work on the fortifications. The superintending of construction was given to Major John Crittenden, Clark's aide-de-camp.[88]

On March 24 Governor Harrison sent an answer to Clark's request for cannon and other equipment for his gunboats. He promised to supply as much as possible and to deliver it to Fort Pitt.[89] On the following day he wrote to Isaac Zane, who operated an iron foundry, and ordered four cannon. He told Zane that the work would have to be done on credit, but he felt that payment could be made by fall.[40] Within a fortnight William Davies of the Virginia War Office wrote to inform Clark that he expected to send two light three-pounders and a quantity of clothing by wagon to Redstone for shipment down the Ohio.[41]

In April a fresh militia company went to Louisville from Lincoln County. This time Ben Logan went along, probably to see for himself just what was being accomplished. Soon after his arrival he was relieved by his second-in-command, Colonel Trigg, who remained throughout the one-month tour of duty.[42]

Small parties of Indians frequently molested the settlers. John Floyd saw this as part of the British plan to capture Fort Nelson and then to overrun Kentucky. The Indians repeatedly stole the settlers horses. This loss would make flight difficult and pursuit of the invaders impossible.

Floyd blamed the frequent failure of militiamen to report when called for duty upon the talk of a possible separation of Kentucky from Virginia. Some of these delinquents may have believed that a division would be effected very soon, and that it would save them from being brought to justice.[43]

The separation movement was being pushed by Arthur Campbell, John Donelson, and other political leaders and land speculators. These men hoped that separation would be accompanied by the invalidating of Virginia land titles in the Kentucky area. With this in view they sought to influence the Congress to deny Virginia's ownership of Kentucky. In this event speculators might acquire from the United States title to lands which Kentucky settlers now held under Virginia law. Some of the advocates of this scheme sought to hold a meeting at Harrodsburg to draw up a petition to be sent to Congress. On the first attempt the meeting was broken up by a group of Kentuckians led by Major Hugh McGary. Two days later a successful meeting was held with John Donelson presiding. Petitions asking for the separation of Kentucky from Virginia were sent both to Congress and to the Virginia Assembly.[44]

Clark believed that the crest of the wave of agitation for a separate state had passed by the first of May. The Kentuckians had begun to suspect that they were being misled. "I believe," he wrote to the governor, "[that] in a short time it will be dangerous . . . to speak of [a] new government in this quarter . . . The body of the people now seem to be alarmed for fear Virginia will give up their interest."[45]

Meanwhile Clark was continuing the work on his gunboats, or row galleys as he liked to call them. Lindsay, his commissary, was still procuring supplies.[46] The fortifications at Louisville were nearing completion, but Clark was putting his greatest hope in the galleys, the first of which he expected to launch by the end of May. It was seventy-three feet long, was to have forty-six oars and would carry one hundred and ten men. Its gunwales were four feet high, and were surmounted by false gunwales on hinges which could be raised even higher. Both the fixed and the false gunwales were bullet-proof. Thus the boat could "lay within pistol shot of the shore without the least danger." Clark's intention was to mount eight cannon, a two-pounder, six four-pounders, and a six-pounder in each boat.[47]

Governor Harrison in his message to the assembly on May 6 stated that Kentucky was expecting a heavy blow from Detroit, and that artillery and supplies had been sent down the Ohio for her defense.[48] Unfortunately some of the stores failed to reach Clark when he expected them. They were sold by an officer who had them in his charge. This officer had not been granted authority to make such a conversion of public property into cash and had failed to report the incident. He was reprimanded by the governor and ordered to replace all that he had sold.[49]

In spite of Clark's hopes, it was not until July 6 that the first of the row galleys, with a few guns mounted, was ready to move up the Ohio. It was to be used to patrol the river around the mouths of the Licking and the Miami. It was decided that regulars or Jefferson County militiamen would take it to the mouth of the Kentucky. There they would be relieved by a militia company from Fayette. Officers of the Virginia line would remain in command.

On June 27 John Todd started forty of his militiamen, about one-fourth of his total strength, to the meeting place. He promised to relieve them within four weeks. This company was commanded by Captain Robert Patterson. When the boat did not appear at the expected time Patterson and his men camped at Drennon's Lick, a few miles from the mouth of the Kentucky, where they could replenish their supply of meat.[50] Word soon came from Clark that the boat was ready to move. Patterson was ordered to march his company down the Ohio until he met it.[51]

Captain Robert George, who commanded the boat, found it necessary to keep his regulars at the oars. The militiamen met the boat, but they were not very co-operative. They demanded and received double rations of flour. They refused to row, insisting that they were soldiers and not sailors. At the mouth of Big Bone Creek, a few miles below the Miami, they declared that they were going home. This they did, although their period of active duty lacked a week of being completed.[52]

After this unsatisfactory experience the galley was placed under the command of Captain Jacob Pyeatt. It was operated by marines who were enlisted for that express purpose. These men were mostly members of Virginia line companies whose period of enlistment had ended.[53]

Although difficulties had been encountered, the galley had a beneficial effect. The British were expecting another American invasion of Canada. They believed that it would be launched by the summer of 1782, and that their enemies would be assisted by Frenchmen and Indians.[54]

On the day that Patterson and his men took leave of the galley, Indian spies were watching from the hills on the north side of the Ohio. They may have been under the influence of liquor, because they reported to their Loyalist leader, Alexander McKee, that they had seen two large boats both mounting cannon. They said also that these boats were accompanied by the largest army of both Indians and whites which ever had approached their villages. McKee concluded that such a host could not be expected to stop with the destruction of a few Indian villages. Surely this was the expected invasion. He promised his superiors that he and Captain William Caldwell, who was approaching the Ohio with a party of Lake Indians, would try to keep their forces between the enemy and Detroit.[55]

At this time there was little likelihood that British and Indian war parties would attempt to cross the Ohio in the vicinity of the galley. If a few more of these gunboats had been ready for action the Kentuckians might have been safe.

By the first of August Clark must have doubted that an attack was imminent. He was considering an invasion of the Shawnee country in co-operation with General William Irvine who expected to make a thrust from Fort Pitt. These plans were known to the British and caused them to increase their forces protecting Detroit.[56]

Caldwell and McKee must soon have realized that the reports concerning the army which was said to be with the row galley were false. The proposed drive against Detroit had not yet been prepared. Their Indians were hard to retain in a state of inaction. Giving the galley a wide berth, they marched to a point on the Ohio nearly opposite the mouth of Limestone Creek. From that location they crossed into Kentucky. The stated purpose of the two officers was to draw a few of the Kentuckians away from one of the forts. In this way they might take prisoners who could furnish information concerning Clark's intensions.[57]

By daylight on the morning of August 16 the war party under Caldwell, McKee, and the renegade, Simon Girty, had surrounded Bryan's Station. This settlement was situated in Fayette County, about five miles northeast of Lexington. It was protected by a stockade and blockhouses in a manner common along the frontier. Attempts to lure some of the defenders outside of the fort failed. Realizing that Bryan's could not be taken without artillery, the attackers withdrew on the following morning.[58]

By August 18 a party of 182 mounted men had been raised and had started in pursuit. It was led by John Todd with Stephen Trigg as his second-in-command.[59] On reaching the Licking River at the Blue Licks the Kentuckians saw some of the Indians on a ridge on the opposite side. The river at this place curves in the form of a horseshoe. Caldwell and McKee had extended their lines from the point where it first changes course to the point where its general course is resumed. The water was deep at all points in the bend except at one spot near the middle of the curve. Here it could be forded without difficulty. Thus a party entering the horseshoe, if beaten, would have but one point of escape.

The Kentuckians crossed the river and advanced in three columns. The one on the right was led by Colonel Trigg. The center was under the command of Major Hugh McGary of Lincoln. The right was commanded by Fayette's lieutenant colonel, Daniel Boone.

When they were within sixty yards of the enemy the men dismounted and tied their horses. Forming their lines parallel to those of the enemy they continued to advance. Heavy firing began on both sides with Boone's men pushing the Indians back nearly one hundred yards. Subsequent events seem to indicate that at least a part of this withdrawal was planned. On the Kentucky right there were some ravines and in these, Indians were hidden. They were overlooked by Trigg's men who soon found that they had the enemy at their backs. In trying to escape from this trap they shifted toward the middle of the ridge. McGary's men then shifted behind Boone's. Within five minutes after the first shot had been fired all was confusion. Escape seemed uppermost in every man's mind. As Major Levi Todd described the scene a few days later: "He that could remount a horse was well off, and he that could not saw no time for delay."

Many were slain while trying to cross the river. The Kentucky losses included Colonels Todd and Trigg, Majors Silas Harlan and Edward Bulger, Joseph Lindsay, the commissary general, four captains, five lieutenants, and about sixty men.

When Benjamin Logan at the head of four hundred and seventy men reached the scene of the battle on August 24 the enemy had departed. Nothing could be accomplished beyond the burial of the dead.[60]

The disaster at Blue Licks occurred at a time when the Revolutionary fighting in the East had ended. The loss of life not only was high, but it included a disproportionate number of officers, both military and civil. In Lincoln County only three of the magistrates were left alive.[61]

As might have been expected there was criticism of those who were responsible for defense. The "roof for Kentucky" had not been completed. There were those who wanted to know why this was the case. Friction between the militia officers and the regulars was in evidence again. As usual it was coupled with a division between Jefferson County on the one hand and Lincoln and Fayette on the other.

Daniel Boone wrote to Governor Harrison and asked that five hundred men be sent out for the protection of Kentucky. He urged that they be stationed wherever the county lieutenants felt that they were most needed. "If you put them under the Direction of Gen: Clark," he continued, "they will be [of] Little or no Service to our Settlement, as he lies 100 miles West of us, and the Indians North East . . ." He complained also that the men of Fayette frequently were called to the Falls to protect the people of that area.[62]

Benjamin Logan was even more critical. "I am inclined to believe," he wrote, "that when your Excellency and Council become acquainted with the military operations in this country . . . you will not think them . . . properly conducted . . ." He then told of attending the council of field officers at the Falls where the decision to build forts instead of attempting a campaign had been made. From that point on, Logan was unfair in his selection of facts. He told of being asked for men to build a fort at the mouth of the Licking. This would have helped to protect Fayette and Lincoln counties. Logan charged that these men had been taken to the Falls instead. Not once did he mention that the first call had been for men to build a fort at the mouth of the Kentucky. On this occasion he and Todd had refused to comply.

Logan next criticized the row galley and accused Clark of "weakening one end [of Kentucky] to strengthen another." He failed to explain that the galley had not remained at the Falls, but had been sent to the mouth of the Miami. Neither did he admit that the refusal of militiamen to serve aboard the galley had been one of the factors which had hampered its activity. Logan concluded by reminding Harrison that "a defensive war cannot be carried on with Indians, and the Inhabitants remain in any kind of safety." Here again he was forgetting that at the officer's council in September, 1781, he had favored defense rather than offense. "Unless you can go to their Towns and scourge them," he continued, "they will never make a peace; but on the contrary [they will] keep parties constantly in your country to kill, and the plunder they get, answers instead of Trade."[63]

Another criticism of the conduct of military affairs in the West was made by Andrew Steel of Fayette, a survivor of the Battle of Blue Licks. Steel objected to the emphasis placed upon Louisville, located as it was upon the northwestern border of Kentucky. He believed that most of the money and effort which had been expended in defending the Western Country had been applied to Fort Nelson, Fort Jefferson, Kaskaskia, and Vincennes. The amount spent upon the three Kentucky counties, thought Steel, would be in comparison "less than a Mathematical Point."[64]

On September 11 Daniel Boone, Levi Todd, Robert Patterson, and other Fayette officers forwarded to the governor a combined request for aid and criticism of Clark. "Our militia," they wrote, "are called on to do duty in a manner that has a tendency to protect Jefferson County, or rather Louisville—A town without inhabitants, a fort situated in such a manner, that the enemy coming with a design to lay waste our country would scarcely come within one hundred miles of it . . ." They then recommended that, if no campaign could be attempted at the time, the plan of erecting forts at the mouths of the Licking and of Limestone Creek be readopted and carried out."[65]

In October Harrison wrote his replies to the letters which he had received from Logan, Todd, Boone, and the Fayette officers. There were expressions of sympathy for the bereaved, implied criticisms of John Todd and Stephen Trigg as commanders, and suggestions to the effect that revenge might be possible. The governor seemed amazed to learn that the Ohio River forts had not been built. He expressed the belief that they could have prevented the disaster, because the settlers could have been warned in time to collect their total strength.[66]

The governor wrote also to Clark condemning his failure to build the forts. He insisted that it still must be done. Harrison's surprise over the situation in Kentucky would seem to indicate that he had not read Clark's letter of March 7, 1782, very carefully. In it the general had explained the change from the building of additional forts to the strengthening of Fort Nelson and the building of gunboats. He had given the expected attack upon the Falls as his reason.[67]

In his letter to the Fayette militia officers Harrison had said: "Kentucky is as much the object of my care as Richmond, and I shall shew it on all occasions." In his message to the assembly on October 21, 1782, the governor questioned the effectiveness of the defensive measures which were being taken for Kentucky's protection. He suggested that a campaign against the Indians be considered.[68]

Clark, Logan, and Floyd did not wait for a decision to be made at Richmond. Forgetting their differences they ordered their men, to a total of about 1250, to meet at the mouth of the Licking on November 1 in preparation for moving into the Indian country.[69] By November 3 this army had crossed the Ohio, had built and garrisoned a blockhouse, and had started northward. It was divided into two regiments. One, which was composed of men from Jefferson and Fayette, was commanded by Floyd. The other, consisting entirely of Lincoln County men, was led by Logan.[70]

The first objective was the Shawnee town of New Chillicothe or Standing Stone on the Miami River. All hope of taking it by surprise was ended when a few mounted warriors discovered the advancing Kentuckians and hastened to give the alarm. Much of the fighting was with retreating Indians who had left their belongings in their cabins. Parties of men were sent out to destroy the neighboring villages. One of these detachments consisted of 150 mounted men under Logan. This party went to the store of a French Indian trader, Pierre Loramie, at the portage between the waters of the Miami and the waters of the Maumee. Here a large quantity of plunder was taken. The building with the remaining contents was burned.

The Kentuckians remained in the Shawnee Country for four days. Fearing that the weather might change for the worse they then decided to withdraw.[71]

When Governor Harrison learned that Clark was leading an expedition into the Indian country without his permission he was considerably disturbed. Only the realization that these were men who friends and kinsmen had died at Blue Licks and that they were seeking revenge modified his criticism. Harrison had heard that after that battle the British had ordered their Indian allies to refrain from taking the offensive. He feared now that Clark's action might cause the war to be prolonged. Thus it is not surprising that he mentioned once more the Ohio River forts and insisted that they be built.[72]

When the governor learned that the campaign had been a success his attitude changed. He congratulated Clark and Logan and praised the officers and men who served under them. "It will teach the Indians to dread us," he said, "and [will] convince them that we will not tamely submit to their depredations." He explained that he always had favored offensive operations, but that he had differed in this respect from those to whom he had to answer. This claim at the least was consistent with his message to the assembly in the preceding October.[73]

Most of the military operations west of the mountains had been conducted on credit. The settlers who had furnished provisions or who had gone out on the various campaigns had received only promises of future payment. By 1782 a commission had been authorized to hear evidence and to approve or disapprove claims. Near the end of April, Logan, who may have been urged by people who were anxious to be paid, asked the governor if he would hasten the formation of the commission and speed its departure for Kentucky.[74]

After several Virginians, including William Preston and William Christian, had declined the appointment, a board composed of William Fleming, Samuel McDowell, Caleb Wallace, and Thomas Marshall was named. The first three arrived in Kentucky late in October.[75]

Although little could be accomplished until Clark, Logan, and the other Indian fighters returned from their campaign, the commissioners held short sessions in Harrodsburg and in Lexington.[76]

When Clark arrived he not only submitted his accounts, but asked the opinion of the board of commissioners on the question of forts along the Ohio.[77] The board realized that the Virginia treasury was not then able to support three additional posts, and the same was true of the people of Kentucky. However, the desirability of a fort at the mouth of the Kentucky was recognized. It would lie in the path of those tribes which were most likely to attack Kentucky. Also it would provide protection for Drennon's Lick, a potential source of salt and a favorite place for Indians to kill and cure game while harassing the Kentucky settlements. Fleming, McDowell, and Wallace agreed that posts at the Licking and at Limestone Creek would be difficult to provision. They advised Clark, however, to establish the Kentucky River post as soon as possible.[78]

Thomas Marshall differed from the other members of the board as to the most desirable location for a fort. He favored the mouth of Limestone Creek. This, he believed, was a logical landing place for people who wished to settle in Fayette, which still was the most thinly populated of the three counties.[79]

There were strong indications that, whatever the British attitude might be, the Indians were not yet ready to make peace. In the preceding November twenty chiefs from four of the tribes around Detroit had visited the Chickamauga branch of the Cherokee. They proposed a joint campaign against Fort Pitt, Fort Nelson, and the Kentucky and

Illinois posts in the spring. The same idea was then carried to the Choctaw and the Creeks. One of Virginia's Indian agents, Joseph Martin, learned of this plan and reported it to the governor. He wrote also to Logan warning him to be on guard.

Fortunately no such dangerous alliance among the tribes as that which Martin had feared was effected. That the Kentucky settlements could have stood against it is doubtful. Although Clark realized the need for additional forts, he denied being able to spare enough cannon even for one. He asked the commissioners to seek assistance for him in the constructing of one or more forts along the Ohio and in the location of a permanent garrison at Vincennes. If more could be accomplished, he favored a campaign against the Indian tribes along the Wabash.

In believing that this much was possible Clark was more optimistic than some of his officers at Fort Nelson. While he was traveling with the commissioners late in February he received a letter from his subordinate, Major George Walls. A meeting of the officers at Fort Nelson had just been held and the concensus of opinion was that, if men and supplies were not sent, that post would have to be abandoned.[80]

In a letter dated April 9 Governor Harrison informed Clark that peace terms with England had been agreed upon and that hostilities were to cease.[81] If the Indians had received this information they apparently were not impressed. On April 8, John Floyd, his brother, Charles Floyd, and Alexander Breckinridge were traveling from Floyd's Station on Beargrass Creek to a point on Salt River. They were attacked by Indians, and John Floyd was seriously wounded. With his death two days later Kentucky had lost two of her three county lieutenants in less than eight months.[82]

The question of forts on the Ohio still was open. Clark, whose request for an early retirement from the Virginia line had been approved, had, at the request of the governor, gone to Richmond to explain alleged irregularities in the accounts of the western military department. On April 30 he wrote to Logan and the two new county lieutenants, Daniel Boone for Fayette and Isaac Cox for Jefferson. He urged their support of his successor, Major George Walls. Then he gave them some information regarding Virginia's latest plan for Kentucky. All state taxes collected in the three counties of Lincoln, Jefferson, and Fayette were to be used for defense purposes. Posts on the Ohio were to be established as had so often been suggested. The first was to be at the mouth of the Kentucky River. It was to be garrisoned by militia units with the addition of one half of the regulars then at Fort Nelson. This could have led to a renewal of the controversy between the state troops and the militia.[83]

It is not too surprising that the proposed "roof" never was constructed. On September 3, 1783, final peace terms with England were signed and the liklihood of an organized Indian invasion of Kentucky was thereby greatly reduced.[84] By the end of the year Virginia's cession of her lands north of the Ohio to the general government had been accepted by Congress. On March 1, 1784, the deed was presented to the Congress by Thomas Jefferson.[85] It was now the property of the United States to garrison as circumstances might demand and funds might permit. A roof for Kentucky no longer was considered a necessity. From time to time, however, the United States located small garrisons across the Ohio; Fort Harmar at the mouth of the Muskingum, Fort Washington opposite to the mouth of the Licking, Fort Finney at the mouth of the Miami, Fort Massac a few miles below the mouth of the Tennessee, and Fort Knox at Vincennes.[86]

Clark was wise in considering Fort Nelson to be the key to the western country. While the peace negotiations were underway in Paris the Northwest was not strongly held by the Virginians. Clark could not spread his small forces over the entire area. By selecting Louisville as his point of concentration he was in a position to discourage a major attack by Indians who were hesitant about leaving their villages undefended. Also he could reach Vincennes or Kaskaskia more quickly than the British could do so from Detroit. No reference was made to Clark's activities in the diplomatic papers prepared at Paris, but his strong position must have been evident to the British negotiators and to the Prime Minister, the Earl of Shelburne. Governor Harrison, a frequent critic, wrote to Clark on July 2, 1783: "I feel called on . . . to return my thanks and those of my council for the very great and singular services you have rendered your country in wrestling so great and valuable a territory out of the hands of the British enemy, repelling the attacks of their savage allies, and carrying on successful war in the heart of their country."[87]

FOOTNOTES

[1] Jefferson to Clark, September 29, 1780, Draper MSS. 50 J 61. The Draper Manuscript Collection is the property of the State Historical Society of Wisconsin and is availble on microfilm at the University of Kentucky and at The Filson Club.
[2] Jefferson to Clark, January 13, 1781, Draper MSS. 51 J 7; James A. James, *The Life of George Rogers Clark* (Chicago, 1928), 231.
[3] See Clark's commission, dated January 22, 1781, Draper MSS. 51 J 18(1).
[4] James, *Clark*, 229-30.
[5] Joseph Crockett to Governor of Virginia, undated, Draper MSS. 60 J 79-81; Draper MSS. 60 J 267.
[6] Clark to Governor Thomas Nelson, October 6, 1781, Draper MSS. 14 J 73; Draper MSS. 13 C 24(1-2), 185; James, *Clark*, 230-41.
[7] Draper MSS. 60 J 267.
[8] Floyd to Clark, August 10, 1781, Draper MSS. 51 J 80; Draper MSS. 51 J 104.

Roof for Kentucky 81

⁹ John Todd to Thomas Nelson, October 21, 1781, Draper MSS. 60 J 63; Draper MSS. 63 J 49.
¹⁰ Draper MSS. 51 J 85; 60 J 63; 63 J 49.
¹¹ Draper MSS. 51 J 84(1-2), 85; 63 J 49.
¹² Draper MSS. 51 J 84(1-2).
¹³ *Ibid.*, 85.
¹⁴ *Ibid.*, 85-85(1).
¹⁵ *Ibid.*
¹⁶ *Ibid.*, 87-87(1).
¹⁷ *Ibid.*, 87(1)-88.
¹⁸ *Ibid.*, 86.
¹⁹ Todd and Logan to Clark, October 13, 1781, Draper MSS. 51 J 93.
²⁰ *Ibid.*, 93-93(1).
²¹ *Ibid*, 93(1).
²² Todd to Nelson, October 21, 1781, Draper MSS. 60 J 66-67.
²³ William Preston to John Floyd, June 17, 1781, Draper MSS. 13 C 21; William Christian to William Preston, June 30, 1781, Draper MSS. 13 C 23-23(1); Mary Logan Smith to Lyman C. Draper, April 25, 1845, Draper MSS. 12 C 45(3); Draper MSS. 13 C 21, 24(1-2), 185; 6 S 149-50; 13 S 185; 5 C 51(3-5).
²⁴ Todd to Nelson, October 21, 1781, Draper MSS. 60 J 66-67.
²⁵ Montgomery to Governor of Virginia (Thomas Nelson), August 10, 1781, *Calendar of Virginia State Papers*, II, 313, cited in Temple Bodley, History of Kentucky (Chicago-Louisville, 1928), I, 294-95.
²⁶ Draper MSS. 51 J 15, 100-100(3). The idea of a "roof" refers to the way Kentucky appears on a map. The Licking fort would be at the ridge or comb. The Falls and Limestone forts would support the eaves. The longer side of the roof, that from the Falls to the Licking, which would measure about eighty miles as compared to forty-five for the side stretching from the Licking to Limestone Creek, would have an additional point of support near its center. This would be the fort at the mouth of the Kentucky River. Some Kentuckians believed this to be the most important of the four.
²⁷ William Davies to County Lieutenants of Jefferson, Fayette, and Lincoln, December 20, 1781, Draper MSS. 13 S 157.
²⁸ William W. Hening (ed.), *The Statutes at Large* (Richmond, 1809-1823), X, v.
²⁹ Harrison to Clark, December 20, 1781, Draper MSS. 51 J 101-101(2).
³⁰ *Ibid.*, Draper MSS. 51 J 100-100(3).
³¹ Clark to Harrison, February 18, 1782, William P. Palmer, Sherwin McRae, and W. H. Flourney (eds.), *Calendar of Virginia State Papers* (Richmond, 1875-1893), III, 68-69; Draper MSS. 60 J 144.
³² Clark to Lindsay, February 18, 1782, Draper MSS. 29 J 54-54(1); Logan to Lindsay, March 11, 1782, Draper MSS. 29 J 57-57(1).
³³ Logan to Lindsay, February 18, 1782, Draper MSS. 32 J 5; Logan to Lindsay, March 11, 1782, Draper MSS. 29 J 57-57(1); Trigg to [Lindsay], February 21, 1782, Draper MSS. 29 J 53-54.
³⁴ William Irvine to George Washington, February 7, 1782, Draper MSS. 11 J 11; Clark to Joseph Lindsay, March 5, 1782, Draper MSS. 11 J 17; Clark to Benjamin Harrison, March 7, 1782, *Calendar of Virginia State Papers*, III, 87-88.
³⁵ *Ibid.*
³⁶ Clark to Lindsay, March 5, 1782, Draper MSS. 29 J 55-55(1).
³⁷ Floyd to Clark, March 8, 1782, Draper MSS. 52 J 9-9(1).
³⁸ Draper MSS. 60 J 134; 63 J 106; 1 00 109; Lincoln County Court Order Book 1, p. 15.
³⁹ Harrison to Clark, March 24, 1782, Draper MSS. 52 J 11-11(1).
⁴⁰ Harrison to Zane, March 25, 1782, Draper MSS. 52 J 11-11(1).
⁴¹ Davies to Clark, April 6, 1782, Draper MSS. 52 J 12.
⁴² Pension statement of Abraham Estis, Draper MSS. 1 00 10.
⁴³ John Floyd to John May, April 8, 1782, Draper MSS. 11 S 137-41.
⁴⁴ John Donelson to John Campbell, April 20, 1782, Draper MSS. 9 DD 34; Thomas Allin to Levi Todd, September 1, 1806, Draper MSS. 16 CC 40; Thomas P. Abernethy, *Western Lands and the American Revolution* (New York, 1937), 302-303.
⁴⁵ Clark to Harrison, May 2, 1782, Draper MSS. 60 J 148-49.
⁴⁶ Clark to Lindsay, April 8, 1782, Draper MSS. 11 J 19; Draper MSS. 29 J 56.

⁴⁷ Clark to Harrison, May 2, 1782, Draper MSS. 60 J 148-51; James, *George Rogers Clark*, 261.
⁴⁸ Draper MSS. 10 S 29.
⁴⁹ Benjamin Harrison to William Harrison, May 22, 1782, Draper MSS. 10 S 31-32.
⁵⁰ Todd to Patterson, June 27, 1782, Draper MSS. 1 MM 105; Draper MSS. 1 MM 36; 29 J 92(1-3).
⁵¹ Clark to Patterson, July 5, 1782, Draper MSS. 32 J 1.
⁵² Robert George to John Todd, July 19, 1782, Draper MSS. 4 J 84; Draper MSS. 4 J 19; 31 J 34, 88(1).
⁵³ Pyeatt to Clark, August 4, 1782, Draper MSS. 59 J 29-29(1); John Floyd to Clark, March 8, 1782, Draper MSS. 52 J 9(1).
⁵⁴ Extract from *Maryland Journal*, July 9, 1782, Draper MSS. 3 JJ 90. This was reprinted from a London newspaper of April 1, 1782. The London paper cited as its authority several letters written by General Frederick Haldimand, British Commander in Canada.
⁵⁵ McKee to Major Arent S. DePeyster, July 22, 1782, "Haldimand Papers," *Michigan Pioneer and Historical Collections* (Lansing, 1908-1912), XX, 32-33.
⁵⁶ Clark to Irvine, August 10, 1782, Draper MSS. 11 J 22; Frederick Haldimand to Sir Guy Carleton, July 28, 1782, "Haldimand Papers," *Michigan Pioneer and Historical Collections*, XX, 34.
⁵⁷ McKee to DePeyster, August 28, 1782, "Haldimand Papers," *loc. cit.*, XX, 49; Caldwell to DePeyster, August 26, 1782, in Reuben J. Durrett, *Bryant's Station*, Filson Club Publications Number 12 (Louisville, 1897), 208-209; Temple Bodley, *George Rogers Clark, His Life and Public Services* (Boston, 1926), 212.
⁵⁸ McKee to DePeyster, August 28, 1782, *loc. cit.*, Caldwell to DePeyster, August 26, 1782, *loc. cit.*; Levi Todd to Benjamin Harrison, September 11, 1782, *Calendar of Virginia State Papers*, III, 300-301; Draper MSS. 52 J 36(1); 60 J 17; 11 S 10, 115-118, 203-205.
⁵⁹ Levi Todd to Robert Todd, August 26, 1782, *Calendar of Virginia State Papers*, III, 333-34 or Draper MSS. 11 S 115-118; Trigg to Logan, August 17, 1782, Draper MSS. 52 J 35.
⁶⁰ Levi Todd to Robert Todd, August 26, 1782, *loc. cit.*; Daniel Boone to Harrison, August 30, 1782, Draper MSS. 60 J 70-71; Logan to Harrison, August 31, 1782, Draper MSS. 11 S 17-18; Caldwell to DePeyster, August 26, 1782, *loc. cit.*; McKee to DePeyster, August 28, 1782, *loc. cit.*; Draper MSS. 52 J 35(1)-36; 60 J 120-21.
⁶¹ Boone to Harrison, August 30, 1782, *loc. cit.*; Logan to Harrison, August 31, 1782, *loc. cit.*
⁶² Boone to Harrison, August 30, 1782, *loc. cit.*
⁶³ Logan to Harrison, August 31, 1782, *loc. cit.*
⁶⁴ Steel to Harrison, September 12, 1782, *Calendar of Virginia State Papers*, III, 303-304; Durrett, *Bryant's Station*, 231.
⁶⁵ Officers of Fayette Militia to Harrison, September 11, 1782, Draper MSS. 60 J 74-77.
⁶⁶ Harrison to Logan, October 14, 1782, Draper MSS. 10 S 64-67; Harrison to Todd, October 14, 1782, Draper MSS. 10 S 55-57; Harrison to Boone and the Fayette Officers, October 14, 1782, Draper MSS. 10 S 57-60.
⁶⁷ Harrison to Clark, October 17, 1782, Draper MSS. 52 J 50-51(1); Clark to Harrison, March 7, 1782, *Calendar of Virginia State Papers*, III, 87-88.
⁶⁸ Draper MSS. 10 S 80; Harrison to Fayette Officers, October 14, 1782, Draper MSS. 10 S 57-60.
⁶⁹ Clark to William Davies, October 19, 1782, Draper MSS. 60 J 160-61; Clark to Harrison, October 22, 1782, Draper MSS. 60 J 160-61.
⁷⁰ "Clark's Orderly Book," Draper MSS. 63 J 116-26; Clark to William Irvine, November 13, 1782, Draper MSS. 11 J 24.
⁷¹ Clark to Harrison, November 27, 1782, Draper MSS. 60 J 161-64; Extract from *Maryland Journal*, January 7, 1783, Draper MSS. 3 JJ 103; Clark to William Irvine, November 13, 1782, Draper MSS. 11 J 24; "[William] Whitley's Narrative," Draper MSS. 9 CC 42-44; Major Arent S. DePeyster to General Allan Maclean, January 7, 1783, "Haldimand Papers," *Michigan Pioneer and Historical Collections*, XX, 87; J. Winston Coleman, Jr., *The British Invasion of Kentucky* (Lexington, 1951), 29.
⁷² Harrison to Clark, December 19, 1782, Draper MSS. 10 S 95-97.
⁷³ Harrison to Clark, January 13, 1783, Draper MSS. 52 J 73; Draper MSS. 10 S 80; 13 S 162.

[74] Logan to Harrison, April 29, 1782, *Calendar of Virginia State Papers*, III, 142.
[75] William Christian to Thomas Nelson, October 10, 1781, Draper MSS. 10 S 205-206; William Fleming to Benjamin Harrison, December 26, 1781, *Calendar of Virginia State Papers*, III, 672-73; Draper MSS. 60 J 371; Bodley, *History of Kentucky*, 319-20.
[76] Draper MSS. 60 J 371.
[77] Clark to Commissioners, December 15, 1782, Draper MSS. 60 J 167-70.
[78] "Journal of William Fleming," January 10, 1783, cited in Bodley, *History of Kentucky*, 323; Commissioners to Governor of Virginia, cited in Bodley, 323n; Draper MSS. 60 J 372; James, *George Rogers Clark*, 282n.
[79] Thomas Marshall to Clark, January 27, 1783, Draper MSS. 52 J 74.
[80] Martin to Harrison, February 2, 1783, Draper MSS. 60 J 172-75; Martin to Logan, February 20, 1783, Draper MSS. 46 J 74-74(1); James, *George Rogers Clark*, 281-83; Walls to Clark, February 21, 1783, cited in Bodley, *History of Kentucky*, 331-33.
[81] Harrison to Clark, April 9, 1783; Draper MSS. 52 J 84; Thomas A. Bailey, *A Diplomatic History of the American People* (New York, 1946), 29, 32; James, *George Rogers Clark*, 283, 283n. The preliminary articles were signed on November 30, 1782. The agreement on the cessation of hostilities was reached on January 20, 1783.
[82] Draper MSS. 12 C 47(3); 6 J 104; "Journal of William Fleming, 1782-1783," in Newton D. Mereness (ed.) *Travels in the American Colonies* (New York, 1916), 672-73; James, *George Rogers Clark*, 288.
[83] Clark to County Lieutenants, April 30, 1783, *Calendar of Virginia State Papers*, III, 478; Draper MSS. 51 J 104(3); 52 J 84; 60 J 113, 118, 230-31, 258-62, 369.
[84] Jefferson to Clark, December 4, 1783, Draper MSS. 52 J 93; Bailey, *Diplomatic History*, 32.
[85] Jefferson to Clark, December 4, 1783, Draper MSS. 52 J 93; Bodley, *History of Kentucky*, 349.
[86] Beverley W. Bond, *The Civilization of the Old Northwest* (New York, 1934), 248; "Journal of General Richard Butler," in Neville B. Craig (ed.), *The Olden Time* (Pittsburgh, 1848), II, 455-56.
[87] James, *George Rogers Clark*, 280-87.

CHARLES G. TALBERT (1912–   ), associate professor of history at the University of Kentucky, was born in Carlisle, Kentucky. His A.B., M.A., and Ph.D. were all earned at the Lexington campus. He taught at Centre College before joining the University of Kentucky faculty in 1951. His best-known works are *Benjamin Logan: Kentucky Frontiersman* and *The University of Kentucky: The Maturing Years*. Talbert has also published a number of articles and reviews.

This article first appeared in *The Filson Club History Quarterly* in April 1955, vol. 29, pp. 145–65.

II.

THE ANTEBELLUM YEARS

ASIATIC CHOLERA'S FIRST VISIT TO KENTUCKY: A STUDY IN PANIC AND FEAR

By Nancy D. Baird*
Bowling Green, Kentucky

Few maladies have struck Kentucky in epidemic proportions in recent years, but the state's first century was plagued with epidemics of smallpox, typhoid, yellow fever, and Asiatic cholera. The most devastating and dramatic, from a medical and historical viewpoint, were the cholera visitations.[1] This "scourge of the nineteenth century" caused the untimely deaths of millions throughout the world, and during its four visits to the United States, thousands of Kentuckians died. Although each visit was severe, cholera's initial visit to the Commonwealth, during the 1830's, was the most severe — and the most frightening.

Originating in India, the scourge passed beyond the Indian borders in 1826 and spread with the direction of man's travels. By 1831 cholera had reached the British Isles, and the following spring it crossed the Atlantic aboard the crowded, dirty immigrant packets. Cases of the disease were reported in New York City in early June, and it soon spread to other densely populated areas throughout the nation.[2] Kentucky's newspapers reported the westward advance of the pestilence, and in late July of 1832 the *Lexington Observer and Kentucky Reporter* concluded that there could be "no doubt" that cholera would "reach every part of the nation."[3] The disease appeared in Cincinnati in the fall of 1832 and probably was spread by stagecoach and riverboat passengers to Maysville, Louisville, and other southern river ports.

Kentuckians were assured by their physicians that the disease was not

---

*NANCY D. BAIRD, a graduate assistant in the History Department at Western Kentucky University, has taught history in the public schools of Cincinnati, and at a private school in New Orleans.

[1] Caused by the *Vibrio Cholerae*, a comma-shaped bacillus, Asiatic cholera differs from all other enteric diseases in the highly explosive character of the epidemic outbreaks, which is attributed to its short incubation period and its high fatality rate. The disease is spread by the ingestion of water contaminated by the fecal discharges of other cholera patients and is characterized by copious and purging diarrhea, vomiting, severe muscle cramps, and general prostration. The rapid loss of fluids results in dehydration, extremely weak pulse, subnormal temperatures, and the suppression of urine. Although many victims die within a few hours after being stricken, the majority of deaths occur 24 to 36 hours after the onset of the disease. Modern drug therapy has been unable to alter the course of the disease, but careful restoration of body fluids and minerals has reduced the death rate from as high as 70 percent to less than 30 percent. The bacillus is destroyed by heat (to the boiling point) and chemical disinfectants. Asiatic cholera should not be confused with a variety of acute diarrheal diseases that have been termed "cholera" incorrectly, *vis* cholera morbus, cholera nostras, and cholera infantum.

[2] For a history of the disease in the United States, see J. S. Chambers, *Conquest of Cholera: America's Greatest Scourge* (New York, 1938). An excellent study of the disease in New York is found in Charles Rosenberg, *The Cholera Years* (Chicago, 1962).

[3] *Lexington Observer and Kentucky Reporter*, July 12, 1832. This newspaper will be cited hereafter as *Lexington Observer*.

contagious and could be cured with prompt treatment in its earliest stages. Most Kentuckians accepted the miasmatic or malarial theory on the cause of cholera. They believed that the disease was the result of poisonous gases produced by rotting vegetable matter and were advised to protect themselves from such airborne gases through the avoidance of night air, mid-day sun, chill, fatigue, crowded quarters, indigestible foods, and "ardent spirits." As an additional ounce of prevention, the citizens of Lexington were requested to set aside August 18 as a day of prayer to implore "the Throne of God to throw its mantle around us and shield us from the desolating scourge...."[4] But despite all the best preventatives of the day, cholera came to Kentucky in the fall of 1832, accompanied by fear, grief, and death.

In early October a cook employed on a regular packet between Cincinnati and Louisville died of cholera in the Falls City, and within several days other cases were reported by Louisville physicians. The majority of the cases appeared in the low areas along the Ohio River and Beargrass Creek. The city council appointed a board of health to keep records of the number of cases and deaths; it reported 122 fatalities during October and early November. However, this figure can be considered only a rough estimate, for most physicians were either too busy or too complacent to report all cases, and many victims probably did not seek medical attention. Feeling that their city council was not taking enough effective measures, a group of the town's citizens met, established a cholera hospital and urged the mayor to secure nursing aid from the Sisters of Charity at Nazareth. A campaign was also begun to rid the city of miasma-producing filth and debris. However, the campaign was short-lived.[5]

Henderson, Maysville, Frankfort, Bardstown, and Lexington were also visited by the pestilence, but except for Henderson, where about 10 percent of the population became cholera victims, few cases were reported. Describing the brief visitation to Lexington, a citizen of the town wrote that cholera "killed five intemperates, frightened our citizens into strict temperance, drove away some of the faint-hearted pupils who were just assembling [at Transylvania] and then took wing itself and troubled us no more."[6] A heavy frost in mid-November ended the 1832

---
[4] *Ibid.*, August 16, 1832.

[5] Lunsford P. Yandell, "Notice of the Diseases of the Summer and Fall of 1832," *Transylvania Journal of Medicine*, V (Oct.-Dec. 1832), pp. 500-506; Theodore S. Bell, "Remarks on Spasmodic Cholera in Louisville," *Western Journal of Medicine*, VI (Oct.-Dec. 1832), p. 326; W.P.A., *Medicine and Its Development in Kentucky* (Louisville, 1940), 14n; *Lexington Observer*, Nov. 1, 1832; Louisville *Journal and Focus*, Oct. 31, 1832.

[6] *Lexington Observer*, Nov. 15, 1832; Edmund L. Starling, *History of Henderson County, Kentucky* (Henderson, 1887), pp. 166-167. The quotation can be found in Charles H. Caldwell to George Hayward, Nov. 25, 1832, Catalogued Collection (Margaret I. King Library, University of Kentucky).

cholera scare in the Commonwealth, where the disease had been comparatively mild. Many Kentuckians doubted that it really was cholera. But the mild outbreak was only a preview, an introduction. The great invader slumbered throughout the winter, and early the following summer it struck Kentucky with renewed force. Few towns were spared, and its victims came from every walk of life.

On the afternoon of May 29, 1833, the citizens of Maysville heard rumors that there were cases of cholera in town; within 24 hours a dozen deaths were confirmed. The populace began to panic, and within 36 hours after the confirmation of the disease, nine-tenths of Maysville's white population had fled. The town remained deserted for nearly two weeks. Only the medical faculty,[7] mayor, and a few relatives of the sick remained. Supplies became difficult to secure, for shops were closed and riverboat crews refused to land at Maysville. The town's postmaster informed a Lexington newspaper that Maysville had "never before been visited by such a calamity." By mid-June 60 persons, including the mayor and the last survivor of Mason County's first settlement, had become victims of the scourge.[8]

Traveling with Maysville's fleeing refugees, cholera soon infected most of the towns along the Maysville-Lexington road. As soon as cholera cases were reported in Flemingsburg, most of the citizens fled. Of the few who remained, one-sixth perished, including three of the town's four physicians. The small village of Elizaville was completely wiped out. Citizens of Sherbourne fled to the mountains on hearing that the pestilence was in the area, and both panic and death visited the fashionable resorts at Blue Lick and Harrodsburg, where many Kentuckians had gathered under the delusive impression that safety could be found there. Seven percent of the population of Paris and four percent of Cynthiana's residents also became cholera victims. Despite these and similar frightening statistics, the citizens of Lexington felt reasonably safe from the disease. Lexington had the reputation of being Kentucky's healthiest town. Her physicians assured the people that theirs was not a likely location to be revisited by the scourge, and the editor of a local newspaper promised his readers that if they kept their premises clean, remained temperate and bought a year's subscription to his newspaper, he could almost guarantee to them safety from the death angel.[9]

---
[7] The term "faculty" was used in the nineteenth century to refer to the town's physicians as well as the teaching staff of a college or university.
[8] *Nile's Weekly Register*, June 27, Aug. 10, 1833; G. Glenn Clift, *History of Maysville and Mason County, Kentucky* (Lexington, 1936), pp. 178-179. The quotation is from the *Lexington Observer*, June 1, 1833.
[9] *Nile's Weekly Register*, June 6, 19, 27, 29, July 6, 1833; *Lexington Observer*, June 22, July 6, 27, 1833; A. Thompson to Thornton K. Thompson, June 24, 1833, Catalogued Collection; "Epidemic Cholera: An Eclectic, Miscellaneous, and Clinical Review," *West-*

Five days after cholera appeared in Maysville, several cases were reported in Lexington. However, the number of cases and deaths was small, and it was hoped that the scourge would soon disappear. On June 7, rain fell in "unprecedented torrents" and privies, city streets, and wells were flooded. The cholera cases increased, and the fatalities soon mounted to 50 a day. To escape the invisible monster, one-third of the town's 6000 inhabitants fled. For several days the streets were filled with the noises of crowded stagecoaches, carriages, wagons, carts, and horses that carried the panic-stricken citizens to hopeful safety. Thereafter the town became abnormally quiet; one could hear the occasional footsteps of a neighbor going to the apothecary or in search of a physician. The routine trips of the death wagon also broke the silence, as it made its grim journey between homes, once filled with gaiety, and the cemetery. Grass grew in the streets, and the newspapers, when printed, reserved more than half of the front page for cholera news. Christ Church, the town's largest church, was open every afternoon for prayer, but few persons ventured out from their homes.[10]

By early June the pestilence was waning in Lexington, and the Fourth of July was observed at the town's churches with mingled tears and prayers of thanksgiving and supplication. On July 13 the *Kentucky Gazette* announced that the disease had ceased to be epidemic in the town, and one citizen noted that "the sore affliction poured on this country may cause every soul spared to prepare to meet our God in Judgement." By early August the newspapers had returned to reporting political events, but more than 500 residents of the state's "healthiest town" would never again read the news.[11]

Versailles and Nicholasville mysteriously escaped the disease in 1833, although the former was to suffer from it the following summer. Frankfort reported only a few deaths, but there were more than 100 in the county. Many of these occurred at the state prison, which was turned into a house of horror when nearly every inmate was stricken. Lancaster reported 116 deaths, Somerset recorded 34, Danville buried 55 of her citizens, and the students at Centre College fled in panic. Richmond suffered more from panic than disease, and all but 17 of Mt. Sterling's 600 residents fled before the presence of the disease was established. In Winchester, 25 died and others fled, "retreating in confusion and fright" from the cholera-producing poisons that were

ern Journal of Medicine, VII (April-July 1833), p. 93; William Perrin, ed., *History of Bourbon, Scott, Harrison, and Nicholas Counties, Kentucky* (Chicago, 1882), p. 100.

[10] *Nile's Weekly Register*, June 22, 1833; *Lexington Observer*, June 6, 1833; George W. Ranck, *History of Lexington* (Cincinnati, 1872), pp. 323-325; Robert Davidson, *History of the Presbyterian Church in the State of Kentucky* (New York, 1847), p. 133.

[11] Charles Short to William Short, June 23, 1833, Charles W. Short Letters (The Filson Club, Louisville). The quotation can be found in James McDowell to Sydney Payne Clay, July 18, 1833, Sydney Payne Clay Papers (The Filson Club).

reported to have filled several homes with a "green vapor" and caused fresh meat to become "putrid within the hour." Bardstown did not suffer severely in numbers lost, but the Hon. John Rowan, one of the town's most distinguished citizens, lost two sons, a daughter-in-law, a sister, and a granddaughter to the relentless destroyer.[12]

There were a variety of opinions concerning the presence of cholera in Louisville in 1833. A visitor from Virginia wrote that the disease was ravaging the town and countryside, but local newspapers reported only 15 to 20 deaths; these deaths were said to be transient cases that were contracted elsewhere. Whatever the origin and number of cases in town, there seemed to be no panic. Believing in the miasmatic origin of the disease, Louisvillians saw no need to flee as long as the cholera did not originate in their city.[13]

By the spring of 1834 cholera had traveled to the southern part of the state. A Bowling Green man wrote in a letter to a relative that cholera cases were reported along the Green River in late March and concluded that the town could not expect to escape the disease, although the health of the area had been "highly favored."[14] Bowling Green, Glasgow, and Greensburg all suffered from the pestilence. However, of all the southern Kentucky towns, it was Russellville, a town of 1400, that was the most severely stricken. In a three-week period during the summer of 1835, 147 of Russellville's several hundred cholera patients died, and most of the other residents fled.[15]

Contemporary accounts provide pictures of fear, confusion, and pathos as Kentuckians awaited "in fear and trepidation" for the disease to strike.

> Great fear fell over the people [of Danville] and paleness spread over every face . . . the profane swearer no longer uttered the blasphemous oaths; the drunkards, with few exceptions, abandoned their vicious courses Many prayers were made and vows repeated . . . which would stand as witness against those who uttered them on judgement day.[16]

Men passed their close friends on the streets in silence, 'staring like

---

[12] *Lexington Observer,* July 7, 10, Aug. 8, 1833; Joseph Huber to Sydney Payne Clay, June 20, 1833, Clay Papers; Perrin, *History of Bourbon . . . Counties,* p. 370. F. Garvin Davenport, *Ante-Bellum Kentucky* (Oxford, Ohio, 1943), p. 146; L. F. Johnson, *The History of Franklin County, Kentucky* (Frankfort, 1912), p. 97; Iona Montgomery, "When Cholera Struck," Louisville *Courier-Journal,* Nov. 28, 1954. The quotations can be found in James Flanagan, "Asiatic Cholera in Winchester," typescript (King Library).

[13] *Lexington Observer,* July 7, 1833; William R. Finn to Felix G. Hansford, June 17, 1833, Felix G. Hansford Collection (West Virginia University, Morgantown).

[14] E. Walker McElrcy to Elizabeth Harrison, March 26, 1834, Knott Collection (Kentucky Library, Western Kentucky University).

[15] *Kentucky Gazette,* July 20, 1834; Jacob Wythe Walker to David Walker, Aug. 1, 1835, W. Lemke, ed., Walker Family Papers [mimeographed collection] (Fayette, Arkansas, 1956), No. 10, p. 14. A list of most of Russellville's cholera victims is included in the papers of the Rev. David Norton (The Filson Club).

[16] J. J. Polk, *Autobiography of Dr. J. J. Polk* (Louisville, 1867), p. 33.

lunatics for fear of contagion being upon them."[17] A Lexington newspaper editor reported that he had never witnessed such panic, alarm, and anxiety as the faces of the citizens generally evinced.

> The stoutest hearts seemed to quail before the relentless destroyer . . . no one pretended to claim immunity from its grasp and no one knew at what moment he, or some member of his family, would be one of its victims. All seemed to be seized with an awful dread.[18]

Wills were drawn up, medications were secured, and farewell letters were written to loved ones. Men who had lived sinful lives were induced to reform as they "prepared for judgement and for eternity and trusted in God's mercy."[19] The health of some became so adversely affected by fear of the disease that they were advised by their physicians to leave the stricken area. Still others were so afraid they seemed to lose all sense of propriety. A resident of Russellville, who had lost two of his children to the disease, became so deranged that he hurried out of town with the rest of his family, leaving two young, unattended apprentices dying in his house.[20] An army veteran summed up the feeling of fear by stating that not even in the bloodiest of battles had he felt such "dread of impending danger" as he had experienced during the cholera epidemic in Lexington.[21]

Cholera tested the moral fiber as well as the physical endurance of the people; fear and panic were often as difficult to arrest as the disease itself. Towns were suddenly vacated, businesses came to a halt, and construction sites were deserted. Farmers were forced to abandon their crops in the fields for lack of laborers, and steamboats were tied at their moorings, because passengers and crews feared these floating pesthouses. Stores, banks, hotels, and taverns were closed; in many towns only the apothecaries remained open. The Maysville newspaper was forced to stop printing during the epidemic, and the presses of both Lexington newspapers remained quiet at the height of the epidemic there.[22] An unidentified Lexingtonian described his city:

> . . . the distress is beyond description! No city police — (at least not visible) — no board of health — no medical reports — and the streets have for the most part the stillness which pervades the ruins of Palmyra.

---

[17] Ranck, *History of Lexington*, p. 326.
[18] *Nile's Weekly Register*, June 22, 1833.
[19] Phillip E. McElroy to Elizabeth Harrison, June 10, 1833, Knott Collection.
[20] Rebecca Washington to Jane and David Walker, Aug. 10, 1835, Walker Papers (Kentucky Library); J. O. Harrison to Jilson Harrison, July 13, 1833, Micajah Harrison Papers (Kentucky Historical Society, Frankfort).
[21] *Nile's Weekly Register*, June 22, 1833.
[22] John Esten Cooke, "Spasmodic Cholera," *Transylvania Journal of Medicine*, VI (Oct.-Dec. 1833), p. 484; A. Thompson to Thornton K. Thompson, June 24, 1833, Catalogued Collection.

> ... I leave you to imagine the picture of dispare. But I must still add that the markets are suspended and the bakers' shops shut, with one exception. Not a pound of beef is to be got — and very little else. Not even a cracker for sale.[23]

A Russellville woman observed that "every description of business made a full stop. The printer and all the magistrates died, the postmaster and clerks were at the point of death, every stor [sic] shut up, their owdners [sic] either dead or fled into the country. I have never seen such a scene of calamity in my life."[24] A rugged army general stated that he would prefer a "seven months campaign in a furious war to undergo another seven days . . ." like those during the height of the epidemic in Lexington.[25] Famine was averted in Lexington and other stricken towns only because of the generosity of a few philanthropic individuals and the few remaining civic authorities, who made generous contributions and appropriations to provide food for the needy.[26]

To many of the fearful, flight appeared to be the only answer to the threat of cholera. A Winchester resident described the flight of the residents of that town as a "perfect stampede. . . . I was often reminded of it afterwards by the stampede of Union men when Morgan's or Scott's cavalry would come along."[27] A few refugees found a haven with friends and compassionate citizens like Cassius M. Clay, the master of White Hall, who had several buildings on his Madison County farm prepared for friends fleeing from Lexington. Many citizens of Russellville were indebted to the Shakers at South Union for succor. But flight held no assurance of safety; many who fled carried the disease with them, spreading it to neighboring towns or areas. Those who sought refuge at healing springs, spas, and fashionable resorts across the state frequently had cause for regret, as cholera also visited there. Many who left home were returned within a day or two on a bier, and others died in the country. A citizen of Lexington wrote, ". . . when I thought of flight, I knew not where to go — the country is filled with cholera."[28]

The services of a nurse were almost impossible to secure at any price. Lexington's attempt to establish a cholera hospital was thwarted by the inability to obtain nurses; local physicians believed that such a hospital would have saved many lives. The Sisters of Charity provided most of the professional nursing care for Louisville, Bardstown and Danville, but the majority of the care was administered by friends, relatives, and

---
[23] "Epidemic Cholera . . . Clinical Review," p. 91.
[24] Rebecca Washington to Jane and David Walker, Aug. 10, 1835.
[25] Robert Peters, *History of Fayette County, Kentucky* (Chicago, 1882), p. 410.
[26] *Lexington Observer*, June 29, 1933.
[27] Flanagan, "Cholera in Winchester."
[28] *Lexington Observer*, Aug. 3, 1833; Julia Neal, *By Their Fruits* (Chapel Hill, 1947), p. 79; *American Journal of Medical Science*, XIII (Philadelphia, 1882), pp. 187-183. The quotation is in "Epidemic Cholera . . . Clinical Review," p. 91.

religious leaders. The Episcopal Bishop of Kentucky, the rector of Lexington's Christ Church, and theology students from Transylvania travailed unceasingly in Lexington, and the Catholic Bishop of Danville worked constantly administering to the sick and burying the dead after most of the Protestant ministers had died or fled.[29] Yet there was never enough nursing care for the ill and dying, and many cholera patients received no care, or minimal care; probably more than one child "buried her mother in the afternoon, nursed her father in the evening, and for lack of help . . . had to close his eyes alone."[30]

Physicians were also in great demand during the epidemic, and there were neither enough physicians nor hours in the day for every cholera patient to receive their professional care. Those troubled with other maladies had no chance to see the busy practitioners. A few medical men, after advising their patients to flee from the infected areas, took their own advice. A Lexington newspaper accused the doctors at Millersburg of running away from the danger; the physicians indignantly replied that they had fled only after nearly every one else had left town. The practitioners who remained in the cholera-ravaged areas were frequently at the point of exhaustion, or, like all but one of Lexington's physicians, seized by the disease. At the height of the Lexington epidemic, the shortage of doctors able to administer to their patients became so acute that aid was requested from Louisville's physicians; three immediately traveled to Lexington to give their help, and others volunteered to go if they were still needed. Not waiting for his help to be requested, Dr. Luke Pryor Blackburn, a future Governor of Kentucky, went from Lexington to Versailles during the 1834 epidemic there and alone answered the town's need for medical attention.[31]

Despite flight and medical and nursing aid, the mortality rate was alarmingly high. A veteran physician, who had spent a lifetime administering to the sick, noted that "its horrors have passed my most

---

[29] Lunsford P. Yandell, "Spasmodic Cholera as It Appeared in Lexington," *Transylvania Journal of Medicine*, VI (July-Sept. 1833), pp. 202-203; *Nile's Weekly Register*, June 22, 1833; M. J. Spalding, *Sketches of the Life, Times and Character of Bishop Flaget* (Louisville, 1852), p. 277. Lexington presented the Episcopal Bishop with $1000 in gold in appreciation for his services during the epidemic; the Bishop returned the money to the city, requesting that it be used for needy widows and orphans. According to the July 20, 1833 issue of the *Kentucky Gazette*, many other ministers also administered to the sick, and the Bishop should not have been singled out by the city for recognition. For a more detailed narrative of the Episcopal Bishop's activities during the epidemic, see Robert Inko, *Kentucky Bishop* (Frankfort, 1952); Francis Swinford and Rebecca S. Lee, *The Great Elm Tree* (Lexington, 1968); and Charles A. Christian to Mrs. Charles J. Smith, Feb. 24, 1941, Catalogued Collection.

[30] "Epidemic Cholera . . . Clinical Review," pp. 91-92.

[31] *Lexington Observer*, June 22, July 15, 1833; Thomas Buford to Sydney Payne Clay, June 27, 1833, Clay Papers; Dr. Hawley to Drs. Firkin [?] Hunt, Dudley, and Cooke, June 14, 1833, reprint; J. N. McCormack, ed., *Some of the Medical Pioneers of Kentucky* (Bowling Green, 1917), pp. 167-168.

horrific conception, and its mortality has baffled the best and most boldly executed practices."[32] Coffin production was unable to keep up with the demand; additional special orders from Louisville and Cincinnati could not fill the needs of Lexington in 1833. During the Maysville epidemic that same year, even crude plank coffins had to be ordered at least 24 hours before they were needed. Cholera victims were frequently buried in trunks and boxes or merely wrapped in the bed linens on which they died. Carts made their daily rounds to collect and bury the dead, without rites of clergy or graveside mourners; those who had remained near their loved ones during life often fled when all hope was gone, for the body of a cholera victim was considered septic. Due to the subnormal body temperature, near absence of pulse and lifeless appearance of the cholera victim during the most severe stage of the disease, it is possible that a few persons were hastened to the grave. The premature interment of a child was averted at Lair's Station only because of the delayed arrival of the undertaker. Coffins were frequently and hastily deposited at the cemetery gates in confused heaps, and among the coffins could be seen a few unincased corpses wrapped in bed linen shrouds. To facilitate rapid burial, many of the dead were buried in long trenches or shallow graves. In Russellville, the stench of those buried in shallow graves could be detected for more than a mile.[33]

The theories concerning the cause of cholera varied during the early nineteenth century. A few Americans saw disease as a form of Divine punishment, a "rod in the hand of God" that would rid the earth of those who contaminated and defiled society. Ministers occasionally preached fiery sermons in which they pointed out God's use of disease to punish the wicked, the non-believers, and those who defied His word. When affluent and respected citizens fell victim to cholera, it was assumed that they either had a secret vice, were one of the rare exceptions, or their disease had been incorrectly diagnosed. The epidemic in Kentucky, however, seemed to prove the prevailing theory of a correlation between sin and disease to be in error; for while cholera struck Louisville in the poorer sections, where filth, poverty, and vice

---

[32] Charles Short to William Short, June 16, 1833, Short Papers.
[33] A. Thompson to Thornton K. Thompson, June 24, 1833, Catalogued Collection; Micajah Harrison to Jilson Harrison, July 13, 1833, Harrison Papers; Chambers, *Conquest of Cholera*, p. 160; Davidson, *History of the Presbyterian Church*, p. 335; Ranck, *History of Lexington*, pp. 325-326; L. Boyd, *Chronicles of Cynthiana* (Cincinnati, 1894), p. 120; Carolyn Berry, "Cholera in Kentucky," *Journal of American History*, VII (Oct.-Dec. 1913), p. 1428; May Belle Morton, "The Plague of Asiatic Cholera," Russellville *Logan Leader*, Aug. 5, 1968. One of the heroes of the Lexington epidemic was the town's chief gravedigger, a vagrant named William but known as King Solomon, who worked day and night during the epidemic to provide burial facilities. Many sources have labeled King Solomon as a Negro. However, according to the portrait painted of him by Colonel Price, he was a blue-eyed, sandy-haired Caucasian. The error is probably due to the fact that he had been sold as a bond servant.

were believed to be companion traits, it also struck Maysville in the town's most affluent area, and hit with its greatest fury in the aristocratic Bluegrass, where living conditions were the best in the state.[34] Devout Christians and law-abiding citizens, as well as the "lower orders" of society, became cholera victims. An eminent physician observed that cholera had "proven more malignant, fatal and indiscriminate in the selection of its victims in Lexington than in any other town in the Union," for they had not come "from the ranks which commonly supply its victims, but from among the most respected, sober and useful citizens . . . I have not heard of the death of a solitary drunk."[35] Another citizen of Lexington agreed that "the intemperate were generally spared."[36]

It is doubtful that any other malady of the early nineteenth century set the pens of so many physicians in motion as did the 1832-1835 cholera visitation. Letters, newspaper editorials, and medical journal articles presented an array of theories concerning the causes of the disease. Miasma produced by filth, decaying vegetation, stagnant ponds, marshy inlets, temperature variations, and even lightning were believed to have some effect on the airborne gases that were said to cause cholera.[37] The immediate or "exciting" causes that precipitated the disease in individuals also received much attention. Indigestible foods, especially green fruits and vegetables, all melons and alcoholic beverages were said to be very dangerous, and some Kentuckians refused to eat fresh fruits and vegetables of any kind during the epidemics. Other frequently mentioned exciting causes included strong emotion, a delicate nervous system, an hemorrhoidal disposition, and the "abuses of the pleasures of Venus."[38]

The bulk of the many articles written about cholera concerned its treatment. Unfortunately nineteenth-century physicians were handicapped by the lack of fundamental scientific knowledge, the lack of an understanding of the pathology of the disease, and the lack of reliable

---

[34] Chambers, *Conquest of Cholera*, pp. 170-171. The quotation can be found in Rosenberg, *Cholera Years*, p. 200.
[35] Charles Short to William Short, June 16, 1833, Short Papers.
[36] J. O. Harrison to Jilson Harrison, June 13, 1833, Harrison Papers.
[37] Chambers, *Conquest of Cholera*, pp. 169-170. Cooke, "Spasmodic Cholera," p. 409; "Epidemic Cholera . . . Clinical Review," p. 93. There appears to have been no mention of the possibility of contaminated water causing cholera. As long as water was clear and cool, it was considered good for drinking purposes. No one realized that fecal wastes that were thrown on the ground or deposited in shallow privies could easily seep or be washed into wells and streams. The deep backhouses that were believed to never need cleaning, the pride of the elite of the Bluegrass, drained into underground limestone sinkholes and subterranean caverns, through which also ran the streams that fed public and private wells.
[38] Phillip E. McElroy to Elizabeth Harrison, July 1, 1834, Knott Collection; Micajah Harrison to Jilson Harrison, June 7, July 10, 1833, Harrison Papers; "Epidemic Cholera . . . Clinical Review," pp. 62, 93; "Miscellaneous Intelligence," *Transylvania Journal of Medicine*, V (Jan.-Mar. 1832), pp. 114.

statistics. Therefore, they were unable to prescribe with any degree of effectiveness for their patients. Any enteric disease was considered cholera, if cholera were known to be in the vicinity. If the medication or treatment used seemed to prevent the patient from developing complete cholera symptoms, the treatment was hailed as a successful preventative. Records were not kept by either the individual physicians or the state and local officials,[39] and it was therefore impossible to know the number of patients who died or the percentage that survived any given treatment. Cures were frequently more deadly than the disease. Many remedies used provided some relief, but not for the reason intended, and other medications had no effect whatsoever.[40] However, if the patient survived, the medication was thought to be responsible; if he died, he probably was beyond all medical help anyway.

The major treatments for cholera were calomel, opium, and the lancet. Calomel, a mercuric chloride compound, was generally used as a cathartic for enteric diseases, and Dr. John Esten Cooke of Transylvania was its best known and most outspoken advocate. Believing that gases produced by decaying masses caused an accumulation of blood in the interior vein of the liver, Cooke urged the use of increasingly larger doses of calomel to act on the organ. Such doses were to be increased until there was a change in the appearance of the patient's discharges or until salivation occurred. Doses once thought fit only for a horse were given routinely to adults and children stricken with cholera. As much as a pound of the deadly mercuric salt might be given in a 24-hour period.[41] One of the few physicians of the midwest who disapproved of the large doses of calomel was Daniel Drake,[42] who surmised that the high death rate in Lexington might have been caused by the excessive doses of calomel. Agreeing with Drake, a Danville resident blamed the deaths of several members of his family on the "ignorant and un-

---

[39] The State Medical Society appointed a Committee of Vital Statistics in 1851 but it was many years before it functioned effectively. Kentucky did not have a State Board of Health until 1878.

[40] Methods used to help the retention of body heat, the stimulation of the circulation by rubbing the skin, regardless of what ingredients were contained in the rubbing compound, and the replacement of body fluids with any sort of liquids, probably helped the cholera patient and gave him a better chance for recovery. Many of the metallic salts ingested by the cholera patients generally passed through the body too quickly to do any harm. Had the stomach contained normal amounts of hydrochloric acid, these medications, especially in large doses, might have produced fatal metallic poisoning.

[41] Cooke, "Spasmodic Cholera," pp. 492-500. The "change" in the discharges was the appearance of a blackish semi-solid, believed to be caused by the presence of bile. This change was more likely due to the presence of blood, for excessive calomel could cause internal bleeding. It is interesting to note that some of the symptoms of metallic poisoning from mercuric chloride are similar to the symptoms of cholera — excessive vomiting and diarrhea, renal failure and circulatory failure.

[42] Drake, a former member of the Transylvania Medical School faculty, was living in Cincinnati during the epidemic. However, as editor of the west's most widely circulated medical journal, the *Western Journal of Medicine*, he was one of the most prolific and widely read authorities on cholera.

skilled faculty" who "stuffed and clogged . . . [them] with calomel."[43]

Opium was used to reduce muscle spasms and cramps and tranquilize the stomach. Some physicians, however, feared that it aggravated the "congestion of the brain." Drake warned against the use of opium in children and suggested the use of one teaspoon of powdered rhubarb in its place.[44] The lancet was another favorite remedy for cholera, for it was believed that bleeding would reduce the "congestion" in the blood vessels. Numerous reports were published of physicians bleeding near terminal cholera patients of a quart of blood, and then prescribing large doses of calomel. Occasionally a patient would survive such radical treatment. Other frequently used treatments included hot packs to retain body heat and salves and ointments made from mixtures of spirits of turpentine, camphor, mustard, brandy, or hot salt to stimulate the circulation.[45]

Not all physicians supported the calomel and opium medications. Complicated preparations were also administered, and a few practitioners believed that the patients who survived owed their remarkable recoveries to these cholera preparations. The manuscript collection of a Hickman resident contains two such remedies.

> 1 oz. opium
> 1 oz. gum of myrrh
> 2 scruples of camphire [sic]
> 60 gr. of musk [?]
> 2 scruples of flower of Benzoin
> 1 scruple of Incense of Irodine [sic]
> 5 pints of French Brandy

A teaspoon of the above mixture was to be taken two to three times a day as a cholera preventative and a teaspoon every few hours for the treatment of the disease.[46] One-half a wine glass of the following, taken every fifteen minutes, was said to be a good cholera medication:

> 1 pound of Bayberries, well pulverized
> 1 tablespoon of [?] berries. Simmer them well together and drain off the excess until you get 1 gallon of the liquor — to that add 1 gallon of good molasses, 1 gallon of Jamaican Rum, French Brandy and [?] African cayenne.[47]

A Louisville newspaper published a similar rum-molasses-brandy cholera

---

[43] "Epidemic Cholera . . . Clinical Review," p. 90. The quotation can be found in Thomas Nicholas to W. S. Nicholas, Aug. 3, 1833, Jonathan Bell Nicholas Papers, microfilm (The Filson Club).
[44] "Epidemic Cholera: Its Pathology and Treatment," *Western Journal of Medicine*, VI (Oct.-Dec. 1832), p. 612
[45] *Ibid.*; Dr. John F. Henry to Charles Short, Nov. 13, 1832, Short Papers.
[46] Dr. Porter's Recipe, 1833, Clark Papers (Kentucky Historical Society, Frankfort). A scruple is equal to 20 grains.
[47] Dr. T. Thompson's Cholera Preparation, 1833, Clark Papers.

medication that promised to provide relief and produce a "determination of the circulation outward."[48] But despite all the favorite remedies and preparations, at least one Kentuckian was not impressed with the skills and medications of the state's physicians, for she wrote that "they do not know how to treat it . . . and it is a more curable disease" than any other malady that frequented the state.[49]

With the appearance of cold weather in the fall of 1835, the cholera epidemic in Kentucky subsided, and the pestilence disappeared from the North American continent for 13 years.[50] Those who had been spared seemed momentarily stunned and stupefied. Whole families had been wiped out, towns deserted, children orphaned,[51] and friends and loved ones buried in common, unmarked graves. Despite the abundance of articles written by the most outstanding medical minds of the day, there was no agreement on the causes of the disease, and no positive cure or preventative had been found. Events of the forthcoming years would date from the cholera visitation, and years would pass before the ravages of the disease were forgotten.

---

[48] Louisville *Journal and Focus*, Oct. 31, 1832.

[49] Polly Harrison to Jilson Harrison, July 19, 1833, Harrison Papers.

[50] The pestilence returned to plague every state and territory of the nation in 1849-1854 and 1866. The 1873 epidemic reached epidemic proportions only in the interior valley.

[51] One of the by-products of the first cholera visitation was the founding of two Kentucky orphanages to care for the children left homeless by the pestilence. Through a series of fairs the women of St. Louis Church in Louisville were able to raise money for an orphanage, and St. Vincent's Orphan Asylum was opened for the waifs of that city. The citizens of Lexington collected $4000 through private contributions and in the fall of 1833 established the first non-sectarian orphanage in the state. Lexington's first free school also opened several months after the 1833 cholera visitation revived attention to the need for such an institution. J. Stoddard Johnston, *Memorial History of Louisville from Its First Settlement to the Year 1896* (2 vols.; Chicago, [n.d.]), II, pp. 120-121; Ranck, *History of Lexington*, pp. 325-327; *Annual Report of the Orphan Society of Lexington: Report of the Board of Managers* (Lexington, 1834), pp. 1-2; *Lexington Observer*, Aug. 8, 1833; Peters, *History of Fayette County*, p. 313.

NANCY D. BAIRD (1935–   ), a native of Ohio, received her A.B. degree at the University of Kentucky and her M.A. and Specialist in History degrees at Western Kentucky University where she has taught. She is now a staff member of the Kentucky Library at Western Kentucky University. She has written several articles for state and national journals. One of her particular areas of interest is medical history.

This article first appeared in *The Filson Club History Quarterly* in July 1974, vol. 48, pp. 228–40.

THE SLAVERY BACKGROUND OF FOSTER'S MY OLD KENTUCKY HOME

By Thomas D. Clark

University of Kentucky, Lexington
Read before The Filson Club, March 4, 1935

Perhaps no state in the Union has taken more pride in a song than has Kentucky. As a matter of fact Kentucky can not claim a monopoly on this song for it has long since become the property of music lovers the world over. The long-standing popularity of *My Old Kentucky Home, Good Night* has stimulated a vast amount of research in American social life of the middle Nineteenth Century, and likewise more or less bitter controversy.

In his *Stephen Foster, America's Troubadour*, John Tasker Howard[1] has painted a careful and complete picture of Foster's early background and life. However, he suggests, on page 177, that "what bearing this (Mrs. Stowe's *Uncle Tom's Cabin*) may have on the Bardstown legends is interesting to ponder." It is not the purpose of the writer of this paper to re-open the controversy of where *My Old Kentucky Home, Good Night* was written, for that is of little or no consequence compared to the actual background of the song.

Howard has suggested a thesis which encourages some interesting investigation into the social background of Foster's songs. It is with that problem that this paper deals.

At the time of the birth of Stephen Collins Foster his father was devoting much of his time to the candidacy of Andrew Jackson of Tennessee for the presidency of the United States. The elder Foster seems to have fed quite freely at the public trough

---

[1] John Tasker Howard, *Stephen Foster, America's Troubadour*, New York, 1934. 445 pages.

when his politics were in harmony with those of the elected powers.² As a result of the disputed election in 1824, the Democrats were sorely disappointed that their beloved hero, General Jackson, was "swindled out of office" by Clay and Adams' "bargain and corruption" ruse.³

Those were stirring times, when friendships were made and broken on the turning of political affiliations. Thus it was that Stephen Collins Foster became a congenital Democrat. Throughout his early and impressionable years he was a silent listener to long and earnest discussions of internal improvements, tariff issues, nullification, Calhoun, and bank charters.⁴ He had listened to his Pennsylvania father recount the valiant deeds of "Old Hickory," and doubtless he learned to hate the opposition from the selfsame source.

Throughout the whole period from 1824 to 1860 the Foster family was very much concerned over matters of national politics. Naturally, Pennsylvanians were vitally interested in the policies of the national government: First, because any internal improvements of a national nature would affect their state, for Pennsylvania was the "jug neck" which separated the North and East from the evergrowing West, and any internal improvements of an intersectional nature were forced, of course, to pass through Pennsylvania. Second, Pennsylvania was the typical border state of the period, it stood as the dividing section between anti-slavery industry to the north and pro-slavery agriculture to the south. Western Pennsylvania, Stephen Collins Foster's home, looked in both directions for its income. To a very large extent, Pittsburgh was the social and economic clearing house for the Ohio and Mississippi valleys. It was the point of origin for a vast amount of commerce, and an important depot for commerce from other sections. Goods shipped over the Ohio River from either the South or the North went by way of Pittsburgh.⁵

American eyes were turned to the South and West as the great American frontiers. The South and West were promising

---

²*Ibid.*, pp. 15, 367.

³Claude G. Bowers, *Party Battles of the Jackson Period*, New York, 1928, p. 31.

⁴For an account of the numerous issues of the Jackson period see William Graham Sumner, *Andrew Jackson as a Public Man, What He Was, What Chances He Had, and What He Did with Them*, Boston. 1883, pp. 164-276.

⁵Balthasar H. Meyer, Caroline Magill and Staff, *History of Transportation in the United States Before 1860*, Washington, 1917, pp. 7, 14, 51, 75, 82-89, 120, 225, 248, 286.

culture which would excel that of the Old World just as soon as lands were cleared and new systems of agriculture established. The following boast from an English magazine published in 1821 clearly illustrates the frontier American's views:[6]

"Other nations boast of what they are or have been, but the true citizen of the United States exalts his head to the skies in the contemplation of what the grandeur of his country is going to be. Others claim respect and honor because of the things done by a long line of ancestors; an American glories in the achievements of a distant posterity. Others appeal to history; an American appeals to prophecy, and with Malthus in one hand and a map of the back country in the other he boldly defies us to a comparison with America as she is to be, and chuckles in delight over the splendors the geometrical ratio is to shed over her story. This appeal to the future is his never-failing resource. If an English traveller complains of their inns and hints his dislike to sleeping four in a bed he is first denounced as a calumniator and then told to wait a hundred years and see the superiority of American inns to British. If Shakespeare, Milton, Newton are named, he is again told to wait until we have cleared our land, till we have idle time to attend to other things; wait till 1900, and then see how much nobler our poets and profounder our astronomers and longer our telescopes than any that decrepit old hemisphere of yours will produce."

This London magazine of 1821 little realized that this impetuous American boast would begin to be true as early as the decades extending from 1830 to 1860. While the Jacksonians and the anti-Jacksonians were in earnest combat over the "peoples' destiny," James Fenimore Cooper was directing the literate American's attention to native sources for their literature. This he did in the *Spy*, *The Last of the Mohicans*, and *The Prairie*. In his novels, Cooper sensed a changing social attitude and he predicted, though unconsciously, the very thing which created a theme for Stephen Collins Foster's songs.[7] In 1837 Ralph Waldo Emerson sounded the nation's cultural declaration of independence when he delivered "The American Scholar" as a

[6] Ralph Volney Harlow, *Growth of the United States*, New York, 1932, quotes a London magazine for 1821, p. 311.

[7] It is interesting to note the reputation which James Fenimore Cooper acquired as an author in his early years. When seeking a consulate position Governor Clinton recommended him to Henry Clay in the following note: "Believing you disposed to encourage American talent I have taken the liberty of commending him (Cooper) to your favorable notice as a gentleman every way worthy of it." Quoted by Henry Wolcott Boynton, *James Fenimore Cooper*, New York, 1931, p. 142. See also pp. 67, 75, 82, 118, 142, 160, 162.

Phi Beta Kappa address. Following these early leads, American literature became purely American in theme.⁸

The twenties and thirties of the Nineteenth Century were years of social ferment. Philosophers dreamed of social Utopias, such as Robert Owen's experiment at New Harmony, Indiana, and the Transcendentalist experiment of Brook Farm in Massachusetts.⁹ Horace Mann and a host of other democratic social leaders conceived the idea of public education and struggled faithfully to develop a democratic American school system. Through this agency these leaders hoped to create an effective and informed American democracy. Thus was set in motion an educational fervor which was to run to many extremes. In a new country where educational training was as yet untried and socialism was rampant it was only natural that many erratic institutions should develop. Some of the new type schools soon became hot beds of social, political and moral reform. Such institutions were Lane's Seminary, established in Cincinnati in 1833, and its offspring, Oberlin College, founded in 1835. These schools laid an effective basis for a powerful abolition movement in the South.

It was with malice aforethought which prompted the location of Lane Seminary and Oberlin College near the border line of slavery. It was from these bases of operation that a successful attack on slavery was conducted. From these points anti-slavery agents and literature were sent into the South with the hope of abolishing the insitution of chattel slavery.¹⁰

When Stephen Collins Foster was only four years of age William Loyd Garrison brought out the first copy of his *Liberator* at Boston, on January 1, 1831. The next year the Anti-Slavery Society was formed.¹¹ It is interesting to note in this connection that the attitude toward slavery underwent a change also. Using Kentucky as a specific example it is easy to see that the local attitude changed from one of peaceful emancipation to one of stubborn resistance of abolition. *The Frankfort Commonwealth* for December 13, 1831, said that public sentiment was stirred to the breaking point when anti-slavery propaganda was

⁸Phillip Russell, *Emerson the Wisest American*, New York, 1929, p. 150.
⁹Donald G. Mitchell, *American Land and Letters*, New York, 1897, p. 159.
¹⁰Asa Earl Martin, *The Anti-Slavery Movement in Kentucky*, The Filson Club Publications No. 29, Louisville, 1918, pp. 98, 110.
¹¹*The Liberator*, Boston, January-July, 1831.

distributed in the State. Two years later James G. Birney, a native of Boyle County, removed to his native state of Kentucky from Huntsville, Alabama,[12] where he had run amuck with slavery forces. In December of that year he called a meeting of the "Kentucky Society for the Relief of the State from Slavery." Thus Birney created much sentiment in Kentucky in opposition to the anti-slavery crusade.[13] Where there had been a considerable tendency among the Kentucky slave holders to emancipate their slaves they now held on to them to spite their protagonists. Had the arguments condemning slavery continued to come from within the State, and had they been based purely upon economic issues there is little doubt that slavery would have ceased peacefully to exist. Instead, the issue was made on the grounds of morality, and the anti-slavery forces went far in condemning indiscriminately the Kentuckians for their mistreatment of slaves.[14]

Unfortunately, Kentucky was a Border State, which placed it in front so far as the views of the anti-slavery group were concerned. Too, the institution of slavery in Kentucky was entirely different from that of the lower Southern States. Kentucky's lands were fertile, but through climate and soil conditions Mother Nature was able to dictate types of agriculture. Despite this unquestioned fertility of the Kentucky soils it was impractical to carry on extensive agricultural operations. Hence few Kentucky planters had overseers, for slavery was purely domestic. Thus whatever evils existed in the local system of slavery were chargeable directly to the owner, and it is very easy to account for the fact that the charges of the Anti-Slavery Society were taken as personal attacks by the domestic owners. This condition naturally created much bitter sentiment.[15]

While Kentucky's slave system was being attacked, first by the church and then by the abolitionists, the lower South was growing in population and economic importance. The 1850 *Census*, edited by James B. DeBow of New Orleans, gave the South 2,137,000 white people and 1,841,000 blacks. That part of the South which was most influenced by slavery produced the

---
[12]William Burney, *James G. Birney and His Times*, New York, 1890, p. 40.
[13]Asa Earl Martin, *op. cit.*, pp. 70-71.
[14]Theodore Weld, *American Slavery as It Is: Testimony of a Thousand Witnesses*, New York, 1839, pp. 87, 93.
[15]Even Henry Clay changed his mind when the Abolitionists began to meddle with Slavery.

My Old Kentucky Home 105

major portion of the $102,000,000 worth of cotton, $14,000,000 worth of sugar, and $2,600,000 worth of rice exported from the United States. The lower South furnished more than one-half of the $203,000,000 of goods exported by the whole country. Thus the South had become money-minded. Cotton, sugar and rice were bringing good prices, and there was plenty of land for future exploitation.[16]

Immigration from Kentucky, Tennessee and Missouri was greatly stimulated by the opening of new territory, and this immigration encouraged the domestic slave trade.[17] As early as 1842 the Webster-Ashburton Treaty between the United States and Great Britain closed the African trade, and made the Southern cotton states definitely dependent upon the border states for their supply of slaves. Travelers throughout the South were impressed with the increasing slave trade.[18] As early as 1818 Henry Bradshaw Fearon, an English traveler, noted barges loaded with slaves from Kentucky landing at Natchez.[19] J. H. Ingraham, in 1834, found the slave market at the Natchez "Cross Roads" both fascinating and shocking.[20] Court records in Kentucky court houses bear mute testimony as to the extent of the "down river trade" in slaves.[21] River boats were common and efficient carriers of slaves to market, for once on board a steamboat there was little chance that a slave would be lost either from exhaustion or from running away. Although this trade was notorious and the dealers were clouded with social opprobrium,[22] the steamboat companies seemed to have had no scruples against hauling such cargo.[23]

Throughout the slave holding counties in Kentucky slave dealers were conspicuous.[24] Robert Wickliffe, the largest slave-

---

[16] James D. B. DeBow, *Statistical View of the United States* (Compendium of the Census of 1850), Washington, 1854, see tables CLXXXIII-CLXXXVI, pp. 169-174.

[17] Winfield Collins, *Domestic Slave Trade of the South and Other States*, New York, 1904, p. 26.

[18] Henry Bradshaw Fearon, *Sketches of America*, London, p. 268.

[19] *Ibid.*

[20] J. H. Ingraham, *The Southwest, By a Yankee*, New York, 1835, pp. II, 192, et seq., especially p. 244.

[21] See Index to Fayette County Court Records, Lexington, 1849-1860.

[22] No self-respecting man dared have it known that he was engaged in the business of buying and selling slaves. If a respectable man socially did engage in the business it was in secrecy.

[23] Sundry Way Bills in possession of author.

[24] *The Observer and Reporter*, Lexington, *The Kentucky Statesman*, Lexington, *The Frankfort Commonwealth*, and *The Louisville Journal* all carried advertisements asking for slaves.

holder in Fayette County, estimated in 1840 that over 60,000 slaves were being taken to the lower South annually. Humane slaveholders were bitterly opposed to this sale of Negroes down the river, but always there were enough unscrupulous, or bankrupt owners, to commit this act. Petitions from over Kentucky were submitted to Congress periodically requesting that interstate traffic be prohibited. Congress, however, refused on the ground that it had no right to go further than the regulation of interstate commerce.[15] Thus the argument over the internal slave trade continued until it was brought to a close in 1865. However, the question of internal slavery was brought to a head in the Compromise of 1850.

At the Whig convention in 1848, Zachary Taylor of Kentucky, and hero of the battle of Buena Vista, won the nomination as his party's candidate for the presidency of the United States. Already an issue was fermenting which was to distinguish the brief administration of the heroic Kentuckian.

On January 24, 1848, a listless California mill foreman discovered a lump of gold in a mill race, and following the announcement that gold had been discovered at Sutter's Mill there followed the maddest struggle in American annals for everyone wished to reach California and gold.[16] This sudden immigration Westward created sufficient population in the California area for the territory to petition for statehood. President Taylor and his advisers were quick to perceive that the sectional struggle would break out anew when California petitioned for statehood unless some efforts were made to prevent such an occurrence.[17]

President Taylor turned to his fellow Kentuckian, the venerable Whig leader, Henry Clay, to bring the Union safely through this morass of sectional bickering. Clay's task was that of producing a definite statement regarding sectional difficulties already apparent and the admission of California. Fortunately the aging Clay had at his command some able young assistants who were anxious to try their wings of leadership. Outstanding among these young men was Stephen A. Douglas of Illinois. Thus, with competent assistants who did most of the work, Clay

[15] Asa Earl Martin, *op. cit.*, pp. 44, 45.
[16] Bayard Taylor, *Eldorado or Adventure in the Path of Empire*, New York, 1855; and Stuart Edward White, *The Forty-Niners*, New Haven, 1921, see chapters IV-V.
[17] George Fort Milton, *Eve of Conflict*, Boston, 1934, p. 50.

was able to lay before the United States Senate, on January 29, 1850, eight resolutions for the settlement of California, the other western territories and the slavery question. The sections of this compromise which dealt directly with slavery were the fugitive slave clause (which guaranteed the Southern slave holder a right to recover his property with federal protection) and the prohibition of the slave trade from the District of Columbia. This discussion attracted more attention, perhaps, than any measure which came before Congress prior to 1860, for the moderates hoped it would bring peace, the slave holders hoped it would insure recovery of their fugitive slave property, and the radical anti-slavery forces hoped they could eventually exclude slavery from the country.[28]

The moderates of both sections believed that the compromise would save the Union, but little did they realize that the agreement was only a lull in what proved to be a disastrous storm. Just when the Union was saved from a civil war, public opinion was stirred to a high pitch by the election of 1852, which was followed by the appearance of Mrs. Harriet Beecher Stowe's *Uncle Tom's Cabin*. This story was effective in creating a storm of public rage; it first appeared as a serial in the *National Era*, and then, in 1852, as a two volume work.[29]

Thus *Uncle Tom's Cabin* is immediately important to the understanding of Foster's *My Old Kentucky Home, Good Night*. Some commentators on Foster's works acknowledge a possibility of the influence of Mrs. Stowe's book, but, so far as is known, no one has thoroughly analyzed this influence. The story of *Uncle Tom's Cabin* did not originate with Mrs. Stowe; it antedates her publication by more than two decades. Perhaps the first publications attracting attention in the Middle West were the various denominational pamphlets issued by the itinerant preachers of Kentucky. Especially was this true of the pamphlet published by Father David Rice, at Danville, in 1792, under the title of *Slavery Inconsistent with Justice and Good Policy*. Even Henry Clay had attacked the institution of slavery in the *Kentucky Gazette* for April 25, 1798, under the pseudonym of *Sccevola*.

Perhaps the first of these anti-slavery works which actually attracted Mrs. Stowe's attention was William Lloyd Garrison's

---
[28] *Ibid.*
[29] *Kentucky Statesman*, December 17, 1852.

Liberator. Doubtless this publication was very influential in planting the germ of righteous protest in her mind.

The next publication of importance was the *Anti-Slavery Record* issued by the Anti-Slavery Society from its 143 Nassau Street, New York, address. This little magazine appeared for the first time in 1834 and carried more anti-slavery propaganda than any other publication of its time. It played very definitely upon the imagination of its readers by the sure-fire method of using quotations. These excerpts range all the way from the Declaration of Independence to speeches of Asa A. Stone, a theological student from Natchez, Mississippi at Lane Seminary.[10]

The *Anti-Slavery Record* devoted a goodly amount of attention to slavery in Kentucky. The next year after the initial appearance of this publication, J. H. Ingraham, a New England school teacher-novelist, published his work entitled *The Southwest by a Yankee*. Ingraham's story of slavery as he found it around Natchez was indeed fascinating. He witnessed the slave trading operation of the dealers at the "Natchez at the Cross Roads" market.[31] Although not writing from the standpoint of a propagandist, his work, which is in two volumes, was soon circulated in anti-slavery circles. It made a very definite impression upon anti-slavery writers who were to express themselves in the future.

Four years after the appearance of *The Southwest by a Yankee* William Jay published his interesting little volume entitled *Jay's View*.[32] Jay perhaps did more solid investigating than any of the protagonists before him. He analyzed slavery from a political and economic standpoint, and many of his findings will still stand fire under the best of historical research. To anti-slavery propagandists *Jay's View* formed the ridge pole of well informed criticism.[33]

At the same time that William Jay expressed himself in his publication Theodore Weld, with the assistance of his South Carolina wife, Angelina Grimke Weld, issued his work *American Slavery as It Is: Testimony of a Thousand Witnesses*.[34] This book, containing 224 pages, is undoubtedly the most exhaustive

---
[10]For some of these quotations see Theodore Weld, *op. cit.*, pp. 35-36, 77-82.
[31]J. H. Ingraham, *op. cit.*, p. 244.
[32]*Jay's View* is cited by many anti-slavery authors.
[33]William Jay, *Jay's View*, New York, 1839.
[34]Theodore Weld, *American Slavery as It Is*, New York, 1839.

study of its kind. The author collected letters, speeches, pamphlets, testimonials and newspaper advertisements to condemn slavery. Kentucky is duly represented; in fact the reader gets the impression that much of the attack was centered upon Kentucky, thus the chief background study for *Uncle Tom's Cabin*. It was from this information collected by Weld that Mrs. Stowe secured a well-digested source for her famous book. If one should take *Uncle Tom's Cabin* and check it against *American Slavery as It Is* he would find that the two would coincide, with only one significant exception: Mrs. Stowe had the advantage of changing national circumstances and additional written materials. Following the battle of Buena Vista, in February, 1847,[15] there was a general expansion of the cotton industry, and consequently an expansion of the slave trade.

Advertisements appeared in the newspapers throughout the country asking for slaves to be sold in the Southern market. The following which appeared in 1852 is typical of these requests:

I wish to purchase immediately, for the South, any number of negroes, from 10 to 30 years of age, for which I will pay the very highest cash price. All communications promptly attended to.
Joseph Bruin,
West End, Alexandria, Va.[16]

During the same time, in Kentucky, John Mattingly's agency was advertising in 1849 for 100 negroes to be sold in the Southern market.[17] There were also other agents, such as P. N. Brent, and J. M. Heady, who were advertising in the Kentucky papers each week for negroes to be sold in the Southern markets.[18]

Thus the expanding slave market gave Mrs. Stowe her central theme. Contrary to popular belief, Mrs. Stowe did not, however, collect all of her material in Kentucky. It is true, as she says in her *Key to Uncle Tom's Cabin*,[19] that she saw slavery in Kentucky and was duly impressed by it. Tradition says she saw the conditions of slavery at the old Kennedy home in Garrard County and at Washington in Mason County. On casual observation it would seem true that Kentucky formed the background for *Uncle Tom's Cabin*, and had this book not attracted

---
[15] Theodore Clark Smith, *Parties and Slavery*, 1850-1860, New York, 1906, pp. 3-13.
[16] *Lynchburg Virginian*, November 18, 1852.
[17] *Kentucky Statesman*, August 17, 1850.
[18] See *Kentucky Statesman and Lexington Observer and Reporter*, 1850-1860.
[19] Harriet Beecher Stowe, *Key to Uncle Tom's Cabin*, 1853, p. 9.

world-wide attention and had it not incurred such bitter criticism the author's many readers might never have been wiser.[40] As it was, Mrs. Stowe felt that she was impelled to make some statement in behalf of her book, and in 1853 she published her *Key to Uncle Tom's Cabin Presenting the Original Facts and Documents upon Which the Story is Founded—Together with Corroborative Statements Verifying the Truth of the Work.* This book throws some interesting light upon just how much influence the writings and utterances of the anti-slavery disciples had upon the making of *Uncle Tom's Cabin.* It is now well known that Mrs. Stowe's book is a composite picture of the whole anti-slavery struggle. The work embodies all of the anti-slavery arguments combined into an appealing drama of the life of Uncle Tom.

The *Key to Uncle Tom's Cabin* is a fine skeleton of the original publication, and completely denounces the belief of local origin. In fact the careful student of slavery is surprised to see how much material was called into service in the creation of the Uncle Tom story. It is quite obvious that Mrs. Stowe set out to present a prejudiced view of the slavery situation, and naturally her works have to be taken judiciously; but at the same time she is to be credited with having utilized the mass of anti-slavery material available. It is especially significant in the treatment of the subject in hand to know that *Uncle Tom's Cabin* was not the figment of a fertile imagination. The story of *Uncle Tom's Cabin* is generally borderland,[41] falling with equal responsibility upon Maryland, the Carolinas, Kentucky and Missouri. Upon careful analysis of the story it will be found that it has three natural divisions: that of a happily situated and trusted domestic servant, a slave unhappily involved in the financial reverses of a beloved master; the sale, and the inevitable movement down the river, and, lastly, despair in this life, but hope that better times are coming in a better land.

Here it is opportune to analyze the theme of *My Old Kentucky Home, Good Night.* In the first stanza, and the one sung most often, is the cheerful picture of what was a slave's Utopia:

"The young folks roll on the little cabin floor,
    All merry, all happy and bright";

---

[40]Mrs. Stowe was enthusiastically praised and bitterly condemned. She felt it worthwhile to publish some comment on the sources for her work. It is possible, however, that many of these sources were unknown to her in 1852.

[41]By border-land is meant Missouri, Kentucky, Virginia, Maryland and North Carolina.

My Old Kentucky Home 111

The second stanza indicates that a veil has passed over this happy situation, and the negroes are seized with the dread of an impending crisis:
"They hunt no more for the possum and the coon,
    On the meadow, the hill, and the shore: . . .
  The time has come when the darkeys have to part";
In the third stanza, one slave moans:
"A few more days, and the trouble all will end,
    In the field where the sugar canes grow. . . .
  A few more days till we totter on the road;—
    Then my old Kentucky home, good night."

There are several angles to my *Old Kentucky Home, Good Night*, which are worthy of serious consideration. First, Foster, truly enough, was a Democrat; but was he a staunch Democrat? Did his Democratic view in politics affect his attitude toward slavery? Many Democrats were opposed to slavery. For instance, Stephen A. Douglas, a staunch Democrat who was ambitious for the highest gift of the party, was not favorably disposed toward slavery.[42] Also, did the fact that the Foster family had a bound girl, Olivia Pise,[43] make of Stephen a pro-slavery advocate? He was not, contrary to some claims, a Southerner, and it is unlikely that Foster was affected vitally by any of these influences. Apparently he took his politics lightly, and doubtless his contact with slavery in his own family was a far cry from that of the lower South. It would not be unreasonable to suspect that the Foster family looked upon the absentee master system of slavery as atrocious, whether they were anti-abolitionists or not.

It is well to go further behind the scenes and analyze the situation socially and politically in American history at the time *My Old Kentucky Home, Good Night*, was written. Stephen Collins Foster went to Cincinnati to become a bookkeeper for his brother Dunning, some time after 1846. During the years 1848, 1849 and early 1850 he was engaged as a clerk in his brother's steamboat business. While there he drew upon southern slavery as the source for several of his early songs. Especially was this true of *Away Down Souf, Camptown Races, Lou'siana Belle,*[44] and

---
[42]It is most doubtful that Stephen Collins Foster's politics in any way influenced his views on human relationships.
[43]There were two servants in the Foster household, but these were indentured, or bound servants, rather than "slaves for life." Howard, *cp. cit.*, pp. 82, 83, 86.
[44]*Lou'siana Belle* was written in Pittsburgh and published in Cincinnati.

Oh! Susanna.[45] These songs show conclusively that at times Foster's inclination in his writings was toward the South. Furthermore, as a clerk in a steamboat office, it is not at all unreasonable to suppose that he saw numerous bills-of-lading for negro traders who were shipping their human wares southward.[46]

At the time young Foster was a resident of Cincinnati the community was upset over slavery, largely due to the activities of the underground railroad, Lane Seminary and Oberlin College. Foster undoubtedly saw much of this in the Cincinnati newspapers, and heard much discussion of the subject in the street.[47]

It is impossible to throw much light upon the next point, but if Foster read any of the works of the contemporary American poets he would have come face to face with some startling selections condemning slavery.[48] Longfellow wrote in his *Slave's Dream:*

> "In dark fens of the Dismal Swamp
>   The hunted negro lay;
> He saw the fire of the midnight camp,
> And heard at times the horse's tramp
>   And a blood hound's distant bay," etc.

John Greenleaf Whittier wrote in *The Farewell:*

> "Gone, gone—sold and gone,
> To the rice swamp dank and lone.
> Where the slave whip ceaseless swings,
> Where the noisome insect stings,
> Where the fever demon strews
> Poison with the falling dews,
> Where the sickly sunbeams glare,
> Through the hot and musty air,—

---

[45]There is a controversy as to whether *Oh! Susanna* was written in Pittsburgh or Cincinnati. It was copyrighted, New York, February 25, 1848.

[46]Undoubtedly Foster saw way-bills passing through the steamboat office of his brother Morris. He also saw slaves being shipped South by boats in 1852. Morrison Foster's *My Brother Stephen*, originally published in 1896, in Pittsburgh, was republished in 1932, in Indianapolis, by Josiah Kirby Lilly, Foster Hall, Indianapolis. 55 pages; p. 51.

[47]Not only was slavery a subject of discussion in Cincinnati and the surrounding area, but Mrs. Stowe's reputation spread abroad in an incredibly short time. The play *Uncle Tom's Cabin* was popular in several foreign languages.

[48]Foster's work book, now in possession of Mr. Josiah Kirby Lilly, Foster Hall, Indianapolis, has a list of classic American titles scribbled on the back of one of the pages.

Gone, gone—sold and gone,
To the rice swamp dank and lone,
From Virginia's hills and waters,—
Woe is me, my stolen daughters!"

It cannot be proved that Foster read the works of the American poets.[49] On this subject both Morrison Foster and John Tasker Howard are mute. That Stephen Collins Foster read Longfellow and Whittier is rather doubtful. They were read and used, however, by Mrs. Harriet Beecher Stowe.[49] John Greenleaf Whittier's *The Farewell* was a strong influence in laying the basis for the latter part of *Uncle Tom's Cabin*.

It is significant that *Uncle Tom's Cabin* was dramatized in many languages, and that Stephen Collins Foster was busily engaged in writing for the minstrels of his day. Chief among these traveling companies was that of E. P. Christy which advertised its appearance in 1847 at Mechanic's Hall, New York:[50]

CHRISTY'S
Far famed and original band of
ETHIOPIAN MINSTRELS
Whose unique and chaste performances have
Been patronized by the elite and fashionable in
All the principal cities of the Union-respectfully
Announce that they will give a series of their
Popular and inimitable concerts, introducing
A variety of entirely new songs, choruses
And burlesques.

The minstrel was a popular form of entertainment during the forties and fifties.[50] As early as 1842 Dan Emmett organized a minstrel company, and that same year the Virginia Minstrels were organized in Buffalo by E. P. Christy. It was not, however, until 1846 that this group became known as Christy's Minstrels.[50]

On September 11, 1850, Phineas Taylor Barnum, the king of American amusement, crowded Castle Garden to more than its

---

[49]Mrs. Stowe quotes John Greenleaf Whittier in her *Key to Uncle Tom's Cabin*, New York, 1858, p. 151.

[50]Meade Minnigerode, *The Fabulous Forties*, 1840-1850, New York, 1924, pp. 230-232.

6,000 comfortable seating capacity when he introduced Jenny Lind, "The Swedish Nightingale."[51] For once P. T. Barnum had produced the real thing, and the American amusement-loving public was spared the ordeal of paying its money to be swindled by the "Master of Colonel Tom Thumb." While "The Swedish Nightingale" was taking her New York audience by storm at Castle Garden, and was being written-up in every tag-end newspaper on the continent, the "divine" English actress, Fanny Kemble, was collecting $1,600.00 in Cincinnati for six interpretations of Shakespeare's plays.[52]

Americans of the forties and fifties craved excitement. The gold rush of the late forties had keyed the public to a high pitch. This was an America which demanded manufactured amusement, and there were showmen to do the amusing. Barnum, Christy, Emmett and scores of others catered to their fellow countrymen's desires. Everything from a fake mermaid, a stupid waterfall called "Niagra," dioramas, and wax figures to the plunk-a-plunk of the minstrels' banjos were called into service. In order to meet the increasing demands there were hundreds of creative artists who, like Stephen Collins Foster, kept their producers supplied with new tunes to tickle the fancies of their fickle audiences.[53] Time has proved that none of these artists were as efficient as Foster, for his tunes are still capable of creating in the American, whether North or South, a nostalgic longing for some sentimental place.

It is significant that *My Old Kentucky Home, Good Night*, was published early in 1853, and certainly written in 1852.[54] Not even the most casual school child can read *My Old Kentucky Home, Good Night* from beginning to end without becoming immediately conscious that the description of a state or region is only incidental to the story. The existence of a personality is as distinct as was the ghost at the death bed of Simon Legree. The first draft of it gives it a personality. That personality is a poor luckless old negro who lives during the first stanza in a

---

[51] Joel Benton, *Life of Honorable Phineas Taylor Barnum*, n. p., 1891, p. 224.
[52] Leota S. Driver, *Fanny Kemble*, Chapel Hill, 1933, p. 166.
[53] See list of songs turned out during these years by Foster, Howard, *op. cit.*, appendix 1, pp. 370-385.
[54] Manuscript copy of Foster's work book, Foster Hall, Indianapolis.

My Old Kentucky Home

happy home—who in the second verse senses trouble—and in the third verse, like Whittier's:

> "Gone, gone—sold and gone,
> To the rice swamps dank and lone,"

Foster makes the soulful plaint:

> "A few more days and the trouble all will end
> In the fields where the sugar canes grow;
> A few more days for to tote the weary load,
> No matter, 'twill never be light,
> A few more days 'till we totter on the road,
> Then my old Kentucky home, good night."

This verse, however, (like the other two verses and the chorus) has been changed from the original draft which admitted a personality in the text and the title. Instead of "My Old Kentucky Home, Good Night" the title was "Poor Uncle Tom, Good Night." The line

> "Den poor Uncle Tom, good night"

appears at the end of each verse in the original draft, also at the end of the chorus.

The last line of the three verses of the finished song, it will be recalled, is

> "Then my old Kentucky Home, good night."

and at the end of the finished chorus the line is

> "For my old Kentucky Home, far away."

The original draft of the song is in Mr. Josiah K. Lilly's Foster Collection and is reproduced in facsimile in *Foster Hall Bulletin*, No. 8, February, 1933. A reduced facsimile is presented in this, the January, 1936, issue of *The Filson Club History Quarterly*.

Perhaps Foster changed the title of his song to dodge prejudices against it in the South. The minstrels were playing throughout the country, and it was from the South that they collected a goodly amount of revenue.[55] Hence it was poor policy to antagonize so important an amusement loving center.

---

[55]See advertisements in southern newspapers. A specific notice appears in *The Kentucky Statesman*, April 19, 1853.

After 1852 the minstrels had competition in *Uncle Tom's Cabin* which was dramatized and appeared on the stage throughout the free states. There were also other slave plays which enticed the showgoing public to patronize their theatres. Although not enjoying anything like the phenomenal popularity of *Uncle Tom's Cabin*, J. T. Trowbridge's *Neighbor Jackwood* had a successful run.[56] Throughout the country the newspapers were crowded with both estimable and critical comments on Mrs. Stowe's work.[57] One commentator said of the book that "When Latin I studied, my Ainsworth in hand, I answered my teacher *Sto* meant 'to stand', but if you asked I should now give the reply 'For Stowe means, beyond cavil, to lie.' "[58]

All of the many and thunderous comments undoubtedly attracted the attention of Stephen Collins Foster. It is well known that he was extraordinarily sensitive to contemporary occurrences. In 1848 he published: *Santa Anna's Retreat from Buena Vista*; in 1856 *The Great Baby Show, The Abolition Show*; in 1861 *I'll Be a Soldier*, and, in 1863, *A Soldier in de Colored Brigade*.[59]

Other writers of the period were sensitive to the happenings of the times. For instance, C. S. Bodley's music store in Lexington, Kentucky advertised the *Gold Diggers' Waltz*, in 1853, a song commemorating the Gold Rush to California.[60]

Foster, like Cooper, found in his American surroundings a super-abundant source of themes for his songs. This fact is well illustrated in his negro songs such as *Away Down Souf* (1848), *Dolcy Jones* (1849), *Dolly Day* (1850), *and Gwine to Run All Night* (1850).

Thus it matters little where *My Old Kentucky Home, Good Night* was written, but it is significant that it mirrors a most interesting background of the nation's history. It is significant, also, that the author's use of a title obscured his context sufficiently to cause Kentuckians, to whom *Uncle Tom's Cabin* was anathema, to take the song to their hearts and claim it as their very own.

---

[56]Meade Minnigerode, *op. cit.*, 160-161, gives a list of other plays which were popular.
[57]See any Southern newspaper for 1853.
[58]*The Kentucky Statesman*, February 1, 1853.
[59]George Cooper wrote the words for *A Soldier in de Colored Brigade*.
[60]*The Kentucky Statesman*, January 18, 1853.

THOMAS D. CLARK (1903–   ), born in Louisville, Mississippi, became one of Kentucky's (and the nation's) most distinguished historians. He earned his B.A. degree at the University of Mississippi, his M.A. at the University of Kentucky, and his Ph.D. at Duke University. Longtime head of the Department of History at the University of Kentucky, he has served also as Distinguished Visiting Professor at Eastern Kentucky University. Clark has been active in numerous state and national historical societies and historical projects. Among his many articles and books are *A History of Kentucky; Kentucky, Land of Contrast; Frontier America; Pills, Petticoats, and Plows;* and *Indiana University.*

This article first appeared in *The Filson Club History Quarterly* in January 1936, vol. 10, pp. 1–17.

THE CODE DUELLO IN ANTE-BELLUM KENTUCKY

BY J. WINSTON COLEMAN, JR.
Lexington, Kentucky

By the turn of the nineteenth century, much of the rawness of the backwoods was passing; men were taking on the more polished ways and manners of the Atlantic seaboard states and duelling became the accepted means for gentlemen of the Bluegrass region to settle their personal disputes. This method of defending one's honor or avenging a personal affront by the code duello superseded the rough and tumble fights of the pioneer era, when backwoodsmen, drunk or sober, scorned such pompous formalities.

A gentleman of this period could demand satisfaction from another gentleman for any grievance, either real or imagined, and the man who refused to accept a challenge was regarded as a coward of the lowest degree who hardly deserved to live. Under this vicious code of honor, personal differences were settled with pistols, often resulting in the death of one or both of the parties. Early attempts were made to suppress this "pernicious practice," but public opinion sustained it and, as a result, the law merely winked at the affray and the press said very little. The best excuse was that the duel prevented informal brawls and street fights, and gave personal encounters an atmosphere of gentility. All too often, however, the wrong man died; the trickier eye or quicker shot, won out.

Meetings that occurred to avenge a personal affront or to satisfy some sensitive gentleman's high sense of honor were conducted according to a tradition that was quite simple; the aggrieved party sent a challenge note in writing through a friend, the choice of the place, distance, and weapons being left, as a rule, to the challenged person. Usually the meetings took place in some secluded spot or place hidden from public view, with seconds and surgeons in attendance. Sometimes each principal had two seconds. Together these men drew up the formal statement of conditions of the affair, even to the smallest details. Pistols were usually at ten paces, or thirty feet; rifles and shotguns infrequently were at farther distances.

There was no formal guide of behavior, no book of etiquette on the code of honor during the early days of the state's history. All the meetings were carried out under the rules then in force and used by custom in Virginia, Maryland, and the Carolinas, as well as in the Deep South, where the Sir Walter Scott tradition of southern honor and chivalry was so rigidly enforced. In 1838, Governor John Lyde Wilson, of South Carolina, published a thin sixteen-page pamphlet titled: *The Code of Honor; or Rules for the Government of Principals and Seconds in Duelling*. This authority on the code which went through a number of editions, became the accepted guide for all affairs of honor in the Bluegrass State.

Encounters between Kentuckians often occurred for trivial reasons or from charges of cowardice; many of which today seem ridiculous in both purpose and practice. When shots were exchanged or blood drawn, most "affairs" were considered settled and the aggrieved gentleman's honor was duly satisfied. It was the desire for "satisfaction," rather than an urge to kill.

However, it was beneath the dignity of a gentleman to engage in a duel with a person not of his own social standing—a *gentleman* could fight only with a *gentleman*. When a person was challenged and refused to fight, he was "posted," as the term went. Flaming handbills were distributed about town and tacked up in conspicuous places loudly proclaiming the accused person a liar, coward, poltroon, vile wretch or slanderer. To be so posted was too much for any hot-blooded and high-strung Kentuckian. Therefore, he sought "satisfaction" in the usual mode, and he quickly called out his opponent.

The code duello was not a new thing in Kentucky. It had, like all other Kentucky institutions crossed the mountains from Virginia, Maryland, and the Carolinas. Hot-blooded and sensitive gentlemen not only brought their honor, but the means whereby it might be defended. With the older and aristocratic families that emigrated from the eastern states came their fine sets of duelling pistols, fitted in elaborate mahogany cases, complete with powder measure, bullet molds, and ramrods. These were treasured heirlooms and guarded with great family pride.

The first time the "code" was invoked to assuage an insult was two years before the Commonwealth of Kentucky was admitted into the Union. Near Danville, on August 1, 1790, Captain James Strong met Henry Craig in this affair of honor. At sunrise, the antagonists lined up facing each other armed with clumsy flintlock pistols of large caliber. Captain Strong received Craig's fire in the right groin, and the missile ripped through his hip leaving a mortal wound, while Mr. Craig himself was struck in the thigh.[1]

Another of the early meetings in the Western Country which found its way into the contemporary press occurred in neighboring Garrard County during the fall of 1794. General Thomas Kennedy, a Virginian and owner of a fine plantation of several thousand acres rolling up from the Kentucky River, became involved in a duel. Kennedy was a large slaveholder, the master of a fine colonial brick mansion where

Harriet Beecher Stowe visited to gather materials for her great antislavery novel *Uncle Tom's Cabin*.

General Kennedy and William Gillespie, a cattle-trader from Madison County, became involved in a business deal, hot words followed and a challenge ensued. The parties met in General Kennedy's front yard on Tuesday, October 21st and, as the *Kentucky Gazette* reported: "Gillespie was on the first fire mortally wounded, who died the next day, but Kennedy escaped, the bullet passing through his clothes under his left arm."[2]

These two personal encounters convinced the Kentucky legislators that the code would take its toll in the state as it had so many times beyond the mountains. In 1799, the General Assembly sought to check the spread of the "honor killings" and accordingly, on December 13th, passed "An Act more Effectually to Suppress the Practice of Gambling & Duelling," which levied a fine of 150 to 500 dollars for each violation.[3] This law was even more stringent by imposing prison terms on offenders and disqualifying duellists from holding public offices for a period of seven years—a provision especially oppressive on politically-minded Kentuckians.

Judge John Rowan was, in time, to make his name synonymous with that of Nelson County. A noted lawyer, owner of Federal Hill, he was a man of great prominence and scholarship. Bardstown also had another highly educated gentleman, Dr. James Chambers, a young physician and son-in-law of Judge James Sebastian, of the Kentucky Court of Appeals.[4]

On the evening of January 21, 1801, these two gentlemen met in an upstairs room of Duncan McLean's Tavern in Bardstown for a round of beer drinking and card playing. They became engaged in a two-handed game of "vigutum" (vingt-et-un), or "twenty-one," as it was popularly known. Playing for stakes and still drinking, Judge Rowan "won about 11½ dollars on credit from the Doctor besides several quarts of beer." After the game had progressed for some time Rowan and Chambers became involved in a heated argument "as to which understood some of the dead languages the best." Each accused the other of being vastly inferior to himself in matters of classical scholarship. Rowan called Chambers "a damned lie," whereupon the Doctor jumped up, "collered him & said he was superior," both being intoxicated. Judge Rowan appeared more so, "for when blows ensued, Mr. Rowan struck the wall of the chimney as often, perhaps oftener, than he struck the Doctor[5]." Two days after the card-playing brawl, Chambers challenged Rowan to a duel.

At dawn on February 3, 1801, the two masters of the dead languages, accompanied by their seconds and a few close friends, met at Captain

Jacob Yoder's plantation on Beech Fork, two and three-quarters of a mile south of town. At the command, both men wheeled around and fired; neither bullet finding its mark. On the second fire, Doctor Chambers slumped to the ground with a pistol ball "near the center of the body in the left side just below the nipple[6]." He expired at his home early the next day.

Although he had acted in strict conformance of the code duello, Judge Rowan was arrested and later tried for murder. At his examining trial, the magistrate announced, after hearing all parties, that there was no evidence sufficient to hold the defendant to the Grand Jury; Judge Rowan walked out of the court-room a free man.[7] This verdict clearly showed that public sentiment in Kentucky strongly favored the code duello; that it was considered no offense for one man to kill another in a formal encounter with pistols at ten paces.

On May 30, 1806, Major General Andrew Jackson, afterwards President of the United States, and Charles Dickinson, an attorney-at-law and handsome, gay young blade of Nashville, met on the field of honor at Harrison's Mills, on Red River, in Logan County, Kentucky. Their differences grew out of a horse race in which Dickinson's father-in-law, James Erwin, lost ten thousand dollars to Jackson, and the aspersions the young lawyer cast upon the General's premature wedding with Rachel Robards.

Two years had elapsed since the husband, Lewis Robards, obtained a bill to permit him to be divorced from his wife. He did not follow it through with court action. In the meantime, Jackson and young Rachel became engaged and, assuming all was well and that the divorce had gone through, took a trip down the river to Natchez and there were married by a Catholic priest, in the summer of 1791.[8]

Jackson's marriage was destined to cause him a great deal of trouble. His charming wife was not welcomed in Nashville society and, all too often, her husband had to resent the charge of living with another man's wife. At length the Court of Quarter Sessions, at Harrodsburg, finally granted the divorce, and in January, 1794, a second marriage ceremony was performed.[9] There circumstances caused a great deal of scandalous talk, and reflections about the irregularity of his marriage or any disparaging remarks about his wife incensed the General more than anything else.

However, it was not long before Dickinson made some slighting allusions to Mrs. Jackson, this being the second time such matters had reached the General's ears. The story stirred his sensitive emotions and relations between the two men became increasingly strained. On May 21st, young Dickinson handed a "card" to the editor of the Nashville *Review*, declaring General Jackson "a worthless scoundrel, a poltroon and a coward." On the following day, Jackson challenged Dickinson and he immediately accepted—pistols at eight paces!

As the hour of seven came, Jackson's second, Thomas Overton called out:

> "Gentlemen, are you ready?"
> "I am ready," replied Dickinson.
> "I am ready," echoed Jackson.
> "F-i-r-e" cried Overton, with a loud shout.

At the word, Dickinson fired almost instantly. A small puff of dust came from the left shoulder of Jackson's coat; he had been hit, but stood steadily on his feet, with his left arm tightly drawn across his chest. Meanwhile, as planned, he had held his own fire. Dickinson, startled, recoiled a pace or two and falteringly muttered: "Great God! Have I missed him?"

"Back on your mark, Sir," cried Overton, as he fingered his own weapon. Dickinson recovered his composure, stepped forward to the peg and turned his eyes away from the cold gaze of his antagonist. Jackson took deliberate aim and pulled the trigger. There was no report; the seconds found that the hammer of his pistol had stopped at half-cock. Under the rules of the code this was not a shot; he could try again. Once more Jackson raised his pistol, took careful aim and fired. Dickinson swayed over backwards and fell to the ground, as his friends sprang forward to catch him. He lingered in great agony throughout the day, dying at five minutes past nine that evening.[10]

When Jackson's big loose coat and waistcoat were removed, it was found that Dickinson's bullet had gone true to its aim; he had sent the ball precisely where he supposed Jackson's heart was beating. The bullet though missing the heart, had hit a spot dangerously near it, and had broken a rib and grazed the breastbone. Jackson's wound never properly healed, and was believed to have been a contributing cause of his death nearly forty years later.

As the laws of Kentucky prohibited duellists from holding public offices and subjected them to heavy fines, they often went beyond the boundaries of the state to settle their affairs of honor. Henry Clay, the "Harry of the West" and a member of the Kentucky House of Representatives, journeyed across the Ohio River at Shippingport, below Louisville, to "an eligible spot" of ground on the Indiana shore immediately below the mouth of Silver Creek, in Floyd County. Here, on January 19, 1809, he met Humphrey Marshall, likewise a member of the Kentucky Legislature, to settle with pistol and ball what they had started with oratory back in the statehouse at Frankfort. Dr.

Frederick Ridgely, of Lexington, was Clay's surgeon, while Marshall took along a Frankfort physician to look after his needs.[11]

At the word both gentlemen fired. Henry's ball gave Marshall a slight flesh wound; the second fire Clay's pistol snapped and Marshall's bullet went wild. On the third round Marshall wounded Clay in the thigh. Then the seconds seeing Clay wounded, terminated the meeting.

Clay later gave a brief account of the affair: "I have this moment returned from the field of honor," he wrote. "We had three shots. On the first I grazed him above the navel—he missed me. On the second my damned pistol snapped, and he missed me. On the third I received a flesh wound in the thigh, and owing to my receiving his fire first, &c, I missed him. My wound is in no way serious, as the bone is unhurt, but prudence will require me to remain here some days."[12] In about two weeks the Master of Ashland returned to his public duties in the House, and he had demonstrated a bravery under fire which in no wise detracted from his public popularity.

As a rule doctors went to the duelling grounds primarily in a professional capacity, with surgical kit in hand. Occasionally a doctor leveled his pistol at a non-professional man, but when a medical man gave battle to one of his own brethren, it was a matter of high interest and widespread attention. Among the duels of this sort was the meeting on the field of honor between Dr. Benjamin W. Dudley and Dr. William H. Richardson, both eminent and learned members of the medical faculty of Transylvania University, in Lexington.

During the summer of 1818, a man was killed in a drunken brawl on the streets of Lexington. Drs. Dudley and Drake were summoned by the coroner to examine the body and report "whether the fall of the Irishman's head upon the curbing, killed him, or some other foul means."[13] Doctor Dudley performed the autopsy and made his medical report. Dr. Drake who failed to attend the postmortem examination insinuated that Dr. Dudley's findings were not sustained by the facts in the case. This professional reflection greatly incensed the noted Lexington lithotomist who then charged Drake "with disregard both of the law and his professional duty." Drake retorted that Dudley was a man without honor and no gentleman. This was too much for Dudley and he challenged Drake to meet him on the field of honor.

The incident over the autopsy of the Irishman which resulted in the challenge, climaxed the long-standing enmity between Doctors Drake, Dudley, and Richardson, which had been smoldering for a number of months over the medical school and its methods of operation. Drake, on account of his opposition to this method of settling differences between gentlemen, declined the challenge, but he was not able to prevent his ardent friend and colleague, Dr. Richardson, from accepting it in his stead. Terms were speedily arranged, seconds and surgeons selected, and the day set for the affair of honor.

Early on Tuesday, August 5, 1818, the two doctors, with their surgeons and attendants and a few close friends, met at the favorite duelling-grounds of central Kentucky, about six and one-half miles northwest of Lexington on the line of Fayette and Scott counties, in the vicinity of present-day Donerail, on what is known as the James K. Duke Farm, now a part of Walnut Hall Farm.[14]

When the word was given, both parties fired. In a few seconds the smoke cleared. Dr. Dudley stood untouched. Dr. Richardson staggered and fell; blood rushed from a serious wound in the groin which severed the inguinal artery.

It was evident that relief must be had speedily or the wounded man would bleed to death. It was further apparent that the efforts of the attending surgeon to arrest the flow of blood with a tourniquet were of no avail. At this moment Dr. Dudley stepped forward and offered his services to save the life of his adversary which was so swiftly ebbing away. By pressing his thumb on the large blood vessel where it passed over the ilium, Dr. Dudley soon had the situation under control and gave time for the ligature of the artery by Richardson's surgeon. Thus, "by the ready skill and magnanimity of Dudley," said an early account, the life of the challenged man was saved.

Popular feeling against duelling expressed itself loudly after the resort to arms between Dudley and Richardson. Several days after the affair of honor, an anti-duelling meeting was held in the courthouse in Lexington, where seventy-six prominent men of the town went on record as opposing this method of settling differences, and voiced the strong opinion "that no circumstances can arise between our citizens where their honor might not better be sustained by a reference to the deliberate opinion of a few judicious and pacific men, than by an appeal to deadly combat."[15] This meeting, however, failed to remedy the situation and "honor killings" continued. Ironically enough, eleven years later, a son of one of the men who attended the anti-duelling meeting was himself killed in a duel.[16]

On Sunday, July 4, 1819, Independence Day was celebrated with a general muster and review of the county militia, in the little town of Frankfort, county seat of Franklin County and State Capital of Kentucky; it was the forty-third anniversary of the Nation's freedom. In the afternoon the three local military companies and a large concourse of citizens repaired to Cove Springs, three miles northeast of the town on the Peak's Mill Road. After the conclusion of several speeches and a bountiful feast, the three companies took the field and began their annual muster and maneuvers. In Captain Alexander Rennick's company were two young subalterns: Jacob H. Holeman, a newspaper man of Frankfort, and Francis G. Waring, also of the Capital city.[17] Both were vain officers, and both were showing off before their admiring audience and friends.

As the raw but eager young recruits were being put through their fancy maneuvers, the strict military decorum of the occasion was disturbed by the appearance of Holeman's pet dog which trotted on the drill-field closely behind his master's heels. Officer Waring, strutting at the head of the column, became so highly incensed at this breach of parade-ground discipline that he gave the animal a fierce thrust with his dress sword and killed it on the spot. A fist fight between the officers followed, and next day Waring, seeking that satisfaction due one gentleman from another under the code duello, challenged the Frankfort newspaperman.

The parties met by arrangement at six o'clock on the morning of July 16, 1819, in the large woodland situated on the farm of the Reverend Silas M. Noel, about one and one-half miles from Frankfort, later the home of Colonel Theodore O'Hara, author of the well-known poem *The Bivouac of the Dead*.

At the word fire both pistols rang out at the same time. Waring slumped forward and fell to the ground, the ball from Holeman's pistol entered the right breast, ranged to the left and passed through his heart. He died instantly. Waring's bullet took effect in Holeman's hip and he fell to the ground seriously wounded.[18]

Following the tragic ending on the field of honor, Jacob H. Holeman and his second, Wilson P. Greenup, were tried in the Franklin Circuit Court for the murder of Francis G. Waring on July sixteenth.[19] A number of witnesses were called and heard; all stating that the meeting had been fair and fought according to the code duello. At length, the jury "having heard the evidence upon their oaths," declared the prisoners at the bar "not guilty" of the charges in the indictment. Holeman and Greenup were set at liberty. Again it was demonstrated that, although duelling was a downright violation of the criminal statutes and generally frowned upon, popular opinion sustained it.

Ten years later, on March 9, 1829, Charles Wickliffe, the young son of Robert ("Old Duke") Wickliffe, shot and killed Thomas Benning, editor of the *Kentucky Gazette* over an article published in his paper. His trial opened on June 30, 1829. Crowds thronged into the old brick courthouse in Lexington to hear the great "Harry of the West" plead the case of the Old Duke's son. The jury had a pro-slavery complexion and Clay's friends claimed he never lost a criminal case in the last thirty years of his practice. The jurors stayed out a little over five minutes, and Charles Wickliffe went free.[20]

Following the death of Mr. Benning, the editorship of the *Gazette* was taken over by George James Trotter, son of the late General James Trotter, a noted soldier in the War of 1812. The impetuous son of the Old Duke, flushed with success of his recent trial, became angered "in consequence of some remarks made in the paper in relation to the death of Benning." This editorial insinuated that young Wickliffe had cowardly murdered the former editor of the *Gazette* without the latter having a chance to defend himself; it hinted strongly at a "packed and perjured jury," and spoke of the undue influence of Henry Clay as senior counsel for the accused.

When Wickliffe read the charges in the paper, he became highly aggrieved and felt his honor should be satisfied according to the code under which Southern gentlemen operated. Several days later, he sent a formal challenge in writing to the editor:

> Mr. George J. Trotter: Lexington, Sept. 28, 1829.
> A wanton and unprovoked attack was made upon my feelings in the *Gazette* of the 18th of the present month, induces me to demand that satisfaction, which is due from one gentleman to another. My friend Dr. Ritchie, is authorized to settle the several points of time, mode and place.
> Your obedient [servant],
> Chas. Wickliffe[21]

A strong and emphatic answer was returned by the challenged man, which read:

> Mr. Charles Wickliffe. Sir: Your note was received on yesterday by the hands of Dr. James Ritchie, and whilst I cannot recognize your right to call upon me in the manner you have, still the satisfaction you ask for *shall not be denied.* My friend Mr. John Robb, is fully authorized to confer with Dr. Ritchie as to the time, place and distance.
> Geo. J. Trotter[22]

Captain Henry Johnson and Dr. James Ritchie, as seconds for their respective parties, signed the terms and conditions under which the duel was to be fought on the following Friday:

1st.   The weapons to be pistols of the size, length and caliber usual on such occasions; the distance to be eight feet; the pistols to be loaded with single balls.

2nd.   The parties to take their positions, presenting the right side to each other, their pistols to be held with the muzzles presented to the ground. The word will then be given, "Are you ready," to which will be responded, "I am." One, two, three, four, five, will be called; after the word *five* each may fire as soon as he can; but neither shall fire [until] after the second giving the word, shall have counted the number to five.

3rd. Each party to demand as many fires as he may think proper; and each to be attended by one second and one surgeon each, and no more.

4th. A snap or a flash to be considered a fire, and each party to have leave to take two brace of pistols to the grounds.

5th. If either of the principals act in violation of these rules, by which his opponent is injured, the second of the injured man has a right to shoot the offender on the spot.

6th. The giving of the word to be determined by lot, and the meeting to take place on Friday, the 9th of October, 1829, at 9 o'clock A.M., at or near the junction of the Scott and Fayette lines.

Henry Johnson

Agreed to and signed: James Ritchie[23]

A little before the appointed time the parties met at the favorite duelling-grounds, with Dr. Samuel B. Richardson in attendance for Wickliffe and Dr. Japtha Dudley for Trotter. At the word *five,* both pistols were discharged. Strange to say, neither bullet found its mark, at the unheard-of distance of eight feet![24] Mr. Wickliffe then said very sharply, "I demand a second fire." Trotter advancing toward him, replied: "Sir, you shall have it *with pleasure.*" On the second fire Wickliffe received a mortal wound above the hips and died three hours later at his father's residence in Lexington. Trotter escaped without a scratch.

The eighteen-thirties and forties of the nineteenth century were years when men's tempers grew short, and their honor was most sensitive. Other duels occurred through the years and fanned the public attention. On May 15, 1841, Cassius M. Clay, the fiery anti-slavery leader of Madison County, and Robert Wickliffe, Jr., of Lexington, met on the field of honor in Indiana, opposite Louisville. Colonel William R. McKee was Clay's second; General Albert Sidney Johnston was Wickliffe's. Flintlock pistols were selected at thirty feet; two rounds were fired and nobody was injured. Friends of the parties interposed and adjusted the difficulty.

Then on January 17, 1848, Lieutenant Roger Hanson, of Clark County, and William M. Duke, of Scott County, faced each other at ten paces, each determined to take the life of the other. They met "at a point in Indiana, opposite the mouth of the Kentucky River," with Dr. French Bush, Dr. Alexander Blanton, and several friends in attendance. At the command *fire,* the pistols cracked simultaneously, Hanson firing too low, Duke too high. The second and third rounds were fired without effect. On the fourth fire, Hanson threw his pistol into the air and fell headlong to the earth, "the large ball crushing through his right thigh bone, making a bad wound, and breaking also the left thigh." He subsequently recovered, but was lamed for life. It was said at the time, that the cause of the duel was a young lady— Miss Caroline Hickman, who later became the wife of William M. Duke, challenger of the duel.[25]

Newspaper editors and lawyers flew at each other with epithets, and met under the code duello to assuage their wounded honor with pistols, rifles, and shotguns. A striking example of this was the tragic affair near Louisville between Captain Henry C. Pope and John Thompson Gray, both prominent lawyers of the city and members of old and distinguished families. Captain Pope, recently out of the Mexican War, and his friend Gray, with two other gentlemen were engaged in a game of cards at the old Galt House. After an hour or so had passed at the card table, young Pope, who was drinking heavily, drew a knife and threatened one of his fellow-players. Gray took the knife away from him and threw it out of the window, remarking: "I won't let you commit murder." This broke up the card game and for a while quieted the former Mexican War captain.

The young captain, getting deeper in his cups and apparently resentful of Gray's offer to help, now turned on him and called him all sorts of vile and abusive names and harshly accused him of mistreating his wife, Anita Thompson Gray. His loud talk, insults, and threats became so offensive that Gray could stand them no longer and "he fell to fighting him with all his might & broke his cane over Pope's head and cut his face & bruised him very much."[26] The fight terminated in the front yard of the hotel.

Nothing but a meeting on the field of honor, reasoned Captain Pope, could atone for the rough handling he received from his friend and fellow-lawyer; he forthwith challenged Gray. Twelve-guage percussion-type shotguns, loaded with single balls, were chosen as the weapons, distance sixty feet. For their meeting-place, a wooded spot was selected in Indiana across from Six Mile Island in the Ohio River, above Louisville; time of the meeting was fixed at 10 A.M., June 14, 1849.

Upon arrival at the duelling-grounds, the usual ceremonies were enacted. Pope, for some strange reason, sported "a white vest &

black pants & coat"—the most conspicuous dress he could have selected; Gray wore an ordinary business suit, with waistcoat removed The principals took their stations, a second gave the word and both guns went off with a loud report. Captain Pope crumpled and fell over backwards, dropping his shotgun to the ground. Gray's bullet "passed through Pope's thigh breaking the bone all to pieces, just below the hip & entering the other thigh." The wounded duellist was placed in a boat and the men at the oars rowed for the city, while Dudley Haydon, his second in the affair, held his head in his lap "bathing him with camphor & giving him brandy & water." After the boat had gone a short distance, Pope attempted to raise up and say something, but "laid down & died without a struggle."[27]

Next morning the funeral of Captain Pope was held at the residence of William Prather, on Walnut Street, attended by his family and a large gathering of friends. Walter N. Haldeman, editor of the *Morning Courier,* paid a fine tribute to the fallen young man, describing him as "one generally esteemed for his fine social qualities, kindness of heart and brilliancy of mind. Yesterday morning," continued the editor, 'he was in good health, and enjoyed fair prospects of a long life as any one in our midst. At noon he was a corpse—another victim to the bloody *code of honor.*"[28]

John Thompson Gray, the challenged man, escaped unhurt, the ball from his adversary's shotgun going wide of its mark. Although he had fought the duel honorably and bravely and strictly by the code, Gray now bore the odium of having killed one of Louisville's most popular and talented young men. He was forced to leave the city and remained in Maryland with his relatives for a number of years. Afterwards, in the late 1850's, he returned to Louisville but never quite lived down the unfavorable comment caused by his participation in the duel.

During the early months of the Civil War, William T. Casto, prominent lawyer and mayor of Maysville was arrested and charged with aiding and abetting "the so-called Confederate States of America." With six other Southern sympathizers he was hustled off to Fort Lafayette, the Federal prison in New York harbor. After remaining in military custody for several months, he was finally released on February 21, 1862, and he lost no time in returning to his home in Mason County, Kentucky.[29]

Colonel Leonidas Metcalfe, son of Kentucky's ex-Governor Thomas ("stone-hammer") Metcalfe, was a Colonel in the United States Army and in command of a regiment stationed near Maysville. It was Colonel Metcalfe who, acting upon orders of his superior officer, had arrested Casto and the six others for treason in the fall of 1861. Becoming obsessed with the belief that Colonel Metcalfe was solely and individually responsible for his arrest and subsequent incarceration at Fort Lafayette, Casto developed a bitter antipathy against the Union officer from Nicholas County and a burning desire for revenge. For the next six weeks or two months, he brooded over what he regarded as his gross mistreatment.

At length, Casto worked himself up to the point of seeking redress from Colonel Metcalfe under the code duello, and on May 6th he sent him a challenge note which read:

> Col. Leonidas Metcalfe: Maysville, May 6, 1862
>
> Sir—Having done me great wrong under circumstances adding indignity to injustice, you cannot deny me what is the purpose of this note to demand the satisfaction due from one gentleman to another. My friend Mr. Isaac Nelson, the bearer is authorized to arrange the terms of the meeting.
>
> Respectfully your ob't serv't,
> W. T. Casto[80]

Colonel Metcalfe lost no time in accepting the challenge, designating rifles at sixty yards; the time, five o'clock P. M., May 8, 1862. In agreeing to do battle with the Maysville attorney, the Colonel explained that "he believed the challenge was designed to take his life without provocation, or to injure him in public estimation."

Colonel Metcalfe, as an officer of the United States army, was likely to be court-martialed for accepting the challenge, while both principals, their seconds and surgeons were subject to the strict Kentucky laws against duelling then on the statute books: $500 fine or 12 months imprisonment for anyone sending a challenge; $250 or six months in prison for accepting a challenge; $150 or three months in jail for any person carrying or delivering a challenge note or for acting as a second or as a surgeon. Furthermore, any and all participants in an affair of honor, as already noted, were excluded from holding public offices in the Commonwealth of Kentucky "for a space of seven years after conviction."

For their rendezvous the parties chose a smooth sandbar in Bracken County, a short distance east of the mouth of Stony Creek, two miles down the Ohio River from Dover. Each principal, with seconds, arrived at the grounds sometime before the affair; each brushed up on his marksmanship. At length, when everything was ready, the seconds carefully checked the condition of the duelling weapons— Colt's 56 caliber revolving (5 shot cap and ball) rifles, and saw that each gun was properly loaded, in one chamber only. The challenger had no surgeon, but Colonel Metcalfe had two doctors in attendance who immediately proceeded to open their kits of surgical instruments and spread them out on blankets. The ground was measured off and the spectators ordered to keep their distances. The two principals were sent to their positions. They were both bearded men, powerfully built and over six feet tall. As a last precaution Metcalfe's second passed his hand over Casto's clothing to make sure that he wore no armor underneath. His pockets were emptied of everything that might stop or deflect a bullet, as it was known that lives had been saved by the presence of a metal match-box or jack-knife. Casto's second made a similar examination of Metcalfe's person.

When the signal was given, both duellists blazed away. Casto staggered and sank to the ground with a bullet through his body, a little below the heart. He lived for about fifteen minutes, though unconscious all the time. Metcalfe was unharmed. "Everything" noted the *Cincinnati Daily Commerce*, "was done in accordance with the code of the duello, and passed off without any difficulty."[31] At the time of the duel Metcalfe was forty-three and Casto was thirty-eight years old.

By the end of the Civil War, the formal duel in Kentucky was much on the decline, although there were still a number of sensitive gentlemen who sought satisfaction under the code duello for a grievance or personal affront, especially where a man's honor was thought to have been assailed. Of the latter-day duels that gained much notoriety at the time and sent one of the principals into exile, the Desha-Kimbrough affair of honor, fought on the James K. Duke farm, on the Scott-Fayette county line, on March 26, 1866, was probably the best known.

Both of these men were born and raised in Harrison County; they attended school together when boys but were never very fond of each other. One of the contestants was Joseph Desha, the handsome young grandson and namesake of an ex-Governor of Kentucky. He was captain in the Confederate army, saw action in a number of major battles and was seriously wounded in the left arm. The other participant in this affair of honor was Alexander Kimbrough, who espoused the Union cause and valiantly served as sergeant of Company K, Fourth Kentucky Volunteer Infantry. He too participated in a number of battles and skirmishes and was badly wounded in the right leg.

A quarrel and fist fight in the lobby of the old Smith House in Cynthiana, in February, 1866, resulted in Kimbrough sending a challenge to Captain Joseph Desha, "late of the rebel forces." The Confederate officer named pistols at ten paces; the time, shortly after sunrise on March twenty-sixth at the favorite duelling-grounds on the Fayette and Scott county lines. This secluded spot on the present-day Lisle Pike and in the vicinity of Donerail, had been the site of a number of other noted duels: the Dudley-Richardson affair in August,

1818; the famous Trotter-Wickliffe duel in March, 1829, and the lesser-known meeting between William O. Smith and Thomas H. Holt, on September 6, 1848. Here also on October 5, 1852, two young students of Transylvania University settled their differences with double-barreled shotguns, loaded with single balls, at forty yards.[32]

Sergeant Kimbrough chose Major William Long, of Covington, to act as his second, and for his surgeon he selected Dr. W. B. Kean, of Georgetown. The challenged man named his cousin, Lieutenant Colonel (Dr.) Hervey McDowell, of Cynthiana, late of the Second Kentucky Infantry, C.S.A., for his second and Dr. John Burk, of Lexington, to be his medical representative.[33] The pistols selected for the duel were once the property of Henry Clay, himself a noted duellist, and were the same ones the Master of Ashland had used years before in his famous meeting with John Randolph, of Virginia.[34] These duelling weapons were of a large caliber and of the smoothbore type, made in Sheffield, England, and were described as being "finely polished and silver mounted."

Everything being in readiness, the seconds pitched up a silver coin for the choice of position which was won by Dr. Hervey McDowell, who represented the challenged man. Likewise, by another toss of the coin, he gained the privilege of giving the word. Each principal was escorted to his position by his second, and a loaded and cocked pistol was handed to him with the admonition to keep it parallel to his right side. "All the while," noted an eye-witness, "the two men stood in their positions with the utmost composure, pistols in hand, body erect, and ready to receive the other's fire."

The principals took aim and fired, but without harm.[35] On the second fire, Sergeant Kimbrough slumped forward and fell face downward; blood rushed from the Union soldier's right hip. Captain Desha escaped unhurt; the ball from Kimbrough's pistol passed through his coat pocket. There was little hope for the wounded duellist to walk again as "he was shot through and through the hips, the ball terribly mashing the hip bones."[36] The wound from Captain Desha's pistol though not fatal, gave the Union sergeant and challenger of the duel a considerable limp which he carried the rest of his life.

The Desha-Kimbrough duel was the leading topic of conversation for years to come, due to the Civil War standing of each man and the prominence of the families involved. This was the last important affair of honor fought in Kentucky under the strict code of the duello. It marked the end of an out-moded system of honor which had been in effect before the founding of the Commonwealth, and one which had needlessly taken the lives of a number of its prominent and most valuable citizens.

FOOTNOTES

[1] *Kentucky Gazette,* Lexington, August 2, 1790.

[2] *Ibid.,* October 25, 1794.

[3] William Littell, *The Statute Law of Kentucky* (Frankfort, 1809-1819), Vol. II, pp. 284-285.

[4] J. Winston Coleman, Jr., *Famous Kentucky Duels* (Frankfort, 1953), pp. 2-14.

[5] *The Palladium,* Frankfort, April 28, 1801.

[6] John Rowan to William Lytle, Bardstown, April 19, 1801. Original in the Historical and Philosophical Society of Ohio.

[7] Coleman, *op. cit.,* p. 11.

[8] *Truth's Advocate & Monthly Anti-Jackson Expositor,* Cincinnati, January, 1828, p. 20.

[9] William G. Sumner, *Andrew Jackson* (Boston, 1899), p. 12.

[10] Coleman, *op. cit.,* pp. 26, 27.

[11] Coleman, *op. cit.,* pp. 31, 32.

[12] This letter was found and published many years later in the *Lexington Daily Press,* August 9, 1873.

[13] Dr. Christopher C. Graham, Louisville, February 12, 1876 to Dr. Robert Peter, Lexington. Original in Transylvania College Library.

[14] Coleman, *op. cit.,* pp. 45, 46.

[15] *Kentucky Gazette,* Lexington, August 7, 1818.

[16] Charles Wickliffe, youngest son of Robert Wickliffe, was killed in the Trotter-Wickliffe duel, October 9, 1829.

[17] *The Commentator,* Frankfort, July 9, 1819.

[18] *Argus of Western America,* Frankfort, July 23, 1819.

[19] Commonwealth of Kentucky vs. Jacob H. Holeman & Wilson P. Greenup, Franklin Circuit Court, file No. 247, October, 1819.

[20] Coleman, *op. cit.,* p. 72.

[21] *Argus of Western America,* October 28, 1829.

[22] *Ibid.,* October 28, 1829.

[23] *Argus of Western America,* October 28, 1829.

[24] Trotter, because he was near-sighted, demanded a distance of eight feet. When the two men faced each other, their pistols almost overlapped.

[25] *The Courier-Journal,* Louisville, March 25, 1894.

[26] Mrs. William C. Bullitt, Oxmoor Plantation (near Louisville), June 19, 1849, to John C. Bullitt, Philadelphia. Quoted in Coleman, *Famous Kentucky Duels,* p. 87.

[27] *Ibid.* Also: *Louisville Journal,* June 15, 1849.

[28] *Louisville Morning Courier,* June 15, 1849.

[29] Coleman, *op. cit.,* pp. 97, 98.

[30] *Tri-Weekly Commonwealth,* Frankfort, May 21, 1862.

[31] *Cincinnati Daily Commercial,* May 16; May 30, 1862.

[32] *Louisville Public Journal,* October 6, 1852. In this meeting, Benjamin Thompson, son of Captain Henry Johnson, killed Thomas White at the first fire, "the ball passing through his brain and killing him instantly. Johnson was not injured."

[33] Coleman, *op. cit.,* p. 115.

[34] The Clay-Randolph Duel was fought near Washington, D.C., on April 8, 1826. Clay fired twice and Randolph once without effect. On the second round, Randolph fired into the air, and called out that he declined to fire on Mr. Clay again. This magnanimity caused a reconciliation.

[35] *Cincinnati Daily Gazette,* March 27, 1866.

[36] *Union Standard,* Lexington, March 27, 1866.

J. WINSTON COLEMAN, JR. (1898–   ), a native of Lexington, received his B.S. degree in engineering at the University of Kentucky. A successful engineer and farmer, Coleman became increasingly interested in Kentucky's history, and by the early 1930s he had begun writing the first of his many books, pamphlets, and articles and assembling a magnificent collection of Kentuckiana in his private library. A list of his best-known works includes *A Bibliography of Kentucky History, Slavery Times in Kentucky, Stage-Coach Days in the Bluegrass, Three Kentucky Artists, Historic Kentucky,* and *Kentucky: A Pictorial History.*

This article first appeared in *The Filson Club History Quarterly* in April 1956, vol. 30, pp. 125–40.

CASSIUS MARCELLUS CLAY AND THE *TRUE AMERICAN*

By Lowell Harrison[*]

Paper read before The Filson Club, January 5, 1947

One of the most determined opponents of Kentucky slavery was Cassius Marcellus Clay, who devoted half a lifetime and sacrificed a career in his struggle to free the state of Negro bondage. Born into a wealthy slaveholding family outside Lexington, young Clay became convinced of the evils of the institution while at Yale, where he was swayed by one of William Lloyd Garrison's fiery denunciations. After his return home Clay entered into the anti-slavery crusade, but his conversion was far from being complete; for a number of years he wavered near the dividing line, and not until 1843 did he free his own slaves. But his violent speech and truculent attitude obscured the essential mildness of his views, and his opposition gradually stiffened under the savage attacks provoked from the slavocracy. One of his most spectacular and most worthwhile encounters occurred in 1845 when he attempted to publish an emancipationist newspaper in Lexington, the very heart of Kentucky slavery.

Clay had begun to experience increased difficulty by 1845 in securing space to express his views in the columns of the local press.[1] The editor of the *Lexington Observer*, a conservative pro-slavery man, had always printed emancipation articles, but Clay's contributions had become "so militant and provocative" that, "in the interests of the public peace," he declined to accept any more.[2] Clay, hoping to use the press in educating the people to the necessity of a legal repudiation of slavery,[3] denied that the current Southern papers were a true reflection of sectional sentiment. "They are the mouthpieces of the slaveholders, who are the property holders of the country; they hold the bread of the press in their hands...."[4] Although he realized

---

[*] Mr. Harrison is a graduate of Western State Teachers College, Bowling Green, Kentucky, and presently is teaching history at New York University.

that the venture would probably be a financial failure, he was ready to supply the deficit from his own resources in order to forward his plan for making Kentucky free.[5]

It seems strange today that such a temperate document as the prospectus for the new paper could arouse so much protest. It merely advised the public that a number of native Kentuckians would publish a paper, the *True American*, in the interest of gradual and constitutional emancipation. They would act solely as a state group, and allegiance to existing political parties would be maintained. Appeal would be "to the interests and the reasons, not the passions, of our people," and the columns would be open for the expression of all shades of opinion. "Our readers shall not be our masters; if they love not truth, they may go elsewhere . . . our press shall be independent or cease to exist. . . ."[6] The influential planters, however, were well acquainted with the temperament of Cassius M. Clay, and they regarded the proposed paper as a direct challenge to their established order. Any journal expressing anti-slavery views would have encountered difficulty; certainly one edited by Clay could not long escape censure.[7]

This introduction was so mild that the *Liberator* could give the new venture only slight praise, although Garrison did agree to collect the $2.50 subscription fee from Northern supporters. He predicted that Clay, still deluded concerning the virtues of gradual emancipation, would be forced to see that "the leviathan of slavery cannot be drawn out with a hook," and that the paper would not be tolerated unless it became an apologist for slavery.[8]

The reaction within the state was even less enthusiastic. *The Lexington Observer* adopted a typical attitude:

"Mr. Clay has taken the very worst time that he could to begin the agitation of that great and delicate question, even for the accomplishment of his object, since it is an admitted truth that the fanatical crusade which has been waged by Northern Abolitionists against the institution of slavery, which never in any degree concerned them, has produced a state of feeling in the minds of slaveholders anything but propitious to the slave or his liberation. . . . We make these remarks not to discourage Mr. Clay, for we know very well that his ardent and enthusiastic temperament never sees an obstacle in his way, and we do not know anyone whom under other circumstances we should welcome to the Editorial Corps with more cordiality than Mr. Clay, but to appraise him in advance, that, from our observation and reflection, he is embarked in a very hopeless undertaking."[9]

The office and press of the *True American* were housed in a three-story, red brick building at No. 6, North Mill Street in Lexington.[10] Clay was well aware of the fate of previous papers with similar views, and threats of mob action had been received long before the rollers were inked for the first issue. So he made careful preparations for the defense of his constitutional right to free expression. With the aid of a few friends who pledged support in any extremity, he transformed the building into a fortress. The outside door and windows were covered with sheet iron, and the office was armed with a stand of rifles, several shotguns, and a dozen Mexican cavalry lances. Two brass four-pounder cannon were purchased in Cincinnati, loaded with Minie balls and miscellaneous nails, and mounted breast high on a table where they commanded the doors. In event of defeat there was a trap door in the roof for the defenders and a keg of powder which could be exploded from outside for the invaders.[11] There is little doubt but that the fiery editor was fully determined to level the building if pushed to the limit.[12]

The first issue of the paper appeared on June 3, and was read by 300 Kentuckians and 1,700 out-of-state subscribers.[13] Clay had appealed to the North for five or six thousand names,[14] but the requested number failed to respond despite the solicitations of a special representative who canvassed New England on a collection tour and secured the support of Daniel Webster.[15] Clay was still considered too ideologically unsound to merit the unqualified support of his radical comrades in the cause; he was definitely on the right flank of the left wing. The circulation continued to improve, however, and before the day of crisis arrived the list contained over 3,400 names.[16] Of even more importance was the influence upon other papers; Clay was widely quoted and reprinted in the North, and a few of the more liberal Kentucky papers also carried some of his writings. He began to have a distinct appeal for the non-slaveholders of his state,[17] and to them he devoted much attention.

The leading articles repeated the same line of argument that the editor had advanced so many times before in speech and print. The primary appeal was to the economic self-interest of the people with emphasis upon the welfare of the laboring, non-slave owning element. There could be no middle ground, he wrote, and he asked the small shopkeepers to compare the amounts purchased from them by two hundred free men and by two hundred of Wickliffe's slaves before making their decision.[18] He compared Southern with Northern states (Clay employed this technique many times), and concluded that the presence of slaves caused the general economic inferiority of the former.[19] The wage laborer was impoverished by the competition of unpaid workers;[20] if the blacks were free "they would require wages; which would prevent you from being underbid as you now are."[21] The crusading editor gleefully invited the public to view a new press—which had to be purchased from a Northern firm employing free labor.[22] Clay worked diligently to arouse a sense of class consciousness within the labor ranks, whose ballots he called the sole hope of Kentucky's becoming free. "Come, if we are not worse than brutish beasts, let us but speak the word, and slavery shall die!"[23]

Clay denied that the freed slaves would constitute a major problem. After all, the whites already exceeded the blacks by over 450,000 persons, and in every instance freedom had resulted in a lower rate of increase for the Negro. The Negro would be as closely bound by civil law as he was by the slave code.[24] Although he was a member of the Colonization Society, Clay did not regard it as a remedy for the ill. Banishment of freed blacks was to be opposed because it was unjust to those who had done nothing to justify removal from their homes and because it would greatly increase the costs of emancipation. Yet he was willing to accept removal if freedom could be obtained only upon that condition.[25]

The new editor was careful to deny any connection with the abolitionists, although his subscription list and the praise of the abolitionist press appeared somewhat contradictory to most Kentucky observers. At the same time he pointed out with considerable logic that it was as unjust to denounce the abolitionists as a group as it was to label all slaveholders murderers because of the actions of a few members of their class.[26] Anyway, it was more dangerous for slaves to read the proslavery papers than the *True American,* for the latter preached the necessity of submission to due process of law, while the former were filled with gory accounts of suggestive outrages.[27] Besides, slaves were permitted to pick up the papers only upon presentation of written authorization from their masters, and circulation had been deliberately curtailed to keep the blacks from gaining access to the pages.[28]

The *True American* was careful to advocate only constitutional means of effecting the desired change unless the occasional manifestos calling laborers to arms are regarded as more than just flaming rhetoric. "No government upon earth can stand an hour upon any other principle than that, 'That which the law makes property is property' . . . Upon the same basis, then, does slavery stand . . ." Existing laws must be obeyed until they could be changed by the regular process of securing the consent of a majority of the people.[29] Clay cited three constitutional propositions which he considered the vital aspects of the problem. First, the states alone had control over slavery within their borders; its status could be altered only by their action. Second, slavery did not and could not legally exist in areas under exclusive Congressional jurisdiction. Third, the Supreme Court should free by writ of habeas corpus anyone held as a slave within a territory.[30] The solution to Kentucky's problem, then, was a constitutional convention which would provide for gradual emancipation.[31]

Although most of the articles and editorials in the new paper were temperate and well balanced, Clay was occasionally goaded into violent outbursts. Irascible old Robert Wickliffe, unmellowed by his threescore years and ten, was soundly chastised in the initial issue after he had been outspoken in opposing Clay's new venture. After recalling the famous Brown affray, Clay warned that the same blade was "ready to drink of the blood of the hireling horde of sycophants and outlaws of the assassin-sire of assassins."[32] When ex-Governor Metcalfe took to public print to belabor Clay as a traitor to his section, Clay published the remarks "of this silly old man" because it seemed the easiest way to dispose of him. But the editor was not content to stop there; he sneered that "we were born into the circle to which he has at length in spite of many vulgarities which attest his origin, forced his way . . . We shall not retort in kind . . . for our moral elevation places us out of reach of his batteries."[33] After an Alabama preacher had called upon the Lord to silence the paper by mob action, Clay turned his wrath upon ministers who "shed crocodile tears over the miseries of men . . . while they uphold this institution . . . these men prostitute to base uses of crime and woe the sanctity of the pure and living God."[34] When he was in the right, he asserted, the pistol and bowie knife were as sacred to his cause as the gown and pulpit.[35]

Perhaps the most arresting feature of the paper was the almost total absence of appeals to moral and humanitarian sentiments.[36] Clay had little faith in their effectiveness, and when they did appear they hinted of afterthought. It was for this lack of moral interest that he was most severely condemned by the Abolitionists.[37]

"Perhaps no journal in Kentucky ever created a more violent storm of protest than did the *True American* . . . . Coming as it did from the heart of one of Kentucky's slaveholding counties . . . it was from its beginning a most potent force in the formation of public opinion."[38]

There were hints of suppression long before printing started, but even after the first issue appeared the *Observer* denied that mob action was justified, although it denounced the propriety of the enterprise.[39] But opposition increased with each issue and with each stride the paper made in influencing the people, so that by the following month the *Observer* queried, "Slaveholders of Fayette, is it not now time for you to act on this matter yourselves . . . ?" Clay was charged with "howling out about slavery, abolition, emancipation . . . until he creates a little excitement and reaps some political profit out of it."[40]

Before the paper was a month old, the editor had received an ominous warning penned in blood or "red turnip juice."

"You are meaner than the autocrats of hell. You may think you can awe and curse the people of Kentucky to your infamous course. You will find, when it is too late for life, the people are no cowards. Eternal hatred is locked up in the bosoms of braver men, your betters, for you. The hemp is ready for your neck.

Your life cannot be spared. Plenty thirst for your blood—are determined to have it. It is unknown to you and your friends, if you have any, and in a way you little dream of.

"Revengers[41]"

Antagonism increased in direct proportion to the influence Clay developed. With the aid of Henry Clay, who made a personal last-day visit to the polls, he ruined Tom Marshall's candidacy for a Congressional seat by reprinting some of Marshall's letters, written when he was not seeking office, in which slavery was branded "a cancer ... a withering pestilence ... an unmitigated curse ...." Opposition became even more fierce after that.[42]

Over in South Carolina, John C. Calhoun, the "Man of Iron," detected a flutter in the steady pulse beat of the South. He requested James H. Hammond to write an article praising Dr. Bascom, president of Kentucky University "It is a powerful antidote to the poison, attempted to be disseminated by C. M. Clay in that State."[43] Hammond replied that Bascom was not sound enough in his opinions to merit the attention. Then he turned to Clay. "He could not be tolerated a moment, if Kentucky was sound or his friends less powerful. The people however are waking up. Abolition entered largely into the canvass between Davis and Marshall and will become a leading question in elections very soon."[44]

The Northern response was naturally much warmer than the one Clay received within the state. As his earnest efforts were rewarded by increased abuse, even the *Liberator* began to entertain hopes that he might ultimately enter the fold of the true faith. When a Boston minister called Clay anti-religious, Garrison retorted that as long as the church was craven enough to leave the task of unmasking slavery to infidels it could at least keep quiet about the whole matter.[45] Garrison even reprinted an article from the *Greenfield Massachusetts Gazette*, which lauded Clay's labors. "This paper, if continued, and we hope it will be, will effect in one year more than can be accomplished by a hundred Garrisons and his coadjutors, in the space of ten."[46] Horace Greeley kept his readers well posted on the Lexington journalistic venture, and he added his voice to the call for additional subscribers.[47] Clay was generally hailed for his part in helping stir the Southern non-slaveholders into a realization of their latent power.[48]

The anticipated crisis finally came when the Lexington readers scanned the August 12 issue. Clay had been ill with typhoid since the twelfth of July, and the editing had been done by ear from his bed or by unskilled friends.[49] The lead story in the fateful issue was prefaced with the explanation that "Our leader today is from one of the very first intellects in this nation; and as he is a large slaveholder, we allow him to speak his sentiments in his own language." The editor, it added, would present his own views the following week.[50] But all explanations of Carolinian authorship were forgotten when the readers came to the last paragraph. For the editor concluded by saying,

"But remember, you who dwell in marble palaces, that there are strong arms and fiery hearts and iron pikes in the streets, and pains (sic) of glass only between them and the silver plate on the board, and the smooth-skinned woman on the ottoman. When you have mocked at virtue, denied the agency of God in the affairs of men, and made rapine your honeyed faith, tremble! for the day of retribution is at hand, and the masses will be avenged."[51]

The outraged citizenry was not too concerned about the safety of the silver plate, but the implied appeal to slave lusts was a flagrant violation of the most sacred taboo of a slave community. That one sentence was directly responsible for the events which followed, although provocation had accumulated over a period of months.

Two days later a handful of men, among them Thomas F. Marshall, ended a casual discussion of the affair by deciding to call a private, non-partisan meeting to frame a remonstrance expressing their common views. Such a course of action would, they asserted, prevent mob or individual action, either of which was almost certain to result in bloodshed.[52] Invitations were therefore extended to twenty-seven men to assemble in the courthouse that afternoon "to take into consideration the propriety of adopting suitable measures to protect the property, and defend the wives and daughters of the citizens of Lexington against the 'strong arms, fiery hearts, and iron pikes' of the so-called *True American*."[53]

Considerable embarrassment developed that afternoon when Cassius Clay crawled out of bed, strapped on his knife, and unexpectedly staggered into the courthouse to defend himself. So weak that he had to lie on a bench, he still found strength to denounce the committee for being composed mainly of personal enemies with but one Whig present. He explained that the offending article had been written by someone else, that his policy was to permit freedom of discussion, and that if a slave revolt should occur, "I feel myself as bound as any citizen in the state to shoulder my musket to suppress it . . . "[54] Clay finally left when the committeemen glumly refused to continue their discussion in his presence. Later that day a committee of three delivered a resolution urging him to discontinue the paper in order to ensure the peace and safety of the community with which he, himself, was so closely connected.[55]

Clay's rejection of this "extraordinary letter," contained in an extra issued the following day, was decidedly not apologetic, despite a denial that he had tried to incite rebellion. Why, he queried bitterly, had no action been taken during the weeks when he had been able to defend himself? He denied the right of "thirty despots" to dictate to his conscience, and he called upon the laborers to rally to his support.

"Laborers of all classes—you for whom I have sacrificed so much, where will you be found when the battle between Liberty and Slavery is to be fought? . . . If you stand by me like men, our country will yet be free, but if you falter now, I perish with less regret when I remember that the people of my native State, of whom I have been so proud, and whom I have loved so much, are already slaves."

He closed on a high note of defiance.

"Go tell your secret conclave of cowardly assassins that C. M. Clay knows his rights and how to defend them."[56]

This answer was almost as bad as the original article, for Clay's foes immediately assumed that he was appealing directly to the slaves for aid. After the committee had considered his scornful rejection and read his handbill, the members decided to call a mass meeting of all interested citizens for the following Monday morning in the courthouse yard, and a thousand copies of the call were ordered printed for distribution.[57] A letter which appeared in a local paper on August 16 summarized the prevailing thought neatly; "Mr. Clay is a fanatic and an incendiary . . . the madman must be chained."[58]

The second of Clay's handbill extras, which appeared the same day, although he had to dictate it from his bed contained his detailed plan for gradual constitutional emancipation. Clay admitted that he might have made mistakes in the distasteful job of editing, but his critics had persisted in misunderstanding his intentions.

"I am willing to take warning from friends or enemies for the future conduct of my paper, and whilst I am ready to restrict myself in the latitude of discussion of the question, I never will voluntarily abandon a right or yield a principle."[59]

It was a distinct gesture of conciliation, but it came too late by weeks.

Another handbill, issued on the morning of the mass meeting, was written in the same moderate vein. In it, Clay tried to dispel the taint of abolitionism from his paper. He cited his refusal to attend a Cincinnati Anti-Slavery Convention in July because he disapproved of unconstitutional methods of freeing slaves,[60] and he reaffirmed his allegiance to the Whig party. As for the abolitionists, "I utterly deny that I have any political connection with them . . . . They form not over one-fourth of my subscription list."[61]

Despite a relapse caused by his fruitless courthouse visit, Clay made final preparations for a last-ditch defense. Cannon were reloaded and sighted carefully to sweep the doors; rifles and shotguns were fitted with new percussion caps; and Clay made his will and sent his camp bed to the office.[62] His mother wrote for him to consider his course carefully, for he had acted imprudently; but, "If you prefer death to dishonor, so do I."[63] There seemed little doubt but that a bloody battle was in the making. A pessimistic Lexington correspondent reflecting on the probable outcome wrote that "everybody understands that the editor will have to be killed first, and that he is somewhat difficult to kill . . . . What effect the killing of C. M. Clay will have on the free states in exasperating the abolitionists and swelling their numbers, you can judge as well as I."[64]

Over 1,200 men assembled before the courthouse on Monday morning to decide what action should be taken in regard to the "filthy abolition paper."[65] They must have had difficulty recognizing Clay's handiwork in the humble letter which was read to open the proceedings. For Clay, pathetically reminding them that he had been unable to hold a pen for over a month, avowed the deepest respect for "a constitutional assemblage of citizens," a group entirely different from the one he had treated with such contempt the previous week. The offending article would never have appeared in print had he been well enough to edit it personally. "I cannot say that the paper from the beginning has been conducted in the manner I could have wished." In the future, discussion would be restricted; "I shall admit into my paper no article upon this subject for which I am not willing to be held responsible . . . . I did not forsee any such consequences as have resulted." The trouble was actually being agitated by selfish men seeking political gain. Clay concluded by announcing that his defenses had been removed, and the office was defended only by law. "You will so act, however, I trust, that this day shall not be one accursed to our country and state."[66]

With that formality out of the way, the meeting proceeded according to plan, climaxed by Marshall's able speech which justified suppression of the press because the safety of the people was the supreme law in such a situation. He conceded Clay's right to establish a paper of emancipationist views, but he argued that Clay had become the organ and tool of the abolitionists.

"Such a man and such a course is no longer tolerable or consistent with the character or safety of this community . . . the negroes might well, as we have strong reason to believe they do, look to him as a deliverer . . . . Who shall say that the safety of a single individual is more important in the eye of the law than that of a whole people? . . . He is a trespasser upon them . . . and they will remove him by force . . . . He may rest assured that they will not be deterred by one nor 10,000 such men as he . . . . A Kentuckian himself, he should have known Kentuckians better."[67]

Six resolutions were then adopted which stated the determination of the people to remove Clay's press, peacefully if possible, but by force if necessary. A committee of sixty was appointed and authorized to seize the press and ship it to Cincinnati.[68] It is probable that but for Marshall's orderly dominance of the proceedings the result might have been brutal mob action.[69]

While the crowd was gathering for the meeting, Clay's opponents had quietly eliminated his legal right of self-defense. With no notice to Clay and with no hearing of the facts, Judge George R. Trotter of the Police Court issued an injunction suspending operation of the *True American* and seizing its plant.[70] The writ of seizure was served at Clay's bedside, and with tears in his eyes he surrendered his keys to the city marshal.[71]

When the Committee of Sixty[72] reached the office, the keys were surrendered to them after the mayor gave formal notice that their action was illegal but that he could not resist.[73] The committeemen resolved to hold themselves responsible for any damage that might be done, and printers went to work dismantling the new press while Clay's personal papers and desk were sent to his home. He was informed of the shipment of his property to Cincinnati with all charges paid by a politely phrased letter.[74] The *Cincinnati Herald* of August 23 reported that a large and curious crowd which collected on the riverfront to see the unloading of the equipment found the press and type in sorry plight,[75] but there is no other evidence of any damage to the equipment.

On September 18 the committee members were arraigned before Judge Trotter on a riot charge. When the defense objected to the severity of the charge to the jury, the judge obligingly added, "That if the jury believe that the *True American* paper was a public nuisance, and could not exist in its then present location and position, without being a nuisance, the defendants were justified in abating it." No one was surprised to hear the verdict "not guilty" pronounced.[76] Upon his return from Mexico over two years later, Clay sued the leaders of the committee for damages. After a change of venue to Jessamine County had been granted, he was awarded a judgment of $2,500.[77]

Such proceedings were certain to create widespread public interest in a day when the battlelines were becoming sharply drawn about the slavery issue. Most Kentuckians approved of the action that had been taken. The *Christian Intelligencer*, a small Methodist paper printed in Georgetown, was also forced to cease publication; the editor stoutly denied that he was an abolitionist, but his condemnation of the Lexington proceedings was considered sufficient evidence to warrant his suppression.[78] An unfortunate aftermath of the excitement was a brutal attack upon several free Negroes in Lexington the day after the mass meeting. Responsible leaders denounced the attacks almost immediately, but most Northern papers linked the two stories in their columns.[79]

A Kentucky correspondent for the *New York Evening Post*, writing during the height of the struggle, indicated the common thought of the Commonwealth.

"By my next you may hear of violence and bloodshed—a tale of terrible retributive justice, which should startle from their horrid purposes those wicked fanatics and traitors who so recklessly trespass upon the constitutional rights of the South, and endanger the lives of their white brethren, in their mad crusade for negro emancipation."[80]

The *Kentucky Compiler* was equally outspoken in its opposition to Clay's work.

"We regard the paper as insurrectionary in its character ... it exposes the sanctity and safety of the homestead to imminent peril, engenders suspicion, distrust and fear between persons standing in a recognized, legal relation, and assails with blind violence legal and vested rights . . . . Its circulation can do nothing but mischief, and may give being to such a train of events as will fill the land with mourning."[81]

Mass meetings were held in counties throughout the State, so that more citizens would have an opportunity to endorse the Lexington action. Opposition developed at the Madison assembly when a considerable minority rejected the resolutions branding the *True American* "intemperate and inflamatory ... unjustifiable and meriting the severest reprobation" as being entirely too mild for the seriousness of the offense.[82]

From Louisville there came a small, courageous note of protest. The *Journal* admitted that Cassius Clay's rashness had led to evil when he had intended good, but it denied that he had ever advocated servile war. Although the Lexington citizens had acted with restraint, their illegal action set a dangerous precedent for freedom of expression. "But the rational and temperate discussion of the question of ultimate emancipation will not be checked ... no human power can stop it." If slavery was at fault for such a situation, then it was time to eliminate slavery.[83] The same issue reported that the Negroes were confident that Clay would break their bonds and lift them to equality with their masters. They sang long songs in his praise, and many were becoming insolent and difficult to control.[84]

Unqualified approval of the result came from the *Nashville Whig*, which doubted that Clay was really sincere in his proclaimed motives,[85] and most of the other Southern papers. A New Orleans editor was surprised that hot-tempered Kentuckians had abstained from personal violence after the provocation they had received,[86] and the *Washington Weekly Union* decided that Clay's efforts could do no good and that the reaction of the people could be justified.[87]

Northern reaction was generally favorable to Clay, but it did not approach the practical unanimity of Southern opinion. The *Cincinnati Gazette* felt that the uproar in Lexington would do more to unsettle the Negroes than would twenty years of *True American* editorials, and that even if all the charges brought against Clay were true the action remained an unjustifiable outrage.[88] The *Gazette* of Chillicothe, Ohio, changed a few of the adjectives but retained the gist of the same views. The South had paved the way for the abolitionists by just such outbursts, it stated, and if slavery and freedom conflicted, the former had to give way.[89]

Clay's discretion was not in proportion to his zeal, confessed the *Philadelphia Public Ledger*, but the denial of free expression by his neighbors "reflects the deepest disgrace upon their intelligence and liberality, and proves how great a blight the institution of slavery produces ...." It was for the law to determine whether or not the editor had overstepped his legal rights.[90] Horace Greeley wondered that the action had been so long delayed, for such a dangerous foe could not be tolerated by the slave power.[91]

Other sections of the New York press were more critical of

the deposed Kentucky editor. He was conceded to be a noble and gallant enthusiast who was fearless in maintaining his convictions,[92] but he lacked the coolness and prudence necessary to ensure the success of such an undertaking. Kentucky was probably ripe for emancipation, but her citizens were too high-spirited to permit the tone of such a paper.[93] In the abstract it was a worthy attempt, but in practice the articles were too offensive to be endured, although the people should have employed legal means of ridding themselves of the annoyance.[94] One paper decided that Clay was but a front for Northern abolitionists and only a plea of insanity would excuse his writings. He was to be held personally responsible for anything that might occur as a result of his misdirected labors, although the mob action was to be condemned.[95] The *New York News* was most caustic in its comments. It gave him credit for brute strength and a willingness to die, but "he is evidently a mere vain and vulgar fanatic . . . . He is a humbug—nor did Aesop chronicle last 'ass in a lion's skin.' "[96]

Even in Boston, accustomed as it was to Garrison's rantings, the *True American* and its editor were condemned in harsh terms. "More inflammatory language was never used by any demagogue; a more direct appeal to the basest passions was never uttered; a more cowardly attempt at kindling the flames of revolt was never made . . . ."[97] The *Liberator* contented itself with reprinting long extracts from other papers while committing itself to a minimum of editorial comment. Garrison must have experienced indecision in reconciling Clay's anti-abolition avowments with his natural desire to attack the pro-slavery mob. In general, however, it was favorable to Clay.

Most anti-slavers hailed Clay as a martyr to the cause, and mass meetings throughout the North showered complimentary resolutions upon him.[98] Frederick Douglass wrote from England that the establishment of the paper in Lexington had been "one of the most hopeful and soul-cheering signs of the time,— a star shining in darkness, beaming hope to the almost despairing bondsman," and he promised to exploit the mob action to the utmost in furthering his own anti-slavery work.[99]

As a matter of fact, the *True American* was not dead. Early in October the subscribers found issues reaching them again. Cassius Clay edited the copy in Lexington while the actual printing was done at Cincinnati, where his press had been reassembled.[100] There was something of grudging respect in the *Observer's* announcement of the reappearance. "There is no man, we believe, but C. M. Clay, who would again attempt this rash procedure. He is . . . deaf to the entreaties of friends, the remonstrances of foes, or the solemn enunciation of public feeling, displayed to him in the most clear, emphatic and decisive manner."[101] Clay continued to spew words, "great, huge, swelling words,"[102] yet something was missing; some vital spark had vanished. No other article appeared to match the August sensation, and with the press safely across the Ohio the good citizens had nothing to vent their resentment upon except a rapidly recovering Clay. There was an attempt in the next legislative session to vote legal censorship in order to exclude all antislavery publications from the state, but the House blocked passage after Senate approval.[103] Cassius Marcellus Clay walked the streets of Lexington unmolested.

The new *True American* was more moderate than its predecessor although the editor continued to boast of permitting free discussion upon all subjects. Clay could even muster a wry smile at the recent episode; "Our printing office was moved one day in our absence . . . by some of our friends. It puts us to some inconvenience, but we are good-natured, and used to ill-usage; we don't say much about it, they can't!"[104] His discussions followed the same general pattern of those in previous issues, with his chief appeals being directed to the economic welfare of both slaveowner and non-owner.[105] He continued to disgust the abolitionists by insisting that slavery in the Southern states was legal,[106] and that the only practical method of abolishing it was through a system of gradual emancipation by constitutional authority.[107] Emancipation would not endanger the peace and security of the state; on the contrary, it was the only way to be sure of safety.[108] The last issue that he edited denied any association with the abolitionists. "They have no more right to come here and declaim against slavery, than we have to go to Russia and denounce despotism of the same sort there."[109]

One of the most savage assaults Clay ever made against slavery was contained in a prayer he composed and printed for those Christians who believed slavery a divine institution. "If it is of God, Christians, pray for it! Try it; it will strengthen your faith, and purify your souls." It became a popular item on programs for abolitionist meetings.[110]

"O Thou omnipotent and benevolent God, who hast made all men of one flesh, thou Father of all nations, we do most devoutly beseech thee to defend and strengthen thy institution, American slavery! Do Thou, O Lord, tighten the chains of our black brethren and cause slavery to increase and multiply throughout the world! And whereas many nations of the earth have loved their neighbors as themselves, and have done unto others as they would that others should do unto them, and have let the oppressed go free, do thou, O God, turn back their hearts from their evil ways, and let them seize once more upon the weak and the defenseless, and subject them to eternal servitude.

"And, O God, . . . let their husbands, and wives, and children be sold into distant lands, without crime, that thy name may be glorified, and that unbelievers may be confounded, and forced to confess that indeed thou art a God of justice and mercy; Stop, stop, O God, the escape from the prisonhouse by which thousands of these 'accursed' men flee into foreign countries, where nothing but tyranny reigns; and compel them to enjoy the unequalled blessings of our own free land!

". . . And, O God, thou Searcher of all hearts, seeing that many of thine own professed followers, when they come to lie down on the bed of death . . . emancipate their fellowmen . . . do thou, O God, be merciful to them, and the poor recipients of their deceitful philanthropy, and let the chain enter into the flesh and the iron into the soul forever!"[111]

Clay had never enjoyed the time-consuming mechanics of editing, and he realized that he was far from being the ideal journalist.[112] It was with a sense of relief that he quit the unwelcome task after the May 27, 1846, issue and rode toward Texas and the Mexican War at the head of a company of Kentuckians. Despite the cancellation of many local subscriptions, the paper was steadily growing.[113] John C. Vaughan, a South Carolinian via Ohio, became the new editor with Cassius Clay's brother, Brutus, having general supervision in his capacity as financial agent for Cassius. Brutus was no believer in his brother's political views, and, when the Northern support declined in protest of Cassius' participation in the war, he ceased publication.[114] Vaughan secured enough backing to start the *Examiner*, a mild emancipationist sheet, in Louisville, and Clay's materials and list of subscribers were transferred with him. Clay wrote that "Those who have seen both papers will not regret the change," and he called for support of the new paper. The *Examiner* and its able editor encountered little opposition; its political foes often used its articles, and the *Journal* tagged it the best paper of its class in the Union.[115] It died peacefully in late 1849 from financial starvation.[116]

Some credit for the toleration of the *Examiner* should be given its predecessor. Clay's spirited campaign for freedom of expression and his ruthless suppression had awakened many liberal-minded Kentuckians more fully to the dangers of the institution they harbored. The pro-slavery group had moved too far, too fast. Public sentiment was directed by this small, active, and able group for over another decade, but its members were more careful thereafter not to chance a public rebuke by such drastic action. By sheer audacity and personal courage a hot-headed Kentuckian won a degree of tolerance that had never been achieved by more moderate and wiser men, and their paths were smoother for his efforts.

NOTES

[1] Clement Eaton, "Mob Violence in the Old South," *Mississippi Valley Historical Review*, XXIX, No. 3 (December, 1942), pp. 351-70.

[2] William H. Townsend, *Lincoln and His Wife's Home Town* (Indianapolis, 1929), p. 115.

[3] Cassius M. Clay, *Life and Memoirs, Writings and Speeches of Cassius Marcellus Clay*, I (Cincinnati, 1886), p. 106. Volume II was never published. Referred to hereafter as *Life*.

[4] Kenneth M. Stampp, "The Fate of Southern Anti-Slavery Sentiment," *Journal of Negro History*, XXVIII, No. 1 (January, 1943), pp. 10-22.

[5] *Life*, p. 106.

[6] Cassius M. Clay, *Writings of Cassius Marcellus Clay*, ed. Horace Greeley (New York, 1848), vi. Referred to hereafter as *Writings*.

[7] Clay engaged T. B. Stevenson of Frankfort to edit the paper at $1,000 per year, but after the prospectus aroused criticism T. B. failed to appear. *Life*, p. 106.

[8] *Liberator*, XV, No. 9 (Boston), February 28, 1845, p. 35.

[9] *Lexington Observer and Reporter*, February 19, 1845, p. 3.

[10] On April 1, 1845, the population of Lexington was 4,999 whites and 3,179 blacks. Lewis and Richard H. Collins, *History of Kentucky* (hereafter cited as Collins & Collins), I (Covington, Ky., 1874), p. 50.

[11] J. Winston Coleman, *Slavery Times in Kentucky* (Chapel Hill, 1940), p. 307.

[12] *Life*, p. 107.

[13] Asa Earl Martin, *The Anti-Slavery Movement in Kentucky Prior to 1850*, Filson Club Publications No. 29 (Louisville, 1918), p. 115.

[14] *Liberator*, XV, No. 13, April 4, 1845, p. 54.

[15] *Ibid.*, XV, No. 17, May 2, 1845, pp. 70-71.
[16] Clay estimated generously that there were twenty readers per paper. *Writings*, p. 302.
[17] Martin *op. cit.*, p. 115.
[18] *True American*, June 10, 1845, p. 3.
[19] *Ibid.*
[20] *Ibid.*, June 17, 1845, p. 3.
[21] *Ibid.*, July 1, 1845, p. 3.
[22] *Ibid.*
[23] *Ibid.*, July 15, 1845, p. 3.
[24] *Ibid.*, June 24, 1845, p. 3.
[25] *Ibid.*, June 17, 1845, p. 3.
[26] *Ibid.*
[27] *Ibid.*, July 15, 1845, p. 3.
[28] *Ibid.*, August 12, 1845, p. 3.
[29] *Ibid.*, July 22, 1845, p. 3.
[30] *Ibid.*, June 24, 1845, p. 3.
[31] *Ibid.*, July 15, 1845, p. 3.
[32] *Ibid.*, June 3, 1845, p. 3.
[33] *Ibid.*, July 22, 1845, p. 3.
[34] *Ibid.*, July 15, 1845, p. 3.
[35] *Ibid.*, July 1, 1845, p. 3.
[36] "We go for the abolition of slavery, not because the slave is black or white—not because we love the black man best, for we do not love him as well, we confess we are full of prejudices—but because it is just—because it is honest—and because honesty is the best policy." *Ibid.*, February 18, 1846, in *Writings*, p. 382.
[37] He overlooked few appeals that might win a convert to the cause. Women of the state were advised to give up their slaves. "Make up your own beds, sweep your own rooms, and wash your own clothes—throw away your corsets and nature will form your bustles . . . You will have full chests, glossy hair, rosy complexions, velvet skins, rounded limbs, graceful tournures, eyes of alternate fire, sweet tempers, good husbands, long lives of honeymoon, and—no divorces." *Ibid.*, June 17, 1845, p. 3.
[38] Thomas D. Clark, *A History of Kentucky* (New York, 1937), pp. 350-51.
[39] *Observer and Reporter*, June 7, 1845, p. 3.
[40] *Ibid.*, July 16, 1845, p. 3.
[41] *True American*, June 17, 1845, p. 3.
[42] Townsend, *op. cit.*, pp. 308-09.
[43] John C. Calhoun, "Correspondence of John C. Calhoun," ed. J. Franklin Jameson, *American Historical Association Report 1899*, II (Washington, D. C., 1899), pp. 667-68.
[44] *Ibid.*, pp. 1046-47.
[45] *Liberator*, XV, No. 25, June 20, 1845, p. 97.
[46] *Ibid.*, XV, No. 31, August 1, 1845, p. 121.
[47] *New York Tribune*, June 11, 1845, p. 2.
[48] John G. Palfrey, *The Slave Power* (Boston, 1846), pp. 54, 57.
[49] Coleman, *op. cit.*, p. 309.
[50] *True American*, August 12, 1845, p. 3. The article was supposedly written by Nathaniel Ward of South Carolina. See William Ritchie, "The Public Career of Cassius Marcellus Clay" (unpublished Ph.D. dissertation, George Peabody College for Teachers, 1934), p. 51.
[51] *Ibid.*
[52] *History and Record of the Proceedings of the People of Lexington and Its Vicinity in the Suppression of the True American* (Lexington, 1845), pp. 1-2. To be referred to hereafter as *Proceedings*.
[53] *Ibid.*, p. 3.
[54] *Ibid.*, pp. 9-11.
[55] *Cincinnati Gazette*, August 19, 1845, p. 2.
[56] *True American*, Extra No. I, August 15, 1845. In *Writings*.
[57] *Proceedings*, pp. 6-9.
[58] *Ibid.*, pp. 13-17.
[59] *True American*, Extra No. II, August 16, 1845. In *Writings*.
[60] *Niles Weekly Register*, Vol. 68, No. 1765 (Baltimore), July 29, 1845, p. 332.
[61] *Proceedings*, pp. 19-20.
[62] *Scioto Gazette* (Chillicothe, Ohio), August 28, 1845, p. 2.
[63] *Life*, p. 109.
[64] *New York Tribune*, August 25, 1845, p. 2.
[65] Coleman, *op. cit.*, pp. 310-11.
[66] *Cincinnati Gazette*, August 22, 1845, p. 2.
[67] Thomas F. Marshall, *Speeches and Writings of Hon. Thomas F. Marshall*, ed. W. L. Barre (Cincinnati, 1858), pp. 198-209.
[68] *Daily National Intelligencer* (Baltimore), August 26, 1845, p. 2.

⁶⁹ Mrs. Archibald Dixon, *True History of the Missouri Compromise and Its Repeal* (Cincinnati, 1899), p. 395.
⁷⁰ Townsend, *op. cit.*, pp. 131-32.
⁷¹ Coleman, *op. cit.*, p. 310.
⁷² James B. Clay, son of Henry Clay, was secretary. Henry Clay himself had hurriedly departed for White Sulphur Springs, Virginia, for a visit which Cassius considered rank desertion. *Philadelphia Public Ledger*, August 28, 1845, p. 2.
⁷³ Collins and Collins, I, *op. cit.*, p. 51.
⁷⁴ E. Polk Johnson, *History of Kentucky and Kentuckians*, I (Chicago, 1912), p. 175. He commented, "It will be noticed that Mr. Clay received notice of the departure of his property 'by letter.' That was the safest method of conveying information to Mr. Clay when his feelings were ruffled."
⁷⁵ Quoted in *New York Evening Post*, August 28, 1845, p. 2.
⁷⁶ Connelley, William E., and Coulter, E. M., *History of Kentucky* (Chicago, 1922), II, p. 812.
⁷⁷ Townsend, *op. cit.*, p. 170.
⁷⁸ *New Orleans Daily Picayune*, September 1, 1845, p. 2.
⁷⁹ *Niles Weekly Register*, Vol. 68, No. 1770, August 30, 1845, p. 409.
⁸⁰ *New York Evening Post*, August 23, 1845, p. 2.
⁸¹ Quoted in *Liberator*, XV, No. 35, August 29, 1845, p. 138.
⁸² Collins and Collins, I, *op. cit.*, p. 52.
⁸³ *Louisville Journal*, August 21, 1845, in *Cincinnati Gazette*, August 23, 1845, p. 2.
⁸⁴ *Ibid.*
⁸⁵ Quoted in *Liberator*, XV, No. 39, September 26, 1845, p. 153.
⁸⁶ *New Orleans Daily Picayune*, September 3, 1845, p. 2.
⁸⁷ *Washington Weekly Union*, I, No. 17, August 21, 1845, p. 261.
⁸⁸ *Cincinnati Gazette*, August 19, 1845, p. 2; August 21, 1845, p. 2.
⁸⁹ *Scioto Gazette*, August 28, 1845, p. 2; September 4, 1845, p. 2.
⁹⁰ *Philadelphia Public Ledger*, August 22, 1845, p. 2; August 25, 1845, p. 2.
⁹¹ *New York Tribune*, August 21, 1845, p. 2.
⁹² *New York Weekly News*, August 30, 1845, p. 4.
⁹³ *New York Evening Post*, August 25, 1845, p. 2.
⁹⁴ *New York Journal of Commerce*, August 22, 1845, p. 2; August 29, 1845 p. 2.
⁹⁵ *Morning Courier and New York Enquirer*, August 23, 1845, p. 2; August 25, 1845, p. 2; August 27, 1845, p. 2.
⁹⁶ Quoted in *Liberator*, XV, No. 39, September 26, 1845, p. 153.
⁹⁷ *Boston Times*, quoted in *Liberator*, XV, No. 36, September 5, 1845, p. 141.
⁹⁸ *Life*, pp. 110-12. *Liberator*, XV, No. 43, October 24, 1845, p. 169.
⁹⁹ Carter G. Woodson, ed., *Mind of the Negro as Reflected in Letters Written during the Crisis 1800-1860* (Washington, 1926), p. 395.
¹⁰⁰ Connelley and Coulter, *op. cit.*, II, p. 812.
¹⁰¹ Quoted in *Liberator*, XV, No. 44, October 31, 1845, p. 173.
¹⁰² *True American*, February 18, 1846, in *Writings*, p. 383.
¹⁰³ Martin, *op. cit.*, p. 117.
¹⁰⁴ *True American*, October 14, 1845, in *Writings*, p. 326.
¹⁰⁵ *Ibid.*, November 4, 1845, in *Writings*, pp. 337-40.
¹⁰⁶ *Ibid.*, November 25, 1845, in *Writings*, p. 352.
¹⁰⁷ *Ibid.*, November 4, 1845, in *Writings*, pp. 337-40.
¹⁰⁸ *Ibid.*, April 15, 1846, in *Writings*, p. 437.
¹⁰⁹ *Ibid.*, May 27, 1846, in *Writings*, p. 473.
¹¹⁰ Lewis and Milton Clarke, *Narratives of the Sufferings of Lewis and Milton Clarke* (Boston, 1846), p. 134. A model program is outlined for members with little originality.
¹¹¹ *True American*, March 25, 1846, in *Writings*, pp. 409-10.
¹¹² *Ibid.*, April 8, 1846, in *Writings*, pp. 429-30.
¹¹³ *Liberator*, XV, No. 49, December 5, 1845, p. 194.
¹¹⁴ Salmon P. Chase, "Diary and Correspondence of Salmon P. Chase," *American Historical Association Report for 1902*, II (Washington, 1903), pp. 111-12. Letter to Charles Sumner.
¹¹⁵ Martin, *op. cit.*, pp. 118-20.
¹¹⁶ Dwight L. Dumond, *Letters of James G. Birney*, II (New York, 1938), p. 728.

LOWELL HARRISON (1922–   ), a native Kentuckian, received his A.B. degree at Western Kentucky State College and his M.A. and Ph.D. degrees at New York University. He taught history at New York University and West Texas State University before joining the faculty of Western Kentucky University in 1967 as professor of history. His publications include *John Breckinridge: Jeffersonian Republican*, *The Civil War in Kentucky*, *George Rogers Clark and the War in the West*, and numerous articles.

This article first appeared in *The Filson Club History Quarterly* in January 1948, vol. 22, pp. 30–49.

MILKSICKNESS IN KENTUCKY AND THE WESTERN COUNTRY

By Philip D. Jordan

Associate Professor of History
Miami University, Oxford, Ohio

Through Kentucky and the western country an insidious disease, somber as forest shadows, struck at settlers and their cattle during the nineteenth century. Hardy frontiersmen who scoffed at "fever'n ager" shunned milksick communities with determined zeal. They knew what it meant when their milch cows trembled and thrust dry nostrils deep into cool creeks; they realized, too, the impending tragedy when the lassitude, weakness, nausea, and extreme thirst fell upon their families. From the Yadkin and the Chattahoochee, through the counties of Kentucky, to the Ohio and the Wabash, the mysterious sickness annually forced many pioneers to abandon settlements, pack up their rifles and spiders, and trudge wearily into the back-of-beyond, leaving behind deserted cabins and fresh-turned graves.

No man knew the cause of the disease which masqueraded under many names. Its etiology was debated for more than a century by emigrants, farmers, hunters, physicians, and botanists. And only within the last twenty years has adequate treatment been determined. Milksickness, indeed, was one of the most baffling and persistent of all the border diseases which conditioned the westward course of empire. In Kentucky, men called it simply "milksickness" or the "sick stomach"; in North Carolina and Georgia it was known as the "trembles"; and in Ohio, Indiana, and Illinois it sometimes received additional and more colorful names—"swamp sickness," "tires," "slows," "stiff joints," "puking fever," "river sickness," "alkali poisoning," "murrain" and "bloody murrain," "distemper," and "Carolina distemper." Folks in Maryland, Virginia, Alabama, Mississippi, Michigan, and Iowa usually referred to it as "milksickness." Frontier physicians advocated a number of scientific titles—*Colica trementia, Paralysis intestinalis, Ergodeleteris, Mukosma, Syro, Lacemesis*—but none of these found their way into reliable materia medica texts. Even today "milksickness" is the accepted descriptive term used by the medical profession.[1]

No one knows exactly when milksickness began to take its toll along the fringe of settlement, but apparently the disease was known in North Carolina during the Revolution. Shortly after the turn of the century, travelers, penetrating the western country, began describing the strange malady in their journals. In 1806, Thomas Ashe recorded the presence of milksickness among settlers on the Ohio River, and less than five years later a Virginia physician, Thomas Barbee, said that frontiersmen living in the Mad River district of Ohio were afflicted. In Indiana, milksickness was noted by William Faux,[2] and S. H. Long found it among residents living along the Missouri River.[3] During the thirties Edmund Flagg, journeying through the Illinois country, wrote graphically of the violence of this "mysterious" disease.[4] Even authors of emigrants' guides felt obliged to discuss the causes and effects of this peculiar and deadly sickness.[5] Veterinarians gave it space in their texts,[6] and medical students prepared detailed case reports. One of the papers submitted for the degree of Doctor of Medicine at Transylvania University on February 20, 1829, was devoted to milksickness.[7]

In 1810 and again in 1815, Daniel Drake, foremost physician of the West and one of the most brilliant medical lecturers ever to fascinate students in Lexington, Louisville, and Cincinnati, published the first definite accounts of the trembles.[8] "On the head waters of the Great Miami, and in some of the adjoining parts of Kentucky," wrote Drake, "a disease called by the people *Sick-stomach*, has prevailed more or less for several years." At that time Drake did not regard the disease as constituting any serious objection to the districts in which it was prevalent. It was not long, however, before he was forced to alter his opinion, for both popular and professional interest increased as region after region reported typical cases which were resulting in a high mortality rate. In the autumn of 1818, for example, the little community of Pigeon Creek, in southern Indiana, was hard hit by milksickness. Among those succumbing was Nancy Hanks Lincoln.[9]

In November, 1838, a family of six persons, traveling westward, put up at a house a few miles east of Terre Haute, Indiana. At breakfast they drank milk and immediately departed on their journey. By the time they reached Illinois, five or six hours later, they were all taken ill and died, every one of them, in from two to six days. Upon inquiry it was learned that the place where they had eaten their breakfast was in a "milksick" region.[10] An early physician of Ohio testified that nearly one-fourth of the pioneers and early settlers of Madison County died from milksickness.[11] A physician who was taken ill himself with the disease testified to its high mortality rate, saying that acute cases usually died between the second and the ninth day,[12] and recent studies show that the death rate may be as high as twenty-five per cent.[13]

With this type of evidence before him, Drake and other frontier physicians began to investigate seriously a disease which actually was conditioning the advance of settlement. The result was a score of independent research programs and the publication of results in the medical journals of the day. It is interesting, indeed, to note that articles discussing milksickness appeared in the first volume of the *Transylvania Journal of Medicine and the Associate Sciences*, of the *Western Journal of Medicine and Surgery*, and of the *Journal of the American Medical Association*, and that the first persistent analyses were done by Kentucky and Ohio physicians. Among these were Lunsford Pitts Yandell, John Terrell Lewis, Charles Wilkins Short, I. E. Nagle, and Daniel Drake. Each published his findings in Kentucky medical periodicals.

In September, 1840, Drake, after having read all available material concerning milksickness, resolved to tour the Virginia Military District in Ohio to see for himself what the disease was which was causing so much consternation among settlers. "This endemic of the West," he wrote, "to which science has not yet given a name, and even sometimes professes to doubt the existence, continues to attract the attention of the people and country practitioners, in various parts of Ohio, Indiana, Illinois, Kentucky, and Tennessee."[14]

He was particularly anxious to learn, if possible, what caused the disease, what the symptoms were, and what preventive or curative measures were being taken, as physicians were in disagreement on all these points. Yandell thought that the etiology was vegetable;[15] Short, in general, held the same hypothesis, although he specified the "mass of vegetable matter growing in the bottoms of stagnant pools of water" and suspected the wild "parsneps";[16] M. L. Dixson was none too specific, although he too leaned to some botanic cause;[17] M. Winans felt that at least some member of the mushroom tribe was responsible;[18] and John Travis, coming close to the real solution, held that a vine, "a species of the Rhus" was the culprit.[19]

During Drake's 150-mile tour of seven counties in Ohio, he interviewed many persons and observed, at first hand, some of the plants suspected of causing the disease. It was rather generally believed that humans became milksick only after drinking milk from a cow which had been poisoned as the result of eating some unknown plant. The great point of difference, however, was the non-agreement among settlers and doctors as to which plant was the active agent. Drake compiled a list of about six suspicious plants. Included were the straight mercury (*Bignonia capreolata*), the poison oak (*Rhus toxicodendron*), the poison sumach or swamp elder (*Rhus venenata*), various fungi and mushrooms, and white snakeroot (*Eupatorium ageratoides* or *Eupatorium urticaefolium*). On October 1, 1838, John Rowe, a farmer of Fayette County, had announced publicly that the white snakeroot was the plant which gave cattle the trembles and humans the milksickness.

Unfortunately, Drake did not feel that the evidence offered by John Rowe was conclusive, and dismissed the truth in favor of the "elm and Rhus slashed of the oak plateaus" which he felt were the "abode of the special cause of the Trembles," although he was careful to add that such had not been conclusively proved and that the "final decision of this question cannot be made without additional facts, the acquisition of which cannot be easily made . . ."[20] The result of Drake's exhaustive monograph was to leave the cause of the disease in doubt, although he leaned toward the vegetable theory. During the next few years he was to scoff at an arsenic hypothesis[21] and to say that, in Ohio, the northern limit of the disease was along the "southern shore of Lake Erie, between Cleveland and Sandusky city, in N. lat. 41° 25'."[22]

Clinically, the symptoms of milksickness which Drake observed compared, almost point by point, with the physical manifestations described in the journal literature. A typical milksick patient would manifest, first, lassitude, dizziness, and loss of appetite, soon followed by nausea and persistent vomiting. Then came pain in the region of the stomach and an intense thirst. The tongue was swollen, coated white, and the lips were dry. Peristalsis was completely absent and obstinate constipation was present. A subnormal temperature, a weak pulse, and slow respiration of the Cheyne-Stokes character indicated approaching death which usually was preceded by prostration and finally concluded in coma. A characteristic diagnostic aid was a pronounced odor on the breath and in the urine.[23]

Some physicians, during the early days, believed the disease to be a low form of congestive fever with all the appearances of an excessive bilious-typhus cast,[24] and a Kentucky physician described it as "severe Bilious remittent fever with a complication of gastro enteritis" with the patient presenting the following symptoms: "Pulse about 145 to 150, feeble; eyes injected; skin of an icterode hue; tongue heavily coated on the back part with a brown fur belt for about an inch and a half, from the tip it was very red and cracked; breathing difficult; thirst was intense; vomiting severe, and the matter ejected was of a dark gumous character, having the appearance of arterial blood mixed with the secretions of the stomach, and similar to the black vomit of yellow fever; complained of an intense burning in the stomach and bowels; epigastrium tender on pressure as was also the right iliac region; bowels were constipated, having had no action for twelve or fourteen hours previously; features were pinched and eyes sunken. His urine was scant and of a brick dust color. His extremities were cold, both superior and inferior."[25]

The Kentuckian who drew this graphic picture came to the conclusion that milksickness was not in itself a disease, but was, as previously indicated, a bilious remittent aggravated with an acute gastritis. This professional judgment, honest as it was,

was attacked sharply by a colleague within a few weeks who said bluntly that true milksickness carried with it no remission or intermission and that there was nothing bilious about it.[26] The result of this professional blast was to bring an apology and an admission that chills were not a part of the regular diagnostic picture.[27] As a matter of fact, chills were foreign to the trembles. Most physicians listed no such symptom, although one did mention cold, clammy sweats.[28] Some men of medicine, in their symptomatology, neglected to mention or to pay due attention to the peculiar odor characteristic of this illness.[29] William Osler's text, the standard of hundreds of students and physicians, ignored this symptom as late as 1907,[30] and government reports were equally lax in this important respect, although fairly reliable with other data.[31]

There was much more uniformity and accord among physicians when they treated the milksick patient than when they attempted to isolate the activating causative agent or when they attempted systematic symptomatology. Drake, during his Ohio tour in 1840, compiled a list of eight different courses of treatment used individually or collectively. These included the time-honored practice of phlebotomy or blood-letting; the administration of cathartics, especially heroic doses of calomel; the use of opium to deaden pain; the application of counter-irritants, especially blisters; the application of cold affusions, an early form of hydrotherapy; the prescribing of antacids to allay the gastritis; and the giving of alcoholic tinctures and demulcent drinks.

A typical course of treatment would begin by an attempt to allay the gastric irritability with opium, administered every one or two hours. This was followed by the application of blisters over the region of the stomach and bowels which, said one practitioner, "besides their revulsive and counter-acting influence over the inflamed structures, are valuable auxiliary measures to opium in allaying the irritability of the stomach."[32] Next calomel was given to overcome the constipation and to alter the morbid condition of the liver. Twenty grains were prescribed every three or four hours. The importance of calomel in the frontier materia medica must not be underestimated. Many frontiersmen swore by it. A home missionary said that it was almost better to be without corn meal than calomel.³³ If, however, calomel failed, the patient was given oleum ricinus and spirits terebinthina, assisted by enemata. After the bowels had been opened, hot brandy toddies were indicated, especially if the patient seemed to be sinking.

The use of opium, however, was not endorsed by all physicians. I. S. Swan expressed his "decided disapprobation" of its use, for, he said, opium only aggravated the torpor of the liver and the stubborn constipation of the bowels, although he admitted that opium might sometimes tranquilize the stomach and thus produce a little momentary relief. His treatment consisted of from ten to thirty grains of calomel, followed in a few hours by a cupful of an infusion of senna containing epsom or glauber salts. At the same time he applied a folded, wet cloth to the throat and stomach, provided there was more than natural heat at the epigastrium. Sometimes he substituted Seidlitz powders or a mixture of cream of tartar and jalap for the calomel.³⁴ Another physician held that very little medicine was indicated in treatment during the early stages of the disease, but recommended bleeding as of great value in later stages and then relied upon calomel, in small but frequently repeated doses, as well as upon oleum ricini, sulphate magnesia alone or in combination with senna tea. He said that he delayed the tendency to vomit by placing mustard poultices over the region of the stomach.³⁵

Botanic physicians and those trained in the hydrotherapy school, of course, treated the trembles according to their learning. John Kost, a successful botanic doctor, utilized the antispasmodic tincture of *Lobelia inflata* or lobelia in powder form, although he did not indicate dosage. In addition, he used charcoal once every three or four hours after the lobelia had accomplished its purpose. He also relied upon the following clyster which, he said, must be repeated at short intervals, until the desired effect was achieved:

Soft soap, 1 tablespoonful; common cathartic, 1 teaspoonful; Lobelia, ½ teaspoonful; Cayenne pepper, ¼ teaspoonful.

His external applications consisted of the oil of spearmint or peppermint applied over the region of the stomach. As the patient recovered, Kost put him upon the usual botanic tonics.³⁶

Water-cure physicians, on the other hand, resorted to the plunge bath, the pouring bath, the sponge or towel bath, the dripping sheet, the sitz bath, the douche or the wet compress, the wet girdle, the wet bandage, or the wet-pack sheet.[37]

As the close of the nineteenth century drew near, treatment was much simplified, although results continued to be unsatisfactory, as was only natural when physicians could administer only to symptoms and not to causes. During the eighties an old-time doctor relied entirely upon four ounces of whisky to one quart of water, given every four hours.[38] Others began to use bismuth and hydrastic and to experiment with strychnine and digitalis.[39] Feeding by mouth was thought to retain strength and absolute rest was insisted upon.[40] Bicarbonate of soda and potassium bicarbonate were also used to counteract what some scientists believed to be the presence of aluminum phosphate in the body.[41]

Meanwhile, even though Drake apparently had forgotten the disease and had not included it in his great two-volume work devoted to the diseases of the Mississippi Valley, persistent, if not too scientific, research was being carried on to determine, if possible, the real origin of milksickness. As early as 1827, a Kentucky legislative committee had been appointed to investigate the trembles,[42] and somewhat later the state medical society of Indiana conducted an investigation.[43] Emphasis swung again to the mineral hypothesis;[44] to a belief in a "microzym which has developed pathogenic properties and can be reproduced indefinitely in the bodies of living animals;[45] to dew accumulating upon plants in the evening;[46] and again to a suspicion of the white snakeroot.[47] However, in 1905, a physician wrote that "after a century's familiarity and knowledge of the symptoms and results, its true origin is as much shrouded in gloom as in the beginning."[48]

But attention was being focused more and more upon the white snakeroot. It was demonstrated in the laboratory that the root, when fed to animals, resulted in the trembles,[49] although two years later government agriculturalists still remained skeptical of the poisonous qualities of white snakeroot, *Eupatorium ageratoides*.[50] About the same time, two University of Chicago bacteriologists suggested cautiously that they believed they had isolated a bacillus—*B. lactimorbi*—which might be the causative agent.[51] By 1917 researchers were accepting both the idea that the white snakeroot was the cause and that a bacteria was responsible.[52] As a matter of fact, the latter view was incorporated in one of the standard texts dealing with a sanitary milk supply.[53] Most scientists, however, turned their attention to isolating the specific poison believed to be present in the white snakeroot.[54]

Finally, more than a hundred years after Drake had first begun his investigations in Kentucky and the western country, a pathologist of the Bureau of Animal Industry reported in 1917 the results of a long chain of laboratory experiments which proved beyond doubt that the active poison in the white snakeroot had been isolated and given the name of "tremetol." The constituent which had killed so many frontiersmen was $C_{16}H_{22}O_3$.[55] It was also demonstrated that the rayless goldenrod (*Aplopappus heterophyllus*) of western Texas, New Mexico, and Arizona, where milksickness had manifested itself after 1900, contained tremetol.[56]

The medical profession now was ready to treat a specific poison, rather than to merely allay symptoms as nineteenth-century doctors had been forced to do.[57] During 1937-38 when twenty-one cases appeared in Illinois with a mortality rate of about ten per cent, treatment consisted of saline purgation, fluids, alkalies by mouth, glucose intravenously, enemata, and honey and whisky.[58] The odor of acetone, which so many early writers had mentioned, now was explained as a ketosis, a condition of faulty metabolism which was a secondary manifestation of chronic tremetol poisoning, and each of the symptoms so carefully recorded for more than a century, beginning with Drake, was proved to be a typical reaction from the same chemical compound. The mysterious milksickness had given up its secret, but too late for the thousands of settlers in the western back-of-beyond who had perished and been buried in such frontier communities as Winchester, Tennessee; Hardinsburg, Kentucky; and near the Minor Breton lead mines of Missouri. No one need ever again write, as did Hanks to Herndon, "we war perplext by a Disese cald Milk Sick."[59]

FOOTNOTES

[1] See, for example, William Osler (ed.), *Modern Medicine, Its Theory and Practice* (Philadelphia, 1907), III, 546-548. Also edition of 1934.

[2] Reuben G. Thwaites, *Early Western Travels, 1748-1846* (Cleveland, 1905), XI, 206. Reprint of *Memorable Days in America* (1823), by William Faux.

[3] *Ibid.*, XIV, 141, 142. Reprint of *An Expedition from Pittsburgh to the Rocky Mountains* (1823), compiled from notes by Major S. H. Long and others.

[4] *Ibid.*, XXVII, 95, 96. Reprint of *The Far West* (1838), by Edmund Flagg.

[5] M. Peck, *A New Guide for Emigrants to the West* (Boston, 1836), 87; R. B., *View of the Valley of the Mississippi, or the Emigrant's and Traveller's Guide to the West* (Philadelphia, 1834), 86.

[6] S. W. Cole, *The American Veterinarian* (Boston, 1848), 212; see also, *The Cultivator* (Albany, New York), VII (1840), 112, 145; *ibid.*, VIII (1841), 117, 133, 143, 160, 187.

[7] John Terrell Lewis, "Cases of Milk Sickness, With Some Remarks on the Treatment," *Transylvania Journal of Medicine and the Associate Sciences* (Lexington), II (1829), 241-245.

[8] Daniel Drake, *Natural and Statistical View or Picture of Cincinnati and the Miami Country* (Cincinnati, 1814), 182, 183.

[9] John G. Nicolay and John Hay, *Abraham Lincoln* (New York, 1890), I, 30, 31; Albert J. Beveridge, *Abraham Lincoln* (New York, 1928), I, 47, 48; for a fictional account of milksickness in the Lincoln country, see Bruce Lancaster, *For Us The Living* (New York, 1940), 194, 195, 199, 201, 206-211. See also 'The Death of Nancy Hanks Lincoln," by Philip D. Jordan, in *Indiana Magazine of History*, XL, June, 1944, 103-110.

[10] Wm. J. Barbee, "Facts Relative to Milk-Sickness," *Western Journal of Medicine and Surgery* (Louisville), I (1840), 176-190.

[11] William M. Beach, "Milk Sickness," *Journal of the American Medical Association* (Chicago), I (1883), 71-75.

[12] Arthur J. Clay, "Personal and Clinical Experience with Milk Sickness," *Illinois Medical Journal* (Chicago), XXVI (1914), 103-108.

[13] Edwin C. Jordan and Norman MacL. Harris, "Milksickness," *Journal of Infectious Diseases* (Chicago), VI (1909), 424, 425.

[14] (Daniel Drake), "Milk Sickness, alias Sick Stomach," *Western Journal of Medicine and Surgery*, I (1840), 84.

[15] Lunsford Pitts Yandell, "An Essay on Milk-Sickness," *Transylvania Journal of Medicine and the Associate Sciences*, I (1828), 309-321.

[16] (Charles Wilkins Short), "Alleged Causes of Milk Sickness or Sick Stomach," *ibid.*, II (1829), 145.

[17] M. L. Dixon, "An Essay on Milk Sickness," *ibid.*, VI (1833), 157-163.

[18] M. Winans, "Practical Observations on the Disease Denominated Milk Sickness or Sick-Stomach," *Western Journal of Medicine and Surgery*, I (1840), 191-193.

[19] John Travis, "Observations on Milk-Sickness," *ibid.*, II (1840), 101-104.

[20] Daniel Drake, "A Memoir on the Diseases Called by the People 'Trembles,' and the 'Sick-Stomach,' or 'Milk-Sickness'; as they have occurred in the counties of Fayette, Madison, Clark and Green in the State of Ohio," *ibid.*, III (1841), 215, 225. Drake also journeyed through sections of Franklin, Pickaway, and Ross counties.

[21] (Daniel Drake), "Arsenic and the Trembles," *ibid.*, V (1842), 236, 237.

[22] (Daniel Drake), "Northern Limits of Milk-Sickness," *ibid.*, VII (1843), 65.

[23] John Kost, *The Practice of Medicine According to the Plan Most Approved by the Reformed or Botanic Colleges of the U. S.* (Mt. Vernon, Ohio, 1847), 166, 167; W. H. Byford, "Milk Sickness, Poison, Tires, &c." *Nashville Journal of Medicine and Surgery* (Nashville), IX (1855), 460; R. L. Anderson, "Sick Stomach—Milk Sickness—Trembles—or Dry Murran," *The Water-Cure Journal and Herald of Reforms* (New York), XII (1851), *passim*.

[24] I. W. Nagle, "Milk Sickness," *Nashville Journal of Medicine and Surgery*, XVII (1859), 289-295.

[25] Thos. R. W. Leffray, "To the Editors of the Western Lancet," *The Western Lancet* (Cincinnati), XVI (1855), 19.

[26] W. M. Chambers, "Editor Western Lancet," *ibid.*, XVI (1855), 352.

[27] Thos. R. W. Jeffray, "Editor of the Western Lancet," *ibid.*, XVI (1855), 410. Note difference in spelling of author's name as given in note 25.

[28] William Dickey, "An Essay on Milk Sickness," *The Western Lancet*, XIII (1852), 392; R. L. Anderson, "Sick Stomach—Milk Sickness—Trembles—or Dry Murran," *The Water-Cure Journal and Herald of Reforms*, XII (1851), 82.

[29] W. J. Collins, "Milk Sickness," *The Medical Standard* (Chicago), XXV (1902), 420-423; J. W. Alexander, "Milk Sickness," *Illinois Medical Journal* (Springfield), VII (1905), 65.

[30] William Osler (ed.), *op cit.*, III, 546-548. (See our footnote No. 1.)

[31] National Board of Health, "Annual Report," *Executive Documents*, 64 Congress, 2 Session, 1879-80 (Washington, D. C., 1879), Vol. XVIII, document 10, page 155; United States Department of Agriculture, Bureau of Animal Industry, *Twenty-fourth Annual Report, 1907* (Washington, D. C., 1909), 155, 156.

[32] William Dickey, "An Essay on Milk Sickness," *The Western Lancet*, XIII (1852), 397.

[33] J. F. Cowan, "Correspondence of the American Home Missionary Society," *The Home Missionary* (New York), IX (1836), 87.

[34] I. S. Swan, "Milk Sickness," *The Western Lancet*, XIII (1853), 671, 672.

[35] J. Newton Smith, "Milk Sickness," *The Western Journal of the Medical and Physical Sciences* (Cincinnati), XLII (1837), 324, 325.

[36] John Kost, *op. cit.*, 166, 167. (See our footnote No. 23.)

[37] James M. Gully, *The Water Cure in Chronic Disease* (New York, 1849), Part III, chapter 2; R. T. Trall, *The Hydropathic Encyclopedia* (New York, 1873), Part V, chapter 2.

[38] William M. Beach, "Milk Sickness," *Journal of the American Medical Association*, I (1883), 71-75.

[39] W. J. Collins, "Milk Sickness," *The Medical Standard*, XXV (1902), 420-423.

[40] J. W. Alexander, "Milk Sickness," *Illinois Medical Journal*, VII (1905), 65, 66.

[41] E. L. Moseley, "Antidote for Aluminum Phosphate, the Poison that Causes Milk-Sickness," *Medical Record* (New York), LXXVII (1910), 620-622.

[42] Cincinnati *Daily Gazette*, December 21, 1827.

[43] R. Carlyle Buley, "Pioneer Health and Medical Practices in the Old Northwest Prior to 1840," *The Mississippi Valley Historical Review* (Cedar Rapids, Iowa), XX (1933-4), 501.

[44] J. B. Evans, "Milk Sickness—A Mineral Poison," *Nashville Journal of Medicine and Surgery*, XVIII (1860), 110.

[45] National Board of Health, "Annual Report," *Executive Documents*, 64 Congress, 2 Session, 1879-80 (Washington, D. C., 1879), Vol. XVIII, document 10, page 155.

[46] J. W. Walker, "Milk-Sickness," *Science* (New York), VIII (1886), 482-484; Alice B. Tweedy, "Mischief-Makers in Milk," *The Popular Science Monthly* (New York), XXXV (1889), 211-215.

[47] W. J. Vermilya, "Milk Sickness," Ohio State Board of Agriculture, *Thirteenth Annual Report, 1858* (Columbus, 1859), 671; N. S. Townshend, "Milk-Sickness," *ibid., 1873* (Columbus, 1874), 489.

[48] J. W. Alexander, "Milk Sickness," *Illinois Medical Journal*, VII (1905), 64.

[49] E. L. Moseley, "The Cause of Trembles in Cattle, Sheep and Horses and of Milk-Sickness in People," *The Ohio Naturalist* (Columbus), VI (1906), 463-470; 477-483.

[50] Albert C. Crawford, "The Supposed Relationship of White Snakeroot to Milksickness or 'Trembles'," United States Department of Agriculture, Bureau of Plant Industry, *Bulletin 121, Miscellaneous Papers* (Washington, D. C., 1908), 5-20.

[51] Edwin O. Jordan and N. M. Harris, "The Cause of Milksickness or Trembles," *Journal of the American Medical Association*, L (1908), 1665-73; Edwin O. Jordan and Norman MacL. Harris, "Milksickness," *Journal of Infectious Diseases*, VI (1909), 401-491; Arno B. Luckhardt, "Additional Notes on the Bacteriology and Pathology of Milksickness," *ibid.*, 492-505.

[52] C. Dwight Marsh and A. B. Clawson, "Eupatorium Urticaefolium as a Poisonous Plant," *Journal of Agricultural Research* (Washington, D. C.), XI (1917), 699-715.

[53] Horatio N. Parker, *City Milk Supply* (New York, 1917), 59.

[54] F. A. Wolf, R. S. Curtis, B. F. Kaupp, "Studies on Trembles or Milksickness and White Snake Root," *Journal of the American Veterinary Medical Association* (Ithaca, New York), LII (1918), 820-827; Walter G. Sackett, "The Connection of Milksickness with the Poisonous Qualities of White Snake-Root (Eupatorium Urticaefolium)." *Journal of Infectious Diseases*, XXIV (1919), 231-259; C. B. Jordan, Julia P. Whelan, W. F. Gridley, "A Study of the Cause of Trembles (in Domestic Animals) and Milksickness (in Man)," *Journal of the American Pharmaceutical Association* (Easton, Pa.), XIII (1924), 206-210; James Fitton Couch, "Acidosis, Trembles and Milksickness," *Science* (New York), LXIV (1926), 456, 257.

[55] James Fitton Couch, "The Toxic Constituent of Richweed or White Snakeroot," *Journal of Agricultural Research*, XXXV (1927), 547-576; *id.*, "Milk Sickness, the Result of Richweed Poisoning," *Journal of the American Medical Association*, LXXXI (1928), 234-236; *id.*, "Tremetol, the Compound that Produces 'Trembles' (Milksickness)," *Journal of the American Chemical Society* (Easton, Pa.), LI (1929), 3617-19.

[56] James Fitton Couch, "The Toxic Constituent of Rayless Goldenrod," *Journal of Agricultural Research*, XL (1930), 649-658.

[57] Fred W. Tanner, *Food-Borne Infections and Intoxications* (Champaign, Ill., 1933), 122.

[58] G. Howard Gowen, "Milk Sickness," *Illinois Medical Journal* (Oak Park), LXXIV (1938), 447-452.

[59] Quoted in Beveridge, *op. cit.*, I, 95n. (See our footnote No. 9.)

PHILIP D. JORDAN (1903–) was born in Burlington, Iowa. He received his B.S. degree from Northwestern University and his M.S. and Ph.D. degrees from the University of Iowa. Jordan taught history at Miami University from 1935 to 1945 and at the University of Minnesota from 1946 until his retirement several years ago. He is the author of eleven books and approximately 250 journal articles.

This article first appeared in *The Filson Club History Quarterly* in January 1945, vol. 19, pp. 29–40.

GENERAL JAMES TAYLOR AND THE BEGINNINGS OF NEWPORT, KENTUCKY

By Robert C. Vitz*

The first hint of the coming winter was in the morning air as the election judges made their way toward the Taylor mansion overlooking the Ohio River. They were paying Newport's most distinguished resident a singular honor by going to the old general's bedside to record his vote on that gray November day in 1848, and as the ailing gentleman cast his vote for his cousin, Zachary Taylor, he supposedly said, "I have given the last shot for my country."[1] Hours later General James Taylor was dead. Although in declining health his last years, James Taylor had led an active life as a businessman, land speculator, town promoter, and agent for the War Department, and during his fifty-five years residence in Newport, Kentucky, he established himself as one of the largest landowners in the Ohio Valley. Indeed, when his will was probated, his Kentucky property amounted to more than 60,000 acres and, in addition, he owned land in twenty-six Ohio counties. The total value of the estate was estimated at four million dollars.[2]

Like so many early Kentucky fortunes, Taylor's was linked to his Virginia background. By the time of the American Revolution, the Taylors were already an old and distinguished family in Caroline County, Virginia, and Newport's Taylor was the fifth person in direct succession to carry the name of James.[3] The first James Taylor in this country migrated from England in 1682 and established the name that was eventually linked by marriage to most of the prominent families in the Virginia piedmont. The future General Taylor grew up a part of a local gentry comprised of Chews, Burnleys, Minors, Lees, and Taliaferros, and he included among his relations two future presidents, James Madison and Zachary Taylor, as well as John Penn, Edmund Pendleton, and John Taylor of Caroline.[4] Taylor's father, James Taylor

---

ROBERT C. VITZ, PH.D., teaches history at Northern Kentucky State College.

[1] Lexington *Observer and Reporter*, November 15, 1848 (quoted from the Cincinnati *Atlas* of November 8, 1848; Cincinnati *Daily Gazette*, November 8, 1848, p. 2; Lewis Collins, *History of Kentucky* (2 vols.; Frankfort: Kentucky Historical Society, 1966), II, 115.

[2] "List of Taxable Property, 1846" in the Taylor papers, folder 8, Manuscript Department, The Filson Club, Louisville, Kentucky; Collins, *History of Kentucky*, I, 67.

[3] For convenience Newport's James Taylor (1769-1848) will be referred to as James Taylor the younger or General James Taylor, his father (1732-1814) will be referred to as James the elder.

[4] "Some Colonial Families—Taylor of Virginia," *The American Historical Register*, II (June, 1895), 1001-02; Colonel Francis Taylor, *Diary, 1786-1799*, the original of which is in the Virginia State Library, a microfilm copy is in The Filson Club, Louisville, Kentucky.

the elder, had been a lieutenant-colonel in the Virginia militia and a high sheriff, chief surveyor, and magistrate of his county. All of which is to say he was a man of considerable means and importance. An acquaintance of George Washington, the elder Taylor had served as chairman of the local Committee of Public Safety just prior to the outbreak of the Revolution, and he then joined his legislative colleagues, which included Thomas Jefferson, Edmund Pendleton, and Patrick Henry, at Rawley's Tavern in Williamsburg in passing the famous Virginia Resolutions of 1775. Although not an active participant in the war, he did organize a volunteer regiment, and his very excited six year old son later recalled strutting around wearing "a cocked hat with a buck's tail for a cockade."[5]

By the time the young James reached maturity, the war was over and interest in the western lands of Kentucky had soared to fever pitch. Like his fellow Virginian of that period, John Breckinridge, Taylor must have heard much about the rich soil and fertile valleys, where the future promised much for one with vision and ambition.[6] Recent years had not been good to Virginia, with wartime disruption and a declining agricultural economy, and, however exaggerated, the bountiful vision of Kentucky beckoned to many. Colonel Francis Taylor, a relative residing in the adjacent county, recorded the constant arrivals and departures of various relations and acquaintances, and by 1790 several Taylors had already permanently settled in the western country. With cheap land providing the major attraction, thousands of adventuresome Americans made the journey down the Ohio by flatboat, and in one twelve month period alone an observer at Fort Harmar, near present day Marietta, recorded 850 flatboats with an estimated 20,000 people. By 1790 Kentucky, still a county of Virginia, claimed a population of 73,000.[7] Removal to Kentucky was not a decision made lightly, however. The heartache of separation, the uncertainty of one's

---

[5] James Taylor, "General James Taylor's Narrative," p. 66. There are several copies of this unpublished manuscript and the pagination differs in several of them due to the inclusion of added material. I have used a xerox copy in the collection of the Northern Kentucky State College Library; there is also a typed copy in the Cincinnati Historical Society, which is in more readable condition. See also Marshall Wingfield, *A History of Caroline County, Virginia* (Baltimore: Regional Publishing Company, 1969), p. 58; this is a reprint of the original 1924 edition which gives some information on the elder James Taylor and other members of the family.

[6] Lowell H. Harrison, *John Breckinridge: Jeffersonian Republican* (Filson Club Publications, Second Series, number 2; Louisville: Standard Printing Co., 1969), pp. 27-31. Another factor which may have encouraged so many Taylors to emigrate to Kentucky was the size of the clan; it would take a genealogical chart of considerable size to include the numerous descendants of the first James Taylor, and James Taylor of Newport could count forty to fifty first or second cousins alone.

[7] William Henry Perrin, *Kentucky, A History of the State* (Louisville: F. A. Battey and Company, 1885), pp. 225-226.

economic future, the risks that accompanied a primitive and isolated life, and, especially, the many reports of Indian attacks often deterred all but the most enterprising. Hubbard Taylor, an elder brother of James, in a letter to James Madison, related several Indian disturbances near the small settlement of Lexington, and another relative, Edmund Taylor, commented on how "troublesome" the Indians were. Hancock Taylor, a surveyor who had entered the Kentucky country as early as 1773, died at the hands of the Indians; and another relation died "of the cholic" soon after moving west.[8]

For James Taylor the desire to go to Kentucky centered around his father's land located at the confluence of the Ohio and Licking rivers. The original land warrant, granted to the elder James Taylor for his services in the American Revolutionary War, comprised 2500 acres (which included part or all of the present day northern Kentucky communities of Newport, Bellevue, Dayton, and Fort Thomas), of which 1000 acres on the upper end was turned over to George Muse and later purchased by Washington Berry, a son-in-law of the elder Taylor.[9] Unmarried, soon to turn twenty-three, and with an ambitious eye towards the future, the young James Taylor made his first trip to Kentucky in 1792. He and a companion, Ensign William Clark, made the arduous journey in about six weeks. Due to General Arthur St. Clair's defeat the previous fall, the Indians had become quite "bold and daring," and Taylor and Clark joined a flatboat flotilla of twenty-five boats to insure their safety down the Ohio. Although they saw several parties of Indians, the only danger came when their boat, lashed to another for added protection, narrowly missed being crushed against rocks. Landing at Limestone, now Maysville, Kentucky, "a muddy hole of a place with two or three log houses and a tavern," the flotilla broke up, and Taylor proceeded overland to Hubbard Taylor's house near Lexington. He spent most of May and the first half of June at his brother's and had the good fortune to be in Lexington when the state's first legislature convened. Along with Hubbard, a member of the new state Senate, and several other legislators, the young James Taylor stayed at the home of Thomas Carneal, the father of Covington's Thomas D. Carneal. In mid-June Taylor bade farewell to the political atmosphere of Lexing-

---

[8] Hubbard Taylor to James Madison, [1792], in James A. Padgett, ed., "The Letters of Hubbard Taylor to President James Madison," *Register* of the Kentucky Historical Society, 36 (April, 1938), 107-13. Francis Taylor, *Diary,* May 9, 1786; August 9, 1786.

[9] James Taylor, "Narrative," pp. 53, 56. Willard Rouse Jillson, *The Kentucky Land Grants* (Louisville: The Standard Printing Co., 1925), pp. 124-26. Various Taylors held land warrants throughout Kentucky and there is some confusion as to how much the elder James Taylor claimed. The chaotic system of land grants, which included English colonial grants as well as Virginia and Kentucky state warrants, involved most of the early speculators, including the Taylors, in an endless travail of litigation.

ton. Joining a battalion of mounted men, escorting supplies to various frontier forts to the north, he made the acquaintance of two already prominent Kentuckians, Judge Henry Innes and the soon to be senator John Brown. Upon arriving at Cincinnati, Taylor gladly accepted an offer to stay at Fort Washington, where he met General James Wilkinson, with whom he maintained a lifelong friendship. Remaining at Fort Washington for two weeks, he spent much of his time examining his father's land on the opposite bank of the Ohio, one-third of which had been promised to him.[10] Although his brother Hubbard had laid out over two hundred lots the previous year and named the site Newport, in honor of Captain Christopher Newport of the Jamestown expedition, there was little to indicate what the future would bring. A few log shanties and a small clearing provided the only indication of settlement, yet with its location on two rivers and Fort Washington as a source of protection, Taylor must have felt confident of the future.[11]

Before returning to Virginia, James Taylor made an extensive trip back through Kentucky to visit relations in Lexington, Frankfort, and Louisville. This quick tour of the state's major settlements proved beneficial for the future. He made the acquaintance of the chief surveyors for the Virginia military lands and of the future governor, General Charles Scott, as well as extending those friendships from his earlier visit. By the time Taylor left Kentucky he had an extensive network of relatives, friends, and acquaintances which he would find quite useful in developing his vast land holdings.[12]

The following spring James Taylor made his permanent move to the west. Accompanied by Washington Berry and his wife, Taylor's sister Alice, two other gentlemen and several slaves, he set out over the usual route. They crossed the Shenendoah Valley and proceeded to Redstone, Pennsylvania, a small port south of Pittsburgh on the Monongehela River, and then went by flatboat to Pittsburgh. After a short rest there, the small party passed an uneventful eight days or so floating down the Ohio to Limestone, where the Berrys and the other gentlemen landed and proceeded to Lexington. In the meantime, Taylor had met a British deserter, Robert Christy, who hired out himself and his wife for three

---

[10] James Taylor, "Narrative," pp. 51-53, 57-58. Hubbard Taylor, who had moved to Kentucky in 1790, lived along Boone's Creek some twelve miles east of Lexington.
[11] Captain Nathan Kelly interview, n.d., Draper Collection, 13 CC 46, Wisconsin State Historical Society; a microfilm copy is in The Filson Club, Louisville, Kentucky. Margaret Hartman, "Jonathan Huling, An Early Citizen of Newport and a Very Busy Man," paper read before the Christopher Gist Society, Covington, Kentucky, January 17, 1970, p. 3.
[12] James Taylor, "Narrative," pp. 55-56, 58.

years in return for Taylor paying their expenses to Kentucky, and on the third of May, 1793 they landed at the mouth of the Licking.[13]

The first task was to establish shelter of some sort, and Taylor, Christy, and the three slaves, Moses, Humphrey, and Adam, set about clearing the land and building rude cabins. Working from the Ohio River back, Taylor soon had erected a cabin on lot number six, and in June planted about fifteen acres in corn. The group spent the first months making the area liveable, but the usual number of misfortunes provided constant interruptions. Toward the end of May the two older slaves, Moses and Humphrey, disappeared while their owner was visiting friends at Fort Washington. Homesick and lonely for people of their own race, the two had set out by way of Limestone for Hubbard Taylor's place near Lexington, where they knew some twenty-five other slaves resided. Taylor and Jacob Fowler, an early Newport settler and acknowledged woodsman, set off in pursuit the next morning, and learned when they reached Washington, Kentucky that the two unfortunate blacks had already been apprehended and sent back. Returning by way of Augusta on the Ohio River, Taylor took the opportunity to purchase a cow, some fowls, and a yoke of young work oxen to aid in clearing the fields. An unfortunate side effect of the trip in pursuit of the slaves was the loss of one of Taylor's thoroughbred riding horses from a case of the "yellow water." This disease, noticeable by the sudden loss of hair, caused a yellow liquid to form in the blood which turned to jelly when cold.

By August time off was needed to look to the area's future. With the assistance of Jacob and Edward Fowler, Taylor marked off the first road to Lexington, but the undertaking proved surprisingly hazardous. Due to stagnant water on Plumb Creek, a small tributary of the Licking, the young town developer fell seriously ill. The proximity of Fort Washington proved a blessing, and a Dr. Brown, sent over by the Surgeon General of the Western Army, diligently attended Taylor. Even with the aid of eighteenth century medicine, however, James Taylor remained bedridden for several weeks and was still too weak to participate in an early October buffalo hunt at Big Bone Lick, some twenty miles to the west. Although he received one hundred pounds of prime buffalo meat —which he preferred to beef—and some fine marrow bones for looking

---

[13] *Ibid.*, pp. 60-61. Among his possessions when he landed Taylor mentioned two blooded horses and a boatload of household supplies that he had obtained in Pittsburgh in exchange for a lame horse.

after his neighbors' families, the young Taylor must have envied the hunters when they returned with twenty-three of the great beasts.[14]

Shortly after regaining his health, smallpox ravaged the Cincinnati area. *The Centinel of the Northwestern Territory,* Cincinnati's first newspaper, announced the death of seven year old David Strong and commented that the dreaded disease "prevails with great virulence in this place."[15] The only physician in the area was overwhelmed with work, so Taylor took his three slaves, a black family in his care, and a boyhood friend out on a visit to a neighbor for inoculation. In spite of this precaution, or perhaps because of it, Boagdell Allcock, the visitor, died a few days after Christmas, and the slave Humphrey never regained his health after contracting the disease. Taylor himself came through the episode unscathed; one presumes that he had been inoculated previously in Virginia, although his health at this time was frequently poor. In his autobiography Taylor makes several references to ill health in his youth, and an uncle by marriage, Dr. Thomas Hinde of Lexington, wrote a short letter to him in 1798, in which he made note of Taylor's "predisposition to consumption."[16]

Despite these time-consuming setbacks, Taylor continued slowly to develop what would become his own estate, and the little settlement of Newport gradually reflected the industriousness of its early citizens. While local sentiment recognizes James Taylor as the founder of Newport, Jacob Fowler had built a cabin there even before Hubbard Taylor had laid out the first lots, and Nathan Kelley claimed to have built the first real house there in 1791. By the time James Taylor settled at Newport, the chief residents of the area included not only Kelley and the Fowlers but Jacob Barrackman, Robert Benham, Uriah Hardesty, and John Bartle. To Benham belongs the distinction of having made the first cash purchase of a town lot from Taylor—lots number three and four for the sum of ten pounds, ten shillings—but he was shortly joined by

---

[14] The number of slaves on Hubbard Taylor's estate is mentioned in Pratt Byrd, "The Kentucky Frontier in 1792," *The Filson Club History Quarterly,* 25 (July, 1951), 200-2 The rest of the information is from James Taylor, "Narrative," pp. 62-64. The choice parts of the buffalo were the rump, tongue, and marrow gut; the buffalo meat, as described by Taylor, was dark with yellow fat and made up the basis of his diet for the next six months.

[15] *The Centeninal of the Northwestern Territory,* November 30, 1793, p. 3.

[16] James Taylor, "Narrative," p. 65. Thomas Hinde to Taylor, April 27, 1798, typed copy in Richard Southgate material, Northern Kentucky State College Library; the original is in the possession of the Kentucky Historical Society, Frankfort. Smallpox inoculation was still a very risky method of avoiding the disease. Hubbard Taylor wrote James Madison in 1794 that the disease had "been very fatal both by the Natural way and by inoculation. Forty or upwards died in Lexington . . . ," and as late as 1804 the town of Cincinnati forbade smallpox inoculations and condemned any doctor using them "as an enemy to the health and prosperity of the town." See Padgett, "Letters of Hubbard Taylor to James Madison," p. 117, and Richard Wade, *The Urban Frontier* (Chicago: The University of Chicago Press, 1964), p. 98.

Bartle, Kelley, and William Christy. Other early lot owners, either by purchase or donation, included William Lytle, Jacob Fowler, David Lewis, James Taylor and his brothers Hubbard and Edmond, and a Taylor sister, Elizabeth Minor.[17] The town proper had been laid off into 180 in-lots (66 feet frontage and 214½ feet deep), 24 out-lots of three acres each on the southern outskirts, and twelve small lots along the esplanade on the Ohio River; the prices paid for these early lots ranged from one pound, sixteen pence to thirty-two pounds, the amount depending on the location and condition of the land. The conditions of the sale were quite specific—one-half of the purchase money immediately, one-half within twelve months, and the buyer had to build a house on the lot within three years or forfeit title. As an added inducement the first eighteen buyers received an out-lot free.[18]

Prior to James Taylor's arrival in Newport, there is no question that John Bartle figured as the area's leading resident. A partner in the Cincinnati firm of Strong and Bartle, he included among his customers several prominent Cincinnatians, as well as the single largest landowner in what would soon become Campbell County, Major David Leitch.[19] Bartle handled northern Kentucky subscriptions for Cincinnati's first newspaper and received the first license to operate a ferry between Newport and Cincinnati. In 1794 Jams Taylor, on behalf of his father, successfully brought suit against Bartle, claiming exclusive right to all river frontage and ferry privileges, and the Taylor control of the river frontage remained intact for over sixty years.[20] Although the northern Kentucky area did provide a few basic commodities for the Cincinnati-Fort Washington market, such as lumber and salt, the main trade route between Lexington and the future Queen City passed through Maysville. Thus, quite early in its development Newport and its neighboring settlements were left in something of an economic backwater. In 1800 the

---

[17] *Record of the Lots in Newport, 1791-1795*. This early handwritten account book is in the possession of the Newport Public Library; also see E. C. Perkins, *The Borning of a Town, Newport, "Cantuckee"* (Ft. Thomas, Kentucky: privately printed, 1963).

[18] *Ibid*. The English monetary system was commonly used in this part of the country until after 1800, and the value of the pound, while never exact, was equivalent to about $2.70 in the Cincinnati area. The original boundaries of Newport, that is, the in-lots, ran from the river (except for the actual frontage which remained in Taylor's control) to Fifth Street, and from Isabella to Washington Street.

[19] Hartman, "Jonathan Huling," p. 4. See also "Account of Major David Leitch on John Bartle, July 24, 1793," Box 19, folder 563, Kentucky Historical Society. Mrs. Leitch, the future Mrs. James Taylor, was apparently a preferred customer if her purchases for January, 1795 are any indication. In that month alone her total bill came to over 25 pounds, or about $70; see "Account of Mrs. Leach [sic]," January, 1795, Box 19, folder 563, Kentucky Historical Society.

[20] *Centinel of the Northwestern Territory*, November 9, 1793, p. 3; Collins, *History of Kentucky*, II, 112; Hartman, "Jonathan Huling," pp. 3-4.

census recorded 106 residents in Newport and as late as 1830 it still remained a sleepy village of less than 800.[21]

This lack of growth was certainly not the fault of James Taylor, who years later expressed just the merest suspicion of regret at not having purchased property in Louisville when he visited there in 1792, instead of directing his energies into Newport. As early as September, 1795 Taylor had put up for auction "a number of valuable and well situated lots in the town of Newport," the auction scheduled for Campbell Court day; at about the same time he advertised for sale "three thousand acres of military land" in present day Clermont County, Ohio, and in the spring of 1796 he listed one thousand acres—"level, well-watered, and of exceeding good quality"—near the junction of the Little Miami and the Ohio.[22] In most of these early land sales Taylor acted as agent for his father or other relatives, but about this same time he commenced his own vast land speculations which provided the basis for his later wealth. Indeed, by the end of the decade he had not only received from his father title to the unsold lots in Newport, but was vigorously acquiring land in a variety of ways in both Ohio and Kentucky.[23]

While Taylor obviously had a good eye for profitable land, excellent family connections, and abundant energy, the land situation was not without its problems and risks. Money was scarce in the Ohio Valley, as was typical everywhere on the frontier, and the shortage of cash often proved to be a major hurdle in the buying and selling of land. Taylor's associate for several years, William Lytle, noted that he had been unable to make many sales and that "money is almost out of the question to collect...." A few years later another of Taylor's associates lamented the "very poor progress in selling land," and made note of the unseasonably low prices for local produce.[24] While the periodic financial recessions often compounded the already tight monetary situation, in some cases the inability to pay debts resulted from natural hazards. Reuben Taylor,

---

[21] G. Glenn Clift, "*Second Census*" *of Kentucky—1800* (Baltimore: Genealogical Publishing Co., 1966), p. 250; Collins, *History of Kentucky*. II, 263.

[22] *Centinel of the Northwestern Territory*, August 15, 1795, p. 1; April 11, 1795, p. 3; May 14, 1796, p. 3.

[23] *Deed Book B*, p. 9 Campbell County records, Alexandria, Kentucky. William Lytle to James Taylor, September 17, 1799, in James Taylor papers, folder 1, The Filson Club, Louisville, Kentucky; John Armstrong to James Taylor, February 27, 1800, Box 1, folder 21, Kentucky Historical Society. Taylor acquired most of his land through direct purchase or by locating other people's land warrants and then receiving a certain amount as his share, although on one occasion he received some acreage through a land lottery.

[24] William Lytle to James Taylor, September 19, 1799, in James Taylor papers, folder 1, The Filson Club, Louisville, Kentucky. Hubbard Berry to James Taylor, November 28, 1816, Taylor papers, Box 1, item 45 Cincinnati Historical Society. Hubbard Berry, the son of Washington Berry, was a nephew of James Taylor.

another brother of James, gave evidence of this in a letter in which he described at length the crop damage done by a "hale storme," as an explanation for his own current financial difficulties. Not infrequently James Taylor found himself short of funds. In 1797 his father-in-law's estate sent him a bill for over fifty pounds, including interest for *six years*, and two years later Lytle commented that he was sorry to learn that Taylor's credit was "suffering." In 1804, after Taylor had been appointed to superintend the construction of the military facilities at Newport, the elder James Taylor hinted that perhaps the son would now be able to pay off the debts he owed his father, but rather wistfully concluded that "you speculators are never willing to part with money but on a prospect of gain."[25]

In 1806 Taylor suffered one of the few major financial losses of his career. After selling some 4000 acres of land near Delaware, Ohio for $16,000 in Treasury notes, he then invested this money in the Bank of Kentucky and the Farmers and Merchants Bank of Lexington. Due to a politically motivated banking law which established the Commonwealth Bank of Kentucky as a state bank, independent bank notes dropped fifty per cent in value. Taylor estimated his ultimate loss at close to $20,000.[26] Additional financial setbacks could also be incurred by the many legal squabbles that resulted from the inaccurate surveys, poor maps, and the ever present squatters, and with increasing frequency after 1800, Taylor found his time taken up by various lawsuits, most of which he won. Squatters in the more remote areas often refused to pay rent, and by the time the courts acted, they had usually disappeared into the endless forests. There were other problems as well. Occasionally the bonds given to Taylor in lieu of cash proved to be fraudulent, counterfeit money or bank notes remained a hazard, and on several occasions, whether for legitimate reasons or not, Taylor's own financial respectability came under attack. Despite the multitude of problems and risks, there is little to indicate that James Taylor ever suffered undue financial reverses. His acreage on both sides of the Ohio River continued to accumulate, his private fortune gradually increased, and his position in the social and economic affairs of the area grew rapidly.

Throughout these early years, which included extensive traveling both in the Ohio Valley and back east, Taylor continued to spend consider-

---

[25] Reuben Taylor to James Taylor, October 23, 1812, Taylor papers, Box 4, item 7, Cincinnati Historical Society. The Estate of Hugh Moss to James Taylor, 1797, Box 21 folder 699, Kentucky Historical Society; Hugh Moss was the father of Mrs. James Taylor. See also William Lytle to James Taylor, September 17, 1799, Taylor papers, folder 1, The Filson Club, Louisville, Kentucky. For the elder Taylor's comment see James Taylor to Major James Taylor, Jr., June 14, 1804, Box 25, folder 945, Kentucky Historical Society.
[26] James Taylor, "Narrative," pp. 70-71.

able time involved with Newport and Cincinnati affairs. In 1795 he had married Keturah Leitch, the widow of Major David Leitch who had owned over 13,000 acres in Campbell County below Newport. Taylor had been acquainted with the Leitchs since his first visit to Kentucky in 1792, and during the next two years the three had relied on each other for social entertainment. Following David Leitch's death, the result of a wet November surveying trip, Taylor became one of the three executors of the estate. A year later he married the widow. A handsome, strong-willed woman of keen intelligence who would live into her nineties, Keturah Leitch proved to be an exceptionally good choice as a wife. Born in Goochland County, Virginia in 1773, the daughter of Major Hugh Moss and Jane Ford Moss, she had come with her widowed mother to Kentucky in 1784, and the family had settled in the vicinity of Lexington. In 1790 Keturah Moss married David Leitch and in the spring of 1792 they moved to Leitch's property, known as Leitch's Station, in Campbell County. As her sister lived in Cincinnati, Keturah Leitch was on close personal terms with several early prominent Cincinnatians and this, plus her friendly relations with numerous Lexington families, proved to be a definite asset to her new husband; and then, of course, she also joined her late husband's large land holdings to those of James Taylor.[27]

The move from Leitch's Station, on the Licking six miles from its mouth, could scarcely have been considered a move into civilization by the new Mrs. James Taylor. The Newport of the 1790s remained mostly uncleared lots, occasional ponds, a scattering of cabins, and several dirt roads. Whatever "society" there was required a trip, usually by canoe, across to Cincinnati. But even the future Queen City remained a raw western outpost for several more years. The town's weekly newspaper printed numerous accounts of theft, personal violence, desertion, and arson. In 1794 the acting territorial governor had called for an inquiry into a riot in Cincinnati involving "a party of lawless men" who had violently assaulted a number of Choctaw Indians under government care. During this same period a Kentuckian strongly protested the practice of Ohioans in "staining the Kentucky bank of the Ohio, with human gore, by duelling"; and in 1799 The *Western Spy* made a note of "an association of wicked men" who had burned four buildings within a week as a device to plunder homes while the citizens fought the fire.[28] Indians remained a menace in the surrounding area until General

---

[27] *Ibid.*, 29-35; Will of David Litch, November 8, 1794; Inventory and Appraisement of the Estate of David Leitch; both in Box 19, folder 563, Kentucky Historical Society.
[28] *Centinel of the Northwestern Territory*, September 13, 1794, p. 3; January 9, 1796, p. 3; *Western Spy* is quoted in Wade, *The Urban Frontier*, p. 91.

Anthony Wayne's victory at Fallen Timbers in August of 1794, and *The Centinel* recorded numerous accounts of Indian sightings and outrages until that date; and at one point anti-Indian sentiment ran so high that local citizens put a bounty system into operation with $136 being the reward for the first ten scalps with "right ear appended."[29]

While the proximity of the Indians provided a certain justification for the violent, rough and tumble manners of some area residents, the most immediate problem the town fathers of Cincinnati faced emanated from Fort Washington. Despite Josiah Espy's rather favorable comment of Cincinnati as "a remarkably sprightly, thriving town," most early visitors painted a far less favorable portrait, particularly of the Fort. William Henry Harrison, a young ensign in 1791, remarked on the number of drunken men, and General James Wilkinson advised one of his officers "to reach Fort Washington in the morning and to leave before night" in order to prevent "disorder and desertion." Lewis Condict simply called it "the most debauched place I ever saw."[30] Lest Kentuckians read too much into these accounts, one traveller left an unforgettable view of the early inhabitants of the Bluegrass state:

> With them the passion for gaming and spiritous liquors is carried to excess, which frequently terminates in quarrels degrading to human nature. The public-houses are always crowded, more especially during the sittings of the courts of justice. Horses and law suits comprise the usual topic of their conversation.[31]

For northern Kentuckians the problems raised by Fort Washington remained north of the Ohio, at least until 1803 when the garrison was transferred to Newport. Indeed, not only did the Taylors and their neighbors enjoy the benefits of military protection and the economic stimulation provided by the Fort, but they also turned to the garrison for much of what passed as genteel society on the frontier. And while the immediate daily problems of clearing and disposing of the land and of developing his own property, occupied most of James Taylor's time,

---

[29] *Ibid.*, April 5, 1794, p. 1; March 22, 1794, p. 3; April 26, 1794, p, 3; May 17, 1794, p. 3.

[30] Josiah Espy, *Memorandums of a Tour in the States of Ohio and Kentucky and Indiana Territory in 1805* (Cincinnati: Robert Clarke and Co., 1870), p. 7. Harrison is quoted in Wade, *Urban Frontier*, p. 25. General James Wilkinson to Major Jonathan Williams, Jr., July 1, 1801 is quoted in Dwight L. Smith, "The Ohio River in 1801: Letters of Jonathan Williams, Jr.," *The Filson Club History Quarterly*, 27 (July, 1953), 203; Lewis Condict, "Journal of a Trip to Kentucky in 1795," *Proceedings of the New Jersey Historical Society*, IV, new series (1919), p. 119.

[31] F. A. Michaux, *Travels to the West of the Alleghany Mountains in the States of Ohio, Kentucky, and Tennessee. . . .* (London, 1805), included in Reuben G. Thwaites, *Early Western Travels, 1748-1846* (32 vols.; Cleveland: Arthur H. Clark and Co., 1904), III, 247-48.

he no doubt agreed wholeheartedly with his older brother's optimistic appraisal that should he live to see the Indians "at peace, the Mississippi open, and the titles to our lands adjusted . . . I shall behold the happiest & richest Country in the world."³²

In terms of James Taylor's personal fortune, the future depended to a great extent on the successful development of Newport, and from 1795 on he devoted considerable time to just that. His expense record, kept as agent for his father, recorded some of the necessary tasks: a re-survey in 1793, a trip to the Mason County Court "to get Ferry established" in January, 1794, a trip to Frankfort in March to get "town and county established," another trip to Frankfort in 1796 "to prevent the Seat of Justice being moved," and later the need to organize subscriptions to build a courthouse and a jail. Interwoven with these major undertakings were added the expenses for smaller surveys, pond drainage, taxes, and even "cash for Liquors and Tavern Bill at sale of lots."³³ Taylor's efforts on behalf of the town's future soon paid handsome returns. Late in 1795 the General Assembly of the Commonwealth passed an act establishing the town of Newport and appointed the first Board of Trustees; earlier Campbell County had been carved out of Scott, Mason, and Harrison counties, and while the no longer existing town of Wilmington served as the first county seat, the newly appointed officials quickly made Newport the political center of the county.³⁴

As the son of the proprietor of Newport and a major landowner in the county in his own right, James Taylor's importance could not be overlooked. Appointed the clerk of both the county and the quarter session court and for the Newport Board of Trustees, positions he would hold for many years, Taylor was able to oversee the political and geographical development of the entire region. For the most part, the County Court busied itself with issuing tavern and ferry licenses, recording land transactions, laying out roads, granting permits for saw and grist mills,

---

³² Hubbard Taylor to James Madison, May 23, 1793, in Padgett, "Letters of Hubbard Taylor to President James Madison," p. 114. *Centinel of the Northwestern Territory*, July 12, 1794, described the Independence Day celebration of that year, a celebration that James Taylor and the Leitchs probably attended. It included a federal salute with cannon, a dinner with venison and turtle as the specialties, and toasts to Washington, The Congress, Governor Arthur St. Clair, the Kentucky Volunteers, and "The San Culottes of France and the Cause of Liberty Triumphant."

³³ *Record of the Lots in Newport, 1791-1795;* the account ledger for the years 1793-1798 is at the back of this lot sales record book, which is in the possession of the Newport Public Library; also see E. C. Perkins, *The Borning of a Town*, pp. 7-14.

³⁴ Campbell County *Court Order Book A*, pp. 1-3, Alexandria, Kentucky Taylor's donation of six in-lots as "a public square" no doubt encouraged the transfer from Wilmington to Newport; this area is now the location of the present Newport city-county building. The original boundaries of Campbell County included not only present day Campbell County but also Boone, Kenton, Bracken, Pendleton, and Grant counties.

and, in general, managing the nuts and bolts of county development; while the Newport trustees turned to the task of transforming a raw settlement into a town, even controlling things so far as to require that all new buildings be erected "on the front of the lot so built on or five inches thereof, except houses built more than twenty feet back."[35]

In 1799 the small community's future noticeably brightened with the establishment of the Newport Academy, one of the earliest educational institutions west of the Appalachian Mountains. Included among the first trustees were Washington Berry, John Grant, Thomas Carneal, Richard Southgate, John Crittenden, and James Taylor, and the initial cost was to be raised by subscription. Taylor was appointed "to superintend the locating and securing of land granted . . . by the act of the last assembly. . . ." The Reverend Robert Stubbs became the first president of the Academy, and the trustees agreed to furnish him with a house, seventeen acres of cleared land, and an annual salary of seventeen pounds for three years.[36] The Academy opened in the spring of 1800, and the *Western Spy* noted that "besides the ordinary branches of education," the school offered instruction in "the dead languages, geometry, plain surveying, navigation, astonomy, mensuration, logic, rhetoric, bookkeeping, Etc." One wonders whether all of this was actually taught. At any rate, whether due to this heavy and varied load or perhaps for personal reasons, the Reverend Stubbs resigned after one year and moved to the country, opening a boarding school for boys two miles south of Newport. Stubbs, however, remained active in the area for many years, and, according to Mary Keturah Jones, a granddaughter of James Taylor, among the young scholars who came under his tutelage either in Newport or earlier in Virginia were Richard M. Johnson, a future Vice President of the United States, John McLean, a future Supreme Court Justice, and numerous sons of locally prominent families. A native of England and an Episcopal minister, Stubbs' talents apparently went far beyond the traditional pedagogical skills, for he also knew "the mystic virtue of the hazel bough as described by Virgil, could discover hidden springs, and was often employed to tell where wells should be dug."

---

[35] *Ibid.*, p. 1. Newport Board of Trustees, *Minutes*, p. 1; the original is located in the Newport Public Library. The first trustees of the town, appointed by the state, included Thomas Kennedy, Washington Berry, Henry Brasher, Thomas Lindsey, Nathan Kelly, James McClure, and Daniel Duggan; and their first meeting was held at Jacob Fowler's house on May 16, 1796. Fowler's house, which may also have been a tavern, served as the meeting place for the town trustees, the county commissioners, and later for the trustees of the Newport Academy.

[36] *Minutes of the Newport Academy*, September 21, 1799, September 10, 1800; the original is in the Newport Public Library. The other trustees appointed in 1799 were William Kennedy, Charles Morgan, Thomas Sanford, Daniel Mayo, and Robert Stubbs.

More importantly, he is frequently given credit for writing the first almanac produced west of the mountains.[37]

Although James Taylor seems to have avoided any direct political involvement during this time, a not altogether easy task considering the political turbulence surrounding Kentucky's first ten years, he definitely considered himself a Jeffersonian Republican. He had conscientiously maintained contact with the network of relations and acquaintances back in Virginia and, as his later correspondence suggests, on occasion cultivated influential connections, at one point going so far as to send fruit trees and strawberry cuttings to President Jefferson. However, as a second cousin to James Madison, and on reasonably close personal terms with him, he no doubt followed the election of 1800 with keen interest, and the resulting election of Jefferson and the subsequent appointment of Madison as Secretary of State soon bore fruit of a different nature for the ambitious Taylor.[38] In April 1803 Taylor received a letter from Secretary of War Henry Dearborn mentioning that the month of the Licking was being considered as the site for a new federal arsenal and asking Taylor if he would be interested in superintending the construction. Although residents of Frankfort made intensive efforts to have the army facilities built in their town, the proposed site at Newport, aided by Taylor's well-timed donation of five acres of land, carried the day. By early summer Taylor had received detailed instructions from Secretary Dearborn as to the size of the buildings, the material to be used and the method of construction; and thus began a fourteen year association between the young proprietor of Newport and the War Department.[39]

---

[37] *Western Spy* quoted in Charles Cist, *Cincinnati in 1841: Its Early Annals and Future Prospects* (Cincinnati: E. Morgan and Co., 1841), p. 169. *Minutes of the Newport Academy*, September 25, 1802. Mary Keturah Jones, *History of Campbell County* (Newport, 1876), pp. 8-9. The Newport Academy apparently expired in 1817, although it may have operated intermittently between 1804 and 1815, since there are no records currently known for those years.

[38] Thomas Jefferson to James Taylor, February 26, 1806, Box 15, folder 480, Kentucky Historical Society. Dolly Madison to James Taylor, March 13, [1808], Box 20, folder 626. Kentucky Historical Society. James Taylor to James Madison, September 25, 1803, in James A. Padgett, editor, "The Letters of James Taylor to the Presidents of the United States," *The Register* of the Kentucky State Historical Society, 34 (April, 1936), 109. In this letter to Madison, Taylor comments that he "cannot fix on anyone but yourself who could have been so good as to name to the Secretary of War to superintend the erection of those buildings." Although there is no acknowledgment of Madison's role in this matter, the letter does imply that Taylor did not actively seek the position with the War Department.

[39] Henry Dearborn to James Taylor, April 12, 1803, Record Group 107, entry 4; Henry Dearborn to James Taylor, June 15, 1803; July 13, 1803; copies in Newport Barracks material, Cincinnati Historical Society. See also James Taylor, "Narrative," pp. 71-72; Newport Board of Trustees, *Minutes*, July 28, 1803.

James Taylor, of course, not only received remuneration for his extensive work in building the arsenal and subsequent facilities, but this position also laid the groundwork for his later appointment as paymaster and quartermaster general of the western army during the war of 1812. The construction of the military installation, along with the transfer of the garrison from Fort Washington, put Newport on the map. The Newport Barracks became the army's chief recruiting center for the upper Ohio valley during the next twenty years, and many prominent officers of both the War of 1812 and the Mexican War spent parts of their careers at the mouth of the Licking. This constant flow of officers greatly stimulated the social life of the small community, and there is little question that the Taylors thrived on this and benefited from it.[40] About the same time, perhaps for social reasons as much as any other, James Taylor embarked on his "military" career. Commissioned a major in the 48th Regiment of the state militia in 1800, he soon dressed himself as befitting an officer and a gentleman, although, his initial choice of a silver mounted sword proved too expensive.[41] During this same period Taylor also began to diversify his business interests. He constructed what would soon be quite profitable saw and grist mills along the Licking near the old Leitch's Station and, at least for a while, attempted to breed mules, perhaps with an eye for selling them to the army. Although he continued to speculate heavily in Ohio lands, he took the opportunity in 1805 to end the sometimes sour partnership with William Lytle that had involved the buying and selling of Virginia military land in that state.[42]

The erection of the Newport Barracks brought to a close the first phase of James Taylor's long and active life. More and more his interests centered on the development of Newport and his own position in that

---

[40] See the interesting letter from Ensign Jacob Albright, at that time in command at the Barracks, to Henry Dearborn requesting "double rations" in order to compensate himself for the increased expenses that resulted from the Barracks location on the Ohio River; January 31, 1807, typed copy in the Newport Barracks material, Cincinnati Historical Society.

[41] G. Glenn Clift, *The "Corn Stalk" Militia of Kentucky, 1792-1811* (Frankfort: Kentucky Historical Society, 1957), p. 125. J. Selleman to James Taylor, January 14, 1802, Box 23, folder 844, Kentucky Historical Society. Selleman was a Cincinnati merchant whose wife was a step-sister to Mrs. James Taylor. James Taylor's granddaughter wrote that Taylor had been commissioned a brigadier general in the 22nd brigade of the Kentucky militia in 1804, but this seems to be in error, as Clift notes his appointment in 1806 as lieutenant colonel and P. G. Voorhies addressed a letter in 1804 to Major James Taylor. See Jones, *History of Campbell County*, p. 11 and Voorhies to Taylor, March 9, 1804, Box 26, folder 1015, Kentucky Historical Society.

[42] Campbell County *Court Order Book A*, November 11, 1802, p. 300. W. Thornton to James Taylor, June 29, 1808, Box 25, folder 975, Kentucky Historical Society. William Lytle to James Taylor, September 17, 1799, Taylor papers, folder 1, Filson Club, Louisville. Lytle to Taylor, April 30, 1805 and December 20, 1805, Taylor papers, Box 2, items 156, 158, Cincinnati Historical Society.

community, and while the town never achieved the growth that its promoters had envisioned—in 1830 it still remained the drowsy village of Daniel Drake's recollection—Taylor's own personal fortune steadily mounted.[43] Following his participation in the War of 1812, which saw him captured with General Hull at Fort Detroit, Taylor involved himself in a variety of economic ventures in both Cincinnati and northern Kentucky. He was active in securing a branch of the Bank of the United States for Cincinnati, and served for a short time as a director of the Lexington branch; as Newport developed its own small but important economic base, he was instrumental in establishing the Newport Bank and the Newport Manufacturing Company, and he worked on several local turnpike commissions. Later he became a director of the Miami Export Company in Cincinnati, and in 1835 he vigorously promoted the never developed Cincinnati to Charleston, South Carolina Railroad. By the time of his death in 1848, General James Taylor, long considered northern Kentucky's wealthiest and most influential citizen, enjoyed a reputation throughout the Ohio Valley for his business acumen, community interest, and civic promotion.

---

[43] Drake is quoted in Charles T. Grave, *Centennial History of Cincinnati and Representative Citizens* (2 vols.; Chicago: Biographical Publishing Company, 1904), I, 350.

ROBERT C. VITZ (1938–   ) was born in Minneapolis, Minnesota, and did his undergraduate work at DePauw University. He received his M.A. degree from Miami University and his Ph.D. from the University of North Carolina. The author of several articles for historical journals, Vitz teaches history at Northern Kentucky State College.

This article first appeared in *The Filson Club History Quarterly* in October 1976, vol. 50, pp. 353–68.

III.

THE CIVIL WAR

GENERAL JOHN HUNT MORGAN
THE GREAT INDIANA-OHIO RAID

By JAMES BELL BENEDICT, JR.*
Cincinnati, Ohio

The spring of 1863 was marked by a feeling of hope and confidence in the Confederacy. General Lee's fighting Southerners had recently succeeded in whipping "the finest army on the planet,"[1] under General Hooker, at the battle of Chancellorsville. Richmond was not yet seriously worried over the safety of Vicksburg, and General Bragg, with his command protecting Chattanooga from Rosencrans' advance, was credited with having a force strong enough to keep the Yankee at bay. Hearing this, Lee decided against re-enforcing Bragg, and led his men northward in search of new successes. The high hopes of the Confederacy rode with him into the hills of Pennsylvania.

In the state of Ohio, farmers watched their fields turn green with corn and wished that the long and drawn-out war would end. For in the Midwest—in Illinois, and Indiana, and Ohio, there was none of the South's whoop and holler optimism. In the last several months there had indeed been little to be optimistic about. Military successes had been few and far between, and enthusiasm for the war had cooled to a point so low that when "King Lincoln" tried to bolster the sagging Union armies with an enforced draft, he was met by rioting in most of the major cities of the North. At this same time, a violent political battle was being waged. "Peace Democrats" made political capital out of the Administration's refusal to let France act as a mediator between the North and South. "The people have been deceived as to the objects of the War," a prominent Ohio Democrat stated. He referred to the war as a struggle "for the liberation of the blacks and the enslavement of the whites." As he spoke, his audience listened intently, carefully digesting the powerful accusations. Above his head there hung unfurled a large banner bearing the slogan, "The Copperheads Are Coming," spelled out with butternuts. Federal detectives sent to report on the speech later testified that hundreds of the assembled citizens wore badges cut from the copper "head" of a penny. Someone shouted, "Jeff Davis is a gentleman, and that is what the president is not."[2]

---

*EDITOR'S NOTE. Mr. Benedict is a native of Cincinnati, Ohio, and the grandson of Hulbert Taft, publisher of the Cincinnati *Times-Star*. He graduated from Phillips Academy, Andover, Massachusetts, in June, 1956. This paper was written in his senior year in competition for the Cates Prize in American History. This competition is open to 220 Andover seniors, and entries are judged by the History Department of Princeton University. Mr. Benedict is now serving with the Marines at Parris Island.

On the twenty-second of December, 1862, Secretary of War Stanton received a communication from Colonel H. B. Carrington, an investigator working jointly for Governor Morton of Indiana and for Stanton himself. Carrington reported that "a secret order exists in this vicinity (Indianapolis) to incite desertion of soldiers with their arms, to resist arrest of deserters, to stop enlistments, to prevent further drafting . . . in short, a distinct avowal to stop this war. There are oaths and signs and watchwords, all to forward the foregoing designs."[3] Three months later Colonel Carrington prepared for President Lincoln a more-lengthy report[4] concerning this "secret order." It was based upon the operations of an organization known as the "Knights of the Golden Circle," but it could equally well have been applied to the "Corps de Belgique," which operated in Missouri, or about the "Sons of Liberty," which took over after the Knights of the Golden Circle had been disbanded.[5] These orders all had one common purpose: to do everything in their power "against the present Yankee abolition, disunion Administration."[6] "It is claimed in their lodges," Carrington stated, "that they have the co-operation of the fraternity in Kentucky, Tennessee, etc.; that at the next raid of Morgan he will leave the command and quietly appear against the standard of revolt in Indiana. Thousands believe this, and his photograph is hung in many houses." The detective went on to warn President Lincoln of the dangerous power possessed by the Indiana "Peace Democrats." "The popular daring of Vallandingham makes him so mischievous that either he or Morgan could raise an army of 20,000 traitors in Indiana. If this Vallandingham counsels resistance or defiance to any U.S. statute in Indiana I wish authority to arrest him."[7]

Carrington would not have long to wait! Late in May, General Burnside, recently given command of the Department of Ohio, issued his famous "General Orders, No. 38." This order stated, in effect, that any person "declaring sympathies for the enemy" in the state of Ohio would be arrested, and either tried or sent out of the country "into the lines of his friends." A roar of anger rose from the rank and file of the "Peace Democrats," and on the 1st of March, Clement Vallandingham challenged the general's action in his famous Mount Vernon speech. "I will not ask David Tod or Abraham Lincoln or Ambrose E. Burnside for my right to speak. My authority for so doing is higher than General Orders, No. 38—it is General Orders, No. 1—the Constitution, George Washington commanding."[8] After finishing his speech, Vallandingham returned to his home in Dayton, but three nights later, some hundred armed and uniformed men surrounded his house, hammered their way through his front door, and carried him to the Dayton jail. "His friends then rang the fire bells and called out the people . . . An attempt was made to rescue him, but failed."[9] The Cincinnati *Gazette* of that date reported that a disloyal mob had cut all the telegraph wires in Dayton and set the *Journal* office on fire.[10]

Copperhead troublemaking continued all over the Midwest. From Indianapolis, Colonel Carrington reported that armed resistance to the arrest of deserters had been made.[11] In Hendricks County, Indiana, at a political rally for the Hon. Daniel W. Vorhees, rioting broke out between a number of armed Butternuts and a group of Union men that had come to observe the festivities. Five or six were wounded, two of them mortally.[12] The *New York Dailey Tribune* for July 7th, 1863, reported that the Knights of the Golden Circle had broken open the depot at Huntington, Indiana, "opening two or three boxes of guns and ammunition, and distributing them among themselves." Farmers rose from their beds in the early hours of the morning to attend secret meetings held in barns and in abandoned quarries. Small groups of men met, exchanged passwords, and left together to burn bridges and destroy sections of railroad track.

Meanwhile, in Sparta, Tennessee, a Southern general was planning to make good use of the Copperhead opposition to "Mr. Lincoln's War." His name was Morgan: General John Hunt Morgan of Kentucky fame. The gentlemen farmers of the Bluegrass Country knew him well, for during the first few years of the war he had paid innumerable "visits" to their racing stables. They called him the "King of the Horse Thieves"[13] and this nickname was richly deserved. His men were always mounted on the finest of Kentucky's thoroughbred racing stock.

What Morgan proposed to do was to lead a raid northward, circling through Kentucky, Indiana, and Ohio, crossing back into Kentucky again, and then rejoining General Bragg somewhere in Tennessee. A raid of this sort would have a threefold purpose.[14] First of all, it would serve to avenge Colonel Grierson's recent insult to the power of Southern arms.[15] Secondly, by drawing General Burnside into pursuit, it would prevent him from carrying out his intention of cutting off Bragg's line of retreat. And finally, it would test the power of the Knights of the Golden Circle, perhaps providing the intiative needed to goad the order into complete and open rebellion. It was with these ends in mind that Morgan approached General Bragg requesting the latter's permission to begin what was later to be known as the "Great Indiana-Ohio Raid." Bragg was perfectly willing that Morgan should lead a raid into Kentucky, even going so far as to suggest the capture of Louisville, but he absolutely refused to give permission for a raid extending across the Ohio.[16] Morgan, however, was convinced that the Confederacy could only maintain its supremacy by carrying the war onto Northern Soil. As he returned from his interview with Bragg, he decided that he must disobey the general's orders; that "the emergency . . . justified disobedience."[17]

So, on the first of June, 1863, General John Hunt Morgan moved north, crossing into Kentucky just south of Burkesville. With him rode Colonel Basil Duke and Colonel Adam Johnson, along with 2,460 well mounted men—the pick of their brigades. The raiders ran into their first organized resistance while crossing the Cumberland River near Burkesville. The river was high, and 12,000 of General Judah's men were guarding the fords. Colonel Duke moved his brigade downstream to Scott's Ferry, and began the difficult task of ferrying men, ammunition, and a pair of three-inch Parrot guns across the swollen, seething river. Meanwhile, at Turkey Neck Bend, Colonel Johnson had lashed several canoes together, and was busy ferrying his men to the far shore. Almost 600 had been successfully gotten across when Judah's Cavalry appeared over the crest of a nearby hill. Colonel Duke's Parrot guns were turned on the enemy, and a charge by the 9th Tennessee quickly put them to rout. The remainder of the crossing was uneventful.[18]

Passing through Columbia on the third, the raiders reached the bridge over the Green River early the next day. Here their crossing was contested by Colonel Orlando H. Moore, who had stationed three or four hundred of his Michigan Infantry in a position overlooking the bridge. When one of Morgan's officers demanded his surrender, Moore is said to have replied good-naturedly that as an officer of the United States he had no right to surrender on the Fourth of July. An attack was immediately ordered, and Colonel Johnson's brigade ran forward with their bayonets fixed. They succeeded in reaching the foot of the earthworks, but, becoming entangled in a network of judiciously placed timber and brush, were forced to withdraw. Another charge was ordered, but it too was beaten back. By this time almost ninety of General Morgan's men had been killed, with an equally large number wounded. Realizing that another assault would cost him half his command, the General "reluctantly drew off," and crossed the Green at a point farther upstream.[19]

It had been a bad Fourth of July for John Hunt Morgan. But the rest of the Confederacy was not worrying about ninety men killed at Tebbs Bend, Kentucky. For on July 4th, 1863, 23,000 Confederate soldiers had been captured at Vicksburg . . . an estimated 10,000 more lay still upon the battlefields of Gettysburg.[20] Gone were Morgan's dreams of joining a triumphant General Lee in his victory march through the North. The "King of the Horse Thieves" would have to fight his way back from the Ohio Country!

On the morning of July 5th, Morgan's column rode into the outskirts of Lebanon, Kentucky. After seven hours of fighting, the rebel forces commenced burning the town, setting fire to the railroad depot and six or seven houses. Colonel Hanson then surrendered, and Morgan's force left in the direction of Springfield.[21] That night an entire company of the Sixth Kentucky Cavalry deserted.[22]

The command passed through Springfield and turned off to the west. At Bardstown a six-hour rest was called, and weary troopers slumped from their saddles into the welcome shade of a stand of sycamore trees. With the fords of the Ohio River lying not far ahead, Morgan sent a detachment of 130 men to "scout in the vicinity of Louisville."[23] By threatening that city, he hoped to divert attention from the river crossing at Brandenburg, Kentucky. Early on the morning of July 8th, Captains Merriwether and Taylor reached Brandenburg with instructions to procure steamboats for the crossing. The raiders concealed themselves on the wharf boat, and, when the *John B. McCombs* landed, seized both ship and captain. In a few minutes the sidewheeler *Alice Dean* churned into sight. Slowly and cautiously the rebels edged the *McCombs* into mid-stream, boarding the *Alice Dean* and forcing the pilot to run her into shore.[24]

Early the next morning, General Morgan rode into Brandenburg with the remainder of his command, and the river crossing was begun. A party of home guards on the Indiana shore were driven back by Lieutenant Lawrence with his Parrot guns, and the Second Kentucky and Ninth Tennessee were ferried across without their horses. The steamboats had barely returned when an unexpected enemy appeared. "A gunboat, the *Elk,* steamed rapidly around the bend and began firing alternately upon the troops in the town and those already across."[25] The ferrying was forced to cease, and, for an hour or two, every available piece of artillery was trained upon the insolent little gunboat. At last it was forced to withdraw, and by midnight the river passage was complete.

The realization that they were standing on Northern soil brought cheers to the lips of the Southern cavalrymen. For at last it was they that were taking the offensive! At last it was the South that was doing the invading! As the raiders climbed up from the river into the darkness, the flames from the *Alice Dean* sent flickering shadows trailing after them.[26]

The raiders rode northward toward the town of Corydon, Indiana. Ahead of them lay broad stretches of fertile corn-land, land occupied by a bare handful of Federal troops. All of the available cavalry and artillery had been sent south to block Morgan's advance through Kentucky; now that the raider had slipped through their trap, the disgruntled Yankees were having trouble keeping up with his twenty-hour marches. When Indiana's Governor Morton first learned that the rebels had crossed the Ohio, there were only a few hundred mounted men in the state. Within twenty-four hours upwards of 15,000 had assembled, and before Morgan left Indiana almost 65,000 had offered their services.[27] There was great confusion in arming and mounting these men. Cannon were almost non-existent, and the soldier that carried a pair of rusty pistols considered himself well armed. A company was raised in Columbus for cavalry service, and the following dispatch was sent to Indianapolis: "We have a company of mounted men. Where shall we get horses?"[28]

Rumors of Morgan's whereabouts spread like a brushfire, and the rebel general used every trick that he knew to keep the Indiana militia guessing. Riding with him was a telegraph operator named Ellsworth, a talented wire tapper who played havoc with the enemy's communications. Swinging aloft with his earphones and notebook, he eavesdropped on the Federal high command, and sent hundreds of false orders and misleading reports. It was thanks to Ellsworth's messages that the city of Indianapolis was thrown into a state of panic. Morgan was coming! The dots and dashes of the telegraph spelled out disaster for the capital! For in nearby Camp Morton were 6,000 able-bodied Confederate prisoners of war, and in the arsenal at Indianapolis were the weapons needed to arm them.

But the "invasion" of Indianapolis was a mere diversionary action. Even with the help of 6,000 prisoners of war Morgan could never have hoped to hold the city for long. It was confusion that he sought to create, and it was confusion, thanks to George Ellsworth's skill with a telegraph key, that he got![29]

Continuing northward, the raiders brushed aside a party of Indiana militia and pushed rapidly on toward Corydon. Morgan had dinner that night, July 9th, in the Corydon hotel.[30] As he ate, his men helped themselves to the comforts of town life, tying bolts of calico onto the backs of their saddles and filling their pockets with freshly-baked biscuits. The well-filled stores and gaudy shop windows of the Indiana towns seemed to destroy all sense of reason in these men "accustomed to impoverished and unpretentious Dixie."[31] "The weather was intensely warm, . . . yet one man rode for three days with seven pairs of skates slung around his neck; another loaded himself with sleigh-bells. A large chafing dish, a medium-sized Dutch clock, a green glass decanter with goblets to match, a bag of horn buttons, a chandelier, and a birdcage containing three canaries, were some of the articles that I saw borne off and jealously fondled," wrote Basil Duke. "Baby shoes and calico, however, were the staple articles of appropriation."[32]

Moving rapidly toward the interior of the state, Morgan reached Salem on the morning of the tenth. Taking possession of the town, he burned a portion of the railroad depot and destroyed several bridges and a section of track.[33] It was in Salem that he began his policy of what today would be called "selling protection." The rebels were about to set fire to three mills and a distillery but, upon entreaty (plus a payment of $1,000 for each building!), Morgan decided to spare them.[34]

From Salem the raiders moved eastward toward Vienna. Detachments were sent to Madison, Versailles, and other points, "to burn bridges . . . and keep bodies of militia stationary that might otherwise give trouble."[35] General Shackleford stated in his report: "Our pursuit was much retarded by the enemy's burning all the bridges in our front. He had every advantage. His system of horse-stealing was perfect. He would dispatch men from the head of each regiment, on each side of the road, to go five miles into the country, seizing every horse, and then falling in at the rear of the column."[36] In this way Morgan swept the countryside of fresh horses, leaving his pursuers to do as best they could with castoff plugs.

Although Morgan's pursuers were poorly mounted, the citizens of Indiana made up for this by making sure that they were well fed. From the moment that Colonel Hobson arrived at Corydon until the end of his pursuit near Buffington Island, his line of march was between two files of patriotic people—men, women, and children—laden with fried chicken and thick slices of blackberry pie. On several occasions, however, General Morgan was able to turn this patriotism to suit his own purposes. In some places he represented himself as a commander of Union troops, and persuaded loyal citizens to point out the finest horses in the neighborhood. "In many settlements Colonel Hobson found his force looked upon with dread," for the inhabitants thought that they had just fed the Union troops, and that Hobson himself was "the terrible Morgan."[37]

The rebels continued through Vienna, helping themselves to fresh horses as they rode on toward the town of Vernon. After destroying a portion of the Ohio and Mississippi Railroad[38] they paid a visit to a packing plant just north of DuPont, Indiana. As they rode away, many of the raiders had replaced their bolts of calico with smoke-cured Indiana hams.[39] From DuPont a squad of sixty men moved on Osgood, burning a bridge and taking the telegraph operator prisoner.[40] The main body of troops made camp at Sunman, Indiana, several miles to the east, and only fourteen miles from the Ohio border.[41]

In Cincinnati, meanwhile, there was great excitement. As it was fully expected that Morgan would be in the city before dawn, General Burnside declared martial law, suspending all business and calling on all citizens to organize for the defense of their city. Federal detectives were on the alert for a pro-southern uprising in the town, and watched with special interest the activities of a young man claiming to be an East Tennessee refugee.[42] He was very inquisitive, inquiring about the number of troops in the city, their strength, and their equipment. "As soon as arrested, papers were found in his possession which confirmed the suspicion that he was one of Morgan's spies."[43]

As the command moved into Harrison, on the Indiana-Ohio border, Captain Taylor and Lieutenant McLain returned from a scouting mission in Cincinnati. They reported that the city was greatly excited, and that troops from Covington and Newport, Kentucky, were being brought across the river to aid in the defense.[44] Morgan wisely decided against an attempt to capture the city—he had no intention of involving his handful of wearied men in a labyrinth of hills and streets.[45] After remaining in Harrison for two or three hours, the general moved with his entire column in the direction of Hamilton. But as soon as he was clear of the town, he cut the telegraph wires and turned southward toward Cincinnati. It was Morgan's hope that, by threatening first Hamilton and then Cincinnati, he would leave the intervening area free of Federal troops.[46] Passing through the outskirts of Cincinnati at about ten o'clock on the night of the fourteenth, the rebels continued eastward, unmolested. The ruse had worked. But by this time the men were too exhausted to appreciate their good luck—stragglers fell out of their saddles and were found the next morning asleep by the roadside. Finally the raiders were safely past the city. They had ridden more than ninety miles in thirty-five hours!

The next morning, after helping themselves liberally to fresh horses, Morgan and his men passed through Reading toward the Little Miami Railroad. On a bend between Miamiville and Branch Hill, the raiders wedged cross-ties end on end in a cattle guard. "They then concealed themselves in a corn field about half a mile above, known as 'Dangerous Crossing.' When the train made its appearance they fired a volley at the engineer, who, discovering the presence of the rebels, put on more steam,"[47] sending the train flying around the curve at the rate of forty miles an hour. In a moment the locomotive struck the obstruction, springing up into the air, and overturning down the embankment. Two hundred unarmed Federal troops were captured and forced to take the pardon oath.[48]

By now the question was how to get safely back across the Ohio. The river was much too high to ford, and Federal gunboats were patrolling a few miles apart up and down the stream. Along the lower Ohio, every description of flatboat, raft, and scow had been removed from the north bank of the river.

To complicate things still further, Generals Hobson, Wolford, and Shackleford were in close pursuit.[49] The *New York Daily Tribune*[50] reported that Morgan was "pretty well hemmed in," and that his chances of escape were "very slight." Twice the raiders' advance guard approached the river, but each time they were driven back by Federal gunboats. Meanwhile, in their front, the local Home-Guards made a persistent nuisance of themselves, felling trees across the road and peppering the raiders from hidden vantage points. The Ohio militia were more numerous and aggressive than those of Indiana. General Duke wrote, "We had frequent skirmishes with them daily, and although hundreds were captured, they resumed operations as soon as they were turned loose."[51]

The raiders continued eastward, heading for the fords of the Ohio at Buffington Island. They had been on the move now for almost three weeks, riding twenty hours a day, and sleeping in the saddle. Orderly ranks were a thing of the past; the men straggled along—two, three, four, and sometimes eight abreast. A hundred or more wore bright blue veils which they had stolen from a clothing store in Jackson, Ohio.[52]

In Winchester, one of the raiders is said to have left the column and, approaching a wide-eyed onlooker, asked her if he could borrow a saddle. The woman replied testily that she didn't have one. "I'll just go have a look-see," the rebel said good-naturedly, as he rode over to a barn on the opposite side of the road. He didn't find a saddle, but there was a shiny new buggy in the barn! With a whimsical "thank you," he hitched up his horse and took his place in the ranks, much to the amusement of his friends.[53]

Farther east, at Springdale, Ohio, the rebels paid an early morning visit to the home of the town butcher, a man named Watson. General Morgan asked for a speedy breakfast, but the butcher began to make excuses—among other things, he had no fire. Morgan suggested that it would be better for Watson to make the fire than for him to do it, as it might be "inconvenient" to put *his* fire out. The butcher took the hint and got the breakfast.[54]

As the raiders advanced through the fertile counties of southern Ohio, the news of their approach spread rapidly ahead of them. Horses and cattle were hidden in the woods, and silver plate and jewelry were hastily buried where "that damned highway-robber Morgan" couldn't lay his hands on them. At Bantam, Ohio, a farmer leaving to join his Home-Guard regiment told a neighbor that he had hidden his life savings in a springhouse near the East Fork of the Little Miami River.

In the ensuing action he was killed and his fortune (if there ever was one) has never been discovered.

As the column appeared in the outskirts of Eagleport, one of the town's more-timid citizens took refuge in a nearby pig pen. A rebel trooper saw him enter, and, following him into the pen, discovered him crouched behind a matronly-looking sow that was in the process of feeding a number of new-born offspring. "Halloa!" shouted the rebel soldier. "How did you get here? Did you all come in the same litter?" The good humor of the raiders seems to have remained with them right to the end.[55]

There was little time for rest as the tired cavalrymen pushed on toward the shoals at Buffington Island. At New Haven, Ohio, where Morgan stopped for an exchange of horses, sleeping riders fell from their saddles without ever waking.[56] However, even in this exhausted condition, they managed to steal more than fifty horses from a two-mile area surrounding New Haven. Tearing down fences, the raiders turned their mounts loose in fields of oats, letting the tired animals eat their fill.[57] "But the crowning, most noticeable circumstance of their stay in New Haven, was the very general shout they raised for Vallandingham, occasionally varied by a cry for Jeff Davis. They inquired with much interest about Vallandingham's followers, whether they were numerous, etc., and by their hurrahs displayed the warmest sympathy for him."[58] The raiders had been led to believe that Morgan's presence in the Ohio country would be the signal for a general revolt among Vallandingham's Peace Democrats. Members of the Knights of the Golden Circle were armed—Colonel Carrington had said that Morgan could easily recruit "an army of 20,000 traitors in Indiana."[59]

Why, then, didn't the Copperheads rally to the standard of revolt raised by General Morgan as he and his raiders passed through the peaceful countryside? One answer might possibly be found in the recent Union victories at Vicksburg and Gettysburg. It would certainly have been an inauspicious moment to jump into the fight in support of the South! But despite these two great northern victories, Copperhead activity continued in those parts of the Midwest that Morgan had not burned and plundered. On the eighteenth of July, 1863, President Lincoln was informed of a meeting of the Knights of the Golden Circle near Chatham, Illinois. Among those present, a number hurrahed for John Morgan—there were cheers for Jeff Davis and for the ashes of Stonewall Jackson.[60]

It would seem, then, that it was only in the southern counties of Indiana and Ohio that the Copperhead movement had lost its vigor. The fact that Morgan gave no special consideration to the so-called

"Fifth Column" probably accounts for the cold reception that they gave him in return. Butternuts had been led to believe that a silver star placed under the eaves of their homes would save them from any pillaging that might take place in a raid of this sort.⁶¹ Great was their disillusionment when they awoke to find their stable doors open, and a crowd of Morgan's hungry troopers milling about downstairs in the kitchen.

The rebel raiders were openly contemptuous of the Knights of the Golden Circle. One old Copperhead, who had lost three horses, protested to Morgan that he was a Vallandingham man. "Then you ought to be glad to contribute to the South," the general replied, taking his wagon from him. As the poor Butternut watched his wagon disappearing in the direction of Jackson, he complained pettishly that his boots were so tight that he couldn't walk. A trooper took his boots from him, and made him limp along barefoot behind the column, singing "I'll bet 10c in specie that Morgan'll win the race."⁶²

On the afternoon of July 18th the raiders reached Chester, eighteen miles inland from Buffington Island. General Judah's cavalry had been brought up the river to Gallipolis, and were now in close pursuit. The combined forces of Generals Hobson, Wolford, and Shackleford menaced Morgan from the rear, and the ever-present gunboats kept him from crossing into West Virginia.

At Chester a two-hour halt was called, to breathe the horses, close up the straggling ranks, and, if possible, obtain a guide. This halt proved to be disastrous—it caused the raiders to arrive at Buffington Ford after night had fallen, and delayed their crossing of the Ohio until the next morning.⁶³ An earthwork had been thrown up to guard the ford. From the piece-meal information that Morgan could gather, it was manned by about three hundred Federal infantry, with two heavy guns. Not knowing the lay of the land, General Morgan was loth to attack in the darkness; instead, he placed the 5th and 6th Kentucky in position about four hundred yards away, with instructions to attack at dawn. Dawn came, but when the two regiments moved against the earthwork, they found that it had been secretly evacuated during the night. Had Morgan's scouts been more vigilant, and had they observed and reported this evacuation, almost the entire division could have been gotten across the river before dawn.⁶⁴

As it was, however, the raiders had barely swung into their saddles when the rattle of musketry announced the approach of General Judah from the direction of Pomeroy. At almost this same time, 3,000 of General Hobson's troopers poured down into the valley from the town of Chester. General Morgan immediately began drawing off upstream, with Adam Johnson and Basil Duke protecting his retreat. Suddenly the gunboat *Moose* loomed out of the fog, and began firing her 24-pounder Dahlgreen guns over the heads of Judah's men into the rebel ranks.[65] The *Moose* and the *Allegheny Belle* had been towed upstream during the night, and now proceeded to steam along parallel to the retreating raiders. This was a problem that Morgan had not anticipated![66] Shells were coming from three directions, filling the air with fragments of shrapnel. As Morgan, with the greater part of his command, passed out of the northern end of the valley, frightened stragglers galloped frantically back and forth behind him. Wagons and ambulances upset—horses broke loose and plunged wildly about the valley floor—terrified riders clung instinctively to bolts of calico that unrolled behind them, streaming like banners in the wind.[67]

Seeing that Morgan had gotten safely out of the valley, Colonels Duke and Johnson began to drop back in orderly fashion. As they neared the narrow gorge leading away from the river, however, a general rush was made for safety. The 7th Michigan dashed into the mass of fugitives, and the gunboats swept the narrow pass with grape. "All order was lost in a wild tide of flight."[68]

More than seven hundred prisoners were taken at Buffington, and perhaps a hundred killed and wounded.[69] Among those captured were Basil Duke and three of General Morgan's brothers: Calvin, Charlton, and Richard. A fourth brother, Tom, had been killed leading a charge upon the depot at Lebanon.

In the meantime, General Morgan limped northward with the remainder of his command—some 1,200 men in all. The ever-present gunboats eased cautiously after him, and Hobson's cavalry, with General Wolford at their head, dogged his every step. About a mile and a half above Buffington Island, a number of the men threw down their arms and plunged headlong into the river. A pair of field pieces had been hastily drawn into position to cover the crossing, but a few judiciously-placed shells from the *Moose* put the rebel gunners to rout.[70] Colonel Johnson, with about three hundred of his men, succeeded in getting safely across, although several were drowned in the swollen, rushing water. General Morgan was in midstream when the gunboats came into sight, but, seeing that the bulk of his command would be forced to remain on the Ohio side, he turned his horse and gallantly rejoined his men.[71]

Fleeing northward through the river counties of eastern Ohio, Morgan succeeded in eluding his pursuers for six more days. After crossing the Muskingum, he found his way blocked by a large body of militia, but managed to make his escape by leading the tired riders down a narrow pass and then up along an almost-perpendicular ridge.

Several nights later he avoided almost certain capture by silently slipping out of camp while the enemy's unsuspecting scouts kept their eyes fixed on the glowing embers of his campfires. But in the end, the combined forces of fatigue and superior numbers proved to be too much for the rebel general. Union detachments under Major Way of the 9th Michigan and Major Rue of the 9th Kentucky Cavalry were being brought up by rail; in a desperate fight with Way at Salineville, Morgan lost almost half of the remainder of his command.

As the raiders straggled eastward, General Morgan overtook a group of local militia, and sent a messenger under flag of truce to request an interview with their captain. A conference took place, at which the militia captain, a man named Burbeck,[72] agreed to guide Morgan to the Pennsylvania line in return for the latter's promise not to do any damage in Burbeck's district. As the pair rode along together, General Morgan noticed a long cloud of dust rolling along parallel to the raiders. Slowly but surely it inched ahead, gaining ground persistently. Major Rue had arrived with his 9th Kentucky Cavalry! Leaving the road that Morgan was traveling, Rue had gone at a gallop down a dry creek bed, through a cow pasture, and onto a private road that joined the main thoroughfare about half a mile ahead of Morgan's advance.[73]

"As soon as we reached the main road we wheeled to the left, and rode to the crest of the hill," wrote Rue several years later. "I found we were ahead of Morgan. I knew then that I had him . . . I had scarcely placed my troops in position for a fight, when over the crest of a hill about a quarter of a mile away, appeared the heads of the horses of Morgan's advance. As soon as they saw me, they halted and drew back, leaving one or two men to watch our movements."[74]

With capture now a certainty, General Morgan was anxious to surrender in the most advantageous way possible. Aware that he was not likely to get "terms" from any officer of the regular troops that were pursuing him,[75] and fearing that, because of the large number of prisoners taken at Gettysburg and Vicksburg, the cartel providing for the exchange and parole of prisoners would be broken, the general decided to surrender to the militia captain that rode at his side. Burbeck was at first taken back by Morgan's offer of surrender, but at last reluctantly agreed. The general wrote his own terms.[76]

Meanwhile, three troopers sent by Morgan to demand Major Rue's surrender returned with the latter's indignant refusal. Word was then sent to Rue that Morgan had himself surrendered. "Burdick?" The name meant nothing to the Major, who suspected a trick, and demanded that the general "surrender or fight." So, on the 26th of July, only fourteen miles from the Pennsylvania line, and a day's ride from Lake

Erie, the great Indiana-Ohio raid came to a close. Men were lying on both sides of the road, and nearly every one of them was asleep. When Major Rue rode into the rebel camp, he found General Morgan mounted on a fine Kentucky mare—the only horse, according to Morgan, that had come the whole way from Kentucky, and that had withstood the strain of twenty-seven consecutive days of travel under the hot July sun. "Morgan was very loth to part with that sorrel mare," Rue later recalled. "He gave her to me, supposing probably that I would take her to Kentucky, where he might someday steal her back from me."[77]

Yes, the great Indiana-Ohio raid had come to a close. Militarily it had been a fiasco. True, it had drawn away and delayed troops which might otherwise have harassed Bragg's retreat from Middle Tennessee, and which might have turned the tide in favor of Rosencrans at Chickamauga. But upwards of 2,000 able-bodied Confederate soldiers had been killed or captured by the Federals—a force that, if added to Buckner's division, might have defeated Burnside and cut Rosencrans' lines of supply and communication.

As for Morgan himself, the raid had been both the high point and low point of his career. The very same raid that made him the idol of Southern womanhood, cost him his future in the Confederate army. Richmond would not easily forget his disobedience in crossing the Ohio, and General Bragg, always one to bear a grudge, would see to it that Morgan was never again given a good command.[78]

As for damage done to property in the states of Indiana and Ohio, Morgan had been extraordinarily successful. The *Cincinnati Enquirer* estimated that the cost of the raid to the people of Ohio would be "not less than $800,000."[79] The Democratic-controlled *Enquirer* went on to say that this unprecedented figure had been "caused mostly by the silly panic of Governor [David] Tod (a Republican), and not by the actual destruction of property by Morgan."[80] Even so, a commission appointed to settle the Morgan raid damages was swamped with claims. In Ohio alone, 4,375 persons asked the government for about half a million dollars in damages.[81] This, added to similar figures in Indiana, and combined with the cost of destruction of railroads, steamboats, and bridges, raises the estimated cost of the Morgan raid to something in excess of $10,000,000.

Although Morgan's own losses were heavy, the Yankees themselves did not escape unscathed. Almost 6,000 Federal soldiers were captured and paroled on the spot, a practice that was the cause of many angry protests from the high command at Washington. Losses were equally heavy among the Home-Guards.

A rebel parole meant little to the farmers of Indiana and Ohio, who "took the oath," were released, and immediately returned to their old habits of bushwhacking and bridgeburning.[82] Even the slumbering patriotism of the Butternuts seems to have been aroused by the presence of an enemy force in their midst. "Morgan's raid into this state," wrote a Cicero, Indiana, correspondent of the *New York Daily Tribune,* "has done more to kill off Copperheads than anything that has transpired so far. A few more similar raids by the guerillas would completely finish them up, and we should all be on one side."[83] But more important even than this was the way in which Morgan's raid served to tighten the defences of Ohio and Indiana; to show the great potentialities lying in the Home-Guard system; and to force these same Home-Guards to organize more efficiently. In this sense, then, the Morgan raid did more harm than good to the Southern cause.

But even though the "Great Indiana-Ohio Raid" was a failure militarily, there was something about it that appealed to the Southerner's sense of adventure—something that let him forget, for a moment, the freshly dug graves at Vicksburg and Gettysburg. Here was a man that had ridden farther north than any other rebel leader during the War. Here was a man that had drawn more than 100,000 blundering Yankee pursuers over a route that passed through three states— presumably protected from invasion by the United States Government. Here was the Southern answer to the embarrassing Colonel Grierson!

But what, meanwhile, had happened to General Morgan and his men? The seven hundred prisoners taken at Buffington were hustled aboard a small steamer and hurried down the Ohio to Cincinnati. Several slipped overboard during the night. As the rebel officers began their trek up the hill from the public wharf to City Prison, a huge crowd of citizens assembled to gawk at these strange creatures that had terrorized the city such a short time before. Along the entire line of procession the interest was immense, and the streets, sidewalks, and buildings were thronged with spectators. "The prisoners seemed cheerful, and frequently raised their hats to the people as they passed along."[84]

While the privates were sent to Camp Morton (Indianapolis) and Camp Douglas (Chicago), all of the officers remained in Cincinnati for three days.[85] Then, on the second of July, the prisoners were transferred to Johnson's Island. "At every station on the railroad, from Cincinnati to Sandusky," recalls Basil Duke, "large and enthusiastic crowds assembled to greet us. . . . There seemed to be 'universal suffrage' for our instant and collective execution."[86]

Meanwhile, a controversy was raging over the question of what to do with Morgan and his officers. Governor Tod claimed them as his own, and, for reasons best known to himself, General Burnside at last agreed that the prisoners should be sent to the Ohio Penitentiary. When Morgan arrived in Cincinnati, he and twenty-eight other officers were therefore sent north to Columbus, where they were turned over formally to Warden Merion. As he stood in line to have his belongings searched, one of the prisoners nervously fingered an old newspaper; he claimed that he used it as a liner for his hat. A suspicious guard, leafing through its pages, discovered that it contained an excellent map of Ohio!

After the prisoners had been thoroughly searched, they were stripped of their clothing and placed, one by one, in huge hogsheads filled with water. A pair of Negro convicts gave them an unceremonious scrubbing, and then the prison barber proceeded to shave away each man's beard, and to pass out "decent haircuts" all around. According to the code of the penitentiary, a "decent haircut" was one in which every scrap of hair (that the scissors could reach) was shorn away. The appearance of the raiders was so changed that, when forty-two of Morgan's officers were transferred from Johnson's Island to the penitentiary at Columbus, one of their number, Basil Duke, did not even recognize the general. "He was so shaven and shorn that his voice alone was recognizeable."[87]

The newcomers were taken to their cells—small, dimly-lighted cubicles that faced out on a central hall. There were five levels of cells, one above the other, with thirty-five cells in each "range."[88] Only about two-fifths of the cubby-holes were occupied. General Morgan was placed in a cell on the second tier; his brother Dick was in the level below him, along with Captain Thomas H. Hines. Hines, a self-styled cloak and dagger man, would later find fame as the leader of a fantastic plot to free rebel prisoners from Camp Douglas.

Soon after they had moved into their new "lodgings," the prisoners were informed by Warden Merion of the regulations to which they would be subject. From five o'clock in the evening until early the next morning they were to be locked into their cells, with no conversation allowed. Between these hours they could exercise together in the narrow hall facing the tier of cells. A military guard of two men with side arms was to be stationed in the hall during the day.

As summer gave way to fall, the terrible weariness of prison life took its toll on the rebel officers. During their long hours of boredom, they grasped at any and all forms of amusement. Marble tournaments were organized, chess games were attended with great interest, and reading became a favorite pastime.[89] General Morgan occupied himself with sending indignant letters to the authorities in Washington, demanding that he and his men be treated as prisoners of war instead of as common felons.⁹⁰ But the answer was always the same. "By direction of the general commanding I am desired to say that no privileges will be granted to your command until official intelligence is received of the release of Colonel Streight's men,⁹¹ now held in confinement at Richmond."⁹²

The purchase of newspapers was strictly forbidden, but the rebels had friends in Columbus who saw to it that every few days a paper was smuggled in to the prisoners. When news of the battle of Chickamauga began trickling through, General Morgan succeeded in getting hold of several newspapers containing full accounts of the victory. "These papers were read to the whole party in detachments—while one listened, the succeeding one awaited its turn in nervous impatience."⁹³

Time continued to drag. On the tenth of October, Major Webber was placed in solitary confinement because of a letter that he had written criticizing the exchange of Negro prisoners of war.⁹⁴ Several days later, Captain Cheatham also had the misfortune of being sent to the "dungeon" for a petty offence.⁹⁵ Under cruel and vindictive treatment of this sort, the prisoners grew more and more restless, and General Morgan determined to escape "at any hazard or labor."⁹⁶ There is no evidence that Morgan had any knowledge of the schemes of Ohio School Commissioner Charles Cathcart.⁹⁷ But he must certainly have given serious consideration to the many other plans for escape, ingenious and desperate, that were suggested. Among these plans, bribery of the guards seemed the most feasible. "We could have commanded, through our friends in Kentucky . . . an almost unlimited amount of money," Basil Duke later wrote. This plan was finally discarded, however, because of the double set of guards, both military and civil, whose watchful jealousy would have made bribery impossible.⁹⁸

Then finally, sometime near the end of October, Captain Hines hit upon an escape plan that caught General Morgan's fancy right from the beginning. Noticing that his cell floor was dry and free from mold, Hines conjectured that there was something in the nature of an air chamber underneath, to prevent dampness from rising up the walls and through the floor. "If this chamber could be reached, a tunnel might be run through the foundation into the yard," from which the prisoners might escape by scaling the outer wall. After consulting with General Morgan it was decided that digging should begin in Captain Hines' cell, and that the five officers whose cells were nearest the point at which the tunnel was to begin, plus Morgan and Hines, should undertake the escape.

On the fourth of November, General Mason sent Sergeant J. W. Moon to the Penitentiary as "prison steward." "I had Sergeant Moon selected as a trustworthy and reliable soldier," General Mason wrote not long afterward. "No instructions were given him . . . with reference to the inspection of cells in the Ohio Penitentiary."[99] The prison authorities, however, later testified that on the fourth of November the complete care, control, and management of the rebel prisoners was put in the hands of the military. From that date on, neither Merion nor the directors of the Penitentiary "had any further care of said prisoners than to furnish food, fuel, etc., . . . and to watch them at night when locked up in their cells."[100] Because of this misunderstanding, cell inspection was stopped not long after Captain Hines and his fellow-plotters began their task of tunneling downward through the floor of Cell #20.

Several table knives had been stolen from the prison dining hall, and these were used in the slow process of digging a hole wide enough for a man to pass through. After six inches of cement had been chipped away, and six layers of brick loosened and removed, Captain Hines slipped feet first into the hole and lowered his body cautiously to the bottom of the air chamber. So far, so good! As he had anticipated, the chamber was about six feet wide, and ran the full length of the range of cells. It was just a shade over four feet high.[101]

The cement and brick that had been cut away during a week of digging was now taken from its hiding place in Captain Hines' mattress and removed to the air chamber. Careful exploration showed that the prisoners were faced with two alternatives. Either they could cut their way through the stone wall of the prison building, or else they could tunnel under its foundation into the yard outside. On the recommendation of Captain Hockersmith, a stone mason by trade, the latter course was adopted.[102]

The work of tunneling under the foundation was tedious and difficult. Two or three of the men would descend and go to work, while the others kept watch; in an hour or so a fresh group would be sent down, and the first shift would return to the surface for a welcomed rest. In this way none of the prisoners was ever out of sight long enough to create suspicion among the guards.

As the need arose, a code of signals was invented by which those above could communicate with those in the chamber below—one knock on the stone floor meant to suspend work; two knocks gave the signal to proceed, and three meant to come up out of the tunnel. While the work continued underground, General Morgan's brother Dick prepared a rope of braided bed ticking, and from the iron poker of the hall stove fashioned a grappling iron to fasten to the end of it.[108] The work was now complete with only one exception. Working from the air chamber, the rebels tunneled upward into the cells of the six other escapees, leaving only a thin crust of cement to deceive the eyes of the ever-watchful guards. Now everything was in readiness!

On the evening of the 27th, as the prisoners filed into their cells to be locked up for the night, General Morgan secretly traded places with his brother Dick. Dick's cell was in the first range, and had been painstakingly prepared for the general's escape. Since both of the Morgans were of about the same weight and height, and since each stood with his back to the cell door as it was being locked, the guard was unaware that a change had taken place.[104]

From newspapers that had run the gauntlet into the prison, General Morgan had been able to ascertain that the train for Cincinnati left Columbus at 1:15 in the morning. At midnight all was still. A guard, making his rounds, thrust a lighted lantern into Captain Hines' cell as he passed. The captain was snoring gently. As soon as the guard had left the building, Captain Taylor rose from bed, broke through the thin crust of cement covering his exit tunnel, and quietly lowered his body down into the dry darkness of the air chamber. At his signal, General Morgan, Captain Hines, and the four other conspirators arranged their bedclothes so as to resemble sleeping prisoners, and followed Captain Taylor down into the tunnel.[105] Before leaving his cell Captain Hines wrote and left, addressed to Warden N. Merion, the following:

> CASTLE MERION, CELL NO. 20, November 27, 1863 . . . Commencement, November 4, 1863; conclusion, November 24, 1863; number of hours for labor per day, five; tools, two small knives. "La patience est amere, mais son fruit est doux."[106] By order of my six honorable Confederates. THOMAS H. HINES, Captain, C.S.A.[107]

"We came out near the wall of the female prison," wrote Hines, ". . . crawled by the side of the wall to the wooden gate, cast our grappling iron . . . over the gate, ascended the rope to the top of the gate, drew up the rope and made our way by the wing wall to the outside wall, where we entered a sentry box and divested ourselves of our soiled outer garments."[108]

Attaching the iron hook to a railing on the outer edge of the wall, the rebels descended to the ground a short distance away from a group of prison guards that stood huddled about a blazing fire. Here they separated, each with a hurried handshake and a whispered good luck. Hockersmith and Bennett found their way to the railroad depot, where they bought tickets on the 1:15 to Cincinnati. They had no sooner seated themselves than Hines strolled casually into the car, followed a few minutes later by General Morgan. Morgan took a seat next to a Federal Colonel, and the pair soon found themselves engaged in an animated discussion, punctuated only by sips at the colonel's bottle of peach brandy.[109]

As the train passed the Penitentiary, the Federal officer smiled, turned to the general and said with a laugh, "This is the hotel at which Morgan stops, I believe."

"And will stop, I hope," Morgan replied. "He has given us his fair share of trouble and will not now be released." He raised the flask. "I drink to him. May he ever be as closely kept as he is now."

"I'll drink to that," the Federal said and did.[110]

At Dayton the train stood motionless in the depot—thirty minutes, forty minutes, a full hour of agonizing delay. The rebels knew that their escape would be discovered before they reached safety, for at 7:00 the deputy warden would make his rounds, unlocking the cells and calling the prisoners out for breakfast. Word would be telegraphed to Cincinnati, and, by 7:30 Federal troops would be stationed at the depot, searching every train coming south from Columbus. There was only one thing to do! As the train moved slowly through the suburbs of the city, Morgan and Hines strode to the back platform, leaned on the brakes, and swung cautiously to the ground.

Going directly to the river, the escapees reached the Ludlow Ferry at about 8:00. "A skiff was being used, and the two men stepped in, desiring to be rowed over at once. The boy in charge of the boat wished to wait a few minutes for a load, telling them that more would soon be along to go over. One of the strangers asked how much a full load would be worth, and was told 'one dollar', whereupon the man gave the boy two dollars," and the bargain was completed.[111]

Meanwhile, in Columbus, officials at the Ohio Penitentiary tried blunderingly to explain the mysterious escape of General John Hunt Morgan and his six compatriots. "There has been bribery somewhere!" raged Warden Merion.[112] "There is no evidence that there has been bribery anywhere," rejoined Governor Tod.[113] Everyone had his own pet theory concerning the general's whereabouts. Secretary of State Stanton held to the opinion that Morgan was lying low somewhere in Columbus,[114] and the *Cincinnati Enquirer* confidently stated that General Morgan had arrived safely in Toronto, via Great Western Railroad.[115]

General John Hunt Morgan 207

The military and civil authorities at Columbus worked frantically to find some trace of the escaped rebel officers. Governor Tod ordered a full investigation of the affair, and posted flyers announcing a $1,000 reward for Morgan's capture.[116] But it was all to no avail. General Morgan had left Ohio and was spending a carefree evening at the home of friends in Boone County, Kentucky. The worst was over, now. The danger had passed. Posing as cattle buyers,[117] and riding horses provided by their Kentucky friends, General Morgan and Captain Hines reached the Confederate lines near Dalton, Tennessee, on the 27th of December. The last chapter of the Great Indiana-Ohio Raid had come to a close!

FOOTNOTES

[1] Edward A. Pollard, *The Lost Cause*, E. B. Treat and Co., New York, 1866, p. 378.
[2] The preceding information has been taken from testimony relating to the trial of Clement L. Vallandingham. *Official Records of the Union and Confederate Armies* (hereinafter referred to as *Official Records*), Series 2, Vol. 5, pp. 633-646. The prominent Ohio Democrat referred to is Vallandingham himself.
[3] Carrington to Stanton: *Official Records*, Series 2, Vol. 5, p. 108.
[4] Carrington to Lincoln: *Official Records*, Series 2, Vol. 5, pp. 363-367.
[5] In Boston, Massachusetts, a man arrested for fitting out a privateer was found to be carrying a set of forms for a secret society known as the "Knights of the Golden Circle." When confronted with a charge of treason, he claimed that it was a loyal instead of a disloyal organization.
[6] A section from the oath for the "2nd Degree" of the Knights of the Golden Circle Colonel Carrington's report to President Lincoln.
[7] *Official Records*, Series 2, Vol. 5, pp. 363-367.
[8] *Official Records*, Series 2, Vol. 5, p. 636.
[9] *New York Daily Tribune*, Wednesday, May 6, 1863.
[10] *Cincinnati Gazette*, May 5, 1863.
[11] *Official Records*, Series 2, Vol. 5, p. 235.
[12] *New York Daily Tribune*, April 24, 1863.
[13] Howard Swiggett, *Rebel Raider*, Bobbs-Merrill Company, Indianapolis, 1934.
[14] *The Cincinnati Gazette* for July 17, 1863, gives four possible reasons for Morgan's raid: 1) to avenge Col. Grierson's raid; 2) to test the loyalty of the Knights of the Golden Circle; 3) to carry out Morgan's boast of being able to go *"where I please, when I please, and how I please"*; 4) to "rob the innocent citizens of Ohio and Indiana."
[15] In the latter part of April, 1863, Col. Grierson led his raiders across the entire Confederacy, starting on the Tennessee-Mississippi border, and re-entering the Union lines at Baton Rouge, Louisiana. He claimed afterwards that the Confederacy was a mere shell, and that "Hundreds who are skulking and hiding out to avoid conscription, only await the presence of our arms to sustain them." *Official Records*, Series 1, Vol. 24, Part 1; quoted in Larned's *History for Ready Reference*.
[16] Basil W. Duke, "A Romance of Morgan's Rough Riders: The Raid," *Century Magazine*, January, 1891, p. 403.
[17] *Ibid.*, p. 404.
[18] Captain Theodore F. Allen of the 7th Ohio Cavalry gives the following account: "Arriving at the Cumberland River above Burkesville, we found Morgan with his division of cavalry occupying the south bank of the river. For a day or two we had skirmishing

'give and take.' It was impossible for us to picket the entire length of the river, and by July 3rd, Morgan had succeeded in transferring his command to the north bank of the Cumberland River." *The Hesperian Tree: An Annual of the Ohio Valley*, 1900.

[19] Among the Federal wounded was a 16-year-old Canadian girl named Lizzie Compton, who was said to have served for eighteen months in the Union army, re-enlisting whenever her sex was discovered. Benson J. Lossing: *Pictorial History of the Civil War*, Vol. III, p. 92.

[20] Pollard, *The Lost Cause*, p. 410.
[21] *Cincinnati Daily Enquirer*, July 6, 1863.
[22] Swiggett, *Rebel Raider*.
[23] Basil W. Duke, "The Raid." *Op. Cit.*, p. 408.
[24] *Cincinnati Daily Enquirer*, July 13, 1863.
[25] Basil W. Duke, "The Raid." *Op. Cit.*, p. 409.
[26] "On leaving Brandenburg, Morgan burned the *Alice Dean*, but gave up the *J. T. McCombs*, which arrived here (Louisville) this afternoon." *Cincinnati Daily Enquirer*, July 10, 1863.
[27] W. D. Foulke, *Life of Oliver P. Morton*, The Bowen-Merrill Co., Indianapolis-Kansas City. 1899. Vol. I, p. 281.
[28] *Ibid.*, ff. 280.
[29] The *Official Records* contain an interesting account of Ellsworth's operations on an earlier Morgan raid (Series 1, Vol. 16, Part 1, pp. 774-781). By cleverly cutting wires and grounding out interfering stations, he managed to give the Federals the impression that he was one of their own operators. His counterfeit dispatches sent whole regiments of Yankee troops on wild goose chases to far corners of the state; by the end of the raid the Federal high command was afraid to trust even the messages of its own operators. . . . As the raider prepared to leave Kentucky, General Morgan gave Ellsworth a list of messages to send to several of the State's more objectionable officers and politicians. "Good morning, Jerry!" he telegraphed to General J. T. Boyle, at Louisville. "My friend Ellsworth has all of your dispatches since July 10 on file. Do you wish copies?" But even more than for his sense of humor, George Ellsworth was known for his cool-headed bravery, and for his thorough knowledge and effective use of the telegraph as an instrument of deception.
[30] Swiggett, *Rebel Raider*.
[31] Duke, "The Raid." *Op. Cit.*, p. 410.
[32] *Ibid.*, p. 410.
[33] *Cincinnati Enquirer*, July 11, 1863.
[34] Swiggett, *Rebel Raider*.
[35] Duke, "The Raid." *Op. Cit.*, p. 410.
[36] Don D. John, *Morgan's Great Indiana-Ohio Raid*, ff. p. 20. (Privately Printed), 1955.
[37] Captain T. F. Allen, in *The Hesperian Tree: An Annual of the Ohio Valley*, 1900.
[38] *Cincinnati Daily Enquirer*, July 16, 1863.
[39] *Ibid.*
[40] *New York Daily Tribune*, July 13, 1863.
[41] Cecil Fletcher Holland, *Morgan and His Raiders*. The Macmillan Co., New York, 1942, p. 241.
[42] *Cincinnati Daily Enquirer*, July 14, 1863.
[43] *Ibid.*
[44] "Kentuckians are in high glee over the present one of Morgan. Northern people have habitually taunted Kentucky with her inefficiency and inability to counteract Morgan." The tables were turned. *Cincinnati Daily Gazette*, July 20, 1863.
[45] Duke, "The Raid." *Op. Cit.*, p. 410.
[46] *Ibid.*
[47] *Cincinnati Daily Enquirer*, July 15, 1863.
[48] *Cincinnati Daily Enquirer*, July 15, 1863.
[49] The raiders were openly contemptuous of their pursuers. About General Hobson they said: "All that we know about him is what we see in the daily papers."
[50] July 16, 1863.
[51] Duke, "The Raid." *Op. Cit.*, p. 411.
[52] *Cincinnati Daily Enquirer*, July 15, 1863, had this to say: "Morgan's men are nearly exhausted for the want of sleep, and only the free use of liquor prevents them from dropping off their saddles."
[53] The *Sciota Gazette*, quoted in *Anecdotes, Poetry and Incidents of the War*, by Frank Moore, New York, printed for the subscribers, 1866, pp. 163-164.
[54] *Ibid.*

[55] Henry Howe, *Historical Collections of Ohio.* State of Ohio, 1900. Vol. 1, p. 458.
[56] *Ibid.,* Vol. 2, p. 312.
[57] *Cincinnati Daily Gazette,* July 18, 1863.
[58] *Cincinnati Daily Gazette,* July 18, 1863.
[59] *Official Records,* Series 2, Vol. 5, pp. 363-367.
[60] *Ibid.*
[61] *Ibid.*
[62] Howe, *Historical Collections of Ohio,* Vol. 1, pp. 458-459.
[63] Basil W. Duke, *History of Morgan's Cavalry,* Miami Printing and Publishing Co., Cincinnati, 1867, p. 446.
[64] *Ibid.,* p. 448.
[65] *New York Daily Tribune,* July 24, 1863.
[66] Under normal conditions the river was too shallow for navigation above the foot of Buffington Island.
[67] Basil W. Duke, *History of Morgan's Cavalry,* p. 451.
[68] Duke, "The Raid." *Op. Cit.,* p. 411.
[69] One of the captives was a young man named Stone, who had been an active supporter of Daniel Vorhees during the latter's first campaign for Congress. The violently-Republican *New York Daily Tribune* had this to say about the matter: "That a Vorhees man, full of what little ideas Vorhees is able to impart, should join the Rebel Army ... is just as natural as that a tadpole should shed its tail and parade as a frog."
[70] A. T. Mahan, *The Navy in the Civil War: The Gulf and Inland Waters,* Charles Scribner's Sons, New York, 1883. Vol. III, p. 182.
[71] Duke, *History of Morgan's Cavalry,* p. 453.
[72] Also seen as "Burbeck," "Burdeck," and "Burbrick."
[73] Major George W. Rue, "Celebration of the Surrender of Gen. John H. Morgan—An account by Morgan's Captor," *Ohio Archeological and Historical Quarterly* (1911), Vol. XX.
[74] *Ibid.*
[75] With the possible exception of General Wolford, "who was as noted for generosity to prisoners as for vigor and gallantry in the field." Duke, *History of Morgan's Cavalry,* p. 457.
[76] The following is taken from a report by General W. T. H. Brooks: "When Morgan saw that his advance was about to be cut off by Major Rue, he said to Captain Burbick: 'I would prefer to surrender to the militia than to United States troops. I will surrender to you if you will agree to respect private property and to parole the officers and men as soon as we get to Cincinnati.' Burbick replied that he knew nothing about this business. Morgan said, 'Give me an answer, yes or no.' Burbick, evidently in confusion, said yes." Don D. John, *Op. Cit.,* note 2, p. 22.
[77] Major George W. Rue, *Celebration of the Surrender of Gen. John H. Morgan Op. Cit.*
[78] After the disaster at Missionary Ridge, Bragg resigned his command of the Army of Tennessee and went to Richmond as "a sort of chief of staff and military adviser to Davis." Thanks to Bragg's influence with the president, Morgan was deprived of his old Kentucky cavalry, which had been reorganized by Adam Johnson.
[79] *Cincinnati Daily Enquirer,* November 29, 1863.
[80] Newspapers controlled by the Ohio Democratic Party took advantage of every opportunity to expose the blustering inefficiency of Governor Tod and his fellow Republicans. Republican controlled newspapers fought back just as fiercely, showering their readers with accusations that Ohio's "Peace Democrats" and "Vallandinghammers" had invited Morgan into the state. "Thank God" wrote a correspondent of the *Cincinnati Gazette* (July 18, 1863), that 'this demonstration has had the effect of causing the scales to fall from the eyes of many honest Democrats, who declare they cannot support a man who has so many ardent admirers going about pillaging stores, stealing horses, and otherwise abusing inoffensive citizens.'
[81] Report of the Ohio Commission on Morgan Raid Claims, December 15, 1864, quoted in *Morgan and His Raiders,* by Cecil Fletcher Holland, pp. 238, 239. According to this report, some of the claims were for damages as insignificant as "one stolen bowie knife," valued at $1.25, and "two sacks of apples," valued at $4.00.
[82] Duke, "The Raid." *Op. Cit.,* p. 411.
[83] *New York Daily Tribune,* August 8, 1863.
[84] *Cincinnati Daily Enquirer,* July 24, 1863.

⁸⁵ The lot of the prisoners at Camp Morton was not a hard one. According to a report in the *Official Records*, they spent the days "conversing with their friends, laughing and enjoying themselves . . . sneering at the Yankees . . . and boasting of their rebel raid and what they will do when exchanged." Series 2, Vol. 6, pp. 162-163.
⁸⁶ Duke, *History of Morgan's Cavalry*, p. 465.
⁸⁷ *Ibid.*, p. 468.
⁸⁸ Desellem-Merion, *Official Records*, Series 2, Vol. 6, p. 665.
⁸⁹ Duke, *History of Morgan's Cavalry*, p. 473. An excerpt from Warden Merion's record book shows that early in August the prisoners were allowed to purchase a set of Waverly novels, *Official Records*, Series 2, Vol. 6, p. 668.
⁹⁰ See Morgan-Stanton, *Official Records*, Series 2, Vol. 6, pp. 495-496, and Morgan to Mason, *Official Records*, Series 2, Vol. 6, p. 448.
⁹¹ The Northern Press had drummed up public opinion over the rumor that Colonel Abel Streight, an Ohio officer captured by Nathan Bedford Forrest, had been placed in a Georgia penitentiary. This rumor later proved to be completely groundless: Colonel Streight and his men were being treated in just the same manner as other prisoners in the South and were being held in Libby Prison, at Richmond.
⁹² *Official Records*, Series 2, Vol. 6, pp. 158-159.
⁹³ Duke, *History of Morgan's Cavalry*, pp. 479-480.
⁹⁴ Letters written by the prisoners were handed over to General Mason for censorship. Since this letter of Webber's was particularly objectionable (it ended by urging the immediate execution of all Negroes captured on the battlefield) it was forwarded to the War Department.
⁹⁵ The dungeon, or "black hole" as it was sometimes called, was a small, dark cell to which prisoners caught reading smuggled newspapers or talking after hours were sent. General Morgan's brother Calvin returned to his cell covered with green mold, after less than twenty-four hours in the "black hole." Visibly shaken, he called it the most terrible place that he had ever seen. (From a letter written by Dick Morgan), *Official Records*, Series 2, Vol. 6, p. 734.
⁹⁶ Duke, *History of Morgan's Cavalry*, p. 480.
⁹⁷ Cathcart, along with five others from the Cincinnati area, was arrested for conspiring to "assemble" at Camp Chase and overpower the guard. They were next to attack the Penitentiary to release Morgan and his officers. A Rebel Campaign in Ohio would commence. (*Cincinnati Gazette*, quoted in *The Rebel Raider*, by Howard Swiggett.)
⁹⁸ Capt. Thomas H. Hines, "A Romance of Morgan's Rough Riders, The Escape," *Century Magazine*, January, 1891, p. 417.
⁹⁹ *Official Records*, Series 2, Vol. 6, p. 670.
¹⁰⁰ *Ibid.*, pp. 676-677.
¹⁰¹ Hines, "The Escape." *Op. Cit.*, p. 418.
¹⁰² *Ibid.*
¹⁰³ *Ibid.*
¹⁰⁴ Duke, *History of Morgan's Cavalry*, p. 486.
¹⁰⁵ Hines, "The Escape." *Op. Cit.*, p. 420.
¹⁰⁶ "Patience is bitter, but its fruit is sweet."
¹⁰⁷ Hines, "The Escape." *Op. Cit.*, p. 420.
¹⁰⁸ *Ibid.*
¹⁰⁹ Duke, *History of Morgan's Cavalry*, p. 488.
¹¹⁰ *Ibid.*
¹¹¹ *Cincinnati Daily Gazette*, December 1, 1863.
¹¹² Merion to Wallace, *Official Records*, Series 2, Vol. 6, p. 671.
¹¹³ Tod to Watson, *Ibid.*, p. 606.
¹¹⁴ Stanton to Tod, *Ibid.*, p. 632.
¹¹⁵ *Cincinnati Daily Enquirer*, December 1, 1863. In Windsor, Canada, a southern sympathizer named Joseph H. Morgan decided to have some fun at the Yankees' expense. His signature in the Queens Hotel register sent Stanton's detectives scurrying north into Canada with instructions to keep an eye on Morgan and to "warn the British authorities" of his presence.
¹¹⁶ The *Cincinnati Daily Enquirer* was delighted with this wonderful new opportunity to criticize Governor Tod. It had this to say about the cell-inspection mix-up: (December 8, 1863) "Tod's Kitchen Cabinet is divided on the subject. His dog believes the military to be the responsible party, while his legal adviser, who does his marketing and other small chores for him, regards the civil authorities as the guilty ones."
¹¹⁷ Hines, "The Escape." *Op. Cit.*, p. 421.

BIBLIOGRAPHY

Allen, Captain Theodore F., "Our Pursuit and Capture of Morgan's Raiders," an article in *The Hesperian Tree . . . An Annual of the Ohio Valley, 1900.*
Boynton, Charles Brandon, *The History of the Navy During the Rebellion*, Vol. II; New York, D. Appleton and Co., 1867-68.
Century Magazine, January, 1891, Vol. 41; *A Romance of Morgan's Rough Riders: The Raid, the Capture, and the Escape*, by General Basil W. Duke (CSA), General Orlando B. Wilcox (USA), and Captain Thomas H. Hines (CSA).
Duke, General Basil W., *History of Morgan's Cavalry*, Cincinnati, Miami Printing and Publishing Co., 1867.
Formby, John, The American Civil War (maps), New York, Chas. Scribner's Sons, 1910. (Not cited.)
Harpers Pictorial History of the Civil War, Harper & Bros., N. Y.
Greve, Charles Theodore, *Centennial History of Cincinnati and Representative Citizens*, Cincinnati, 1909. (Not cited.)
Holland, Cecil Fletcher, *Morgan and his Raiders*, New York, MacMillan Co., 1942.
Horan, James David, *Confederate Agent*, N. Y. Crown Publishers, 1954. (Not cited.)
Howe, Henry, *Historical Collections of Ohio*, Published by the State of Ohio, 1900.
John, Don D., *Morgan's Great Indiana-Ohio Raid*, Louisville, privately printed. 1955.
Larned, Josephus Nelson, *History for Ready Reference*, Springfield, Mass., The C. A. Nichols Co., 1894-95.
Lossing, Benson John, *Pictorial History of the Civil War*, Hartford, Thomas Belknap, 1874. (Not cited.)
Mahan, A. T., *The Navy in the Civil War*, Vol. III, *The Gulf and Inland Waters*, N. Y. Charles Scribner's Sons, 1883.
Moore, Frank, *Anecdotes, Poetry, and Incidents of the War*, N. Y., printed for the subscribers, 1866.
Pollard, Edward Albert, *The Lost Cause*, E. B. Treat and Co., 1856, N. Y.
Rue, Major George W., "Celebration of the Surrender of Gen. John H. Morgan"; *Ohio Archeological and Historical Quarterly*, Vol. XX, Oct. 1911.
Rhodes, James Ford, *History of the United States*, N. Y. MacMillan Co., Vol. V, 1904. (Not cited.)
Swiggett, Howard, *The Rebel Raider*, Bobbs-Merrill Co., Indianapolis, 1934.
Vallandingham, Rev. James L., *A Life of Clement L. Vallandingham*, Baltimore, Turnbull Bros., 1872. (Not cited.)
Cincinnati Daily Enquirer.
Cincinnati Daily Gazette.
New York Daily Tribune.
Official Records of the Union and Confederate Armies, Washington, Government Printing Office, 1880-1899.
W. D. Foulke, *Life of Oliver P. Morton*, The Bowen-Merrill Co., 1889. Vol. I, p. 279.

JAMES BELL BENEDICT, JR. (1938–) is a native of Cincinnati. He received his B.A. from the University of Colorado and his Ph.D. from the University of Wisconsin. Since 1970 he has been a faculty affiliate in the Department of Anthropology at Colorado State University, doing geological research and mountain archaeology in the Colorado Front Range.

This article first appeared in *The Filson Club History Quarterly* in July 1957, vol. 31, pp. 147–71.

QUANTRILL'S MISSOURI BUSHWHACKERS IN KENTUCKY

THE END OF THE TRAIL

By Albert Castel

Western Michigan University, Kalamazoo, Michigan

On the morning of January 22, 1865, several dozen heavily armed men, attired in Federal uniforms, rode into Hartford, Kentucky. Their leader, a tall, slender man in his late twenties with reddish brown hair and drooping eyelids, identified himself to the commander of the Union detachment stationed in the town as Captain Clarke of the Fourth Missouri Cavalry. He further stated that he was heading for the Ohio River to search for guerrillas, and that he would like to have the services of a guide. Lieutenant Barnett of the Hartford post at once volunteered to act in that capacity, and two other men, a discharged veteran and a soldier on furlough, asked to go along also.

Three miles from the town Captain Clarke ordered his column to halt. Then, before the horrified eyes of Barnett and the furloughed soldier, Clarke's men hanged the discharged veteran from a tree by the roadside. Nine miles further on they shot the other soldier, and after another six miles they killed the lieutenant.[1]

The Federal troops in Kentucky did not realize it yet, but the man responsible for these atrocious, cold-blooded slayings was none other than William Clarke Quantrill, the notorious guerrilla chieftain and bloody scourge of the Kansas-Missouri border. And with him were a picked group of the toughest, most desperate of his Missouri bushwhackers, including Frank James, elder brother of Jesse. For over three years these men had ridden rampant through the West. It had been they who had carried out the famous Lawrence Massacre, in which a Kansas town of nearly 3,000 had been utterly destroyed and 180 of its male inhabitants ruthlessly murdered. It had been these men, too, who had slaughtered scores of helpless Union soldiers at Baxter Springs and Centralia. In the words of a Confederate general who had encountered them in Texas, they regarded "the life of a man less than you would that of a sheep-killing dog."[2]

Their leader, Quantrill, was a native of Ohio who after a wandering career as schoolteacher, teamster, gambler, and gold prospector, had become an outlaw in Kansas prior to the war. Most of them came from the region around Independence, Missouri, which was also their main center of operations or "stamping ground." Skilled horsemen and deadly revolver shots, they had successfully defied all efforts of the Federal troops and Missouri Unionist militia to suppress them. Although they professed to serve the Southern cause, and although Quantrill had a Confederate captain's commission, their first loyalty was to themselves, and their primary object plunder and revenge for personal wrongs.[3]

Quantrill's most sensational exploit, the Lawrence raid, had occurred in 1863. During most of 1864 he laid low in a private hideout in Missouri while his lieutenants, George Todd and "Bloody Bill" Anderson did the real fighting. But following the deaths of Todd and Anderson in October, he resumed active command. A Confederate invasion of Missouri had just ended in disaster, and he concluded that the Southern cause in the state was lost. Hence he proposed to his men that they shift their theater of operations to Kentucky. The numerous Southern sympathizers there would be glad to provide them with food, hideouts, and information, and they would have fresh fields of plunder. Moreover, if worse came to worse, it would be much safer for them to surrender in Kentucky, where they were not so well-known, than in Missouri, where they were known only too well and under sentence of death.[4]

Quantrill also led some of his followers to believe that he had still another purpose in heading east: The assassination of President Lincoln![5] However, if this ever was a serious objective (which is doubtful), Quantrill abandoned it soon after arriving in Kentucky.

With about fifty men, Quantrill left West Missouri early in December and marched southeastward into Arkansas. On the night of January 1 he crossed the Mississippi River in a yawl at Devil's Elbow, fifteen miles above Memphis. His gang then passed through Tennessee, and on January 15 entered Kentucky near the little town of Canton.[6]

Here the first in a series of mishaps which were to make Quantrill's venture into Kentucky a complete disaster occurred. His favorite horse, a magnificent steed which he had taken from a Union officer and named "Old Charley," suffered a cut tendon and had to be destroyed. Quantrill was badly shaken by the loss of this mount. He had ridden "Old Charley" through most of the war and the horse had saved his life on numerous occasions. He felt, therefore, that now that "Old Charley" was gone, so was his luck. He was right.[7]

Two days later the Missourians had their first battle in Kentucky as they clashed with a small force of Union cavalry. They routed the enemy, but during the fighting Jim Little was mortally wounded. Little was Quantrill's closest friend and his death further depressed him.[8]

The guerrillas continued on to Houstonville, where they stole a number of horses. One of the horses belonged to a militia lieutenant, who ran up just as Allen Parmer, one of the most vicious of the bushwhackers, started to ride the steed out of a stable. Grabbing hold of the bridle, the lieutenant cried, "If this horse leaves here, it will be over my dead body."

"That is a damned easy job!" sneered Parmer, who then drew a revolver and shot the lieutenant dead.[9]

The Missourians next made their presence in Kentucky felt at Hartford, in the manner already described. Most likely Quantrill had the three luckless soldiers murdered in revenge for the death of Little.

A week after the Hartford atrocity the bushwhackers raided Danville in the central part of the state, plundering a bootstore, gutting the telegraph office, and robbing the citizens. They then rode to a point five miles west of Harrodsburg, where they went to three different houses in the vicinity to get supper and find places to sleep. But while they were eating, a company of Kentucky militia under Captain J. H. Bridgewater, which had pursued them from Danville, surrounded a house containing twelve guerrillas, and called on them to surrender.

The trapped men tried to break out, but three of them were killed and the survivors captured. Also slain was another bushwhacker who came from a nearby house to see what all the shooting was about and found out the hard way. Quantrill and the other Missourians, warned by the firing, escaped by scattering into the woods.[10]

This was a terrible setback for Quantrill. Not only did he lose a third of his band, but some of his oldest and toughest followers. The Federals placed the captives in a prison at Lexington and on three different occasions took them out into the yard as if to hang them. Each time, however, they came out defiantly cheering for Jeff Davis and daring the "blue-bellies" to hang them, at the same time warning that their deaths would be avenged. Eventually in April eight of them were taken to a Louisville jail, from which they soon escaped with the aid of friendly Kentuckians. The one who remained at Lexington, Tom Evans, was kept there because the Federals believed that he had killed the militia lieutenant at Houstonville. He did not get out until after the war, when one of his comrades swore out an affidavit declaring that Parmer was the person guilty of the murder.[11]

Following the Harrodsburg fiasco, Quantrill went into Nelson County, where he joined forces with the Kentucky guerrilla chieftain, Sue Mundy. Together they burned a railroad depot at Midway, west of Lexington, on the night of February 2. Six days later they captured a Union wagon train at New Market, killing three of the guards and capturing four others, whom they subsequently murdered also.[12]

Meanwhile, Captain Bridgewater's company doggedly pursued the guerrillas. The night after the New Market raid he overtook them west of Houstonville, killed four of them, captured four more, and chased the remainder, mostly barefooted, into the woods. According to his report, Quantrill, whose true identity was now known to the Federals in Kentucky, was among those forced to flee horseless and bootless.[13]

This was the second severe, even humiliating, blow administered the bushwhackers by Bridgewater's company. Such disasters had rarely, if ever, befallen them in Missouri. Either the Kentucky Federals were more formidable than their Missouri counterparts, or else Quantrill's followers had lost their zest for fighting now that the war was lost and they were operating on alien soil.

During the next several weeks the bushwhackers kept low while obtaining fresh horses and new equipment. Many Kentuckians proved willing to aid them. Part of the time Quantrill stayed at the home of one such friend, Jim Dawson, a prosperous farmer who lived near Wakefield.

February went by and so did March. The Missourians confined their activities to petty raids and robberies, plus an occasional skirmish with the militia. Their main "stamping ground" was Spencer County, south of Louisville, a region strongly pro-Southern in sentiment. On April 15, the day after Lincoln's assassination, they turned up, drunk and merry, at Judge Jonathan Davis' house in Spencer County. "Excuse us, ladies," hiccupped Quantrill. "We are a little in our cups today. The grand-daddy of all greenbacks, Abraham Lincoln, was shot in a theater at Washington last night."[14]

The continued and constant depredations of Quantrill's gang ultimately stirred the Union commander in Kentucky, Major General John M. Palmer, to take special action against it. Because pro-Southern civilians always kept the guerrillas posted on Federal movements, regular troops had proved incapable of catching and destroying them. Therefore he decided to fight fire with fire. He commissioned a young Kentuckian named Edwin Terrill, leader of a band of so-called "Federal guerrillas" in Spencer County, to pursue Quantrill until he got him dead or alive.[15]

Terrill, who had served in the Confederate army earlier in the war, then defected to the Union side, had his first brush with Quantrill on April 13. In conjunction with some militia he found and attacked the Missourians near Bloomfield, killed two of them, and wounded three others. Thereafter, throughout the rest of April and into May, he chased and harassed the bushwhackers, but never quite caught up with them.[16]

Quantrill's main hideout in Spencer County was James H. Wakefield's farm near Bloomfield. Wakefield was a Confederate sympathizer, and he gladly provided the Missouri guerrillas with food and shelter. In addition, a number of Kentucky youths joined Quantrill, attracted by his fame and the prospect of exciting adventure.

The morning of May 10 found Quantrill and about twenty followers at Wakefield's farm. It was raining and they had taken shelter in a barn. Their horses were hitched in an adjoining shed. Quantrill and several others were asleep in the hayloft. The remainder sat around talking and amusing themselves by flinging corn cobs at each other.

Suddenly a large body of horsemen crested a slope to the east and charged full tilt towards the barn, yelling and firing carbines. It was Terrill's outfit, which had tracked Quantrill to the Wakefield farm.

"Here they come!" cried one of Quantrill's men. The bushwhackers, taken completely by surprise, attempted no resistance. Instead they ran to their horses. Most of them quickly mounted and galloped off down a bridle path. Others, however, were not so fortunate. Their horses, frightened by the firing and shouting, broke loose and they were forced to flee on foot.

Quantrill was one of those unable to mount his horse. He had obtained the steed only a few days previously from a young Kentucky lady as a gift, and it was not accustomed either to gunfire or to its new master. It bucked and reared wildly, and finally broke away from Quantrill and galloped about the shed snorting with terror.

Abandoning his futile attempts to mount, Quantrill ran after his men, frantically calling on them to wait up. Two of them, Dick Glassock and Clark Hockensmith, halted their horses and opened fire with their revolvers to hold back Terrill's men, who were now swarming through the farmyard. Quantrill caught up and started to climb on behind Glassock. But just at that moment a bullet struck Glassock's horse and it became unmanageable. Quantrill then ran to Hockensmith and tried to mount his horse. As he did so a bullet pierced his back and he pitched forward into the mud on his face.

The pursuers came pounding by, nearly trampling the prostrate body. One of them fired at Quantrill again and by some freakish chance shot off his right index finger — the trigger finger. They soon overtook and killed Glassock and Hockensmith, both of whom would have escaped easily had they not tried to save their leader.

Quantrill was conscious, but the bullet had lodged against his spine and he was paralyzed from the chest down. After a while Terrill's men came back and took his revolvers and boots. They then rolled him onto a blanket and carried him to Wakefield's house, where they placed him on a couch.

Terrill asked the wounded man who he was. Quantrill, still clinging to his customary alias, replied that he was Captain Clarke of the Fourth Missouri Cavalry. Terrill remained silent on hearing this, and it is doubtful if he was deceived. Quantrill then asked Terrill to let him stay at Wakefield's. Terrill, noting that Quantrill was unable to move, consented. However, he warned Wakefield that he would hold him responsible if "Clarke" was not there when his company returned. Quantrill thereupon gave Wakefield his word that he would not let his men take him away.

Terrill then departed to report his victory. He had accomplished with thirty men in one month what ten thousand Union troops in Missouri and Kansas had failed to do in four years: Capture the dread William Clarke Quantrill.

Wakefield sent for a local doctor to look at Quantrill's back wound. After examining it, the doctor shook his head sadly and said that it was fatal.

That night some of the bushwhackers returned to the Wakefield farm. They wanted to carry Quantrill to a place where he would be safe and his wound tended. But the guerrilla chieftain refused to be moved — he had given his word to Wakefield, and besides he was going to die anyway.

The following day Southern sympathizers in the neighborhood came to see Quantrill. Two girls brought him a beautiful bouquet of flowers, to which was attached a card bearing the inscription, "Compliments of Miss Maggie Frederick and Sallie Lovell to Mr. Quantrill."

During the second night at Wakefield's his followers again came to urge that he let them take him away. But as before he refused to be moved.

On the morning of May 12 Terrill returned. His men lifted Quantrill into a farm wagon, stuck some pillows and straw under him, and then headed for Louisville.[17] Terrill stopped for the night at Jeffersontown, where the prisoner's wounds were treated by two physicians. The following day he took Quantrill into Louisville and turned him over to the Federal authorities, who placed him in the hospital of the military prison.[18]

The Louisville newspapers noted his arrival. The *Daily Union Press* was brief:

> *Quantrill.* — The noted guerrilla who has been operating in Kentucky under the name of Quantrill, and whose capture was noted Saturday, is in the Military Prison hospital. There is very little hope of his recovery, as his whole body is perfectly paralyzed.

The *Daily Courier*, however, provided fuller coverage:

> Quantrill, the notorious Kansas guerrilla, arrived in this city yesterday morning about 11 o'clock. He was conveyed in a country wagon a bed of straw, and a few pillows, and guarded by Terrill's men disguised as guerrillas. He is wounded through the left breast, and it is thought that

he will die. All the honor of his capture is due to Captain Terrill and his company — "Terrill's guerrillas."

. . . Quantrill has been sailing under the name of Captain Clark and it is supposed by many that it is not the veritable Kansas outlaw, but we understand that Terrill and part of his company are intimately acquainted with him. One fact that strongly corroborates their assertions is that a picture of a young lady was found in his possession, which one of the parties recognized as Miss Hickman, who resides within five miles of the Kansas line. Quantrill also stated that the three followers of his who were killed were from Missouri. The news of his capture will cause great joy throughout the Union. The inhuman outrages that he committed years ago, such as burning the town of Lawrence, etc., are still fresh in the memory of our people.

The *Daily Democrat,* on the other hand, denied that the prisoner actually was Quantrill:

Captain Terrill and his company arrived here yesterday from Taylorsville. They brought with them the guerrilla who bears the name of "Quantrill." It is not the Quantrill of Kansas notoriety, for we have been assured that he was at last accounts a colonel in the rebel army under Price. This prisoner was shot through the body in a fight in a barn near Taylorsville on Wednesday last. Five others were killed on the spot by Terrill's men, but what their names were we could not ascertain. The prisoner brought down is confined in the military prison hospital and is said to be in a dying condition.[19]

Terrill did not enjoy his trumph long. A few weeks later he was killed by a posse of infuriated citizens while "shooting up" the little town of Shelbyville.[20]

A number of persons visited Quantrill as he lay paralyzed in the prison hospital, among them some of his Missourians. But he was little interested in talking to callers, and seemed resigned to dying. As the end drew near he turned to religion, embracing the Catholic faith and receiving its last rites.

On June 6, at four o'clock in the afternoon, Quantrill died. A woman who saw him shortly before his death later charged that his passing was hastened, if not caused, by neglect on part of the hospital staff.[21] The Louisville papers published only short notices of the notorious guerrilla chieftain's demise. In fact, one paper, the *Daily Union Press,* even insisted that he was not *the* Quantrill![22]

The body was buried in the Louisville Catholic Cemetery in an unmarked grave. It remained there until 1887, when Quantrill's mother and a boyhood friend succeeded through some rather devious means in obtaining it for reburial in Ohio. However, the friend kept out several bones, which later passed into the custody of the Kansas State Historical Society in Topeka, where they are now to be found.[23]

Quantrill's remaining followers continued to operate in a half-hearted way until July. On the twenty-sixth of that month sixteen or eighteen of them, including Frank James, voluntarily surrendered to the Federal post commander at Wakefield, Kentucky. They were released on parole and no attempt was made to punish any of them, not even Parmer, the slayer of the militia lieutenant at Houstonville.[24] Quite probably they were the last organized Confederate soldiers (if such they can be truthfully called) to surrender, at least east of the Mississippi. In any case, the career of the Ohio renegade Quantrill and his Missouri gunmen in Kentucky had been brief, bloody, and inglorious, and now it was the end of the trail.

FOOTNOTES

[1] *The War of the Rebellion: A Compilation of the Official Records of the Union and Confederate Armies* (128 vols., Washington, D.C., 1881-1901), Ser. I, XLIX, Part 1, p. 657. (Hereafter this work will be cited as OR).
[2] *Ibid.*, XXXIV, Part 2, p. 542.
[3] For a brief account of Quantrill's career, see Albert Castel, "The Bloodiest Man in American History," *American Heritage*, XI (October, 1960), pp. 22-24, 97-99. A good general history of the Missouri bushwhackers is provided by Richard M. Brownlee's *The Gray Ghosts of the Confederacy* (Baton Rouge: Louisiana State University Press, 1958).
[4] Manuscript Memoirs of Frank Smith (Copy of original in possession of author), p. 134; OR, Ser. I, XLI, Part 4, pp. 715, 782, 960; John McCorkle, *Three Years With Quantrill* (Armstrong, Mo., 1910), pp. 129-33; Statements of Sylvester Akers and M. T. Mattox, in William E. Connelley, *Quantrill and the Border Wars* (Cedar Rapids, Iowa, 1910), pp. 456-59; John N. Edwards, *Noted Guerrillas; or, The War on the Border* (St. Louis, Mo., 1877), pp. 383-89.
[5] Statement of F. Luther Wayman, in Connelley, p. 456.
[6] McCorkle, pp. 133-35; Connelley, pp. 458-59.
[7] McCorkle, pp. 134-36.
[8] *Ibid.*, pp. 136-40.
[9] *Ibid.*, pp. 140-41; Statement of Akers, Connelley, pp. 463-64.
[10] OR, Ser. I, XLIX, Part 1, pp. 17-18, 626, 673-77, 684, 694, 698, 788; McCorkle, pp. 141-42.
[11] *Ibid.*, pp. 141-43.
[12] OR, Ser. I, XLIX, Part 1, pp. 35-37, 634-35.
[13] *Ibid.*, pp. 35-37.
[14] Connelley, p. 465.
[15] Statement of R. T. Owen, *ibid.*, pp. 467-69; Statement of J. M. Ridlow, *Kansas Historical Collections*, VIII (1905-1908), pp. 544-45.
[16] OR, Ser. I, Part 1, p. 512.
[17] The account of Quantrill's capture is based on a letter written by Wakefield in 1888 to W. W. Scott and published in Connelley, pp. 475-77.
[18] *Ibid.*, pp. 480-81.
[19] Louisville *Daily Union Press*, May 15, 1865; Louisville *Daily Courier*, May 14, 1865; Louisville *Daily Democrat*, May 14, 1865 (Clippings in Kansas and Civil War Scrapbook, Volume III, Kansas State Historical Society, Topeka, Kansas).
[20] Statement of R. T. Owen, Connelley, p. 468.
[21] *Ibid.*, pp. 480-82.
[22] Louisville *Daily Union Press*, June 7, 1865 (Clipping in Kansas and Civil War Scrapbook, Volume III, Kansas State Historical Society, Topeka, Kansas).
[23] Memorandum of W. W. Scott, Connelley, pp. 35-36.
[24] *Ibid.*, pp. 478-79; McCorkle, p. 149.

ALBERT CASTEL (1928–   ) was born in Wichita, Kansas, received his B.A. and M.A. degrees from Wichita University and his Ph.D. from the University of Chicago. He has taught at Western Michigan University since 1960. A specialist in Civil War history, Castel has written many journal articles. His books include a biography of William Quantrill and *A Frontier State at War: Kansas, 1861–1865*, which received an Honorable Mention for the Albert J. Beveridge Award in 1957.

This article first appeared in *The Filson Club History Quarterly* in April 1964, vol. 38, pp. 125–32.

LOUISVILLE, KENTUCKY
DURING THE FIRST YEAR OF THE CIVIL WAR

By WILLIAM G. EIDSON
Nashville, Tennessee

During the first eight months of 1861 the majority of Kentuckians favored neither secession from the Union nor coercion of the seceded states. It has been claimed that since the state opposed secession it was pro-Union, but such an assertion is true only in a limited sense. Having the same domestic institutions as the cotton states, Kentucky was concerned by the tension-filled course of events. Though the people of Kentucky had no desire to see force used on the southern states, neither did they desire to leave the Union or see it broken.

Of course, there were some who openly and loudly advocated that their beloved commonwealth should join its sister states in the South. The large number of young men from the state who joined the Confederate army attest to this. At the same time, there were many at the other extreme who maintained that Kentucky should join the northern states in forcibly preventing any state from withdrawing from the Union.

Many of the moderates felt any such extreme action, which would result in open hostility between the two sections, would be especially harmful to a border state such as Kentucky. As the *Daily Louisville Democrat* phrased it, "No matter which party wins, we lose." [1] Thus moderates emphasized the economic advantages of a united country, sentimental attachment to the Union, and the hope of compromise. In several previous crises the country had found compromise through the leadership of great Kentuckians. Hope prevailed that such might be accomplished again.

Eventually Kentucky decided to declare itself neutral. In this manner it could most nearly keep the *status quo* of the state. Neutrality would help preserve political good will with both sections, would maintain Kentucky's economic connections, and thus would secure all the real benefits of a united country.[2]

The city of Louisville virtually mirrored the feeling throughout the state. Some Louisvillians praised the merits of secession; others emphasized the need for quick coercive action, but most desired neither.

Captain Thomas Speed, a Union officer who wrote *The Union Cause in Kentucky, 1860-1865* and some of the Civil War history of Louisville in the massive two-volume *Memorial History of Louisville*, maintains that the city was overwhelmingly Unionist. However, some of the incidents which he labels as pro-Union were in reality measures for the protection of Louisville from either side.

On April 19, 1861, the mayor sent a message to the city council urging measures of defense for the city and the making of necessary appropriations. The council responded by appropriating $50,000 and by appointing a military board to regulate and disburse the funds. Then on May 19, the mayor reported that eighteen companies of men (later called the Home Guard) had been voluntarily organized and offered themselves for the defense of the city.[3] These measures were not pro-Union or pro-Confederate. Rather they were to prepare the city to defend itself against any oppressor.

Despite this, the fact remains that there was a considerable amount of secessionist feeling and activity in the city. This is reflected by the number of young Louisvillians who joined the Confederate army.

On April 16, 1861, Colonel John Allen published a call in the Louisville papers for volunteers for the southern cause, and soon Colonel Philip Lee began to raise troops for the same purpose. Two days later Blanton Duncan announced that he and his company would leave in a few days for the South, and later in the month Captains Ben M. Anderson and Fred Van Alstine left with their troops by steamer for New Orleans. Shortly thereafter Duncan and Captain Michael Lapeille each left the city by rail with companies of one hundred each, and Captain John D. Pope of Louisville left with 114.[4] Similar recruiting continued until September when the First Kentucky Brigade of the Confederate Infantry was organized in the city and immediately went south where it distinguished itself as the "Orphan Brigade."[5]

Besides this, there were several "Southern Rights" meetings held in Louisville in the spring and summer,[6] and by the admission of the *Louisville Daily Courier* there were at least two thousand "Southern Rights" voters in the city in August.[7] Later, after the neutrality had been shattered and the Union troops had moved into the city, there were so many arrests that William Tecumseh Sherman remarked, "As you can well understand, we would soon fill all the places of confinement in Louisville were we to arrest and imprison all who may be dangerous."[8] Also General Lorenzo Thomas, the Adjutant General, quotes Sherman as saying, "The young men were generally secessionists and had joined the Confederates . . . ."[9]

The most outspoken and influential secessionist spokesman in the city was Walter N. Haldeman, the editor of the *Louisville Daily Courier*. Repeatedly this paper urged the citizens of the state to resist the encroachments of the North and to unite with the South. It clearly denounced each trade restriction put on the city by federal officials, urged the people to rise up in arms against Cincinnati for interfering with the river traffic, predicted that General Robert J. Anderson would set aside the laws of the land, lamented that all the Associated Press dispatches were full of lies because they first passed through the hands of northern officials, beseeched all "Southern Rights" men in the city to vote against Lincoln men, and claimed that it would be foolish and reckless for Kentucky not to unite with the southern states.[10]

With such bold assertions, it is not surprising that the federal government took steps to suppress this southern sympathizer. The government, however, confined itself at first to preventing the sale of the paper in St. Louis since the administration was cautious not to do anything that might chase Kentucky into the rebel camp;[11] but once Kentucky abandoned its policy of neutrality, the federal officials acted swiftly. On the same day Kentucky cast its lot with the North the *Courier* was excluded from the mails and was suppressed by military force because it had been "found to be an advocate of treason and hostility to the Government and authority of the United States . . . ."[12]

Soon the newspaper reappeared in Bowling Green while the Confederates were in the southern part of the state, and it was said to be twice as reckless as when published in Louisville.[13]

Such pro-southern sentiment actually reflects only a small percentage of the people in the city. A larger number, though how many is impossible to ascertain, were for remaining in the Union but not necessarily for coercing the seceded states.

Both the *Louisville Daily Journal* and the *Daily Louisville Democrat*, the other leading newspapers, fit this category. The *Journal*, a newspaper which became a mighty force in the state during the war, was edited by George D. Prentice. Prentice ardently denounced secession and referred to it as "a wild, unpatriotic, and insane idea."[14] Even though he eventually had two sons in the Confederate army, he never was able to write anything favorable about the Confederacy. Once Kentucky abandoned neutrality the paper lent its full support to the Union cause, though Prentice violently condemned Lincoln for his slavery policy.

John H Harney was editor of the *Daily Louisville Democrat*, a paper which strongly supported efforts at compromise and declared secession to be a very dangerous experiment.[15] Harney felt that most of the people in the North, as well as in the South, were for the union of the whole country; but the politicians, who were only for themselves, were the ones really causing the trouble. He wrote, "Shall the country be plunged into civil war by the action of political tricksters? Forbid it, heaven!"[16]

Like the *Journal,* once hostilities began the *Democrat* supported the Union; but with the coming of the Emancipation Proclamation and various military rigors, it became more critical of the administration than the *Journal* and assumed the leadership of the Peace Democrats.[17]

The majority of the voters in Louisville certainly agreed with Prentice and Harney that the state should remain in the Union. In the May 6 city election John M. Delph, a Union candidate for mayor, defeated his "Southern Rights" opponent by better than three to one; and in June, Robert Mallory, a Union man who favored coercion of the southern states, was re-elected to Congress by a majority of 6,224 votes.[18] Then in the August state-wide election held two weeks after the battle of Bull Run, Louisville elected Union men over "State Rights" candidates by substantial majorities. Of six men elected from Louisville for the state legislature, the Union men received a total of 16,172 votes as compared to 2,547 for the "State Rights" candidates, which is better than a six to one majority.[19]

This Union sentiment is further shown by the spontaneous formation of the Union Club in Louisville in the spring of 1861. This was a secret organization in which each member was bound by a solemn oath to support the flag and the government of the United States. It is estimated, though perhaps without sufficient evidence, that within six weeks this society had 6,000 members in the city and became a most effective agent in the formation of the Home Guard and in securing enlistments for the Union army.[20]

These enlistments began around the end of April and continued until the war was over. According to Thomas Speed a great body of enlisted men and commissioned officers from Louisville were in the 5th, 6th, 15th, 28th, and 34th Infantry, the 2nd and 4th Cavalry, and three batteries raised at Louisville for its own protection.[21] With so many enlisting on both sides, "it was no uncommon sight in Louisville shortly after this, to see a squad of recruits for the Union service marching up one side of a street while a squad destined for the Confederacy was moving down the other." [22]

Perhaps the strongest pro-Union group in the city outside of the Union Club was the city council which became increasingly more Unionist as the months passed. In April a resolution was proposed by one member of the council that the true position of Kentucky was with the South, but this motion received only two votes.[23] Later when it was announced that General Robert Anderson would come to the city, the council voted to welcome him and extend the hospitalities of the city. In July it took steps to prevent persons from inducing minors to join the Confederate army, and the next month it appropriated $200,000 to be used to encourage volunteering into the Union army.[24] In September the board of aldermen passed a resolution inquiring into the loyalty of its members[25] and is alleged to have soon become a center of Union enthusiasm and military activities. From this time on the city council cooperated thoroughly with federal officials in the city.

While the Union Club and city council were strongly Unionist, the citizens engaging in trade and commerce presented a different and far more complex story.

In 1861 Louisville was an extremely strategic city for both the South and the North. As a result of its location on the Ohio River and great advances in river trade, the city was sometimes called the "mistress of the commerce of the South." [26]

Louisville was also strategically important because of the Louisville and Nashville Railroad which was completed shortly before the war began. Since this was the only operating railroad which passed through the state to the South and was the only channel of rapid communication from the Ohio to the South and Southeast, it was considered extremely important to both sides.

For several months prior to and after the actual outbreak of hostilities, the L&N carried on a very profitable trade in provisions with Tennessee, Alabama, Georgia, and other southern states. This trade was especially heavy in 1861 because there had been crop failures in these states the preceding year which meant more provisions had to be shipped in from other markets. Also the Mobile and Ohio Railroad, the only other railroad connecting the North with the South in this area, was deprived of its ultimate outlet on the Ohio River at Cairo, Illinois, by the concentration of northern troops there and thus ceased to carry provisions southward. This then left the entire business to the L&N.[27]

Once the hostilities began, the Confederates feverishly began buying supplies of all sorts north of the Ohio and rushing them south before it was too late. Naturally prices spiralled upward, and some northern traders made fortunes overnight. Speed was essential to the southerner, and the only fast way to get the provisions was over the L&N.

Frantically the road strove to cope with the situation, but it simply was not able to do so. So many provisions came to the depot to be shipped southward that goods were piled in and around the depot and anywhere space could be found. Ultimately the L&N declared a temporary embargo between April 29 and May 8 in order to give the company ten days to clear the line.[28] As shipment after shipment went south, Louisville citizens began to fear that not enough would be left in the city for food. Alarmed by such rumors, attempts were made to tear up the tracks south of the city in order to prevent further shipments. Some crowds became so unruly that James Guthrie, president of the line, found it necessary to send armed guards ahead of the trains to protect them from violence.[29]

Throughout the month of May the provisions continued to be carried at a record-breaking pace. An anonymous individual is quoted as summing up the situation as follows:

> Day and night for weeks past, every avenue of approach to the depot has been blocked with vehicles waiting to discharge their loads, while almost fabulous prices have been paid for hauling and the road has been taxed to its utmost capacity to carry through the enormous quantities of freight delivered to it.[30]

This was the situation despite the fact the United States Government had decided to restrict such shipments.

On May 2, 1861, Salmon P. Chase, Secretary of the Treasury, issued a circular to all customs officials on the northern and northwestern waters to search all water craft, railroad cars, and other vehicles "laden with merchandise the ultimate destination of which you have good reason to believe is for any port or place under insurrectionary control" and to seize all "arms, munitions of war, provisions, or other supplies . . . ."[31]

This circular had little effect in Louisville. The customs establishment in the city was too small (only one surveyor, one chief clerk, and one messenger)[32] to stop the southern traffic unless the L&N voluntarily agreed to stop, and the railroad had no intention of stopping so lucrative a trade. President Guthrie justified this action by maintaining that Chase's order did not apply to his road since it was in a neutral state.[33] Secretary Chase was aware that the rules in Louisville remained unexecuted, but he feared any more drastic course would drive Kentucky into the Confederacy.[34] Thus the traffic rolled merrily on.

By the end of May Secretary Chase changed his mind. He concluded that by allowing Louisville to continue this trade, the federal government was losing too much. Thus, on May 25 he ordered the Louisville surveyor to stop the "treasonable trade" with the insurgents.[35] Three days later in a letter to George D. Prentice, Chase stated that it seemed "indispensable that supplies to the Rebels from Louisville shall cease." Also he said that he hoped such cessation would be a voluntary act of the people but that Robert J. Anderson, the former commander of Fort Sumter, was being ordered to the city to help the customs officers just in case he was needed.[36]

The surveyor, however, refused to enforce the circular "upon the ground that it would cause such an excitement . . . . that a mob would interfere."[37] Other prominent men in Louisville denied that such would take place,[38] whereupon the federal government quickly appointed a new surveyor, Charles B. Cotton.

Acting upon federal orders, Cotton announced that after June 24 no shipments would be allowed over the L&N without a permit from his office.[39] When this news reached Guthrie, he immediately filed suit before a federal judge in Louisville against the government for damages to the railroad.[40]

Prevented from shipping directly from Louisville to the South, the merchants quickly resorted to other measures in order to continue their profitable trade. Since the customs officials were only at Louisville, it was decided to have the goods moved by wagon to some point south of the city and there load them on the railroad. Thus immense quantities of goods were hauled by wagons night and day to Shepherdsville, a town eighteen miles south of Louisville, where they were then loaded on the L&N and shipped south.[41]

Soon, however, the merchants improved on this. Since the federal trade restrictions dealt only with items shipped to seceded states, the merchants began to send their goods from Louisville to Kentucky towns on the Tennessee line. Tennesseans could then get the goods there and ship them wherever they pleased.[42]

The federal government made several new attempts to halt these evasions of the law. A closer watch was kept on the cargo shipped over the L&N, and troops were sent to enforce the regulations.[43] Trains were ordered to leave by day to prevent smuggling, and inspectors were sent to the interior railway towns to prevent suspicious goods from being loaded.[44] Wagons were watched and goods which appeared to be destined for the Confederacy were removed.

Some shipments captured by treasury aides were later forcibly recovered by armed men and sent to Tennessee. Such action led William P. Mellen, a special agent of the Treasury Department, to advise local treasury aides to seize goods only if their communities were pro-Union and would sustain them. Otherwise the goods should be allowed to proceed unless they were arms or munitions. This was all that could be done until military aid was available.[45]

This illicit trade was known to all, but the L&N had no interest in stopping it, and the federal government was reluctant to use military force. Such military force would stop much, though not all of the illicit trade, but what the federal government feared was that such a display of force might drive Kentucky into the Confederacy.

Ironically it was Confederate action which eventually stopped this traffic southward. In May the Confederate Congress placed an embargo on the exportation of cotton to the North; and later this was extended to include sugar, rice, molasses, tobacco, syrup, and naval stores.[46] On July 4 Governor Isham Harris of Tennessee placed an agent on the L&N at the Tennessee line to prevent contraband goods from being shipped north and also confiscated all the L&N rolling stock in Tennessee. Harris then demanded that Guthrie cooperate with the Confederacy in maintaining train service, but the L&N president steadfastly refused the Tennessean's demands.[47]

Then on September 18, 1861, Brigadier-General Simon Bolivar Buckner of the Confederate army seized the entire line of the L&N up to Lebanon Junction, which is only thirty miles from Louisville. Buckner issued a manifesto to Guthrie suggesting that the road's agents and employees continue to work but under Buckner's military control.[48] Once again Guthrie refused, declaring that such action would be giving aid to the enemy.

Referring to the South as "the enemy" was something new for Guthrie, but it is indicative of his changed policy. Whereas previously he had espoused Union sentiment, he nevertheless used every means available to make a profit for the L&N by trading with the South even when such action was forbidden and by charging the federal government higher rates than other roads charged.[49] Now when southern officials threatened to bankrupt his line by confiscation and attempted to dictate the policy of the road, he became one of the strongest Unionists in the state.

Of course, the problem is that no one knows exactly where Guthrie stood prior to this time. He was a prominent national figure having served as Secretary of the Treasury under Pierce and having been a favorite son candidate for President in the Democratic Convention of 1860. Contrary to some of his speeches, many agree that his sympathies basically lay toward the South. Though he opposed secession, he felt that the South had the right of revolution. He strongly believed, however, that had the South stayed in the Union it could have rendered Lincoln powerless to harm. Nevertheless, whatever his views may have been, it appears that in the end it was his business concern rather than his political ideals which dictated his choice.

By March, 1862, Union forces had driven the Confederate army out of the state and had reopened the entire line of the L&N. From this time on the road was a great line of supply for the armies and the chief avenue of communication with the front,[50] though it continued charging higher rates and giving the War Department many headaches.

It is important to remember, however, that it was not the L&N alone which made Louisville so important, but also the large amount of river traffic which the city controlled.

The Confederates hoped by their economic policy regarding the Mississippi River to induce the Northwest to enter the Confederacy. Thus on February 18, 1861, in its first tariff act, the Confederacy provided that all products of the farm, manufactured or raw, plus munitions of war should be admitted duty free. Louisville was very pleased with this act, for it meant that there would be free trade both to the North and South. As a result, in the spring of 1861 there was an immense amount of trade that went to the Confederacy from the Ohio River Valley, and Louisville made herself the great collecting and shipping center for this commerce.[51]

Though many in the North were not pleased by this traffic to the South, they did tolerate it as long as there were no indications of immediate conflict. However, once Sumter was fired upon, many in the North became incensed by what was being shipped down the Ohio River for the South. One shipment of bacon and guns headed for the South via Louisville was seized by a group of enraged Cincinnati citizens. Following this irate action, the city of Cincinnati commissioned two steamers to patrol the river.[52]

The news of this action so angered the citizens of Louisville that some were ready to march against Cincinnati with armed forces and compel the city to relinquish its hold on the river.[53] Headlines in the *Louisville Daily Courier* screamed: "To Arms! To Arms! — Cincinnati Seizes Southern Property! Kentucky Will You Stand Back?"[54]

A group of Louisvillians decided not to stand back. By way of retaliation they took possession of an armory, seized two small cannons, dragged them to the bend in the river, and prepared to confiscate a steamer from St. Louis loaded with arms for Pittsburgh. They desisted only after Simon B. Buckner, commander of the Kentucky State Guard, assured them the arms were for his men.[55]

Though foiled in this attempt, a delegation of Louisville businessmen did go to Cincinnati on April 23 to present a protest against such interference with the river trade. There they were considerately received and were assured by the mayor, who read a statement from the governor, that except when absolutely certain a cargo contained munitions for the South, there would be no further seizures.[56]

It was not long after this that the Chase circular with its trade restrictions was issued; but unlike the railroad restrictions, those on the river commerce were effectively carried out. Many of the boats were pressed into military service, and the river traffic was so restricted that at times the wharf looked quite desolate.

But by the end of 1861 the city began to show a few signs of its former river commerce as more and more boats began to arrive; and as the Confederates were pushed out of the state, a distinct trade revival took place. In fact so much trade came that by March, 1862, it could be said that the wharf "was completely blockaded with the tobacco, cotton, and corn brought up from below by the Henderson and Cumberland river boats."[57] From this time on, the wharf was habitually crowded with army and medical supplies, wagons, ammunition, foodstuffs, refugees, prisoners, and wounded soldiers.[58]

The actual hostilities in Kentucky did not begin until September 3, 1861, when General Leonidas Polk of the Confederate army occupied Columbus, Kentucky. Immediately General Ulysses S. Grant and his army occupied Paducah; and on September 7, Brigadier-General Robert J. Anderson removed the headquarters of the Department of the Cumberland from Cincinnati to Louisville.[59]

Soon after this Albert Sidney Johnston, commander of the Confederate forces in the West, ordered Simon B. Buckner, formerly the commander of the Kentucky State Guard, with five thousand Confederate troops to proceed by rail to occupy Bowling Green, Kentucky.[60] This was accomplished by September 18, and advanced detachments were sent to within thirty miles of Louisville.[61]

Great excitement prevailed in Louisville, for most felt that Buckner intended to occupy their city. As General William T. Sherman later wrote, "The city was full of all sorts of rumors . . . . Many of the rebel families expected Buckner to reach Louisville at any moment." [62] The fact that no trains from the South arrived in Louisville and that telegraph communication south of Louisville was impossible for the next three days added greatly to the rumors about Buckner's movements and the size of his forces.[63]

These rumors undoubtedly exaggerated the size of Buckner's troops, but there was good reason for apprehension. Although General Anderson was in the city and at his request William T. Sherman had been sent to join him, they had no troops.[64] The only men they could immediately use were Lovell H. Rousseau's two thousand recruits at Camp Joe Holt across the Ohio River and the Home Guard of Louisville, but neither was ready for the field. Nevertheless, they had to be used.

General Anderson and James Guthrie felt that Buckner would try to reach Muldraugh's Hill, a spot about twenty-five miles southwest of Louisville which Buckner knew to be a very strong position. Thus it was decided that Sherman would take all available troops there in an effort to secure a position on the hill before Buckner could reach it.[65]

By shortly after midnight over two thousand men from Camp Joe Holt and the Home Guard had boarded the L&N and were being transported south. The next morning they disembarked at Lebanon Junction and marched the remainder of the distance to Muldraugh's Hill.[66] Sherman's army was a motley crew since the Home Guard did not wear regulation uniforms and Rousseau's men were not well equipped,[67] but as rapidly as fresh troops reached Louisville they were sent to Sherman.[68]

Buckner, however, never seriously considered marching to Louisville or dislodging Sherman from the hill. He estimated his own strength at not more than 6,000 but believed Sherman would soon take the offensive with 13-14,000.[69] Sherman, on the other hand, estimated that Buckner had at least 15,000 whereas Sherman had only 4,000,[70] though later this number was increased. Consequently, the Union general had no intention of undertaking an offensive. Thus, Sherman and his men remained between Muldraugh's Hill and Elizabethtown while Buckner remained near Bowling Green with neither seriously engaging the other in battle.

Meanwhile, the Union command at Louisville underwent a change. General Anderson had not been in good health when he assumed command in the city. In fact his physicians had advised him to refrain from active duty; but he declared that the Union men of Kentucky were calling on him to lead them, and he must make the attempt.[71]

It was soon apparent that the pressures of his command and the fact that his native state was being torn asunder by split loyalties was too much for him. Sherman stated that while at Muldraugh's Hill, "the daily correspondence between General Anderson and myself satisfied me that the worry and harassment at Louisville were exhausting his strength and health, and that he would soon leave."[72] Finally on October 6, 1861, Winfield Scott relieved Anderson of his command so that he might have his health restored and turned over the command of the Department of the Cumberland to General Sherman.[73]

Sherman, however, remained in command only until November 15 when Brigadier-General Don Carlos Buell replaced him and assumed the enlarged command of the Department of the Ohio.[74] During his month of command Sherman complained frequently and bitterly of the disloyalty of the Kentuckians, asserting that many joined the Confederate army but few the Union.[75] Then too, he saw the necessity of huge Union forces if the Confederates were to be beaten in the West. Ultimately it was probably his request for 200,000 men,[76] which seemed ridiculous or even insane to many, that led to his removal.

Buell quickly realized that Buckner was not going to attack Louisville but was fortifying himself at Bowling Green instead. Thus he wrote to General McClellan in November, "As for his attacking, though I do not intend to be unprepared for him, yet I should almost as soon expect to see the Army of the Potomac marching up the road."[77]

There were no other threats on Louisville or no more fighting near the city until the fall of 1862, but there is one other feature of the life of Louisville during the first year of the war that needs to be told.

On September 21, 1861, the first troops returning from the field, the 49th Ohio, passed through Louisville. With them came a considerable number of soldiers who were ill and could not be left behind, but no hospital arrangements had been made for them in the city. The sick of Rousseau's brigade had already been taken from Camp Joe Holt to the Marine Hospital;[78] but since it was very limited in accommodations, no new soldiers could be taken there. Louisville was in the process of organizing two new hospitals, but they could not be used yet. Then too, since several of the men were sick with measles they could not be taken to the city hospital nor the infirmary. Eventually arrangements were made with a lady who kept a large boarding house near the depot, and the sick were taken there. From September 21 to October 22, sixty patients made use of these arrangements; and although several were very ill, none died.[79]

This was merely the beginning of a new problem for Louisville. During the fall of 1861 the sick accumulated rapidly. Trains brought them almost every evening. Sometimes they arrived in very large numbers, and at other times they arrived without previous notice having been sent to the Medical Director who was thus often obliged to extemporize hospital accommodations.[80] School buildings, churches, and even a few factories were made into "make-shift" hospitals and soon were filled to capacity with sick and wounded men.

In a seven-week period during the early part of 1862 (January-March) 265 soldiers died in these hospitals;[81] and according to Isabel McMeekin, more than one thousand died within the first nine months of the war.[82]

Nevertheless, there is ample evidence that considering the limitations of space, equipment, and personnel, the soldiers were well taken care of. According to newspaper reporters the rooms were kept clean and well ventilated with separate areas for the various diseases.[83] Also the shortage of medical personnel was partially compensated for by the voluntary services of many Louisville ladies who furnished provisions, prepared and served meals, and even took some patients into their homes.[84]

By March, 1862, the situation was well enough in hand that the twenty hospitals had been reduced and centralized into eight with approximately two thousand patients.[85] As the resources at the command of the Medical Department increased, the necessity for the direct services of the ladies greatly decreased; but many continued their work.[86]

Thus is concluded this short account of Louisville during the first year of the Civil War. Although the fighting did not actually reach the city, its effects were felt very deeply.

Economically the city profited from the war. The L&N during the period of neutrality and throughout the war carried more freight than it had ever done before and at the end of the war was bigger, wealthier, and in better condition.[87] Though the river commerce suffered for a few months in 1861, it was reaching capacity by the spring of 1862 and continued that way throughout the war. Then, of course, the merchants made exorbitant profits from trading during the period of neutrality and later from war contracts.

Socially the city suffered, as did all cities in the country, from the death of many of its native sons. The tragedy of the Louisville situation was that regardless who won, many Louisvillians would be killed; for many fought on each side.

During this first year of the war the majority of the citizens remained moderate with respect to the sectional controversy. It is obvious from the material presented that some were strongly pro-Secessionist while others were equally strong for the North. However, most of the citizens of Louisville desired to remain in the Union, though they were opposed to any attempt to coerce a state which desired to secede.

FOOTNOTES

[1] *Daily Louisville Democrat*, 17 April 1861.
[2] E. Merton Coulter, *The Civil War and Readjustment in Kentucky* (Chapel Hill: U. of North Carolina Press, 1926), p. 57.
[3] Thomas Speed, "Civil War History—Federal," *Memorial History of Louisville from its First Settlement to the Year 1896*, ed. J. Stoddard Johnston (Chicago: American Biographical Publishing Co., 1896), I, p. 163.
[4] *Ibid.*, pp. 162, 200.
[5] Isabel M. McMeekin, *Louisville: The Gateway City* (New York: Julian Messner, Inc., 1946), p. 133; also see Albert D. Kirwan, ed., *Johnny Green of the Orphan Brigade; the Journal of a Confederate Soldier* (Lexington: U. of Kentucky Press, 1956).
[6] Wilson Porter Shortridge, "Kentucky Neutrality in 1861," *Mississippi Valley Historical Review*, IX (March, 1923), pp. 286-7.
[7] *Louisville Daily Courier*, 5 August 1861.
[8] U. S. War Department, *The War of the Rebellion: A Compilation of the Official Records of the Union and Confederate Armies* (hereafter cited as O. R.), Series I, Vol. IV (Washington: Government Printing Office, 1882), p. 327, Brigadier-General W. T. Sherman, Commanding, Department of the Cumberland, Louisville, 2 November 1861, to General W. T. Ward, Campbellsville, Kentucky.
[9] *Ibid.*, p. 313, L. Thomas, Adjutant-General, Washington, 21 October 1861, to Hon. Simon Cameron, Secretary of War.
[10] *Louisville Daily Courier*, 18 April 1861, 20 April 1861, 17 May 1861, and 5 August 1861.
[11] *Ibid.*, 21 August 1861.
[12] *Cincinnati Daily Gazette*, 19 September 1861.
[13] Coulter, *op. cit.*, p. 255.
[14] *Louisville Daily Journal*, 26 April 1861.
[15] *Daily Louisville Democrat*, 12 February 1861.
[16] *Ibid.*, 8 February 1861.

17 Coulter, *op. cit.*, p. 255.
18 Speed, *op. cit.*, pp. 131, 133, 160, 161.
19 *Ibid.*, p. 161.
20 R. M. Kelly, "Holding Kentucky for the Union," *Battles and Leaders of the Civil War*, ed. Robert U. Johnson and Clarence C. Buel (New York: The Century Co., 1887), I, p. 375, hereafter cited as *Battles and Leaders;* and Speed, *op. cit.*, p. 165.
21 Speed, *op. cit.*, p. 168.
22 *Battles and Leaders*, I, p. 377.
23 Speed, *op. cit.*, p. 163.
24 *Ibid.*, p. 165.
25 Frank Moore, ed., *The Rebellion Record: A Diary of American Events* (New York: G. P. Putnam, 1861 ff), III, p. 26, hereafter cited as *Rebellion Record*.
26 J. Stoddard Johnston, ed., *Memorial History of Louisville from its First Settlement to the Year 1896* (Chicago: American Biographical Publishing Co., [1896]), I, p. 103.
27 Thomas Weber, *The Northern Railroads in the Civil War, 1861-1865* (New York: King's Crown Press, 1952), p. 95; and R. S. Cotterill, "The Louisville and Nashville Railroad, 1861-1865," *American Historical Review*, XXIX (1923-1924), p. 702.
28 George R. Leighton, *America's Growing Pains: The Romance, Comedy, and Tragedy of Five Great Cities* (New York: Harper and Brothers, 1939), p. 62; Kincaid A. Herr, *The Louisville and Nashville Railroad* (3rd printing; Louisville: L & N Magazine, 1959), pp. 16-17.
29 Cotterill, *op. cit.*, p. 702; Herr, *op. cit.*, p. 17; and Weber, *op. cit.*, p. 95.
30 Leighton, *op. cit.*, p. 62.
31 *Illinois Weekly State Journal*, 15 May 1861.
32 Coulter, *op. cit.*, pp. 68-69.
33 Cotterill, *op. cit.*, p. 703.
34 J. W. Schuckers, *The Life and Public Services of Salmon Portland Chase* (New York: D. Appleton and Co., 1874), p. 319, Salmon P. Chase, Washington, 29 May 1861, to William P. Mellen.
35 Robert Frank Futrell, "Federal Trade with the Confederate States, 1861-1865: A Study of Governmental Policy" (unpublished Ph.D. dissertation, Vanderbilt University, 1950), p. 15.
36 Schuckers, *op. cit.*, p. 425, Salmon P. Chase, Washington, 28 May 1861, to George D. Prentice, Louisville, Kentucky.
37 Futrell, *op. cit.*, pp. 13-14.
38 *Ibid.*, p. 14.
39 *Cincinnati Daily Gazette*, 24 June 1861.
40 Futrell, *op. cit.*, p. 14; and Leighton, *op. cit.*, p. 63.
41 John Leeds Kerr, *The Story of a Southern Carrier: The Louisville and Nashville* (New York: Young and Ottley, Inc., 1933), p. 21; and *Illinois Weekly State Journal*, 12 June 1861.
42 Coulter, *op. cit.*, p. 74.
43 *Illinois Weekly State Journal*, 24 July 1861 and 28 August 1861.
44 *Cincinnati Daily Gazette*, 22 July 1861 and 31 July 1861.
45 Futrell, *op. cit.*, pp. 20-21.
46 Herr, *op. cit.*, p. 17; and Weber, *op. cit.*, p. 96.
47 Weber, *op. cit.*, p. 96; and Leighton, *op. cit.*, p. 63.
48 *O. R.*, IV, pp. 414-415, Brigadier-General Simon B. Buckner, Bowling Green, 18 September 1861, to James Guthrie, Louisville.
49 Weber, *op. cit.*, p. 180.
50 Johnston, *op. cit.*, I, p. 103.
51 Coulter, *op. cit.*, pp. 58-60.
52 *Ibid.*, pp. 61-62.
53 *Ibid.*, p. 62.
54 *Louisville Daily Courier*, 18 April 1861.
55 *Louisville Daily Journal*, 18 April 1861.
56 Coulter, *op. cit.*, p. 64.
57 *Daily Louisville Democrat*, 3 May 1863.
58 *Cincinnati Daily Commercial*, 6 January 1862; and McMeekin, *op. cit.*, p. 131.
59 *O. R.*, IV, p. 257.
60 *Ibid.*, IV, pp. 407-408, W. W. Mackall, Assistant Adjutant-General, Nashville, 15 September 1861, to Brigadier-General S. B. Buckner.
61 *Ibid.*, IV, pp. 413-414, Brigadier-General S. B. Buckner, Bowling Green, 18 September 1861, to Adjutant-General S. Cooper.

⁶² William T. Sherman, *Memoirs of General William T. Sherman* (New York: D. Appleton and Co., 1875), I, p. 197.
⁶³ *Cincinnati Daily Gazette*, 20 September 1861; and *Battles and Leaders*, I, p. 379.
⁶⁴ *Battles and Leaders*, I, p. 380; and Speed, *op. cit*, p. 166.
⁶⁵ Sherman, *op. cit.*, I, p. 198.
⁶⁶ *Ibid.*; and *O. R.*, IV, pp. 278-279, Brigadier-General W. T. Sherman, Muldraugh's Hill, Kentucky, 27 September 1861, to Captain Oliver D. Greene, Assistant Adjutant-General, Louisville.
⁶⁷ *Battles and Leaders*, I, p. 380.
⁶⁸ Sherman, *op. cit.*, I, p. 199.
⁶⁹ *O. R.*, IV, p. 437, Brigadier-General S. B. Buckner, Bowling Green, 4 October 1861, to W. W. Mackall, Assistant Adjutant-General.
⁷⁰ *Ibid.*, IV, p. 279, Brigadier-General W. T. Sherman, Muldraugh's Hill, Kentucky, 27 September 1861, to Captain Oliver D. Greene, Assistant Adjutant-General, Louisville; and p. 295, Anson Stager, Louisville, 7 October 1861, to Eckert.
⁷¹ *Louisville Daily Courier*, 15 August 1861.
⁷² Sherman, *op. cit.*, I, p. 199.
⁷³ *O. R.*, IV, p. 296, Winfield Scott, Washington, 6 October 1861, to Brigadier-General Anderson.
⁷⁴ *Ibid.*, IV, p. 358.
⁷⁵ *Ibid.*, IV, p. 313, L. Thomas, Adjutant-General, Washington, 21 October 1861, to Simon Cameron, Secretary of War.
⁷⁶ *Ibid.*
⁷⁷ *O. R.*, VII, p. 444, D. C. Buell, Louisville, 22 November 1861, to Major-General George B. McClellan.
⁷⁸ *Ibid.*, IV, p. 261, Brigadier-General Robert Anderson, Commanding, Department of the Cumberland, Louisville, 18 September 1861, to W. M. Bricken.
⁷⁹ J. S. Newberry, *The U. S. Sanitary Commission in the Valley of the Mississippi During the War of the Rebellion, 1861-1866* (Cleveland: Fairbanks, Benedict, and Co., 1871), p. 301.
⁸⁰ *Ibid.*
⁸¹ *Cincinnati Daily Commercial*, various dates January through March, 1862.
⁸² McMeekin, *op. cit.*, p. 137.
⁸³ *Cincinnati Daily Commercial*, 9 January 1862.
⁸⁴ Speed, *op. cit.*, p. 190; and Newberry, *op. cit.*, p. 304.
⁸⁵ *Cincinnati Daily Commercial*, 1 March 1862.
⁸⁶ Newberry, *op. cit.*, p. 304.
⁸⁷ Leighton, *op. cit.*, pp. 64-65.

WILLIAM G. EIDSON (1936–   ) was born in Alton, Illinois, and received his B.A. and M.A. degrees from Southern Illinois University. He has a B.D. from the Southern Baptist Theological Seminary and a Ph.D. from Vanderbilt. He taught at Southern Illinois University and is now professor of history at Ball State University in Muncie, Indiana. Eidson has contributed to such scholarly journals as *Mid-America* and the *Tennessee Historical Quarterly*.

This article first appeared in *The Filson Club History Quarterly* in July 1964, vol. 38, pp. 224–38.

SOUTH UNION SHAKERS DURING WAR YEARS

By Julia Neal
Western Kentucky State College, Bowling Green

It was August 15, 1861, when General Bedford Forrest, with a company of eighty-six cavalry, rode into the South Union Shaker village and pitched camp at the head of the mill pond. This visit and many others were to be set down by Eldress Nancy Elam Moore, a member of the Shaker ministry, who got a "feeling to record . . . the destruction, distress, and desolation . . . of the unnatural war." Her two-volume diary, which began with Forrest's arrival, ended on September 4, 1864. It was Nancy's journal that would be sent later to the head ministry in New Lebanon, New York, as the official record of how South Union was drained of its strength and property. Being as objective as she could, the eldress gave a candid account of how the 223 society members tried to maintain their neutrality even though both armies were surging back and forth across their land.

One reason for the constant passing of the troops was the society's location. The main street of South Union was a state road, which connected Bowling Green and its military fortifications, held alternately by the Confederates and the Federals, with Russelville, the organizational site of the Kentucky Confederacy. Further on, this road led to Forts Donelson and Henry. Just west of the village, the road was intersected by another main road which led to the Green and Ohio rivers.

The Memphis branch of the L & N railroad, offering the fastest rail service then in the South, crossed the Shaker farm and angled through an edge of the village. Since this was the first time in American history that the railroad determined troop movements, the "cars" passed constantly.

As a Shaker pacifist, Nancy knew the difficulties and dangers of trying to maintain a neutral position. Not only the Northern troops but also their Federal Kentucky neighbors could not understand the Shakers' refusal to take up arms to support the government. On the other hand, the secessionists were intolerant of the Shaker abolitionists who refrained from war and went about their normal business.

For most of the war the society was harassed by soldiers of both armies who came demanding food, cloth of all kinds, fresh horses and forage, or shelter for the night. Often the dust had not settled after the departure of one group before another group came into sight.

Almost every page of Nancy's Journal contains entries such as:

> Decr. 9th 1861 Captain Taylor came early in the morning and called for breakfast to be ready by eight o'clock for two hundred and fifty Cavalry who had camped at Covington's this side of B. Green.
> Decr. 10th Captain McLemore with one hundred and fifty cavalry called in at the office horse lot . . . The captain called on us for forty pounds of bread for his men; and dinner for himself and four other Officers.
> Decr. 19th The Southern Pickets rode up about seven o'clock at night and called for supper to be prepared for four hundred soldiers. We were to have it ready by eight o'clock . . . After working hard and getting the victuals cooked they did not arrive at the appointed time but came about midnight with five hundred Cavalry all expecting supper.

In the early months of the war, the visitors were mostly Confederates — but later when the Federals also came making demands, the eldress observed, "These men are as unreasonable as the Rebels. War imbrutes instead of refines."

The Shakers realized early that they would have to treat both armies the same. In the beginning they furnished the soldiers fruit and food without charge. When it became clear that their policy of free food would bankrupt them, they began charging a nominal sum. However, it became increasingly difficult to collect from either army. The leaders wrote numerous letters to the military authorities and made many trips in an attempt to collect the money due them.

Even though the society suffered financial losses, not only from the armies but also from the marauders of the time, the members continued to live by their millennial law of charity. Often the brethren went to Bowling Green with pies, fresh fruits, or dried beef to distribute at the army hospitals. Once the sisters contributed four baked turkeys and ten baked chickens, along with doughnuts, apple butter, and homemade catsup to the soldiers' New Year's dinner.

The sisters found it hard to turn away any of the hungry soldiers who came to the village. Eldress Nancy wrote: "We believed we would save more by being kind and accommodating to them than we would lose." When one officer remarked, "Madam, I fear you will kill us with good victuals," Sister Hannah's answer was, "Better that than with a bullet," which seemed to "take him by the heart."

The general serenity of South Union was broken in many ways. It was not uncommon to hear "wild, hideous, savage yells, come roaring from the Cars" as a train would pass "filled inside and outside with Infantry." At night the quiet might be broken by the "clincking of the soldiers' weapons on the floor, and the thumping of their boots as they turned over thro' the night." At other times the society members were disturbed by the light chatter of "those young women who were escorted by the officers." Nancy described a group of them as being "of the secesh die . . . very light minded and real squealers."

Many nights the Shakers could see "camp fires blazing and sparks flying in high winds." The fires were doubly disturbing since they were often laid from the good Shaker fences.

Events themselves could be disturbing. Such was the case when two of General Buckner's Medical Department came down from the Bowling Green headquarters to request that the Shakers take care of some five hundred sick soldiers. The brethren pointed out their own crowded conditions due to a recent loss of a large dwelling by fire, but agreed to take as many as twelve at a time. Buckner's men left hinting that the General's request would be changed to an order. However, the order did not materialize since the Confederates were soon to lose the Bowling Green fortifications to the Federals.

Nancy retold many stories which came out of the Bowling Green occupation. It happened that when the Rebels first took possession of Bowling Green General Buckner had ordered one of the soldiers to haul down the United States flag. Not satisfied with tearing it down, the soldier trampled the flag under his foot. In relating how the soldier fell from the roof and broke both legs, Nancy wrote "he died in a few days and no doubt received the reward of his works."

Another story concerned the Rebels when they were being routed from Bowling Green. The generals gave word for all to save themselves as best they could. It was then a young woman called out to the men, saying "I've heard of Bull Run, but what sort of a run do you call this?" Nancy never learned whether anyone took time to reply.

Atrocity stories also came from the fort. One James Pike told of having seen a man left in the round house, handcuffed and burnt to death.

With the exception of one slight skirmish, no fighting occurred on the Shaker land, so Nancy gave no firsthand account of any military engagements. But she often commented on the war news she got from the newspapers or from the trustees when they returned from business trips throughout the territory. Many rumors, often false ones spawned by the tensions of the time, were recorded by the eldress, who was particularly disturbed by the constant talk concerning the activity of both Morgan's Raiders and of the many neighboring guerrillas.

Throughout the war, Nancy shared the anxiety felt by all Shakers everywhere as to whether or not their position as pacifists would be recognized officially. She recorded the persistence with which the leaders appealed directly to the military authorities, the Kentucky Legislature, and President Lincoln.

Finally, on December 31, 1863, the South Union society was relieved to receive a telegram from Secretary Stanton giving all the Shaker brethren an indefinite parole. Earlier in the war, the Shaker trustees had gone to Russelville to give the Confederate government the only two guns in the society. According to the law every man worth $500 had to furnish a gun or pay $20. When the officers learned that the Shakers had only two guns for the use of so many people, they let the brethren bring "the most indifferent one back."

Nancy felt distressed as she saw her world of gentle manners and humanitarian impulses giving way to one of laxness and insensitiveness. By March, 1863, she was writing:

> I fear we are becoming too much under the influence of the spirits that accompany the armies which causes a hardness of heart towards our fellow mortals; For certainly the time has been in this place, that we could not have suffered a well man to lie down on the bare floor without bed or covering, much more to let one who is sick with ague chills and fevers to come in dripping wet, and then have to dry his own clothes; and then rest the best he could by the fire.

It is probable that the gentle eldress never realized how the roughness of the times colored her own language, causing her to use such expressions as "he fell dead and never kicked" or "This same Bostick . . . threatened to let out bro. Urben's guts."

That Nancy should have been disturbed by the changes in her Shaker way of life is not surprising for she had been living at South Union for fifty years. Born in nearby Warren County, September 1, 1807, she had been brought to the colony when she was four. When the South Union Society drew up its Church Covenant in 1830, twenty-three-year-old Nancy was one of the signers. At forty-two, she was appointed to the ministry where she served forty years until her death December, 1889.

During the 1,068 continuous days that she recorded "the perilous and awful times," Nancy may have sensed that the promise of Utopian living, which had seemed so bright in the 1850's, would never be fulfilled.

It is true that the South Union Shakers never fully recovered from the losses incurred from both the war and the several disastrous fires believed to have been set by some of their jealous neighbors. Other factors which contributed to the decline of the society were the hard Reconstruction times, the inability of the Shaker craftsmen to compete with the new, large-scale steam manufacturing, and the general waning of all communal experiments.

Never re-capturing its pre-war vigor, South Union came to a close in 1922.

JULIA NEAL (1905–   ), born in Auburn, Kentucky, has had a lifetime association with the Shaker community at South Union, the subject of most of her research and writing. Educated at Bethel College, Hopkinsville (A.A.), and Western Kentucky State College (B.S., M.A.), she did additional graduate work at the universities of Michigan, Denver, and Syracuse. After teaching English at Western and Florence State University, Neal served as director of the Kentucky Library at Western Kentucky University from 1964 until her retirement in 1972. In addition to many articles and papers, Neal is known for *By Their Fruits: The Story of Shakerism in South Union*, *The Journal of Eldress Nancy*, and *The American Shakers and Their Furniture*.

This article first appeared in *The Filson Club History Quarterly* in April 1965, vol. 39, pp. 147–50.

INCIDENTS IN THE LIFE OF FRANK WOLFORD, COLONEL OF THE FIRST KENTUCKY UNION CAVALRY

By HAMBLETON TAPP

Instructor of American History, Louisville Male High School

An address before The Filson Club, January 6, 1936

Colonel Frank Wolford fought to save the Union and after the Civil War he worked to save the South. He was a lion in battle and a giant in debate.

Few things pleased Colonel Wolford as much as speaking in public. In fact, so inordinate was his pleasure in forensics that he often spoke for three and four hours. Equally fond was he of praying in public, to which laudable function was transferred his penchant for lengthiness. One hot Sunday morning in July at the Baptist Church in Liberty, Kentucky, he had been called upon to pray and was getting well under way when the village drunkard, one Raul, who had aroused himself from a Saturday night's alcoholic slumber, staggered into the church. The derelict very respectfully refrained from sitting during the prayer, which proved to be interminable. Minutes passed; a sermon was preached in the prayer, while the luckless Raul reeled dizzily to and fro. Suddenly, without warning, there was a keen peal of thunder, and simultaneously Colonel Wolford uttered an A-men. Poor Raul was heard to mutter: "The Lord sure had the turtle hold on him; if it hadn't thundered, he never would have stopped."[1]

Unlike Colonel Wolford, thunder excites no trepidation on my part; however, I do dread brickbats. My talk, therefore, will be presented with some consideration in mind of the evils of verbosity. In candor, however, it must be said that my intention is to present a few facts of Colonel Wolford's career, his appearance,

---

[1] This story was related to me by Mr. George Stone, of Danville, Kentucky, August 22, 1935. During the late seventies, Mr. Stone was a law partner of Colonel Wolford at Liberty, Kentucky.

his characteristics, and some of the outstanding incidents of his life.

Frank Lane Wolford was born in Adair County, Kentucky, September 2, 1817, of Irish and of Scotch lineage.² His father, John, a very intelligent man, was a surveyor and school-teacher.³ Young Wolford received an average frontier education—perhaps a bit above the average for his locality. Having become well grounded in "the three Rs," he took up the study of law, serving principally as his own instructor, and was admitted to the bar in Casey County, at Liberty, to which place John Wolford with his numerous children and wife had moved in 1825. Frank Wolford served as a private in the famous Second Kentucky Regiment during the Mexican War. At the Battle of Buena Vista two of his officers, Colonel W. R. McKee and Lieutenant Colonel Henry Clay, Jr., were killed, and he, although wounded, risked his life to bear the body of young "Harry" Clay from the field.⁴

By 1860 Frank Wolford had established a reputation of being one of the best criminal lawyers in the Green River Country.⁵ At the outbreak of the Civil War, however, he cast aside his legal work and recruited the First Kentucky Union Regiment, a cavalry organization,⁶ and served as its Colonel until the spring of 1864, when he was dishonorably dismissed from the army for criticizing President Lincoln in a public address. That year, 1864, Colonel Wolford ran on the Democratic ticket for elector to strengthen General George B. McClellan in his race for the Presidency, doing more, perhaps, than any other man in the campaign in Kentucky.⁷

In 1865 he was sent from the Casey-Russell District to the State Legislature, where he played an active part in securing the repeal of the Expatriation Laws, which had been passed during

---

²Interview with Mrs. Nancy Wolford Barbee, of Columbia, Kentucky, a daughter of Colonel Wolford, July 29, 1935.

³Interview with Mrs. Barbee, July 29, 1935. See also L. B. Cox, "History of Education in Casey County," a master's thesis, University of Kentucky, 1932, page 61. See also *Proceedings of the Kentucky State Bar Association*, 1921, an article by Judge Rollin Hurt, of Columbia, Kentucky, on the life of Colonel Wolford entitled "Some Great Lawyers of Kentucky," pages 124-149. See page 130.

⁴*The Louisville Courier-Journal*, August 2, 1895, contains a sketch of Colonel Wolford's life by "Savoyard" (Eugene Newman).

⁵*Proceedings of the Kentucky State Bar Association*, 1921, page 127.

⁶Eastham Tarrant, *History of The First Kentucky Cavalry* (R. H. Carothers, Louisville, Kentucky, 503 pages, 1894), page 8 *et seq.*

⁷*Lexington Observer and Reporter*, July 2, August 10, and September 24, 1864. Also, *The Louisville Daily Journal*, September 30, October 1, and October 3, 1864. See also *The Cincinnati Daily Gazette*, November 17, 1864.

the bitter struggle between the States.[8] Wolford, in 1867, was appointed by Governor Stevenson, of Kentucky, to the office of Adjutant General. The duties of that position at that particular time were strenuous in the extreme: Guerillas were still terrorizing the land; and the Regulators, who had risen to exterminate lawlessness, had become as terrible as the Guerillas themselves[9]. From 1871 until 1879 the "Old Warrior" practiced law at Liberty, and during the latter year moved to Columbia, in Adair County, where he continued to pursue his profession. In 1882 at the Democratic Convention Colonel Wolford's name was unsuccessfully, though eloquently, presented by his friend Colonel Thomas B. Hill, of Stanford, for the nomination for the office of Clerk of the Court of Appeals of Kentucky.[10] In the State Legislature that same year, however, the Democrats, feeling that the party owed a debt to Colonel Wolford, carved out what became known as the Old Eleventh District, in order that he might be sent to Congress. He was elected Congressman in 1882 and re-elected in 1884. His death occurred on August 2, 1895, at Columbia, where he was buried.

Physically, Frank Wolford was a powerful man, but not graceful. He was perhaps 5 feet 10 inches tall. He had a powerful chest, a short, large neck, a thick, long body, and comparatively short, sturdy legs. His was not a handsome figure. His head was wide and high, unusually high and wide behind and above the ears[11], and was crowned by a thick suit of crisp black hair, which, as the years passed, became iron grey. His nose was a huge beak; his mouth, unusually wide and perfectly firm, was supported by a powerful chin. But the most unusual of all his features was his very clear and very grey eyes. They were sharp and hawk-like, fairly glowing with perceptible fire, and, like those of Marius, "could pierce a corselet or gaze an eagle blind."[12]

[8]*The Louisville Daily Journal*, December 4, 1865. Also *Daily Kentucky Yeoman*, Frankfort, December 13, 1865. Also *Journal of The House of Representatives of The Commonwealth of Kentucky*, 1865, pages 75-77.

[9]E. Merton Coulter, *The Civil War and Readjustment in Kentucky* (University of North Carolina Press, Chapel Hill, North Carolina, 468 pages, 1926), page 359. Also *Annual Cyclopedia*, 1870, page 427.

[10]*The Courier-Journal*, Louisville, January 12, 1882.

[11]Interview with Judge Rollin Hurt, of Columbia, Kentucky, September 14, 1935. Both Judge Hurt and his brother, Mr. Lucien Hurt, were personal friends of Colonel Wolford while he resided at Columbia. Both kindly imparted to me a large amount of information concerning the career of Colonel Wolford.

[12]*The Courier-Journal*, August 3, 1895. Also interview the writer had with Mr. John Gabehart at Liberty, Kentucky, June 26, 1935. Mr. Gabehart, age ninety-two, is one of the few surviving members of "Wolford's Cavalry."

Usually, however, there was a twinkle in them, accompanied by a facial expression of mild amusement which extended to the corners of his mouth. The quick twinkle and the amused expression softened somewhat his ruggedness and grimness. One receives the impression of unlimited strength upon studying a picture of Colonel Wolford; he sees not only physical strength but also unusual mental and moral strength. Strength—superb strength—seems to have been the key to his character.

One hesitates to attempt an analysis of Wolford's character because he was not only a man of marked individuality but also a man made up of contradictions. He was one of the most original and unique characters, perhaps, that the State has produced. He did not aspire to be any other body than himself. He was a diamond in the rough, and just a little different from all other diamonds.[13] His manner of speech was broad, archaic, and provincial. "Hit" for it, "sot" for sit and set, "fetch" for carry, "thar" for there, and a dropping of the final "g"; these were a part of his means of expression.[14] Yet, occasionally, his diction in speaking and writing was as pure and poetic as Lincoln's Gettysburg Address.

Sartorially, Wolford was extremely odd. Perhaps never in his life did he wear a suit which could be called a fit, nor did he care. His clothes always gave one the impression of having been thrown at him, they catching and hanging on to his frame as best they could.[15] Nor were uniforms to his taste. At the Battle of Mill Springs "he rode the frame work of an ugly roan horse, wore an old red hat, homespun brown jeans coat, and his face had been undefiled by water and razor for sometime."[16] His taste in foods was simple: his favorite dish being, as he told a friend, "drapped dumplins and biled hen."[17] And simple and temporate, too, were his habits; he never swore nor drank, nor smoked or chewed tobacco.[18]

In his home Colonel Wolford was an odd mixture of the ideal

---

[13]*Adair County News*, September 25, 1918, contains a sketch of Colonel Wolford's life by the late Judge Herschel C. Baker, of Columbia, who knew Colonel Wolford intimately.

[14]*Proceedings of the Kentucky State Bar Association*, 1921, page 129.

[15]*Ibid.*, page 128.

[16]Tarrant, *First Kentucky Cavalry*, page 61.

[17]*Proceedings of the Kentucky State Bar Association*, 1921, page 132.

[18]Interview with Judge Rollin Hurt, at Columbia, July 29, 1935. Colonel Wolford, according to Judge Hurt, was at times a public advocate in the cause of temperance—temperance as applied to the use of intoxicating beverages.

and the ridiculous. He was twice married—the first wife having died before the War between the States—and was the father of eleven children, to whom, it is said, he was always kind, loving, and generous.[19] Particularly noble was his deep love for his white-haired little mother, "Aunt Mahalie." Often late at night when unable to sleep he would rise, dress himself, and walked across the town, Liberty, to see her. She always recognized his footsteps, and neither the infirmities of age nor the ravages of disease could diminish the eagerness of her welcome.[20] The rugged old soldier, however, was not domesticated in the sense in which modern husbands are: If he chanced to buy a bushel or two of new potatoes, he might dump them into the parlor or the front hall. One of his greatest pleasures was derived from taking his razor to the front yard, and there, under the shade of a fine tree, enjoying a good shave.[21]

Kindness to his neighbors was one of Wolford's characteristics. This story has been told: There was to be held a few miles from Liberty a big social function, and a large number of the citizens of Casey County had planned to attend. Wolford's wife, Betsy, eager for the occasion to arrive, had cooked the food in advance, and her new side-saddle was in readiness. The morning of the big day came. A neighbor, a poverty-stricken woman, having procured in some way a horse, appeared at the Wolford house and requested the use of the saddle. Mrs. Wolford was torn between two desires. The Colonel came along, saw the poor neighbor and, patting his wife, said, "Let her have it, Betsy. You can go any time, and she can't."[22]

Financially, Frank Wolford was not successful. Although for years he was the leading criminal lawyer of the Green River Country[23] and might have become wealthy, he had, at the time

[19] Interviews with Judge Rollin Hurt, Mr. Lucien Hurt, and Mrs. Nancy Wolford Barbee, at Columbia, in July, August, and September, 1935.

[20] Interview with Mr. Lucien Hurt, at Columbia, Kentucky, July 29, 1935.

[21] Interview with Mr. W. S. Stone and Mr. O. P. Bowman at Liberty, September 11, 1935. Both gentlemen knew Colonel Wolford while he resided at Liberty. They related to me a number of anecdotes relative to Colonel Wolford's oddities.

[22] Mr. Lucien Hurt related another story to me to illustrate Colonel Wolford's generosity. According to Mr. Hurt, Mrs. Wolford early one cold winter evening chanced to go to the back of the house, in Columbia, and while there discovered someone in the act of stealing firewood. She hurried to the living room and notified Colonel Wolford. The Colonel sympathetically remarked that anyone who would come out to steal wood on such a bitter-cold night certainly must be in dire need of something with which to keep himself and his family warm. The thief, therefore, was not molested.

[23] *Proceedings of the Kentucky State Bar Association*, 1921, page 127. Also *The Courier-Journal*, August 3, 1895.

of his death, practically no property.[24] Extreme leniency in the matter of collections is probably the explanation. If his clients had money, they could pay him if they wished to do so; if they did not pay, Wolford seldom troubled them. On the other hand if he had money, his obligations were discharged promptly; if he had none, he appears never to have been troubled, nor were his creditors.[25]

Possessing a fine Irish sense of humor, Colonel Wolford kept it in readiness for every occasion; even the Civil War did not diminish it. Soon after the outbreak of that conflict, while his regiment was on the march southward, an hysterical wife, whose husband had enlisted shortly before, rushed to Wolford, and amid sobs begged that her "man" not be taken away, tragically wailing that he might be killed in battle. With a twinkle, the Colonel bade her not to worry, saying that he, being a widower, would gladly return and marry her if her husband happened to be killed.[26] Other traits of his character were an unusual degree of bravery and an admirable magnanimity, both of which traits will be illustrated further along.

Colonel Wolford's most notable public services took place during the stirring periods of Civil War and Readjustment. I shall attempt, therefore, to present a few of the incidents of those times in which he played a prominent part. The first of these incidents was at the Battle of Lebanon, Tennessee, fought May 5, 1862. This battle was for the most part fought between Kentuckians: General John H. Morgan's grey cavaliers of the Bluegrass and Frank L. Wolford's blue knights of the Green River.[27]

General Morgan and his men, who slept in Lebanon on the night of the fourth, were taken almost completely by surprise at

---

[24]Interview, September 9, 1935, with Mr. William A. Coffee, of Columbia, the lawyer who appraised the property left by Colonel Wolford at the time of the Colonel's death. Mr. Coffee is now (1935) Commonwealth's Attorney of the district in which Adair County is located.

The circuit court records, county court records, and deed books of both Casey and Adair counties were studied in the search for material bearing upon the career of Colonel Wolford. A casual glance at these records is enough to convince one of Wolford's lack of business acumen, perhaps also his lack of interest in business affairs.

[25]*Proceedings of the Kentucky State Bar Association*, 1921, page 131.

Judge Hurt's statement relative to the lack of concern of Wolford's creditors did not hold good in every instance, as the case of Thomas F. Barber vs. Frank Wolford indicates. See Casey County Circuit Court Records.

[26]Tarrant, *First Kentucky Cavalry*, page 35.

[27]Tarrant, pages 81-92. See also Basil W. Duke, *History of Morgan's Cavalry* (Miami Printing and Publishing Company, Cincinnati, Ohio, 578 pages, 1867), pages 159-163.

4 o'clock in the morning of May 5 by Wolford's swift-moving cavalry column.[28] Through a driving rain Lieutenant Silas Adams led the Federal advance, entering Lebanon from the south by way of the Murfreesboro Pike. He and his company galloped by General Morgan's pickets and plunged through a few sleepy Confederate companies, hastily forming on the north side of the town square. Colonel Wolford leading the main Union column entered the town also by the Murfreesboro Pike, but before reaching the town square his right flank was struck by an irritating fire from a college building situated on an eminence to his right. Placing himself at the head of one or two hundred men he charged the college grounds, surrounded the building, and captured a number of prisoners.[29]

The rain had ceased, but the atmosphere was heavy, and the smoke from the guns hovered low, and, after a short time of firing, little could be seen except flashes from the muzzles of guns. The din was terrible. Amid the crack of rifles, the report of pistols, and the clatter of hoofs on the hard wet streets, could be heard the hoarse shouts of fighting men and at times, the shrill shrieks of frightened women and children in the houses.[30] Colonel Wolford, after taking the college building, rode with the main column into the public square and faced a withering fire from the main body of General Morgan's men who, by this time, were ready for battle. From the buildings about the square, especially from the hotel on the northwest corner of the square, an irregular though rapid cross-fire was poured into the First Kentucky's column. Near the hotel, Wolford was heard giving orders, and while bullets rained about him as if he had been singled out for slaughter, he was struck in the left side just above the hip, the bullet inflicting a dangerous wound.[31] Seeming scarcely conscious of the rapid flow of blood, he ordered his men back to reload and reform, and immediately again charged the square.

Reeling from the dash, Colonel Wolford saw a line formed a short distance to the north and rode to give orders. That line,

---

[28]Tarrant, page 83. The Union force which attacked General Morgan at Lebanon, Tennessee, consisted of detachments of three regiments under the command of Brigadier General Ebenezer Dumont. These detachments were from the First Kentucky under Colonel Frank Wolford; the Seventh Pennsylvania under Major John Wynkoop, and the Fourth Kentucky under Colonel Green Clay Smith.

[29]Duke, *Morgan's Cavalry*, page 160. Tarrant, *First Kentucky Cavalry*, page 84.

[30]*The Louisville Daily Journal*, May 14, 1862, an article by Kirkwood.

[31]Tarrant, *First Kentucky Cavalry*, page 85.

although partly blue-clad, was Confederate. He rode into the arms of Captain Frank Leathers, who immediately claimed him as his prisoner. Upon learning the identity of his captive, the joyous Leathers shouted: "This is glory enough for one day." [32] General Morgan appeared upon the scene and offered Colonel Wolford a parole, but Wolford refused, saying that he preferred to take chances on being rescued by his own men.

By this time the Federal troopers had cut off all the exits from Lebanon, excepting the road leading to Carthage on the Cumberland River. Morgan, with a small remnant of his badly beaten squadron, galloped into this road, closely followed by Wolford's "Wild Riders." [33] The badly wounded and almost exhausted Colonel Wolford was pressed into the fleeing column near General Morgan, and a desperate flight and chase was begun. One of the prisoners, W. H. Honnell, chaplain to Wolford's Cavalry, later commented: "We were on the wildest race a soldier ever experienced. Sometimes we would jump clear over a fallen horse, and horses would sometimes shy around a man on hands and knees struggling to escape from the road." Colonel Wolford, steadily becoming weaker from the loss of blood, fell behind Morgan's fleeing troops and was soon overtaken by two of his own officers. Mr. Honnell describes the scene when Wolford was overtaken: "He sat on his horse urging Captains Carter and Fishback to leave him and press to the capture of Morgan, whom he pointed out in the distance, before he could cross the river. The blood was dripping from his wound into the road as he offered to take care of himself till they could make the dash . . . " [34] General Morgan with twenty of his men seized a skiff at the Cumberland's edge, and crossed the river to safety. Colonel Wolford, too weak to sit a horse longer, was placed in a buggy and taken back to Lebanon. That night his men celebrated a victory. That same night Morgan and the remnant of his squadron sat in defeat at Rome, Tennessee; the great Raider shed tears; it was his first defeat. [35]

Astride Kentucky steeds, Morgan and Wolford, through the summer and fall of 1862, played the glamorous game of war over

---
[32] *Ibid.*, page 87.
[33] Duke, *Morgan's Cavalry*, page 161.
[34] Tarrant, *First Kentucky Cavalry*, page 88.
[35] Howard Swiggett, *The Rebel Raider*—a life of General John H. Morgan (The Bobbs-Merrill Company, Indianapolis, Indiana, 341 pages, 1934), page 56.

the fertile fields of Kentucky and Tennessee—played it as romantically and as chivalrously as did ever Coeur de Lion and Saladin in the days of the Crusades.[36] They met for the last time, face to face, north of the Ohio in the summer of 1863, at the end of the boldest raid and perhaps the grimmest pursuit in the history of cavalry warfare. The great raid began about the first of July. By the time General Morgan and his squadron reached Lebanon, Kentucky, Colonel Wolford and the First Kentucky, having been stationed at Jamestown and Columbia, took up the chase.[37] Day after day, under a scorching mid-summer sun, through Southern Indiana, through Southern Ohio, the indomitable Old Warrior galloped, twenty-one hours a day, always at the head of his dust-covered column.

The daring grey raiders paused before bewildered Cincinnati; some of them counciled that the city be captured and burned unless safe passage across the Ohio be vouched, but Morgan refused, saying that Wolford was too close in pursuit, and continued the flight.[38] On both sides, horses fell from sheer exhaustion, and men, addled from weariness, dropped from their saddles and slept in the dust by the road. Morgan galloped on. Wolford—his saddle soaked with blood from the unhealed wound in his side—pressed on.[39] At last when endurance seemed no longer possible, Federal volunteers were called for. Doughty Old Wolford continued to lead his thin but gallant column in pursuit of the gallant foe.

The day came when General Morgan realized that further flight and resistance were humanly impossible. He stopped and

[36]Judge Herschel C. Baker, in the *Adair County News*, issue of September 25, 1918, tells this story relative to the friendliness between Morgan and Wolford: The two cavalry leaders were raiding and scouting in Southern Kentucky, along the Cumberland River. A number of Colonel Wolford's men had been captured by General Morgan's troopers. It so happened that Morgan did not wish to be encumbered by the prisoners, but was in dire need of salt. Wolford needed all of his soldiers, but had an abundance of salt. A trade was agreed upon: salt for soldiers.

[37]Tarrant, *First Kentucky Cavalry*, page 174.

[38]*Lexington Observer and Reporter*, April 6, 1864. In this issue is quoted an article from *The Louisville Daily Journal*, written by Kirkwood. It describes a council of war held by General Morgan and his officers as they approached Cincinnati in July, 1863. Kirkwood states: "A pause follows the daring proposition [to set fire to Cincinnati if safe passage is not guaranteed across the Ohio River]. General Morgan breaks the stillness by saying: D-n me, it won't do! I know Wolford too well. We halted at Lebanon, Tennessee, and he charged into our columns at day break and killed, wounded, and captured nearly all my men. He will be on us again before we can burn the city or cross the Ohio, and we must push forward at once and avoid all obstruction in front.'" Kirkwood states that General Morgan's squadron feared Colonel Wolford more than any other of its pursuers.

[39]Tarrant, *First Kentucky Cavalry*, pages 181-188. Duke, *Morgan's Cavalry*, pages 252-254.

sought Colonel Wolford, whom he considered the most magnanimous of the Union officers, to surrender to him as he was most likely to give the most generous terms.[40] The "Old Meat-axe," as Wolford was called, could not be found. He did appear later, however, in the full flower of knightliness. He prevented his superior officer from inflicting insults on the captured Raider, and in gratitude Morgan presented Wolford with the beautiful silver spurs which had been given him by Lexington admirers.[41] Later, after escorting General Morgan and his officers from Salinville back to Wellsville, Ohio, Colonel Wolford left them at the hotel to rest. Before leaving them he said: "Gentlemen, you are my guests. This hotel, together with its bar, cigar stand, and other accessories, is at your service and at my expense. Do not go off the square in front of the hotel."[42]

One of the most notable episodes in the life of Colonel Wolford was his controversy with President Lincoln during the summer of 1864. It was the result of a speech delivered on March 10 in Lexington, Kentucky. Early in March, following his brilliant actions in the campaign around Knoxville, Tennessee, the Old Warrior was invited to Lexington to receive, at Melodian Hall, the gift of a jeweled saber, sash, pistols and spurs—tokens of appreciation—from admiring Kentucky Union sympathizers. The award was made Thursday, March 10, 1864, in the presence of a large audience of distinguished people, including Governor Thomas E. Bramlette.[43] Colonel Wolford rose to accept the gift, and, the mood for speech being strong upon him, took occasion to deliver an address of more than an hour's duration. He reviewed the trend of affairs in Kentucky since the autumn of 1861. He charged Mr. Lincoln with "wantonly trampling upon the Constitution and crushing under the iron heel of military power the rights guaranteed by that instrument." He charged the President with violating his solemn pledge that he had repeatedly enunciated at the commencement of his administration as to the purposes of the war. He charged the President, further, with a "violation of the rules of civilized warfare in the indiscriminate, widespread ruin which he was sowing broadcast throughout the South." And, finally, he bitterly resented the recruiting of

---

[40]Duke, *Morgan's Cavalry*, page 457.
[41]Tarrant, *First Kentucky Cavalry*, pages 187, 188. When General Morgan surrendered his horse and sword, he, by request, handed them over to Colonel Wolford.
[42]Swiggett, *Rebel Raider*, page 152.
[43]*The Louisville Daily Journal*, March 14, 1864.

Negro soldiers.[44] The effort, although a long one for a speech of acceptance, received the most respectful attention and at times brought forth tumultuous applause. The leading newspapers of the State, such as *The Louisville Daily Journal* and *The Lexington Observer and Reporter*, expressed admiration for the fearless address, and there is perhaps little doubt but that Wolford's opinions represented those of the majority of his fellow Kentuckians.[45] However, because of his speech, Wolford, a few days later, was dishonorably discharged from the Union Army by order of President Lincoln.[46]

If the candid Old Warrior had not been the most popular man in Kentucky immediately after the Lexington speech, he, in all probability, achieved that distinction following President Lincoln's order of dismissal.[47] Everywhere he chanced to go, curious crowds flocked to see and hear him and to do him honor. At Louisville, for example, a friend took him to the theater. The two occupied a box. Colonel Wolford received more attention than did the actors on the stage.[48]

Politics and the forum were now open to him, and in both he took a delight. Thousands of people throughout the State had been suffering at the hands of what they termed Union Military Tyrants and Dictators. Indignation and wrath had been smoldering in their breasts since 1861. They needed a leader who was aggressive, masterful, and unafraid, as well as popular, and one who loved the Union. Such a man they found in Colonel Wolford.

Although before the War he had been a Whig and a Know-Nothing successively, he now became a Democrat. Fusing together conservative Union men, conservative Democrats, and Southern-sympathizing Democrats on the issues of Constitutional Liberty, Opposition to Negro Recruiting, and to Lincoln Tyranny, Colonel Wolford revived the weakened Democratic party in the State, inspired it with new hope, and gave it a determined belligerency. In this he was vigorously aided by both

---

[44]*Lexington Observer and Reporter*, March 12, 1864. The quotations are from this newspaper's report of Wolford's speech. If this extemporaneous speech was ever published in full, I failed to find a copy.

[45]E. Merton Coulter, *The Civil War and Readjustment in Kentucky*, page 173 et seq.

[46]*Lexington Observer and Reporter*, April 6, 1864.

[47]See *The Louisville Daily Journal* and *Lexington Observer and Reporter* for April and May, 1864. See also *The Louisville Daily Journal*, Editorial Section, October 15, 1864.

[48]*Lexington Observer and Reporter*, March 19, 1864.

The Louisville Journal and *The Lexington Observer and Reporter*. His eloquent voice and persuasive power were everywhere in demand, and crowds listened for hours without tiring, drowning almost his every sentence with thunderous applause.⁴⁹ The Radical Federal military leaders of the State, realizing with dismay his powerful effect on the hustings, determined to silence him by means of arrests, and to base their charges on criticisms of the Federal administration which would be made in the course of his speeches.⁵⁰ On Monday, June 27, following a speaking campaign in the Green River counties, he was arrested at Lebanon, by order of General Stephen T. Burbridge, Military Head of Kentucky, and sent under guard to Washington, D. C., for trial before the Judge Advocate.⁵¹ Soon after reaching the Capital, however, he was ordered back to Louisville for trial, being given a parole by President Lincoln before leaving Washington—a parole that merely relieved him from being jailed. While waiting trial at Louisville Colonel Wolford received from President Lincoln, through his Attorney General James Speed, another parole under which all charges would be dismissed if he expressed no further opposition to Negro enlistments. The old champion of Liberty under the Constitution, now realizing that the authorities had no intention of giving him a trial, refused to accept the new parole upon such basis. His letter of refusal to President Lincoln contains, among other things, a powerful defense of the Individual's Liberty under the Constitution. A few lines from that letter as printed in some of the newspapers, are quoted here:

"I have frankly to say that I cannot bargain for my liberty and the exercise of my rights as a freeman on any such terms.

---

⁴⁹*Lexington Observer and Reporter*, April 6, 1864; also April 13 and 23, 1864. Also, *The Louisville Daily Journal*, October 3 and 7, 1864. In an interview with Mr. George Stone, at Danville, August 22, 1864, this venerable and interesting gentleman related a rare anecdote relative to Colonel Wolford's "long-windedness." The gist of the story is to this effect: When a young man, in 1864, Mr. Stone attended a "Wolford speaking" at Somerset, Kentucky. The occasion was an all-day combination politics-picnic affair. The ladies of the neighborhood brought baskets filled with country provisions to satisfy the hunger of the throng, and the gentlemen brought bottles and jugs of beverages to quench any thirst which might arise. Colonel Wolford mounted the platform about ten o'clock in the morning and began his speech. At noon he halted the address that the people might appease their appetites. Toward two in the afternoon, the loquacious and eloquent Wolford continued his speech, amid rapturous applause. Mr. Stone said that when the sun was dipping to meet the western horizon he, although fascinated by the masterly address, was obliged to leave the enrapt throng, who did not appear, in the least, to have grown weary during the hours of spellbinding oratory.

⁵⁰*The Louisville Daily Journal*, October 1, 1864. Colonel Wolford, exasperated by the actions of the Union leaders of the State, wrote in this issue: "If they do not intend to give me a trial, I hope, for the sake of common decency, if not for the sake of justice, that they will let me alone."

⁵¹*Ibid.*, Friday, September 16, 1864.

I have committed no crime. I have broken no law of my country or of my State. I have not violated any military order or any of the usages of war ... You, Mr. President, if you will excuse the bluntness of a soldier, by an excess of arbitrary power, have caused me to be arrested and held in confinement contrary to law—not for the good of our common country but to increase the chances of your election to the Presidency ... You ask me to stultify myself by signing a pledge whereby I shall virtually admit your right to arrest me, and virtually support you in deterring other men from criticizing the policy of your administration ... No, Sir, much as I love liberty, I shall fester in a prison or die on a gibbet, before I will agree to any terms that will not abandon all charges against me and fully acknowledge my innocence."[52]

Receiving no reply to his animated letter, Wolford, after waiting in Louisville a few days, decided that he was under no further obligation to Mr. Lincoln and again took the stump in the interest of General McClellan's candidacy for the presidency. The final arrest of Wolford was made at his home in Liberty a few days after the fact was known that the Democrats had carried Kentucky overwhelmingly. This final arrest again was ordered by General Burbridge[53] and made by a squad of soldiers, who, with great secrecy, spirited Wolford away to Covington, where he was incarcerated in a filthy dungeon.[54] His friends could not learn where he was confined; nor was he permitted to send his old friend, Joshua F. Bell, a letter requesting legal aid. Finally, United States Senator, Lazarus W. Powell, of Kentucky, introduced a resolution in the Senate, calling upon the President

---

[52] *Ibid.*, Friday, September 16, and October 1, 1864. Also *Lexington Observer and Reporter*, September 21, 1864.
It appears likely that Wolford's Lincoln correspondence is among the Lincoln papers presented to The Library of Congress by Robert Lincoln. These manuscripts, as requested by the donor, are not to be open for public perusal until about 1945 and therefore I am unable to quote from the original documents.

[53] In an open letter written by Lieutenant Governor Richard T. Jacob to the Reverend Dr. Robert J. Breckinridge and published in *The Louisville Daily Journal*, November 3, 1864, Lieutenant Governor Jacob accuses Dr. Breckinridge of inspiring the arrests of Colonel Wolford. The following is an excerpt from that letter: "You (Dr. Breckinridge) in common with a few other blood-thirsty but cowardly Jacobins, hounded on the military to arrest Colonel Wolford and myself. No, Sir, it was not your fault that arrests were delayed. Colonel Wolford was arrested. The noble old patriot who is worth ten times ten million such men as you!" Lieutenant Governor Jacob's pen does not become less vitriolic as the letter continues.

[54] *The War of The Rebellion, A Compilation of The Official Records of The Union and Confederate Armies*, published by the Government Printing Office, Washington, 1898. The reference here is to Series I, Vol. 39, Part 3, page 726.

to disclose the place of imprisonment, and to give the reason for detention.[55] The result was that Colonel Wolford was released by order of President Lincoln, who had not been aware that General Burbridge had ordered the arrest.[56] And thus this controversy, caused by the violent passions engendered by the War, came to a close.

During the summer of 1865, Colonel Wolford made the race on the Democratic ticket for the State Legislature from the Casey-Russell District. The main issue of the campaign was amnesty, especially amnesty for the Kentucky Confederates. The magnanimous Old Warrior, although he had received seven wounds at the hands of Confederate soldiers, championed amnesty with his entire zeal. He fought against apparently insurmountable difficulties. The District was overwhelmingly Union in sentiment, had furnished no soldiers to the Confederacy, and was not inclined to forgive the loss of scores of its sons who had fallen in battle.[57] Wolford's opponent was Colonel Silas Adams, who had succeeded him as colonel of The First Kentucky Regiment. Colonel Adams was an impressive figure, a handsome, dashing, brave, eloquent, and unusually popular man. He opposed general amnesty, thereby representing what seemed to be the sentiment of the District. On the Saturday preceding the election a joint debate was held between the two candidates at Liberty. A huge and excited crowd was present, including a large number of ex-Federal soldiers, most of whom had served under both Wolford and Adams.[58] Colonel Adams spoke first. During the course of his speech he turned to his opponent, and propounded the following question: "Colonel Wolford, you claim to be for complete and unconditional amnesty for unrepentant Rebels. Now, Sir, no dodging; tell the people if you are willing to discharge that arch-traitor, Jeff Davis, from his prison quarters at Fortress Monroe?"

"I'll answer you, Colonel Adams, when your time is up," said Wolford, rising.

"I want an answer now," roared Adams.

Shuffling to the front of the platform, Colonel Wolford delivered this brief speech: "Fellow citizens, I was at Buena Vista.

[55]*Adair County News*, June 20, 1906.
[56]*Official Records*, Series I, Vol. 45, Part I, page 994.
[57]*Proceedings of the Kentucky State Bar Association*, 1921, page 137.
[58]*Ibid.*, pages 138, 139.

I saw the battle lost and victory in the grasp of the brutal and accursed foe. I saw the favorite son of Harry of the West, and my Colonel, weltering in his blood. I saw death, or captivity worse than death, in store for every surviving Kentuckian on that gory field. Everything seemed hopeless, when a Mississippi regiment, with Jefferson Davis at its head, appeared on the scene. I see him now as he was then—the incarnation of battle, a thunderbolt of war, the apotheosis of victory, the avatar of rescue. He turned the tide; he snatched victory from defeat; his heroic hand wrote the words Buena Vista in letters of everlasting glory on our proud escutcheon. I greeted him then as a hero, my countryman, my brother, and my rescuer. He is no less so this day, and I would strike the shackles from his aged limbs and make him as free as the vital air of heaven and clothe him with every right I enjoy, had I the power."[59]

Although the men attending the debate apparently were strongly Union in feeling, they could not resist the fascination of such sublime courage, of such superb sportsmanship, and of such clever eloquence. They sent "Old Wolford" to the Legislature.

The Legislature convened at Frankfort early in December, 1865, and the Representatives immediately turned their attention to the question of amnesty. During the War an excited and punitive Legislature had passed a series of measures known as Expatriation Laws, which deprived Kentucky soldiers in the Confederate army and navy of their State citizenship. These Kentuckians had returned to their native state during the summer of 1865 to find that they, politically, were outcasts. Amnesty in Kentucky, therefore, would mean repealing the Expatriation Laws.

Perhaps the most colorful description of the occasion of the voting to repeal these measures in the State Legislature is found in a speech delivered by the Honorable Thomas B. Hill in January, 1882. That address, because it deals principally with the activities of Colonel Wolford, is here freely paraphrased and quoted:

Robert Davis, Representative from Bourbon County, the young son of United States Senator Garret Davis, had brought forward the bill to repeal the Expatriation Laws. This bill was opposed

---

[59]This speech is quoted from an undated newspaper clipping which Mrs. Barbee, of Columbia, showed to the writer.

in a powerful address by "the leader of the House, who was justly regarded as one of the finest orators of his day." It was thought that a majority in the Legislature was opposed to repeal, and "trepidation and fear hung like a cloud over the proudest homes of Kentucky." It was known, however, that Wolford favored Davis's bill and that he would make the closing argument; "it was known that the most splendid soldier that Kentucky had furnished to the Union cause would speak for the men whom he had so often faced in the 'perilous edge of battle,' and at whose hands he had received the honorable and unhealed wounds he still bore on his person."

The day came; it was bitter cold. The Representative chamber was filled from "base to dome." It was a notable audience, the equal of which Kentucky has seldom known. "The proudest homes of the Commonwealth were there represented. The proudest of her matrons, whose sons were outcasts, the most beautiful of her maidens, whose brothers and sweethearts were under the ban of that law, were there in the full radiance of that beauty which not even the rigors of that day could diminish." Sons of Clay, of Crittenden, of Marshall, of Breckinridge—"names that had carried the fame of Kentucky around the world as the home of eloquence, of courage, of genius"—were there, all "anxious, silent, foreboding." In the midst of that audience sat the rugged form of Wolford. All eyes were turned on him. He arose in his place, and, supporting himself by his desk, he began his oration. His theme was somewhat as follows:

"The Southern soldiers were the children of Kentucky—the common mother of us all—they were his brothers; they were entitled, not by grace, but by heritage and by right, to every privilege which he enjoyed."

For hours he dwelt upon this grand theme. "For hours he thrilled and swayed the bosoms of that audience as the storm-king sways the bosom of the ocean. It was indeed a storm in which the Speaker's gavel and threats of clearing the hall were unnoticed and unheard. It was, in truth, a whirlwind of eloquence and patriotism, which again and again swept to their feet that vast audience in a tempest of plaudits and tears, and which swept forever from the statute books every vestige of the laws which had restricted the rights or stigmatized the honor of the Southern Kentucky Soldier. . . From that day to this there has been no bad blood between the Federal and the Southern Soldier of Kentucky."⁶⁰

Another incident, and I shall close this short sketch of Colonel Wolford. It is an incident that illustrates Colonel Wolford's tactics and his effectiveness in a political "rough and tumble." As in war a soldier sometimes pushes his cap into view to draw the fire of the enemy, so Wolford in debate often adopted a similar stratagem. He would present a harmless issue to try his adversary and to amuse his audience; in other words, he often would use a mis-statement as a decoy.⁶¹

On one occasion he practiced this scheme upon General Speed S. Fry, of Danville, Kentucky. The General was sent to Casey County soon after the Civil War to fill some political engagements, and he and Colonel Wolford met in joint debate. General Fry spoke first, waving the "bloody shirt" vigorously and bitterly indicting the "rebels" for attempting to destroy the Union.

Wolford arose immediately after General Fry had concluded his speech. He described, in his unique way, the cruelty practiced by the Radicals, Carpetbaggers and Scalawags on the helpless South following the War. He severely abused them for hanging Robert E. Lee and Jefferson Davis.

Fry listened for a while in amazement, and at last, being unable to keep his seat longer, rose and denied that Lee and Davis had been hanged.

Wolford remarked that it was not the first time he had heard the statement denied; that it was the way of Republican speakers to deny all the cruelty of which they had been guilty in the South. He said that he was not in the habit of making statements which could not be substantiated, and that, fortunately, there were persons in the audience who were eye-witnesses to the facts. He further stated that he would ask them to stand up and say whether or not it was true. Knowing every man in the audience by his first name, Wolford had little difficulty in getting response. In fact, the audience was delighted with the trend of the debate.⁶²

---
⁶⁰*The Courier-Journal,* January 12, 1882. See also *Daily Kentucky Yeoman,* December 13, 1865. Also *Journal of the House of Representatives of the Commonwealth of Kentucky,* 1865, pages 75-77.
⁶¹Interview with Judge Rollin Hurt at Columbia, July 29, 1935.
⁶²*Adair County News,* October 9, 1918.

Pointing to the left he said: "You, Jim, were a soldier; state whether or not you were present at the time." Jim promptly testified that he was "thar" and it was a fact that both Lee and Davis were hanged.

Then to another: "And what do you know about it, John?" Said he: "It's the God's truth, Colonel, I was right thar, and saw'm when they tied the rope."[63]

One after another gave testimony to the same effect, while the audience roared with laughter. And then a man appearing by his staggering to be considerably inebriated reeled down the aisle and in stentorian tones shouted: "Yes, General Fry, G-d d-n you, don't you deny it; I was thar and seed you when you done it."[64]

It was more than General Fry could endure. He stalked from the platform, and in righteous indignation turned his back upon the crowd and left the country.[65]

Death came to Colonel Frank L. Wolford, August 2, 1895. The funeral services were held in the Court House at Columbia, Adair County. Judge James Garnett, Sr., and Governor Proctor Knott, also Colonel Silas Adams (his enemy in politics and often at the bar, but withall his dearest friend) were the funeral orators. Colonel Adams, who made the last address, was deeply moved, and spoke with difficulty. He told of the saddle incident, quoting Colonel Wolford's words: "Let her have it, Betsy, you can go any time, and she can't." Then paused; resuming he said: "He was the bravest man I have ever known . . . I loved him as I have loved no other man."[66]

Rugged, plain, Old Wolford who had bled for the Union, pled for the South, and lived his eventful life for men and for principles, was laid to rest in the beautiful Green River Country, where the summer air is perfumed by the scent of pennyroyal, and the hush is broken by the notes of birds singing amid the hickories and the redbuds.

---

[63]*Ibid.*
[64]*Proceedings of the Kentucky State Bar Association*, 1921, page 142. Judge Hurt's account of the debate differs somewhat from that of Judge Herschel C. Baker, in the *Adair County News*. The last quotation is from Judge Hurt's paper.
[65]*Adair County News*, October 9, 1918.
[66]Interview with Mr. Lucien Hurt, at Columbia, Kentucky, July 29, 1935.

HAMBLETON TAPP (1900–   ), a native Kentuckian, earned his bachelor's degree at Centre College, his M.A. at George Peabody College, and his Ph.D. in history at the University of Kentucky. After teaching and administrative positions in the public schools of Louisville and Eminence, he was assistant professor of history and executive assistant to the president at the University of Kentucky and, later, director of the university's Kentucky Life Museum. In 1971 he joined the Kentucky Historical Society as assistant director and editor. He has been active in many historical projects and organizations with a particular interest in George Rogers Clark. His best-known work is the four-volume *A Sesqui-Centennial History of Kentucky*, and he has written many articles and reviews.

This article first appeared in *The Filson Club History Quarterly* in April 1936, vol. 10, pp. 82–99.

THE DELICATE TRACK
THE L&N's ROLE IN THE CIVIL WAR

By John E. Tilford, Jr.
Jacksonville University, Jacksonville, Florida
Paper read before The Filson Club, June 5, 1961

I

When Federal Troops marched into Atlanta on September 2, 1864, the Confederacy had been mortally wounded. It was only a matter of time until the death rattle. About the expedition leading to Atlanta's capture, the world's outstanding authority on the subject had this to say:

> The Atlanta campaign would simply have been impossible without the use of the railroad from Louisville to Nashville — one hundred and eighty-five miles — from Nashville to Chattanooga — one hundred and fifty-one miles — and from Chattanooga to Atlanta — one hundred and thirty-seven miles. Every mile of this "single track" was so delicate, that one man could in a minute have broken or removed a rail . . .

The authority was William Tecumseh Sherman, who was in charge. The railroad from Louisville to Nashville, of course, was the Louisville and Nashville. The railroad from Nashville to Chattanooga was the Nashville and Chattanooga, later the Nashville, Chattanooga and St. Louis, and now part of the L&N system. The railroad from Chattanooga to Atlanta was the Western and Atlantic, now also part of the L&N system by lease from its owner, the State of Georgia.

Here I should like to discuss some aspects of the L&N's role in the Civil War, especially the events leading up to the Atlanta campaign. But rather than attempting to rehash battles or to analyze grand strategy, or becoming too much diverted by the dashing John Hunt Morgan, I think it might be useful to beat our way back up the delicate track from Atlanta and pay some attention to the L&N as a railroad company, trying to stay in business in a border state, to fulfill its responsibility to its stockholders, to pay its debts if possible — but inevitably becoming involved in the conflict. In short, I should like to consider its role mainly from the point of view of the Company itself.

Doing that, of course, takes us first to the leadership of the railroad at that time. That leadership rested primarily upon James Guthrie, President, and Albert Fink, Engineer and Superintendent of Roads and Machinery — the one to direct the overall policies of the Company, the other to keep the road operable and the rolling stock in good repair. Both, incidentally, had joined the railroad the same year — 1857. Fink's achievements as engineer, designer and builder of bridges, and railroad executive have been pretty well recognized both generally and by members of The Filson Club. But Guthrie's achievements, perhaps, have been a little neglected.

When Sumter was fired upon, James Guthrie, then in his 69th year, had officially been President only six months. But he had already had a distinguished career, of which a brief reminder might be in order.

Guthrie was born in Bardstown in 1792, of an Irish father who had settled there in 1788. After local schooling and being admitted to the bar, young Guthrie began his public career by running twice — and unsuccessfully — for the General Assembly. He was appointed commonwealth attorney in Louisville in 1827, however, and later served in both houses of the Assembly, representing Jefferson and Bullitt counties in the Senate. In 1835 he was a candidate — unsuccessful again — for the U. S. Senate. In the Kentucky Assembly, he was especially active in committee work dealing with the improvement of roads and rivers and with the establishment of railroads. In 1849 he presided over the convention which made Kentucky's third constitution. He also built up a considerable fortune in Louisville banks and real estate and in railroad promotion.

Guthrie was an outstanding citizen of Louisville: he was a member of the City Council, was active in organizing public schools and the University of Louisville, and served as president of the University from 1847 to 1869. By 1850 he had become one of the leading industrialists and financiers of the South. His political stature, too, is indicated by President Pierce's appointing him Secretary of the Treasury in 1853 (as Secretary he was known as a ruthless reformer, a reducer of debt, and a weeder of incompetents). Retiring from the Treasury in 1857, he was elected Vice-President of the L&N; and, after a controversy between John L. Helm, then President, and the Board of Directors, he succeeded Helm as President October 2, 1860 (though he had actually assumed presidential duties upon Helm's resignation February 21, 1860). He was, incidentally, a prominent candidate for the presidential nomination at the convention of the Democratic Party in Charleston, 1860.

Guthrie was Southern in political sympathies. He believed in states' rights and strongly opposed Lincoln (a fact which did not prevent Lincoln, shortly after he was nominated, from considering Guthrie as a member of his cabinet). But Guthrie was a businessman above all, and he knew that a conflict would be detrimental to his railroad, no matter how Kentucky went. Representing his state both at a futile peace conference in Washington and at the Border State Convention called by Kentucky, he supported the neutrality of Kentucky, and he tried to keep the L&N neutral as long as he could.

"In personal appearance," R. S. Cotterill points out in the *Dictionary of American Biography*, "he was uncouth and unprepossessing . . . He was a man of many eccentricities, of a domineering and arrogant personality, and wholly lacking in the usual graces of a politician. His success in business and politics was chiefly due to his sound judgment and to his reputation for absolute honesty and integrity."

In April 1861 Guthrie's L&N, though chartered in 1850, had sent its first train through to Nashville less than a year and a half earlier. It had just completed its Memphis Branch from Bowling Green to Guthrie, for through service to Memphis (via the Memphis, Clarksville and Louisville Railroad to Paris, then the Memphis and Ohio Railroad to Memphis); and it had a branch line from Lebanon Junction to Lebanon. It had 269 miles of track, 34 locomotives, 28 passenger-train cars, 6 cabooses, 297 freight cars, and a heavy debt. Its equipment was inadequate; much of its roadbed was poor, with considerable track unballasted; and many bridges were more or less temporary (though not, of course, Fink's world-famous bridge over the Green River). Its track, as it were, was indeed in delicate condition.

But the L&N was one of two western north-south lines completed just before the war. The other, the Mobile and Ohio, ran from Mobile to Columbus, Kentucky, 20 miles below Cairo, which was the southern terminus of the Illinois Central. The M&O was paralleled by rivers, however, and Louisville was far more favorably located than Columbus. So upon the L&N fell the main burden of furnishing land transportation of people and goods to and from the South.

II

Before and after the outbreak of hostilities, the South was eager to lay in supplies of all kinds. For a while the L&N throve; sometimes it even had more than it could carry — e.g., on August 31, 1861, Broadway between 9th and 10th was reported piled with freight waiting to go south. The *Annual Report* covering operations from October 1, 1860, to June 30, 1861, states that revenue freight forwarded south during those ten months was 83% of the total hauled. On through business, Louisville to Nashville, of every 100 cars sent, 95 returned empty. Shipments by the L&N during this period, ironically, contributed materially to the South's preparations for war as well as to its own operating revenues.

At first the Federal Government was reluctant to prohibit such traffic, fearful of jolting neutral Kentucky, which had strong Confederate sympathies, toward the South. (Lincoln is reported to have said that he would like to have God on his side, but he must have Kentucky). States on the northern border of Kentucky, however, did try to stop the flow of supplies. In April 1861 Ohio made it treason to furnish enemies of the state or nation with munitions; and Indiana passed a similar law.

Then, on May 2, Secretary of the Treasury Chase forbade shipping munitions and provisions to points controlled by the Confederacy. The three customs officers in Louisville were hard put to enforce the order, and when Cairo was seized by the Federal Government in early May, southbound traffic over the L&N, much of it still illegal, increased. So swamped was the L&N about this time, indeed, that it accepted no shipments from April 29 to May 8. Louisville was the busiest city in the entire Ohio Valley.

During May and early June, Guthrie contended that the Treasury order could hardly apply to a neutral state, and the L&N continued to accept freight to go south. But on June 21, a new Surveyor of the Port of Louisville began requiring permits to ship any articles to points in the area of secession. Guthrie called a Directors' meeting, including those from Tennessee, and arranged a friendly suit to get the matter before a court; and on July 11, Judge Muir, of the Jefferson Circuit Court, ruled the order constitutional. Guthrie, of course, complied. But shippers used many devices to get their contraband south. They carried freight by wagon to smaller stations on the L&N — e.g., to Strawberry Station, Shepherdsville, and Elizabethtown — where it was put aboard trains. Goods were mislabeled or were shipped to towns (like Franklin) just north of the Tennessee line and then smuggled across the border. In August 1861 enough merchandise was billed to Hadensville, near Tennessee, to last the inhabitants of the surrounding countryside a year or more.

Meanwhile, however, all hell had broken loose on the southern end of the railroad. On July 4, by order of Governor Isham Harris of Tennessee, all L&N property in the state was seized by Tennessee State Troops under General Anderson. The reason was suspicion that Guthrie was concentrating the rolling stock in Louisville and not sending Nashville its fair share. Anderson said he would release a passenger train in Nashville for every one sent from Louisville, or would keep all trains seized but not molest others. Guthrie refused both offers.

Then followed an exchange of telegrams between Guthrie and Harris, via Nashville Depot Agent Baldwin (all printed in a supplement to the *Annual Report* for 1861). Guthrie maintained that Tennessee was getting its proper share of rolling stock. Harris, fearful that the L&N would be "occupied by Federal troops," was apprehensive "at any demonstration that threatened to make what [the people of Tennessee] conceived to be a bond of affection an instrument of their destruction." Guthrie stoutly insisted that the charter granted the L&N by Tennessee should be held sacred and that General Anderson was vested with no power to control the management of the L&N or to determine the amount of equipment in Tennessee. He wanted his railroad's property restored, with compensation for losses. The tone of both exchanges was dignified, conciliatory, and firm. But Tennessee won — at least it kept the property seized, including 5 locomotives, 3 passenger-train cars, 67 freight cars, 45 miles of track, and buildings, tools, and supplies. The Company evaluated the property at $110,277.14.

The delicate track had been violated. War had come directly home to the L&N, to stay as an unwelcome guest for nearly three years.

III

Railroads had been used in war before, in a limited way (e.g., in the Mexican War, 1846; in the Crimean War, 1853-55; and in the Italian War, 1859). Some Confederate troops had even been taken to First Bull Run by rail. Though at first neither the North nor the South seemed much aware of the significant part railroads could play in this struggle, railroads and especially railroad junctions soon became major military objectives; and campaigns were planned to destroy or capture lines of value to the enemy. The North began the war with great advantages — 21,000 miles of lines, with adequate rolling stock, repair facilities, and manufactories, as opposed to the South's 9,000 miles, with far poorer organization, equipment, and facilities for upkeep.

The L&N itself soon had its second introduction to the military's realization of the importance of railroads. On September 18, 1861, General Simon Bolivar Buckner, "of the so-called Confederate States," as Guthrie put it, with a small army (about 4,000 men) seized the L&N from the Tennessee state line to Lebanon Junction, plus about half of the remaining rolling stock. Buckner proposed that traffic be resumed on the part of the line under his control, with Guthrie continuing its management and with accounts kept so that the L&N would be fairly recompensed. Buckner even had the depot agent at Russellville write

Guthrie demanding that he, the agent, be authorized by the Board to operate that part of the road. Guthrie declined both propositions without thanks.

On September 20, the Home Guard, under Brigadier-General William Tecumseh Sherman, cleared the track to Elizabethtown, though not before the Confederates had burned three bridges, including one over the Salt River. This was the only part of the Main Stem operated the rest of the year, with constant protection by the Home Guards against raids from Buckner's forces, now established at Bowling Green.

Fink estimated the value of the property taken by Buckner at over $247,000 (the rolling stock included 11 locomotives, 11 passenger-train cars, and about 160 freight cars). Add to this the cost of repair work and the value of the property in Tennessee, and the L&N's total losses in the first six months of war — a neutral railroad in a neutral state — amounted to nearly $378,000. Moreover, it was losing net earnings per annum of some $600,000. Guthrie said that "the profitable business of the road is entirely destroyed."

The result of these activities was that neutrality no longer made sense. Guthrie perforce tied the L&N's fortunes to the Union. Accepting Buckner's demands, he had said, would be "giving aid and comfort to the enemy"; moreover — and here the businessman speaks, a little unrealistically, perhaps — it would be "a violation of the Charter."

Guthrie thereafter worked with Union authorities on plans to invade the Confederacy and — the businessman again — to regain his railroad. Indeed, in October 1861 Secretary of War Cameron came to Louisville and conferred with Guthrie and Sherman. Undoubtedly, Guthrie played an important part in the decision of Federal military authorities to invade the South from Louisville along the line of the L&N, with a flanking movement down the Tennessee and Cumberland Rivers. (Grant's capture of Forts Henry and Donelson in February 1862 opened these rivers to Federal gunboats.) An army was slowly concentrated in Louisville, with General Don Carlos Buell commanding. Locomotives and cars from Northern railroads were diverted to the L&N, many of them being shipped from Cincinnati on flatboats, then pulled to the 10th street depot over a temporary track laid to the canal.

So: the fire to consume Atlanta in the summer of 1864 was laid here in Louisville in the fall of 1861, with James Guthrie, President of the L&N, playing no small incendiary part, while the greater portion of his railroad was occupied — or harassed — by Conferate forces.

IV

The next two and a half years the L&N continued as a private business — it was never taken over by the Federal Government, as were all other roads in the South. But it was, in effect, at war with the Confederate States of America, first defensively, then offensively. Its property was occupied alternately by both sides, as their armies chased each other up and down the line. Retreating Confederates made very sincere efforts to keep the Company from operating, as the *Annual Reports* from 1861-65 vividly show. (Most of what follows here, incidentally, comes from these *Annual Reports,* especially Fink's own accounts entered under the heading of "Reconstruction.")

Late in the fall of 1861 Buell's Federal forces from Louisville began retaking the line south of Elizabethtown and reached the Green River by mid-December, closely followed by Superintendent Fink with his repair crews and bridge builders.

At the Green River, Fink found his renowned bridge — 1000 feet long, 115 feet above the river — partially destroyed: the two southern spans had been deleted by the Confederates. His forces set to work on December 17, installed "tressel" work 390 feet long, 100 feet high (at the highest place), and got the bridge ready for trains three weeks later (January 8, 1862).

On February 15, 1862, Buell's army entered Bowling Green; less than two weeks later he led his advance guard into Nashville; and, as Fink said, "the road south of the Green River passed again into the hands of the Company." But nine depots and the machine shop and engine house at Bowling Green had been burned, and the track had been torn up in many places (for one instance, between mile 87 and mile 91, 3¾ miles of track had been destroyed). All rolling stock had been either destroyed or left in bad repair; of 16 locomotives purloined ten were recovered, but only two were available for service.

Wrote Fink: "On the last day of February, the track was repaired and the road in running order to the Barren River [at Bowling Green]." Unfortunately, the day before the Federal forces reached there, the Confederates had blown up the bridge. But on April 8, 1862, the first trains from Louisville to Nashville since July 4, 1861, were operating. Actually, they stopped at Edgefield across the Cumberland from Nashville. The fine new 700-foot L&N bridge there, destroyed by the Confederates, had to be rebuilt by the Government and was not opened until June 11.

Meanwhile, the principal predator of the L&N had made his appearance. On March 15, Colonel John Hunt Morgan had suddenly turned up at Gallatin, 26 miles to the rear of the Federal army; there he captured a train, damaged the locomotive, and burned 13 cars and the water house. On May 11, he appeared at Cave City, 100 miles north of Nashville, destroying both a freight and a passenger train. From these practice missions, apparently, he became addicted to a very annoying habit — i.e., of tearing up the L&N at every opportunity.

The L&N's total loss so far in the war, as of June 30, 1862, was estimated at $663,307.42: $386,971.04 for damage and repair, $281,336.38 for estimated losses in traffic revenues. A staggering sum it was for a small debt-and-war-ridden railroad.

While Albert Fink, with some help from the Federal Army, was restoring the delicate track to Nashville in the first half of 1862, James Guthrie was looking after the Company's business iterests back home. In May he received orders from the Government that soldiers and government freight should be carried at reduced rates; but he protested vigorously. The L&N, he said, had not been represented in the conference of railroad presidents in Washington the previous February, when these rates were made. Moreover, unlike most railroads in the North, the L&N had practically no two-way traffic as nearly everything went south. Such rates would not even meet expenses, especially as the L&N was heavily burdened by war damage and continually open to attack. Quartermaster-General Meigs was not amenable; but in March 1863, Guthrie's third protest was successful. The Government would allow the L&N higher rates if it would pay for rebuilding the temporary bridge over the Cumberland built by Buell's engineers. Guthrie agreed, and the L&N ultimately paid $33,000 for it.

The L&N had hardly reopened the road in the summer of 1862, however, before the Confederates again manifested their destructive talents. Indeed, as Fink said in the *Annual Report* of 1863 (ending the fiscal year at June 30), the L&N had been open its entire length only seven months and twelve days during the past year. Parts of the Main Stem and all branches had been at one time or another in possession of Confederate forces, except 20 miles north and 20 miles south of Bowling Green. For a period of two weeks, trains dared not even leave Louisville. All bridges and trestles on the Main Stem and branches except four had been destroyed and rebuilt during the year, some twice, and some even thrice (only four of the original bridges were left). Exactly 7,263 lineal feet of bridge and trestlework had been destroyed, not counting additional for that destroyed several times.

A few samples from Fink's "Reconstruction" report of 15½ pages may suggest how railroading looked to the management of the Company, from July 1, 1862, to June 30, 1863.

On July 11, Morgan captured the Federal forces at Lebanon, destroying government stores. On August 12, he took Gallatin, including the Federal garrison. A train of 29 cars and two nearby bridges he carefully annihilated. He also overcame the Federals at Tunnel Hill, seven miles north of Gallatin, and set the timberwork support of the roof and sides of the tunnel afire (by pushing burning box cars into the tunnel). The resultant cave-in filled 800 feet of the tunnel with debris to the average height of 12 feet.

Two days later L&N workmen sent out to begin repairing were driven off by Confederates. Fink himself went out the 15th, but the workers would not stay without protection. Fink tried to get help, but Federal forces were too pressed at that time to spare a sufficient guard.

On September 1, General Kirby Smith's army, invading Kentucky from Knoxville, defeated the Federals at Richmond, took Lexington, and threatened Cincinnati. His raiders partially destroyed the newly rebuilt Salt River Bridge at Shepherdsville on September 7. On September 8, however, Fink and his forces were on the scene and reopened the bridge on the 13th.

Meanwhile, the western prong of the Confederate invasion under General Braxton Bragg had left Chattanooga and started up the L&N. On September 12, Bragg was at Cave City; on September 17, he captured the Federal garrison at Munfordville and burned the rebuilt Green River Bridge. General Buell, with his Federal Army from Nashville, began racing Bragg to Louisville. But Bragg diverged east to Bardstown; and on the 25th, Buell's army began arriving in Louisville.

On September 28, Confederate raiders took Shepherdsville, and in a leisurely three-day period destroyed the Salt River Bridge again. Buell retook Shepherdsville October 3 — and on October 11 trains passed over the bridge (450 feet long, 46 feet over the stream), which Fink and his crew had rebuilt. They continued their rebuilding journey southward until they reached the Green River on October 19, ready to begin on that bridge. Then word came that Morgan had turned up behind them, nullifying several other bridges. But Fink opened the Green River Bridge on November 1, got the rest of the line in operation to Tunnel Hill by November 11, and had the tunnel cleared by November 25. And again trains were running from Louisville to Nashville.

Exactly one month later, December 25 — to no one's surprise, probably — Morgan's addiction became apparent again. (It was, I suspect, less a matter of season's greetings than a celebration of his recent promotion to Brigadier-General.) This time, from Bacon Creek, eight miles north of Munfordville, he worked his way up the line, meticulously demolishing the L&N for a stretch of 35 miles. He captured the Federal garrison at Elizabethtown; he overcame the guard at Muldraugh's Hill and burned all the heavy trestles there; he sent squads to within 28 miles of Louisville to knock out bridges. (This was, incidentally, Morgan's last visit to the Main Stem. He called only once more on the L&N, at Lebanon on July 4, 1863.)

But by February 1, 1863, trains were running to Nashville — and pretty regularly, says Fink, except for guerilla raids, which were the main bother after that.

Fink's estimate of damage to Company property during the past fiscal year was $135,808.30, with $229,470.07 spent for repairing it. He ended his report with a tribute to the employes, who, he said, "thus have not only deserved the thanks of the Company, but also the thanks of their country, in whose service this Road has been almost exclusively operated since the beginning of this war."

V

The L&N's main service to its country during this period was supplying the Federal Army of the Cumberland in Tennessee. All available rolling stock, plus government cars and engines, were put to full use. As the course of the Federal invading armies swung toward Chattanooga in mid-1863, more and more supplies, troops, and prisoners were carried by the L&N. The government helped by transferring increasing amounts of equipment to the L&N, especially from captured Southern lines (which had the same five-foot gauge as L&N). And in July 1863 Guthrie's pleas for greater protection for trains and properties was answered; a fifty-man military guard was assigned to each train.

Everyone worked hard, said Fink, and praise instead of complaint should have been forthcoming. But Federal military authorities in the South nonetheless complained. "It seemed to be taken for granted," Fink observed, "that because the Road could not carry as much freight as the Army of the Cumberland then chanced to require, it must necessarily be badly managed." Despite the Company's attempts to do all it could to improve service, General Rosecrans wrote Guthrie in the fall of 1863 that he would confiscate the entire line if supplies were not transported more quickly. In November, Grant himself grumbled about the service. Guthrie, not one to be pushed around by anybody, insisted that the L&N was doing all in its power. (Throughout this controversy, incidentally, he retained the confidence of Lincoln and Stanton.) In any event, Guthrie kept the management, and the Federal armies in Tennessee continued to depend on the lines from Louisville for troops and supplies.

Problems increased, however, when the Government seized L&N equipment for service on roads further south. From July 1863 to July 1864, it took 25 locomotives and 191 cars; in July 1864 — while the Battle of Atlanta was raging — it had 218 L&N cars in its possession, half the entire number owned by the Company. The main reason, of course, was that when Sherman began advancing from Chattanooga to Atlanta in May 1864, he grabbed every L&N car he could find. When

Guthrie remonstrated, Sherman suggested that he might borrow cars which came to Jeffersonville on Northern Roads. Guthrie followed the suggestion.

The crucial part the L&N and its connecting lines played in Sherman's invasion of Georgia is indicated by these data: every day for 200 days, by the time of the Atlanta campaign, an average of 160 cars rolled over delicate track of the L&N, the N&C, and the W&A to supply Sherman's men, horses, and guns. Sherman well knew his hazardous position, hundreds of miles deep in enemy territory, dependent almost wholly on this single railroad line, as indicated in the quotation at the beginning of these remarks. But it was not merely that the campaign would have been impossible. Should the delicate track be completely severed, his whole force faced isolation and, in all probability, annihilation. In the entire countryside, moreover, there was simply not enough food and forage — not to mention ammunition, hospital supplies, and other military necessities — to support his huge force of 100,000 men and 35,000 animals. But the railroad line held. And, as Colonel Robert S. Henry says, "The campaign which resulted in the fall of Atlanta . . . was the final deciding factor of the Confederate War."

The Atlanta campaign involved the most extensive, most carefully planned, and most dangerous use of railroads in the war, which, as Colonel Henry says, was "the first real railroad war." And, should anyone think I am exaggerating the L&N's participation in it, let me quote another railroad historian. Says Stewart Holbrook in his *Story of American Railroads:* "Possibly, in view of its great help in Sherman's final campaign, as well as the continuous aid it had given to other Northern commands, the L&N could be rated as a major factor in winning the war so far as transportation was concerned." Sherman himself said: ". . . I have always felt grateful to Mr. Guthrie, of Louisville, who had sense enough and patriotism enough to subordinate the interest of his railroad company to the cause of his country."

Considering all it had to go through, the L&N came out very well indeed — not only because of its strategic location but because of the superb leadership of an elderly man (Guthrie was 73 when the war ended) and a young one (Fink was 38). The L&N had done its job, served its country, and made money. Though its total war damage was estimated by Fink as over $688,000 (including $94,000 worth by guerillas the last year of the war), its net profits, 1861-65, were a little better than $6,000,000. It was ready to carry on its peacetime business by improving its equipment and lengthening its track, now getting over its delicate quality. In the *Annual Report* for 1865, for example, Fink noted that during the past year the L&N had bought eight new locomotives and had built 139 new passenger and freight cars in its shops. He also hoped that the U. S. Government would replace 67 freight cars destroyed south of Nashville, "for which," he said rather wistfully, "we have as yet received no compensation."

Governmental recognition of Guthrie's managerial abilities had been attested to by his being again invited to become Secretary of the Treasury when Chase resigned in July 1864. He had declined, saying he could be of more use where he was. But after hostilities ended, he was finally elected to the Senate where he supportd Johnson's policies and strongly opposed the reconstruction measures of Congress. Resigning because of ill health in February 1868, he died a year later (March 1869).

Fink was elected Vice-President of the L&N in 1870 and, after resigning from the Company in 1875, became one of the ablest transportation economists and statesmen of his day.

As for one of the other principals in this story, Brigadier-General John Hunt Morgan, everyone knows of his famous excursion into Indiana and Ohio; his capture, imprisonment, and escape; and his death in Greeneville, Tennessee, in September 1864. But I cannot resist mentioning here one of the many ironies of that war and ultimate peace: Brigadier-General Basil Duke, Morgan's brother-in-law and second in command, later became a valued member of the L&N's Law Department — in fact, its chief lobbyist in Frankfort. There he was constantly alert to forestall attempts to impede the operation and prosperity of the L&N by the peaceful means of hostile legislation.

The L&N today, with nearly 6,000 miles of main line in 13 states, over 730 diesel locomotives, almost 60,000 freight cars, and 450 passenger-train cars, scarcely resembles the little railroad whose delicate track helped end a war almost a century ago. But it is still a proud railroad, with strong track — and it is by no means unaware of its significant role in that lamentable struggle.

BIBLIOGRAPHY

Bibliographical Note: I list below the principal sources consulted in the preparation of this paper. I should also like to express my gratitude to my former colleague, Mr. Kincaid Herr, for many valuable suggestions.

Black, Robert C., III, *The Railroads of the Confederacy*. Chapel Hill, 1952.

Brown, Dee Alexander, *The Bold Cavaliers*. Philadelphia, 1959.

Chanute, O., Rudolph Fink, and H. G. Prout, "Memoir of Albert Fink." *Transactions of the American Society of Civil Engineers*, XLI (June 1899), 626-638.

Cotterill, R. S., "The Louisville and Nashville Railroad; 1861-1865." *The American Historical Review*, XXIX (July 1924), 700-715.

Dictionary of American Biography. 22 Vols. New York, 1928-1958.
Henry, Robert Selph, *This Fascinating Railroad Business.*
   Indianapolis, 1942.
Herr, Kincaid A., *The Louisville & Nashville Railroad:* 1850-1940, 1941-1959.
   Louisville, 1959.
Holbrook, Stewart H., *The Story of American Railroads,* New York, 1947.
Louisville & Nashville Railroad Company, *Annual Reports,* 1861-1865.
Memoirs of Gen. W. T. Sherman, Written by Himself. 4th Edition. New York, 1891.
Milton, Ellen Fink, *A Biography of Albert Fink.* Rochester, 1951.
Needham, Charles K., "The Life and Achievements of Albert Fink." A paper presented to The Filson Club, Louisville, October 4, 1920.
Tanner, James F., "The Louisville and Nashville Railroad to 1866."
   Bloomington: Unpublished Master's Thesis, Indiana University, 1932.
Tilford, John E., Jr., "The Three Railroad Careers of Albert Fink." *The Filson Club History Quarterly,* XXXIII (October 1959), 296-303.
Turner, George Edgar, *Victory Rode the Rails.* Indianapolis, 1953.

JOHN E. TILFORD, JR. (1912–   ), a native of Georgia, received his B.A. and M.A. degrees from Emory University and his Ph.D. from the University of Michigan. Tilford taught in the Georgia public schools and at Emory. From 1957 to 1961 he worked as an assistant to the president of the L & N. Since 1961 he has been at Jacksonville University. He is the author of several articles dealing with literary and historical topics in various professional journals.

This article first appeared in *The Filson Club History Quarterly* in July 1962, vol. 36, pp. 209–21.

IV.

THE LATE NINETEENTH CENTURY

WILLIAM GOEBEL AND THE CAMPAIGN FOR RAILROAD REGULATION IN KENTUCKY, 1888-1900

By Nicholas C. Burckel*
Racine, Wisconsin

William Goebel has been an enigma to historians since his assassination in 1900. Detractors have painted him as the unscrupulous politician whose overweening ambition drove him to sponsor undemocratic and partisan legislation that paved the way for his illegal ascension to the governorship after his defeat at the polls. Goebel's admirers, on the other hand, have seen him as the youthful David pitted against the corporate Goliath who sought to exploit the people. Such rhetorical polarity does little to set the record straight and the fact that none of Goebel's manuscripts have survived makes the job of evaluating the man difficult. As any non-partisan might assume, a reconstruction of the events surrounding Goebel's State Senate career and his gubernatorial campaign reveals Goebel as neither devil nor angel. He was, in fact, a transitional figure in the turn-of-the-century politics of state and nation, for he combined elements of populism of the 1880s and '90s with aspects of progressivism which characterized the first two decades of the twentieth century. That he was also a hard-headed politician who rode railroad regulation into office should not be a startling revelation to historians familiar with recent studies of progressivism in Wisconsin.[1]

Goebel came to Kentucky from Pennsylvania at a time when Democracy ruled the Bluegrass state. Not only had Democrats managed to control the state in the years immediately following the Civil War, but they had successfully fought off the political threat of radical Republicans, and intimidated black voters. As is frequently the case when a single party is in the ascendancy for a long time, the Democratic party began to show signs of internal stress between emerging New South advocates and conservative Bourbons. These New South Democrats, led by Henry Watterson, editor of the Louisville *Courier-Journal*, wished to de-emphasize the racial issue and the importance of a Confederate background for political preferment, and to emphasize instead industrialization of the state.

---

*Nicholas C. Burckel, Ph.D., is Director, University Archives & Area Research Center at the University of Wisconsin—Parkside, Kenosha, Wisc.

[1] Stanley P. Caine, *The Myth of a Progressive Reform: Railroad Regulation in Wisconsin, 1903-1910* (Madison: The State Historical Society of Wisconsin, 1970); David P. Thelen, *The New Citizenship: Origins of Progressivism in Wisconsin, 1885-1900* (Columbia: University of Missouri Press, 1971).

Although Democrats continued to win elections, the internal problems steadily reduced their margin of victory. In 1895 the Republicans capitalized on Democratic division to elect William O. Bradley governor. Bradley's Democratic opponent was free silver advocate P. Wat Hardin, and his narrow defeat was a prelude to a Republican presidential victory the following year. When William Jennings Bryan won the Democratic presidential nomination with his "Cross of Gold" speech in 1896, many of Kentucky's New South Democrats bolted the party. Men like Watterson believed the free-silver issue was an unsound Populist idea that had no place in the Democratic party. In the ensuing election, therefore, McKinley carried the state over Bryan because of this defection of gold Democrats.[2]

This set the stage for the horripilating gubernatorial campaign of 1899 between Republican State Attorney General William S. Taylor and Democratic State Senator and majority leader William Goebel. Seething from the twin defeats of 1895 and 1896, Democratic leaders tried to reconcile their differences in an effort to reassert their accustomed hegemony by 1900. In 1899 the issue of free-silver, while not resolved, receded into the background and gold Democrats returned to the party. In place of free-silver, Democratic gubernatorial contender Goebel emphasized the necessity of governmental regulation of corporations.

In particular, railroad regulation had been a touchstone of Goebel's political career. By the time he won his party's gubernatorial nomination, he had served twelve years in the Kentucky State Senate, representing the Covington area in northern Kentucky. While still a young man he established himself as a prosperous attorney, but he also nurtured political ambitions. In 1887 he sought and won a seat in the State Senate running on the Democratic ticket from Kenton County. From that time until his gubernatorial race, he built a reputation as a leading proponent of state regulation of big business, specifically, railroad regulation.

During Goebel's first term in the Senate, the State Railroad Commission drastically increased to over three million dollars the tax valuation on the property of the Louisville and Nashville Railroad Company, the largest rail network operating throughout the state. Disturbed by so abrupt an action, the Louisville and Nashville, through its president Milton H. Smith and chief lobbyist General Basil W. Duke, reacted with expected pressure on the legislature at Frankfort. In response, one legislator introduced a bill to abolish the Railroad Commission and overturn its ruling. After heated debate the bill narrowly passed the

---

[2] Thomas D. Clark, *A History of Kentucky* (Lexington: The John Bradford Press, 1950), pp. 409-413, 426-434.

House, but met strong opposition in the Senate. Democratic Senator Cassius M. Clay of Bourbon County presented a resolution providing for the establishment of a joint investigatory committee to take testimony and report to the General Assembly on the question of the railroad lobby and its influence on legislation.[3]

Goebel supported the resolution, served on the investigating committee, and drafted the report based on the committee's hearings. The legislative committee found that the L&N hired lobbyists who operated open houses in Frankfort during the legislative session. They spent lavishly, furnishing drinks and dinners at saloons and restaurants, and, of course, gave anyone of probable influence free railroad passes. The committee returned a unanimous resolution seeking an indictment of these lobbyists by a Franklin County Grand Jury. Although the General Assembly failed to take positive action on the committee's recommendations the report had the effect of killing the pending bill which would have abolished the Railroad Commission.[4]

Goebel's action at the Constitutional Convention of 1890 sheds added light on his attitude toward the railroads. He had been instrumental in procuring a favorable Senate vote for holding a convention to write a new constitution to replace Kentucky's inadequate and cumbersome ante-bellum constitution. During debates in the Frankfort convention, Goebel took the lead in shaping that part of the constitution dealing with corporations. He typified many of the delegates' agrarian, anti-corporation bias and singled out the railroad as their most menacing enemy. Convention debates were hottest on the issue of rate regulation, elimination of rebates, and pooling.[5]

Goebel wished to provide specifically for a railroad commission in the new constitution. He reasoned that if the commission were part of the constitution, the legislature could not then abolish it by legislative fiat, as had nearly happened at the preceding session. Abolishing the commission under Goebel's scheme required a popularly approved constitutional amendment. By this provision Goebel hoped to vitiate the influence of the railroads over the legislature.[6]

Mindful of the influence of railroads in the legislature and seeking to forestall efforts to delete his proposal, Goebel argued persuasively for incorporation of the railroad commission into the constitution:

---

[3] *The Courier-Journal* (Louisville), October 17, 26, 1899.
[4] *Journal of the Regular Session of the Kentucky Senate, 1887*, pp. 1751-1754; Jesse Sewell Hunter, The Kentucky Constitutional Convention of 1890 (unpublished M. A. thesis, University of Louisville, 1947), p. 57.
[5] *Official Report of the Proceedings and Debates in the Convention Assembled at Frankfort, on the Eighth Day of September, 1890, to Adopt, Amend or Change the Constitution of the State of Kentucky* (IV vols., Frankfort: E. Polk Johnson, 1890), I: pp. 1506-1509; IV: pp. 4979-5182, 5382-5386.
[6] *The Courier-Journal* (Louisville), October 26, 1899.

> When the law establishing the present system was enacted, it was assailed in the first place by the railroads in the Courts. . . . When the railroads failed in their assault upon that system in the Courts, they came to the General Assembly and undertook to abolish the system, and the Railroad Commission also by repealing the law establishing them. The largest and most aggressive lobby that Frankfort has seen within a quarter of a century was brought here to accomplish that end. The effect succeeded in the House, but failed in the Senate. If the effort had been to enact the law, instead of repeal it, it would have failed, because one branch of the General Assembly was hostile to the law. . . .[7]

Goebel carried the vote preserving the Railroad Commission as part of the new constitution. Along with a majority of the convention, he also supported the method of railroad property tax valuation that other states were not to adopt until the turn of the century. Voters endorsed the constitution in 1891 by a majority of nearly 150,000 votes.[8]

During the legislative session of 1893, Goebel helped guide through the Senate a bill further extending state control over railroads. The proposal forbade unreasonable passenger and freight rates and prohibited rebates and long and short haul rates which arbitrarily discriminated against certain localities. The Railroad Commission was empowered to investigate all complaints against the roads and file its evidence with the appropriate circuit courts. Arguing that the bill was too restrictive, Democratic Governor John Young Brown vetoed it. The General Assembly ignored Brown's admonitions and repassed the bill over his veto.[9]

Senator Goebel not only supported legislative efforts to regulate railroads, but also worked to abolish railroad companies' abuses of employees. When representatives of the Brotherhood of Locomotive Engineers and Conductors sent a delegation to Frankfort seeking support for labor union legislation, he became their advocate on the Senate floor. One of the bills Goebel supported limited the number of hours per day that railroad employees be required to work. Another bill required that conductors and engineers meet certain qualifications designed to guarantee their own safety and that of their passengers and freight.[10]

In 1894 when the American Railway Union inaugurated a sympathy strike supporting Pullman workers, the state court issued injunctions against many railroad employees who honored the strike. Goebel sided with the jailed railway workers, posted bond for several, and se-

---

[7] *Official . . . Debates in the Convention. . . .*, IV: p. 5809.
[8] Hunter, The Kentucky Constitutional Convention of 1890, pp. 41-42.
[9] *Kentucky Acts of 1893*, Chapter 171, p. 612; Thomas D. Clark, "The People, William Goebel, and the Kentucky Railroads," *Journal of Southern History*, Vol. V, No. 1 (February, 1939), pp. 36-37.
[10] *The Courier-Journal* (Louisville), October 26, 1899.

cured their release during investigation of the charges. He successfully defended them in court without charge.[11]

To end what he considered another railroad abuse of labor, Goebel introduced a "fellow-servant" bill. The bill stipulated that, in the event of injury to a worker through no fault of his own, the injured person would be justly compensated by his employer. Previously, the railroads had investigated such accidents, and if they found that injury was a result of another employee's negligence, he, not the railroad, became liable. Thus the railroads often had not borne the financial burden of the many accidents that occurred on their lines yearly.

Arguing his case before the Senate, Goebel reasoned that "the liability of railroad corporations to their own employees should be exactly the same that it is to the tramp upon the highway."[12] By this he meant simply that the railroad should do for its employees at least what, in law, it was bound to do for anyone injured on its property. The bill passed both the House and Senate, but after the legislature adjourned, Republican Governor William O. Bradley vetoed it.

During the 1898 session of the legislature, Senator Goebel continued his campaign against the railroads. He supported a bill submitted by Charles C. McChord, Democratic Senator from Washington County, which subsequently became known as the McChord Bill. Previous to his election to the Senate, he had served as a member and chairman of the Railroad Commission and had supported Goebel in the 1890 convention debates on railroad issues. McChord's Bill was "a masterpiece of legislative drafting," which evidenced his extensive knowledge of the intricacies of railroad operation and related state and federal laws.[13]

The McChord Bill gave the Railroad Commission the power to call hearings on any written complaint the Commission received after a ten-day notice to the parties involved. The Commission would then determine the validity of the case and adjust the rates accordingly. In addition the bill gave the Commission authority to determine the guilt of the railroad companies. The McChord Bill produced violent arguments and heated exchanges both in and out of the legislative chambers and even Democrats differed among themselves over the stringency of the bill. Much of the editorial reaction in the state press was negative. Colonel W. C. P. Breckinridge of the Lexington *Herald* wrote a series of editorials castigating the bill and its two major supporters, Goebel and McChord. The influential and regularly Democratic Louisville *Courier-Journal* indicated its lack of enthusiasm for the bill by making only perfunctory reference to it in the course of news reporting, and

---

[11] *Ibid.*
[12] *Ibid.*
[13] Clark, "The People, William Goebel, and the Kentucky Railroads," p. 39.

avoiding significant editorial comment. In spite of this lack of support, Goebel persuaded the Democratic caucus to vote for the McChord Bill and send it on to the Governor. Governor Bradley exercised his veto and the Democratic legislature failed to overrule him.[14]

Aside from railroad regulation, Goebel's reform record was uneven. Nothing illustrates this better than his support in the 1898 legislature of the controversial Chinn Textbook and Goebel Election bills. It is doubtful that Goebel consciously formulated the McChord Bill and these last two bills as planks in a platform upon which to seek the governor's office the following year. But these bills did form an important part of the Democratic state platform which his supporters wrote at the Louisville convention a little over a year later.

Senator J. Morton Chinn, Goebel's close friend and later personal bodyguard, introduced the first of these bills. Chinn's bill sought to end an alleged monopoly of the American Book Company which supplied the state public school textbooks. Its major provisions were similar to those of an Indiana law which set the price of textbooks and stated that any bookseller who charged more was guilty of a misdemeanor and was punishable by fine or imprisonment. After a warm debate which at one point threatened violence, the Chinn Bill failed, all Republicans and some Democrats opposing it. A milder alternative bill, proposed by fellow Democrat C. J. Bronston of Lexington, also failed because of a squabble among the Democrats. The fact that even Democrats were divided on the Goebel-supported Chinn Bill, however, did not stop the Democrats from making it a campaign issue in the next election.[15]

The last of three bills which Goebel championed during this session was the election bill bearing his name. Goebel sought to outlaw the practice of locally appointing election officers which he felt had robbed Bryan of Kentucky in 1896. Democrats were quick to point out that in areas where McKinley was strong, as in Jefferson (Louisville) County, Bryan men had been denied representation on election boards, either as inspectors or official challengers. The critical balance which gave the state to Governor Bradley in 1895 and to McKinley the following year appeared in these counties.[16]

Rankled by these narrow losses, Democratic legislators wanted to modify the law regulating appointment of election officers. Goebel's bill proposed that the legislature select the three state election commissioners. These commissioners would in turn name the county election commissioners who would then select the officers to preside at the poll-

---

[14] *Lexington Herald*, January-March, 1898.
[15] *The Courier-Journal* (Louisville), October 26, 1899; Clark, "The People, William Goebel, and the Kentucky Railroads," pp. 41-42.
[16] *The New York Times*, September 2, 1899.

ing places. Ostensibly the aim of the bill was laudable, but in practice, it proved as discriminatory as the law it replaced. There was no provision in the bill for equal party representation on the county boards. Thus a Democratic legislature could control the statewide network of election officers merely by appointing Democratic state election commissioners. The Goebel Bill became law when the legislature, on a strict party vote, passed it over Governor Bradley's veto in 1898.[17]

So partisan a law was bound to stir strong feelings, and it tarnished Goebel's image as a reform spokesman. Why then did he so vigorously support it? Goebel's opponents charged he planned to use it as a rear door to the governor's office. If that were true, then why did the bill provide that a majority of the State Board of Election Commissioners had the authority to determine any contested election *except* for governor or lieutenant governor? That section of the law remained as Goebel had originally submitted it, and he was too experienced a legislator not to have intended that exception.[18]

In addition, Goebel's authorship and original enthusiasm for the act are questionable. An editorial in the Louisville *Courier-Journal*, a Democratic newspaper which opposed the bill, suggested that the "Goebel Election Law" was a misnomer. The editorial suggested that Goebel sponsored it only because certain elements in the Democratic party so vehemently argued for it. Rather than risk losing his party leadership over the issue, he reluctantly introduced the election bill.[19]

In a letter to the editor, fellow Democrat and sponsor of a rival bill to the Goebel-supported Chinn Textbook Bill, C. J. Bronston recalled a long conversation with Goebel. In that two-hour exchange, Bronston became convinced that Goebel sponsored the bill only to gain support for his own reforms which he was unwilling to see scuttled by a coalition of Republicans and Democrats. Defending Goebel, Bronston wrote:

> He still adhered to the end desired to be accomplished, namely, the restriction of corporate power to such an extent as to place corporations as nearly as possible upon the same footing as individuals in bearing the burdens of government and enjoying its privileges; to adopt a uniform and economic system of internal affairs, generally, and not to incumber legislation with personal matters. . . . The election law, which was not only originated, but prepared, by one of those friends . . . met with such a disapproval on his part that it was not until a very late state in the session that he [Goebel] at last yielded. . . .[20]

Outvoted in the legislature, Republicans appealed to the courts which

---

[17] Urey Woodson, *The First New Dealer: William Goebel* (Louisville: The Standard Press, 1939), pp. 198-202.
[18] *The Courier-Journal* (Louisville), October 30, 1899. Italics added.
[19] *Ibid.*, February 5, 13, 1900   [20] *Ibid.*, February 19, 1900.

declared the law constitutional. By then the law had become a campaign issue for both parties. Goebel recognized its inequity but defended it as a Democratic measure. In fact, following the 1899 election, Democratic Senator-elect J. C. S. Blackburn said that the law had worked against Goebel and had cost the state ticket some 20,000 votes.[21]

After the legislature adjourned, William Goebel returned home to mend political fences and to determine his chances of success in the forthcoming Democratic gubernatorial campaign. In early spring of 1899 the three avowed candidates, Goebel, P. Wat Hardin (whom Goebel had supported for the governorship in 1895) and ex-Confederate soldier-turned-politician, William J. Stone, stumped the state for county convention support. By the time of the state convention in Louisville during the latter part of June, Goebel trailed both his rivals.[22]

Each candidate had his obvious strength: Hardin attracted a large following on the basis of his free silver stand in the 1895 gubernatorial campaign and was the best known of the candidates; Stone came from the solidly Democratic first district and, as a crippled ex-Confederate soldier, had the sympathy of the southern-oriented Democracy. To counter-balance these attractions Goebel needed something bold and new to win sizable Democratic support. After all, he was only forty-two years old, had not served or been in sympathy with the Confederate cause, had come to Kentucky from Pennsylvania, and was not widely known outside his own senatorial district. During his pre-convention campaign he played down the Goebel Election Law, concentrating instead on the necessity of governmental regulation of corporations, railroads, and trusts. All three Democratic gubernatorial candidates endorsed William Jennings Bryan for President and J. C. S. Blackburn for United States Senator.[23]

At the riotous nine-day "Music Hall" convention in Louisville occasional fist fights or song fests interrupted normal proceedings. All of the hoopla, however, did not cloud Goebel's thinking. He realized his only hope of winning the nomination was through a coalition with Stone to prevent Hardin's first ballot nomination. Under this arrangement Stone and Goebel delegations dominated the convention and wrote a platform based largely on the reform measures which Goebel had supported in the Senate or which he had proposed on the hustings.[24]

---

[21] R. E. Hughes, F. W. Schaefer, and E. L. Williams, *That Kentucky Campaign; or the Law, the Ballot and the People in the Goebel-Taylor Contest* (Cincinnati: The Robert Clarke Company, 1900), p. 8; Woodson, *William Goebel*, pp. 201-202.
[22] Clark, "The People, William Goebel, and the Kentucky Railroads," p. 42; Woodson, *William Goebel*, p. 141.
[23] Hughes, *et al.*, *That Kentucky Campaign*, p. 12; Woodson, *William Goebel*, p. 141.
[24] *The Courier-Journal* (Louisville), June 22-24, 1899; Hughes, *et al.*, *That Kentucky Campaign*, pp. 16-42; Woodson, *William Goebel*, p. 148.

The Goebel-controlled platform committee wrote planks calling for an end to tariffs which discriminated in favor of corporate wealth, and for the endorsement of major Democratic legislation of the last session, including the Chinn Textbook Bill; the prison reform bill; the McChord Railroad Bill; and the Goebel Election Law. Aside from reference to specific trusts in other planks, one plank addressed itself to anti-trust legislation generally:

> We believe the . . . anti-trust law, should be so amended as to make unlawful any arrangement . . . whereby in carrying on any business the prices charged are to be thereby fixed, controlled or regulated. We believe the law should be further amended so as to provide that all contracts and agreements made by combinations, generally known as trusts . . . with the view to fix or regulate prices, should be void and not enforceable as to such trust or combination.[25]

After the convention voted adoption of the platform written mainly by Goebel men, Hardin realized that Stone and Goebel had combined against him, and to avoid certain defeat, he quietly withdrew his candidacy. In the ensuing turmoil of balloting which saw the subsequent reentry of Hardin into the race and frequent charges of political dealing, Goebel won the nomination on the twenty-sixth ballot.[26]

After the Louisville convention ended, opposition to Goebel's nomination continued. John Young Brown, former governor and Goebel supporter, led a revolt of dissident Democrats who called themselves "Honest Election Democrats" and who received major financial support from Goebel's most powerful corporate opponent, the Louisville and Nashville Railroad. The Honest Election Democrats met at Lexington to nominate Brown in early August shortly before the Republican state convention met there. For governor the Republicans nominated William S. Taylor, attorney general under Governor William O. Bradley, in a quiet convention, and they wrote an equally innocuous platform, praising the administrations of Governor Bradley and President McKinley.[27]

While Republicans were holding their state convention, Goebel formally opened his gubernatorial bid in the western Kentucky town of Mayfield. His initial speech indicated the type of campaign he was to pursue. Launching into a diatribe against his old enemy, the Louisville

---

[25] Copy of platform recorded in typescript "History of Goebelism," in the *Temple Bodley Collection*, The Filson Club, Louisville, Kentucky; *The Courier-Journal* (Louisville), June 25, 1899; Hughes, *et al., That Kentucky Campaign*, pp. 22-23.

[26] *The New York Times*, June 24-29, 1899; *The Courier-Journal* (Louisville), June 22-29, 1899; Hughes, *et al., That Kentucky Campaign*, pp. 16-42.

[27] *The New York Times*, June 30, July 25, 26, 28, August 2, 3, 4, 1899; Hughes, *et al., That Kentucky Campaign*, xiv (Introduction); Woodson, *William Goebel*, pp. 164-165; *The Courier-Journal* (Louisville), August 3, 4, 5, 12, 13, 14, 1899; *Lexington Herald*, August 2, 3, 4, 12, 13, 14, 1899.

and Nashville Railroad, he ended with a defense of the vetoed McChord Bill and a plea for the voters to decide "whether the L&N is the servant or the master of the people."[28]

During a speech at Danville he took the L&N to task, reviewing his own efforts at railroad regulation. He mentioned that Louisville attorney Theodore Hallan was one of several lobbyists at Frankfort, who, along with railroad president Milton Smith and Basil Duke, worked assiduously and spent lavishly to convince the legislature to repeal the law creating the State Board of Railroad Commissioners. They failed then, as they had failed in the Constitutional Convention of 1890, to abolish the Railroad Commission, Goebel stressed. Concluding his attack on the railroads he declared, "I believe that the railroad corporations should have a bit in their mouths and the Democratic party should hold the bridle."[29]

In mid-September, while speaking before a large crowd at Carlisle, Goebel linked his own campaign against railroad monopoly with Andrew Jackson's battle with the Bank of the United States:

> We have in Kentucky in this campaign a parallel to the campaign in the United States which made Jackson President a second time. The bank at that time had only one-tenth the capital that the Louisville and Nashville has, and it was owned in the United States, and not in Europe. I believe that as the people of the United States crushed Nicholas Biddle and the United States Bank, the people of Kentucky will not submit to the domination of this foreign-owned corporation. . . . You should remember, too that all the matter in those two papers [*The Louisville Dispatch* and *Post*] . . . is an expression of the will and the wish of a corporation which is owned in Lombard Street, London.[30]

Goebel used this same xenophobic attack on the L&N at other times, as for instance, at Elizabethtown, just south of Louisville. He read a letter from August Belmont, Chairman of the Board of L&N, in which Belmont accused Goebel of deception in calling the railroad a foreign corporation. Goebel countered by asserting that nearly half of the stock in the lines was held in Europe, if not London.[31]

As the campaign intensified and speaking engagements increased, Goebel continued to hammer away at the Louisville and Nashville. While touring the state with William Jennings Bryan, Goebel declared in a speech at Bardwell:

> I have no doubt that if in the Louisville convention I had permitted Mr. Milton H. Smith and Mr. August Belmont to run the Louisville and Nash-

---

[28] *The Courier-Journal* (Louisville) August 13, 1899; Clark, "The People, William Goebel, and the Kentucky Railroads," pp. 43-44.
[29] *The Courier-Journal* (Louisville), September 2, 1899.
[30] *Ibid.*, September 12, 1899.
[31] *The New York Times*, August 27, 1899.

ville political locomotive engine over me, in their judgment I would be an entirely proper person, not only to be Governor of Kentucky, but to hold any other place within the gift of the people.[82]

Goebel only occasionally directed his verbal attack against his Republican opponent in the election, William Taylor. When he did speak of the Republican record during the previous four years, he merely complained about Governor Bradley's vetoes of constructive legislation introduced and supported by Goebel and his lieutenants. The campaign, therefore, was less one between Goebel and Taylor, or even Goebel and Brown, than it was between Goebel and the L&N. He openly characterized the campaign as such in a speech at Hopkinsville:

> Ladies and Gentlemen: There are only two candidates for Governor of Kentucky. There are more than that number who pretend to be candidates, but the only real candidates are the Louisville and Nashville Company and the person who address {sic} you.[83]

In a period when oratory was the major political instrument for rallying voters, frequent speeches were typical, and Goebel hammered the railroads at every opportunity. Whether in Morgantown, Paducah, Henderson, Hardinsburg, Maysville, Versailles, Winchester, Pineville, Corbin, Leitchfield, Hodgensville, Louisville, Lexington, or Covington, the message was the same. In speech after speech Goebel defended his efforts to regulate railroads, his support for the prison reform, Chinn and McChord bills, his opposition to the L&N, and his appeal to the "common man," the farmer-labor bloc of voters.[84]

Newspapers throughout the state divided their support in the gubernatorial campaign, but those which openly declared for Goebel usually did so on the same grounds on which he campaigned. One Democratic newspaper told its readers that Milton H. Smith, President of the L&N, had "openly avowed every effort of that corporation would be arrayed against Goebel in this campaign. And why did he do it? Simply because the L&N knows that if Goebel is elected Governor the special privileges they now enjoy will be curtailed." The article decried the railroad's frequent use of free passes to persuade and control convention delegates and legislators, concluding that the campaign was clearly "a case of the people against a railroad corporation...."[85]

---

[82] *The Courier-Journal* (Louisville), October 17, 1899; Hughes, *et al.*, *That Kentucky Campaign*, p. 90.
[83] *The Courier-Journal* (Louisville), October 17, 1899; *Lexington Herald*, October 17, 1899.
[84] *The Courier-Journal* (Louisville) September 6, 7, 9, 10, 13, 26, October 1, 6, 7, 12, 15, 18, 24, 26, 27, November 7, 1899; John H. Fenton, *Politics in the Border States*, New Orleans: The Hauser Press, 1957, pp. 42-43; Clark, "The People, William Goebel, and the Kentucky Railroads," pp. 43-44.
[85] *The Bardwell News*, quoted in *The Courier-Journal* (Louisville), October 17, 1899.

An editorial in the *Franklin Favorite* was a typical example of small town newspaper support for Goebel. Here Goebel was a representative of the people fighting the lobbyist:

> Every lobbyist in the State is against Goebel. . . . He is naturally against the man he can't 'influence.' Lobbyists work for special favors to special interest and against the people. Are the people with the lobbyists and against themselves in this race, or are they for Goebel?[36]

Another small town newspaper complained that the L&N was obviously spending huge sums of money to oppose Goebel's election, and that the people would later have to bear the campaign costs through increased freight and passenger rates.[37]

An editorial in the *Mt. Vernon Signal* reviewed its past pleasant relationship with the L&N, then concluded with an admonition:

> But we regret to see that the great corporation has taken such an active part in Kentucky politics for the last few years, and especially are we pained to see its strenuous endeavors and methods used to defeat Goebel for Governor. We have not, nor shall we, say one harsh word against the L. and N. We do say that no State should be dominated by greedy and selfish corporations, and the important part this great monopoly is now taking in our State politics forbodes consequences of the gravest significance to the business interest of Kentucky. If these great and powerful monopolies may boldly nominate and elect a Governor they can likewise elect a subservient Legislature. . . . And by doing this they can fix their own rates for the carriage of passengers and freights, and thereby compel every business interest in this great State to pay tribute to their insatiate greed.[38]

The appeal here was less to the common man or laborer than to the business community which depended on the transportation industry. The message was obvious: uncontrolled and uncontrollable monopolies and trusts were not only harmful to the small town merchant, but also to the business community generally.

While some editorials tried to assuage businessmen who might be annoyed or frightened by Goebel's rhetoric, other editorials emphasized the rationality of his approach. Arguing that Goebel was interested in public improvements, including building railroads, and opening coal fields and timber lands, one newspaper editorialized that Goebel opposed only the railroad policy of "all the traffic will bear."[39]

Louisville's *Courier-Journal* was the largest and most prestigious

---

[36] *Franklin Favorite*, quoted in *The Courier-Journal* (Louisville) October 17, 1899.
[37] *The Morganfield Sun*, quoted in *The Courier-Journal* (Louisville), October 17, 1899.
[38] *Mt. Vernon Signal*, quoted in *The Courier-Journal* (Louisville), October 25, 1899.
[39] *West Liberty Messenger*, quoted in *The Courier-Journal* (Louisville), October 17, 1899.

paper in the state. Under the editorial direction of Henry Watterson, proponent of the New South, the paper consistently supported the Democratic ticket. The most notable exception to this was its support for McKinley over Bryan and free silver in the presidential campaign of 1896. By 1900, however, with free silver a less urgent issue, the *Courier-Journal* returned to the Democratic column. Its editorials linked the L&N with the opposition to Goebel:

> The question which we are to answer at the polls is whether we are to govern ourselves or to look to the Louisville and Nashville railroad for our government.
> Nothing should be allowed to subordinate or obscure that question. ... The road is not likely to let us forget it. ... It is avowedly out to beat Goebel, at all cost. It went into the Louisville convention to beat him, and failing there, it got up the Lexington convention. Failing to beat him with Hardin or Stone, it is now bent upon beating him with Taylor. ...[40]

In a letter from L&N's chief lobbyist, Basil Duke, to William Lindsay, Duke emphasized that they must "beat Goebel for the gubernatorial nomination and commit the party to a repeal of his bills."[41] The railroad spared no pains to insure Goebel's defeat. In Louisville alone, the L&N bought control of two moribund newspapers, the *Louisville Post* and the *Louisville Dispatch*, to vent its opposition to Goebel. The railroad delivered thousands of these two dailies freely throughout the state in an effort to influence voters. Writing years after the campaign, Goebel's personal secretary recalled that August Belmont, Chairman of the Board of the L&N, later admitted to him that the company had spent over $500,000 to defeat Goebel and added that, "We would have spent twice that much had we thought it necessary." Goebel's supporters even alleged that the L&N fired anyone on its road who openly supported their candidate.[42]

Mainly because of his stand on governmental regulation of corporations, Goebel gained the support of some prominent Populists in the state. Although they had their own party nominees, some Populists, realizing they had no realistic chance of winning in the state, threw their support to Goebel. Judge E. H. Threlkeld, Owen County Populist, saw the opposition of "monopolies, trusts, and combinations" to Goebel's election as proof that he was a reform candidate. Threlkeld also praised Goebel's advocacy of the Chinn Book Bill which he felt would reduce the price of school books by half and the McChord Railroad Bill. He thought the new railroad commission—backed by the state courts—

---
[40] *The Courier-Journal* (Louisville), September 2, 14, October 26, 1899.
[41] Quoted in Clark, "The People, William Goebel, and the Kentucky Railroads," p. 43.
[42] *Ibid.*, p. 44; *The Courier-Journal* (Louisville), November 2, 1899; Woodson, *William Goebel*, pp. 162-163.

would "control the railroad traffic of the State and guarantee to us reasonable and just rates and insure us against the present unjust discrimination."[43] A wealthy Lewis County farmer declared his support for Goebel and promised to campaign for him in the county. He cited Goebel's "fine reputation in bitter warfare against the abuses of monopoly" as his chief reason for backing the Democratic gubernatorial nominee. Similarly, John H. Keys, nephew of Populist nominee for Secretary of State, Ben Keys, supported Goebel and actively stumped for him in Murray.[44]

State regulation of the trusts was the core of Goebel's campaign appeal, and his vigorous stand probably brought him many Populist votes. To be elected, however, he needed to broaden his base of support, and to achieve this he tailored his speeches to his particular audiences. Speaking in the heart of the Burley tobacco growing region, Goebel attacked the tobacco trust, but offered no specific remedy to the farmers' problems:

> Until within the last two years you, my farmer friends, were able to carry your tobacco to the market in Louisville and Cincinnati where you would meet twenty or thirty buyers, representing . . . different manufacturers. Now all the manufacturers are combined in one trust, and when a farmer carries his tobacco to the market he is met by one buyer, who fixes the price he will pay him for that tobacco.[45]

Without explaining how, Goebel pledged to restore a competitive market to the farmers.

His appeal to the laboring class was more specific. In a speech at Cloverport, Goebel expressed support for a law which would bar employers from entering into binding agreements with employees or prospective employees which forbade them from joining or continuing membership in labor unions. These "yellow dog" contracts were not outlawed by the federal government until the Norris-LaGuardia Act of 1932. Speaking in behalf of such a law, Goebel declared, "I believe that the labor unions have just as much right to organize and protect themselves as have the operators and manipulators of the trusts."[46]

On several different occasions he argued his case for the Fellow Servant Bill which he had introduced in the Senate. He favored a law which would limit the number of hours a railroad employee could work each day, arguing that if the federal government had the power to restrict the number of hours federal employees could work, the state

---

[43] *The Owenton Herald*, quoted in *The Courier-Journal* (Louisville), September 8, 1899.
[44] *The Courier-Journal* (Louisville), September 29, November 3, 1899.
[45] *Ibid.*, September 12, 1899.
[46] *Ibid.*, September 9, 10, 1899.

could legislate similar laws for various other jobs. He never made the distinction between federal legislation which applied only to government employees and his own proposal which applied to private corporations. To help relieve railroad workers, Goebel emphasized the need for a law which would outlaw "double-headers," two trains coupled under a single operating crew. Because of the reduction of manpower, "double-headers" invariably increased the risk of accidents since smaller crews had to man more stations.[47]

Senator Goebel sought not only farm and labor support, but also the Negro vote. Blacks spoke in his behalf throughout the state, but Goebel seldom mentioned the Negro in his campaign speeches. In any case, in Kentucky as in the other Border States except Maryland, the Negro question was never a serious issue in the campaigns or in the state legislature. Goebel's personal position on the Negro's civil rights was similar to the Supreme Court ruling in *Plessy* v. *Ferguson*. While favoring separate accommodations for the two races, he wanted to amend the state law to make more clear the requirement of the railroads to provide truly equal accommodations. He blamed Republicans, who had been in office since the court decision, for taking no action to secure equal accommodations for blacks. He pledged that if elected governor, he would guarantee equality since both black and white paid the same price for the privilege of riding the trains.[48]

Realistically, however, such discussions, whether of the rights of black people or of his opposition to the use of "double-headers," were for local audience consumption. They served to complement his basic position enunciated in the Democratic platform and in his speeches throughout the campaign. Goebel wished to win or lose on the issues of railroad regulation, the McChord Bill, the Chinn Textbook Bill, and on the broader idea of monopoly opposition and corporation control. By the time the campaign closed in early November, most people knew where he stood on those issues. Whether they would elect him governor on that basis was the real question.

On election evening, both major parties claimed victory, but for the next few days the results remained in doubt. Goebel maintained a razor-thin lead until the traditionally Republican mountain counties of eastern Kentucky finally reported their returns. By the end of the week the count officially stood at 193,714 for Republican Taylor; 191,331 for Goebel; and 12,140 for former Democratic Governor John Young Brown. Though Goebel had not made an official concession, he seemed to have failed in his attempt to forge a farmer-labor coalition within

---

[47] *Ibid.*, September 14, October 7, 26, November 2, 1899.
[48] *Ibid.*, September 9, 1899; Hughes, *et al.*, *That Kentucky Campaign*, p. 105.

the Democratic party which would have given him control of the party and election as governor.⁴⁹

The Democratic State Central Committee voted unanimously to contest the election. Whether Goebel actively sought the Central Committee's backing in overturning the election or whether he merely abided by their vote is open to question. Once the battle was joined, however, he seemed disinclined to withdraw. In a statement to the legislature he and his partner in the race, J. C. W. Beckham, filed charges of bribery, intimidation, and fraud in the election, demanding a recount and the invalidation of several counties' votes.⁵⁰

Goebel contested the election on ten specific grounds, including one which linked the Republicans and the corporate interests, claiming that Republicans

> ... corruptly and fraudulently entered into an agreement and conspiracy with the chief officers of the Louisville and Nashville Railroad Company, and other corporations and trusts ... to furnish large sums of money to be used in defeating contestant at said election by bribing and corrupting the voters and election officers of this Commonwealth and debauching the public press thereof....⁵¹

Democrats further charged that Governor Bradley's use of the militia at certain polling places intimidated voters, that returns from the mountain counties were invalid because they were written on translucent tissue paper, and that the L&N had pressured its employees to vote against Goebel.⁵²

One specific charge involved the L&N in bribery. Logan County Democratic Senator S. B. Harrell, in a dramatic Senate session, produced two keys to a Louisville bank deposit box which contained $4,500. The money was allegedly the balance of a payment he was to receive from the L&N for not supporting Goebel in the Democratic caucus and encouraging others to follow suit. The state Supreme Court later dismissed the case, and the truth of the accusation was never established.⁵³

Republicans themselves accused Democrats of wholesale vote buying and corruption but, of course, were willing to let the official results stand. According to the constitution the state legislature, not the courts, however, had the authority to review the allegations. With Democrats in control of both houses of the General Assembly, there was little

---

⁴⁹ Fenton, *Politics in the Border States*, pp. 42-43; Clark, "The People, William Goebel, and the Kentucky Railroads," pp. 44-45; *The New York Times*, November 9-16, 1899.
⁵⁰ Woodson, *William Goebel*, p. 204; Hughes, *et al.*, *That Kentucky Campaign*, pp. 152-153.
⁵¹ *The Courier-Journal* (Louisville), January 3, 1900.
⁵² *Ibid.*
⁵³ *Ibid.*, January 2, 3, 4, 7, 16, 25, 1900; Woodson, *William Goebel*, pp. 208-209; Hughes, *et al.*, *That Kentucky Campaign*, pp. 167-170.

William Goebel 291

doubt of the outcome: the legislature invalidated the disputed election returns and declared Goebel the winner. Such bold action provoked an equally bold response from Republicans. Newly-elected Republican Governor William Taylor addressed several letters to his friends throughout the state urging them to hurry to the capital. Responding to Taylor's plea and to the unprecedented action of the Democratic legislature, contingents of Republicans, many of them mountain men, converged on Frankfort with rifles and pistols. Most came on L&N trains.[54]

While Goebel was walking toward the capitol the day before he assumed office, an assassin fatally shot the Senator from a window of the Executive Offices Building, then occupied by Republicans. Although Goebel was sworn into office the following day, he died three days later, on February 3, 1900. The subsequent trials of several suspects over the next six years cost the state several thousand dollars and settled no questions. A jury convicted Republican Secretary of State Cabell Powers of Goebel's murder and sentenced him to prison, but the next Republican governor pardoned him.[55]

Eulogies of Goebel were expectedly extravagant and partisan, but they also confirmed his image as foe of railroads and unrestricted corporate power. Cassius M. Clay, Jr., former president of the State Constitutional Convention of 1890 in which both he and Goebel were prominent, characterized Goebel as "a radical . . . eminently fitted to be a great tribune of the people . . . in the fierce fight for the protection of the plain people against the colossal corporate power. . . ." *Harper's Weekly* praised Goebel as "the pioneer progressive of the South . . . the pioneer of railroad rate regulation in the country." Newspaper tributes also represented Goebel as, "the bitter enemy of corporate power."[56]

Goebel's assassination briefly served the cause of reform. An aroused legislature repassed the vetoed McChord Bill, and J. C. W. Beckham, who had succeeded to the governorship, signed it into law. To prevent the recurrence of violence at Frankfort, Democrats introduced bills outlawing free transportation of anyone for the purpose of intimidating

---

[54] *The New York Times*, January 10, 21, 26, 28, 1900; *The Courier-Journal* (Louisville), January 9-28, 1900; Hughes, *et al.*, *That Kentucky Campaign*, pp. 189-197; Woodson, *William Goebel*, pp. 204-225; William S. Taylor to Jn. Franklin, January 10, 1900, xeroxed copy in the possession of the author.
[55] *The New York Times*, February 1-11, 19, 22, 27, 1900; *The Courier-Journal* (Louisville) January 31, February 1-15, 1900; Hughes *et al.*, *That Kentucky Campaign*, pp. 241-323; Woodson, *William Goebel*, Appendix.
[56] Hughes, *et al.*, *That Kentucky Campaign*, p. 250; *Harper's Weekly*, LIX: p. 3, quoted in William Elsey Connelley and E. M. Coulter, *History of Kentucky* (V vols., Chicago: The American Historical Society, 1922), II: p. 1012; *The Courier-Journal* (Louisville), February 4, 5, 1900; *Lexington Herald*, February 4-7, 1900; *Toledo Commercial*, quoted in *The Courier-Journal* (Louisville), February 6, 1900.

officers of the state in the discharge of their duty, and preventing common carriers from interfering with conventions or elections. Democrats also introduced a stringent bill against lobbyists and one regulating the issuance of capital stock and preventing overcapitalization.[57]

But the new governor was no Goebel, and during Beckham's incumbency the reform tempo slowed considerably. At least for a time, the momentary spate of legislation became the conclusion, rather than the beginning, of reform in Kentucky. What Goebel might have accomplished in four years as governor is conjectural.

No one questioned that Goebel was always a vigorous and outspoken person; his strenuous campaign indicated as much. His friends admitted that he was also an ambitious man. At his death he was only forty-four years old. All of these qualities: youth, ambition, vigor, when coupled with his political record and rhetoric suggest that he might have led Kentucky to confront corporations as progressive reformers urged throughout the first few years of the 20th century.

---

[57] *The New York Times*, February 24, 1900; Clark, "The People, William Goebel, and the Kentucky Railroads," p. 46.

NICHOLAS C. BURCKEL (1943–   ), born in Evansville, Indiana, received his B.A. degree from Georgetown University and his M.A. and Ph.D. degrees from the University of Wisconsin at Madison. He has served as director of the University Archives at the University of Wisconsin at Parkside, where he is now executive assistant to the chancellor. Burckel has written several articles for historical and archival journals.

This article first appeared in *The Filson Club History Quarterly* in January 1974, vol. 48, pp. 43–60.

JOHN M. HARLAN IN KENTUCKY, 1855–1877
The Story of His Pre-Court Political Career

By Louis Hartz
Omaha, Nebraska
Harvard University, Cambridge, Massachusetts[1]

I

Overshadowed by his long and significant service on the United States Supreme Court (1877–1911), the Kentucky career of John Marshall Harlan remains virtually unexplored. Yet few bore a more consistently significant role in the swift-moving drama of deepening crisis and Civil War and Reconstruction in the border state.

The early years of that drama reveal the Whig party in Kentucky set adrift by the death of Henry Clay and the impatient challenges of the slavery question, never again to reconquer the unity and strength it possessed under the leadership of the Great Commoner from Ashland. Indeed it was a cruel thrust of history that cast young Harlan, with Whig affiliations inherited from his father, James Harlan, twice Attorney-General and twice Congressman under the Whig banner, into the political arena at the moment of party collapse. But only eagerness and confidence streamed through the mind of the strapping six-foot, two-hundred-pound young man who emerged from Clay's own congressional district. Fresh from Centre College and legal study at Transylvania University, he flung himself, with an energy characteristic of his whole living, into the first adventure of the wandering Kentucky Whigs who now sought to recapture with new alliances and new appeals the strength of years past.

The adventure was Know-Nothingism. While the disintegration of the Whig party was sweeping many Northerners into the Republican fold, in the South the forces traditionally arrayed against the Democrats were compelled to seek another road.

---

[1] The materials here presented form part of a larger biographical study undertaken at the suggestion and with the continuous encouragement of my friend, Professor B. F. Wright of Harvard. I am indebted, too, to Miss Laura and Miss Ruth Harlan of Washington, D. C., daughters of the late Mr. Justice Harlan, for their kindness in discussing the Justice's career with me.

John M. Harlan was born in Boyle County, Kentucky, June 1, 1833. He was appointed to the United States Supreme Court in 1877, and served in that capacity until his death, in Washington, D. C., October 14, 1911.

The majority of them, especially throughout Kentucky with its large and swiftly-mounting immigrant population, discovered it in the expanding ranks of the American organization. The Whig-American alliance forged, its first test of strength occurred in 1855, with John Harlan's father fighting for reëlection as Attorney-General on the new ticket.[2] Striving principally to outdo the Democrats as champions of the peculiar institution, the Whig-Americans thrust forward again and again the charge that immigrants "come here almost invariably prejudiced against the institution of slavery."[3] They resurrected the traditional indictment of pauperism and criminality against the newcomers[4] and charged that "the immaculate rulers of the Catholic world claim or seek political supremacy in America."[5] The Germans especially they condemned for "war against religion and the rights of property,"[6] an accusation underscored by specific planks in the American platform devoted to affirming the existence of God and demanding the reinforcement of biblical teaching in the schools.[7]

How seriously young Harlan and his father took these arguments it is difficult to say; to them they were probably little more than tools to be exploited by the realistic politician for the purpose of restoring a great political organization. Yet the religious note doubtless struck a sympathetic chord in the mind of John, who had but recently emerged from the orthodox Presbyterian atmosphere of Transylvania and who throughout life revealed a vigorous piety, teaching a class in Sunday school until his death in 1911 and acting as delegate to many important meetings of the Presbyterian Union.[8] Moreover, he was at this time an officer of the Younger Brothers of Temperance Society, Capital Fountain No. 31, which probably did not relish the beer drinking of the immigrants any more than their free-and-easy approach to the Sabbath.[9]

Whatever his motives, Harlan, who was but twenty-two years old at the time and held no official position in the party network, astonished the battle-scarred political veterans of Kentucky by proceeding vigorously to stump the state on the accepted Whig-

[2] *Frankfort Tri-Weekly Yeoman*, June 26, 1855.
[3] *Paris Western Citizen*, July 6, 1855.
[4] *Lexington Observer and Reporter*, August 1, 1855.
[5] *Ibid.*, June 27, 1855; see *Louisville Daily Journal*, July 18, 1855.
[6] *Louisville Daily Journal*, July 25, 1855.
[7] *Ibid.*, July 18, 1855.
[8] *Louisville Herald*, October 5, 1911.
[9] *Frankfort Commonwealth*, May 7, 9, 1856.

American ticket, which demanded modification of immigration and naturalization laws and the repeal of state legislation permitting foreigners not naturalized to vote.[10] Handsome and commanding in appearance he at once captured the attention of Kentuckians.

Party leaders at Georgetown reported one of his early speeches there to be "the clearest and ablest exposition of American principles which has been given in that place,"[11] while at Danville they joyfully noted that "his speeches are calculated to do much good for the American cause."[12] As news of Harlan's work sped through party ranks, official organs such as the *Lexington Observer and Reporter* and the *Louisville Daily Journal* commenced to carry regular schedules of his appearances, urging mass turnouts for the youthful, newly-discovered Whig-American champion.[13] With enthusiasm the Columbia correspondents of the *Frankfort Commonwealth* declared that Harlan's speech there was "one of the best I have listened to for a great while. . . . He traversed the whole range of discussion between the American and anti-American parties, and left the poor anties prostrate at the feet of his 'Holiness' and the foreigner begging for office."[14] Put concisely, the tale of young John Harlan's entry into politics is found in the comment of a reporter in 1855 that he "came amongst us unknown to fame, and utterly unheralded, but he left an impression behind him that will not be effaced for a long time."[15]

Thus early did young Harlan taste the fruits of political victory, for the Whig-Americans in the campaign of 1855 defeated the Democrats for every state office on the ticket. But it was an achievement not unmixed with apprehensive evidences because election day—August 6, 1855—had been reddened by bloody riots in Louisville so that it settled into history as "Bloody Monday." Nevertheless, success pumped confidence into the ranks of the Whig-American alliance and swiftly campaign machinery was constructed for the presidential election of 1856. Known by now as "the young giant of the American party,"[16] Harlan was allotted the relatively important office of Assistant Elector for

---

[10] *Paris Western Citizen*, July 6, 1855.
[11] *Frankfort Commonwealth*, July 10, 1855.
[12] *Ibid.*, July 16, 1855.
[13] See *Lexington Observer and Reporter*, July 11, 1855; *Louisville Daily Journal*, July 18, 1855.
[14] *Frankfort Commonwealth*, July 23, 1855.
[15] *Lexington Observer and Reporter*, July 25, 1855.
[16] *Louisville Daily Journal*, July 29, 1856.

the state at large on the American slate, which put forth the Fillmore–Donelson combination.[17] Systematically he canvassed the northern and southern counties in Kentucky, his tirelessness time and again receiving comment. "After Mr. Harlan . . . had spoken three hours at Cynthiana, he went to Paris and there addressed another large crowd at night for two hours with great success. Everywhere his praise was upon every American tongue."[18]

Vigorously he refuted the Democratic charge that the Americans were agents of abolitionism. "He triumphantly vindicated the American party from the charge of religious proscription, proving clearly that it denounced none but those who owed allegiance to a foreign power." Marshaling all of his acknowledged oratorical strength he invoked Jefferson, Madison, and Randolph as the true authors of the American party's objectives and boldly he "proclaimed his belief that 'Americans should rule America' and said that in all cases he would vote for the son of the soil in preference to a foreigner."[19] Said the violently American *Frankfort Commonwealth* of a Harlan speech: "It was orthodox, every word of it—it was in fact, Know-Nothing Scripture. We are ready to stand by and swear to every word he uttered."[20]

But this time it was a losing battle. Damaged by the American defeat in the neighboring state of Virginia early in 1856 and the growing realization in Kentucky that division of the proslavery ballot might lead to the election of a Republican president, the Fillmore forces were defeated by more than six thousand votes. The victory of the Democrats combined with the fact that Know-Nothing slogans appeared increasingly artificial beside the great shadow of the slavery issue, to sound the deathknell of the Whig-American coalition. And with its death young Harlan quickly deserted the American doctrines. But if he believed that the Know-Nothing chapter was permanently closed, he was soon to be disillusioned as it came to be reopened again and again to serve as powerful campaign ammunition for future political opponents.

The collapse of Americanism set the majority of old Whigs in Kentucky once more adrift. Soon, however, sentiment crystallized for the formation of one great union of all forces opposing

---
[17] *Louisville Daily Journal*, July 4, 1856.
[18] *Lexington Observer and Reporter*, July 2, 1856.
[19] *Frankfort Commonwealth*, May 21, 1856.
[20] *Ibid.*

the Democracy on a platform rooted largely in the issues of slavery and political corruption. Although Harlan won the Franklin County judgeship in 1858,[21] he did not allow sentiments of judicial disinterest to interfere with vigorous participation in the new Whig drive. Indeed in the Opposition convention in 1859 he held a position of recognized leadership as delegate from the Ashland district.[22] And one of the major upsets of that convention was the passing over of many oldtimers to give the nomination for Congress in the Clay district to the dynamic, twenty-six-year-old county judge. Some Democratic papers hinted that the veterans felt so certain of defeat that they did not wish to risk their reputations on the new slate, but the fact is that many were antagonized by the elevation of Harlan to the candidacy.[23] Speedily, however, the antagonism melted away as it became clear that the youngster was waging one of the most brilliant campaigns that the state had ever witnessed.

Old men from the Ashland district compared Harlan with the young Henry Clay[24] and even his opponents were compelled to admit that he "is clever personally and in point of talent respectable."[25] As before, the newly organized Whigs strove to surpass the Democracy in championing slavery, but little now remains of the anti-immigrant doctrines of the American platform. Indeed Harlan and his associates are now vigorously defending the rights of naturalized Americans included in army drafts by their home governments while journeying abroad,[26] and vigorous effort is being released to capture the immigrant vote. But Harlan's opponents quickly retort, "The naturalized citizens will remember his inflammatory tirades against their political rights and when, as an agent of the Frankfort Clique, he traversed a portion of the state in advocating the proscriptive heresies of the Know-Nothing order."[27]

Though, as I have said, Harlan deserted the anti-foreign doctrines of Know-Nothingism, the orthodox religious vein in his character already described succeeds in finding expression now as before. This time the attack is leveled against the Mormons and their practices in what appears to be his own personal one-

---
[21] *Frankfort Tri-Weekly Yeoman*, June 2, 1859.
[22] *Louisville Weekly Journal*, February 23, 1859.
[23] *Ibid.*, June 1, 1859.
[24] *Ibid.*
[25] *Frankfort Tri-Weekly Yeoman*, May 21, 1859.
[26] *Louisville Daily Journal*, July 28, 1859.
[27] *Frankfort Tri-Weekly Yeoman*, May 24, 1859.

man crusade against the new sect.[28] Doubtless with plenty of exaggeration one of his opponents writes in summarizing his speech at Paris: "He is for destroying the Mormons without law or form; thinks that Brigham Young ought to be hung by the Federal Government for having sixty-four wives."[29] Nor was this to be the last expression of the religious note in Harlan's political outlook.

But it was the slavery issue and not the question of immigrants or Mormons that occupied the spotlight in the 1859 campaign of John Harlan for Congress. Arguing that he was unqualifiedly in favor of positive national intervention in behalf of slavery in the territories, Harlan attempted to demonstrate a greater support of the institution than could be offered by his Democratic opponent Simms,[30] whom he tagged with Douglas doctrines of squatter sovereignty. "He charged Southern Democratic traders with having sold the rights of the Southern people to squatter sovereigns of the North to procure a union with Douglas Democrats."[31] He persistently pressed upon his Democratic rival embarrassing questions such as, "If Douglas received the Charleston nomination would you vote for him?"[32]

Nor was he content to attack squatter sovereignty from the viewpoint alone of its immediate implications. He argued that it was based upon the wider theory of majority despotism, upon "the mobocratic idea which levels destruction at all written contracts by which the weak are protected against the strong, that majorities can make and set aside constitutions at pleasure."[33] However, it is doubtful whether this deeper excoriation of the Douglas doctrine as a standing threat to "individuals or minorities in the enjoyment of private property, freedom of conscience, freedom of speech, freedom of the press, and the other privileges which are the birthright of American freemen"[34] appealed as strongly to Kentuckians as the simple fact behind it all that Harlan was going the limit in his defense of slavery. As I have suggested he also exploited the charge of Democratic

[28] *Frankfort Tri-Weekly Yeoman*, July 23, 1859.
[29] *Lexington Kentucky Statesman*, July 20, 1859.
[30] Early in the campaign a third candidate named Trabue, clinging to the Old Know-Nothing platform, fought both Harlan and Simms, but when it became clear that he could win only small support he resigned in favor of Simms. *Frankfort Tri-Weekly Yeoman*, May 26, June 21, 1859.
[31] *Frankfort Commonwealth*, July 29, 1859.
[32] *Louisville Weekly Journal*, June 3, 1859.
[33] *Ibid.*, February 23, 1859.
[34] *Ibid.*

political corruption, linking the "Douglassites of Illinois" with the notorious "Martin and Forneyites of Pennsylvania" to symbolize the unity of alleged Democratic opposition to slavery and Democratic graft.[15]

The battle in Ashland district between the youthful Opposition champion and the Democrat Simms became so close and bitter that it attracted statewide attention. Two weeks before election day the *Louisville Daily Journal*, an Opposition organ, charged the Democrats with importing into the district "outlaws from Owen and elsewhere" to bolster the Simms vote.[16] And when Harlan was defeated by the bare margin of fifty votes,[17] a howl went up from the Opposition ranks and an abortive campaign swung under way for recount and investigation.[18] Even the *Frankfort Tri-Weekly Yeoman*, fiery Democratic paper, had to admit that "we have before seen party struggles here and elsewhere but never anything to compare with the one that has just passed."[19]

Disheartened by defeat young Harlan now saw the clouds of civil war gathering fast. Through his first five years in politics had played all the forces of final Whig collapse and he knew now that he was a man without a party. But, under the deepening impact of the sectional cleavage, party lines were already disintegrating in Kentucky, border state torn between conflicting attachments to North and to South. In 1860 he threw his energies behind the efforts of the Constitutional Union Party politically to smother the deep-rooted sectional clashes via the Bell-Everett ticket. Nor did the victory of Lincoln or the facts of secession end his struggle for peaceful settlement.

In March of 1861, with horror at the thought of bloodshed written deep into its lines, Harlan dispatched a letter to Joseph Holt, Kentuckian influential in administration councils, pleading for "an immediate withdrawal of the Federal troops from the seceding states." Elimination of the threat of Northern coercion, he argues, would be followed by two results of great importance: "first, in the border slave states the Union cause would be placed upon an immovable foundation; second, a formidable party would immediately spring up in the seceding

---
[15] *Louisville Daily Journal*, June 13, 1859.
[16] *Ibid.*, July 27, 1859.
[17] *Frankfort Tri-Weekly Yeoman*, August 4, 1859.
[18] *Ibid.*, August 13, 16, 27, 1859.
[19] *Ibid.*, August 6, 1859.

states in favor of a return to the national union."[40] Thereupon, he continues with confidence, "the eyes of the country would be directed alone to a National Convention as the only peaceable mode to settle our present troubles."[41] Desperate refusal to face the deeper issues involved, probably more than an inability to understand them, explains this pathetic eleventh-hour plea of young Harlan. Indeed at this moment his fear of war clearly transcends his attachments to national solidarity for he writes: "It must be conceded that whenever it becomes a settled fact that the people of the seceding states are unalterably opposed to the Federal Government they should be allowed to go in peace."[42]

One month after Harlan communicated his proposal to Holt the guns boomed out against Fort Sumter. However much he may have preferred peaceful secession to bloodshed, Harlan knew now that he must choose one military camp or the other and that his choice could only be Unionist. Yet he did not then realize how ruthlessly the vicissitudes of war and concomitant social revolution were to tear him away from the framework of values and beliefs he had hitherto cherished. Like our own generation of young men he had been flung by history upon a road the social directions of which he could not envision.

II

The firing on Fort Sumter—April 12, 1861—initiated a critical period of plot and counterplot within the divided state of Kentucky. Encouraged by the gubernatorial proclamation of neutrality, leading Confederate sympathizers at Frankfort mapped plans for a state convention which would either secure the proclamation as permanent or bind Kentucky to the South. But they were outwitted by Union leaders, with young Harlan deserting his Louisville law practice to aid in defeating the convention scheme. Upon his return he discovered in the virtual closing of the courts the signal for full-time labor in the desperate drive to stem the Confederate tide in Kentucky until the Union ranks were equipped with arms.[43]

Events caught momentum as the summer of 1861 brought with it crucial state elections. Forsaking campaign dignities, speaking on street corners and on store-boxes, and hiring a band of

---
[40] Letter to Joseph Holt, March 11, 1861, Holt Mss. in Library of Congress.
[41] *Ibid.*
[42] *Ibid.*
[43] Harlan Mss. printed in Captain T. Speed, *The Union Cause in Kentucky*, with a Foreword by Justice Harlan (1907), page 117.

musicians to attract listeners, Harlan stumped Louisville for the Union slate.⁴⁴ Vigorously he fought Southern propaganda for "an acknowledgment of the independence of the Confederate states" disseminated in the belief that when "all hope is lost for the restoration of the Union, Kentucky will drift into the Southern Confederacy."⁴⁵ Parallel with these efforts at mass persuasion ran the grim business of importing armaments and at a dawn in May, Harlan, with an associate, heavily armed, met the first shipment of Union guns at the Louisville wharf and sent them to Lexington, whence they were distributed to Unionists throughout the state.⁴⁶

In September Harlan announced his intention to raise a regiment,⁴⁷ establishing his headquarters in Lebanon and traveling to "several adjoining counties making speeches for the Union cause and inviting men to join my regiment."⁴⁸ But national solidarity was apparently not the only principle enunciated in those talks. Five years later the *Frankfort Tri-Weekly Yeoman* declared: "When he was raising his regiment he pledged himself to the people that if he saw any decision on the part of the Government to turn the war into a struggle for the destruction of slavery he would not only resign his commission but he would go over to the Confederates and take his regiment with him, and help them to fight their battles against the Government. This is what he promised."⁴⁹ A similar report on Harlan's speeches during this period is found in the *Louisville Daily Courier*.⁵⁰ Nor is it astonishing that in entering the Federal ranks Harlan, who since 1855 had been striving to outdo his political opponents in championing slavery, should make important reservations with respect to the peculiar institution. These reservations doubtless account in part for his extraordinary success in recruitment throughout a dominantly proslavery region, the group that he brought into camp within two months numbering about a thousand.⁵¹

---
⁴⁴ *Ibid*, page 117.
⁴⁵ Letter from Harlan to John J. Crittenden, June 25, 1861, Crittenden Mss. in Library of Congress.
⁴⁶ Harlan Mss. in Speed, *op. cit.*, pages 118–121; "General Nelson, Kentucky and Lincoln Guns" in *The Magazine of American History*, August, 1883.
⁴⁷ *The Union Regiments of Kentucky*, published under auspices of Union Soldiers and Sailors Monument Association (1897), page 337.
⁴⁸ Harlan Mss. in Speed, *op. cit.*, page 195.
⁴⁹ *Frankfort Tri-Weekly Yeoman*, July 21, 1866.
⁵⁰ *Louisville Daily Journal*, July 18, 1866. I have been unable to discover any denial by Harlan of this allegation.
⁵¹ Harlan Mss. in Speed, *op. cit.*, page 195.

Commissioned a colonel at the age of twenty-eight, Harlan commanded his Tenth Kentucky Infantry in the Federal division formed under General Thomas. While he played important roles in the Battle of Mill's Spring,[52] in the advance on Corinth,[53] and in the skirmishes at Lavergne,[54] it was Harlan's victory over the raider John H. Morgan at Rolling Fork Bridge—September 18, 1861—that was responsible for his military fame in Kentucky. For that victory prevented the utter destruction of railway lines by which an important sector of the Union forces were mainly supplied and contributed significantly to the final retirement of Morgan from the state.[55] Wrote Brigadier-General Fry: "Colonel Harlan, for the energy, promptness, and success in pursuing and driving rebel forces from railroad, is entitled to the gratitude not only of the people of Kentucky, but of the whole Army of the Cumberland."[56]

Far-reaching was the impact of war experiences upon the developing mind of young John Harlan. Out of the spirit of cameraderie emerging from dangers and hardships met in common with soldiers of all creeds and classes, there flowed powerful egalitarian influences. The sympathy which Harlan bore for the soldiers of his regiment lingered strong throughout life[57] and finds expression through his war dispatches in repeated praises of "their willingness, even eagerness, to endure any fatigue or make any sacrifice."[58] If Know-Nothingist antipathy for Catholicism remained at all in Harlan, it must have been hammered away by the valor and self-sacrifice of his Catholic soldiers; for years after Appomattox he recalled: "It was a magnificent sight to see how the boys struggled through mud and rain to reach the field of battle. The ground was so wet and muddy under them that their feet slipped at every step. I see now with great distinctness old Father Nash pushing along on foot with the boys. Equally earnest with him was a Catholic priest from Washington County, who had come with Catholic soldiers from that county. There were many Catholics in my regiment."[59]

Primarily it was sympathies for lower-class men that were sharpened in camp and on battlefield. Small farmers, mechanics,

---
[52] *War of the Rebellion: Official Records*, Series I, Volume 7, pages 85, 88.
[53] *Ibid.*, Series I, Volume 16, Part II, page 236.
[54] *Ibid.*, Series I, Volume 23, Part I, pages 20–22.
[55] *Ibid.*, Series I, Volume 20, Part I, pages 137–141.
[56] *Ibid.*, page 141.
[57] Miss Laura Harlan, Washington, D. C., *Per Coll.* of Harlan.
[58] *War of the Rebellion: Official Records*, Series I, Volume 7, page 90.
[59] Harlan Mss. in Speed, *op. cit.*, page 197.

workers made up the bulk of Harlan's regiment; and he insisted again and again during the Reconstruction era: "When war menaced the country it was the poor and the sons of the poor who sprang to its defense."[60] "The war . . . was in the main fought by the poor man. . . . The poor had to fight that war to the end. . . . "[61] And it was they who fell into line "with commendable alacrity" despite being "entirely destitute of provisions,"[62] who deserved "the thanks of the country for the cheerfulness with which, with insufficient food and rest, they bore up under the severest privations,"[63] who stood ready to "make any sacrifice" for the Union cause.[64] In their valor and in comradeships shared with them is doubtless discoverable a segment of the roots of that compassion for common men which emerged to prominence in Harlan's thinking immediately after the war and which profoundly conditioned his judicial outlook.

War, too, cemented with blood and hardship the lesson Harlan early learned from "the Sage of Ashland, who taught me that . . . I owed primary allegiance to my country."[65] How attachments to national solidarity were thus reinforced is dramatically revealed in Harlan's military dispatches when, defying the usual pattern of emotional restraint, he lashes out at "those wicked and unnatural men who are seeking without cause to destroy the Union of our fathers."[66]

Thus was the war a crucible in which were molded new directions of thought for Harlan and in which others previously acquired were reinforced. But early in 1863 Harlan was torn from military life by the death of his father. Forced to return to Louisville to settle family affairs, he gives vent to his Unionist thoughts at floodtide in his letter of resignation: "If, therefore, I am permitted to retire from the army, I beg the commanding general to feel assured that it is from no want of confidence either in the justice or ultimate triumph of the Union cause. That cause will always have the warmest sympathies of my heart, for there are no conditions upon which I will consent to a dissolution of the Union. Nor are there any conditions, consistent with a republican form of government, which I am not prepared to make in order to maintain and perpetuate that Union."[67]

---
[60] *Cincinnati Daily Gazette,* June 28, 1871.
[61] *Louisville Daily Commercial,* July 29, 1871.
[62] *War of the Rebellion: Official Records,* Series I, Volume 7, page 89.
[63] *Ibid.,* Series I, Volume 20, Part I, page 140.
[64] *Ibid.,* Series I, Volume 7, page 90.
[65] *Cincinnati Daily Gazette,* May 25, 1871.
[66] *War of the Rebellion: Official Records,* Series I, Volume 7, page 90.
[67] *Union Regiments in Kentucky,* page 371.

Returning from the army with that powerful appeal which successful military leaders have always had for Americans, Harlan once again entered the political arena. At the 1863 convention of the Union Party in Kentucky Harlan's only opponent for nomination as Attorney-General withdrew, rendering the choice unanimous.[68] The ex-colonel "responded briefly, earnestly recommending our earnest prosecution of the war with all the energies of the nation and discarding the idea of peace on any terms other than submission of the rebels to the laws which they had outraged and coming under the authority of the government."[69]

Yet national unity was by no means the only principle upon which John Harlan waged his victorious campaign for the Attorney-Generalship in 1863.[70] Parallel with their excoriation of the secessionists, Harlan and the Union Party vigorously condemned Lincoln for suspending the writ of habeas corpus and with even greater violence attacked the Emancipation Proclamation of 1862 as unconstitutional and null and void.[71] Indeed it is not surprising that Harlan, who since 1855 had been championing slavery politically, and who in 1861 apparently issued radical views as to his position were the war to become an instrument of abolition, should rise to a position of leadership in the attack upon the emancipation move.

In 1864 Harlan flung his support behind McClellan and the Democrats in their campaign against Lincoln.[72] Not only did he discover time, while Attorney-General, to fight the administration in Kentucky, but he traveled to Indiana to combat the re-election of the Republican leader Morton as governor. For this the *Frankfort Commonwealth*, now a Lincoln organ, lashed at him bitterly:

"Is it not inconsistent and ungrateful for any citizen of Kentucky professing Unionism—much more so for an incumbent of State office—to take an active part in the attempt to defeat Governor Morton? On every occasion when Kentucky was threatened by rebel hordes, Governor Morton has sent promptly to the State thousands of Union troops to defend us. And three times he has sent troops promptly to protect Frankfort when the property and interests of Colonel John M. Harlan . . . were threatened. . . . We can assure the Union men of Indiana, the

---
[68] *Louisville Daily Journal*, March 20, 1863.
[69] *Ibid.*
[70] See 62–66, *Kentucky Reports*.
[71] *Louisville Daily Commercial*, July 8, 1863.
[72] *Frankfort Commonwealth*, September 30, 1864.

UNION men of Kentucky are not to bear the blame of an apparent ingratitude. Col. Harlan, once an unconditional union man has cast in his lot with those who were from the first with the rebellion. . . . "[73]

Little use for Harlan to plead that he was fighting not unconditional unionism but the war measures of emancipation. As events were to hammer home to him with increasing force, the two issues were inextricably bound together.

With summary emancipation of Kentucky negroes via military channels initiated by General Palmer and social havoc traveling in its wake,[74] Harlan was less than ever prepared to accept the administration move. His twin attack upon both secessionist and radical emancipationist he carried into the year 1865, when Kentucky sentiment for this approach was moving toward renewed organizational expression preparatory to the summer campaigns. In a letter to Colonel John Combs, of Versailles, refusing to run as Conservative Union candidate for Congress because of "considerations . . . of a private nature,"[75] Harlan presents his views in extensive outline.[76]

At the outset he re-emphasizes "that I am now, as I have ever been, opposed to the dissolution of the Union in any event." With the chaotic results of Palmer's policy evidently keen in his mind, he condemns "the subsistence of large bodies of negro men, women, and children in this State, at the expense of the Nation, and with a watchful care which has never been exhibited for the wives and families of the white soldiers of Kentucky." Vigorously he denounces the policy whereby Kentucky's "large slave population is suddenly freed in our midst, and the power taken from the State by proper legislation to effect the removal of the blacks to other localities or protect her white citizens from the ruinous effects of such a violent change in our social system." Declaring that adoption of the emancipation amendment "will destroy the peace and security of the white man in Kentucky," and in fearful anticipation of the ultimate direction of events, he pleads that "there should be a thorough union of all citizens who . . . are opposed to the admission of the negro to the ballot-box or to the enjoyment of other political privileges."[77]

---
[73] *Ibid.*
[74] E. Merton Coulter, *Civil War and Readjustment in Kentucky*, pages 264-270.
[75] *Lexington Observer and Reporter*, June 10, 1865, speaks of Harlan as the "Conservative Candidate for the Legislature," but this is apparently an error.
[76] *Ibid.*, June 1, 1865.
[77] *Ibid.*

But Harlan's condemnation of the Thirteenth Amendment was not based solely on the practical damage he charged it would bring to Kentucky society. In a fiery speech at Lexington in 1865, branded by the Republican *Cincinnati Gazette* as "Harlan's Harmless Harangue," he declared that "if there were not a dozen slaves in the state of Kentucky, I should oppose the amendment,"[78] and elsewhere in the same year he declared that Kentucky must abolish slavery herself within seven years.[79] Basically, Harlan argued, he opposed the amendment because of "the dangerous character of the principle embodied in it—a principle which in some shape, and at some future day in the history of our country, may eventuate in the destruction of our present form of government."[80]

What that sinister principle is Harlan partially reveals in his condemnation of the Emancipation Amendment as "a direct interference, by a portion of the States with the local concerns of other States, and . . . at war with the genius and spirit of our republican institutions."[81] Though this declaration is plainly an appeal to the traditional states rights theory and illumines sharply the limits at this time of Harlan's nationalism, its roots seem to lie in a deeper attitude central to his whole philosophy of government.

That attitude is an ingrained fear of unlimited majority supremacy with respect to individual rights. I have already demonstrated how it found forceful expression as early as 1859, when the twenty-six-year-old Harlan attacked the squatter sovereignty theory as based upon "the mobocratic idea which levels destruction at all written contracts" and upon the alarming theory of "the divine inalienable rights of majorities."[82] Now he lashes out at the principle in the pending Thirteenth Amendment which "confer[s] upon a bare majority of Congress the power to enforce" abolition of rights in slavery. "If three-fourths of the states and two-thirds of each branch of Congress can by amendment of the National Constitution, abolish slavery in Kentucky," he argues in revealing the basic arbitrariness of majority rule, "the same power can establish slavery in Ohio. . . ."[83] Crystallized in 1859, extended now, this anti-

---

[78] *Cincinnati Gazette*, August 2, 1865.
[79] *Lexington Observer and Reporter*, June 10, 1865.
[80] *Ibid.*, June 1, 1865.
[81] *Ibid.*
[82] *Louisville Weekly Journal*, February 23, 1859.
[83] *Lexington Observer and Reporter*, June 1, 1865.

majoritarian outlook was to find expression later in Harlan's vigorous defense of individual rights while on the Supreme Bench and doubtless accounts for his standing disapproval of the majoritarian Jefferson.[84]

In 1866 the Conservative Union party in Kentucky supporting the Harlan viewpoint mobilized once again for electoral struggle, facing on one side the now dominant Democratic party ruled largely by old secessionists and on the other the radical Republicans. The first meeting, called in February by John Harlan and other Conservative Union leaders,[85] convened but two months after Secretary Seward had announced the Thirteenth Amendment duly ratified by three-fourths of the states and a part of the fundamental law of the nation. Struck with the inevitable futility of further opposition to national emancipation, Harlan and his associates accepted under the pressure of facts accomplished the amendment which they had so bitterly opposed, and focused their attack upon the other measures being pressed by the Radicals. Here they seized upon Johnson as a symbol, expressing their gratitude to him "for the bold and patriotic stand he has taken against the Radicals in the Congress of the United States and the Revolutionary measures, especially shown by his recent veto message of the Freedman's Bill."[86]

Though he ran for no office, Harlan fought continuously in the 1866 campaign. He charged the Northern radicals with "aiming by amendments to the Constitution and laws of Congress to disfranchise almost the entire white population of the insurrecting States and to enfranchise the negroes. . . . The permanent triumph of those who in the North are following the lead of Sumner and Stevens in their series of Constitutional Amendments would work a complete revolution in our Republican system of Government, and most probably the overthrow of constitutional liberty."[87] With almost equal vigor he condemned the Democratic leaders as "the Disunionists of 1861" and declared emphatically that the Conservative Unionists "denounced the heresies of secession and rebellion while, at the same time, they denounced the fanaticism of the North."[88]

[84] Miss Laura Harlan, Washington, D. C., *Per Coll.* of Harlan, "Kentucky: United We Stand; Divided We Fall," in *Chicago Legal News*, December 28, 1907.
[85] *Lexington Observer and Reporter*, February 24, 1866.
[86] *Ibid.*
[87] Quoted, *Louisville Courier-Journal*, June 3, 1871.
[88] *Cincinnati Commercial*, July 20, 1866.

Significant as a signpost in Harlan's intellectual development is his speech at Elizabethtown near the end of the campaign when, quite apart from the great reconstruction issues of the day, he is reported independently to have "amplified some upon the aristocracy of the South; depicted in glowing terms the difference between the rich man and the poor man and told, pathetically, of the property qualification in South Carolina to enable a poor man to vote. . . ."[89]

The middleway approach which Harlan and the Conservative Unionists sought to follow was at the outset doomed to failure. As the *Cincinnati Weekly Gazette* declared early in the campaign: "There are but two parties in Kentucky. You must go to the one or to the other. . . . If you choose to attempt a middle party, well and good. In some places the rebels will beat you; in others, the Radicals."[90] There was little hope in Kentucky for the anti-Democratic forces in any event, but the splitting of the opposition vote among Conservatives and Radicals rendered the defeat in 1866 disastrous.[91] Logic as well as Republican bias spoke through the words of the *Gazette*: "The Conservative party have lived their day. . . . They have failed, miserably failed, and henceforth must get out of the way. There is no room . . . for these parties. The issues before the people won't admit of being split into three sets of principles; and these Union Conservatives henceforth must go over and join the rebel camp or come out like men and fight for positive, tangible Union principles."[92]

Indeed, as the Conservative Party disintegrated, Harlan realized that he must enter either the Republican or the Democratic fold. Against affiliation with the latter weighed his whole political heritage and career; nor could he bear connection with the old secessionist group. But the road to Republicanism was not an easy one. Consistently he had championed slavery in the political arena and had fought inch by inch the Republican measures of negro emancipation and enfranchisement. Yet the Thirteenth Amendment he had already been forced to accept, and as he pondered the inevitable victory of the Radical measures and as he reconsidered many of the basic social principles upon which his approach had been based, he reconstructed his atti-

[89] *Louisville Daily Courier*, July 18, 1866.
[90] *Cincinnati Weekly Gazette*, March 21, 1866.
[91] *Ibid.*, August 15, 1866.
[92] *Ibid.*

tudes, as he had reconstructed them after the Know-Nothing adventure, in the light of new reflections and new demands. Worthy of mention, too, is the re-emergence of the religious note to condition Harlan's political outlook. For when the violent cleavage within Kentucky Presbyterianism occurred, Harlan with his brother was induced to support the anti-secessionist camp, led largely by the radical Republican Rev. Robert J. Breckinridge.[93] If that affiliation did little in itself to win him over to the Republican ranks, it at least rendered more difficult affiliation with the old secessionists.

In 1868 Harlan was reported "hard at work for Grant" and the Republicans.[94]

III

Entrance into the Republican party was a turning mark of epochal significance in the political career of John Harlan. Having embarked upon political life as a vigorous champion of slavery, he now discovered himself in the party which had executed the measures of Negro emancipation and enfranchisement under Radical domination. Having begun with a forceful attack upon foreigners, he discovered himself in a party which drew much of its support from German immigrants and which fought continuously for the foreign vote in Kentucky. Under the shifting impact of events the change had been wrought; and now the newly-embraced attitudes of Republicanism were to be reinforced by a decade of strenuous battle in their behalf on the political fronts of Kentucky.

The first major skirmish in that battle occurred in 1871 when, after but three years within the Republican ranks, the thirty-eight-year-old Harlan was nominated unanimously for the Governorship.[95] With all the fire he had previously displayed in attacking Black Republicanism, he now campaigned in its defense; and a dramatic commentary upon the whole twist of affiliation is found in Governor Morton's repayment for Harlan's attack upon him in 1864 with a speech in Harlan's support in 1871.[96] Immediately the Democratic forces lashed out at

---

[93] Letters of Harlan and Harlan, Attorneys, to Rev. Robert J. Breckinridge, October 6, 23, and November 16, 1866. Letter of John M. Harlan to Rev. Breckinridge, December 5, 1866. Memorandum of Rev. Breckinridge sent to Harlan and Harlan, October 17, 1866. Breckinridge Mss. in Library of Congress.
[94] *Cincinnati Semi-Weekly Gazette*, July 24, 1868.
[95] *Louisville Courier-Journal*, May 24, 1871.
[96] *Cincinnati Daily Gazette*, July 29, 1871.

Harlan as a "political weathercock" and hounded him with lengthy quotations from his previous anti-Radical speeches.[97] Declared his opponent Leslie: "The people of Kentucky were told by . . . Harlan that" the Republican policy "was revolutionary, and if carried out would result in the destruction of our free government. . . . That was a correct view of it. . . ."[98]

Brazenly Harlan threw overboard the idea of reconciling past with present, and fought to reveal the practical futility of further opposition to the war amendments, emphasizing that he had but "acquiesced in the irreversible results of the war."[99] Branding the Democratic policy of further opposition as "suicidal and ruinous,"[100] Harlan pleaded with Kentuckians not to "enter upon a career of agitation which can bring the state no good, which would be obviously useless, and can only tend to isolate us from the balance of our countrymen."[101]

Nor was appeal to the actual ineffectiveness of the Democratic attack the sole basis of Harlan's campaign plea. Fully as significant was his vigorous defense of the war amendments as desirable and just in principle. Declaring that he would rather be "right than consistent"[102] and that "it can be said of no man that he has changed no opinions within the last ten years," he fearlessly admitted "regret that I ever advocated the sentiments which I expressed . . . in 1859."[103] And subsequent dissents on the Supreme Court were to prove the sincerity of his claim that "there is no man on this continent, from the lakes on the North to the gulf on the South, that rejoices more than I do at the extinction of slavery on this continent."[104]

Yet Harlan is quick to emphasize that the legal equality wrought for the Negro by the Reconstruction amendments can never mean common social footing in all of its implications. Impatient with repeated Democratic charges that he must in logic support every equality, including intermarriage, Harlan retorts: "What do they mean by this cry of Negro equality? Do you suppose that any law of the State can regulate social intercourse of the citizen?" The Negro "is your equal before the law . . . but he is not your equal socially. . . . We do not

[97] *Louisville Courier-Journal*, July 28, 1871.
[98] *Cincinnati Daily Gazette*, June 3, 1871.
[99] *Louisville Daily Commercial*, June 3, 1871.
[100] *Ibid.*, July 28, 1871.
[101] *Ibid.*, July 29, 1871.
[102] *Ibid.*, June 3, 1871.
[103] *Ibid.*, May 26, 1871.
[104] *Ibid.*

declare as the Democratic orators well know, in favor of social equality. No law ever can or will regulate such relations. Social equality can never exist between the two races in Kentucky."[105] Thus he declares that in the public schools "it was right and proper" to maintain the "whites and blacks separate."[106]

If it was the broad provisions of the Reconstruction amendments that were centrally at issue, it was the specific congressional measures enacted under them that struck immediately at Kentucky life. The state turbulent with lynchings and intimidation,[107] Harlan vigorously championed the Ku Klux Klan Act against the violent attack of the Democracy, although he admitted some doubts as to the constitutionality of a section of the bill.[108] "For myself," he declared, "I have no terms to make with that band of murderers and assassins denominated Ku Klux, nor shall I have any terms to make with them if I shall have the honor to become Chief Magistrate of this Commonwealth."[109] Again and again he charged the gubernatorial pardon with sheltering "lawless bands" and condemned the restrictions on Negro testimony in Kentucky courts as being "directly promotive of outrage";[110] and he demanded an immediate convention to remedy these evils constitutionally.[111] But here too the Democracy resurrected the past to embarrass Harlan, charging him with participation in the Bloody Monday riots at Louisville in the Know-Nothing elections of 1855, despite the fact that Harlan, as he repeatedly pointed out, was residing in Frankfort at the time.[112]

Though Harlan doubted the constitutionality of parts of the Ku Klux Klan Act, he had no reservations with respect to the Civil Rights Bill, which he lauded with particular vigor. "Thousands of gallant men in the State of Kentucky," he argued, "owe their lives to that bill and to the fact that it opened the doors of

---
[105] *Ibid.*, July 29, 1871.
[106] *Cincinnati Daily Gazette*, June 3, 1871. *Cf.* Harlan's dissents in *The Civil Rights Cases*, 109 U. S. 3; *Plessy* v. *Ferguson*, 163 U. S. 537; and *Louisville, New Orleans and Texas Railroad Company* v. *Mississippi*, 133 U. S. 587, in which the validity of separation is challenged. The difference measures the extent to which Harlan's convictions with respect to Negro equality were cemented by subsequent years of struggle in their behalf and deeper reflection; or the extent to which judicial office emancipated him from practical considerations of political appeal limiting the full expression of his views.
[107] *Cincinnati Daily Gazette*, July 21, August 9, 1871.
[108] *Louisville Daily Commercial*, July 29, 1871.
[109] *Louisville Courier-Journal*, May 28, 1871.
[110] *Louisville Daily Commercial*, July 29, 1871.
[111] *Louisville Courier-Journal*, May 24, 1871.
[112] *Ibid.*, May 28, 31, 1871.

the Federal Courts for the protection of their lives, their liberty and their property." Had "the Federal Government, after conferring freedom on the slaves, left them to the tender mercies of those who were unwilling to protect them in life, liberty and property, it would have deserved the contempt of freemen the world over."[113] Twelve years later Harlan was to issue substantially the same view from the Supreme Bench.[114]

Primarily it was a defensive battle that Harlan waged with his Democratic opponents over the Reconstruction measures. Nor could much of the tactical value of the offense be drawn from the already hackneyed charge that the "Democratic Party of Kentucky is in its management, nothing more or less than the old Southern Rights Party of 1861 which sought to drag this state out of the union."[115] An issue more vital and more compelling was needed if the Republicans were to seize a vigorous offensive, an issue that would turn the eyes of Kentuckians away from the bitternesses of war and reconstruction.

Harlan and his associates discovered it in the vast undeveloped resources of the state. They mapped a comprehensive program for the exploitation of Kentucky's economic wealth and coined slogans urging a shift of interest from past to future. Of primary significance in that program was the plea for increased immigration to Kentucky that her great "agricultural, mineral, and manufacturing resources may be developed."[116] Charging that "Democratic policy had driven immigration to other states"[117] Harlan revealed how Illinois and Ohio were outstripping Kentucky in population and hit at the last legislature for refusing to appropriate funds for the assistance of a German society which sought to induce immigrants to Kentucky from abroad.[118] Yet once again the past rises up to hinder him. His Democratic opponent Leslie "reminded . . . Harlan that it was only so long ago as 1857 that he as a Know-Nothing opposed all kinds of emigration," and opposition papers made immense capital of the Know-Nothing experience.[119] Again seizing the issue head-on, Harlan frankly admitted his earlier nativistic connections, pointed out that he was a young man of but twenty-two years at

---
[113] *Louisville Daily Commercial*, July 29, 1871.
[114] See his dissent, *The Civil Rights Cases*, 109 U. S. at 34.
[115] *Louisville Daily Commercial*, July 28, 1871.
[116] *Ibid.*, May 18, 1871.
[117] *Louisville Courier-Journal*, May 31, 1871.
[118] *Louisville Daily Commercial*, May 24, 1871.
[119] *Louisville Courier-Journal*, May 28, 1871.

the time, and that he was now fully convinced of his error.[120] The *Louisville Courier-Journal* was cynically to say of Harlan in the next campaign that "no one can laugh off inconsistency better than he, for his youth, the passions of the time, for which he was not responsible, are always at hand to excuse forever positions that to his present view are incorrect."[121]

Hand in hand with the plea for increased immigration went the Republican campaign for the extension of railroad facilities throughout the state. Kentucky transportation advance had been choked for years by the virtual monopoly maintained for the Louisville and Nashville Railroad by the refusal of the state legislature under its domination to grant other charters. Seeking to break Louisville's grip upon the Kentucky interior, Cincinnati and Lexington thrust forward plans for a rival road, but their plea for franchise had been flatly denied by the last session of the assembly. Hence this sector of the Republican economic program comes to revolve around the broader issue of monopoly; and Harlan, now with a principle upon which he can clearly seize the offensive, vigorously strikes out at "railroad monopolies, absorbing the capital of the state and controlling its politics."[122]

Repeatedly he branches off upon an attack against monopolies everywhere, charging that New York was "rolling in corruption" under the influence of the Central and Erie.[123] With his repeated plea that monopolies should not be permitted to "stifle the powers of industry and national wealth,"[124] Harlan argues that the values of free industrial competition be enforced by building "up rivals to" the railroad "monopoly and every other monopoly in this commonwealth."[125] Years later on the Supreme Court when Harlan issued a series of memorable opinions with respect to the Sherman Anti-Trust Act, he may well have recalled these strenuous days of struggle against "a monopoly which is gradually overshadowing the greater portion of this state."[126]

Allied to the general stream of economic controversy running through the campaign of 1871 was the issue of taxation with respect to the debt emerging from civil war. Maintaining that

[120] *Ibid.*, May 31, 1871
[121] *Ibid.*, July 7, 1875.
[122] *Louisville Daily Commercial*, July 29, 1871.
[123] *Cincinnati Daily Gazette*, May 24, 1871.
[124] *Louisville Daily Commercial*, May 24, 1871.
[125] *Cincinnati Daily Gazette*, May 24, 1871.
[126] *Ibid.* See *United States* v. *E. C. Knight Co.*, 156 U. S. 1 (dissent); *Northern Securities Co.* v. *United States*, 193 U. S. 197.

the Democratic platform of 1868 would substitute "direct taxation" on property for the indirect income tax of the Republicans, Harlan forcefully charged his opponents with desiring to shift unjust burdens upon poor men. Before masses of Kentuckians he pointed out that the proposed Democratic system of direct taxation would tax "your farms, houses, land, implements, and tools . . . equally with the incomes . . . of the wealthy."[127] Harlan declared that the national government "foresaw that the poor man would have to fight the battles of the country and hence determined to make the rich man pay the taxes. . . . The lawyer and the physician were taxed on their income over and above $2000, but the poor mechanic who only made $1000, or $1500, a year was not taxed on his income at all."[128]

In Harlan's vigorous defense of the income tax and in his opposition to the "direct taxation" of the Democracy as shifting upon the masses "burdens which would be hard indeed to bear," there are discoverable relationships running both to the past and to the future. To the past in the plea for the emancipation of common men from undue civil burdens already emergent in 1866; to the future in the Income Tax Case, in which Harlan issued one of his most vigorous dissents, arguing primarily what he assumed in 1871, that a levy on incomes is not a direct tax.[129]

Harlan lends further support to the principle of taxation according to ability to pay in his attack upon Leslie for favoring poll instead of property taxes for school maintenance and in his plea for a tax equalization fund to assist education in the poorer regions of Kentucky.[130] Throughout the campaign he attacked the newly-enacted rate-bill system, which provided that deficits in school districts be made up not from the property of the state but from assessments upon local families in proportion to the number of children they had enrolled in the schools. This measure meant "that a poor man blessed in the number of his children but unprovided with the world's goods, is taxed while the rich who are able to educate their children in private schools, are exempt from taxation."[131] Referring to the valor of poor men on the battlefields of the civil war, Harlan charged that

---
[127] *Louisville Daily Commercial*, July 29, 1871.
[128] *Louisville Courier-Journal*, May 31, 1871.
[129] *Pollock v. Farmer's Loan and Trust Co.*, 157 U. S. 429; 158 U. S. 601.
[130] *Louisville Daily Commercial*, June 3, 1871.
[131] *Ibid.*

"the rich owed it to the poor to contribute to the education of the latter."[132]

As Harlan hammered away at the new issues of economic progress and the equalization of tax burdens, it became increasingly clear that the Republicans were to capture a record vote in Kentucky. Speaking every day except Sundays throughout the whole campaign, he marshaled an astonishing amount of energy in what it seemed reasonably clear would at best be a losing battle.[133] For history had not yet slated Harlan's platform of newer and more challenging social issues for victory; it was still to be overshadowed by the accumulated hates of civil war and Reconstruction. Despite his defeat by over thirty thousand votes, however, Harlan succeeded in virtually doubling the Republican ballot in Kentucky and everywhere Republican papers hailed the accomplishment. Said the *Cincinnati Gazette:* "The election of the entire Republican ticket in almost any other state in the union would have been no greater victory than was won in Kentucky."[134]

So strong had Harlan's appeal become nationally as a result of the campaign that, in August of 1871, when Colfax announced his intention to withdraw from public life, the *Gazette* put forth Harlan for the next Republican vice-presidential nomination, praising his "spirit, pluck, and tact" and arguing that his nomination would mean a Republican victory in Kentucky in 1872.[135] But if the movement in this direction died, the national Republican convention of the next year was nevertheless of tremendous significance for Harlan because it was there that he shifted the support of the Kentucky delegation to Hayes at a critical hour, a move which succeeded in capturing Hayes' everlasting gratitude.

1875 saw Harlan once again carrying the Republican banner in the gubernatorial contest. Again he defends the Reconstruction amendments and the congressional enactments in behalf of Negro civil rights[136] and once more he is swamped by the ineradicable prejudices of Kentuckians and by the resurrected inconsistencies of his career.[137] Once more he thrusts forth his

---
[132] *Cincinnati Daily Gazette,* June 28, 1871.
[133] *Ibid.,* August 5, 1871.
[134] *Ibid.,* August 9, 1871.
[135] *Ibid.*
[136] *Louisville Daily Commercial,* August 1, 1875.
[137] *Louisville Courier-Journal,* July 7, 1875.

vision of economic progress and the principle that "each and every citizen should be made to bear the burdens of the government in proportion to his ability to pay."[138] Now, however, there is traceable a note of weariness in his speeches entirely absent in 1871, expression of an underlying realization of the immensity of the social forces working against Republican success in post-war Kentucky.

Defeated again, Harlan was offered an ambassadorship to England by the grateful Hayes and, refusing it, he was appointed to the electoral investigating commission dispatched to Louisiana. In 1877 he was nominated by Hayes for the Supreme Court. It was doubtless with a hardened reaction that he heard news of opposition to his confirmation by some Republicans who brought out his one-time opposition to Negro emancipation;[139] yet his championship of Republicanism in Kentucky had won the admiration of influential Republicans everywhere and he was easily confirmed.

As the forty-four-year-old John Harlan entered upon what became almost four decades of Supreme Court labor, he had behind him a record of thought and action that was profoundly to condition his approach to the momentous social problems thrust before the Court by the swift-moving industrial developments of the latter Nineteenth Century. In the turbulence of Kentucky life, through crisis, Civil War and Reconstruction, basic social attitudes had been hammered out and ideas on specific problems articulated. Again and again they were to speak through the legal framework of Supreme Court opinion.

[138] *Louisville Daily Commercial*, June 13, 1875.
[139] *Louisville Courier-Journal*, October 8, 1877.

LOUIS HARTZ (1919–   ) was born in Youngstown, Ohio, and received his B.A. and Ph.D. degrees from Harvard University. He has taught at Harvard since 1945. A winner of several prizes (including the Woodrow Wilson prize of the American Political Science Association), Hartz is the author of many articles in scholarly journals. His books include *Economic Policy and Democratic Thought* and *The Liberal Tradition in America*.

This article first appeared in *The Filson Club History Quarterly* in January 1940, vol. 14, pp. 17–40.

BASES FOR CONFLICTS IN THE KENTUCKY CONSTITUTIONAL CONVENTION 1890-91

By Rhea A. Taylor*
Lexington, Kentucky

Paper read before The Filson Club May 3, 1971

After four years of civil war, in which Kentucky suffered as a border state, her people passed through a short period of optimism, followed by one of confusion and disorder. These divergent periods were caused by the war and complicated by the unfriendly attitude of the Federal Government. These experiences produced bitter factional feelings. New industrial, commercial, and agricultural developments contributed greatly to the rehabilitation of the state, but they added conflicts to the partisan political outlook. Changed social practices, which lowered moral principles, created problems of great magnitude. Educational concepts suffered under the weight of state-wide handicaps which remained for a long time. Religious identifications for which Kentuckians had been famous for decades were broken and twisted.

When General Joseph E. Johnston's army surrendered to General William T. Sherman on April 26, 1865, near Durham's Station in Orange County, North Carolina, a feeling of joy came over the people of Kentucky. The end of military conflict had come. It had been a bloody struggle, the major part of which it seemed to them had taken place on their soil. Heartaches caused by property losses, brother fighting against brother, and deaths of thousands of brave Kentucky men were forgotten for the moment and the minds of the leaders were filled with anticipation of renewed growth and prestige for the state. The losses had been large but they were not too large, they reasoned, to prevent Kentucky from serving the country on practically the same scale as she had done in the past. There was a feeling on the part of most people that a rapid return to normalcy was the only course; in fact, many thought that all their trials were over.[1]

The Frankfort *Tri-Weekly Yeoman*, December 15, 1866, said that Kentucky had no "rankling wound in her heart." It added that peace

---

*Editor's Note: Dr. Rhea A. Taylor, Associate Professor of History at the University of Kentucky, is the author of "The Selection of Kentucky's Permanent Capital Site" and "Abraham Lincoln, The Man," both published in previous issues of *The Filson Club History Quarterly*. Dr. Taylor represented the University of Kentucky at the International History Meeting in London, England, 1962.

[1] N. S. Shaler, *Kentucky: A Pioneer Commonwealth* (Boston: Houghton Mifflin Company, 1912), pp. 361-362.

had extinguished the resentments of war; that the pending struggle for national reconstruction presented a common danger; and that a common defense united the state, the South, and the nation. Much emphasis was placed upon the thought that the "rebellion" was a thing of the past, and the Kentuckians who supported it, as well as those who opposed it, were now for the Union and the Constitution.[2]

But when the major part of a state's population is dead, wounded, or worn out by the fatigue of hard military campaigns there are often chronic troubles that are more destructive to vitality than those encountered in actual warfare. Thus problems arose that kept the state disturbed for many years.

Most Kentuckians who fought in the battles on Kentucky's soil, as well as those who campaigned outside the state, returned with a desire to be friendly toward their former foes.[3] The differences separating the Union soldier from his Confederate opponent soon grew dim, and a feeling arose that since Kentucky did not secede, her position in the Union was unlike that of the states that broke from the national moorings. As early as 1863, Governor Bramlette expressed the idea that in Kentucky it would not be a question of a restored Union nor a reconstructed Union, but rather a preserved Union along old conventional lines.[4] Hence the Government's attitude was that Kentucky's position in the Union was like it was before; perhaps it was different to a small degree, but nothing that a little time would not heal.

But the first impressions held by governmental officials that everything would be like it was before the war, that the desires of the majority to return to a condition of normalcy were honest ones, that the intentions of business men to forgive and forget were sincere, and the desires of neighbors, cousins and brothers to patch up differences were on the level, were destined to be incorrect.[5] The national politicians stood in the way of continued advancement in Kentucky. Their purpose was to keep the people stirred up, and they were successful.[6] Fortunately, it was not possible for the party in power in the nation to sink the state to those depths of political degradation into which most of the seceding states were at once plunged. There was no valid excuse to overthrow Kentucky's government, but there was a desire to do so, and an effort was actually made to do it because the victorious war party in the United States saw the necessity of keeping Kentucky in a status like that of the other Southern states.[7]

---

[2] Frankfort *Tri-Weekly Yeoman*, December 15, 1866.
[3] *Lexington Observer and Reporter*, November 26, 1866.
[4] *Frankfort Commonwealth*, September 2, 1863.
[5] *Lexington Observer and Reporter*, April 10, 1869.
[6] Shaler, *op. cit.*, p. 364.
[7] *Ibid.* Confederate soldiers were barred from voting in the general elections in 1865.

This change of attitude by the Federal government, which the people were now aware of for the first time, had developed gradually during the war years. It was largely caused by the 35,000 soldiers that Kentucky furnished to the Confederacy. Many of the leaders of the state endeavored to justify Kentucky's contribution to the Southern war effort by saying that 70,000 of her boys had served with the Union forces in order to preserve the federal government.[8] By a process of rationalization these leaders arrived at the conclusion that without Kentucky's military aid the federal Union would not have been preserved. Thus, throughout the period immediately following the war there was much discontent which gave rise to disillusionment and confusion that was reflected for years in the slow progress of the state.

Had this disillusionment not come there would have been an entirely different Kentucky. The feeling of uneasiness soon changed into one of anger. A number of unfortunate incidents caused the optimist to become a pessimist. Martial law was continued in Kentucky long after it was suspended elsewhere; a minister of the gospel was imprisoned without trial for opposing a union between the northern and southern branches of his church; and the Freedmen's Bureau created bad feelings because it took material wealth from citizens without due process of law, although the Bureau accomplished many beneficial results. The friction between the provost marshal and a resisting people bred a spirit of lawlessness that found expression in the Ku Klux Klan, which, to some degree, preserved some things to which the latter were accustomed. There was a "considerable amount of social rubbish in the state, both black and white. The blacks, as a rule, behaved well, but some who were under the influence of bad white, caused trouble."[9] At first under the Ku Klux Klan the idea was to punish only the transgressors of local customs and laws. The organization was tolerated because it protected the citizen in his property, in his way of thinking, and in his way of living. But Governor Leslie called upon the legislature to pass laws for the detection, apprehension, and punishment of the offenders. This type of lawlessness ran its course and went out after sufficient changes were made in the attitudes and practices of the government.[10]

Thus there were certain fundamental bases for political conflict which arose in Kentucky after the war. It is true that some conditions had their beginnings before that struggle, but it magnified them, and the intensity of feeling during the years to 1890 caused the pre-war period largely to be forgotten. Among the most important were those

---
[8] *Ibid.*
[9] *Ibid.*, p. 366.
[10] Lewis and Richard Collins, *History of Kentucky* (Covington: Collins and Company, 1882), II, p. 28.

concerning industry, social concepts, politics, agriculture, and education.

The industrial problems after 1865 changed in scope and demanded so much attention that they can be assumed to have arisen principally out of the revolution which resulted from the war. A sharp decline in industrial development came during the early post-war years; then it experienced a rapid increase. This was caused by the opening of markets, the construction of transportation lines, and the desire of the people to acquire the financial returns made possible by the National *laissez faire* system. It was not, however, until after 1890, that the general exploitation of Kentucky's natural resources began on a large scale.[11]

Economic conditions were changing rapidly and the keenest observer was taxed to understand them. Before the war Kentucky carried on commerce with the Southern states in plantation supplies, including slaves.[12] The commodities of trade were shipped to the plantation owner who distributed them. But after the war the system was changed. The manufacturer dealt with the community merchant.[13] This latter system incorporated a middleman's profit which caused an increase in prices, and thus the volume of trade was decreased for a few years because of a scarcity of ready cash with which to purchase goods.

The Reconstruction Period witnessed a rehabilitation of existing railroads and the construction of new ones. The repairing of existing roads was accomplished in such a manner as to arouse no suspicion by the way in which it was done, but the building of new roads, especially the Southern Railroad, did arouse suspicion and caused competition between cities.[14] Interstate roads felt this condition more keenly since the cities in which factories were located strove to become feeder points in the commerce race. By 1870 Louisville and Cincinnati were competing against each other for the commerce of the deep South. In 1869 Louisville spent large sums to impress the delegates who attended a commercial convention here that she was the legitimate trading point for the South. During 1870 Cincinnati sent a commission throughout the Southland to study commercial and financial conditions and possibilities with the objective to outbid Louisville. Finally, when a railroad was built from Cincinnati across Kentucky, Louisville lost a great por-

---

[11] E. Merton Coulter, *The Civil War and Readjustment in Kentucky* (Chapel Hill: The University of North Carolina Press, 1936), p. 386.

[12] J. Winston Coleman, "Lexington's Slave Dealers and Their Southern Trade," *The Filson Club History Quarterly*, XII (January, 1938).

[13] Thomas D. Clark, *Pills, Petticoats and Plows: The Southern Country Store* (Indianapolis: The Bobbs-Merrill Company, 1944), Chs. xvi, xvii.

[14] E. Merton Coulter, *The Cincinnati Southern Railroad and the Struggle for Southern Commerce*, 1865-1872 (Chicago: The American Historical Society, Inc., 1922), pp. 27-64. Also Elmer G. Sulzer, "Kentucky's Abandoned Railroads," *The Kentucky Engineer*, IX (August, 1947), pp. 15-46.

tion of her trade. But she resorted to all kinds of schemes to thwart her sister town up the river. A bridge was built across the Ohio River at a low height so river boats could not pass under it. For a while Cincinnati became a bridge-locked city wholly at the mercy of Louisville as far as downstream shipping was concerned. The issue became so heated that relief was sought in the national Congress.[15] The construction of the Southern Railroad was the answer, but before that project was completed a swollen Ohio River washed away the bridge which was never replaced at such a low height.

Cincinnati, by a vote of 15,438 to 1,500 issued $10,000,000 in city bonds on June 26, 1869, to build a "trunk line" railroad between that city and Chattanooga. A little more than a month later some counties in Kentucky began to subscribe to the Cincinnati project, especially those through which the right of way ran, and from which branch or feeder lines could be constructed.[16] Such actions caused alignments of Congressmen from Kentucky. Those from the areas adjacent to Louisville sided with her, while those from the counties through which the road ran south from Cincinnati sided with the Queen City. This grouping of interests was plainly discernible when the Constitutional Convention convened, and the delegates from Covington and Newport followed a policy which helped, not only the internal interests of the Bluegrass regions, but of Cincinnati as well.

Several small independent lines were developed during this surge of industrialism. Among them were the Short Line Railroad which was completed between Covington and Louisville at a cost of $3,933,401 and was opened for business in June, 1869. On August 2, Bourbon County authorized a $2,000 subscription to build a line from Paris to Maysville. Eight days later Lexington and Fayette County voted $450,000 to aid in the construction of the Elizabethtown, Lexington, and Big Sandy Railway. On September 6, by a bare majority of twelve votes, Shelby County subscribed $400,000 to the Cumberland and Ohio Road. Even though most of the efforts to support the building of railroads were successful, there were some failures. On August 10, 1869, for instance, the people in Henderson County refused to approve a bond issue in behalf of the Henderson and Nashville Railroad.[17]

A law was passed in 1884 over Governor Knott's veto, to encourage the building of railroads in Kentucky by exempting them from taxation for a period of five years. This law included all roads to be built by companies already chartered as well as those yet to be chartered. The

---

[15] Thomas D. Clark, *A History of Kentucky* (Lexington: The John Bradford Press, 1950, p. 190.
[16] Collins, *op. cit.*, I, p. 197.
[17] *Ibid.*, p. 198.

period of exemption began with the start of construction.[18]

These are examples of the interest cities, counties, and the legislature had in this type of development. They were contrary to good judgment since economic barriers soon arose between the towns and areas as a result of capital invested in these projects and their exemption from taxation. Not only were the railroad companies eventually fought by agricultural interests because of the exorbitant rates charged for carrying and storing of products when they knew no taxes were paid by them, but other industrial corporations vied with them both in the field and in the legislative halls. This economic competition grew into huge corporations.

Economic progress in Kentucky after the Civil War, when compared with that of the Northern states, could, at best, be described as backward and slow. Kentucky lacked industrial plants, thus her economy was based upon agriculture. This type of economy made Kentucky different, and although many Kentuckians recognized this difference, conservatism prevented a change for a long time. Marse Henry Watterson, editor of the *Courier-Journal*, recognized the damaging condition and tried to lead the people and legislature to change it, but to no avail. Some years after the war a Cincinnati paper taunted that one who traveled south through Kentucky went backward toward the dawn of history at the rate of 500 miles an hour.[19] This statement was a bit exaggerated, to be sure, but there were some grounds upon which to base such a contention.

Many people believed that when the slaves were freed every part of the system which had shackled the progress of government, education, social life, and even the religious life would be erased.[20] It was felt by many of the state's leaders that if the natural resources of the state were utilized Kentucky could soon rank among the topmost and more progressive states in the Union.[21] Some of the governors were among the leaders in this crusade. They extolled the value of the wealth to be found on and in the hills, mountains, and meadows of the commonwealth.[22]

Another phase of the industrial development was the program followed by the legislature in the generous chartering of business companies. The session of 1865, for example, chartered numerous oil companies and mining companies. Likewise water works companies,

---

[18] *Acts of the General Assembly of the Commonwealth of Kentucky* (Frankfort: S. I. M. Major, Printer, 1884), I, p. 195.
[19] *Cincinnati Commercial*, April 24, 1867.
[20] Coulter, *The Civil War and Readjustment in Kentucky*, p. 367.
[21] *Lexington Observer and Reporter*, December 9, 1865.
[22] *Daily Kentucky Yeoman* (Frankfort), January 4, 1867; January 8, 1884. The first date refers to effort by Governor Bramlette, and the second refers to that of Governor Knott.

turnpike companies, insurance companies, fruit companies, and fish companies were incorporated by the dozens.[23] This practice was continued through the 1870's and 1880's without any appreciable let up.[24] A Cincinnati paper criticized the Kentucky Legislature for losing sight of the real objective needed and suggested suitable names for some of the chartered companies in a mood of derision.[25]

Many of these ill-planned-for companies laid the basis for conflicts which burst into full bloom by the time the Constitutional Convention convened in 1890. Coal corporations fought those of oil; oil companies vied with those of whiskey; whiskey companies strove with those of timber, and timber units disagreed with those of coal. Thus the circuit was completed, and sometimes these conflicts cut across lines whenever the legislature seemed to be more favorably inclined toward any one corporation.

Some prominent historians have concluded that the Civil War "led to mechanization and standardization of social life, modified social institutions such as the family, and changed the intellectual outlook of the people."[26] This conclusion referred to the nation as a whole, to be sure, but when applied locally to Kentucky was true only in a general way. In the first place the war did not lead to a standardization of social life and of social institutions in Kentucky to any appreciable degree greater than what existed prior to 1860. There were too many divisions among the people: some had favored the North and some the South during that conflict and, regardless of all efforts to reunite the people, such had not been done. In the second place such great national movements as turning from Europe to develop the west after 1815, the struggle for states' rights during the decades prior to the Civil War, the rise of the abolition issue, and the recognition that Americans could stand alone in the world had shaped a general policy for the nation. Kentuckians could not agree as to the importance of these movements. Consequently, there were many opinions held by them which prevented uniform development.

The keeping alive of Confederate and Federal conflicts; the reliving of memories of hardships, trials, and physical sufferings; the continued bitterness toward the national governmental attitude and actions concerning Kentucky; the appearance of national and state scandals; the practice of feuding; the differences between the geographical divisions

---

[23] *Acts of Kentucky*, 1865, *et passim*.
[24] *Ibid.*, 1865-1881, *et passim.* Waterworks (1865), p. 14; turnpike (1865), p. 369; manufacturing (1873), p. 104; coal (1873), p. 410; race and fair, p. 579; and lands (1881), p. 69.
[25] *Cincinnati Gazette*, February 23 and March 10, 1865.
[26] Samuel Eliot Morison and Henry Steele Commager, *The Growth of the American Republic* (New York: Oxford University Press, 1942), II, p. 124.

of the state; the development of special interests; the financial upheaval and its slow readjustment during the 1870's and 1880's, and the increasing demands of farmers and laborers caused differences of opinion among the people. These conditions were basic, and gave rise to problems which were exemplified in disunited statesmanship, sordid business manipulations, parvenu rich, and resulted in a sense of humiliation and apology oftentimes.

The wreckage of a social organization, the devastation of a labor system built during many generations, and a change of attitude by the Federal government entered into the picture to help mold the lives, direct the actions, and shape the thoughts of the people.

Such changes had obvious effects on Kentuckians and resulted in alignments which reached their peak in 1890. One school of thought embraced a large majority which clung to fundamentalism—the acceptance of old customs and beliefs—while another was more anxious to accept the changes then in progress, and was called pragmatism. The pursuit of wealth, by practices sometimes slightly shady, in which the legislature often acquiesced, tended to drive society into separate cliques. Edward Bellamy popularized his revolutionary theory—that eventually a more even distribution of goods and values would come and, because of the stinging presence of poverty, gained converts by the hundreds. Likewise many disciples of Henry George, who advocated that only land should be taxed, lived in the commonwealth. These ideas helped to bring about changes in the social and economic concepts of 1890.[27]

Keeping alive the Confederate and Federal causes gave rise to mingled feelings in a people who suffered from a lack of sympathy, patience, and foresight on the part of national politicians who could have led them toward a progressive existence. School books, on the whole, sympathized with the Southern point of view and were studied by youngsters who were fired with enthusiasm for a cause which lived on in their minds. Teachers found it easy to arouse their pupils. Perhaps there has never been a period in our history when the shaping of ideas of the youth was more important. A student at the State University in 1870 gave vent to his feelings by destroying a United States flag and confessed his action was prompted by the constant waving of the bloody shirt in the press.[28] Such incidents aroused the "fighting blood" in Kentuckians and those who fought on both sides were quick to defend the North or the South. Organizations sprung up throughout the state to preserve the memories of those who paid the supreme sacrifice upon the fields of battle. One of these was the Ladies' Memorial

---

[27] Frankfort *Weekly Yeoman*, January 1, 1884. This paper changed from tri-weekly to weekly publication at the end of Reconstruction Period.
[28] *Louisville Commercial*, October 21, 1870.

and Monumental Association. The reburying of the dead was one of their activities. At Cynthiana, Crab Orchard, Frankfort, Lexington, and other places these sad rites were performed. An outstanding example was the reburial of John Hunt Morgan. A massive crowd attended his reinterment in 1866, among whom were hundreds of his former troops.[29] Coulter described the rites as follows:

> Amidst elaborate ceremonies the body was placed on a funeral car, drawn through the street, and lowered into a grave . . . while cadets . . . fired a parting volley to honor this hero and end a day of sincere mourning.[30]

The effects of such activities are hard to estimate, but if editorials can be taken as reflecting the general sentiment, the people relived a period which would have been better forgotten.[31]

Not only were dead heroes memorialized but also those who returned alive were honored. When John C. Breckinridge returned from exile in Canada he was perhaps the most loved Kentuckian of the day. He had fled from the Federal government after ordering the people of Kentucky to join the Confederate army. The Louisville and Lexington papers openly advocated his pardon.[32] It was not until the last weeks of Johnson's presidency that he was free to return to his home in Lexington.[33] He barely participated in the parades, speakings, and celebrations, and refused to enter politics again. He determined not to help keep the antagonisms alive against the North. He realized the sooner the prejudices were permitted to die the earlier progress could return to Kentucky. It was unfortunate that his philosophy was misunderstood until some years after his death. When he died in 1875 the General Assembly declared his death left "the impartial judgment of history to place him among the actors of his time "[34] Another Kentucky son who returned from exile was Simon Bolivar Buckner; he was elected Governor in 1888 and served as the state's chief executive during the Constitutional Convention.[35]

Thus Kentucky society and politics became permeated with that intangible but real something—the Confederate tradition. During the first ten years after the war this tradition was built up to sufficient strength to insure Democratic domination of the government until 1896. After 1876, however, a lessening of war and reconstruction

---

[29] *Cincinnati Semi-Weekly Gazette*, May 8, 1868.
[30] Coulter, *The Civil War and Readjustment in Kentucky*, p. 368.
[31] *Lexington Observer and Republic*, April 15, 1868.
[32] *Louisville Courier*, January 31, 1868; *Lexington Observer and Recorder*, February 8, 1868.
[33] *Lexington Observer and Recorder*, March 19, 1869.
[34] *Acts of Kentucky*, 1875, I, p. 144.
[35] *Appleton's Annual Cyclopedia and Register of Important Events* (New York: D. Appleton and Co., 1888), XII, p. 411.

antagonisms were noticeable. Perhaps "Marse" Henry Watterson was the greatest leader in promoting the change. He advised the people to forget the past and face the future with confidence.[36]

In the realm of politics there was a dogged contest between the conservatives, sometimes called the Bourbons, and the Radicals who later became Republicans. After 1871, when the birth of the Republican Party officially occurred in Kentucky, the campaigns boiled down to hot contests between that party and the Democrats. Twenty-five years passed before the Republicans carried the state for a presidential or gubernatorial candidate.[37] All of the nine Democratic governors between 1865 and 1895 carried the state by comfortable majorities.[38] Only once was there a serious threat to the Democratic rule. This occurred in 1871, the year the Republican party became official, when Henry Watterson led one faction of the Democrats along the road to a "New Departure"—a split in the Bourbons to form the "New South" wing, a group who advocated changes in practices such as methods of nominating, campaigning, and electing as well as adopting a constructive legislative program. Watterson demanded that the voters should judge the candidates for all public offices on the principles they supported rather than accept views released by party machines, and that they accept amendments to the Constitution for the betterment of the entire population rather than retain its old, outmoded sections which retarded governmental reform and progress.[39]

One faction of the Conservative party refused to follow the Democracy. They broke away on the grounds that they were permitted to play only a minor part in the party's organization, that discrimination against men who fought on the side of the Union was unfair, and that the doctrine of secession had been solved by the contest of arms.[40] But by 1875, most of this group had reaffiliated with the Democratic party.[41]

The Democrats won in the elections of 1868 and 1869 by the largest majorities in the state's political history.[42] The national press said much about the victories of democracy over radicalism, while the de-

---

[36] Louisville *Courier-Journal*, May 14, 1875.
[37] Coulter, *The Civil War and Readjustment in Kentucky*, p. 438. William McKinley for President, and William Bradley for Governor.
[38] Z. F. Smith, *History of Kentucky* (Louisville: The Courier-Journal Printing Company, 1889), p. 223. Governors: Thomas E. Bramlette, 1863-1867; John L. Helm, September 3 to 8, 1867; John W. Stevenson, 1867-1871; Preston H. Leslie, 1871-1875; James B. McCreary, 1875-1879; Luke B. Blackburn, 1879-1883; J. Proctor Knott, 1883-1887; Simon B. Buckner, 1887-1891, and John Young Brown, 1891-1895.
[39] Clark, *A History of Kentucky*, pp. 409-425, *et passim*.
[40] Louisville *Courier-Journal*, September 18, 1867.
[41] Frankfort *Tri-Weekly Yeoman*, June 13, 1875.
[42] *Appleton's Annual Cyclopedia and Register* . . . ., p. 405.

feated forces continued to criticize their opponents.[43]

Some of the bases for later political rivalries were indelibly outlined in these elections and their immediate results. The Radicals were willing to listen to comments made by papers outside the state and to accept their statements as truth. A New York paper viewed the election results as nothing but an affront of the worst kind to the national government. Democratic victories, it warned, might spread to other states.[44] A Cincinnati paper said that the Radicals could never win in Kentucky because too much prejudice existed against them. It complained that the Radicals were not treated as political opponents but as something to be shunned like poisonous reptiles, since the "whole force of society, in all its relations, social, civil, religious, commercial, was arraigned against them."[45]

Henry Watterson reminded outside partisan papers that Kentucky's position was unique in that she did not secede from the Union. The trend of events was somewhat natural since undeserved impositions had been made by outside influences. Kentucky would protect her integrity, he argued, and since the war she had "proscribed" no one. She had given welcome to all who wanted to come into the state, and would continue to do so. Because of this attitude Kentucky was regaining her prosperity, and political conditions seemed to be peaceful and happy.[46] He further maintained that the laws were enforced better in Kentucky, and there was less crime committed, than elsewhere. Kentuckians had as much right to do their own thinking as others, and if they could not see their way clear to vote for Republican candidates no one had the right to criticize them for their political actions.[47]

This outside interference fostered among most Kentuckians a defense of their state officials and institutions. Only the party of opposition agreed with the outside criticisms. They took a firm stand against the things they did not approve. These differences were not to be ironed out during one generation. They were still in evidence when the Constitutional Convention assembled late in 1890 to write Kentucky's fourth Constitution.

Some bases for conflict arose out of the sordid conditions found in the realms of agriculture and education. Both of these entities suffered greatly during the war and reconstruction years. The yield of tobacco was cut in half, that of wheat by two-thirds, and the hemp crops never reached a normal yield for a dozen years.[48] By 1890, however, ap-

---

[43] *Cincinnati Semi-Weekly Gazette,* August 8, 1868.
[44] New York *Tribune,* August 19, 1868.
[45] *Cincinnati Semi-Weekly Gazette,* August 28, 1868.
[46] Louisville *Courier-Journal,* September 9, 1868.
[47] *Ibid.*
[48] Coulter, *The Civil War and Readjustment in Kentucky,* p. 381.

proximately four times as much tobacco was grown as in 1870, nearly twice as much wheat, about ten times as much hemp, and twice as much corn.[49] With the introduction of the white burley type of tobacco drastic changes came about not only in the production of the plant, but in the marketing processes as well. Louisville and Cincinnati were the marketing places immediately after the war. By 1883 inroads had been made on this monopoly when large warehouses were hastily constructed in towns such as Shelbyville, Frankfort, Maysville, Paris, and Lexington. The changing from the old method of selling through one or two markets to a new way of dealing more directly with the farmers in the vicinities where tobacco was grown gave rise to urban rivalries which have not as yet subsided.

The war caused many schools to be discontinued. The sessions of those that did continue to function averaged about three months in length. Not until the superintendency of Edward Porter Thompson in the early 1890's were school terms as long as five months.[50] The funds for educational purposes in 1872 were slightly more than $960,000 as compared with almost $2,000,000 in 1891.[51] Superintendent Zachary Smith in 1867 instituted a plan for better teachers, the establishment of high schools, and the constant discussion of school needs in the press. This program called for an increase in appropriations by the legislature. Many of the politicians were not in favor of increasing taxes, but they were forced to try to meet this need.[52] By 1890 the number of pupils increased from 169,477 in 1869 to 370,913. The number of children of school age was 376, 868 in 1869 and 618,-791 in 1890. The number of school districts increased from 4,477 in 1869 to 6,815 in 1891, the length of the sessions jumped from three months to five, and teachers' salaries rose from twelve to thirty dollars per month to thirty and fifty dollars a month. County teachers received thirty dollars and city teachers made fifty.[53] Even this small increase in salary induced most teachers to take more professional interest in their work. The Society for the Advancement of Education in Kentucky was organized in 1874. County superintendents were elected by the people after 1884, which made these offices political. Many people believed this step was in the wrong direction, which was later changed.

---

[49] *Ninth Census of the United States: 1870.* Compendium, p. 691; and *Eleventh Census of the United States: 1890.* Agriculture, pp. 64-65, 367-368, and 512-513.
[50] Barksdale Hamlett, *History of Education in Kentucky* (Frankfort: Kentucky Department of Education, 1914), VII, No. 4, p. 271.
[51] *Report of the Superintendent of Public Instruction,* 1872, pp. 5-7; *ibid.,* 1891, p. 691.
[52] *Lexington Observer and Reporter,* January 23, 1869.
[53] *Report of the Superintendent of Public Instruction of the Commonwealth of Kentucky, 1892,* p. 81. Also *Eleventh Census of the United States; 1890. Compendium,* II, pp. 214-252, *et passim.*

The Superintendent of Public Instruction for the state is still elected by popular vote. Not until after the turn of this century were education reforms of great magnitude instituted in the state.

Prior to 1890 bases for conflict were deep-seated. They were apparent when our present Constitution was written, many were not solved in its provisions, and some of them still exist to plague you and me in our efforts to have a better state.

RHEA A. TAYLOR (1902–   ), a native of Virginia, received his A.B. degree from Emory and Henry College, his M.A. degree from Ohio State University, and his Ph.D. from the University of Chicago. A contributor of articles to several historical journals, Taylor taught history at the University of Kentucky until his retirement several years ago.

This article first appeared in *The Filson Club History Quarterly* in January 1972, vol. 46, pp. 24–36.

HENRY WATTERSON AND THE "TEN THOUSAND KENTUCKIANS"

By Joseph F. Wall

Grinnell College, Grinnell, Iowa

Henry Watterson, who for fifty years was editor of the Louisville *Courier-Journal*, has won for himself a lasting place in American journalism's Hall of Fame. His adroit phrases such as "the Boy Orator of the Platte" to describe Bryan, and "the long grey wolves of the Senate" to describe certain predatory members of the United States Senate are still remembered and quoted a quarter of a century after his death. His place in American politics, however, during those same eventful five decades has been curiously slighted or misinterpreted by recent historians and largely forgotten by the American people. Although Henry Grady of Georgia and L. Q. C. Lamar of Mississippi have won deserved honor for their contribution to Southern reconciliation in the Union, Watterson's earlier and equally effective efforts in the same cause have been underestimated. If he is remembered by the general historian at all, it is usually as a Southern "hothead" or Bourbon Kentucky colonel.

This unfair estimate of Watterson can be explained in great part by one speech that he delivered in the winter of 1877, following the Hayes-Tilden election, when the nation waited in suspense to learn the name of the next president and talk of another civil war was loud in the land. Invariably it is this speech by Watterson that is quoted by historians to prove his "recklessness" and "irresponsibility," and it is high time that the speech as well as Watterson's role in the whole election crisis be reevaluated in the interest of historical truth as well as in the interest of Watterson's personal reputation.

Although prominent in Democratic politics for over fifty years, in no other campaign did Watterson play so important or so dramatic a role as in the Tilden campaign of 1876. From 1874, when Samuel J. Tilden won the governorship of New York and thus became a symbol for a revived Democratic party, Watterson had been booming him for the presidency in the editorial columns of the *Courier-Journal*. When Watterson went as a delegate from Kentucky to the National Democratic Convention at St. Louis in June of 1876 and was chosen temporary chairman of that convention, his selection was everywhere regarded in the press of the nation as a victory for the Tilden forces; and so it proved, for on the second ballot Tilden received the nomination.

In the ensuing campaign, Watterson devoted all of his abundant energy to securing Tilden's election, for in the cautious, reserved New York governor, Watterson had found his *beau ideal*, his ideal of the perfect statesman. And although temperamentally poles apart, the two men had from the first found themselves in happy accord on all political issues of the day. Watterson regarded Tilden, because of his record of reform in New York State, as the one man who could redeem the nation from the corruption of the Grant administration and rescue the South from the long-experienced evils of Radical Reconstruction.

It was in the interest of Tilden that Watterson, in the summer of 1876, for the only time in his life, agreed to run for public office to fill the unexpired term in the House of Representatives of Edward Parsons of Louisville. In a special election in August, Watterson overwhelmed his weak Republican opposition, and thus it was as the newest member in Congress that he took his part in the crisis that followed the election.

By midnight on election night, nearly every paper in the country, Republican and Democratic, had conceded the election to Tilden, and Watterson and his staff at the *Courier-Journal* office were happily preparing the morning headlines which would proclaim ecstatically, "Thank The Lord! Boys, We've Got 'Em."[1] Watterson went to bed in the small hours of the morning convinced that his campaign efforts in behalf of Tilden had been successful and that after twenty years the nation had again elected a Democratic president.

It was not until the following day that Watterson and the rest of the nation awoke to the realization that the shrewd managers of the Republican party, Oliver Morton, of Indiana, and Zachariah Chandler, National Chairman, and others, had thrown the election in doubt by claiming for Hayes the three Southern states of Louisiana, South Carolina and Florida, in which Republican carpet-bag governments were still being maintained by Federal troops. It is not necessary to go into the familiar details of how the Republican managers devised or proposed to carry out this scheme. Suffice it to say that although Tilden had a popular majority throughout the nation of over a quarter of a million, if Hayes could be given the electoral votes of the three Southern states in question, he would have a majority of one in the Electoral College, and would thus be the duly elected President.

Upon hearing of what he and other Democrats were henceforth to call "the Hayes conspiracy," Watterson's first reaction, and a correct one, was to act quickly, to meet this threat head on, to stop it before it had changed from an impious wish into unalterable reality. He at once wired to Tilden one of the most sensible pieces of advice that any Democrat would offer in the confused weeks ahead. He proposed that Tilden at once confer with Governor Hayes on the course of action to follow in the threatening crisis, and he suggested that both agree on a committee of eminent citizens to go to Louisiana to supervise the canvass of votes by the notoriously corrupt Returning Board there.[2] It was good advice. If Tilden, at this stage of the game, had made an overture to Hayes, who was an honorable man, the plans of Chandler might well have been thwarted. As it was, Tilden did nothing, and Hayes, under pressure of his advisors, soon rationalized his defeat into a deserved victory. Watterson sent another urgent telegram to Tilden: "Our friends in Louisiana need moral support and personal advisement have bayard thurman barnam randall macdonald dorsheimer and others go to New Orleans at once a strong demonstration will defeat designs of returning board. Beck McHenry and I start tonight you must reinforce us Answer."[3] Thus the so-called "visiting statesmen" plan was born. In forty-eight hours, the city of New Orleans was overflowing with the greatest conclave of political dignitaries, both Republican and Democratic, that the Crescent City had ever seen.

The "visiting statesmen" idea, which might have had merit had Watterson's first proposal to Tilden of a joint committee been accepted, became a farce, a school boy's game, as Republicans appointed by Grant, and Democrats appointed by Abram Hewitt, National Democratic Chairman, raced each other to Louisiana. When they were all assembled at the St. Charles Hotel, it quickly developed that they were there more to watch each other than to inspect the official returns. Watterson, being one of the first on the scene, quickly learned that the four members of the Returning Board, whose duty it was to supervise the returns and throw out illegal votes, although all of them Republican, did not have closed minds exactly and were open to "reason." He was approached in the hotel lobby by a state senator who stated as casually as if he were selling a horse that the price for their conversion to Democracy was two hundred and fifty thousand dollars. "Senator," Watterson replied, "the terms are as cheap as dirt. I don't happen to have that amount about me at the moment, but I will communicate with my principal and see you later." Two or three days later the man was back and Watterson told him that he had never had any intention of accepting the proposal.[4] The Returning Board then proceeded to change an eight thousand majority for Tilden to a four thousand majority for Hayes, by casually tossing out some twelve thousand Democratic votes as being fraudulent.

As no action was forthcoming from Tilden in New York, Watterson became discouraged. "The chance had been lost," he later wrote. "I thought then, and I still think, that the conspiracy of a few men to use the corrupt Returning Boards of Louisiana, South Carolina, and Florida to upset the election and make confusion in Congress, might, by prompt exposure and popular appeal, have been thwarted."[5] He stayed in New Orleans until November 17, sending an occasional dispatch to the *Courier-Journal*, but otherwise accomplishing little. When it had become apparent as to what decision the Returning Board would make, he returned home to spend a few days at his much neglected desk in the *Courier-Journal* building before going on to Washington for the opening of the second session of the Forty-fourth Congress.

Congress convened on December 4 in an atmosphere that was strained and hostile. In many respects, the situation was not unlike that of December 1860, and the threat of war was no idle talk. Great recognition was paid by the House of Representatives to its newest member when Watterson was appointed to the important Ways and Means Committee filling the vacancy caused by James Blaine's election to the Senate to finish the unexpired term of Senator Morrill. Of far greater moment, however, in this troubled time was his appointment by a party caucus to a place on the Democratic Advisory Committee to deal with all proposals concerning the disputed election. His colleagues on the committee were such distinguished Democratic figures as Randall, Hewitt, Lamar, Payne, Hunton, and Warren of the House, and Bayard, Thurman, McDonald, Kernan and Stevenson of the Senate. The committee met frequently, sometimes at Hewitt's home, more generally in the Speaker's room at the Capitol, so that Watterson was at all times fully informed as to legislative proposals in both chambers.[6]

The only real interest in this second session of the Fortyfourth Congress lay in determining who had been elected president. All other legislative matters were largely ignored as the seemingly insolvable problem was turned over, twisted and attacked from every conceivable angle. Like an intricate Chinese puzzle, it grew more complicated with the handling. South Carolina and Oregon had each submitted two sets of electoral votes, while Florida and Louisiana had submitted three. Who had the authority to decide which set was valid? The maddeningly vague clause in the Constitution regarding the counting of electoral votes was read and re-read, and it meant nothing. "The President of the Senate shall, in the Presence of the Senate and House of Representatives, open all the Certificates, and the Votes shall then be counted." But by whom? There was no answer. And so the matter stood—seemingly a hopeless deadlock. Precedent was appealed to, but there no answer could be found. In previous cases of disputed electoral votes, the vote of the state in dispute in some instances had simply been discarded; in other instances it had been counted both ways. And in any case, the election of a president had never before been dependent upon any electoral vote that had been questioned. There were serious proposals to have Hayes and Tilden flip a coin for the Presidency. The most constitutionally-minded people in the world had become hopelessly ensnared in their own Constitution.

What of Tilden in this crisis? There had been no public statement from him since the beginning of the trouble. Did he want arbitration, compromise, surrender or war? His closest advisors in Congress did not know.

On December 19, Congress adjourned for the Christmas holiday with no solution of the problem in sight. Watterson did not go back to his family in Louisville but spent the Christmas week with Tilden in New York. There, with John Bigelow and Manton Marble of the New York *World*, he spent long hours talking with Tilden, trying to reach some sort of decision for action to be taken. Robert McLane of Maryland came to visit Tilden while Watterson was staying at Tilden's home in Gramercy Park. As a boy, McLane had been in England with his father, Lewis McLane, the American Minister to Great Britain, during the excitement over the Reform Bill of 1832. The youth had been much impressed by the effect that an aroused public opinion had had in forcing the Reform Act through Parliament. It seemed to McLane now that a similar situation had arisen in America and he urged a similar demonstration on the part of a determined public to see that justice prevailed here in this crisis. And so a plan was conceived that was to have unfortunate consequences for Watterson. It was decided that Watterson would make a speech in Congress in which he would suggest that "a mass convention of at least one hundred thousand peaceful citizens exercising the freeman's right of petition" should assemble in Washington on February 14, the day the electoral votes were to be counted, to see that the will of the majority was not thwarted. It was this speech that was to affect so greatly later historical judgment of Watterson. Watterson himself had no great faith in the idea, but his loyalty to Tilden was such that he was willing to do anything that Tilden thought advisable. Moreover, this at least was a decisive move, and anything was better than the inaction of the past weeks.[7]

The idea was neither particularly original nor so drastic as it sounded. There had been several such proposals in the public press in the past few weeks, and even the cautious and conciliatory Hewitt had suggested early in December that "while the people are yet free and independent, we invite them to assemble at their usual places of meeting in every city, town and hamlet in the country on the 8th day of January next to consider the dangers of the situation and by calm, firm and temperate resolutions, to enlighten their representatives in Congress now assembled as to their duties in this great crisis of our institutions . . ."[8] a suggestion to be sure, that incurred less danger of an explosion but which was based on the same general idea of a mass protest as the McLane proposal. It is interesting to note that Tilden had vetoed Hewitt's earlier suggestion as being too radical whereas now he agreed, even to the extent of writing to Speaker Randall about it, to the more dangerous proposition of a huge mass meeting in Washington where Grant had assembled troops. The reasons for Tilden's reversal are obvious. Hewitt's appeal was to be an official declaration by the Democratic party of which Tilden was the head. If the proposal should backfire or lead to open conflict, he would be directly implicated; whereas the McLane proposal had the great advantage, which the shrewd quick mind of Tilden immediately perceived, of coming not from Tilden but simply from an individual in the Democratic party. If the appeal caught on and proved effective, well and good; but if it should fail or lead to trouble, Tilden could repudiate it and protest clean hands. To make sure that it could not possibly be considered as an official statement emanating from Tilden's headquarters, the plan at the last minute was changed so that Watterson was to make the proposal not in the Halls of Congress as an official representative of the Democratic party, but in an open meeting in Ford's Opera House purely as a private citizen.[9] Watterson, to be sure, ran the risk of being the scapegoat, which was unfortunate but, to Tilden's mind, unavoidable.

Watterson who never questioned the motives of his chief, even after this trial balloon had blown up in his face, returned to Washington the first week in January with the speech, which had been thoroughly scrutinized and then approved by Tilden and McLane, in his pocket. Speaking to an excited audience at a Jackson Day celebration in Washington on the night of January 8, Watterson said, "If it should become necessary that they [the people] should have a leader, another Jackson stands ready to take his life in his hand and make their cause his own." He then issued his call for the one hundred thousand unarmed citizens, of which number he expected ten thousand Kentuckians. So was launched Tilden's trial balloon. Watterson was followed by Joseph Pulitzer, who, carried away by the excitement of the moment, asked that these one hundred thousand citizens be armed.[10]

Tilden did not have long to wait for an answer. Immediately such a blast went up from the Republican press, that the balloon was burst even before the frightened Democrats could draw it back down. It was easy to mix Watterson's statement with that of the then relatively unknown Pulitzer, and to change his demand for an assembly of peaceful, unarmed citizens to a call for a wild, revolutionary mob, armed to the teeth. Upon Watterson's head descended the most violent abuse of the whole bitter struggle. Here was the overt call for Revolution from a well-known Southerner for which the Radicals had been waiting. They played it up for all it was worth. Thomas Nast, America's most noted cartoonist, depicted Watterson as a wild-eyed Southern rebel with unkempt, Medusan locks of hair twisting savagely and with fire bursting from his nostrils. So malicious were Nast's cartoons, in fact, that Watterson protested vigorously to Nast's publisher, Joe Harper, and the latter ordered Nast to make some sort of an apology. Making use of the fact that Mrs. Watterson had just given birth to a boy, Nast drew a humorous cartoon depicting Watterson walking the floor with his newborn son, and a caption below quoted Watterson as saying, "Let us have peace." This cartoon along with the widely quoted remark of some wit, that Watterson's son was "the only one of the hundred thousand in arms who came when he was called" helped take some of the sting out of Nast's earlier cartoons.[11]

But, in the main, Watterson was left to face the attack alone. Granted that the proposal was unwise and that Watterson was hasty in making it, still it had not been his idea originally, and the least he might have expected was some word of support from his own party. But no word came from Gramercy Park, only a silence so icy that one might suppose that Tilden had never heard of any proposal so shocking in nature. The other Democratic leaders followed suit. When, during a session of the Joint Congressional Committee to draw up a plan of arbitration, Senator Edmunds made some slighting allusion to "Henry Watterson's one hundred thousand Democratic men who are said to be coming," a virtual chorus of Democratic voices answered him with "Oh, they are not coming; we've telegraphed them not to come!" followed by much laughter.[12] Watterson had become the obliging court fool whose antics were meant to amuse only and not to frighten. Let the scapegoat get out of the affair as best he could.

Even Watterson's own paper treated the whole affair most gingerly. The new editorial policy under W. N. Haldeman's direction was that of compromise, and the paper specifically warned the special Democratic state convention meeting on January 18—the convention that was supposed to provide the ten thousand Kentuckians—against making any "rash and intemperate declaration."[13]

The unfortunate victim of Tilden's one faltering gesture of defiance wrote to Editor Whitelaw Reid to express his thanks for the N.Y. *Tribune's* kindness in printing something in his defense. "It seems to me that I have been berated beyond my offenses as to the 100,000. The speech of the 8th of Jan'y was decorous, the outgiving preconcerted and *by authority*. You know me not to be an extremist. And yet: if I were a mad dog, I could not have come in for greater disparagement."[14] The condemnation of Watterson, however, had only begun.

By far the most serious aspect of the incident was not the immediate storm of criticism and slander that raged about Watterson. In a moment as politically tense as was that January day, Watterson undoubtedly expected a violent reaction to his words. What is serious is the fact that for that one speech, Watterson received an undeserved reputation for being the leader of those who sought war to prevent political defeat in 1876. Later historians seemed to have confused his speech with a Rebel yell for war, with the same disregard for facts that his contemporaries had. Forgotten were the long years of labor for sectional reconciliation. He became a symbol for "irresponsibility" and "hot-headedness," and in some standard texts of American history the only mention of his name has been in connection with "the ten thousand *armed* Kentuckians." Certainly he has been "berated beyond his offenses."

In the long weeks following his unfortunate speech, Watterson played a conspicuous part among those who favored arbitration and a peaceful settlement of the explosive issue. He was at first opposed to the Electoral Commission plan which was finally devised as the only possible way out of the deadlock. The commission was to be composed of five senators, five representatives and five Supreme Court justices who would decide which set of returns from each of the disputed states should be accepted. Watterson later gave support to this plan when assured by Colonel Pelton, Tilden's nephew, that Tilden saw no other alternative except war. When his colleague, Representative Blackburn of Kentucky, and several other Southern members attacked it in the House, Watterson defended the measure in one of the most brilliant speeches of his whole career. "The sole hope left the people—a choice of evils, I grant—is the proposed commission," he said in conclusion.[15] Later when the commission, voting along straight party lines, by a vote of 8-7 gave to Hayes the Republican electoral votes of all three states, and thus the Presidency, Watterson refused to join other Southerners in a filibuster to delay the final count. Once again he arose in Congress to counsel sanity and to urge his Democratic colleagues to accept the results of a bad bargain peacefully.[16] Years later old Joe Cannon, Republican Speaker of the House, would remember that as a young Republican representative, he had seen Henry Watterson "save the country from revolution." Largely through Watterson's, Hewitt's and Speaker Randall's efforts, the filibuster movement with its incalculable dangers was thwarted and the count proceeded to the inevitable conclusion.

At four o'clock in the morning on March 2, less than forty-eight hours before the inauguration of the new President, Thomas Ferry, President of the Senate, arose to announce before a joint session of Congress the results of the count of the electoral votes. At the last moment someone yelled across the room to Watterson to bring on his ten thousand.[17] Not even in that bitter moment nor forever afterward was Watterson allowed to forget his sensational speech.

It is Watterson's last dispatch to the *Courier-Journal* from Washington after Hayes' election had been made certain, however, that history should have remembered, for it gives a true insight into Watterson's statesmanlike and moderate behavior throughout the whole tense crisis. In that dispatch, although making no pretense to hide his sore disappointment, he advised his readers and the nation to accept the results as final.

> "The deed is done, and there is in this, as in most matters, a certain inexpediency, not to say unwisdom, in weeping over spilled milk. . . . The inauguration of Hayes, under these circumstances, is something of a calamity. But the world will not stop on its axis; the people will live, move, and have their being. . . . I hope that I shall never be so weak, that our Southern men and women, who have borne so much, will never be so weak as to hang all earthly hope on any public or political event. . . . For my part, I mean to accept it as I have accepted many things, 'on faith,' . . . faith in the people and faith in the future. I earnestly advise everybody to do the same."[18]

Here Watterson gave consolation, courage and hope to the American people who had submitted to peaceful settlement of a grave dispute. Although the final decision was unjust, it was accepted by the Democrats because the method of settlement had been agreed to by their chosen representatives. Watterson's attitude in this bitter defeat is an expression of his lifelong devotion to peaceful reconciliation between the sections.

Watterson's dispatch, then, and not his "ten thousand Kentuckians" speech, belongs to the American political legend, for it illustrates what Hewitt said after Hayes was inaugurated without one show of violence throughout the nation: "We have proven to the world that we are capable of self-government." Because of the efforts of men like Watterson, Hewitt and Tilden and because of the essential law-abiding spirit of the American people, the horrors of another civil war had been averted.

FOOTNOTES

[1] *Courier-Journal*, Nov. 8, 1876.
[2] Watterson, "The Hayes-Tilden Contest for the Presidency," The *Century Magazine*, Vol. 86, No. 1, May 1913, p. 8.
[3] Watterson to Tilden, Nov. 9, 1876, *Tilden Papers*. New York Public Library.
[4] *Century*, May 1913, op. cit., p. 14. This story is confirmed by W. C. Hudson of the *Brooklyn Eagle* as reported in Alexander C. Flick, *Samuel J. Tilden*, p. 341.
[5] *Century*, May 1913, op. cit., p. 15.
[6] Allan Nevins, *Abram S. Hewitt*, p. 351.
[7] *Century*, May 1913, op. cit., pp. 15 and 17.

8   Allan Nevins, *op. cit.,* p. 352.
9   *Century,* May 1913, *op. cit.,* p. 17.
10 *Courier-Journal,* Jan. 12, 1877.
11 *Harper's Weekly,* March 10, 1877, p. 188; *Century,* May 1913, *op. cit.,* p. 17.
12 Milton H. Northrup, "A Grave Crisis in American History," *Century Magazine,* Vol. 40, No. 6, Oct. 1901, p. 931.
13 *Courier-Journal,* Jan. 18, 1877.
14 Watterson to Reid, Feb. 2, 1877, *Whitelaw Reid Papers.* The italics are the author's.
15 *Cong. Record,* 44th Cong., 2nd Session, Vol. V, pp. 1005-1007.
16 *Ibid.,* p. 1690.
17 Paul Haworth, *The Disputed Presidential Election of 1876,* p. 282.
18 *Courier-Journal,* Feb. 20, 1877.

JOSEPH F. WALL (1920–   ), a native of Iowa, received his B.A. degree from Grinnell College, his M.A. degree from Harvard University, and his Ph.D. from Columbia University. He is Parker Professor of History at Grinnell College, where he has taught since 1947. Wall is the author of several books, including *Henry Watterson: Reconstructed Rebel* (1956) and *Andrew Carnegie* (1970) for which he won the Bancroft prize in 1971. He is currently working on three other books including a history of Iowa for the Bicentennial States of the Union series.

This article first appeared in *The Filson Club History Quarterly* in October 1950, vol. 24, pp. 335–45.

LOUISVILLE'S LABOR DISTURBANCE, JULY, 1877

BY BILL L. WEAVER*
Bowling Green, Kentucky

The year 1877 proved to be a turbulent one both for American labor and for the nation's railroads. Strikes occurred on railroad lines across the nation, and in many locations violence caused the loss of lives and massive destruction of property. Unlike many cities hit by the strikes, Louisville escaped without deaths and with a minimum of property destruction. The disturbance at Louisville differed also in that few, if any, railroad employees participated in the disruptive events.

For many workers, as for Samuel Gompers, who later founded the American Federation of Labor, the year 1877 "dawned on a world of unrest and gloom."[1] By 1877 it was estimated that one-fifth of the nation's workingmen were completely unemployed, and two-fifths worked no more than six or seven months a year.[2] Unemployment was low among railroad workers, but they faced other problems. The Panic of 1873, followed by a widespread depression, had strongly affected the railroads of the United States. The competition between railroads in the early 1870's for the decreased traffic had resulted in rate wars, which necessitated a strict economy to maintain the dividends which stockholders expected. To achieve this economy many roads reduced wages of employees.

Employees and officials of struggling labor organizations[3] found the railroad companies' justification for wage reductions to be insufficient. Workers could not accept the contention that wages must be lowered because of the depression while uniformly high stockholders' dividends were being paid by the same roads. They could not understand why the workingman should be required to bear the full burden of a faulty economic condition. Furthermore, employees expressed displeasure at railroad management's hostility toward labor organizations as expressed through dismissal of employees who dared to serve on grievance committees. The workers were, according to Gompers,

---

*BILL L. WEAVER is a member of the history faculty at Western Kentucky University and staff assistant to the Dean of the Graduate School.

[1] Samuel Gompers, *Seventy Years of Life and Labor* (2 vols., New York, 1925), I, p. 138.
[2] J. G. Rayback, *A History of American Labor* (New York, 1959), p. 129.
[3] No single union or group of unions spoke for the railway worker at this time. The Brotherhood of Locomotive Engineers, the Brotherhood of Locomotive Firemen, and the Order of Railway Conductors attracted only a minority of skilled workers. The Trainmen's Union, formed in June, 1877, tried to unite all railway labor, skilled and unskilled, but it fell apart and died with the strikes of 1877. Gerald G. Eggert, *Railroad Labor Disputes* (Ann Arbor, 1967), pp. 6-7.

"made desperate by this accumulation of miseries, without organizations strong enough to conduct a successful strike. . . ."[4] Despite growing dissatisfaction in the ranks of railroad employees during the early 1870's, the fact that they had steady employment when others did not helped bring compliance with management's decisions.

Railway workers rebelled in early 1877 when additional ten per cent wage reductions and a considerable reduction in employees were announced. According to Gompers, their rebellion was "a declaration of protest in the name of American manhood against conditions that nullified the rights of American citizens."[5] The protest, which involved the largest number of persons of any labor conflict in the nineteenth century and halted traffic on nearly two-thirds of the nation's rail mileage, began at Martinsburg, West Virginia and spread to Baltimore, Philadelphia, Pittsburgh, Buffalo, Cleveland, Toledo, Columbus, Cincinnati, Indianapolis, Chicago, St. Louis, Kansas City, Omaha, and Louisville as well as to many smaller cities.

Confrontations occurred between strikers, who attempted to halt rail transportation, and management officials, who personally operated the trains when strikebreakers were unavailable. These confrontations frequently ended in violence and with disastrous results to both sides. Local police, state militias, and, on occasion, federal troops were dispatched to scenes of disturbance where they battled the enraged laborers. Not since slaveholders had ceased to be "haunted by dreams of a slave uprising" had the propertied class been so horror-stricken.[6] Frightened businessmen formed militias to protect property, and alarmed citizens expressed fear of a revolution triggered by "communist orators." Such was the tenor of the nation by that turbulent and torrid month of July, 1877.

The Louisville *Courier-Journal* began reporting disturbances at the eastern rail centers on July 18. It predicted a westward extension of difficulties while urging the replacement of violence with moral agitation.[7] To the dismay of the local citizenry, the prediction came true as the Louisville, Cincinnati, and Lexington Railroad, commonly known as the Louisville Short Line, announced ten per cent wage reductions to become effective August 1, one month after the Louisville and Nashville Railroad had enforced a similar reduction. In the wake of the announcement of the proposed wage reduction and in view of the disturbances which similar announcements had caused elsewhere, the *Courier-Journal* urged the working people of Louisville to unite with management to better conditions, rather than to wage war against

---

[4] Gompers, *Seventy Years*, I, p. 140.
[5] *Ibid.*
[6] Rayback, *History of American Labor*, p. 135.
[7] Louisville *Courier-Journal*, July 18-21, 1877.

each other and make conditions more intolerable. Complimenting the working class of Louisville, the *Courier-Journal* reminded them that disorders were the result of "universal conditions," but assured them that these conditions did not exist in Louisville or elsewhere in Kentucky. The newspaper emphasized that the outbreaks that had occurred were an "outgrowth of modern civilization acting upon the situation of modern society. . . . We have had trouble enough on this side of the Ohio of other people's making without adding to our misfortune trouble of our own making."[8] Allan Pinkerton, founder of the detective agency of the same name and writing from reports submitted by his detectives, saw these comments by the *Courier-Journal* as having a "wonderfully beneficient effect."[9] These admonitions were to go unheeded, and, according to Pinkerton, "a small percentage of thoughtless and inconsiderate workmen, a sprinkling of howling communists, vicious tramps, mischievous boys, and idle city riff-raff, determined that the popular anticipation of disturbance should not be disappointed, and then accordingly proceeded to give the citizens of Louisville a breezy bit of excitement."[10]

Informal groups of railroad workers discussed their problems on Sunday, July 22, and on Monday a committee of Louisville Short Line employees was formed. Inasmuch as John MacLeod, Receiver for the Short Line,[11] was out of town and could not be contacted, the committee called on Chancellor H. W. Bruce in Chancery Court and requested that he rescind the order establishing the wage reduction. Bruce acceded to their request, whereupon the employees of the Louisville and Nashville line met that evening at the Falls City Hall. This meeting, open to all railroad employees in mechanical trades outside of firemen and engineers, drew approximately 500 workmen.[12] They appointed a committee and instructed the members to meet with Dr. E. D. Standiford, President of the Louisville and Nashville, the next day and present three demands: (1) all laboring men should receive a minimum of $1.50 per day, (2) all brakemen and switchmen should receive $2.00 per day, and (3) all other employees should have restored to them the wages allowed prior to July 1. The committee was instructed to inform Dr. Standiford that he would have until 5:00 p.m. to answer; if the demands were refused, the Louisville and Nashville employees would quit work.[13]

---
[8] *Ibid.*, July 23, 1877.
[9] Allan Pinkerton, *Strikers, Communists, Tramps, and Detectives* (New York, 1878), p. 379.
[10] *Ibid.*, p. 380.
[11] This is an indication that the Louisville Short Line had fallen victim of financial difficulties.
[12] Louisville *Courier-Journal*, July 24, 1877.
[13] *Ibid.*

On the morning of the 24th the Louisville and Nashville employees' committee met at the St. Nicholas Hotel to phrase the resolutions, and at 11:00 a.m. approximately forty of the employees went to Dr. Standiford's office in the Farmers and Drovers Bank, of which he was also president. There, according to the *Courier-Journal,* "they were courteously received" by Dr. Standiford and other officials of the Louisville and Nashville Railroad.[14] They listed their grievances and Dr. Standiford, whom Pinkerton characterized as a "gentleman of broad and enlightened views on all subjects,"[15] responded unhesitatingly. Standiford stated that he would accede to their requests, and, although they did not represent firemen and engineers, he was prepared to raise their wages also.[16]

That same warm, misty morning some "idle Negroes," led by a Cincinnati man called "Buffalo Bill," made the rounds of sewer construction projects located on Ninth, Thirteenth, Fifteenth, and Hancock streets and persuaded or forced the workers to strike for $1.50 per day.[17] The *Courier-Journal,* pointing out that very few whites were involved, described the group as "half-dressed, dirty-looking persons, evidently belonging to the worst class of colored men, . . . armed with picks, shovels, and some with pieces of wood and sticks."[18] Pinkerton, further emphasizing the predominance of Negroes in the group, stated that anyone understanding the "mercurial nature of that childish and ignorant race" should know that Negroes require "but the veriest trifle to stimulate them into making a show of themselves."[19]

Around noon the striking sewer workers reached the water works project at Crescent Hill where approximately 370 men were employed for various tasks at wages ranging from $1.00 to $1.28 per day.[20] There the strikers announced that the men would not be allowed to work if they were not receiving $1.50 per day. Workers stopped, and a few joined the ranks of the marchers. From the water works the group marched back to the center of town, dwindling in size to approximately 50 persons, and by 4:30 p.m. they dispersed.

At noon, while the strikers were making their rounds of sewer construction projects, Mayor Charles D. Jacob, whom Pinkerton described as a "gentleman of wealth and culture, whose life of elegant ease hardly fitted him for a rough grapple with a turbulent mob,"[21] issued

---

[14] *Ibid.,* July 25, 1877.
[15] Pinkerton, *Strikers, Communists,* p. 381.
[16] To the contrary, R. V. Bruce states that Standiford "balked" at the laborers' request for a raise. R. V. Bruce, *1877, Year of Violence* (Indianapolis, 1959), p. 264.
[17] Sewer workers did not receive uniform wages, but a considerable number were drawing $1.00 to $1.15 per day. Some contractors offered them a raise to $1.25 per day, but they refused.
[18] *Ibid.*
[19] Pinkerton, *Strikers, Communists,* p. 381.
[20] Louisville *Courier-Journal,* July 25, 1877.
[21] Pinkerton, *Strikers, Communists,* p. 379.

Labor Disturbance 345

a proclamation to the workingmen of Louisville. He admonished them to preserve order, to listen to no incendiary language, and to "heed not the talk of idle and worthless creatures who, unwilling to work themselves, would gladly get you in trouble, that they may feast upon your misfortune."[22] He informed them that in other cities it had been "vagrants and tramps" who had caused the trouble and the "poor workingmen" who had to bear the "odium of the outbreak."[23]

During the afternoon a number of citizens, including such renowned persons as General Benjamin Helm Bristow and Colonel Basil Duke, met at the request of Mayor Jacob and Police Chief Colonel Isaac W. Edwards and organized to help defend the city against any attack. In preparation for a major disturbance, they requested arms and ammunition from Frankfort and dispatched a detachment of several hundred men to Anchorage, a small town on the route to Frankfort, to pick them up. However, they were unable to return to the city with the arms until 12:30 a.m., and the violent behavior had been quelled by that hour. City Hall was converted virtually into an arsenal, and Mayor Jacob, Police Chief Edwards, General Bristow, Sheriff William H. Able, and others used it as an information center. It was apparent that, as the New York *Times* reported, there was "a determined spirit among good citizens to quell any disorder."[24]

By evening the light rain, which had fallen during the afternoon, had stopped, and 2,000 excited persons gathered in front of the Court House. The *Courier-Journal* reported that a pretty good humor seemed to prevail among the group, which Pinkerton describes as "Negroes, half-grown rowdy boys, and dirty, disgusting tramps, and many communists," and there appeared to be very little interest in hearing the speakers.[25] Finally, someone called for the Mayor, who obligingly came over from his office in City Hall to address the group. Before he could conclude his remarks, the crowd shouted him down. After Mayor Jacob departed several persons tried to be heard, but none was successful until a man named Taylor spoke in "rather inflammatory tones."[26] Someone suggested that a procession be formed. An estimated 500-600 persons immediately joined such a formation, and at the shouted suggestion, "Let's go to the Nashville depot," they headed west on Jefferson to Seventh where they turned south. Someone threw a rock through a large plate-glass window of the Home Sewing Machine Company, and apparently the "tinkling and crunching of glass came to the ears of the mob as Christmas candy to the teeth of a child."[27] With ammunition

---
[22] Louisville *Courier-Journal*, July 25, 1877.
[23] *Ibid.*
[24] New York *Times*, July 25, 1877.
[25] Louisville *Courier-Journal*, July 25, 1877; Pinkerton, *Strikers, Communists*, p. 382.
[26] Louisville *Courier-Journal*, July 25, 1877.
[27] Bruce, 1877, *Year of Violence*, p. 264.

laying at hand near street excavations, few houses escaped without broken windows.

Turning west at the corner of Seventh and Broadway, the mob, according to the Owensboro *Examiner,* "yelling like fiends,"[28] began shattering street lamps one by one. Upon reaching Ninth and Broadway, they opened a "terrific fusilade" upon the freight depot of the Louisville and Nashville Railroad and succeeded in smashing all the windows before a contingent of police arrived, and, with considerable difficulty, arrested two white men and one Negro accused of being the leaders.[29] Turning eastward, the remaining rioters proceeded up Broadway boisterously wrecking stores and private residences.

When the mob reached Third Street, it turned north and severely damaged businesses and private residences between Broadway and Walnut. Included in the private residences which came under fire were those of Mayor Jacob and Dr. Standiford. The Standiford residence, a half block from Walnut on Third, became the victim of a special effort on the part of the boisterous element. The Standiford family, taking refuge in one of the upper rooms, escaped uninjured, but windows were destroyed and much furniture was severely damaged.[30] The group, having dwindled to approximately fifty persons, further divided at Third and Walnut with some continuing down Walnut in the direction of the Short Line depot while others scattered in different directions. Upon its arrival at the Short Line depot, at the corner of Floyd and Jefferson streets, the small group was faced with fifty armed policemen. When someone cried out to attack the police, the officers opened fire.[31] This action resulted in a permanent dispersal of the rioters, and by midnight the streets were quiet except for patrols of volunteer militia. Pinkerton claimed that there never would have been trouble had Police Chief Edwards attacked the "vile rabble" when "a squad of a dozen determined policemen could have driven it before them or scattered it to the winds in five minutes."[32]

That evening 700 militiamen, many of them "influential and wealthy citizens," were on duty to assist the 175 policemen.[33] At 1:00 a.m. fire was discovered in the basement of the Louisville and Nashville depot. The *Courier-Journal* surmised that the fire "could not have been otherwise than the work of an incendiary."[34] However, the blaze was

---
[28] Owensboro *Examiner,* July 27, 1877.
[29] Louisville *Courier-Journal,* July 25, 1877.
[30] Bruce, *1877, Year of Violence,* p. 264.
[31] The *Courier-Journal* first announced that officers were using blank cartridges, but later, in claiming that some persons were wounded, admitted that officers had live ammunition. The New York *Times* alleged that officers shot over the heads of the rioters. Louisville *Courier-Journal,* July 25, 1877; New York *Times,* July 25, 1877.
[32] Pinkerton, *Strikers, Communists,* p. 380.
[33] New York *Times,* July 26, 1877.
[34] Louisville *Courier-Journal,* July 25, 1877.

Labor Disturbance 347

discovered early and was extinguished without difficulty.

At 2:30 a.m., July 25, Mayor Jacob issued a proclamation condemning the "brutal, cowardly mob," which he characterized as "too cowardly to do more than break a few windows." He commended the veteran soldiers, men who had "adorned the Blue and honored the Gray," for subduing "these creatures" who were "brutes lower than those of the animal creation."[85] The *Courier-Journal* saw the group as of no particular laboring class (certainly not railroad men) but as men without character or identity who had pillage as their only object and devastation as their motive.[36] Supporting Mayor Jacob's orders to use prompt means to suppress disturbance, the *Courier-Journal* complimented the laboring men who did not participate in the violent activities and reminded them that as a group they would lose because of the turmoil. The newspaper encouraged them to enlist in the effort to suppress such disgraceful proceedings as those of the previous evening. The editorial urged the city authorities to recognize that Louisville contained "a body of thieves and thugs" who needed to be disciplined with "powder and bullets."[37] Although some employees, especially at the Louisville and Nashville, were not satisfied with their wage settlements, the Mayor and the newspapers had been careful to point out the absence of railroad men in the disturbances.

On the morning of the 25th, Mayor Jacob sent a telegram to Governor James B. McCreary requesting additional men, ammunition, and guns, and the Governor responded by sending several hundred rifles by special train. In addition, 400 troops were ordered to proceed to Louisville to afford protection against further disorder.[38] No trouble was expected until the evening, and, in an effort to forestall difficulties, the Mayor issued an order closing all liquor saloons.

By 7:00 p.m. more than a thousand armed citizens patrolled the city, and the *Courier-Journal* became almost poetic in its exuberance on the establishment of tranquility.

> The silver moon is shining with luminous serenity upon homes peaceful and secure, while the only sounds that break upon the midsummer night air are the steady tramp of the patrol and the occasional hoof-clatter of the mounted guard.[39]

The *Courier-Journal* concluded by assuring citizens that with the local military organization and the expected arrival of United States troops, there was "no longer a possibility for thieves and bummers to take

---

[85] *Ibid.*
[36] *Ibid.*
[37] *Ibid.*
[38] Louisville *Courier-Journal*, July 25, 27, 1877.
[39] *Ibid.*, July 26, 1877.

advantage of the public excitement and prey upon the community unprepared."[40] One factor helping to assure the existence of tranquility in Louisville was the security added by employees of both the Short Line and the Louisville and Nashville who, in the words of Dr. Standiford in a report to the Louisville and Nashville stockholders, "flew to our assistance, and with arms in their hands, were day and night most vigilant in the protection of your [stockholders'] property."[41]

Thursday, July 26, brought a rash of strikes among coopers, textile and plow factory workers, brickmakers and cabinetmakers. That morning the striking Louisville and Nashville employees requested immediate consideration by Dr. Standiford of an advance in wages. Dr. Standiford, after arguing at length, firmly declined, and the men left "satisfied" and "enthusiastically" guarded the company's property.[42]

The *Courier-Journal*, presenting a basic employer point of view, urged the workers to request reasonable wages in comparison with the employers' ability to pay and to recognize that workers' problems could not be separated from other problems of society. Concluding with phrases that could easily have been drawn from a social Darwinist like William Graham Sumner, the newspaper stated:

> Each one has his vote, each his quantum of power according to his capacity to use it. The fittest survive and move forward in every craft. . . . The man who does not get on, high or low, college-bred or factory-bred, may charge it to himself. Nobody else is to blame. . . . In this country all men start out even in the race.[43]

Along the same line of thinking, Dr. Standiford stated that

> the workingman now realizes that his present distress originates from sources and causes that have been in operation for years, and that any correction of the evils which now bear so heavily upon him is only to be brought about by patience and a true understanding of the relations between capital and labor. He certainly believes no longer in communism and destruction of property, which would only augment the very evil from which he is endeavoring to extricate himself.[44]

The Louisville *Commercial*, the Republican spokesman in Kentucky, expressed willingness to maintain the "indefeasible right of men to strike if they are dissatisfied with their wages, and to prevent by all legal and proper means others from going to work in places they have vacated. The right goes no further, however, and as soon as strikers

---

[40] *Ibid.*
[41] *Annual Report to the Stockholders of the Louisville and Nashville Railroad,* 1877, p. 9.
[42] New York *Times,* July 26, 1877.
[43] Louisville *Courier-Journal,* July 27, 1877.
[44] *Report to Stockholders of Louisville and Nashville Railroad,* 1877, p. 9.

resort to violence against the person or property of others, they come under the ban of just laws, ..."[45]

Pinkerton saw the disturbance in Louisville as "merely a tempest in a teapot, which boiled itself away after a few hours of mob antics," and with very little more destruction of property than annually accompanied the "Sophomore 'breakout' of many Eastern colleges."[46] In fact, the mildness of the situation is demonstrated by the fact that, although 30-40 persons were arrested, the most severe action taken against those persons was the levying of $20 fines and placing them under $1,000 peace bonds for a period of one year. Edward Winslow Martin's *History of the Great Riots,* published in 1877, did not even mention the Louisville disturbance.[47]

One cannot fully appreciate Pinkerton's statement that the "meagerness of evil results" in Louisville is attributable to the fact that the city had been affected only slightly by the economic problems, and, as a result, the streets were not filled with "gaunt, hollow-eyed men, asking for bread or work."[48] Louisville obviously had its share of unemployment, for employers, frequently justifying an existing wage rate, stated that large numbers of workers were available on short notice to replace strikers. Louisville possessed the necessary ingredients of a violent reaction. It merely possessed them in smaller quantities than a number of cities which endured greater violence.

In determining results of the confrontations, one must look at the overall effect on the labor movement as well as the effect on the laboring population of Louisville. While most persons who expressed themselves viewed strikes and certainly violence as unjustifiable, they were willing to admit that problems existed which caused concern to employees. The business community became aroused as never before to the potential power of industrial workers, and many businessmen attempted to suppress labor activity by reviving the old conspiracy laws, intimidating workers from joining unions, requiring oaths denying union affiliation, and enlisting strikebreakers whenever trouble developed.[49] The agitation awakened the nation to the danger of allowing relations between labor and management to deteriorate.[50] Furthermore, the strikes convinced labor that local, state, and national government was essentially hostile to its aims and that resort to politics was necessary.[51]

Economically, the threat of a strike by railroad employees brought

---
[45] Louisville *Commercial,* July 24, 1877.
[46] Pinkerton, *Strikers, Communists,* p. 379.
[47] Edward Winslow Martin, *The History of the Great Riots* (Philadelphia, 1877).
[48] Pinkerton, *Strikers, Communists,* p. 379.
[49] Foster Rhea Dulles, *Labor in America: A History* (New York, 1949), p. 122.
[50] Philip Taft, *Organized Labor in America* (New York, 1964), p. 82.
[51] Rayback, *History of American Labor,* p. 136.

a near-capitulation by railroad companies in Louisville. The violence that occurred, though not by railroad men, may have helped the labor movement in Louisville indirectly by graphically demonstrating the destructiveness of mob action whether justifiably or unjustifiably begun. Socially, in the shadow of a common danger, the distinction between "Yankee" and "Rebel" disintegrated, and, followed by the cohesive effect of President Rutherford B. Hayes' trip to Louisville in September, the distinction was never as sharply defined again. Politically, the laboring man was to be more adequately represented after the August election in which five of seven candidates of the Workingmen's Party were elected to the Kentucky Legislature.[52]

On the national level, the doctrine of laissez-faire had prevented governmental interference with labor problems,[53] but the railway strikes of 1877 launched a new era. From 1877 on, effective railway strikes were generally viewed as intolerable and the "necessity for ending them proved to be the mother of federal intervention."[54] Good or bad, the disorder in Louisville may have had a small part in shaping that policy.

---
[52] Bruce, *1877, Year of Violence*, p. 317.
[53] Eggert, *Railroad Labor Disputes*, p. 1.
[54] *Ibid.*, p. 19.

BILL L. WEAVER (1941–   ), a native of Barren County, Kentucky, received his A.B. and M.A. degrees at Western Kentucky University where he has taught history and served as an administrator. He is currently a doctoral candidate at Indiana University. Weaver has published several articles in various journals.

This article first appeared in *The Filson Club History Quarterly* in April 1974, vol. 48, pp. 177–86.

V.

THE TWENTIETH CENTURY

STONEY POINT, 1866-1969

By J. W. Cooke*

Stoney Point[1] is a rural, black community a few miles northeast of Smiths Grove in Warren County, Kentucky. It has been in existence for about 112 years, although blacks, both bond and free, farmed some of the Stoney Point lands before the Civil War. The boundaries of Stoney Point, which are not fixed but change as the amount of roughly contiguous land owned by blacks changes, have shrunk in the twentieth century. This is also true of the membership of the Stoney Point Baptist Church (founded in 1866). In 1880, for instance, the membership of the church was 255 (91 male and 164 female), and the usual attendance at Sunday services probably averaged between seventy and eighty. In 1969 the total population of the settlement was less than one hundred, and the number present at Sunday services averaged between thirty and forty. Several of the most faithful members no longer live in the community but still drive from nearby Smiths Grove and Bowling Green each Sunday for services. The middle aged and the elderly now comprise the majority at Stoney Point; there are still children but they are a much smaller proportion of the population than was the case a few years ago.

The landscape, too, has changed. Originally, the farms at Stoney Point were covered with a hardwood forest, principally of red, scarlet, post, and shingle oak, shaggybark and mockernut hickory, red cedar, sassafras, chestnut (now extinct although there are said to be some seedlings about), sycamore, dogwood, redbud, Southern hackberry, and

---

*J. W. Cooke, Ph.D., is a professor of history at the University of Tennessee at Nashville. He is a native of Bowling Green which is some 15 miles from Stoney Point.

[1] I would like to thank the American Philosophical Society for a grant which helped make this study possible. I would also like to express my thanks to the following residents of Stoney Point, Smiths Grove, and Bowling Green, Kentucky, for their kindness and cooperation: Mr. and Mrs. Joseph Cook, Mr. and Mrs. Herschel Cooke, Mrs. Daisy Board, Mrs. Katy Preston, Mrs. Mary R. Board, Mr. and Mrs Buford Cook, Mr. L. D. Britt, Jr., Mr. Bus Cooke, and Mrs. Edna Cashman. The different spellings of the surname "Cooke" (or "Cook") are in accord with local usage.

black locust. Much of this forest was cut and replaced by cultivated land in the last third of the nineteenth century. The timber was used for houses, barns, fences, and firewood, and the cleared land for corn, wheat (in very small quantities), vegetables, sorghum cane, and, later, dark and burley tobacco. Only remnants of the original forest cover are still visible; an occasional huge oak that somehow escaped the initial and later clearings, and slender second and third growth of oak, hickory, black locust, cedar, dogwood, and wild plum. There are also a few maples that were planted around some of the homesteads and some remnants of osage orange fences planted in the late nineteenth century as a substitute for chestnut rail fences but now turned into "little lines/ Of sportive wood run wild" (Wordsworth). Hundreds of acres at Stoney Point can be called neither forest nor field. They are covered with sawbriers, blackberries, broom sage (an inevitable sign of acid soil), honeysuckle, short, scraggly cedars, and a large variety of weeds. Some of these areas are almost tropical in their density. There are occasional spots of bare red earth which not even hardy weeds and broom sage can reclaim: they testify to the losing battle the Stoney Point farmers fought with the wind, the rain, and the recalcitrant earth. When the land was first cleared, there were several springs, ponds, and a number of caves. Today the springs have ceased to flow (with one partial exception), many of the ponds have dried up or shrunk, and the caves have been filled in with earth. Gullies have appeared, to be filled in with tin cans, rusted-out car chassis, old wash tubs, and other artifacts of high civilization. Natural drainage was and is provided by sinkholes, collapsed openings in the earth which provide a means for water to reach the underground streams below. Many of the sinkholes have been filled or partially filled with rocks (so very abundant at Stoney Point) and assorted household trash.

Spotted about this landscape are over a dozen abandoned cabins or their limestone rock foundations. Where cabins once stood there are still shade trees, rose bushes, beds of iris and other flowers, and the remains of grassy yards. A few of the remaining cabins were closed and their doors latched when the last resident died or moved away, but most are now open to the elements. The best built of these structures have limestone chimneys, tight log or clapboard covering, glass windows, and a tin roof. They are usually small; the largest remaining has a kitchen, living room, and bedroom on the first floor and an attic on the second. Most of the cabins are smaller; usually there are only three rooms. Nearby is a cistern or a well and a privy. The walls of the cabins are covered with old newspapers (Louisville *Courier-Journal*, *Park City Daily News* [Bowling Green], *Louisville Defender*), pages from old magazines, and some wallpaper. Old, broken down chairs and tables are still to be found in many of the cabins; sometimes there are bed frames and mattresses also. In the kitchen there may be a decrepit stove or icebox and an occasional jar of preserves or jelly now turned green and rancid. One of the attics contained quantities of cancelled checks, letters, and postcards covering a period of fifty years. Books are almost entirely absent from the cabins and there is only an occasional farm magazine. Some of the cabins have been put to use by the present owners of the land. Hay is stored there, and a part of the tobacco crop may be stripped (the leaves taken from the stalk, graded according to color, and tied together in preparation for sale) in the best lighted of the rooms. Otherwise, the cabins are unused.

The soil at Stoney Point was and is poor, thin, and acid. Continued misuse has contributed significantly to its comparative sterility today. Agronomists classify this soil as one of the Baxter series. It is characterized by a moderate permeability; rainfall can be absorbed at the rate of from .63 to 2 inches an hour. The slopes are from 2% to 30%, and water runoff is consequently medium to rapid. Solid rock is usually found about six feet under the surface of the soil, along with many underground streams. There is much subsoil showing at Stoney Point; it is cherry red clay and very rocky. Almost all the land presently under cultivation has at least a few inches of topsoil; it is hardly possible to raise anything on the subsoil without prohibitive expense. The average rainfall in that part of Kentucky is between 48 and 50 inches a year and the growing season is usually between 180 and 210 days a year. Given the nature of the climate, the steepness of the slopes, and the kind of row crops grown, severe sheet and gully erosion is inevitable.[2]

The history of Stoney Point as a separate black community properly began with the death of John White, a comparatively wealthy white landowner on December 24, 1848. He had emigrated from near Manassas, Virginia, to Kentucky in the 1790s and had acquired several

---

[2] See *Description of Soil Associations for the General Soil Map of Warren County* (Bowling Green, Ky.: n.p., n.d. [1969]), pp. 5-7; *A Survey of Agriculture in Warren County Prepared for Warren County Agricultural Council by John A. Perkins Division Farm Service Adviser Kentucky Utilities Company, Inc. Lexington, Kentucky Cooperating With Kentucky Chamber of Commerce Published January 1955* (Lexington, Ky.: n.p. 1955), p. 4; Carl Ortwin Sauer, *Geography of the Pennyroyal: A Study of the Influence of Geology and Physiography upon the Industry, Commerce and Life of the People* (Series VI; 35 Vols.; Frankfort, Ky.: The Kentucky Geological Survey, 1927), XXV, 6-7, 123-42, 185-88, 233-49 The influence of the richer soil to the southwest of Stoney Point upon the farmers at Stoney Point has been considerable. These soils belong to the Pembroke-Crider Association; they are comparatively level, well-drained, and fertile. The white farmers who owned these lands were able to give extensive employment to many of the inhabitants of Stoney Point. Only this permitted many of the latter to remain on the land.

thousand acres in Warren, Edmonson, and Barren counties, Kentucky. At the time of his death he held over fifty slaves. His will, written just twelve days before his demise, freed at least six: "Amelia—alias Mely—and her daughter Catherine Charlotte, Calom, Victoria Richardilla or Richard Dilla and Matilda and Eliza a daughter of Matilda" plus all their issue. The six blacks were given a tract of about 1,810 acres along with necessary horses, oxen, cattle, sheep, farming and cooking utensils, and a year's supply of provisions. Surveying the land described in John White's will began on February 12, 1849 and was completed five days later. There is no indication of how the land was initially divided among the freedmen, nor can it be learned whether all of them remained in the country, or how they lived. The Warren County Census of 1850 lists a Matilda White as fourteen and a mulatto, John C. [Colom?] White, fourteen and mulatto, Eliza White, thirty and mulatto, and John, three and mulatto. Ten years later census records list a Matilda White as twenty-one and mulatto [why the discrepancy in age? Is this the same Matilda White listed in the earlier census and in the White will?], Victoria White, twenty and mulatto [where had Victoria been ten years before?], and Sarah, eight and mulatto. Apparently the other freedmen were either overlooked by the census takers, had married and thus lost their surnames (although their marriages are not recorded in Warren County records), had died, or emigrated.[3]

In any event, Matilda White was the first of the freedmen to sell the lands allotted to her by the late John White. In November and December, 1859, she transferred all her acres to L. P. Smith, a white man, for $700.00. A little less than five years later Smith also acquired a part of Victoria White's land for another $700.00. Eliza was the third to sell: R.A. Crump, a white man, paid her $400.00 for 175 acres and the deed was registered on November 12, 1875. She had already sold a part of her land to Wilkerson Mitchell and [?] Graham. Both Eliza and Victoria retained a part of their inheritance. In 1880 Ike and Lucinda Larue, both black, sold L.D. Shobe, also black, a tract of 34 acres for $100.00; it is described in the deed of conveyance as being "the life estate of Eliza White of color." Three years later Anthony and Matilda Rone, both black, sold R.A. and Robert Crump, white, 50 acres for $350.00; according to the deed this tract had originally been given to Matilda by Victoria White. Two recorded marriages may indicate that some of the original beneficiaries of John

---

[3] *Warren County Deed Book 22*, pp. 17-20; *Warren County Will Book D*, pp. 253-57; *Warren County Census of 1850, District 1* [Louisville Public Library, Louisville, Ky.], no page number; *Warren County Census of 1860* [Louisville Public Library, Louisville, Ky.], p. 273.

Stoney Point 357

White's munificence were still living in the vicinity of Stoney Point. Permelia [Amelia?] White married Maliki Dunn, a black who had been freed before 1860. Permelia was fifty years old at the time. Later land transfers indicate that Maliki and Permelia owned a farm at Stoney Point. On October 14, 1869, Mely Jane White, possibly one of the original slaves freed or one of the issue, married Wesley Preston, a farmer with descendants living today at Stoney Point.[4]

Another source of land for the Stoney Point farmers was also connected, although indirectly, with John White's will. The latter, although he married a second time late in life, left a substantial part of his estate to his adopted daughter Nancy Hailey White, who had married Israel Alexander Cooke. Both died in 1852, leaving three underage boys, John W. (named for John White), Peyton A., and William. These three in turn began to dispose of land inherited from their parents and land which they had purchased from the second wife of John White in the 1870s, and this dispersion continued for about two decades. Other white landowners also sold small amounts of land to blacks. The Stoney Point Church was built on an acre of land purchased from Eli and W.B. Rasdall for $50.00 in 1876; the names of Stanford Jones, R. J. Hays, J. C. Walton, and John Hazelip also appear in property transfers. Significantly, all sales were for a small amount of money and they always involved relatively few acres. After the initial sales by Matilda, Eliza, and Victoria White, the average number of acres transferred was less than thirty-five; the largest recorded sale was of 105, the smallest sales were of less than an acre. The price per acre was also quite low; the average taken from twenty-six randomly selected but typical sales was $8.99.[5]

The original settlers at Stoney Point were, with a few exceptions, of local origin. Most had been slaves who subsequently worked for years as tenants and field hands before accumulating enough money to buy their farms. Several were Civil War veterans. James Ledman, for instance, was mustered into Company K, 109th U.S. Colored Infantry

---

[4] *Warren County Deed Book 45*, pp. 207-8; *Warren County Deed Book 52*, pp. 98-99; *Warren County Deed Book 57*, pp. 384-85; *Warren County Marriage Bonds A-B (Colored)*, pp. 58, 258. Maliki (or Malachi) Dunn was also one of the pioneer black preachers in the community. Already a landowner with real estate and personal property worth $3,100.00, he probably preached at Icy Sink, a black congregation about 2½ miles as the crow flies from Stoney Point, before the Civil War. See *Warren County Census of 1850, District 1* and J.H. Spencer, *A History of Kentucky Baptists from 1769 to 1885 Including More Than 800 Biographical Sketches*, ed. Mrs. Burrilla B. Spencer (Rev. ed.; 2 vols.; Cincinnati: J.H. Spencer, 1885), II, 664.

[5] See, for instance, *Warren County Deed Book 43*, pp. 433-36; *Warren County Deed Book 41*, pp. 206-7; *Warren County Deed Book 65*, pp. 61-62; Warren County Deed Book 77, pp. 87-88, 462; *Warren County Deed Book 100*, pp. 589-90; *Warren County Deed Book 106*, p. 307; *Warren County Deed Book 115*, pp. 93-4, 99, 419-20; *Warren County Deed Book 117*, pp. 465-66.

on June 19, 1864; the next day William Cook joined the same outfit. Another William Cook joined Company D, 108th U.S. Colored Infantry and was listed as a Corporal on July 6, 1864. Thomas Cook joined Company I of the 6th U.S. Colored Cavalry on September 19, 1864. Henry and Fountain Cook were members of Company E, 115th U.S. Colored Infantry; both had joined on August 22, 1864. Richard Board (although not of local origin he acquired land at Stoney Point) joined Company B, 115th U.S. Colored Infantry on August 2, 1864 and rose to the rank of Sergeant before receiving his discharge, and Anthony Rone joined Company H of the 123rd U.S. Colored Infantry on April 6, 1865. Additional biographical information can be gotten from a genealogy prepared by Herschel Cooke, a Stoney Point farmer whose ancestors helped to found the community, and from the fragmentary records of the Smiths Grove Baptist Church, a predominantly white institution founded in 1812. Herschel Cooke is a descendant of Edmond Cooke, born a slave on November 19, 1836, and Susan Murrell, also born a slave on May 1, 1840. Both joined the Smiths Grove Baptist Church on the third Saturday in May, 1859. Edmond remained a member of the church (which had at least 52 black members out of a total of 148 in 1851) until at least June, 1868, some years after his marriage. He and Susan had eleven children, not an especially high number for the farming families at Stoney Point. Herschel's father, Hute, was also born a slave on December 17, 1860 and farmed at or near Stoney Point all his life although, like so many of his generation, he did not buy any land there until the 1890s.[6]

The center of the community's life is still the Stoney Point Missionary Baptist Church. It was organized in 1866, the first full year of freedom for Kentucky's blacks. Today, the church is located about a mile from the site of the original structure. Trees shade the white frame building and grounds, and there is a graveyard behind the church. Nearby stands the unused Stoney Point School. Church records, which are now in the keeping of Mrs. Rich Board, are incomplete, but they give a good deal of insight into the social and economic life of the community and also some indication of the changes in the black population of the area.

One of the principal functions of the church was to discipline wayward members. A regular procedure was followed in all such cases. During the course of the Sunday morning meeting the alleged offender

---

[6] *Report of the Adjutant General of the State of Kentucky* (2 vols.; Frankfort: John H. Harney, 1867), II, 17, 39, 52, 61, 64, 118; *Smiths Grove Church Minutes, December, 1849-June, 1885* [Southern Baptist Theological Seminary, Louisville, Ky], pp. 28, 126-27, 130.

would be accused of some infraction of church rules and a motion would be made to exclude him from communion. If present the accused could respond to the charge or charges and the assembled church would make its judgment. If found innocent, the threat to fellowship was put to rest. If found guilty, however, the offender was to be excluded from fellowship until he or she had acknowledged guilt and pledged repentance. The most common offenses were drunkenness, fighting, gambling, adultery, and fornication. On March 18, 1885, for instance, William Armstrong was charged with drunkenness; a similar charge was made the next February against Charles Dunn. In January, 1897, Luoda Mury was also charged with this offense; only a month before she had been accused of dancing. During 1896 Sister Bell Arnold was twice accused of fighting; that same year Janny Webs received "parton" for this infraction of church rules. Even as late as October, 1930, George Cooke was reported for fighting.

Profanity was also punished. Henry Murrell, for instance, was informed in December, 1897, that he "Shall Come Before the Church and mak his Statement for Swaring and Cursing . . . . " Presumably he was restored to fellowship after acknowledging his guilt and asserting repentance. In January, 1897, a motion was made to exclude a female member for "an Adulty"; the next month the same charge was made against another member, also a female. In June, 1930, a female member of the church was charged with fornication. Interestingly, no male members were ever accused of either offense. Card playing was the most common form of gambling brought to the attention of the church. In November, 1896, Charles Jenkins, James Carder, Cora Ferguson, Allas Arnold, and Addy Arnold were allegedly guilty of this offense. That same year both Cy Arnold and Brother Hade Carter were similarly impeached. More obscure infractions were also brought to the attention of the church. Brother Campbel was accused of having blown out the church's lights before those attending services could leave the building in July, 1896. In March, 1897, a motion was made to exclude Ellen Richision "for publick Rumer and not to be Restored untill the Rumer is Stopted." James Carter was charged with "Slowfulness"; Lester Williams with stealing eggs. In August, 1913, Rotney Britt drew the ire of the faithful for "too Stepping." Even the one successful attempt at business enterprise ever to exist at Stoney Point ran afoul of the church. Twice during 1912 Sam and Henry Cook were charged with keeping a barber shop and grocery open on Sunday. Occasionally, religious disputes erupted in the church. Sister Sally Cook, according to a motion made in March, 1897, ought to be excluded from communion "for claiming she had no Religion." In March, 1914, Annie Shobe was charged with "Preaching with out a Thority." Less than a year later a motion was made that Sister Shobe be charged "for Sowing the Seed of Discord by Claiming She Had to tell a lie to Stay in the Church." Sister Shobe was present when the accusation was made. She stated that the charge was true and asked the church's pardon.[7]

An unusual feature of the Stoney Point Church was the sale of church tickets, a practice begun by the Rev. Alexander Williams in 1884 (Rev. Williams and Rev. Eugene Evans were the co-founders of the Union District Association of which the Stoney Point Church is still a member). Under this system of meeting the necessary expenses of the church, male members originally paid 20¢ monthly and women 15¢ monthly. Each man or woman was given a card with twelve 20¢ or 15¢ symbols on it. When the monthly donation was made the card was punched. At the last meeting of the year any dues still owed were to be paid. If they were not, the offending member received church discipline. Additional monies were collected at the Sunday meeting by passing the collection plate. The earliest reported collection was $4.20 for May 15, 1882. On February 8, 1890, it was $4.35. Things were not much better in 1896; on July 11, the collection was $4.69. The financial condition of the church improved later in the year, perhaps after the yearly tobacco crop of the Stoney Point farmers was marketed, and on two successive Sundays it totalled $19.25. Collections began to rise in 1897, probably because of higher prices for farm products. In 1904, for instance, one typical collection was $11.75; two more in November totalled $28.02. A late August collection in 1914 was $8.50. The agricultural depression which began in May, 1920, adversely affected the prosperity of the Stoney Point Church; even so the collection for November 9, 1930, was $13.00. Later collections in November and December, 1941, ranged from $4.78 to $18.50.[8]

A major part of the collection went to pay the pastor. In 1890, the Rev. Alexander Williams of Bowling Green was paid $104.00 for his preaching at Stoney Point. In 1896 and 1897 the Rev. B. P. [?] Whitesides received $8.00 a month for his services. In 1904 the Rev. L.D. Britt, Sr. began his forty-three year service to the Stoney Point Church. His initial salary was $6.00 a month, but by 1912 it had risen to $9.00.

---

[7] *Stoney Point Church Records, Book II, Book III, Book IV, Book V;* hereinafter cited as *Stoney Point Records.* These records were in the possession of Mrs. Mary R. Board, Stoney Point.

[8] See a rare pamphlet in the possession of Herschel Cooke, Rev. Alexander Williams, *Life Pastorate of Rev. Alexander Williams* (Bowling Green, Ky.: n.p., 1914), p. 28; The Rev. Williams also taught school at Stoney Point for one year in the 1880s while preaching at Rich Pond, about twenty-six miles away. See *Ibid.,* pp. 12, 17, and *Stoney Point Records, Book I, Book II, Book III, Book IV, Book V, Book VI.*

In 1919 the Rev. Britt's compensation was raised to $10.00 a month and in 1920 to $12.00 monthly. The latter salary was constant throughout the 1920s and 1930s, although there was talk of reducing it to $10.00 again during the depth of the Depression. The highest salary the Rev. Britt ever received was $15.00 for a Sunday's preaching. The Stoney Point Church could never afford a regular pastor; on other Sundays the Rev. Britt preached at nearby Smiths Grove and at Rockfield and Horse Cave.[9]

The other center of community life was the Stoney Point School. No certain date for its beginning can be established, but it was probably begun rather soon after emancipation to teach the freedmen at least the rudiments of literacy. It was, for many years, held in the Stoney Point Church but a separate white wooden structure was built on the church grounds in 1908, where it is to be seen today. Mrs. Daisy Board, the oldest living member of the Stoney Point Church, remembered that when she was a child the school term was about five months, beginning in August and ending in December. Geography, arithmetic, language (English grammar), and spelling were taught. Parents had to buy all the textbooks used. The single room of the school was heated by a coal burning stove in the center. There was a blackboard on the wall and slates for use by the children. Later, the slates were done away with and textbooks provided by the state. The school term was extended in the 1920s to seven or eight months.

Several, but not all, of the school censuses survive, and they reveal the changing pattern of population and age distribution at Stoney Point and nearby farms. In the census of 1897, seventy children were listed in the age group 6-20, although there is no way of knowing how many were actually enrolled and attending school. In 1906, the census listed seventy-two children in the same age category. By 1909 there were ninety-three children listed; sixty-four were enrolled in school, but there was an average attendance of only thirty. Stoney Point's juvenile population apparently peaked in 1910; there were ninety-five children present in the school district, sixty-six were enrolled in school, but there was an average attendance of only twenty-five. After 1910 the school census reveals a slowly declining school age population at Stoney Point. By 1918 the census takers could find only fifty-six children in the district, but average school attendance was up to twenty-nine. Three years later there were only forty-three children of school age in the district, but again the average attendance at Stony Point

---

[9] *Stoney Point Records*, Book I, Book II, Book III, Book IV, Book V, Book VI; L.D. Britt, Jr., Smiths Grove, Ky. interview with the author, August 23, 1971; hereinafter cited as L.D. Britt, Jr.

School had gone up, this time to thirty-eight. This is the last year in which school census figures are available. The Stoney Point School was finally closed in the late 1930s and the remaining children bused to school at Smiths Grove.[10]

Salaries for the teacher were always pitifully low. In 1922, for instance, the teacher, who usually boarded with some family in the community, received $76.00 a month for the months when the school was in session.[11] By 1924, the salary had risen to $93.00 and the length of the school year had been extended to seven or eight months. Expenditures per pupil also changed rather drastically during the period recorded; in 1909 the average amount spent per pupil was $7.00; the average rose to $12.00 in 1910, to $50.00 in 1911, and then, by 1921, to $83.00.[12]

The one business venture at Stoney Point was a restaurant and barber shop run by Sam and Henry Cook between 1910 and 1918. It was called by at least some local inhabitants the "Last Chance." The restaurant and barber shop catered to the Stoney Point farmers and to the section hands who worked on the Louisville and Nashville Railroad which ran close by. Fish, sardines, and cold drinks were sold during the warm weather, and chitterlings and pigs feet during the winter months. The drinks were kept cool by placing them in a barrel buried in the ground and immersing them in cold water carried from a nearby well. "Long Life" bitters, a nostrum with a high alcoholic content, was also sold. Although apparently profitable, the restaurant was eventually closed because its owners turned over the building to a relative whose house had been destroyed by fire.[13]

Mrs. Daisy Board, born August 12, 1887, is the oldest living member of the Stoney Point Church and, although she now lives in Bowling Green some twenty miles away, usually attends Sunday services there. Her grandfather, Dick Board, was one of the original settlers at Stoney Point and a Union veteran. Her father was Charles Board. She remembers that as a child she helped to clear the land and that her

---

[10] Mrs. Daisy Board, Bowling Green, Ky., interview with the author, August 14, 1969; hereinafter cited as Mrs. Daisy Board; *Warren County School Census of 1897; Warren County School Census of 1906; Warren County School Census of 1909; Warren County School Census of 1910; Warren County School Census of 1918; Warren County School Census of 1921.*

[11] Notation on the margin of the *Warren County School Census of 1919, 1920, 1921; Warren County School Census of 1909; Warren County School Census of 1910; Warren County School Census of 1911; Warren County School Census of 1912.*

[12] Mrs. Daisy Board; Mr. and Mrs. Herschel Cooke, Stoney Point, Ky., interview with the author, July 17, 1971; hereinafter cited as Hershchel Cooke. The Len Board school may have been used to teach the basics of literacy to blacks going North to work in the Detroit factories.

[13] Herschel Cooke; Mr. and Mrs. Herschel Cooke, Stoney Point, Ky., interview with the author, August 12, 1969; hereinafter cited as Herschel Cooke (2).

Stoney Point

father once told her that in the 1870s, when the Stoney Point farmers were in the process of getting their farms into cultivation, some tracts sold for as little as 25¢ an acre. Times were hard when she was a child; as a young woman she received $1.00-$1.50 a day for a full day's work off her father's farm. Once she dropped tobacco plants for 10¢ a day, the standard wage paid to a child. The Board family grew almost everything that they ate; even sorghum cane was planted to provide something sweet. Most clothes were homemade. Farm implements were few and simple; a plow, one team (two) of mules, a wagon, a double shovel plow, a harrow, and, perhaps, a buggy or buckboard. Corn was planted by hand when she was a child. All water was drawn from a cistern. Mrs. Board has always voted, usually Republican, but has never seen jury duty. She could recall no one at Stoney Point whom she believed to have either Indian or white ancestors except, perhaps, Aunt Tildy (Matilda) Rone, who may have been part Indian. Although the numerous descendants of Dick Board and his wife are now scattered widely throughout the country they still return to Stoney Point or to some nearby location for a family reunion each year on the Sunday before Labor Day.

Most of the Stoney Point farmers, Charles Board included, spent a good deal of their time farming for some nearby white landowner; their wives, too, often worked for the husband's employer or for some nearby white family as domestics doing laundry, cooking, house cleaning, caring for the children, and occasionally, working in the fields. In the time remaining the husband and wife tended their own acres and raised their children. The Boards usually worked for the Kirbys, a nearby white family with extensive acreage around Smiths Grove. The Kirbys were also a source of assistance in times of financial crisis and they provided the Board family with a form of vicarious prestige. One person interviewed thought that, if anything, the Board and Cooke families, both of whom enjoyed a rather close relationship with local white families, were rather more favored than were the other black families at Stoney Point. Another Stoney Point resident remembered hearing his father quote Dick Board as saying that his family threw away the kind of food other families in the community usually ate.[14]

Mrs. Mary R. Board, clerk of the Stoney Point Church, underscored the economic dependence of most of the black farmers upon white landowners. Her father, Lewis Wallace, owned sixty acres at Stoney Point (all cleared by him) and he, too, worked most of his adult life for the Kirbys. Mrs. Board remembered hearing her father say

---

[14] Mrs. Daisy Board; L.D. Britt, Jr.; Herschel Cooke (2).

that in 1897 and 1898 he was earning 50¢ for a full day's work. It was her opinion that, with one possible exception, everyone at Stoney Point had some white ancestors and that several had Indian forebears. She expressed admiration for Booker T. Washington but said that she did not pay much attention to men like "Rap" Brown and Malcolm X.[15]

Herschel Cooke also remembered helping to clear land for cultivation, and he worked for 10¢ a day when a boy and for 50¢ a day as a grown man. The staple foods of his boyhood were pork, corn meal, beans, milk, and sorghum, all grown on the farm. There was much hunting to supplement the family's food supply; Herschel remembered one particularly poor family that depended almost entirely on their guns and traps for food. Most clothing was homemade and the children got one pair of shoes a year when the tobacco was sold, usually the last of November or the first two weeks in December. Wooden buckets, wooden barrels, and wooden-beam turning plows were commonly used. Corn was planted by hand, two or three kernels to a hill, and then covered with a hoe. Sorghum cane seed was planted the same way and wheat was scattered on the ground and lightly harrowed. The houses at Stoney Point were originally log or clapboard with fieldstone foundations. The barns were usually log and covered with red oak boards; the most common fencing material was white oak palings. Women usually had the task of carrying water from the cistern, well, or spring in buckets and crocks. One would be carried on the head, and the other in the hand.[16]

Mr. and Mrs. Joseph Cook have lived at or near Stoney Point nearly all their lives. Born and brought up at Stoney Point, Joseph has spent most of his adult life as a tenant farmer, but in the late 1950s he bought the farm where he now lives. He remembers that as a boy water for the household was gotten from cisterns and springs (today, there is only one small spring still flowing). Dark tobacco was the money crop until about 1917, when burley was first grown. There was, so far as he remembers, no moonshine made at Stoney Point. Times were especially hard during the Depression, which began for the farmers at Stoney Point in 1920. Joseph worked for 50¢-75¢ a day and was paid by being credited for this amount at the grocery. His employer promised to pay the bill. Times were hard, too, when he was a boy: there was no electricity, no telephone, just low wages and hard work. The bowels of the earth yield more abundantly at Stoney Point than does the soil.

---

[15] Mrs. Mary R. Board, Stoney Point, Ky., interview with the author, August 11, 1969.
[16] Mr. and Mrs. Herschel Cooke, Stoney Point, Ky., interview with the author, August 10, 1969; Herschel Cooke (2).

Stoney Point

During the 1920s oil was discovered there and some of the farmers still receive a small income from their wells. Joseph is one of these.[17]

Mrs. Edd Preston has lived at Stoney Point since 1907. As a child, she reminisces, most of the land was cleared. The farmers grew tobacco and a little garden. From the early 1940s raw milk could be sold to the Pet Milk Company in Bowling Green and dairying became, for some of the Stoney Point farmers, a second source of cash income. When she attended the Stoney Point school there were 40-50 students in the one room building. She could not recall anyone in the community with either white or Indian blood. Like many another wife she walked for many years to work at Smiths Grove, about four miles away. The road she used was cut through Stoney Point in 1910; before that time the only way out was to walk the railroad tracks or follow a wagon track across a neighboring white farmer's land until a dirt road leading to Smiths Grove or Rocky Hill could be struck. She has been registered to vote all her adult life and has usually voted the Republican ticket. She has never served on a jury. Like the other residents of Stoney Point who were interviewed, she had no recollection of overt anti-black activity although the Ku Klux Klan enjoyed a brief, minimal popularity in that section of Warren County in the 1920s. She expressed great admiration for some of the teachers and preachers she had heard at Stoney Point, but said that she had never paid much attention to such contemporary black leaders as Martin Luther King, Jr. or Malcolm X.[18]

Buford Cook also remembered the hard times of the 1930s; once four acres of Burley tobacco sold for only $88.00. Today, it might bring him as much as $4,800.00. He recalled that Stoney Point land once yielded 15-20 bushels of corn to the acre and that the land was rested between crops by allowing it to grow back up in weeds and small trees. Not until 1922 or 1923 was commercial fertilizer used for this crop. Buford did not recall any overt anti-black activity although he heard about it at Smiths Grove. He has been registered to vote all his adult life as a Republican and once served on a federal grand jury. He expressed great admiration for both Ralph Bunche (for whom one of his sons was named) and for Martin Luther King, Jr.[19]

From its beginnings Stoney Point has been, in large part, a dependent community. The acres bought by the freedmen and their descendants were sold to them by white men. Neighboring white farmers hired the

---

[17] Mr. and Mrs. Joseph Cook, Stoney Point, Ky., interview with the author, August 13, 1968; Mr. and Mrs. Joseph Cook, Stoney Point, Ky., interview with the author, August 9, 1969.
[18] Mrs. Edd Preston, Stoney Point, Ky., interview with the author, August 12, 1969.
[19] Mr. and Mrs. Buford Cook, Stoney Point, Ky., interview with the author, August 12, 1969.

labor of the freedmen, their wives, and sometimes their children, thus permitting black farmers to sustain themselves in times of economic stress and to pay for their farms. Further, if they bought more land, it was through borrowing from white men, by saving money gotten from labor done for white men, or by a combination of the two expedients. The Stoney Point farms simply were not big enough or fertile enough to support adequately the owners and their frequently large families. Even Stoney Point's location, about halfway between the two farming communities of Rocky Hill and Smiths Grove, contributed to this dependency because it permitted the community's inhabitants to live at home and yet work somewhere else during the day.

This dependency also helped to keep relations with the surrounding white community comparatively tranquil. The quasi-patriarchal connection which once existed between the Cooke and Kirby families at nearby Smiths Grove and some of the Stoney Point farmers permitted easy relations as long as both groups played their customary roles. Seemingly, this arrangement set the pattern for the years between the end of the Civil War and World War I. The Ku Klux Klan, admittedly of little force even in the 1920s, left the people of Stoney Point alone and none of the community elders remembered (or acknowledged remembering) instances of racial prejudice that were not, in some sense, customary. Associations with whites were not, of course, always good. In one bloody series of events, a white man killed a Stoney Point farmer and then subsequently made a black woman his mistress. One morning, while drunk, he knocked the woman down and dragged her around the yard of the cabin where she lived. He son, coming up through the early morning fog, saw the incident and killed the white man with his shotgun. He was tried for the murder and given two years in the county jail. After serving out his term the young man went to Toledo, Ohio, and later died there. Such conflict was quite unusual. For whatever reasons, politeness, surface geniality, and informality have been and are the best words to describe the usual black-white relationship. There was also some miscegenation. A few of the Stoney Point inhabitants are reputed to have one or several white ancestors, and in one case there is good reason to believe than Indian blood was present. Indians were, after all, both slaves and slaveholders for a good 250 years. In another instance, a neighboring white girl and one of the young men at Stoney Point were alleged to have had an affair that resulted in the birth of a daughter and the young man's leaving the country.

The old, semi-patriarchal relationship which existed between some of the black families at Stoney Point and certain neighboring white families has, of course, ended. The community is less dependent than formerly upon nearby white farmers because so many of its inhabitants are on Social Security and thus have no need to work off their own farms. And the consolidation of acres that inevitably followed emigration, has meant that those who remained acquired farms large enough to occupy most if not all of their time.

Despite the shrinking boundaries of Stoney Point, one new house has been completed [Summer, 1972] and two more are being built. Some of the younger generation remain, or have returned, although they are not farming, but commuting to work in factories located from eight to fifteen miles away. Still, there are many more people born at Stoney Point living in Louisville, Indianapolis, Detroit, and Bowling Green than at Stoney Point. Why did they leave? The usual answer is, there wasn't enough work. The Stoney Point land is rather unproductive; the farms small, the families large, and the surrounding white community was unable to hire all who wanted to work. Stoney Point's other name, "Scufftown," makes the point neatly: "You had to scuff [struggle] to make a living," explained Herschel Cooke. Or, as Bus Cooke put it in describing his childhood: "Just hard times all the time." You got paid on Saturday, then went to the store and bought the necessities. Most of the money was spent there, and a little bit more on Sunday. By Tuesday following the money was gone and it was necessary somehow to make it until the next Saturday. Then the process began again. It is understandable that so many of the young left when factory jobs in the northern cities (or elsewhere) became available.

Perennially low farm prices, the continued rise in land prices, and agriculture's lack of attraction as a way of life make the future of Stoney Point problematical. Many rural, black communities like Stoney Point have already ceased to exist. Yet the "old settlers," as Joseph Cook calls them, have shown a remarkable tenacity in holding on to their acres. And it may be that a combination of stubbornness and the fortunate location of light industry within driving distance of Stoney Point will enable the community to survive.[20]

Postscript, June, 1976

Several of the "old settlers" have died and their land has passed into the hands of descendants. Other acres have been sold to nearby white farmers. Bulldozers have been busy and some of the jungle-like growth has been replaced with fescue pasture interspersed with clumps of stumps, brush, and pokeberry. One new oil well has been brought

---

[20] Herschel Cooke (2); Mr. Bus Cooke, Smiths Grove, Ky., interview with the author, August 1, 1970.

into production. Wind, weather, and time have further altered the landscape. A number of the abandoned cabins are reduced to hulks and their contents exposed to the elements. Although its membership continues to shrink, the Stoney Point Church still meets on Sunday. The community persists.

J. W. COOKE (1929–   ) received his A.B. from Western Kentucky University and his M.A. and Ph.D. degrees from Vanderbilt University. The author of several articles in scholarly journals, Cooke won a research grant from the American Philosophical Society in 1969. He teaches history at the University of Tennessee at Nashville.

This article first appeared in *The Filson Club History Quarterly* in October 1976, vol. 50, pp. 337–52.

THE BANCOKENTUCKY STORY

By ROBERT T. FUGATE, JR.*
Louisville, Kentucky

On the evening of November 16, 1930, an official of the National Bank of Kentucky posted a notice on the bank's door. The message solemnly proclaimed that the bank had been closed by an order of its board of directors. Simultaneously the Louisville Trust Company and the Security Bank, two smaller institutions controlled by the Banco-Kentucky Company, were closed by their respective directors. The shock wave spread across the city and out into the state. The affairs of the BancoKentucky Company were of vital importance to numerous communities all over Kentucky and the Ohio Valley region. The chain reaction from this event caused panic, additional bank closings, and even suicides. Not only did BancoKentucky control a number of banks outside Louisville, but many small county banks used the National Bank of Kentucky as a depository for their monies. In Louisville the Bank of St. Helens, the American Mutual Savings Bank, and the First Standard Bank all closed in rapid succession.[1] These banks had used the National Bank as a depository for their money. Fear spread across the city, and all banks were rapidly becoming suspect. In order to stem the rising tide of public concern, Louisville bankers took out large newspaper advertisements proclaiming the soundness of their institutions.

These bankers feared that other bank runs might result in the total destruction of the entire Louisville banking system. This feeling of impending disaster was so strong that vigorous contermeasures were instituted. For its part, the *Courier-Journal* printed front-page warnings to those who would, in its words, spread "baseless rumors" about the unsound condition of local banks. The paper cautioned its readers that Kentucky laws fixed penalties against individuals who made such statements.[2]

It is sad that civil liberties are often treated as privileges to be taken away in times of crisis. A few days after the warning appeared, Albert Iveson, manager of a local A & P Food Store, was arrested on the charge of spreading false rumors about the soundness of the Stock Yards Bank.[3] It is interesting that a liberal newspaper like the *Courier-*

---

* MR. ROBERT FUGATE has a M.A. in history from the University of Louisville. Formerly a high school teacher, he is now a stockbroker in a local firm.

[1] *Courier-Journal* (Louisville), November 17, 1930; November 20, 1930; November 19, 1930.

[2] *Ibid.*, November 18, 1930.

[3] *Ibid.*, November 22, 1930.

Journal did not protest the arrest of local citizens for voicing unpopular statements.

It should be pointed out that the Louisville bank closings were not unique phenomena. In fact, during November 1930, 143 American banks failed. Of these bank failures, 129 could be traced to the collapse of Caldwell and Company of Nashville, Tennessee and the panic it spread.[4] Unfortunately for the city of Louisville, the BancoKentucky Company was one of those institutions which received the "kiss of death" from Rogers Caldwell.

It would be wrong, however, to single out one man for sole blame. It took the unwitting efforts of a number of individuals to bring about the final collapse. Most prominent of these were James B. Brown, BancoKentucky's colorful, careless, and reckless president. Brown was a truly interesting character. Born in Lawrenceburg, Kentucky, in 1872, he received his education in the Shelbyville public schools before coming to Louisville in 1887. As a young man with great ambition and drive, he first went to work for the Southern News Company as an office boy. Ten years later, when he left Southern News, he was cashier. Brown was chiefly interested in finance and after a brief period of working for the Tax Receiver's office, he became cashier of the First National Bank in 1906. Brown's mastery of the intricacies of finance, plus his personal magnetism, propelled him in two short years to the presidency of the bank. Three years later, he was elected president of the National Bank of Commerce. In 1919 he managed to merge his bank with the American Southern National Bank and the National Bank of Kentucky. The two surviving entities of this consolidation were the National Bank of Kentucky and James B. Brown.[5]

The National Bank of Kentucky was a venerable institution that had been formed in 1834. It was a state bank known as the Bank of Kentucky until 1900 when it received a charter under the National Banking Act and became the National Bank of Kentucky of Louisville. When Brown consolidated his control in 1919, the bank was the largest south of the Ohio River, with resources estimated at more than $50,000,000. The Bank of Kentucky had survived many calamities, including financial panics and the Civil War, and was the trusted bank of thousands of Kentuckians, both urban and rural, as well as the main depository for numerous state banks, small cities, and counties throughout Kentucky.[6]

---

[4] *Time*, December 1, 1930, p. 41.

[5] *Who's Who in Louisville, 1926*, compiled by W. T. Owens (Louisville, Ky.: The Standard Printing Co., 1926), p. 28.

[6] Keys v. Akers *et al*., United States District Court, Western District of Kentucky, Number Eq 649 (1931), Plaintiff's Petition, p. 10. This and future citations in this paper refer to printed transcript published by Judd and Detweiler, Inc., Washington, and found in the Kentucky Room of the Louisville Free Public Library. Hereafter cited as Keys v. Akers *et al*.

In 1925 Brown bought a controlling interest in the Louisville *Herald* and the Louisville *Post*. Later that year he consolidated these papers into the Louisville *Herald-Post*. This newspaper published both morning and afternoon editions and was a strong competitor of the *Courier-Journal* and *Louisville Times*. Brown also became a director of many of Louisville's most important businesses, including Standard Oil Company (Kentucky), the Southern Bell Telephone and Telegraph Company, and the Louisville Gas and Electric Company.[7]

A flamboyant, self-made man in the Horatio Alger tradition, Brown spent lavish sums of money on himself and his friends. He once admitted that between 1928 and 1930 he had personally spent more than two and one-half million dollars.[8] Much of this money was spent entertaining friends and business associates. For example, Brown stated that he would invite guests to French Lick, Indiana, to gamble at the Casinos. He would then reimburse all losses sustained by the members of his party.[9] Brown's personality exuded those qualities which enabled him to dominate other men. He possessed the aura of a winner, and few dared to question his business acumen. Brown was able to run the various businesses that he dominated without any serious attempt on the part of the company directors to make sure the affairs of the various firms were being conducted in a business-like manner.

E. P. Lock, counsel for the Receiver of the National Bank of Kentucky, once described the attitude of the directors of the various Brown-dominated companies as completely trusting of any thing their president did or said. The real reason, of course, for the directors' unwillingness to assert proper control over Brown was that they genuinely admired him. They felt that Brown was going to make millions of dollars for them and they were not going to antagonize him.[10] Beginning in the mid-1920's, Brown became almost inaccessible to his employees and the officers of the bank. As the years passed, his eccentricities became more pronounced. Brown rarely visited the bank during the day. Instead, he preferred working alone in his office from midnight to dawn.[11] His impressive bearing and business ability covered a fatal flaw in his character; at heart he was a reckless gambler, possessed of unbounded optimism in himself and in the American economy.

The seeds of destruction were sown long before the financial panic of 1929. In fact, as early as 1925 worried federal bank examiners had con-

---

[7] *Who's Who in Louisville, 1926,* p. 28.
[8] *Herald-Post* (Louisville), January 16, 1931.
[9] *Courier-Journal,* January 17, 1931.
[10] *Ibid.,* October 18, 1933.
[11] Keys v. Akers *et al.*, p. 25.

tacted the directors of the National Bank of Kentucky, asking them to assert themselves against the one man rule that Brown had established over the bank. The examiners were particularly concerned about the increasing numbers of bad debts that the bank was incurring. John W. Pole, federal comptroller of the currency, later stated that between 1925 and 1930 the bank was a constant source of concern to his office. He went on to detail his charges against the management of the bank. Beginning in 1925, Pole's office advised the officers of the bank that loans in excess of established limits had been granted. The record indicates, however, that the government took no action against the bank other than verbal scoldings.[12] The next year a bank examiner described the National Bank of Kentucky as an institution completely dominated by one man—James B. Brown. In November 1926, examinations disclosd that the bank was receiving very slow payment on outstanding loans of more than $4,000,000.

By 1927, the Comptroller's Office took the extreme position of telling the directors of the bank that Brown was an unsafe banker. Apparently, however, the directors paid little attention to these allegations. The following year an increasingly concerned comptroller asked his examiners to contact individual directors in order to determine if they were giving any consideration to the warnings from his office. In December 1929 another examination revealed even more glaring irregularities. Slow assets, that is, loans repaid at a slower than agreed upon rate, were reported at $5,000,000; doubtful paper was listed at $725,-000; and outright losses were placed at $386,000.

Even more spectacular accounts of large-scale banking irregularities were disclosed by Hugh A. White, an accountant appointed to investigate the bank after its closing. White's audit uncovered instances where a local brokerage firm had been given special borrowing privileges far in excess of its net worth. The firm in question, Wakefield and Company, had handled Brown's various stock market transactions. It was subsequently disclosed that some clerks employed by Wakefield and earnings less than $2,500 a year had been able to borrow sums in excess of $100,000 from the bank. It can be assumed, however, that the loans were not used for the personal benefit of these employees. It seems far more likely that these monies were actually channeled into various speculative investments of interest to Brown. In other words, Wakefield and Company was used by Brown as a front to conceal certain business activities. At the time of the closing of the national bank, Brown personally owed Wakefield $3,500,000.[13] At the same time,

---

[12] *Courier-Journal*, March 5, 1931.
[13] *Ibid.*, March 5, 1931; February 9, 1932.

Wakefield and Company had loans outstanding with the National Bank of Kentucky for $1,000,000.[14]

An examination of other loans sheds additional light on the lax banking practices of James Brown. For years Kentucky Wagon Manufacturing Company had incurred continuing deficits. Despite this fact, the National Bank of Kentucky continued to lend the company monies far in excess of its saleable assets. Paul Keys, Receiver for the National Bank of Kentucky, estimated that the bank sustained a loss, counting principal and interest, of $3,000,000 when Kentucky Wagon went into receivership shortly after the collapse of BancoKentucky.[15]

In a similar vein, loans made to E. B. Norman and Company proved equally damaging. The Bank of Kentucky lost over $525,000 due to Norman's inability to repay its loans. This company owned timberland and operated a small sawmill in Louisiana. The company was located well outside of the bank's normal trade area. Apparently E. B. Norman was unable to obtain any other creditors than the bank. Throughout the late 1920s the records show that the company did not pay off or even amortize previous loans. Despite this fact, the bank continued to lend large sums of money to the company.[16]

The bank also lost over $800,000 in loans made to the Murry Rubber Company. Originally incorporated as the Rubber Company of America, Murry Rubber's principal asset was a contract with Sears, Roebuck to supply that firm with automobile tires. When Murry Rubber lost the Sears contract, its market outlet vanished. Located in New Jersey, again well outside the bank's normal trade area, and in dire financial straits, Murry Rubber was not a likely candidate for the bank's credit. And yet the National Bank of Kentucky did extend it loans. One possible explanation for this situation was the fact that the company was owned by personal friends of James B. Brown. This is not the only instance of Brown assisting friends with the bank's money. Paul Keys pointed out many occasions when Brown lent unsecured monies to personal friends. At the same time, the bank was forced to borrow large sums of money in order to meet heavy customer withdrawals. In fact, the bank often borrowed to the limit of its pledgable assets. The lending policies of the bank were so lax that huge amounts of slow and overdue paper accumulated. This, plus outright losses, increased until it "aggregated as much as the capital and surplus of the Bank."[17] The favorable business climate of the late 1920s had enabled the bank to survive without any discernible difficulties. However, Brown's reckless-

---

[14] Keys v. Akers, *et al.*, pp. 53-54.
[15] *Ibid.*, pp. 39-40.
[16] *Ibid.*, pp. 72-74.
[17] *Ibid.*, pp. 64-65, 31.

ness and irresponsible business practices weakened the bank and left it much more vulnerable to deflationary economic cycles than it would have been under conservative management.

In 1929 Brown conceived the idea of merging the National Bank of Kentucky and the Louisville Trust Company into a holding company known as the BancoKentucky Company. Apparently he believed that he could raise large sums of money through public subscription of the new company's stock. Brown then hoped to engage the company in enterprises forbidden to banks. This new corporation was to be run under the same management as was the National Bank of Kentucky. BancoKentucky Company would not even have a separate place of business. The day-to-day corporate business was conducted by clerks of the bank.[18]

On July 20, 1929, the Louisville *Herald-Post* announced with great fanfare the creation of the BancoKentucky Company. The newspaper undoubtedly under Brown's direction, hailed the company as a milestone in Louisville's economic development. Claiming that the new company had resources of $170,000,000, the newspaper proceeded to state that BancoKentucky was a type of financial organization that would bring various banks into close cooperation for the benefit of both the stockholder and the community.[19] The publicity surrounding the birth of the holding company was not merely boasting or pride. There was a serious, practical purpose behind all the hoopla. The success of this scheme depended upon the ability of BancoKentucky to raise large sums of money by the sale of its stock. Brown had to convince the investing public that BancoKentucky was a very promising investment. The creation of this enterprise preceded by three months the Wall Street panic of October 1929 and it proved to be the apex of James B. Brown's financial career. No one could have guessed the dramatic and traumatic events that would leave Brown's empire in utter ruin. The BancoKentucky Company had less than eighteen months of life. Its collapse proved to be one of Louisville's most painful experiences during the great Depression.

The collapse of the BancoKentucky Company began in an unlikely manner. In January 1930, Brown received a letter from Rogers Caldwell, president of the prestigious Nashville banking and investment house, Caldwell and Company, The letter stated:

---

[18] *Courier-Journal*, October 18, 1933.
[19] *Herald-Post*, July 20, 1929.

My Dear Mr. Brown:

I have been wondering lately whether it would be feasible to consider a consolidation between the BancoKentucky corporation and the banks in which we are interested. If I could discuss the matter with you I have a suggestion to make which, in my opinion, might be very helpful to the market situation of BancoKentucky stock. As you know, the banks in which we are interested already have deposits of above 150,000,000 and I believe that a combination of our interests would make one of the most formidable situations in the country.

I am leaving tonight for St. Louis to attend the annual meeting of the Missouri State Life Insurance Company and if you think this suggestion is worthy of our getting together you might wire me there, care of the Missouri State Life Company and I could come back by the way of Louisville.

With assurance of my regards and looking forward to discussing this matter with you, I remain

Very truly yours,
Rogers Caldwell.[20]

The letter struck a receptive cord in Brown. In fact he became intrigued with the idea that such a merger would open up tremendous avenues of growth, both for his company and the Caldwell firm. Brown quickly agreed that a meeting should be arranged in order to discuss the possible merger. Brown did not realize, however, that he was being led into a trap set by Rogers Caldwell. These men were much alike. Dewitt Carter, an executive of Caldwell and Company, once described his boss as a man of resource, vigor, supreme self-confidence, boundless ambition, and, interestingly, of little moral restraint.[21]

No record exists of the conversation between these two men. However, from the results, it is apparent that Caldwell must have used great charm and negotiating skill on the unsuspecting James Brown. Even given his great talents, it is still surprising that Caldwell could have persuaded Brown to merge the two companies without an audit or even the exchange of balance sheets.[22] But that is exactly what happened.

After their meeting, Brown presented the merger plan to the directors of the BancoKentucky Company. In justifying the merger, he pointed out the many benefits that it would bring. He talked at great length of the various insurance companies that Caldwell and Company

---

[20] Laurent v. Akers *et al.*, Jefferson Circuit Court, Chancery Branch, First Division, Number 206688 (1931), I, 229. This and future citations in this paper refer to printed transcript of testimony and evidence given published by The Standard Printing Co., Inc., Louisville, Kentucky. Hereafter cited as Laurent v. Akers *et al.*

[21] *Courier-Journal*, February 27, 1931.
[22] *Ibid.*

controlled and stressed in particular the reputed $5,000,000 monthly income of the Missouri State Life Insurance Company. To Brown, this was a most important factor, because BancoKentucky was often hampered by liquidity problems that would be solved quickly with the availability of a steady cash flow. As usual, the board of directors acquiesced to Brown's wishes and voted twenty-six to one in favor of the transaction. The lone opposing vote was cast by Ben Robertson, who pointed out that they were giving away good stock for a company whose assets had never been accurately appraised. While the board of directors of the BancoKentucky Company were meeting to discuss the merger, the executives of Caldwell and Company were, in the words of T. G. Donovan, a Caldwell official, literally walking the floor waiting for the deal to be approved. The reason for this nervousness on their part was that Caldwell and Company and the Bank of Tennessee were completely insolvent.[23]

At the time of the merger discussions between Brown and Caldwell the BancoKentucky Company had amassed considerable assets. Brown had pursued an aggressive policy of acquiring numerous banks throughout the Ohio Valley region. Besides the National Bank of Kentucky and the Louisville Trust Company, BancoKentucky controlled seven other banks. These included the Brighton Bank and Trust Company of Cincinnati, Ohio, the Pearl-Market Bank and Trust Company, also of Cincinnati; two Covington, Kentucky, banks—the Central Savings Bank and Trust Company and the Peoples Liberty Bank and Trust Company; the Ashland National Bank, Ashland, Kentucky; the First National Bank of Paducah, Kentucky; and, finally, the Security Bank of Louisville, Kentucky.[24]

On June 2, 1930, the official announcement of the merger of the two companies was made in the Louisville *Herald-Post*. In large headlines the paper proclaimed "Huge Bank Deal Completed, Caldwell & Company is merged with BancoKentucky." Ironically, the newspaper added that the merger was a result of careful negotiation carried on over a period of months, and that the two companies each acquired substantial interests in the other.[25]

The actual terms of the agreement called for the exchange of one-half of the shares of stock of Caldwell in return for approximately 900,000 shares of BancoKentucky stock. However, 100,000 shares were to be returned to BancoKentucky in consideration for Caldwell and Company's receiving notes of obligation from the Kentucky Wagon Company and National Motor Company. By this method BancoKen-

---

[23] *Ibid.*, October 8, 1932; February 14, 1931.
[24] Laurent v. Akers *et al.*, I, 539.
[25] *Herald-Post* (Louisville), June 2, 1930.

tucky was able to rid itself of questionable assets that had been highly criticized by federal bank examiners. In addition, another 200,000 shares of BancoKentucky stock were held in escrow pending a certification of the true worth of Caldwell and Company.[26]

Now that Brown had, in effect, become a partner, Caldwell decided to disclose to him the true financial position of Caldwell and Company. This unhappy task fell to Dewitt Carter, who was dispatched to Louisville to give Brown the real balance sheets of the ailing company. When Brown discovered that he had been tricked, he reacted angrily and accused Caldwell of cheating him. His anger was only partly alleviated when Carter returned an additional 200,000 shares of BancoKentucky stock. However, Caldwell and Company retained 400,000 shares of BancoKentucky, which at the time had a market value of approximately $15 per share. At the same time BancoKentucky held 10,000 shares of Caldwell and Company supposedly worth $100 per share.[27] In reality, of course, the Caldwell stock was worthless unless, somehow, the company could be made solvent again. It then became imperative for the BancoKentucky Company to shore up the sagging fortunes of its new partner. During August 1930, Brown confided to a colleague that Rogers Caldwell had "us sewed in and I've got to protect Caldwell and Company for the bank's sake." Now both BancoKentucky's money and reputation were in the greatest of peril, and Brown was forced to lend additional sums to Caldwell and Company in a vain effort to ward off the inevitable.[28]

However, by early November 1930 neither Brown's dwindling financial resources nor Rogers Caldwell's cunning could stave off the continuing rumors concerning Caldwell and Company's financial health. On November 5, 1930, a committee of the Nashville Clearing House, representing the Tennessee Banking Commission, after a secret meeting with representatives of Caldwell and Company, decided to step in to protect Caldwell's fast diminishing resources.[29]

The news that Caldwell and Company had been placed in receivership caused consternation throughout the mid-South. Brown immediately issued a public statement to the effect that the merger between the BancoKentucky Company and Caldwell and Company had never taken place.[30] It is unlikely that Brown really believed that he could continue this ruse for any length of time. But it was possible that he might gain enough time to work out some agreement that would pre-

---

[26] John Berry McFerrin, *Caldwell and Company* (Chapel Hill: University of North Carolina Press, 1939), p 135.
[27] *Courier-Journal*, February 27, 1931.
[28] *Ibid.*, March 5, 1931.
[29] *Ibid.*, November 6, 1930.
[30] *Herald-Post*, November 6, 1930.

vent insolvency. During the last few days in the life of the Bank of Kentucky, Brown sought out various means to save his holdings, including talks with the TransAmerica Company, hoping to merge his banks with that powerful banking and insurance company.[31]

During this hectic period, Caldwell and Company officials attempted to contact Brown and inquire as to how he could possibly claim the merger had not taken place. BancoKentucky representatives informed them that Brown had used the word "consumated" in referring to the merger. Later Dewitt Carter stated that whether or not the merger had in fact been legally consumated, there was no doubt that BancoKentucky owned half of the stock in Caldwell and Company, and Caldwell possessed 400,000 shares of BancoKentucky.[32]

Time was quickly running out for the National Bank of Kentucky. Almost immediately after the difficulties of Caldwell and Company became known, a quiet run began on the bank. The run was not initiated by the small depositors. News of the impending disaster passed by word of mouth among the more influential and financially sophisticated Louisvillians. This was not surprising considering the fact that directors of the BancoKentucky had connections with many other firms in the city. Corporations, including Standard Oil (Kentucky) and the Louisville and Nashville Railroad, withdrew large sums from the bank shortly before its collapse.[33]

A detailed breakdown of deposit shrinkage at the bank during the final week of its existence shows that on November 12, 1930, $1,798,000 was withdrawn; on November 13, $751,000; November 14, $1,833,000; and on November 15, the last day the bank would open, a huge $2,565,000 was withdrawn.[34]

On November 12, two Louisville bankers—Ralph C. Gifford, president of the First National Bank, and John R. Downing, president of the Citizens Union National Bank—asked Robert H. Neill, chief National Bank Examiner for the Eighth Federal Reserve District, to come to Louisville to discuss the growing crisis associated with the National Bank of Kentucky. Although they had no connection with BancoKentucky, these two men were concerned as to whether the Federal Reserve would stand behind their own banks in the event that a general run might begin upon all the banks in the city. Accompanying Neill on his trip to Louisville was William M. Martin, governor of the St. Louis Federal Reserve Bank. Upon their arrival, the two men entered into

---

[31] George R. Leighton, *Five Cities* (New York: Harper & Brothers, 1939), p. 95.

[32] *Courier-Journal*, February 27, 1931.

[33] Interview with Joseph H. Ganz, former employee of the National Bank of Kentucky, April, 1971.

[34] Laurent v. Akers *et al.*, p. 332.

an all-day conference with the local banking group and certain directors and other officials of the National Bank of Kentucky. Toward evening, Neill learned that Brown was currently negotiating with representatives of the TransAmerica Company for the sale of the BancoKentucky Company. When Neill discovered this new and potentially important development, he telephoned Stuart Duncan, chairman of the National Bank of Kentucky's Executiv Committee, and asked for a meeting to discuss the likelihood of an agreement between TransAmerica and BancoKentucky. Duncan, however, declined to meet with Neill because of a previously scheduled dinner party. Neill, angry and frustrated, called another of the bank's directors, William S. Speed, who came immediately to Neill's hotel room. Speed, upon being informed of the urgency of the matter at hand, himself called Duncan and demanded that he join them in the discussion.[35] The three men proceeded to evaluate the position of the bank and talked about the possible remaining options. Neill urged the directors to take an active part in the merger talks and not let Brown alone handle the negotiations.

Impressed by Neill's argument's, the directors telephoned Brown and invited him to join in the discussions. Brown agreed to meet with Neill and the other directors. He confirmed that merger talks were indeed being held and said that preliminary negotiations were progressing well. Actual completion of the merger depended, however, on whether three shares or two shares of BancoKentucky stock would be given in exchange for one share of TransAmerica stock. Brown claimed that he was determined to hold out for an agreement of three shares.

Neill could hardly believe his ears. With the BancoKentucky Company and its affiliated banks tottering on the edge of bankruptcy, Brown's words sounded like the babble of a man who had lost contact with reality. Neill strenuously implored him to reconsider his position, stating over and over that BancoKentucky was simply in no position to haggle.[36] This argument seemed to have little effect upon Brown, who left the meeting without inviting the other directors to participate in the merger discussions. Because it was highly unlikely that Brown had suddenly taken leave of his senses, the most probable explanation for his unconcerned attitude is that the merger talks were not near the final stages he had indicated.

It seems most likely that Brown was again attempting to buy precious time. Neill returned to St. Louis on November 13. Before leaving however, he gave instructions to William T. Zurschmied, the cashier of the National Bank of Kentucky, to report to him on the bank's cash

---

[35] *Courier-Journal,* Februray 9, 1932.
[36] *Ibid.*

balances at the close of each business day. On Friday, November 14, Zurschmied reported that losses were becoming intolerable and urged Neill to return to Louisville at once. Neill arrived on Saturday to find that the situation had become hopeless.[37]

The bank had almost completely exhausted its borrowing power. Very quickly thereafter a meeting of the Louisville bank clearing house was called. As a result of this action, a committee was appointed to appraise the assets of the bank. On Sunday, November 16, about seventy-five persons, some no more than curious onlookers, crowded into the meeting room to hear the report of the special committee. Brown later compared the meeting to a "Roman Circus" rather than a sober business gathering. The committee reported that in its opinion the National Bank of Kentucky was indeed insolvent. Brown angrily retorted that the bank was not insolvent but rather had $55,000,000 in net assets. He went on to remind them that if the bank were closed, the closing would cause the greatest financial disaster ever to occur in the city of Louisville.[38]

After listening to the discussion, the governor of the Federal Reserve Board took the position that the federal government could not advance money unless it was guaranteed by the other banks in Louisville. The other banks were unwilling to give any such guarantee unless the directors of the National Bank of Kentucky first pledged $5,000,000 of their personal assets in order to secure the loan.[39] The directors refused to make such a pledge. Feeling that there was no other course of action, the directors then voted to close the bank and place it in receivership.

At 5 o'clock the following afternoon the directors of the BancoKentucky Company met in a special session. There was a general feeling of urgency, bordering on panic, that somehow the remaining corporate assets had to be protected for the creditors and stockholders of the company. The directors decided that the best course of action would be to sell the remaining banks while they were still solvent. The board authorized three directors—R. Lee Calahan, T. Kennedy Helm, and Saunders P. Jones—to leave immediately for Cincinnati and negotiate the sale of the Pearl-Market Bank and Trust Company and the Brighton Bank and Trust Company.[40]

Less than twenty-four hours later a special emergency meeting of the board of directors was called to consider some especially disturbing

---

[37] *Ibid.*

[38] *Herald-Post*, January 8, 1931.

[39] McFerrin, *Campbell and Company*, p. 185.

[40] Laurent v. Akers *et al.*, the following material was taken from the Minute Book and Organization Records of the BancoKentucky Company, Inc., p. 546, introduced as evidence and exhibited as "Zurschmied No. 42." Hereafter cited as Minute Book.

news. Helm had called from Cincinnati to report that a run was in progress upon two smaller BancoKentucky banks located across the river in Covington, Kentucky. The two banks in question were the Peoples—Liberty Bank and Trust Company and the Central Savings Bank and Trust Company. He also reported that it was possible to sell these two banks to Cincinnati interests if an immediate purchase could be negotiated. When questioned about the price involved, Helm was less than optimistic. He stated that BancoKentucky would have to take the best terms available. Helm then proceeded to read over the telephone a hastily drawn option contract outlining in detail various provisions for the sale of the banks in Covington and Cincinnati. The other directors, believing that their was no real alternative, agreed to the sale.[41]

Anticipating more emergencies, the directors requested that Helm contact various officials in Ashland, Kentucky, to see if a profitable sale of the Ashland National Bank might be possible. The reason for the urgency was that the bank in Ashland, because of its proximity to the Covington-Cincinnati area, might also be in grave danger.

Helm's overtures to various Ashland bankers fell upon receptive ears. A syndicate of Ashland capitalists dispatched two directors of the Ashland National Bank to Louisville to discuss the possibilities of purchasing the bank. The Ashland syndicate knew that the BancoKentucky directors were desperate to dispose of the holdings. Realizing this, the Ashland group felt that they could get control of the bank very cheaply. The two sides met at a hastily called meeting in the Inter-Southern Building, later known as the Kentucky Home Life Building.[42]

After the exchange of pleasantries, the two sides began serious bargaining. The Ashland directors went into extended detail about the way the BancoKentucky Company had originally purchased the bank by an exchange of stock and that now, of course, the stock was worthless. The Ashland team went on to state that their bank was still basically sound and that, all things considered, they were prepared to offer $30.00 a share for four thousands shares of stock in the bank. The four thousand shares in question represented about 60 per cent of the bank's capital stock. For their part, the directors of the BancoKentucky Company rather angrily pointed out that they had originally purchased the stock for $200 a share. Furthermore, a BancoKentucky director pointed out that he was not prepared to let the company give away any more

---

[41] *Ibid.*, p. 550.
[42] *Ibid.*, p. 553.

banks that might be, in his opinion, liquidated for three or four times the amount that they were offering.[43]

At this point the two sides adjourned to different meeting rooms in order to discuss strategy. The BancoKentucky directors were clearly at a disadvantage, or at least, they so perceived themselves to be. From their point of view, time was not in their favor. For the moment the Ashland bank was sound, but there was serious question as to how long it would continue to enjoy the public's confidence.

Returning to the meeting, BancoKentucky directors countered the Ashland proposal with an offer to sell the four thousand shares for $100 per share. This was rejected by the Ashland representatives, but both sides agreed to hold another meeting the next day. Finally, the two sides compromised their differences. BancoKentucky agreed to sell the four thousand shares for $50 per share. Another three thousand shares would be turned over to Paul C. Keys, the receiver of the National Bank of Kentucky, to be sold at a more advantageous time.[44] Rightly or wrongly, the directors of BancoKentucky believed the best course of action was to liquidate all banks controlled by the company as quickly as possible, while the banks were still in operation.

Later the directors would be strongly criticized for the "panic" selling of BancoKentucky assets All told, the BancoKentucky Company suffered a loss of $8,147,719.71 due to the sale of bank stocks after November 17, 1930. On September 27, 1929, for example, 44,290 shares of Brighton Bank and Trust Company were purchased for $4,109,884.90. At the same time, 47,854 shares of Paerl-Market Bank and Trust Company were bought at a cost of $3,573,788.30. This was a total price for the two banks of $7,683,773.20. On November 18, 1930, the directors of the BancoKentucky approved the sale of these banks for $1,107,250. This action resulted in a staggering net loss of $6,576,423.20

The quick sale of the two Covington banks resulted in a smaller but not insignificant loss of $660,759. And finally, another large loss was suffered in the sale of the four thousand shares of Ashland National Bank, which had been originally purchased for $1,110,537.50. BancoKentucky sold out for $200,000, a net loss of $910,537.50.[45]

The collapse of the BancoKentucky Company and its affiliated institutions had both immediate and long-term effects upon the city. In the short run it meant financial loss to the stockholders and creditors of the bank and also caused the public to lose confidence in the other local banks. The greatest financial losses were not suffered by the depositors, because they eventually received their deposit monies. The real brunt of

---

[43] *Ibid.*, p. 555.
[44] *Ibid.*, pp. 555-556.
[45] Laurent v. Akers *et al.*, the following information obtained from typed brief submitted as evidence and filed with the previously noted Laurent evidence No. 206688, pp. 41-42.

the losses was sustained by the stockholders. BancoKentucky stock was primarily held by people living in Louisville or in the immediate trade area of the company. Many middle-class Louisvillians had eagerly purchased shares of BancoKentucky at prices ranging as high as $25 to $30 a share, believing that their holdings would rapidly appreciate in value. In a very short time, they saw their investment completely wiped out. This, however, was not the total extent of their misfortune. It was later determined that the stockholders were also liable for the losses suffered by the depositors of the bank. After considerable litigation, it was finally determined that the stockholders of record at the time of the collapse would be assessed slightly more than $5 a share.[46] Hard pressed, also, were those persons who had been extended credit by the various banks controlled by BancoKentucky. The receivers for the banks refused to extend loans and put great pressure on them to repay their debts. This action resulted in increased foreclosures and bankruptcies.

Even for those individuals who had no direct connection with the BancoKentucky Company or the closed banks, the failure posed serious questions about the safety of all banks. The banks were the very foundation of the capitalistic system and if they could not survive the Depression, could any business hope to? The stock market crash of 1929, and the failure of the BancoKentucky Company, reinforced the growing belief in Louisville that this Depression would be the most serious yet encountered by the American economy.

The long-term effects of the bank failures upon the city were more subtle and yet more important. The failure of the National Bank of Kentucky, the city's largest bank, left lasting scars upon the community's bankers. An article which appeared in the February 26, 1971, edition of the *Louisville Times* was addressed to this point. The reporter, Geoffrey Brown, conducted an in-depth study under the title "Who Decides Where Louisville Is Going." The purpose of the article was to single out the most powerful and influential men in the community. In doing so, Brown brought out the interesting point that the failure of the Bank of Kentucky acted as a restraint upon the future development of the city. According to Brown, the real power in Louisville today resides with the major banks. This is due principally to the fact that there are no other large concentrations of wealth in the community. But this power was applied only in the most conservative manner until approximately five years ago when through death and retirement a new generation of bankers assumed control. The older bankers, Brown theorized, never got over the shock of witnessing the largest bank in the city collapse. From the BancoKentucky failure in 1930 until the late

---

[46] Interview with Joseph H. Ganz, former employee of the National Bank of Kentucky, April, 1971.

1960s Louisville banks were noted for their stout conservationism and lack of enthusiasm for new and venturesome projects.

Local businessmen, as a rule, bypassed Louisville banks when seeeking financing for high-risk ventures and turned to the more receptive banks of New York, Atlanta, and Nashville. It was not until the last few years that local banks began to push actively for the development of the city. As a result, the skyline of Louisville is rapidly changing. It is significant that many of the new building projects, such as Village West, the University of Louisville Medical Center, the River Front project, and the high-rise office buildings owe their genesis either to direct or indirect support by the local banks. Whether or not the failure of the Bank of Kentucky directly resulted in the stifling of Louisville development is an arguable point. But it cannot be denied that in 1930, the year of the BancoKentucky collapse, the city of Louisville was the twenty-fourth largest city in the country and the second largest city in the South. Louisville, then, surpassed such important cities as Atlanta, Denver, and Portland, Oregon. In 1970 Louisville ranked thirty-ninth in size among American cities. In the last forty years Louisville was supplanted as a major American city.

Curiously, the men responsible for the failure of the banks received only mild censure. Brown and a number of the directors declared bankruptcy shortly after the collapse. However, Brown was still able to maintain a comfortable standard of living due to the fact that his wife had considerable assets completely out of the reach of his creditors. A large number of law suits were filed against Brown and the other directors of the BancoKentucky Company. The two most important actions were brought by Joseph S. Laurent, receiver for the BancoKentucky Company and Paul C. Keys, receiver for the National Bank of Kentucky. However, neither of these nor subsequent action were successful in redressing the loss suffered by stockholders and creditors of the closed institutions. A criminal action was brought against Brown, charging him with deliberate fraud, but a jury found him not guilty. It is surprising, in view of the enormity of the losses and the disclosures of large-scale banking irregularities, that no really successful court actions were sustained against the executives of BancoKentucky. It should be remembered, though, that the pre-Roosevelt period was still a time when big businessmen were glorified. Brown was not generally condemned for his banking practices, rather, he was condemned for his failure to succeed.

The failure of the BancoKentucky Company raised two fundamental questions. Why in fact did it happen and who was responsible? Basically the failure can be ascribed to three factors. First, the National

Bank of Kentucky had for years engaged in speculative loans—a highly questionable practice for a supposedly conservative institution. This mistake was compounded by the bank's decision to carry and even increase those loans after it had become obvious that their repayment was in considerable doubt. Instead of cutting short their losses, the bank continued throwing good money after bad. This alone should not have caused the bank to fail, bearing in mind that the Bank of Kentucky had been the largest bank in the city, with resources of more than fifty million dollars. It is also likely that these banking irregularities were not unique among local banks. It can be assumed that these highly questionable practices were common before 1929.

The second factor was the Depression itself. The survival of any bank depended upon its ability to grant loans backed by secure collateral. The realities of the Depression operated to negate this practice. The stock market crash and the subsequent recession produced two damaging trends. First, there was a marked increase in slow repayment and outright defaults; secondly, the collateral backing the loans began to depreciate rapidly in value. This resulted in the sustaining of even larger losses. At the same time the bank's liabilities, principally in the form of demand deposits, salaries, and interest, remained at the same level.

The third and most important factor was the effect of the Caldwell merger. The merger cost the BancoKentucky Company its money, and most importantly, its reputation. At the time of the merger and the subsequent abortive effort to keep Caldwell and Company solvent, BancoKentucky gave its partner millions of dollars in both stock and outright loans. But the critical consideration was that the survival of both companies was inseparable. At the time of the merger, Caldwell and Company was moribund and its collapse doomed BancoKentucky to a similar fate. The merger took from BancoKentucky one of its last important assets, its reputation as a sound institution, capable of safeguarding the public's monies.

The responsibility for this catastrophe must rest primarily on the shoulders of James B. Brown. He was the man who made the critical decisions that set the company on its path to destruction. There have been attempts to single out others for equal or perhaps stronger blame. It was fashionable at that time to picture Rogers Caldwell as the evil influence who ruined the company. The directors of BancoKentucky were also castigated for their ineffectual overseeing of stockholder interests. It cannot be denied that the directors were negligent in the performance of their duties. Time after time they refused the urgent requests of federal banking officials to assume a more active roll in the management of the National Bank of Kentucky. The directors were also aware of the large amounts of overdue paper and the increasing outright losses suffered by the bank and yet they apparently did nothing to correct this situation. They allowed themselves to be completely dominated by James Brown. In fact, their sole function appeared to be merely to affirm actions already taken by the president. The directors did not destroy the BancoKentucky Company; their failing was that they did nothing to save it.

In assessing the responsibility of Rogers Caldwell, it must be remembered that his special case of villainy occurred before he had any connection with the company. In fact, Caldwell was simply trying to prevent the total collapse of his holdings. If one were to attempt to build a case of unethical conduct against this man, his actions preceding the merger would lend credence to this assumption. However, Rogers Caldwell was not legally or, for that matter, morally bound to protect the interests of the stockholders or creditors of BancoKentucky. The same could not be said for James B. Brown, This man was, in effect, the BancoKentucky Company because he dominated it so completely. Brown neither sought out nor encouraged others to participate in important policy decisions. His unusual personality quirks tended to increase his isolation from the other officers of the company.

It was Brown's gambling instinct that caused the bank to make the highly speculative loans which resulted in heavy losses. Brown used the bank to promote his own interests and ambitions. In short, Brown was a reckless gambling banker. His vigor, daring, and optimism helped him to build a great financial empire during the prosperous years following the First World War. These same traits caused his downfall in a different time, one which called for caution and restraint. Brown's actions during the merger discussions between himself and Rogers Caldwell were very curious. How was it that Caldwell was able to talk Brown into merging their respective companies with only verbal assurances as to the financial health of the Caldwell Company? Was it merely a weak moment, or had James Brown become so arrogant and egotistical that he felt he could not be bested in such negotiations? Whatever the answer, the basic fact remained that Brown violated one of the most elemental tenets of business practice when he agreed to the merger without ever bothering to ascertain the true financial picture of Caldwell and Company.

ROBERT T. FUGATE, JR. (1942–) is a native of Louisville, Kentucky. He received his B.A. and M.A. degrees from the University of Louisville. He has taught history in the Louisville school system and served as vice president of the Louisville and Jefferson County Federation of Teachers. He is now a stockbroker with a Louisville firm.

This article first appeared in *The Filson Club History Quarterly* in January 1976, vol. 50, pp. 29–46.

THE NIGHT RIDERS' RAID ON HOPKINSVILLE

By WILLIAM WALLACE HENDERSON
Hopkinsville, Kentucky

Paper read before The Filson Club on February 6, 1950

"A Hot Time in the Old Town." Since the song containing these words became popular during the Spanish American War, many, in a convivial spirit and otherwise, have threatened to create just such a state of thermal intensity. But it remained for a band of from two hundred to two hundred fifty farmers to do just that in Hopkinsville, Kentucky, during the early hours of Saturday morning, December 7, 1907.

The period preceding and following this eventful date, known as the Night Rider Days, encompasses perhaps the darkest hours experienced throughout the confines of the dark tobacco belt, the Civil War Days not excepted. It was a time to try the hearts and souls of stout-hearted men; when brother was arrayed against brother and neighbor against neighbor; when lawlessness ran rampant throughout the land; when no man, whether living in town or country, felt safe; when homes were invaded, property destroyed, and lives taken in cold blood.

But to begin at the beginning. The turn of the 20th Century found the farmers of the section in a deplorable state. For the most part farming in those days was strictly raising tobacco. Diversified farming, rotation of crops, the raising of livestock, co-operative marketing, and all the other innovations now followed by the modern farmer were entirely unknown. He raised tobacco year after year and hauled it off to market, hoping to get a fair return for his labor. The tobacco market was completely dominated by the large companies who bought their needs at the lowest possible price. It was the general practice for a farmer to have his tobacco prized, and then to offer it for sale through a local warehouseman. In about 1903 the large companies withdrew from this system under pretense of doing business directly with the farmers, and started sending their buyers directly to the barns. This was followed soon after by an arrangement among the companies whereby the country was districted, and only one buyer would call on a farmer. The result was that there was no competition among the buyers, and the grower was forced to take what the buyer offered, or take his chances in selling to some of the smaller buyers or "pinhookers." Under such a system, the price continued to fall until it was realized that something had to be done or the whole section would be bankrupt.

In 1903 the farmers organized a crude type of Association and endeavored to secure the agreement of all tobacco raisers to put their tobacco into the Association, where it would be sold and the proceeds distributed. The first year the sign-up was as high as 85%; but the companies had large reserve stocks, so did not rush to buy. The result was that the members received less than the non-members. As contracts were on an annual basis, it became harder and harder to secure signatures in succeeding years, and in the spring of 1906, when three year contracts were advocated, many of the leading farmers refused to sign. To add to the confusion, many who had signed would violate their contracts by selling directly to the buyers, there being no law or provision in the contracts to penalize those who did so. The result was that the Association farmer was lined up against the non-association farmer; against the member who violated his contract; against the buyers who represented the "trusts"; against the trusts and independent buyers who bought from non-member farmers, or from members who violated; and each of these factions was, in turn, arrayed against the others. Feeling became intense, meetings were held at some place in the county nearly every night in the week, and the kindling was laid for the conflagration which was to follow.

The first outbreak of lawlessness occurred in May, 1906, when the plantbeds of L. L. Leavell and J. T. Garnett, prominent non-members, were scraped and destroyed. This set the pattern. Within a few nights other beds were scraped, and the war was on. Throughout the summer and fall of 1906 numerous acts of violence of a minor nature were reported, but the tension was rising and reached its peak on the night of December 1, 1906, when a band of two hundred rode into Princeton, Kentucky; took possession of the town; and burned two stemming houses from which the flames spread to and destroyed three private residences.

Public sentiment strongly condemned the acts. The press was outspoken in condemnation, and the Association officials disclaimed any responsibility or sympathy for the lawlessness. Insurance companies began to cancel policies on tobacco. The people were soon divided into two opposing classes, those condemning such acts and those not condemning or, in some instances, justifying them. The City of Hopkinsville, Kentucky, was itself divided in sentiment, some of the people thinking it unwise to antagonize the Association in any way. The city officials took a firm stand for law enforcement. The local company of the National Guard was kept in readiness to be called out in case of trouble, and the police force was increased to sixteen men.

During the winter of 1906 an agreement looking to peace was entered into by which tobacco crops already sold might be delivered, provided future crops were put in the Association. But such feeble efforts were futile to stay the rising tide. Letters were written and tied to gate posts ordering crops already sold to be put in the Association. Reports of hostile meetings, at which people assembled at night and organized into companies and were inflamed by incendiary speeches, came thick and fast. Night processions were frequent, with masked riders passing through the small towns and creating a state of terror among all not in sympathy. A demonstration against Hopkinsville was reported from Princeton by telephone on the night of January 4, 1907, and the local militia company assembled in the Armory and spent the night. The invasion did not come, but it was reported that a body of men had come to within twelve miles of the city and had turned back.

Throughout the year of 1907 acts of violence increased in tempo as the months passed. Hogsheads of tobacco were rolled into the river; men who refused to sign up were called out of their homes in the middle of the night and brutally beaten; some who refused to come out had their homes fired into and burned; others had dynamite planted in their wheat thrashers and the machines destroyed when they were operated. Tobacco buyers were overtaken in the country and whipped and warned that they would be killed if they continued to buy Association or non-member tobacco. On November 26 a press report sent out from Hopkinsville spoke of the apparent peace in the Dark district, and on December 2 the Executive Committee of the Christian County Association held its meeting and reported things in fine shape. It was the lull before the storm.

At 2:00 o'clock on Saturday morning, December 7, 1907, the City was invaded by an armed and masked band numbering between two hundred and two hundred fifty men. They entered the town marching in military formation, coming in over the Illinois Central railroad tracks and proceeding up Ninth Street to Main, at the corner of which they divided into six squads, according to a pre-arranged plan.

Squad No. 1 turned left at 9th and Main and proceeded north on Main to the Police office. Officers E. N. Miller, W. I. Broderick, and Joe Claxton were on duty. Booth Morris, night chief, had gone home and Miller was in charge. Broderick and Claxton had just come in when the phone rang. It was one of the night operators at the Cumberland Telephone office calling to tell the police that the night riders were there. Officer Miller turned to cross the room to the Home phone to turn in the alarm; Claxton started for the door and was met by a band of at least 30 men, who ordered him back and began shooting at the door. The officers took refuge in the back of the building while the mob proceeded to shoot up the building. Leaving a detail on guard, the remainder marched up 6th Street to the Louisville and Nashville depot and joined the main body at 9th and Campbell streets.

Squad No. 2 went to the Cumberland Telephone office (now Southern Bell), broke open the door and eight men went up to the switchboard room and brought the night operators, Miss Annie Curtis and Miss Lillian Boyd, down to the street, where they remained in custody. When one of the men began cursing, the leader ordered him to "cut out the cursing and remember you are in the presence of ladies."

Squad No. 3 had gone on up 9th Street to the Fire Station where John Lawson, Lee Morris, Bob Tunks, Ennis Morris, John Hines, and Ernest Haydon were on duty. Haydon, being awakened by the shooting, went to the window just as a load of buckshot warned him back. The firemen were warned that any man or horse leaving the building would be killed, after which the mob proceeded to shoot out all the windows and amused themselves by trying to shoot out the light in the town clock. Fire Chief E. H. Hester left his home and started to the station, but was taken a prisoner. He begged his captors to allow him to save the private property which had caught fire. This they refused to do until they had received the sign to assemble.

Squad No. 6 had meanwhile gone south on Main and captured the Home Telephone Company office, located on the present site of the A & P parking lot, and had then gone across the street to the old Hopson House, a famous landmark located on the southwest corner of 11th and Main streets, where the Gulf filling station now stands. The house was used at the time as a boarding house and was the residence of Lindsey Mitchell, a prominent tobacco buyer for the Imperial Tobacco Company. The raiders called for Mr. Mitchell to come out, and one account states that his wife came to the door and told them that they had a very sick child and asked them to go away. They replied by demanding him to come out and by shooting through the window. When he came out one man told him he would not be hurt, but another said, "Yes, he will," and struck him on the head with a gun barrel several times until he had several bad cuts on his head. Another account says that they went into the house and disarmed him, just in time to keep him from shooting into their comrades. He was brought down to the street and beaten, the captain of the squad looking on until he decided that he had had enough—when he stopped the beating and escorted Mitchell back to his door. This same group also proceeded to demolish the office of the *Hopkinsville Kentuckian,* a newspaper published by Mayor Charles M. Meacham in the building now occupied by the Cayce Gift Shop. In his official capacity as mayor, and through the columns of his newspaper, he had been outspoken in denouncing the Night Riders, and had warned them that a "warm reception" awaited them if they ever came to Hopkinsville. In connection with Mayor Meacham there occurred an incident which has been repeated with great humor through the years. His honor the mayor, being awakened by the noise of the firing, got up, dressed, and started to town regardless of the fact that he had been warned by the Night Riders that when they visited Hopkinsville they would also pay a call on him. Whether the group that he met near 14th & Main streets was on its way to call upon him or not will never be known. However, he decided against meeting them face to face, so took refuge in the vestibule of the First Baptist Church, where he stayed until all danger had passed. This gave rise to the saying which is current to this day, that the Baptist Church has shown that it can save a man, for look what it did for Charlie Meacham!

Details from all these squads, having accomplished their first objective, had hurried to strategic points about the city and, as the aroused citizens came from their homes, promptly took them prisoners and held them until the signal was given that the raid was over. A corral was established at the intersection of 9th and Liberty streets, and all citizens reaching the downtown section were held there.

As the various groups went through the streets a continuous fusillade of firing, designed to terrorize, kept all but the bravest within doors. But even this was not enough, for at every residence or business house where a light was seen a hail of lead was immediately directed. For weeks the town was filled with tales of bullets flying into sick rooms, and of the wanton destuction of private property in no way connected with the tobacco situation. The wonder of it all was that only one person, a colored woman living on the bluff overlooking the I. C. railroad yards, was injured, and she not fatally. There was only one other casualty, J. C. Felts, an L. & N. switchman, was purposely shot by a raider when he attempted, against orders, to move some box cars from the siding between the L. & N. depot and the Latham warehouse. But all these things were preliminary to their objective.

The main body, Squads 4 and 5, had gone up Ninth Street across the L. & N. railroad to the warehouse of M. H. Tandy & Company, owned by John C. Latham of New York, and located on the eastern half of what is now Peace Park. They quickly beat down the door and, with the aid of a liberal application of coal oil, soon had the building afire. They next marched up Campbell to 14th Street, where the same treatment was administered to the Tandy and Fairleigh warehouse, which was the local buyer for the Italian government. Both buildings and their contents were totally destroyed. Flames from the Tandy warehouse spread to the building of R. M. Wooldridge, an Association warehouse situated on the western half of Peace Park site, and practically destroyed this building and its contents. The incendiary work having been done, the main body reformed in military order, marched across 17th Street to Virginia, down Virginia to 14th, thence to Water (now Bethel) and on to 9th and Water streets.

At about 3:30 a signal was given by gunfire and at once all the other squads assembled at 9th and Main. After a roll call by squads and by number, they marched out of town in the glare of the burning buildings by the route by which they had entered singing "The Sun Shines Bright in My Old Kentucky Home."

The raid was over. The town that had boasted what it would do had been surprised and taken with ease. Property to the extent estimated at from $50,000 to $200,000 had been destroyed. But one of the most exciting episodes was yet to occur.

At the first alarm Major E. B. Bassett, later Colonel, left his home at 9th and Coleman streets, just two blocks from the Latham warehouse, and made his way through side streets to the Company D Armory in the Moayon Building at 9th and Virginia. Several other members of the guard company reached there soon after the raid was over. Major Bassett, Mayor Meacham, and the sheriff held a hurried conference and agreed that they should not let the blow go unanswered, and that a pursuit posse should be organized. Men were not readily available for such a posse, however, and more than an hour passed before the posse (composed of five soldiers, Lt. Stanley Bassett, Sgt. Bernice Gooch, Sgt. Riley Butler, Pvts. John C. Lawson and E. W. Clark; four citizen volunteers, John Stites, R. M. Fairleigh, Edgar Elgin, and Charles M. Meacham, Jr.; and Deputy Sheriff Lucien Cravens, with Major Bassett in comand) headed out West 7th Street. Six were on horseback and five were in a two-horse "carry-all." They attempted to head off the raiders at the railroad crossing two miles from town, but got there a few minutes too late. The posse followed them for several miles, with the carry-all staying behind and the horsemen gradually catching up. The raiders, having no fear of being followed and considering the horsemen as part of their party, allowed them to ride into their midst and along with them. Major Bassett said they were in a fine humor, talking and laughing over the raid and considering their job well done. He led his party on through the ranks, hoping to overtake and capture their leader. Not finding him, they turned into a side road to await the coming of the five in the carry-all and to continue the pursuit together. When the raiders divided at the forks of the road that went to Wallonia, the posse followed the group going toward Cadiz with the idea of giving battle. They soon overtook the rear of the column, and Major Bassett, riding up to a surrey carrying four or five, reached in and grabbed one of the occupants by the hair and pulled him out. In the fighting that followed, George Gray, of the Blue Springs section of Trigg County, was killed and Clancy McCool was badly wounded. Other raiders, hearing the firing, came back to the aid of their comrades and a pitched battle followed. The posse retreated toward Hopkinsville without injury and, although it was never proven, the statement was widely published and is current to this day that there were at least two secret funerals in the Night Rider country a few days thereafter.

But Major Bassett and his posse were not the only heroes of the night. In the *Kentucky New Era* of December 8, 1907, we find the following, which we quote:

ONE MAN ONLY RESISTS

While the mob was at police headquarters, Joe Mc-Carroll, Jr. stepped from his house at 2nd and Main streets, and fired ten times at the Night Riders with a repeating rifle. They returned the fire, and McCarroll quickly retreated into the house.

It was only natural that the story of the raid and of the chase of the raiders by the posse would be big news all over the country. Reporters and special writers from many big city papers and magazines visited Hopkinsville, and some of them wrote articles overdrawn and exaggerated in the extreme. All played up the heroism of Major Bassett, and his picture appeared in the Louisville, Philadelphia, New York, Boston, and many other papers. Artists pictured the riders in Ku-Klux regalia in scenes littered with the bodies of fallen men. The most ludicrous story appeared in the February 8, 1908, issue of *Harper's Weekly*, a publication of nation-wide fame which depicted "the spectacle of fellow-Kentuckians, perhaps neighbors, shooting at each other with deadly intent, was painted red by the flames of the burning warehouses; shrieks of terror-stricken women were heard above the rattle of shots, and the cries of the wounded answered the shouts of new recruits to the ranks of the defenders. Slowly fighting each step of retreat, the Night Riders were forced from street to street and alley to alley and finally to the outskirts of the city." The article carried a picture of the ruins of the Tandy and Fairleigh warehouse and explained: "In the rear are the ruins of Acme Mills and Elevator Company [a flour mill] which had a daily capacity of 1200 hogsheads of tobacco."

Interesting sidelights on the Hopkinsville raid are contained in the excellent history compiled by Dr. James O. Nall of Clay, Kentucky, *The Tobacco Night Riders of Kentucky and Tennessee, 1905-1909*, published in 1939. The incidents which he portrays were not given in any of the newspaper reports of the period, and evidently were gleaned by him from the testimony in the various court proceedings which concluded the Night Rider days. Because of their interest, I quote from his book as follows (pp. 74-77):

"... a raid on Hopkinsville was definitely contemplated by the Night Rider leaders in October, 1907, but local men familiar with the situation opposed it until they could make their organization still more complete. So it was deferred, but a date was set—November 19, 1907; and on that night, Night Riders from Calloway, Lyon, Caldwell, Trigg and (West) Christian counties assembled eleven miles from Hopkinsville, just west of Gracey, preparatory to 'riding' on the city. Telephone wires were cut, but not until after the news of the Night Rider gathering had reached the city. A raid was again anticipated, and again extra policemen were put on duty, Company D was assembled, and a hundred or more citizens were notified to be ready.

"The Riders turned back. A stiff wind, which had started blowing with nightfall and had developed into a gale, was given as an excuse by the leaders. They said they had no reason to burn all of Hopkinsville, and that if they set fire to the factories in such a wind it would be impossible to control it. That was true, *but they turned back because they received word that the city was ready to defend itself and they had better not come in...*

"The Hopkinsville raid occurred two and one-half weeks later, on December 6-7, 1907. By that time, enough citizens in and around the city had joined the Night Riders to so control the situation locally to make the raid effective. There was no opposition. The citizens who had formerly been on hand with their guns were at home; the members of Company D were conspicuous by their absence; there were no extra policemen on duty...

"During the afternoon, a Night Rider spy from Wallonia rode into Hopkinsville, contacted local Riders and gave them definite assurance that the raid would be made as planned. He was told, 'Come on. Everything's ready.' Meanwhile, Riders were on the road to Wallonia from Eddyville and Princeton, and other parts of Lyon and Caldwell counties. They met there, shortly after dark, with the local Riders, the lieutenant commander and the General, who gave these squads and their leaders instructions as to their particular duties. These directions consumed an hour, after which a minister is said to have prayed that the raid would be successful without bloodshed. The Riders then started toward Gracey. The majority were on horseback. A few were in buggies. The roads were good—winter weather had not yet set in—and they made good time.

"During the same hours, Riders from Calloway county and the western and southern parts of Trigg county rode toward Cadiz where they joined a local contingent and passed on to meet with the Wallonia squads at the road junction just west of Gracey. The combined force continued through that community toward Hopkinsville. They rode quietly, being joined by parties from Roaring Springs and points in West Christian from time to time. At a point about two miles west of Hopkinsville, where the Cadiz road then crossed the I. C. Railroad, the Wallonia spy met the Riders and told the General that the 'road was open,' that he had but to march in and raid the city. About fifty local recruits joined the party at that place.

"The Riders hitched their horses, and fed them to prepare for the long trip back, except for about 25 horsemen who rode on toward the city to enter and patrol it as general protectors of the main raiding party. About 25 men were left in charge of the horses, the other 250 forming in line along the railroad to adjust their sleeve badges, get their masks ready, and review their orders with their leaders. According to Milton Oliver and Arthur Cooper, final instructions were given in person by Dr. Amoss. The Riders then began their march into the city. . . . In the meantime, unrecognized Night Riders from various places in Christian county had entered the city to be on hand to join the main body. Some came on trains; some on horseback and in buggies, putting up at the livery stables and boarding houses; some stopped with friends, while others killed time in saloons and hotel lobbies. About 11:00 P.M., fifteen Riders hitched their horses on the Greenville road, met nine others from within Hopkinsville and patrolled the L. & N. Railroad until the raid began. Small groups gathered at various places in the city—one on West Seventh street about 11:00 P.M., and another near the Imperial [Tobacco] factory about the same time."

In addition to the wounding of the colored woman and the L. & N. brakeman, Dr. Nall states that there was one other casualty, that of Dr. David Amoss, of Cobb, Kentucky, the alleged commander in chief of the Night Riders, and the brains of the organization. He says:

". . . the next, and most important, casualty was Dr. Amoss himself who was struck in the head by some glancing gunshot while directing the activities near the L. & N. depot. He sustained three wounds in the scalp, one starting a minor but persistent hemorrhage. According to Arthur Cooper, he said, 'I am shot, but I am not shot bad.' He then released command to Colonel Dunning and took charge of a passing livery stable rig in which he drove west on Ninth street to await assembly. . . ." (p. 78)

"Dr. Amoss left the city in the livery stable rig, driving out West Seventh street to the railroad crossing. The troublesome wound continued to bleed, but he remained at the hitching place until the Riders reached their horses. Seeing that his men were safe, and *cautioning them to maintain an alert rear guard in event of pursuit,* he then took stock of himself. A small artery had been severed and a compress was not sufficient to control the hemorrhage. Unable to ligate the artery himself and not daring to return to Hopkinsville for medical attention, he drove fifteen miles to Wallonia (as fast as the 'borrowed' horse could take him) where a young physician closed the artery with a suture-ligature. It was not considered a serious wound, but, under the circumstances, it is probable that he saved the General's life." (p. 79)

"The horse and buggy, which Dr. Amoss had appropriated, were returned that evening by an unknown driver and left in Little River near the Seventh street bridge. The owner 'found' them there about 7:00 P.M. The rig was being driven by Ben Decker, Negro, when the General hailed it, and he drove it on out of the city. He was put out a half-mile from the city limits and told to run; and, as he commented on it later, 'I did, suh.' Dr. Amoss was up and about as usual during the day, but he visited his patients with a cap pulled down close to his ears to hide his wounds. The rumor was out that he had been killed. The community understood that he had a 'severe headache'." (p. 82)

This story clears up the mysterious commandeering of a horse and buggy from Gray and Gates stable, located where the Coca-Cola Bottling Company now stands, and the equally mysterious finding of the horse and buggy tied to a post at the Fifth Street ford across Little River behind the city jail on Sunday morning following the raid on Saturday.

The days following were hectic ones as the rumor persisted that the Night Riders planned to return in force and wipe Hopkinsville off the map in retaliation for the action of the Bassett posse. Company D, the local National Guard Company, was ordered on duty and patrolled the city twenty-four hours a day. They were later relieved by Company H of Louisville, also the troops were re-inforced by a Gatling gun, which was set up on the sidewalk in front of the court house. The Louisville Company was composed principally of untrained boys of 18 and 19 years of age, and they contributed very little to the stability of the community. They were young, badly scared, and made it their policy to shoot first and look afterwards. At least one person was severely injured by their promiscuous shooting. They were later relieved by a company from Eastern Kentucky. These were men of mature age, excellent soldiers, but it was said that they were Night Riders of a different sort. To supplement the National Guard troops a "Law and Order League" was formed with a civilian guard unit, which was sworn to defend the town against all invaders. Night after night the citizens assembled, were issued regulation military rifles, and walked guard all night. A story was told of Mr. Ira L. Smith and Rev. George C. Abbott, both of sainted memory, standing guard all one bitter cold night, armed with Springfield rifles, but without any shells. By degrees the tension subsided as the tide of violence moved into Trigg, Lyon and Caldwell counties.

The first break in the Night Riders' ranks came with the confession of Sanford Hall, Milt Oliver, and others, who gave away all the secrets of the organization. Numerous attempts were made to kill these traitors to the organization, and they would have been killed had not the Governor placed a military guard at the home of each for protection. Various reasons for their betrayal were advanced, but at this late date it is generally conceded that the State paid them to do so and promised them protection. It was largely upon evidence of these men that suits in Federal Court in Paducah, Kentucky, brought by persons who sustained damages against those whom they claimed had participated, resulted in verdicts for damages against the individual members, which made Night Riding very unpopular.

The final chapter of the Night Riding days, insofar as Hopkinsville was concerned, occurred in the indictment and trial of Dr. David Amoss on charge of "willfully and feloniously confederating, conspiring, and banding together for the purpose of molesting, injuring, and destroying the property of other persons." It was an imposing legal battle. The late Judge Jack Hanberry presided. Attorneys for the prosecution were: Commonwealth Attorney Denny P. Smith of Cadiz, J. C. Sims of Bowling Green, S. Y. Trimble, Douglas Bell, and County Attorney John C. Duffy, of Hopkinsville; for the defense: C. H. Bush, Thomas P. Cook, and W. T. Fowler, of Hopkinsville, John W. Kelly of Cadiz, and S. T. Hodge of Princeton. The trial began on March 6, 1911, and ran for ten days. All the so-called state evidence witnesses testified that they were members of the organization, and most participated in the Hopkinsville raid. But it all went for naught when Judge Hanberry instructed the jury:

"If the jury believes that Dr. Amoss entered the conspiracy to destroy the warehouse of John C. Latham, and did carry out this object, you should find him guilty. But you cannot convict him on the unsupported testimony of accomplices."

The jury took one ballot and turned in a verdict of "Not Guilty."

The era of the Night Riders was over. Although they failed as a militant order, they attracted the nation's attention to the conditions which they fought, and it remained for the Supreme Court of the United States to accomplish in a large measure what they had failed to accomplish. In October, 1910, that Court ruled that the American Tobacco Company, as then organized, was a violation of the Sherman Anti-Trust Act and ordered its dissolution. In retrospect it is easy to visualize the Night Riders engrossed in their activities, for many men are still living who resorted to the match, mask, and gun in their fight for the tobacco-grower who could not fight alone. They staged a revolt for a just cause. War is war whether on the battlefield or the tobacco field, and so it was in Kentucky and Tennessee in 1906-07-08.

BIBLIOGRAPHY

The scrap book and personal files of the late Colonel E. B. Bassett.
Meacham, C. M., *A History of Christian County*. Marshall & Bruce Co., Nashville, Tenn. 1939.
The files of the *Hopkinsville Kentuckian*.
Nall, James O., *The Tobacco Night Riders of Kentucky and Tennessee 1905-1909*. The Standard Press, Louisville, Ky., 1939.

WILLIAM WALLACE HENDERSON (1897–   ) is a native of Hopkinsville, Kentucky. A graduate of the Hopkinsville public schools, Henderson runs a lumbering and building-materials business which has been in his family for three generations. He serves as chairman of the board of the First Federal Savings and Loan Association of Hopkinsville. Henderson has written many historical papers on local subjects for The Athenaeum Society of Hopkinsville.

This article first appeared in *The Filson Club History Quarterly* in October 1950, vol. 24, pp. 346–58.

AMAZING BEST SELLERS BY KENTUCKY WOMEN WRITERS

By Mariam S. Houchens
Louisville, Kentucky

Some of Kentucky's most popular women writers have made their mark not by writing novels, but by portraying the wholesome, quaint, human appeal of people and places in short stories, essays, diaries or letters.

Eliza Calvert Hall back at the end of the last century was told by eight New York publishers that her *Aunt Jane of Kentucky* could not be accepted because "short stories in dialect would never sell." Little, Brown and Company of Boston finally took a chance, and in 1910, "Aunt Jane" had sold 80,000 copies.

Mrs. Lewis H. Mayne of Bowie, Maryland found a diary of her mother, Mrs. Kirtley S. Cleveland, in the attic of the family home at 1453 St. James Court, Louisville. It was the diary that her mother had kept when she was 10-year-old Virginia Cary Hudson in school at Margaret Hall in Versailles. Mrs. Mayne took the book to many publishers with no success. MacMillan finally published it, and as *O, Ye Jigs and Juleps*, the little book sold some 400,000 hard-cover copies, without benefit of book club boost, and remained on the best-seller list for nearly 30 weeks. Considerably more copies have been sold in the paperback edition, and the book is still selling. When Mrs. Mayne was ready to publish some of the letters that she had received from her mother as a book entitled *Flapdoodle, Trust and Obey*, Harper and Row, who had refused *O, Ye Jigs and Juleps*, was anxious to get the manuscript.

Back in 1921 Cordia Greer-Petrie brought out a little book of dialect called *Angeline at the Seelbach*. Angeline was a typical Kentucky hill woman, a skillfully executed comic character, and "Lum," her husband, was equally as good. Mrs. Petrie knew the Kentucky hill country, for she had lived in various mining towns with her physician husband, Dr. Hazel Graham Petrie, originally from Fairview, Kentucky. Angeline's and Lum's trip to the Seelbach with Jedge Bowles on a lawsuit case produced some puzzling situations for them, which still make hilarious reading. The fact that the book was in dialect seemingly did not stem the tide of its popularity. In May, 1962 it was in its 27th edition.

Cordia Greer-Petrie died on July 15, 1964, at 92, in Louisville. She was still a delightful personality and an authentic recorder of the dialect of the Kentucky mountains early in this century. Miss Adelaide Bostick, with whom she spent her last years, has remaining some few copies of *Angeline at the Seelbach* and later stories in the Angeline series.

The first chapter of *Aunt Jane of Kentucky* (mentioned earlier) was called "Sally Ann's Experience." This tale first appeared in *The Cosmopolitan Magazine* in July, 1898. It had been rejected for two years by one magazine after another. Not many weeks after it appeared in *Cosmopolitan*, it re-appeared in a woman's paper in far-off New Zealand, and finally there was not an English-speaking country where Sally Ann had not told her experience. The *Woman's Journal* of Boston published the story three times, and each time the edition containing it became exhausted.

It appeared as the first chapter of *Aunt Jane of Kentucky* in 1908, and a few months later President Theodore Roosevelt recommended it as "a charming little book written by one of your clever Kentucky women."

Then, through the *Ladies' Home Journal*, Sally Ann preached her gospel to a million readers. What was her experience? It was actually a prayer meeting talk—the plain tale of plain people told in the plain dialect of a plain old woman. It was a plea for women's rights, pointing up the injustice of the old common law of England in regard to the property rights of married woman. In 1888, at the time that agitation for reform began, Kentucky was the only state in the Union where a married woman could not make a will. No married woman could buy or sell with the freedom of the single woman.

In July, 1908, ten years from the date of its first publication, the *Cosmopolitan* republished the little tale. It was used for years by dramatic readers and teachers of elocution.

For at least 12 years Eliza Calvert Hall continued to receive letters from doctors, lawyers, editors, business men and women in various walks of life, all endorsing Sally Ann and thanking her for her experience.

Eliza Calvert Hall's parents were Dr. Thomas Chalmers and Margaret Younglove (Calvert) Hall of Bowling Green. In private life she was the wife of Maj. William Alexander Obenchain, a professor at Ogden College in Bowling Green. The couple had four children. Their youngest, Cecilia, was born in the same March that *Aunt Jane of Kentucky* came out. Later the Obenchains lived in Dallas, Texas. The "Goshen" used as the locale for "Sally Ann's Experience" is evidently not the Goshen out U.S. 42 from Louisville, but a fictional hamlet.

Amazing Best Sellers

The fourth author whose book became an unexpected best seller was Fannie Caldwell Macaulay (in some references spelled Macauley). Published under the pen name of "Frances Little," her first book, *The Lady of the Decoration*, was brought out in 1906 by the Century Company of New York. There is an interesting little story about its publication.

Fannie Macaulay was the young aunt of Alice Hegan Rice, famed author of *Mrs. Wiggs of the Cabbage Patch*. From 1899 to 1902 Fannie Macaulay had taught kindergarten in Louisville. Then, partly in an effort to forget an unhappy marriage, she steamed away to Hiroshima, Japan to teach kindergarten at a mission school. Gay-hearted, she had never missed a Kentucky Derby, and had serious inner doubts as to what her adjustment would be to missionary life. Her worries were needless. Despite long bouts of aching homesickness, she adored "her children" in Japan, and grew to love also the quiet "half-medieval town" of Hiroshima with its towering castle and lotus-filled moat.

Her letters back to Mrs. Rice were "too entertaining, too sparkling, to be kept for private consumption," said the creator of Mrs. Wiggs in her autobiography, *The Inky Way*. She felt that they would make an excellent book, despite the prejudice against novels in the form of letters. Continuing, Mrs. Rice said, "I cut out the more personal parts, provided the thread of a love story, reversed her family name 'Little Fan,' and gave her the family name of 'Frances Little'." Mrs. Rice presumably found a publisher with ease. "The book was accepted in both England and America and leaped into immediate favor, holding its place among the best sellers for two years," she said.

Mrs. Macaulay's enthusiasm for the Orient fired Mrs. Rice and her husband, Cale Young Rice, with the desire to join her in Japan. Even though the Russo-Japanese War was in full swing, they put out from San Francisco in April, 1906, carrying Fannie Macaulay's book which she did not even know had been published. One morning in Yokohama Harbor they found Mrs. Macaulay bobbing about in a sampan to welcome them. "Her amazement at seeing her book was excelled only by her joy at seeing us, and a happier reunion cannot be imagined."

Each time that Fannie Macaulay pinned on her little enameled watch, her Japanese children called her their "Lady of the Decoration." From that appellation the book's title came. Whether she was teaching Little Japan to skip (the children had never skipped before) or wipe its nose, she loved each child. She remained there until 1907.

By that time, her book was at the top of the nation's best seller list, and she came home. Melville O. Briney, writing about her in the Louisville *Times* December 8, 1949, says that on December 21, 1907, *The Courier-Journal* quoted from *The New York Times:* "A book whose popularity . . . seems destined to break the records of all the big sellers is *The Lady of the Decoration* . . . published about 20 months ago. In that space of time many a good book is born and dies, but 'The Lady' still goes on at a pace that outdistances all rivals. Last Christmas the book was a big seller but this season it has attained a popularity far ahead of what it had then. It is now in its 21st edition. Last week, 15,000 copies were sold, and there is never a day that the sales fall below 1,000 copies . . ."

She lectured on Japan here in Louisville, and wrote other books, but for 20 years her heart was in Japan, and she spent the greater part of her time there, making five trips to the Orient.

She had been born in Shelbyville and educated at Science Hill Academy. During her Louisville years she lived for a time at least in St. James Court, one of the colony of poets, writers and artists who made the lovely Court their home. Mrs. Marguerite Gifford mentions her in her book, *St. James Court in Retrospect,* which was brought out in 1966. In 1936 Mrs. Macaulay was living at the Cortlandt Hotel. Besides *The Lady of the Decoration* her better-known books were *The Lady and Sada San, Little Sister Snow, Jack and I in Lotus Land,* and *The House of the Misty Star.*

She died in Louisville in 1941, four years before the bombing of her beloved Hiroshima.

REFERENCES

Books:
Hall, Eliza Calvert, *Sally Ann's Experience.* Little, Brown, and Company, 1910.
Hudson, Virginia Cary, *O, Ye Jigs and Juleps.* Macmillan and Company, 1962.
Little, Frances, *The Lady of the Decoration.* The Century Company, 1908.
Petrie, Cordia Greer, *Angeline at the Seelbach.* John P. Morton and Co., 1922.
   Also 1962 edition, published by Angeline Publishing Company.

Other References:
Gifford, Marguerite, *St. James Court in Retrospect.* McDonald Business Service, Louisville, Kentucky, 1966.
Rice, Alice Hegan, *The Inky Way.* D. Appleton-Century Company, 1940.

Magazines, clippings and collections:
Briney, Melville O. — "A Louisvillian Made Pre-Atomic Hiroshima Famous." Louisville *Times,* December 8, 1949.
Kentucky Authors' Scrapbook, 1909 (Kentucky Room, Louisville Free Public Library).
Louisville Library Collections — Biography Series, Vol. II. (Kentucky Room, Louisville Free Public Library).
Saturday Review, May 28, 1966, Trade Winds column (Publishing information about *O, Ye Jigs and Juleps*).
Southern Folklore Quarterly, June 1965. "Cordia Greer-Petrie and *Angeline at the Seelbach*" by Mariam S. Houchens. Based on personal interviews with Mrs. Petrie.
Townsend, John Wilson, *Kentucky in American Letters,* Vol. II, pp. 181-184. The Torch Press, Cedar Rapids, Iowa, 1913
Who's Who in Kentucky, 1936 edition.

MARIAM S. HOUCHENS (1904–) was born in Owen County, Kentucky. She received her B.A. degree from Georgetown College and her M.A. degree from the University of Louisville. Houchens has taught in the high schools of Louisville and Jefferson County. She has done free-lance writing for the *Louisville Courier-Journal*, edited a genealogical book entitled *The Cobbs of Owen County*, and written several articles for historical journals.

This article first appeared in *The Filson Club History Quarterly* in October 1967, vol. 41, pp. 353–56.

THE KENTUCKY WPA: RELIEF AND POLITICS, MAY-NOVEMBER 1935

By ROBERT J. LEUPOLD*
Cooperstown, New York

The song birds are the sweetest in Kentucky
The thoroughbreds are the fleetest in Kentucky
Mountains tower proudest
Thunder peals the loudest
The landscape is the grandest —
And politics — the damnedest, in Kentucky.[1]

Prior to 1935 it was generally recognized in Kentucky that the Republicans won during years marked by intense factional strife within the Democratic ranks. In the Democratic primary and the gubernatorial election of 1935, the Democrats were divided, partially as a result of interference by President Franklin D. Roosevelt. Hoping to make a Democratic defeat reflect dissatisfaction with the national administration and the New Deal, the Republicans publicized the contest as a barometer for the 1936 presidential campaign.

While Kentucky's Democrats waged political warfare, Roosevelt launched the largest and most ambitious of the federal relief agencies, the Works Progress Administration (WPA). However, as the election approached and the national spotlight focused on Kentucky, the Roosevelt administration drew charges that "United States Treasury checks sprinkled over the state like a snowfall" had put 150,000 voters "under direct obligation to the Federal Administration."[2] The Republican gubernatorial candidate published a letter sent from Washington to relief recipients which urged them to vote Democratic, and the Republican Congressional Committee accused the newly-formed Works Progress Administration of injecting forty-two million dollars into Kentucky, enough to pay every eligible voter forty dollars.[3] Were these accusations true? What role did the WPA play during its formative months, and was it capable of shifting smoothly from relief to relief politics when votes were needed for the New Deal?

---

* ROBERT J. LEUPOLD, a former member of the Peace Corps serving in Thailand, is a Ph.D. candidate at the University of Kentucky where he was awarded a dissertation year fellowship.

[1] Poem by Judge Mulligan quoted in Malcolm Jewell and Everett W. Cunningham, *Kentucky Politics* (Lexington: University of Kentucky, 1968), p. 1.
[2] *Cincinnati Enquirer*, October 28, 1935.
[3] *Kentucky Herald-Post*, November 4, 1935; *Louisville Courier-Journal*, November 3, 1935, November 8, 1935; *New York Times*, November 4, 1935, December 31, 1935; *Mt. Sterling Gazette*, November 22, 1935.

I

Standing before the Kentucky General Assembly at Frankfort on August 22, 1933, Harry L. Hopkins, outspoken director of the Federal Emergency Relief Administration (FERA), censured the legislators for providing only seventy-seven dollars in relief funds during March, while the federal government had contributed over one million dollars. Speaking without notes, Hopkins told them that he did not expect the state to raise relief funds "like a magician pulling rabbits out of a hat," but advised the lawmakers that ingenuity must be used to discover fruitful sources of revenue.[4] The state administration did not respond with either revenue or "rabbits." Instead, on November 6, 1933, Governor Ruby Laffoon requested that the federal government take full responsibility for relief in Kentucky.[5] Two days later Hopkins sent a brief note informing Laffoon that he was "unwilling to allow the unemployed to suffer because of neglect on the part of state authorities."[6] Needless to say, the relationship between Hopkins and Laffoon was not an amiable one. The animosity spilled over to Thorton Wilcox, Hopkins' appointed head of the new Kentucky Emergency Relief Administration (KERA).

Kentucky was a relief administrator's nightmare. Divided into 120 counties, it had more than any state in the Union except Texas and Georgia, despite being only thirty-sixth in size. In fifty-seven of these counties the assessed valuation of all property was less than the assessed valuation of three office buildings in Louisville.[7] Largely rural and mountainous, many areas like Clinton County, with forty percent of its population on relief, were barely accessible in winter.[8] In addition to administrative and geographical difficulties, Wilcox also faced the usual human ones. Within a month of taking office he ordered an investigation of Magoffin County based on reports that relief rolls were padded. Although fifty-eight percent of the county population was on relief, a member of the local relief commission candidly admitted the "pressure" to keep "relatives, friends, and business associates on the relief rolls is terrific."[9]

---

[4] *Courier-Journal*, August 23, 1933.
[5] *Lexington Daily Leader*, November 6, 1933.
[6] *Lexington Herald*, November 8, 1933.
[7] J. W. Manning, "Kentucky — Looking Toward Consolidation," *The National Municipal Review*, XXIV (January 1935), p. 47.
[8] Only forty miles were paved of Clinton County's 400 miles of country roads. Albany, the largest town and County seat, had a population of 600, and was forty-seven miles from the nearest railroad. Clinton was one of twenty-four counties with between 31 and 45 percent of its population on relief. There were thirteen counties in the 46-60 percent range, and five over 60 percent. See, Kentucky, Works Progress Administration, *1st Annual Report — 2nd District, July 1935-July 1936*, p. 128; Kentucky, Emergency Relief Administration, Work Division, "Percentages of County Population Receiving Relief," *Annual Report 1934-1935*.
[9] *Salyersville Independent*, December 22, 1933.

These obstacles, sufficient in themselves, were compounded by political opposition from the state government and all eleven Congressmen.[10] Wilcox, described as a political independent, was denounced as a "vehicle for Republican politicians" and criticized for the excessively high administrative cost of the KERA.[11] By August, 1934, Senator Marvel M. Logan was calling for Hopkins to "take the administration of jobless relief out of the hands of Thorton Wilcox. . . ."[12] The following month Hopkins initiated an investigation and in October he ordered a complete recheck of relief rolls.[13] Although Hopkins publicly supported Wilcox, the hostility of the state administration combined with eleven congressional votes apparently forced his hand, and at the end of October he appointed a new state director for the KERA.[14]

Logan generally deferred to Senator Alben Barkley in matters of patronage, and it was Barkley who suggested the man to replace Wilcox. George H. Goodman, a lifelong Democrat and boyhood friend of Barkley's, was the man he recommended.[15] Born in 1876, the son of a Paducah riverfront ginmill operator, he was reportedly given ten dollars by his father at the turn of the century, and sent out into the world to make his fortune. In Memphis, Tennessee, he opened a mail order whiskey business and within a few months had branch offices in five southern states. He sold out just before prohibition, later being celebrated in Washington as the "man who ran a ten-dollar bill into a million."[16] In 1922 Goodman bought the Paducah News-Democrat, which he operated until 1929. After selling the newspaper he devoted himself to managing his property, valued at approximately $91,000.[17]

Although Goodman lacked prior experience administering relief and had never held public office before, he did have several very valuable assets. Governor Laffoon, State Highway Commissioner Thomas S. Rhea, and Senator Barkley were all natives of Western Kentucky and had substantial electoral support there. Goodman, as editor and owner of a large Western Kentucky newspaper, had supported all three of them during previous local and state campaigns. Laffoon called Goodman "an outstanding man of Kentucky" and indicated his long con-

---

[10] *Courier-Journal*, October 30, 1934; *Leader*, October 30, 1934.
[11] *Leader*, October 30, 1934.
[12] *Courier-Journal*, August 8, 1934, September 4, 1934.
[13] Kentucky, Emergency Relief Administration, *Bulletin No. 159*, October 8, 1934; Hopkins also informed Wilcox that:
> There have been some reports reach this office which would indicate that a few families are receiving relief wherein the head of the family is employed on full time. I wish to advise you that it is contrary to our policy to supplement the wages of full time employees with relief funds.

[14] *Courier-Journal*, October 30, 1934.
[15] Barkley MSS, University of Kentucky Library, Scrapbook, "A Kentuckian's Advice to Kentuckians Here"; *Herald*, October 31, 1934.
[16] "WPA and the Politicos: Activity in Kentucky," *New Republic*, LXXXXV (July, 1938), p. 249.
[17] *Courier-Journal*, October 30, 1934. Goodman MSS, 1932 Income Tax Form.

troversy with the KERA was at an end. He also made a point of mentioning that he was certain Goodman would not let "politics enter into relief."[18] Barkley, of course, was also laudatory in his statements on Goodman.[19]

Goodman also appears to have had what Barkley called the "gift of tact." Writing to his friend Thomas R. Underwood, editor of *The Lexington Herald,* he pointed out the miserable conditions in Muhlenberg and Hopkins counties, and reminded Underwood that they were only a "stone's throw" from his birthplace, while asking support for the KERA.[20] Goodman also established a Public Relations Bureau, began issuing news bulletins, and moved to counteract charges of high administrative expenses by publishing statistics showing an increase in case loads and a corresponding decrease in expenses during his first two months in office.[21] When he announced that the "dole is not the American way" and stated his first objective would be "to reverse the trend in Kentucky and put more on work relief and less on direct relief," it was not just an attempt to echo Hopkins and gain support.[22] Within seven months Goodman did reverse it, reducing the number on direct relief from 78,000 to 41,000, and increasing the work relief roll from 41,000 to 75,000.[23]

His background as a Democrat helped bring the administration of relief into harmony with the political trend in Kentucky that had given Roosevelt his overwhelming victory in 1932. For the first time a KERA administrator had both national and state support. But when Goodman accepted the new post he had made it known he would not tolerate "any character of petty politics in Kentucky relief."[24] For almost a year there were no complaints from Republicans that the KERA was a Democratic organization. On the contrary, the only protest of a political nature came from a Democrat who argued that "it is a fact generally well known in Lexington that no Democrat holds any executive position under your Fayette County administrator."[25]

II

The political pot came to a rapid boil in the Spring of 1935 as Democrats, Republicans, and factions in each party eyed the November

---

[18] *Leader,* October 30, 1934.
[19] Barkley MSS, Scrapbook, October 24, 1934.
[20] *Ibid.,* Letter, Goodman to Underwood, March 27, 1935, Underwood MSS, General File, Kentucky Emergency Relief.
[21] *Herald,* January 18, 1935.
[22] *Herald,* March 26, 1935, March 27, 1935.
[23] KERA, Work Division, "K.E.R.A. Work Relief-Relation to Direct Relief-and Total Case Load," *Annual Report 1934-1935.*
[24] *Herald,* October 30, 1934.
[25] Letter, Underwood to Goodman, No Date (1935?) Underwood MSS, Gen. File, Kentucky Emergency Relief.

gubernatorial election. The "damnedest" in Kentucky was about to swing into action with the most colorful Kentucky politician of the twentieth century, A. B. "Happy" Chandler, as its standard bearer.

Kentucky governors cannot succeed themselves. As the end of Laffoon's term of office neared, he groomed Thomas S. Rhea, his Highway Commissioner, as the Democratic nominee to be chosen in convention as was Laffoon. Senator Barkley, former governor J. C. W. Beckham, and Ambassador to London, Robert W. Bingham, all powerful in Kentucky politics, disapproved of Rhea and the projected method of nominating him. They spoke to Roosevelt about it. Roosevelt, thinking that a candidate chosen by primary would be more in line with the New Deal Democratic image as a popular party, wrote a widely publicized letter indicating his hope that Kentucky Democrats would choose their candidate by primary rather than convention.[26]

Laffoon, ignoring Roosevelt, decided to go on with the convention. He then took Rhea to Washington to sell him to the President and other national leaders. During his absence Lieutenant Governor Chandler called the legislature into special session and enacted a compulsory primary law.[27] Laffoon rushed back and revoked the special call, but the local circuit judge, then under consideration for appointment to the federal bench, "and subsequently selected on Senator Barkley's recommendation," invalidated Laffoon's action.[28] It appears that when Laura Blackburn, Postmistress of Versailles, wrote that "Seanatar [sic] Barkley holds the key to the situation as far as Happy is concerned," she was not far from the truth.[29]

Laffoon, seeing that a primary was inevitable, called for a double-primary hoping to produce a deadlock and allow him to adjourn the Assembly. Chandler, faced with a choice between two or none, yielded and the bill was passed.[30] Roosevelt's interference and Chandler's quick action in capitalizing on it, had split the Democrats and given the Republicans an opportunity to win. Since Kentucky was one of the few states holding an off-year election in 1935, and because the state had become something of a political barometer, the Republicans hoped not only to win control of the state administration but to discredit Roosevelt and the New Deal in the process.

Chandler ran as a reformer, centering his campaign against Laffoon's sales tax which in the midst of the depression provided the perfect

---

[26] J. B. Shannon, et al., *A Decade of Change in Kentucky Government and Politics* (Lexington: University of Kentucky, 1943), p. 10; John T. Salter, *The American Politician* (Chapel Hill: University of North Carolina, 1938), pp. 178-181.
[27] Jewell, *Kentucky Politics*, p. 134.
[28] Salter, *The American Politician*, p. 179.
[29] Letter, Laura B. Blackburn to A. O. Stanley, No Date, Stanley MSS, University of Kentucky Library, Box No. 5.
[30] Salter, *The American Politician*, p. 179.

issue. However, Rhea won the first primary on August 3, 1935, but did not get the necessary majority. A third candidate, Fredrick Wallis, running with the slogans "work relief for all unemployed" and "jobs, not bread lines," was eliminated and joined Chandler.[31]

Born in Kentucky, Wallis moved to New York in his thirties and made a fortune selling life insurance. He worked as a fund raiser for the Democrats, was appointed Commissioner of Immigration for the Port of New York, and later served as Deputy Police Commissioner and Commissioner of Corrections in New York City. During his term as Commissioner of Corrections he announced the discovery of a cure for drug addicts called "narcossin," which he publicized nationally and profited from personally. The drug later proved to have the same curative qualities as sugar and water. An unnamed writer researched his activities in New York and concluded:

> The concensus of opinion here is that he is an out-and-out unscrupulous faker. He has, as I have said heretofore, a good presence and an attractive personality, and makes a temporarily favorable impression, but his veneer is so thin and his purpose so obvious, that people soon get wise to him.[32]

After his exploits in New York he returned to Kentucky, bought Walliston Farm, near Lexington, and entered into local politics. He became familiar with relief in Kentucky, serving as Chairman of the State Board of the National Recovery Administration. In 1933 he presided over the National Convention of the Red Cross, at which he was introduced by Harry L. Hopkins. Chandler, in 1935 asked him to put his abilities to work as Chairman of his Finance Committee. After the election he would be appointed head of the newly-formed State Welfare Board, and in the 1938 Senatorial primary became Barkley's chief fund raiser.[33] Public office eluded Wallis, and little has been written about him, but apparently his talent for collecting campaign funds was in demand. "Happy," with the support of Barkley and Wallis, won the run-off primary on September 7, and turned to face a unified Republican party. How was relief administered during this first period of political turmoil?

III

On April 8th President Roosevelt approved the Emergency Works Relief Act of 1935, which appropriated over four billion dollars for works projects. He next established the Works Progress Administration (May 6, 1935), and placed Harry L. Hopkins at its head. To Hopkins

---
[31] Underwood MSS, University of Kentucky Library, Politics, Name File, Wallis.
[32] *Ibid.*
[33] *Ibid.*

he delegated the responsibility for the removal from the relief rolls of the "maximum number of persons in the shortest time possible."[84]

On the national level Hopkins retained his most competent FERA administrators.[85] The same process, where possible, was applied to the states. Goodman had proven his ability to run a sound relief program, and was the logical choice as head of the State WPA.[86]

Goodman now faced a complete reorganization of relief in Kentucky. The old KERA would gradually be liquidated and all workable men and women placed on work projects, while all non-workers would revert once more to state and local responsibility. Hopkins' target was to have three and one half million employed by December 1, and the Kentucky quota was set at 67,000.[87] The Work Division of the KERA already had over 75,000 employed on approximately 3,000 projects, and the change-over was expected to proceed swiftly.

The Kentucky WPA built along the same lines as the KERA. At Washington's suggestion Goodman retained the six districts the KERA had operating, and moved only the district offices so they would be closer to the geographical center of their administrative area. But due to the large number of counties and the lack of facilities for mail and transportation, particularly in the mountainous sections of eastern Kentucky, it was also proven practical to establish branch district offices, about one per three counties.[88] This was the same procedure the KERA had followed. Wilcox, in July 1934, had used forty branch offices, which Goodman reduced to twenty in February 1935.[89] Under the WPA forty branch offices were again used initially to insure efficient management in the early stages. Later, in February 1936, the number would again be reduced.[40] What actually took place over the next few months was that 75,000 men were put out of work so their projects, which had already been approved and funded under the KERA, could be approved and funded by the WPA. To handle the work twenty new branch offices were created, so that eight months later, when the 75,000 were back at work, the number of offices could be reduced by nineteen.

The state and district offices were organized in accordance with instructions from the federal administration.[41] The one exception was at the positions of assistant state and assistant district administrators.

---

[84] U.S. Works Progress Administration, Division of Research, Statistics, and Records, *Report on the Works Program*, March 18, 1936, p. 25.
[85] Charles Searle, *Minister of Relief: Harry Hopkins and The Depression* (Syracuse: Syracuse University, 1963), p. 129.
[86] *Ibid.*, p. 177.
[87] Kentucky, WPA, *Semi-Monthly Narrative Report*, November 16-30, 1935.
[88] *Ibid.*, September 1-16, 1935, p. 1.
[89] KERA, Work Division, *Annual Report 1934-1935*, pp. 1-2.
[40] Kentucky, WPA, *Monthly Narrative Report*, January 16-February 20, 1935, pp. 1-2.
[41] Kentucky, WPA, *Semi-Monthly Narrative Report*, September 1-15, 1935, pp. 1-2.

These positions were filled by state and district engineers and were not paid by the WPA.[42] The directors of the Divisions of Operations, Projects and Planning, and Labor Management, were all responsible to the state administrator through the assistant administrator. The same line of authority was followed in the district offices. The official reason for this administrative change was to insure that there would be someone in the organization who was directly responsible for the operation of the program from an engineering standpoint.[43]

Although not specifically mentioned, it appears the district engineer was also important as a concession to local governments. He gave the local governments a direct voice in the operation of the WPA and this was important in light of Goodman's policy of shuffling his administrators and filling jobs with people from counties other than the one they worked in. During July, he shifted Jesse O. Creech, KERA supervisor in Lexington, District three, to London, District four, and appointed him the new WPA supervisor there. Arthur Gamble, who had been the supervisor in District four, was moved to District five at Paintsville.[44] Ernest P. Rowe moved from his former position to head the Lexington office. Judging by the complaint of a Hazard newspaper that of nine employees in the local branch WPA office, eight were from other counties, the policy was also successfully applied at the lower levels.[45] Although the engineers were responsible for the project execution arm of the organization, both the Divisions of Finance and Certification remained in the hands of Goodman's appointed administrators. With the exception of these engineers the administration of relief under the WPA was totally in the hands of federal employees.

On June 12, 1935, the KERA notified its personnel that all employable men and women receiving relief from the public funds were to be registered with the National Re-employment Service (NRS).[46] Two weeks later, district supervisors were warned that all Work Division projects might be transferred to the WPA.[47] On the same day it was publicly announced that the change-over was contemplated and that the Louisville office was awaiting the necessary forms from Washington. As soon as the forms arrived, old projects would be submitted first, and then new ones applied for.[48]

While these events were taking place, Goodman traveled to Wash-

---

[42] *Ibid.*, See also: Kentucky, City of Lexington, *Budget, 1936*, p. 34.
[43] Kentucky, WPA, *Semi-Monthly Narrative Report*, September 1-15, 1935, pp. 1-2.
[44] *London Sentinel Echo*, July 18, 1935; July 4, 1935.
[45] *Hazard Plain Dealer*, October 24, 1935.
[46] KERA, *Bulletin No. 300*, June 12, 1935.
[47] *Ibid., Bulletin No. 305*, June 25, 1935.
[48] *Mayfield Messenger*, June 25, 1935.

ington for a meeting of State WPA Directors. There Roosevelt urged that politics be "outlawed" in the works program.[49] Two weeks later Goodman emphasized the President's words:

> I have it straight from President Roosevelt himself and certainly my entire organization is going to bend over backwards to carry out the last order the President gave me before I left Washington recently. The President's exact words were: "If anybody asks you to discriminate because of politics you can tell them that the President of the United States gave you direct orders that there is not to be any such discrimination. That applies both ways. It means we cannot hurt our enemies or help our friends. We have to, and will, treat them all alike. In carrying out this work, consider it purely from a human point of view. Do everything you can to prevent the use of political considerations one way or the other...." It needs no amplification (said Goodman) and it means to the letter what it says. Political influence shall have no consideration in the new order of things — that I shall certainly see to.[50]

In eastern Kentucky he was more blunt and simply warned that political activity by relief workers would result in immediate discharge.[51]

All activity on KERA work projects ceased on July 11, and the process of transferring them to the WPA began. The 75,000 men employed on these projects were told that work would resume when the projects were approved in Washington and funds allocated. It was estimated the procedure would take several weeks.[52] At the same time Goodman urged local governments to submit new projects, telling them that "the starting of projects . . . will be exactly in proportion to the energy and cooperation of the various local governmental units filling the necessary applications."[53] He stressed that he expected the KERA to go out of business within ninety days, and warned that if counties and towns were delinquent in requesting projects they would have to care for the unemployed themselves.[54] On July 17, area administrators were told to release office employees, keeping only a disbursing officer, area relief supervisor, home economics advisor, and one stenographer. A janitor could also be retained but for "not more than three hours a day — $.30 per hour."[55] The KERA was closing down.

By August a total shutdown of relief was imminent when the $800,000 allocated for direct relief for that month fell far short of the need. Goodman rushed an emergency request to Washington for an additional million dollars and received it on August 9.[56] A week

---
[49] *Ibid.*, June 18, 1935.
[50] *Ibid.*, July 1, 1935.
[51] *Harlan Daily Enterprise*, June 30, 1935.
[52] *Mayfield Messenger*, July 12, 1935; July 16, 1935; July 17, 1935.
[53] *Ibid.*, July 17, 1935.
[54] *Ibid.*, July 16, 1935; July 17, 1935.
[55] KERA, *Bulletin No. 321*, July 17, 1935.
[56] *Herald*, August 9, 1935.

later he acknowledged that the change-over involved considerable delay, but insisted that the various "kinks" had been ironed out, and optimistically predicted that by November 1, 1935, every employable man in Kentucky would be on a constructive job at a fair rate of pay.[57] A month later, on September 15, less than 5,000 men were working.[58]

The "kinks" that needed to be worked out were not in Kentucky but in Washington.[59] Projects accepted by the WPA were sent to the Advisory Committee on Allotments, The Treasury Department, and President Roosevelt for approval. To this point the flow was relatively rapid. But they also needed the signature of Comptroller General John R. McCarl, and there the flow slowed to a trickle. The Comptroller's office would return projects because they were not satisfactory. No explanation was attached why the projects had been refused. Hopkins asked for a list of projects that were acceptable but was turned down. Hence, by trial and error the WPA learned what was wrong with each rejected project. The result was a considerable amount of paperwork, confusion, and delay.[60] In Kentucky it meant no money, no work, and a great deal of dissatisfaction with the WPA.

While Chandler and Rhea were campaigning for the second primary, the Kentucky WPA reported to Washington that "the feeling of unrest is growing more apparent all over the state and may result in labor difficulties unless we can obtain approval of projects . . . and funds with which to operate."[61] The report warned that sponsors who had had projects in Washington since July without official treasury authorization were distressed over the delay and responsible for "considerable adverse criticism of the program and the entire national administration."[62]

The criticism was justified; local sponsors had been enthusiastic about the WPA and were furnishing locations for district and branch offices without charge.[63] In some cases it was urgent that projects start as soon as possible. Hopkinsville, the largest unsewered city in the state, needed a sewerage system, and city officials had applied for it in July. The Secretary of the State Medical Society reported that inadequate sewerage disposal was responsible for the prevalence of typhoid fever in that

---

[57] *Mayfield Messenger*, August 19, 1935.
[58] Kentucky, WPA, *Semi-Monthly Narrative Report*, September 1-15, 1935, pp. 2-3.
[59] Kentucky still had a few "kinks" to iron out. A major problem was the slow progress being made in getting workable clients registered with the NRS. In August, social workers were told: "A number of counties have failed to complete registration of relief clients with the National Re-employment Service . . . we do not wish you to threaten any client by with-holding relief; however, home visitors should clear up any misunderstandings about this registration." KERA, *Bulletin No. 331*, August 8, 1935.
[60] Searle, *Minister*, pp. 139-140.
[61] Kentucky, WPA, *Semi-Monthly Narrative Report*, September 1-16, 1935, pp. 5-6.
[62] *Ibid.*
[63] *Ibid.*, pp. 3-4.

city.⁶⁴ A local high school complained it could not maintain sanitary conditions and the Rotary Club passed a motion calling for a mass meeting. After the Christian County Medical Society demanded that construction begin immediately, city officials announced that the Hopkinsville sewerage project was still in Washington and its fate was "entirely out of their hands."⁶⁵ In some cases public pressure or the necessity of completing projects before winter had forced local authorities to begin construction with their own funds, which by September were running out.⁶⁶

The frustration of sponsors and workers was compounded by announcements in local newspapers of projects approved by the President or the Allotment Board. By September 30, Kentucky had submitted project applications worth $110,068,256. Of that amount, the Allotment Board approved $67,000,000, but only $3,876,553 had reached the state administration in signed warrants from the Comptroller General.⁶⁷ Consequently, only 5,309 men were working. The results of this were evident in the report of Arthur Gamble, the WPA administrator in District five:

> The fact that in many cases Presidential approval has been reported in the newspapers leads them (sponsors) to believe that the subsequent delay is deliberate on the part of the Works Progress Administration.⁶⁸

As can be seen from the events just described, the WPA was in transition during the months July through October 1935. The result was confusion and considerable conflict with local authorities. On July 21, *The Lexington Leader* commented that political observers were wondering if the delay in transferring the work-relief program to the WPA meant that the national administration intended to follow a "hands-off" policy in relation to the party strife within the state.⁶⁹ If Barkley, Chandler, or Wallis had hoped to capitalize on the WPA for support, they were sorely disappointed. A "hands-off" policy, whether intentional or not, was the only wise course of action possible. The statewide criticism of the WPA also partially explains why both sides, Chandler and Rhea, campaigned on local issues and stayed clear of any reference to relief other than general support for Roosevelt and the New Deal.

The voting record in the primary contributes additional evidence that relief had little effect on the election. Chandler's greatest strength was

---

⁶⁴ *Daily Kentucky New Era*, July 15, 1935; September 2, 1935.
⁶⁵ *Ibid.*, July 17, 1935; September 4, 1935; September 17, 1935; October 19, 1935.
⁶⁶ Kentucky, WPA, *Semi-Monthly Narrative Report*, September 16-30, 1935, p. 4.
⁶⁷ *Ibid.*, p. 9.
⁶⁸ *Ibid.*, p. 3.
⁶⁹ *Leader*, July 21, 1935.

not in the poor mountain counties where over fifty percent of the population was on relief, but in the wealthy bluegrass area close to his home county of Woodford.[70] It also appears that when Goodman said that "Political influence shall have no consideration in the new order of things — that I shall certainly see to," he was sincere in his determination to obey Roosevelt's command.[71] For that matter, judging by Roosevelt's note to Hopkins on August 31, 1935, in which he commented "relief in Ky. — too much in Repub. hands — see Fred Vinson & talk with him about it," Goodman may have been too determined.[72]

IV

After winning the second primary, Chandler's efforts were directed at healing party divisions and defeating the Republican candidate, Judge King Swope.

Born in Danville, Kentucky, Swope earned his Bachelor of Law Degree at the University of Kentucky, made his home in Lexington, and was appointed Circuit Judge in 1931. He won the Republican primary by over 100,000 votes and harmony was the keynote in his party.[73] He did not attack the national administration, on the contrary, his platform called for "cooperation."[74] The brunt of his campaign was directed at partisan politics within the state administration, based on material supplied by Chandler and Rhea. He discussed how "after two weeks labor Papa Happy and Mama Ruby presented an anxious public with twin primaries," promised a non-partisan government that would end political activity in the Highway Commission, and guaranteed an end to the practice of using state employees as a source of campaign funds.[75]

In reality the platforms of both Chandler and Swope were almost identical. Both were critical of the sales tax, and both voiced their willingness to work with the federal government. However, Chandler was at times candidly partisan, arguing that "Kentucky must go Democratic . . . if it is to remain in that party's column next year."[76] But the real contest hinged on the personalities of the "King" and the "Woodford Warbler."[77]

The difference between the two men was striking. Chandler, a young man with an infectious smile and optimistic spirit, seldom gave a cam-

---

[70] Jewell, *Kentucky Politics*, p. 134; John H. Fenton, *Politics in the Border States* (New Orleans: Hauser Press, 1957), pp. 30-33.
[71] *Mayfield Messenger*, July 1, 1935.
[72] Searle, *Minister*, p. 195.
[73] *Irvine Times*, August 16, 1935.
[74] Swope MSS. Misc. 1919-1935, Platform, p. 6.
[75] *Herald*, August 25, 1935; Swope MSS. Misc. 1919-1935, Platform.
[76] *Herald-Post*, November 4, 1935; *New York Times*, November 4, 1935.
[77] *New York Times*, November 4, 1935; November 2, 1935.

paign speech that lasted over fifty minutes. He spiced his talks with short, humorous quips, and promised that he would not wear a dress suit at his inaugural. Swope, on the other hand, was a descendant of one of Kentucky's oldest families and projected the image of a dignified aristocrat. He was cold and irritable, lacked the spontaneity of "Happy's" smile, and had a reputation as a severe judge. His speeches were delivered in a concise legal style, had few jokes, and were unusually long. In Boyle County he set a record for the campaign, keeping his restless audience in their seats for two hours and forty minutes.[78]

Swope refused to force the issue on the New Deal, regarding it as better strategy to fight it out on state questions and not run the risk of alienating Democratic malcontents, on whose support he pinned his hopes for victory. But, as the November 5 election neared, Republicans became concerned that he had made a mistake and urged a new approach.[79] By the end of October he was ready to listen.

During a two-hour speech at the Covington Library Auditorium on November 1, Swope charged the Democratic party with soliciting the votes of relief recipients. He produced an unsigned circular letter, sent from Washington, and several on relief that had received them. Under a picture of the United States Capitol were words praising Roosevelt as "a friend of the working man . . . a friend of the poor . . . and true friend of all, white, and colored alike. . . ."[80] It ended with the statement:

> "Happy" Chandler has pledged himself to carry out the Roosevelt program. The President wants and needs Chandler as Governor of Kentucky. Won't you help your President Roosevelt and YOURSELF by voting for Chandler on the Democratic ticket.[81]

Swope asked how the names of relief recipients had been obtained and suggested the letter implied that if relief clients did not vote for Chandler they would lose their checks. A few days later a Republican newspaper, under the heading "Relief Clients Feel Pressure of Politicians," noted that "the heat has been turned on in Chandler's behalf by the national administration."[82]

Coincident with these events the WPA underwent a radical change

---

[78] *Courier-Journal*, November 4, 1935; *New York Times*, November 4, 1935; Salter, *The American Politician*, pp. 175-181.
[79] *Cincinnati Enquirer*, October 28, 1935.
[80] *Herald-Post*, November 4, 1935; *Courier-Journal*, November 3, 1935.
[81] *Herald-Post*, November 4, 1935.
[82] *Ibid*. Signed letters were also sent to Democrats and state employees by James A. Farley requesting support, and Fredrick Wallis asking for campaign funds. When Wallis was criticized by Swope for his actions he defended himself by saying: "It is merely opening the door of opportunity for loyal democrats to support their party ticket in a heated campaign." Letter, Wallis to Underwood, October 21, 1935, Underwood MSS, Politics, Name File, Wallis.

of direction. Hopkins, in October, finally obtained an agreement with the Comptroller, whereby he was informed when a project was rejected and upon what basis the rejection was made. The WPA staff could then make the required corrections and have the project approved in a few days. *The New York Times,* October 23, 1935, under the headline "McCarl Breaks Jam in WPA's Projects," reported $1,500,-000,000 of authorizations released, with approvals going forward at the rate of $100,000,000 or more a day.[83] The effect was felt almost immediately in Kentucky.

At the end of October the Kentucky WPA had over sixteen million dollars to work with, 367 projects operating, and almost 14,000 men at work.[84] The next two weeks, spanning the November 5 gubernatorial election, brought a substantial increase. The state totals jumped dramatically and on November 15 there were 32,257 men at work on 787 projects. District administrators now reported "public opinion has been somewhat moulded in favor of the WPA program in the last fifteen days," and "a more mutual understanding of the President's wishes is evidenced by all."[85] This substantial increase in size continued through November. At the end of that month there were 50,845 men working on over 1,000 projects.[86]

The election was an overwhelming victory for Chandler, and after the results were final a new series of attacks were leveled at the WPA, this time by the Republican Congressional Committee. On November 8 they charged that WPA employees were selected from Democratic ranks and that a flood of funds and projects had been released just prior to the election.[87] Columnist Frank R. Kent, writing under the heading "Game of Politics" was critical of the "frightful confusion and inefficiency of the Works Progress Administration" and expressed concern over the use of Federal "power" and "dough" in the gubernatorial election. He also repeated Republican assertions that forty-two million dollars had been poured into the state by the WPA shortly before the election.[88]

At the end of November or early in December, Ohio Republican Representative Chester R. Bolton consolidated the accusations in a pamphlet entitled "Read the Record." As Chairman of the Republican Congressional Committee he reiterated the charge that ten days before the election forty-two million in WPA money entered Kentucky and noted that "Mr. Roosevelt time and again has refused to take notice

---

[83] *New York Times,* October 23, 1935.
[84] Kentucky, WPA, *Semi-Monthly Narrative Report,* October 16-31, 1935, pp. 1-2.
[85] *Ibid.,* November 1-15, 1935, pp. 1-2, 5-6.
[86] *Ibid.,* November 15-30, 1935, pp. 1-3.
[87] *New York Times,* November 8, 1935.
[88] *Leader,* November 8, 1935.

of factual information that his New Deal lieutenants have deliberately sought to buy votes with the taxpayers' money."[89] When Hopkins was asked about the charges in November, he commented:

> This office is not political and the politicians can yell their heads off as to what this office does or does not do. You can assume that we are going to get a lot of criticism from partisan sources.[90]

Goodman was strangely silent throughout the whole controversy. None of the accusations were leveled at him or members of his organization, and no specific cases of interference in the election were pointed out. All of the charges came from Republicans and were printed in Republican newspapers. No individual was ever cited as having used WPA funds illegally and no verifiable facts other than the figure "42 million" had been supplied. Only one news release on the subject was issued by Goodman's office and it was headlined "Relief Fails to Figure in Election."[91]

Although it is obvious that the complaints came from a partisan source and were motivated largely because the political "barometer" forecast stormy weather for the Republicans in 1936 rather than smooth sailing, a more detailed look at the situation is warranted. The Democrats did have the potential to use WPA funds; Chandler did win; and the WPA did conveniently undergo a period of expansion at the time of the election. Wallis was certainly not above tapping any potential source of funds or votes; Goodman was a staunch Democrat; and the national administration was anxious that the Democratic candidate win the election. Barkley, late in December 1935, answered the Republicans.

Barkley said that a check of WPA records showed only $16,238,053 in Treasury warrants had been issued for Kentucky prior to the election rather than the forty-two million claimed by the Republicans.[92] Actually, $16,783,445 was received up to October 31.[93] More important, during the period spanning the election (November 1-15), this figure was raised by only $52,924 worth of new projects.[94] Although Barkley's figure is slightly less than the real total, he is much closer to the truth. A check of the national trend shows that from November 1 through November 9, the Comptroller signed warrants for one half billion dollars and that expansion in Kentucky was comparable to that of other states which did not have elections in progress.[95]

---

[89] *Herald*, December 31, 1935; *New York Times*, December 31, 1935.
[90] *New York Times*, November 8, 1935.
[91] *Harlan Daily Enterprise*, November 5, 1935.
[92] *New York Times*, December 31, 1935.
[93] Kentucky, WPA, *Semi-Monthly Narrative Report*, October 16-31, 1935, p. 4.
[94] *Ibid.*, November 1-15, 1935, p. 8.
[95] WPA, *Report on the Works Program*, p. 25.

The dramatic increase in the number of workers employed, adding almost 18,000 people, also coincides with the national trend. On October 26, there were only 777,000 men employed by the WPA nationally. By November 9, the number had jumped to 1,265,000. It must also be remembered that the two-week period after the election registered an increase of over 17,000 men. It would seem foolish for the Democrats to have waited so late to add these potential voters.[96]

Barkley also reminded Bolton that McCarl had held Bolton's position as Chairman of the Republican Congressional Committee before he became Comptroller. Barkley concluded that "surely Mr. Bolton would not assume that Comptroller General McCarl would have expedited the approval of expenditures to facilitate a Democratic victory in Kentucky."[97] Here Barkley's argument is less sound, for as we have seen, McCarl actually did attempt to hold up WPA funds until October. Harvey C. Mansfield, in his *The Comptroller General: A Study in the Law and Practice of Financial Administration*, concludes that McCarl's actions were not related to his Republican sympathies, but were based on his desire to abolish the Treasury emergency accounting system and work within a system that allowed him to deal directly with the spending agencies without the interposition of the Treasury.[98] His insistence that all project authorizations be submitted for his approval was an attempt to maintain personal control over Treasury authorizations. The result was a bottleneck in the Comptroller's office. Hopkins found a partial solution to the problem, and as time passed it became apparent, even to the Comptroller, that no useful purpose was served by his review and no objection was raised when the WPA abandoned it in 1938.[99]

Probably the most convincing argument, but also the hardest to document, is to be found in the attitude of the sponsors and workers themselves. Of the 75,000 men who had lost jobs when the KERA stopped work on July 11, less than half were back at work by election time. For every man who received a job, another was waiting and had been idle for over three months. Whereas sponsors had over 3,000 projects operating in July, by November only 787 had been restarted. Although Hopkinsville eventually did get authorization for the construction of a sewerage system, it was after the election.

Perhaps the most dramatic example of the anxiety Kentucky's unemployed suffered during the period of transition from the KERA to

---

[96] *Ibid.*, p. 11; Kentucky, WPA, *Semi-Monthly Narrative Report*, November 16-30, 1935, p. 1.
[97] *New York Times*, December 31, 1935.
[98] Harvey C. Mansfield, *The Comptroller General: A Study in the Law and Practice of Financial Administration* (New Haven: Yale University, 1939), pp. 218-223.
[99] *Ibid.*

the WPA is that of Joe Goodwin from Owensboro. Goodwin, age 54, had found a job in the Spring of 1935 and was dropped from the relief rolls. But in the Fall his work was exhausted. When he reported for relief he was told that the WPA-KERA could not help him. Later, relief worker Robert Huie called at Goodwin's home. When he arrived, Goodwin met him at the door with a pistol in his hand. Pointing it at the relief worker Goodwin reportedly shouted, "I would rather die in the electric chair than starve to death," and pulled the trigger. The shot, fortunately, was deflected by a button on Huie's coat, and the pistol jammed during a second attempt.[100] Although Goodwin's extreme actions were not representative of Kentucky's unemployed, his frustration probably was.

In closing, it appears safe to conclude that rather than an asset the WPA from July to November 1935 was a liability for the national administration and Chandler. His overwhelming victory was not due to the surreptitious use of relief funds, but was a result of Chandler's shrewd use of the sales tax as an issue and the publicity of a closely contested double-primary, as well as a reflection of a trend toward the Democratic party that had its start with Roosevelt in 1932. The warmth and smile of the "Woodford Warbler" radiated hope and optimism, and the people of Kentucky had had enough of the sober and serious that was a part of the depression and the personality of Judge King Swope. Rather than providing support for Chandler the WPA furnished disgruntled Republicans with an explanation for their defeat. A defeat all the more frustrating because of its publicity as a harbinger of things to come in 1936.

---

[100] *Daily Kentucky New Era,* November 22, 1935.

ROBERT J. LEUPOLD (1941–   ), a native of Brooklyn, New York, received his B.A. at Morehead State University and his M.A. and Ph.D. degrees at the University of Kentucky. A former member of the Peace Corps serving in Indonesia and Thailand, Leupold has had extensive teaching experience in secondary schools and at the college level. He is now an instructor in the Department of History at the University of Kentucky.

This article first appeared in *The Filson Club History Quarterly* in April 1975, vol. 49, pp. 152–68.

PAUL SAWYIER: KENTUCKY ARTIST
SOME RECOLLECTIONS OF HIM

By John Wilson Townsend
Lexington, Kentucky

The renaissance regarding the lovely oils, water colours, and other media of Paul Sawyier, which began with his death in 1917, and has continued to grow and broaden throughout Kentucky and other states, is a joy to me, an old friend and always an ardent admirer of his beautiful work. I have even given birth to the idea that I should set down my recollections of him. Perhaps this became apparent to me one snowy night when I read in the Lexington press that November, 1958, was the fiftieth anniversary of the first comprehensive "show" of his work ever held. Somebody, I said to myself, should say something about Sawyier and say it soon.

May I say that I first became acquainted with Paul Sawyier's exquisite drawings and paintings of old Frankfort and the Kentucky and Elkhorn rivers (Elkhorn was a little river once), a long time before I met him face to face. From these I had visualized the artist as a tall, long-haired, unkempt, carelessly dressed fellow something in the fashion of his famous fellow townsman, Robert Burns Wilson, also a painter plus a poet, a fine one, and a novelist, a fair one. So one may well imagine the shock I received when I actually saw him for the first time. He looked less like an artist than any man that ever lived, in all probability, being more of the business-man type and having no paint in his hair or on his hands.

I saw Sawyier for the first time in the winter of 1909, in the offices of Dr. Orin Leroy Smith in Lexington. I saw a little fellow, sunk deep in the folds of the doctor's biggest and softest great arm chair of black leather, climb upward and outward to extend his hand in hearty greeting. He had been reading a magazine, and he came forward with it in one hand while he put out the other in my direction. Removing his small nose glasses, he smiled graciously and warmly. He moved quickly, gingerly. He wore a grey suit and grey accessories which synchronized with his grey eyes, grey hair, and rather dark, almost olive, complexion. He was a smallish man, say five feet eight inches and weighed about 160 pounds. (Of course, I'm guessing now.)

"Here's the fellow I've been telling you about," said Dr. Smith.
"Which one?" I asked.
"Both of you," returned the doctor as we all laughed.

Sawyier and I were seeing Dr. Smith about our glasses, but he was far more interested in Sawyier's art than in our eyes, at the moment. The doctor was an avid art lover of rabid acquisitiveness, and he was collecting Sawyier even then. So was I, but in a very small way. He had discovered Sawyier, the man, about the time I was discovering Sawyier, the artist. It was a happy meeting and as fresh in memory today as though it had taken place this morning. We were actually old friends from that day onward; and, while the artist and the doctor have long since left this unartistic world, they are very green in my memory—and growing greener all the time.

I remember the first of many Sundays Dr. Smith and I spent with Sawyier at High Bridge in Jessamine County, when his houseboat (a tiny tug), on which he lived the whole year round, was tied up there. To Paul it was always "The Bridge." He painted it in oils and water colours from many angles, and he never tired of looking at it. Dr. Smith and I went down on the old Southern railway (Sunday excursions $1 round trip), and Sawyier met us at the little station. He seemed to take us to his heart at once, and I rather think that he did.

"I want you to see the old stone towers first, because I have an oil of them I like a little," Paul put forth timidly as we passed the pillars of the bridge. The little settlement at the place then was almost a perfect picture, but the new bridge, erected some years later, took care of that very nicely, it now being nothing more than a buried hamlet.

We were a gay company as we went down the hill to the river's edge and hopped across the gang-plank to the boat's interior. I think Paul built it himself, but of this I am not sure now. At least he painted it and kept it in good order. He was a fine housekeeper and an excellent cook. (He had had plenty of training at his home in Frankfort in both departments, for years having taken care of his aged mother and father, the old doctor, who died in the winter of 1910, and whom I was to help carry to his grave in the State cemetery on the hill.)

The first thing on the boat we saw was Paul's crayon sketch of Bishop Henry B. Bascom, celebrated pulpit orator of the Methodist Church, and onetime president of old Augusta College and Transylvania University. He was painting a portrait in oils of Bascom for the walls of Morrison College in Lexington, and its foundation was this crayon study. This was at my instance, I having assumed the very delightful task of raising by private subscription the money for it— one hundred dollars. To see this crayon was largely the purpose of our visit. It was done from the frontispiece plate of Bascom, in one of his several volumes of sermons, which blew off the easel one morning and drifted down the river. This amused Paul no end, causing him to write me: "His Reverence blew off the boat with a sudden brush of wind this morning, and is now drifting towards Frankfort, but don't worry as I won't need him further. He's fixed in my mind and I'll have him in oil soon, perhaps tomorrow."

Those were the days, really, before the world went mad—before the world wars, Russia, and other international nuisances. Life on the swaying little tug ran along as gently as the river's sixth pool, not far away, which Paul had painted again and again. One of these I had purchased some months earlier—a really lovely water colour now faded somewhat but still a precious possession. It was the first thing of his that I had.

After dinner Paul produced his box of thumbnail sketches in oils from which he painted larger pictures. Dr. Smith selected the finest one, which Paul priced at $5 and the former Chicago physician whipped out his billfold from a back pocket and paid him so fast that Sawyier gasped forth: "That's the quickest sale I ever made!"

Then I took a little oil of the inner walk of one of the old Shakertown houses (Pleasant Hill), and the one of his houseboat in blue and gold. Later I sold both of these pictures to my old friend, William Kavanaugh Doty, a native of Richmond and for many years a member of the English Department of the United States Naval Academy at Annapolis. After Doty's death I purchased them from his brother, and they are now looking at me as I write, trying to recapture something of the old days with Sawyier on the river, and finding it hard—much harder than I had thought it would be.

I wish I had space for another group of memories of Paul Sawyier. I visited him many times on the river when he was tied up at Camp Nelson, Brooklyn Bridge, and at Frankfort. I had many letters from him, and I saved them and they are now at the University of Kentucky, Transylvania College, and in my old Kentucky collection which went to Eastern in Richmond in 1930.

They await the coming of his biographer, who may be me (before some "Johnny-come-lately" does the job) now that I have shaken the shackles of fifty years of recollections from my sleeping brain. This, then, may be the first chapter or at least the introduction of a little life of him.

Soon, before it's too late, I must set down tales: of our trips on the river; of our venture into business, the formation of the Shaker Ferry Boat Co., with Paul as president, old Boone Terhune as vice-president, and me as secretary-treasurer, and of what happened to my two hundred dollars; of Paul's admiration for the bouquet of that famous Boone's Knoll whiskey—then seventy-five cents a quart—and how I would fetch it to him from Lexington to Nicholasville on the interurban line, where I would change to the rickety "one-hoss shay" of the corpulent coloured mail-carrier for the ride to Camp Nelson; how the C. F. Brower Company would treat him about the prices for his pictures; what $27 meant to Paul when we were down to our last old country ham, half pan of soda biscuits, and half pint of, of course, Boone's Knoll; of the 1910 snow storm in Frankfort when we walked from the old state house to the new, and he made his first criticisms of the water colours of his fellow townsman, Robert Burns Wilson: "They are muddy," he said—and many of them, nearly all of them, are; and finally, how I "missed the boat" in not urging him to write his autobiography for the Kentucky Historical Society magazine, *The Register,* for which I was then associate editor.

These are a few of the things that come stalking back in my memory, and I hope I live long enough to set some of them down. I always liked "the little guy" as Woodford Longmoor often called him, and "the sweet old town," Frankfort, of Paul Sawyier's happy youth and struggling maturity. He was always "broke" and looking for someone to buy a picture; and about the only man in town who would buy one was John Joseph King, without whose interest he may have been hungry more often than he was. Well, perhaps he was not actually hungry but wondering, if not worrying, about the origin of his upcoming meal.

But Paul Sawyier's wondering, wandering, worrying days are over. He sleeps well on the highest hill of the State cemetery as the river below, which he loved most of all things earthly, continues its never-ending journey to join the Ohio. Not far from Boone, Wilson and Willie Price, and at the edge of the governors' plot, he dreams eternally. He may even be unmindful of the Sawyier Renaissance still in full swing and gathering strength every day. If he is aware of it, I'll wager what's left of that two hundred dollars I invested in the ill-fated (they never even laid the keel!) Shaker Ferry Boat Company, he is vastly amused. What was it old George Rogers Clark is alleged to have said? ". . . . . . now I need bread." Paul could add: "Me too, but they gave me a stone." So it goes, old friend, in this world and, maybe, in the next.

JOHN WILSON TOWNSEND (1885–1968), author, speaker, raconteur, and collector, was born in Lexington, Kentucky. Educated at Transylvania and Harvard, his varied career included teaching, journalism, farming, business, editing, government service, and a number of other activities. His major work was the two-volume *Kentucky in American Letters*, but he also wrote *Richard Hickman Menefee*, *Kentuckians in History and Literature*, *Life of James Francis Leonard*, and *James Lane Allen*, in addition to many pamphlets and articles.

This article first appeared in *The Filson Club History Quarterly* in October 1959, vol. 33, pp. 310–13.

THE CHARM OF KENTUCKY FOLKLORE

By Allan M. Trout

Columnist of the *Courier-Journal*, Frankfort, Kentucky
Paper read before The Filson Club, April 7, 1947*

Definitions of Folklore

To the ballader, folklore means old foot-pattin' fiddle tunes around which is improvised such doggerel as:

> Somebody stole my old hound dog,
>   I wish they'd bring him back;
> He chased big hogs through the fence,
>   And little 'uns through the crack.

To the historian, folklore is the spice that enlivens the dull pudding of heavy events.

To the artist, it is the weather lines in an old man's face, or the sunbonnet on a wrinkled old woman's head.

To the sociologist, folklore is the cold classification of warm human emotions into Roman headings I to IX inclusive, with alphabetical subheadings of a, b, and c.

But to me, folklore is the irrepressible cussedness inherent in a robust people. My brand of folklore does not mean anything. It does not solve problems, but neither does it create problems. It does not add leaves to a man's laurel, but neither does it wither the leaves already there.

---

*The paper here presented will be a chapter in Mr. Trout's forthcoming book, *Greetings From Old Kentucky*, to be published by the *Courier-Journal* late this fall. The illustrations are drawings by Edwin A. Finch, *Courier-Journal* and *Louisville Times* artist.

Examples of "Unalloyed Purity"

"Pure Cussedness"

Take a case in point. Lon Sherman used to run a poolroom at Campton, in Wolfe County. It was a small room, always crowded. Two of Mr. Sherman's customers got into a fight one night.

"Hey, there," yelled the proprietor. "This room is too small to fight in. Get out there in the road. It is 40 feet wide and God knows how long."[1]

Now Mr. Sherman did not challenge the right of his customers to fight upon the proper provocation. Whether it was right or wrong to fight never occurred to him. His only point was that the poolroom was too small to accommodate a fight. And to demonstrate he was not the man to stop a fight in deference to the abstract amenities of peace, Mr. Sherman suggested there was plenty of room in the public road out front.

The irrepressible cussedness, pure cussedness, inherent in a robust people, which I call folklore, is as fluid as quicksilver. It is produced by the formula of hit and miss. The same set of circumstances will not produce the same reactions twice in succession.

People who are compelled to work hard for a living do not have much time for organized fun. They seldom laugh out loud for the simple reason they do not see many funny situations. A man's wife is always complaining. His children are subject to croup, measles, and the seven-year itch. The elements conspire against him, and crops are uncertain. He sells low and buys high.

But a streak of inherent cussedness keeps most men from acknowledging defeat. The combination of adverse circumstances at last reaches the point where the only thing left to do is to grin and bear it. At the moment an overburdened man grins he invariably says something that contains a trace of wisdom and truth. That is how my brand of folklore is born.

Now wisdom and truth in the words of a tired, unlettered man are unusual. That is why somebody who hears them repeats the phrase to his neighbors. Children overhear and remember. They repeat the phrase to their children, and so on.

That is how my brand of folklore flows from one generation to the next.

Yes, life is a grim proposition to people who are compelled to keep their nose to the grindstone. Like the tongue-tied woman down in Lincoln County. She opposed her husband, who wanted to move to another neighborhood. A family named Gross lived over there, and she didn't like the Grosses. At last, the distracted woman laid down her ultimatum in these words:

"I'm not doin' to move over there among them Drosses, where you have to drit and drind on a handmill and not have no drease."[2]

Because the streak of cussedness in people is irrepressible, it cannot be cut and dried into academic classifications. But we can apply the rule of thumb. We can say my brand of folklore relates to the fundamental reactions of plain people to the propositions they rub against—such propositions as life and death, religion and politics, railroads and jurisprudence.

"Pure Ignorance"

A small part of it may be defined as "pure ignorance." For example, back in the days when the streets at Jackson, in Breathitt County, were masses of mud in wet weather, a mountain boy fetched a razorback hog to town to sell. The hog became hard to manage in the muddy streets. The boy finally lost his temper, grabbed a stick, and began to club the hog without mercy. A schoolteacher happened to pass.

"Don't beat that poor hog," she said. "It hasn't got any sense."

"I'll l'arn it some," the boy replied.[3]

Another incident of pure ignorance occurred back in 1923 while a fishing party from Pulaski County floated down the Cumberland River on two flatboats from Cumberland Falls to Burnside. The fishermen carried a big supply of sugar and coffee in one-pound bags. This they bartered to mountain farmers for fresh roasting ears, garden vegetables, eggs, butter, milk, and the like.

A bartering party went ashore one day in McCreary County. While the others were trading a farmer one pound of sugar for a day's supply of fresh vegetables, Ambrose Dudley, now of Frankfort, walked over to the front porch of the

Kentucky Folklore

little log cabin. A wrinkled old woman sat there in the sunshine. She was dressed in calico, with a cane-stemmed pipe in her toothless mouth, and a sunbonnet on her pert little head.

"Too bad about Harding dying, wasn't it?" Mr. Dudley began.

"Who?" inquired the old woman.

"Harding," replied Mr. Dudley. "President Harding. He went out West and died before he got back to Washington."

"Lord God," exclaimed the old woman. "I thought Cox got it."[4]

"Pure Sagacity"

Lest you think pure ignorance has got it, let me now give you two examples of "pure sagacity."

Uncle Tom Jett was an esteemed citizen of Breathitt County in the long ago, but was afflicted with rheumatism that almost bent him double.

One of the Hargis boys, who knew Uncle Tom, left Breathitt County and went down to Lexington. He studied at the University and learned many facts and theories of life. He met Uncle Tom one day while on a visit back home.

"Uncle Tom," he said, "there is no need for you to walk bent over that way. Don't you know mind is supreme over matter?"

"Young man," replied Uncle Tom, "observe that wheat field over there. Notice that only the stalks with heads are bent over."[5]

My other example of pure sagacity occurred in Louisville, but the background lies in the Kentucky River country around Irvine, in Estill County.

Jesse Baker, called Boat Man Baker, was a familiar character around Irvine for many years. He lived in a shanty boat on the Kentucky River and was a handy man with everything pertaining to the river—such as fishing, log rafting, and small craft of all kinds. But Boat Man progressed with the times. He next became an expert mechanic on gasoline launches.

At last two Government steamboats, the Gregory and the Kentucky, made their appearance on the Ohio and Kentucky rivers. Boat Man was entranced with the steamboats. He finally got a job on the Gregory. After working on the steamboat several years, Boat Man decided he had picked up enough knowledge to pass the Government examination for a pilot's license.

Boat Man could not read or write, but he came to Louisville and submitted himself to the examination. Among other questions, the Federal examiner asked him:

"Mr. Baker, if you looked up and saw your water gauge empty, then went below and found your water injector working, what would you do?"

"I'd stick my head out the window to see if the river had run dry," Boat Man replied.[6]

"Pure Frustration"

Consider now another example of undefiled purity. This one can be headed: "Pure Frustration."

The first passenger train in Laurel County was called Jane, because the letters J, A, N, and E were painted on the single coach. The train ran on the Rockcastle River Railway between Bond, in Jackson County, and the L. & N., at East Bernstadt.

Uncle Aaron Elkins, an old bachelor, lived with his brother and his brother's wife near the railroad. Uncle Aaron had never ridden a train, but the daily spectacle of Jane puffing up and down the tracks stirred within him the yearning to take a rail trip to Letcher County to visit some kinfolks. Uncle Aaron announced his plans, but his sister-in-law said he would have to wait until she could get some material to make him a new pair of long underwear.

So Uncle Aaron set about to speed the day of his forthcoming train trip to Letcher County. He gathered a basket of eggs and walked 2½ miles to the nearest store. There he tried to trade the eggs for two yards of brown domestic, the basic requirement for one pair of long drawers. But the store was out of brown domestic.

Uncle Aaron walked back home, ate his dinner, then took his eggs to another store, 3½ miles down the road in the other direction. That store, too, was out of brown domestic.

Tired and disappointed, Uncle Aaron cut through the fields on his way back home. As he was climbing a rail fence near the railroad, he heard the engine blowing around the bend. He stood there on the fence until the little one-coach train rolled into view. Uncle Aaron glared at the train, then he shook his fist at it and yelled at the top of his voice:

"Blow, Jane, blow. I'll ride you tomorrow, drawers or no drawers."[7]

"Pure Politeness"

My next example of undefiled purity can be headed "Pure Politeness."

A big spotted bull belonging to a Pike County farmer strayed away from home one morning. The farmer started down the road in search. Upon meeting a neighbor, or coming to a house, the farmer would ask:

"Have you seen a big pied'ed bull pass this way?"

His friends all answered in the negative. At last he came to a house where a woman unexpectedly stepped to the door in response to his call. Not wanting to mention the subject of bulls in her presence, yet anxious to find trace of his fine specimen, the farmer amended his question and asked:

"Ma'am, I don't reckon you saw a big pied'ed cow pass this way?"

"No," she replied, "but I saw a big pied'ed bull pass here a while ago."

"That's her, that's her!" exclaimed the farmer.[8]

"Pure Amazement"

"Pure Amazement" is the proper title, I believe, for our last example of unalloyed purity.

Around 1900, the first telephone line was built in north LaRue County from Hodgenville to Roanoke. There were 16 boxes on the line and it terminated at Spencer & Redmon's store.

One of the partners in the store put in a call to Louisville one day. A crowd quickly gathered to watch a man talk that far away. Aunt Roxie Spencer, who was standing by, summed up her reactions to time, speed and travel.

"Lord have mercy!" she exclaimed. "You can git in a buggy and go to Louisville in two days. You can git on a train and go in two hours. But you can git on the telephone and you are there right now!"⁹

EXAMPLES IN THE FIELD OF RELIGION

Let us now turn to the field of religion for several enlightening examples of irrepressible cussedness. On the surface, it seems paradoxical that a people so inherently religious as Kentuckians should bring their faith within the bounds of folklore. But the paradox disappears when you detect in their apparent irreverence an undercurrent of deep reverence.

Let me emphasize this point with a classic story that exaggerates it. Back in the old days, a family migrated from Indiana to Kentucky in one small wagon. They had to leave behind such non-essentials as pets.

Just before leaving, the little girl jumped off the wagon, hugged her cat, and cried out:

"Goodbye, dear kitty. We're moving to Kentucky and I'll never see you again."

Her brother next jumped off the wagon and embraced his dog.

"Goodbye, Old Shep," he said. "We're moving to Kentucky and I'll never see you again."

Their good mother watched the sad scenes from her seat on the wagon. She choked to the bursting point. The brave woman could stand it no longer. She quickly arose, stretched her arms to heaven, and sobbed in anguish:

"Goodbye, dear God. We're moving to Kentucky and I'll never see you again."[10]

Now that my point has been exaggerated, let us consider a little incident of the meetinghouse.

Uncle Dan Lilly, one of the devout members of the Pleasant Ridge Baptist Church, once owned the only tuning fork in Owen County. He always started the hymns with his fork, thus giving him a head start on the song, a start he invariably held right on through the fourth stanza.

One Sunday Uncle Dan got off to an unusually good start on the old hymn, "In the Sweet Bye and Bye." He observed a bug crawling on Brother Jasper Beck, who occupied a seat in front of him. Rather than relinquish the advantage of his lead, Uncle Dan kept right on singing but in these words:

"Brother Beck, there's a bug upon your neck."

And Brother Beck, being hard put to keep up with the lead Uncle Dan had gained, sang right back in reply:

"Knock it off, Brother Dan, knock it off." [1]

Another nice little story is told against the background of Owen County. The Rev. Clark Riley was an old-time Baptist preacher in those parts. He was not a graduate of the seminary, but was a great preacher, dearly beloved by all who knew him.

At the height of his exhortation from the pulpit, Brother Riley was afflicted with a peculiar sound, much like a man blowing his nose.

A young preacher from the seminary once came to the community where Brother Riley preached. He took dinner that Sunday with a good sister of the congregation. A large gathering was seated at the table. Brother Riley's name was mentioned.

"Yes," said the young visitor, "Mr. Riley is a good preacher, considering his poor education."

"Young man," snapped his hostess, "I'll have you know I'd rather hear Brother Clark Riley blow his nose than listen to an educated young upstart from the seminary."[12]

Still another incident occurred at an old-time meeting in the hill country. The brethren knelt in mass prayer. One of the supplicants for grace was a giant raw-boned fellow. He was barefooted, hence when he knelt his big heels were exposed behind him.

The preacher called upon an old deacon to lead off. As the venerable patriarch waxed fervent he reached out his hands and placed them on the bare heels of the supplicant in front of him. In the course of his prayer he asked the Lord to bless everything he could think of, and then he added:

"And, oh Lord, bless these dear little boys upon whose heads my hands rest."[13]

One of the greatest stories of the faith that passes understanding is told against a background of the Kentucky mountains. An old man and his wife lived there at the head of an isolated hollow. They were about ready for the long, sweet sleep, but neither of them had ever traveled far from home. They knew nothing about the outside world.

The old couple had engaged in a lifetime of quiet argument about how Christ would come the second time. The old man thought he would come on a fodder sled. His wife opposed that viewpoint. She did not know exactly how Christ would come, but she was sure he would not come on a fodder sled.

One day an airplane flew over the hollow. The old man and his wife went to the yard and gazed upward in amazement. It was the first airplane they had ever seen or heard of. They watched it in silence, watched it as the plane melted into the distant horizon of green trees and blue skies. Then the old woman turned to her husband and remarked quietly:

"Henry, I told you that when Christ comes he wouldn't come on a fodder sled."[14]

Examples Inspired by Death

Nowadays, the rattle in a dying man's throat is lost in the soundproof walls of a hospital room. The care of his corpse is entrusted to the professional hands of an undertaker. The grief of his loved ones is carefully controlled in the air-conditioned refinements of a private chapel. Laborers hired for the job shovel clay upon his coffin.

But death is perhaps the greatest inspiration of folklore in Kentucky. That is because death was an intimate experience in the old days. A man died in his own bed at home, and his death rattle was mingled with cries of grief from the loved ones at his bedside.

Neighbors gathered silently to wash his body, lay it out, and then sit by it through the long hours of the dark night. They preached his funeral at the neighborhood church. They opened the coffin to give friends a last view of the remains before the family gathered for a heart-breaking farewell.

He was lowered to rest by neighbors in a grave dug by them that morning. Everybody stood at the graveside until the last song was sung, the last prayer was prayed, the last clod firmly tramped into place on the sad mound of moist clay.

When a great man dies, a secretary is usually standing by to catch his last words, accurately and precisely. Historians undoubtedly cherish dying phrases, else they would not sprinkle so many of them on the pages of history.

But to get the dying words of a plain man, we must rely upon the elusive annals of folklore. The last words of plain men rarely are set to paper. The recollections of loved ones at the bedside too often are obscured by the tears they shed there. But I will give you two authenticated examples of deathbed statements, both yielded to me from the word-of-mouth records of folklore. Neither of them is funny, unless we impute humor to the great truth of the first, and to the great wisdom of the second.

The spring of 1904 was long and late. William Lyon, an old man in Elliott County, was taken down with the grippe. He grew worse from day to day, and the old man at last realized his time on earth was about up.

But the old gentleman was tough, and he lingered on. He grew impatient. He said over and over he wished his time to go would hurry along.

Weeks passed, and the old man's son and grandsons put in their crop. They were hoeing corn one morning about 11 o'clock when the dinner bell rang at the house a quarter of a mile away. The father and his sons knew what the bell meant. They dropped their hoes and hurried to the house.

The old man was dying. There was nothing left to do but stand at the bedside until the end came. But the old man was still conscious. With the last ounce of his waning strength, he turned a tired face to his family and said:

"Boys, I hate to die."[15]

In his long lifetime, William Lyon had been called Honest Bill. The honesty of his dying words was eloquent testimony to the character that inspired such a name.

Jesse O. Wells was a sage of the hill country of Pulaski County. He lay dying one day in 1912. He had been a mighty man in his time, but he now lay on his deathbed at the ripe old age of 85.

The friends of Mr. Wells, his children, grandchildren, and great-grandchildren had gathered at the little mountain home where the patriarch was about to make his peace with God.

The old man's breathing grew harder, and he knew the hour of his death was at hand. He announced he wanted all his friends and kinsmen to gather in the room where he lay.

Everybody gathered around the bed. The old man raised himself from the pillow and looked into their faces.

"I want to tell you," he said, "the wisdom I have learned in my lifetime. I want to leave you the experience I have gained in 85 years."

The silent crowd around the bed leaned forward to catch the last words from the old man's tired lips.

"This is what I have learned," he said. "First, when you are out carrying a gun, never let your dog travel the road ahead of you. Second, always bring your maul and wedges in at night."

And then the old man sank back to his pillow and passed to the Great Beyond.[16]

There are times when folklore yields authenticated quotations, such as the two examples I have recited. But there are other times when folklore hides in that mythical realm where the columbine twineth and the whangdoodle mourneth for her firstborn. Let us now invade that mythical realm and see what we can find on the subject of death.

An old couple once lived in a section of Bourbon County known as "The Pocket." Time passed, the old woman was seized with a mighty illness, and she fell into a sleep of death. The day of her funeral arrived. The coffin was loaded on a wagon, friends and acquaintances fell in behind it on foot and horseback, and the procession wound slowly and solemnly to the graveyard gate.

The coffin was unloaded from the wagon at the gate. As the pallbearers started up the rough, steep path to the grave, one of them slipped and the coffin fell to the ground. The old woman rolled out, came to life, was taken home, and lived seven more years.

The next time she died, the funeral procession wended its way to the same graveyard, over the same rough road. But when the gate was reached, and the pallbearers lifted the coffin out of the wagon to carry it up the steep path to the grave, the bereaved husband quickly stepped to the head of the procession. Then he turned and admonished the pallbearers:

"Steady, men, steady."[17]

Let us now consider an incident of death from the distaff side. An old man in the hill country had been lingering in his last illness for weeks and months. One day in the late fall his wife asked the family doctor to tell her honestly what he thought about her husband's chances to pull through. The old doctor stroked his beard, peered over his glasses, made a few sympathetic remarks, and then said:

"He won't be here after the sap rises next spring."

The days wore on through a long winter. Early spring found the old man still lingering. A few days before he finally died, his tired wife turned wearily to a friend and remarked:

"It seems to me the sap is rising later this spring than it has for 60 years."[18]

Death, of course, wins out in the long run. But the grave sometimes is robbed of an early victory. And how we chortle at such a momentary triumph of man over odds so everlastingly long against him!

Join me now in the happy ending I am about to recite, a happy ending the Grim Reaper himself would have enjoyed had he overheard it.

Down in Metcalfe County in the long ago, Mrs. Sam Hill and Mrs. Henry Hamilton were good friends from girlhood days to their death at ripe old ages. Both were great talkers, and each thoroughly enjoyed the other's company. One night while sitting up with a sick neighbor, they fell into a discussion of unusual births they had witnessed. Mrs. Hill said:

"Don't you know, when I was born I weighed only two pounds? I was so little they put me in a coffee pot and closed the lid."

"You don't say," exclaimed Mrs. Hamilton. "And did you live?"

"Yes," replied Mrs. Hill, "they said I lived and done real well."[19]

Examples in the Field of Politics and Jurisprudence

We now come to the field of politics and jurisprudence, where native wit flows like a wild mountain stream, and the charm of Kentucky folklore unfolds like spring daisies on a sun-kissed upland ridge. If you want to get straight to the heart of Kentucky, go to a public square where politics is argued in the courthouse yard and jurisprudence is practiced in the big room upstairs. Let us now glance in at the big room, the learned judge upon his seat, a spittoon handy at his feet.

There once lived in Christian County a small, thin man with a long beard. He carried a heavy cross, because he was dominated by his overbearing wife and everybody knew it. He was summoned to serve on the jury one day, but his wife made him stay home and hoe the garden. He was yanked before Judge Thomas P. Cook at Hopkinsville on a bench warrant. The defendant tried to excuse himself by saying his wife was sick.

"What's the matter with her?" sternly asked Judge Cook.

"Judge, I don't exactly know," he replied, "but the doctor says she's got something like the worms."[20]

Let us now move over to the Bluegrass country. David Jones, an extremely fat man, was elected Justice of the Peace in a Central Kentucky district. First court day rolled around and Squire Jones decided to hold court in a storage shed attached to a country store. A crowd collected at the door, but Squire Jones told his constable, Joe P. Nave, not to let them in until court was ready to open in a legal manner.

A slight delay followed, due to the fact there were no chairs in the storage shed. But the accommodating storekeeper rolled in a nail keg, set it on end, and told the squire he could take his seat there.

Squire Jones more than covered the keg with his immense proportions. He folded his hands across his ponderous abdomen and, with a look of pride and satisfaction, turned to his constable and said:

"Now, Joe, go to the door and tell the boys I'm a-settin'."[21]

Let us swing down now to the Green River country, to a session of the Casey Circuit Court, at Liberty, in the long ago. Judge Fountain Fox, of Danville, was down there defending a man named Larkin, accused of stealing a side of meat.

The evidence was that the thief had put the side of bacon on his wagon seat and rode away on it. The prosecution deduced, therefore, that the seat of the thief's pants would be greasy. He demanded that Larkin display the seat of his pants to the jury. Larkin turned to his lawyer for guidance, whereupon Judge Fox said:

"Arise, Larkin, and show your integrity to the jury."[22]

Let us now descend to the courthouse yard, where trained experts gather to decide the undecided issues of the day.

Some 25 years ago, a man was tried in the lower court of Metcalfe County for a minor offense. A jury heard the case, rendered its verdict, then retired to the courthouse yard until time to go home.

Somebody asked one of the jurymen what verdict they reached. The juryman, a lanky farmer dressed in overalls, put one foot in advance of the other at an angle of about 45 degrees. He drew a big twist of homespun tobacco from his pocket, bit off a big chew, spat on the ground and, with an air of importance, replied:

"We turned him loose. They didn't have nothin' on him but substantial evidence."[23]

Let us now move over to the courthouse yard at Morgantown, in the fabulous country nourished by Green River. Frank Snodgrass had been the jailer of Butler County for several terms. When he got excited, Mr. Snodgrass had the untidy habit of scattering spit over everything within arm's length. At last, a friend advised him to keep better control of his ambeer while campaigning for re-election.

"Oh, that's all right," replied Mr. Snodgrass. "When I spit on a man he's mine."[24]

Now pick another courthouse yard. Take one at random. Nine times out of ten, a political orator will be on the stump. Like the old Confederate veteran who was canvassing Warren County for a seat in the Legislature. A farmer whose sheep had been killed by dogs wanted the politician to express himself on the dog law. The politician hesitated, so the farmer began to follow him and interrupt his speeches by shouting:

"How do you stand on the dog law?"

One day the politician unexpectedly replied: "I'm in favor of a dog law."

"What kind of a dog law?" the farmer yelled back.

"A law that will protect the sheep and not hurt the dogs," the politician replied.[25]

From what I can gather, Uncle Samp Demunbrun was beloved by more people in his time than any other sage in Edmonson County. Uncle Samp, among other interests, was an old-time member of the local school board.

In the course of a campaign for re-election, Uncle Samp attended a rally in the Forks section of Edmonson County. He was told a certain young man had promoted the rally in the hope of getting himself elected county superintendent by the new school board.

Uncle Samp, of course, was invited to make a speech. He arose and began a political declamation with the poise of an Edwin P. Morrow and the presence of an A. O. Stanley. Uncle Samp at last reached the point where he was compelled to take notice of the young man's initiative in promoting the rally.

"It looks to me," Uncle Samp declaimed, "like a mighty high kick for such a low cow."[26]

Let us stay in Edmonson County a little while longer. Good company never wears itself out in that hospitable home county of the illustrious, the late Senator Marvel Mills Logan. Politics was never lukewarm in Edmonson County, Senator Logan always said. A man was either red-hot on the Democratic side, or he was red-hot on the Republican side. This is the illustration Senator Logan never tired of telling:

A Democratic farmer in Edmonson County killed hogs one winter day. The next morning he loaded his hog heads into a wagon and told his half-grown son to drive them to market at Brownsville. He pulled up in front of a store and asked the merchant if he wanted to buy some hog heads. The merchant was a Republican, and several of his Republican cronies were standing by. Thinking to have a little fun at the boy's expense, the merchant asked him:

"What kind of heads are they, Democratic or Republican?"

"Democratic, I reckon," replied the boy.

"Can't use 'em," said the merchant. "Republican hog heads are the only kind that sell around here."

"Well," answered the boy, "I reckon I could make Republican heads out of 'em."

"How?" asked the merchant.

"By cuttin' 'em open an' takin' out the brains," replied the boy.

And speaking of partisanship, one of the greatest Republican partisans of Kentucky lore was Uncle Gran Philpott, who represented Clay County in the House of Representatives in the long ago.

Uncle Gran's admiration of Caleb Powers was unlimited. He once rode a mule from Manchester to London to hear Mr. Powers speak. Upon his return to Manchester, after riding all night, a friend noted Uncle Gran's crestfallen countenance. He asked:

"What's the matter, Uncle Gran? Didn't Caleb Powers outspeak Henry Clay?"

"He done purty well," Uncle Gran replied, "but he ain't as good as he used to be. He shore dampered me. The son-of-a-gun denied killin' Goebel."[27]

Uncle Gran was a giant of a man, and he had a peg leg. Aunt Millie, his wife, was a little woman. Aunt Millie came with him to Frankfort for sessions of the Legislature. Aunt Millie was his constant companion, but she always walked about 10 paces behind him. They were great favorites in Frankfort.

Uncle Gran and Aunt Millie were entertained at a sumptuous banquet one night in Frankfort. The first course was consomme, which Uncle Gran drank. Then somebody passed him a bunch of tender hearts of celery, which he ate.

At last the main course was brought in. The waiter set a plate in front of Uncle Gran. On it was a lobster. Uncle Gran arose, stomped his peg leg for attention, and said:

"Gent'men, I drunk the dishwater, and I et the bouquet. But I'll be durned if I eat this bug. Take 'er away!"

On another occasion, friends took Uncle Gran and Aunt Millie to a vaudeville show at the Opera House in Frankfort. They had seats on the front row. At last the curtain went up and a line of pretty chorus girls came dancing onto the stage. They were clad in pink tights.

Aunt Millie took a long look at the glittering spectacle, then reached over and slapped Uncle Gran on his good leg and exclaimed:

"Lord God, Gran, ain't they got purty hides?"[28]

William O. Bradley, the prince of Kentucky story tellers, left so deep an impression on political humor that men still relate anecdotes in honor of his memory. An incident is still remembered, for example, that occurred in the course of a speech by Bradley at the Opera House in Frankfort.

Bradley was an old man at the time, and his memory was not as good as it used to be. Early in his speech, he told the story about a blind man who went to the race track, bet on a horse named Bolivar, and then was compelled to rely upon a friend to keep him informed on Bolivar's progress during the race.

"How is Bolivar at the quarter?" asked the blind man.

"Going good," replied his friend.

"And how is Bolivar at the half?" inquired the blind man a few seconds later.

"Running strong," the friend replied.

A few more seconds passed. "How is Bolivar at the three-quarters?" anxiously asked the blind man.

"Holding his own," the friend responded.

"Now how is Bolivar in the stretch?" the blind man asked eagerly.

"In there running like hell," replied his friend. "He's heading for the line, driving all the other horses in front of him!"

The crowd at the Opera House roared with laughter and settled down to enjoy the rest of Bradley's speech. But the grand old orator forgot he told the story and proceeded to tell it again. The crowd was somewhat embarrassed by the beloved old statesman's regrettable lapse of memory, but sat patiently during his second recital of the story. Toward the last of his speech, Bradley again forgot he had told the story and began to relate it the third time.

A strange hush fell upon the audience, but the tension was broken by Dud Richardson, who was sitting down front. Half rising from his seat, and turning to the crowd, Richardson said:

"Danged if somebody don't stop him he'll run old Bolivar to death."[29]

Still another incident is remembered from Bradley's great career in the hustings of old Kentucky. Some 50 years ago, Bradley, a Republican, and P. Watt Hardin, Democrat, were rival candidates for governor. They spoke in joint debate at Paintsville one night and left early the next morning on mule-back for Salyersville, 19 miles away, to fill a joint speaking engagement at 1 p. m.

The day was hot and sultry. About 10 o'clock that morning they stopped to rest and cool their mules in the big grove of trees at Paint Springs in Barnett's Creek Gap. After unsaddling and picketing the mules, Hardin unbuckled his saddlebags and brought forth an attractive package wrapped in an old issue of the *Courier-Journal*.

Hardin removed the newspaper and exposed to the keen eyes of Bradley a quart bottle exactly old enough to vote. Bradley took the bottle and drew the cork. He smelled the contents, and then casting a glance at the newspaper from which it had been unwrapped, remarked dryly:

"Watt, this is the first good thing I have ever known to come out of the *Courier-Journal*."[30]

ACKNOWLEDGEMENTS

[1] Told by Elmer Drake, Lexington.
[2] Told by Mrs. V. W. Baker, Stanford.
[3] Told by R. C. Eversole, London.
[4] Told by Ambrose Dudley, Frankfort.
[5] Told by Jake Stapleton, Paintsville.
[6] Told by Coleman Benton, Irvine.
[7] Told by Grace Baldwin, East Bernstadt.
[8] Told by John M. Moore, Pikeville.
[9] Told by Jed Miller, Elizabethtown.
[10] Told by Cal S. Johnson, Brownsville.
[11] Told by H. P. Pryor, Louisville.
[12] Told by E. G. Jesse, Waddy.
[13] Told by James T. Philpott, Tompkinsville.
[14] Told by Elmer Drake, Lexington.
[15] Told by Dr. A. M. Lyon, Frankfort.
[16] Told by H. C. Kennedy, Somerset.
[17] Told by Mrs. George Wyatt, Jr., Cynthiana.
[18] Told by L. M. Scott, Center.
[19] Told by Willis H. C. Pedigo, Edmonton.
[20] Told by Judge Ira D. Smith, Hopkinsville.
[21] *Stories and Speeches of William O. Bradley*, by Maurice H. Thatcher.
[22] Told by J. C. Fogle, Liberty.
[23] Told by J. B. Smith, Sulphur Well.
[24] Told by Clint Raymer, Reedyville.
[25] *Kentuckians Are Different*, by Marmaduke B. Morton.
[26] Told by R. A. Demunbrun, Brownsville.
[27] Told by Paul M. Williams, Carrollton.
[28] Told by Mike Pennington, London.
[29] Told by Herbert Jackson, Frankfort.
[30] Told by W. L. Hammond, Pineville.

ALLAN M. TROUT (1903–1972), born in western Tennessee, earned his B.A. degree from Georgetown College. He was political reporter in Frankfort for the *Louisville Courier-Journal* and for many years wrote a column for that paper. Trout was recognized as one of Kentucky's foremost authorities on folklore. A selection of his columns has been published as *Greetings from Old Kentucky*.

This article first appeared in *The Filson Club History Quarterly* in July 1947, vol. 21, pp. 179–96.

www.ingramcontent.com/pod-product-compliance
Lightning Source LLC
Chambersburg PA
CBHW020632230426
43665CB00008B/139